The Secret Zodiacs of Washington DC

By the same author

The Secrets of Nostradamus
The Zelator: A Modern Initiate Explores the Ancient Mysteries

The Secret Zodiacs of Washington DC

Was the city of stars planned by Masons?

David Ovason

CENTURY · LONDON

This edition published by Century Books Limited 1999

1 3 5 7 9 10 8 6 4 2

Century
Random House UK Ltd, 20 Vauxhall Bridge Road, London SW1V 2SA

Arrow Books Ltd
Random House UK Ltd, 20 Vauxhall Bridge Road, London SW1V 2SA

Random House Australia (Pty) Limited
20 Alfred Street, Milsons Point, Sydney,
New South Wales 2061, Australia

Random House New Zealand Limited
18 Poland Road, Glenfield,
Auckland 10, New Zealand

Random House South Africa (Pty) Limited
Endulini, 5a Jubilee Road, Parktown 2193, South Africa

Random House UK Limited Reg. No. 954009

A CIP catalogue record for this book
is available from the British Library

Papers used by Random House UK Limited are natural, recyclable products made from wood grown in sustainable forests. The manufacturing processes conform to the environmental regulations of the country of origin.

ISBN 0 7126 7909 X

Typeset by MATS, Southend-on-Sea, Essex
Printed and bound in the United Kingdom by
Creative Print and Design (Wales), Ebbw Vale

Contents

Acknowledgements

I owe thanks to many librarians who have made their specialist books available to me, and to the many Masonic scholars who have listened with such patience to my questions. Yet, for fear of associating these individuals with any imperfections in my work, I think that it will be best to allow them the protection of anonymity. I would, however, like to thank the staff of the Library of the Freemasons' Hall, in London; the staff of the Masonic Library (that marvellous collection of arcane books, started by the genius Albert Pike) in the Supreme Council (Southern Jurisdiction) in Washington DC; the librarian of the delightful specialist library in the George Washington Memorial Monument, in Alexandria; the staff of the Office of the Architect of the Capitol, and the staff of the Library of Congress, whose beautiful building figures so largely in the following pages. And finally, in a sad valediction, I must thank that ancient institution, the British Library, which, even while I worked on this book, moved from a vast space shielded by a celestial dome to a far more austere setting in Euston.

My thanks go to all those Masons and Masonic Lodges of present time who have helped me with questions which must surely have amused those privy to the deeper secrets.

On a personal level, I would like to express my gratitude to Mark Booth, my publisher at Random House, who encouraged the writing of this book. For very personal reasons, I would like to thank the typesetter, Michael Harrington of MATS, whose attention to detail saved this book from foolish textural errors.

Chapter One

Come let me lead thee o'er this second Rome . . .
This embryo capital, where Fancy sees
Squares in morasses, obelisks in trees;
Which second-sighted seers, ev'n now, adorn,
With shrines unbuilt and heroes yet unborn . . .

(Thomas Moore, 'To Thomas Hume, from the City of Washington' 1804, in *The Poetical Works of Thomas Moore*, 1853, vol. II, p.296.)[1]

The shrouding mists have gone, and with them the frogs and the mud-turtles, yet their presence still lives on in the name. Foggy Bottom is the area where the western reaches of Washington DC used to meet with the Potomac River to the south-east of Rock Creek. In modern times, it includes the once-infamous Watergate Complex, and its evocative name has survived in a Metro station, south of Washington Circle.[2]

If you were to walk or drive from this Metro, down to the Watergate Complex and on to the John F. Kennedy Center for the Performing Arts, even as far as the western edge of Constitution Avenue, you would be unlikely to discover the reason for the name Foggy Bottom. The drainage engineers, the landfill experts and the architects of the late 19th century have done their work well, turning pestilential mudflats into habitable land.[3]

Foggy Bottom was originally called Hamburg by a Dutch gunmaker named Jacob Funk, who had settled the area in the mid-18th century with grandiose plans for its development.[4] However, Nature proved intractable, and the plans he had drawn up for a township came to nothing of real substance. The place remained almost uninhabited because of its deafening frog choruses and cough-inducing mists: settlers were deterred, and only duck-hunters and fishermen found the mudflats of use.[5] Incredibly, when, almost 100 years later, in 1859, a gasworks was built in the area, the few householders of Foggy Bottom were delighted:

they imagined that the gas fumes would disinfect the muddy land, and somehow make the fogs kinder on their throats.

Although officially Hamburg, it was called Funkstown by the early residents for a considerable time, yet it was scarcely even a village, and certainly not a town. Only a few wood-frame buildings and even fewer brick houses are recorded at Foggy Bottom, as late as 1800. Surprisingly, a pair of red-brick, two-storey houses have survived from this time, to the south-west of George Washington University. These were built originally by John Lenthall (who was in charge of the construction of the US Capitol) on 19th Street. At that time, they must have been near the northern edge of the ancient Foggy Bottom. In the 1970s they were moved, brick by brick, to their present location on 21st Street, and in spite of this enforced reconstruction are sometimes said to be among the oldest surviving dwellings in Washington DC.

About 1800, a large glass-making factory – essentially for the windows of the new city buildings – was constructed on the southern edge of Foggy Bottom from bricks kilned in Holland. This factory was located on the square sold as lot 89 in the sales map of 1792 (I have marked this position in black on the map below) which had been drawn up at the behest of George Washington to attract capital and speculators to the

new federal district. For a while, the site proved to be an excellent one for a factory, as it faced directly on the Potomac and offered useful wharfage for unloading glass-making materials.

By one of those curious coincidences with which the history of Washington DC is punctuated, this is exactly the site where, nearly 200 years later, a bronze statue of the mathematical genius Einstein was erected, outside the National Academy of Sciences (plate 1). The great man is shown contemplating a star-spangled marble horoscope for 22 April 1979, which is spread out at his feet: he is casually resting his right foot on the stars of two cosmic giants – Bootes and Hercules. As we shall see, this is probably the largest marble horoscope in the world.

The surprising link forged between Foggy Bottom and the stars does not end with Einstein. Behind his statue, in the National Academy of Sciences building, are 12 signs of the zodiac, along with their corresponding symbols, which have been built into the structure of the metal doors (plate 2). In the adjacent building to the east – the Federal Reserve Board building – are two other zodiacs, cut by the great glass designers Steuben, as decorative flanges for light-bulbs (plate 3 and figure 11). These zodiacs – the marble floor of the Einstein statue, the metal doors of the Academy and the glass light fixtures of the Federal Reserve – are just four of the 20 or so zodiacs in central Washington DC.[6]

At a later point, I shall examine each of these zodiacs more closely, but even at this stage we must stop and ask the obvious question: why do we find zodiacs in the formerly unhealthy stretches of Foggy Bottom, where frogs croaked night and day, and where young boys would hunt for mud-turtles?

Today, the air around Einstein is fresh and wholesome, and even the River Potomac has disappeared. The silting of the waters, and the extensive landfills of the late 19th century, explain why the Potomac wharfage has been moved, and why, from the windows of the Academy, one looks on to a greensward extension of the Mall, landscaped with trees and dotted with a variety of war memorials, including that of the Vietnam Veterans. In many ways, this extension of Foggy Bottom, born of the waters of the Potomac, has witnessed greater change than almost any other part of Washington DC.

It would be pleasant to think that Einstein would know that behind him there had once been a site called Observatory Hill. Had perhaps the earlier inhabitants – first the Algonquins, and later the early settlers from Elizabethan England – studied the stars from this rise?[7] The reality is probably more prosaic, for in 1843 the site had been taken over by the US Naval Observatory (overleaf), and an enormous viewing-dome was constructed with a movable frame that swung easily on bearings of huge cannon-balls, mounted on greased cast-iron grooves.

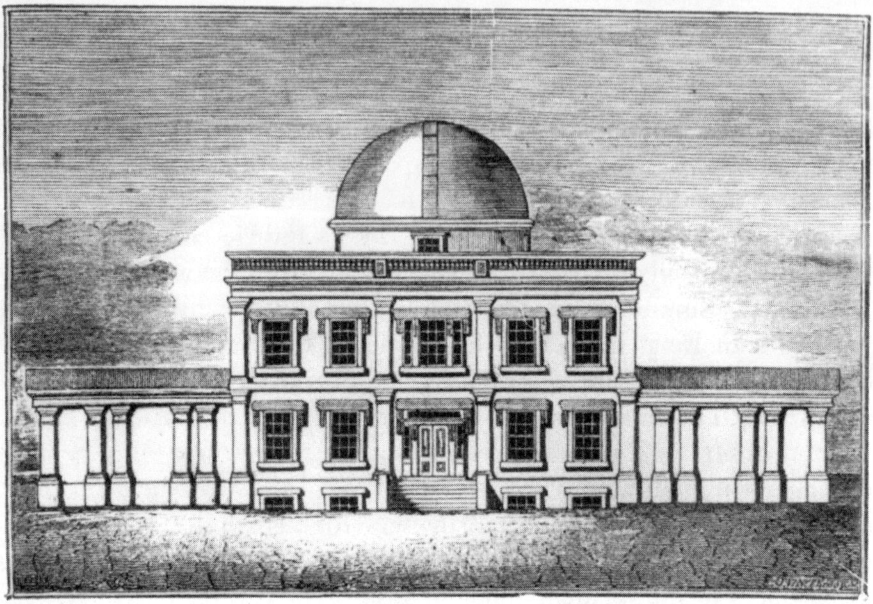

Fifty years later this same site, which had been earmarked by George Washington not for an observatory but for a university, would be proposed for an extraordinary museum by a scarce-remembered architect named Franklin W. Smith, whose highly original architectural ideas would help revolutionize the appearance of the city.[8]

If one of the night-shift workers in the glass factory had chosen to step out to look into the clear night skies in winter-time, he would have seen much the same stellar pattern in the skies as Einstein now contemplates on the marble at his feet – in the skies on Christmas Eve, 1800, at about 7.30 in the evening, he would have seen the gibbous Moon almost overhead, with bright Venus setting over the Potomac, in the west.

The constellation of Canis Major, the Greater Dog, would have risen over Jenkins Heights, where the north wing of the Capitol was almost completed. Dominating this part of the skies would be the scorching dog-star, *Sirius*, a brilliant white and yellow star. In 1800, this was the only star known to have been represented in the Egyptian hieroglyphics. Some modern scholars trace the name of the star in the hieroglyphic of a dog, evoking the god Anubis; however, the ancient Egyptians tended to call Sirius *Spdt*, and represented it with hieroglyphics that resembled an obelisk and a five-pointed star 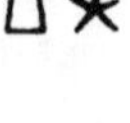.[9] The ancient Greeks, who took over so much of the Egyptian Wisdom, called *Spdt* by the name *Sothis*, yet it remained the dog-star in their calendars, and it was used by both Greeks and Egyptians in the orientation of important temples.[10] I pay attention to the five-pointed hieroglyphic here because, as we shall see, it seems to have been the source of the five-pointed star adopted for the American flag.

Sirius is 23 times as luminous as our own Sun, and even though its distance from the Earth of eight and a half light years dims this luminosity, it is still the brightest star in the sky. The ancient Egyptians *may* have known that it was a double – a two-star system – yet this was forgotten for centuries, until the invention of powerful telescopes. Its companion, known as *Sirius B*, seems to have a density more than 90,000 times greater than our own Sun, and has become one of the great mysteries of modern occult literature.[11]

To the north-west the cross-stars of the constellation of the Swan, the *Cygnus*[12] of the ancients, would be visible, seeming to mark Masons Island (which is now called Theodore Roosevelt Island) with the sign of the cross.[13] The two great stars *Castor* and *Pollux*, distinguishing the constellation Gemini, would have been rising over Jenkins Heights, where the new Capitol building was still being erected. A little higher, the mighty constellation of giant Orion would be hovering in the south-eastern skies – marked by that tight triple belt of stars to which the ancient Egyptians are supposed to have oriented their pyramids. Its orange star *Betelgeuze*, which marks the armpit of the giant, has a diameter about 400 times larger than our own Sun, yet because it is 470 light years from our Earth, it seems to be no larger than a red pin-prick in the skies. It is moving away from Earth at the rate of over 10 miles *per second* , yet so illusory is the cosmos that the ancients wisely called it 'fixed', and the star seems scarcely to have moved since Babylonian astrologers named it *Gula*, about 4,000 years ago.

Two hundred years separate the marble chart of Einstein from the night sky of the glass-worker, yet it would seem as though nothing had changed in the heavens in a period which Man must measure in less than a dozen generations.[14] It was this promise of stellar immutability which had first led the ancient Egyptian priests, and their pupils the Greek architects, to orientate their temples to the stars. It was this same promise which led the designers of Washington DC to ensure that their own new city was also laid out in accordance with a geometry which reflected the wisdom of the stellar lore.

Had you stood on this water-edge of Foggy Bottom on 3 April 1791, before the glass factory was built, you would have witnessed a most remarkable event – one which seems to have been involved in the magic of the building of Washington DC. On the morning of that day, an 'Afric-American' astronomer named Benjamin Banneker was making observations not very far from this spot. Wherever he stood, he would have been looking directly to the east, watching the Sunrise, knowing full well that within a few minutes there would be an eclipse, when the Sun, newly risen over the hill which was then called Jenkins Heights, would be blacked out by the body of the Moon.[15]

This is not poetic fantasy: Banneker was a historic personage (in modern Washingon DC he has a city park named after him) and *did* record that eclipse in his own notebooks.[16] He was working on this land with the surveyor Andrew Ellicott, making the preliminary observations so essential to laying out the boundaries for the new federal district. Ellicott was following the instructions of George Washington himself, and Banneker was his temporary assistant: the two were taking the first giant steps towards designing the city which would be named after the most famous man in America.

Banneker worked on the project for only a few months: it seems that his age told against him in such a strenuous and demanding enterprise.

Besides knowing a little about surveying, Banneker was a self-taught mathematician and astronomer, with some knowledge of astrology: indeed, in the following year he published an almanac, containing planetary positions, and observations on lunar and solar eclipses for the year to come.

In one of his ephemerides, Banneker published a crude woodcut of a zodiacal man (see opposite) – an image depicting the cosmic human being marked with the 12 signs of the zodiac that rule parts of the body. This woodcut (from the almanac for 1795) was borrowed by Banneker's printers from a design used by the almanac-maker, Benjamin Franklin.[17] The image displays one item which relates it to a symbolism that still proliferates in Washington DC. The flower in the hand of Virgo (on the right of the image) has five petals, or leaves. This may not sound very important at this stage, but as our investigation of Washington DC proceeds, the implications will become very clear. It is entirely fitting that, at the end of the 18th century, an American image of the ancient zodiacal sign of the Virgin should hold a five-petalled flower.

As Banneker witnessed the predicted eclipse, he would have known full well that the ancients had always insisted that such a cosmic event would have a profound influence upon earthly events. He would have known,

too, that the nature of that influence would depend upon the planetary patterns in the skies at the time when the eclipse took place.[18] The eclipse of 1791 was in Aries – a certain portent that the destiny of Washington DC would be filled with pioneering endeavour and excessive (not to say belligerent) enthusiasms. Aries had been the golden Ram of the ancient mythologies – the Argonauts of myth and poetry were the ancient Greeks who chose to face the savagery of the guardian dragon, in an attempt to steal the magical golden fleece of this celestial Ram. The Latin word *Aries* means Ram – yet, for astrologers, it is the *courage* of the Argonauts which is signified by the word.[19]

In fact, the augury on that morning of 3 April 1791 was remarkable. The Sun and Moon were not the only pair in Aries at that time: *no fewer than five of the known planets were in that zodiacal Ram – the sign which favours brave undertakings.*[20]

Such cosmic curiosities are a sign that the city had begun in a kind of dream – as a vision. Some historians will tell you that it began as a dream in the mind of George Washington.

When George Washington first rode over the woody site he had visualized as the future federal capital, the highest hill was owned by Daniel Carroll. In his youth, Washington had trained as a surveyor, and he would have perceived immediately the importance of these heights as the federal heart for the new nation. He may even have learned, from local gossip in Georgetown, that at the foot of this hill had been held the tribal grand councils of the Algonquins. Perhaps he had even heard rumours of the most curious thing about Jenkins Heights – that in earlier times the hill had been called Rome.

Other historians will tell you that the beginnings of this second Rome may be traced to a much earlier dream, in the imaginative 'second-sight' faculty of a man who lived on this land long before George Washington was born. In 1663, the owner of this tract of land had been one Francis Pope. It has been suggested that Pope was slyly joking with his own name when he called the hill Rome – and the inlet marking the western boundary of his land the Tiber, after the famous river of the ancient city. That may have been the case, but local tradition twisted the story into something altogether more marvellous. From such tradition, we learn that Francis Pope had the power of prophecy: he predicted a more mighty capital than Rome would occupy the hill, and foresaw that

> later generations would command a great and flourishing country in the new world. He related that he had had a dream, a vision, in which he had seen a splendid parliament house on the hill . . . which he purchased and called Rome, in prophetic honor of the great city to be.[21]

It would be reasonable to take this as a quaint yet entertaining story – sufficiently charming, perhaps, to excite the imagination of the Irish poet, Thomas Moore, who probably heard a version of the tale when he visited Washington DC in 1804.[22] Indeed, the story might easily be taken for the stuff of myth were it not supported by a long manuscript in the Maryland State Archives, at Annapolis. The deed, dated 5 June 1663, is

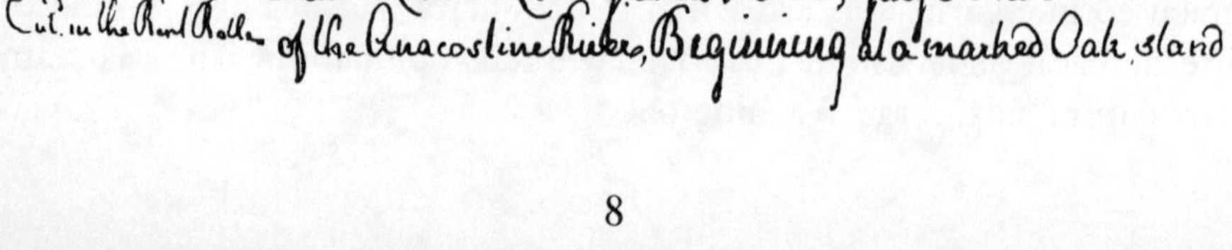
June 5 1663 To the Hon:ble the Lieut: Generall
Francis Pope Laid out for Francis Pope of this Province Gent. a Parcell of
400 Acres Land in Charles County, called Roome, lying on the East side
of the Anacostine River, Beginning at a marked Oak standing

in the name of Francis Pope, and sets out the basis for a survey and granting of a strip of land called Rome, bounded by the inlet called Tiber.[23]

This tenuous link between Pope and Rome was to resurface in Washington DC during 1851, but in a more humorous form. The United States Legation in Rome had been approached by the representatives of the Pope, who was prepared to share with other nations in contributing a block of marble (taken from the Temple of Concord in Rome) to help in the building of the Washington Monument. The official in charge of the operation, George Watterson, accepted the proposal, but a little later this was opposed by a Mr J. T. Weishampel of Baltimore, who interpreted the inscription on the marble (which read, 'Rome to America') as pointing to the aim of the papacy to move lock, stock and barrel to the United States.[24] Weishampel was not the only one to object to this supposed profanation of religious freedom in America, and a 'deed of barbarism' was enacted when a group of men (who were never identified) broke into the storage shed near the Monument and carried off the stone: they broke it up, eventually dropping its remains over the side of a boat in the manner of a latter-day Bostonian tea party.[25]

Records in England show that an Englishman called John Pope had settled at Dorchester, Massachusetts, in 1630.[26] It would be pleasant to think that this John Pope was related in some way to our own visionary Francis Pope, because the family name would then tie together two noteworthy strands of history in Washington DC. As a matter of fact, this John Pope of Dorchester *was* a distant forebear of the architect John Russell Pope, who, besides designing the Jefferson Memorial which stands on land liberated from the marshland of the Potomac across from Foggy Bottom, also built the most esoteric structure in Washington DC, once known to Masons as the House of the Temple, or the Supreme Council, Southern Jurisdiction (figure 1). This has rightly been called by an American historian of architecture 'one of the most vital buildings erected in modern times here or in Europe'.[27]

What is most remarkable about this merging of history with mythology is that ancient Roman astrologers had linked the foundation of their own city with a fixed star in Leo. This was *Regulus*, whose name means 'little ruler' – perhaps a reasonable association for a city that was to rule the world for so many centuries. The star Regulus is said to have entered the zodiacal sign Leo in 293 BC, and has been taken ever since by astrologers as the guiding star of the Eternal City.[28] Perhaps Francis

Pope, or whoever named the parcel of land Rome and the river Tiber, was interested in stellar things, and perhaps he even knew about this ancient connection between the star and the city whose name he adopted for the hill. However, what Francis Pope certainly did not know – and what no one has realized until modern times – is that this same star, Regulus, was also adopted by the early founders of Washington DC as one of their prime marking stars. *As we shall see, Regulus is one of three stars which link the federal city indissolubly with the stellar realms.*

It seems, then, that history-making and stellar mythologizing meet in the beginnings of Washington DC. One consequence of this meeting of dreams is very concrete, very tangible. It is a matter of historical fact, as I have said, that there are more than 20 zodiacs in the centre of the city: I know of no other city in the world with such a multitude of public zodiacs displayed in so small a space. In London, for example, there are presently four public zodiacs of which the Bracken House zodiac, in Cannon Street, is probably the most beautiful. In Oxford (England) there is only one – that on the Fitzjames Arch in Merton College which, by its very placing, should not really be called public. In Boston, Massachusetts, I know of three zodiacs – the two most impressive being the atrium zodiac in the floor of the Public Library, and the Egypto-Babylonian zodiac in the ceiling painting by John Singer Sargent, on the second floor. In New York, the most beautiful public zodiac is that encircling the statue of Prometheus by Paul Manship, in the Rockefeller Plaza. Even Florence – that ancient city which gave birth to the Renaissance in the 15th century – has only three public zodiacs.[29]

As we shall see, the mythology of the stellar lights plays an essential part in the foundation and history of the federal city. The deeper meaning of the zodiacal symbolism which radiates through Washington DC is so subtle that it has remained hidden until even today – secretly enshrined in zodiacs set in marble, plaster, concrete, glass and paint within the fabric of the city. This raises a number of vital questions. Is there some secret behind the efforts of the builders of this city to ensure that so many stars should fall to Earth? Why should astronomers and astrologers make so much effort to weave their magic art in this city?

Furthermore, what is it about Washington DC that, in 200 years of colourful history, has made it the focus of zodiac-builders, and, so far as arcane lapidary symbols are concerned, the richest city in the world? Could the zodiacs have been set in place to remind those who run the United States that the Spiritual World, which the light of the stars symbolizes, is all around, and may never be ignored with impunity? Or is it possible that the city is still embryonic – still secretly being prepared for some future time when the stars will be seen as the living mysteries they really are?

Chapter Two

> According to one of these [prophecies] the World is to end in the year 1881. The 'end of the world' is the end of an Aeon, Age or Circle of Time . . . It now remains for Scientific Astronomy to determine the length of this particular Cycle of Time . . .
>
> (4 March 1881 – note by Gerald Massey as preface to his work, *The Book of Beginnings*, 1881)

In Washington DC, the evening of 4 March 1881 was surprisingly warm. Top-hatted gentlemen and their elegantly dressed ladies were pouring into the newly opened purpose-built museum – the Arts and Industry building of the Smithsonian. Once inside its rotunda, the assembled rich and famous gazed in awe at the giant allegorical female statue of *America*. Their amazement was directed not so much at the statue herself, as at the splendid lamp which she held aloft in her right hand. This was the first electric lighting in Washington DC.

A single photograph of this statue has survived, and it reminds one of the more famous Statue of Liberty, which was completed by the sculptor Frédéric Auguste Bartholdi five years later, and raised on the pedestal which had been founded with a special ceremony on 5 August 1884, under the direction of William A. Brodie, during an incredible downpour of rain.

The giant arm of the lady in New York harbour held up a burning torch, and she had stars around her head, whereas the lady in the new museum in Washington DC, who also held up a light, had stars upon her shield; in each case, however, the message was much the same. The light of the stars around them was turned into an earthly light of liberty, to illumine the pathway to freedom.

Electric lighting was new not merely in Washington DC, but in the world as a whole. The eccentric inventor, Thomas Alva Edison, had made the first working 'incandescent lamp' two years earlier, in 1879. This first lamp, with its ingenious filament of carbonized cotton thread, set in a vacuum, burned for 46 hours. Edison and his assistants are said to have stared at it spellbound for its entire period of incandescence.[1]

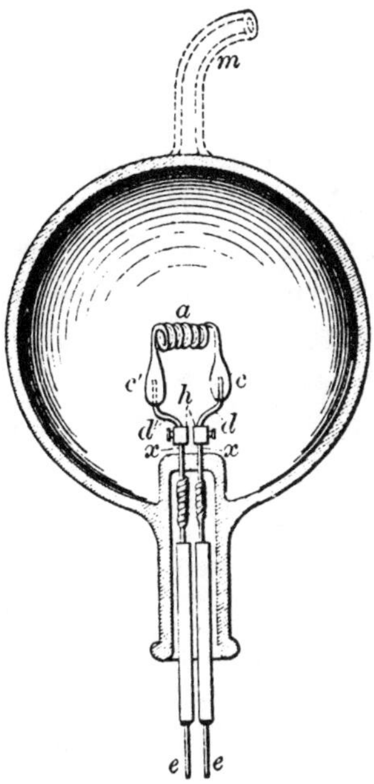

Thomas Edison wisely patented his light-bulb, on 27 January 1880. In 1929, when the largest office in the world was built in Washington DC, between Pennsylvania and Constitution Avenues, Edison's was among those famous patents copied and placed in a recess of the cornerstone of the new building, before the ceremonial laying was conducted by President Hoover. Although sealed in the zinc box inside the foundation stone less than 50 years after the invention of the bulb, the patent was already a paper memorial for electricity past. The largest office in the world straddled the site of the fortress-like United States Electric Lighting Company Power House, which had been built in 1897 to serve the city with electricity.

It was extraordinary how quickly Edison's invention was accommodated into the lifestyle of the United States, which then had a population of just over 50 million. By 1882 Edison had a generating station running in Pearl Street, New York, serving downtown Manhattan. In that same year, the State, War and Navy Department building in Washington DC, designed by A. B. Mullett, had been adapted to include electric lighting. Mullett's building saw another hint of things to come, for in 1899 some of the workers of the General Services Administration (the federal agency set up to administer and clean the building) laid down their tools – the first recorded strike of federal workers. They were objecting to the proposed introduction of newfangled mechanical cleaners, run by electricity. The Administration won: electro-mechanical tools were introduced, and the cleaners were given other jobs.

Back in 1881, at the Garfield inaugural ball, a journalist working for the *Washington Evening Star* remarked on the 'contrast between the whiteness of the electric lights in the rotunda . . . and the yellowness of the thousands of gas burners elsewhere'. Perhaps he had been justified in seeing the figure holding up the lighted bulb in the new museum as prophetic of the future – 'indicative of the skill, genius, progress, and civilization of the 19th century'. The museum itself was a manifestation of a similar cultured progress. Designed by the influential architect Adolf Cluss, and finished in that momentous year of 1881, it was not only the Smithsonian's first separate museum building, but also certainly the first building in the city to be serviced with electricity. This light did not have the power to illumine the future, yet one could feel a frisson of change in the air: at that moment, in distant Europe, Gottlieb Daimler was building his first petrol engine, powered by sparks from an electric battery, and, nearer home in Chicago, plans had been drawn up to build the first skyscraper. Without electricity to drive the lifts, architecture of such a kind would scarcely have been viable. It was clear to everyone that electricity had opened vast vistas on a new age: it was, in the minds of many, the most important contribution made by science to the 19th century.

This idea, that electricity would promote a new life for mankind, was endorsed in a thousand books and works of art. The Masonic writer L. E. Reynolds, who had an interest in astrology, had already seen the symbolic potential in electricity, and set out to explain the motions of the heavenly bodies in terms of its forces.[2] He was not alone in such endeavour, for electricity was used by many of those interested in the hidden world to explain the unexplained. But the harnessing of electricity to give light had happened at a very strange time: it had been recognized for some years by the esoteric Schools that a change in the nature of humanity was due, and that what was called 'intellectual electricity' would be the cause of this change. So excited was one anonymous writer at the prospect that he sketched an 'Electric-Oxygenous Pindaric Ode' on the subject, and offered it for sale from the Office of Mystics and Intellectual Electricity.[3] The author of this piece, composed on 18 July 1798, was of the opinion that this kind of electric shock would galvanize and enlighten mankind in the year 1888.[4] At that point, he foresaw that the later year would mark the time when mankind would make steps into a new spirituality:

> Then th'ELECTRIC SPARK clashes,
> With OXYGEN flashes,
> Expanded genius flows,
> Each gen'rous Spirit glows,
> And mortals to heaven advance.

*

Ordinary mortals might well have criticized the quality of his verse, but the more learned esotericists would have told him that his future history was out by a year or so. In fact, the great spectacle of the ELECTRIC SPARK, which might change the world, would begin earlier, in 1881. This would be the most famous year in occult annals.

Twenty years after the Garfield inaugural ball, the composer Francesco Fanciulli entitled the piece he wrote for the Pan-American Exposition of 1901 *The Electric Century*. No doubt his title referred to the newborn 20th century, rather than to the one just past – but it was an expression of what Fanciulli's contemporaries expected of things to come. Fanciulli is almost forgotten now, but in Washington DC where he lived for a number of years he was once well known. He had succeeded the most famous of all Washington-born composers, the 'March King', John Philip Sousa, as band-leader of the United States Marine Corps (alongside). In one bizarre outpouring of army bureaucracy which delighted Sousa (and puzzled those who did not know the ways of the military), Fanciulli was court-martialled for not playing enough of the popular marches of his rival.[5]

During the 1880s, Sousa's name crops up in even the most obscure corners of the history of Washington DC, for he seems to have known everyone involved in the cultural life of the city. He was to become even more famous in later years, when his piece, 'The Stars and Stripes Forever', was adopted as the national march of the United States (see over).[6]

In his fascinating autobiography, *Marching Along*, there are two photographs which are almost a silent commentary on the power invested by electricity in the future. Sousa was a friend of Edison, and on one occasion they had their picture taken together in a photographer's shop

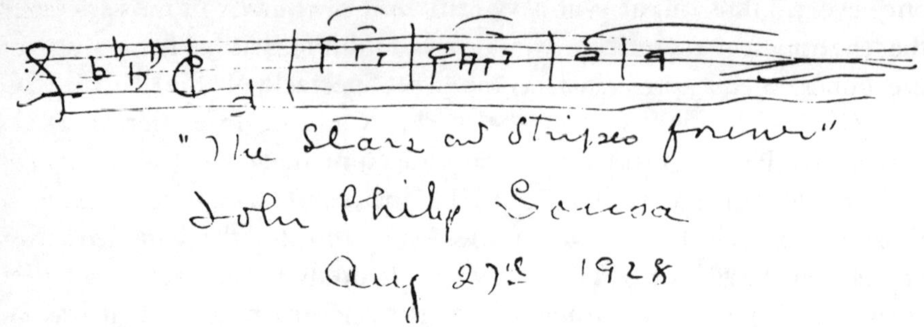

in Pennsylvania Avenue, the main thoroughfare of Washington DC.[7] Sousa reproduced this picture in his book. Below, on the same page, is another photograph of Sousa with the youthful Charlie Chaplin. Edison had been born in 1847 and died in 1931 – in what might be called 'the year of darkness and light' in cinematography. That same year saw the screening (among other masterpieces of cinema) of Chaplin's *City Lights*.[8] Chaplin's title – let alone the film – would not have been possible without the Edison invention.

Besides being an augury of an electrifying future, the new Smithsonian building of 1881 was also a sign of the times. The decade was starting out expansive and secure after a bad recession, and a programme of construction, almost unparalleled since the heady days of the foundation of the federal city, was transforming Washington DC. The founding of the Smithsonian Institution itself had been officiated by Benjamin French, in the presence of the President, James K. Polk, in 1847. Now, just under 40 years later, history, science and culture had become so important to the city that a mere extension was not enough – a new building was required to satisfy the cultural needs of Americans, and take the overflow of exhibits from the Centennial Exposition.

The statues above the main entrance to the new building were – and still are – ranked among the most beautiful neoclassical designs in America (plate 4). These, too, announced an expansive futurity born of this marriage of culture with science. Cast in zinc by means of a new technical process, and painted white in imitation of marble by the sculptor Casper Buberl, the statues had been hoisted in place just in time for the celebrations. Beneath the protective arms of Columbia, Spencer F. Baird, the Secretary of the Smithsonian, would shortly be reading the draft of his co-workers' account of the discoveries of astronomers in that year. He would report that the beautiful comet which appeared as 'an object of general observation' on 23 June would probably appear only once every 3,000 years.[9] Was he perhaps too much of a scientist to recall that the appearances of such comets were supposed to herald the death of great ones, such as presidents?

It seemed that the entire nation had resolved to make this Smithsonian event of 1881 the most magnificent display ever witnessed. The cream of Washington society was assembling in the museum for the inaugural ball of the new President of the United States, James Garfield. Famously born in a log cabin, his life story personified that fairy-tale rise from obscure poverty to influential fame that fed the popular image of the United States as a land of opportunity, a magical country paved with gold, and lighted with electric bulbs.

Garfield had never expected – or indeed wanted – to be President. When, in June 1880, the news that his name had been proposed for the honour flashed down the electric wires of the telegraph, he hesitated. He knew exactly what his youngest son meant when he pointed out that the cherries in their Mentor orchard would be finer than those in the White House gardens. Even so, Garfield shouldered the responsibility: he stood for election, and received a popular majority of Republican votes. From that moment, his private life was swept aside by a tumult of political intrigues, and by the importuning of swarms of people who thought nothing of invading his private house unannounced.

Within a few months, at this peak of his political career, he would die by an assassin's bullet. But, for the moment, it seemed that the whole of Washington DC rejoiced beneath this electric light, which everyone perceived as a symbol of the beacon that the United States had become to the rest of the world.

The Garfield Dining Rooms, which were opened at 908 F Street the year following the assassination of the President, were not a tacky play on his name. The establishment was set up by William T. Crump, who had been Garfield's main support during his short presidency, and who had been in charge of such things as catering at the White House. To ensure that the mortally wounded President remained comfortable, Crump had lifted his heavy body more than 20 times a day. In consequence, he strained his back muscles, and was permanently injured.

In those days, there were no official pensions for such injuries, and shortly after Garfield died, on 19 September 1881, his successor quietly dispensed with the faithful retainer. For want of something better to do, the unemployed Crump opened his dining rooms, which made 'a specialty of the serving of refreshments, dinners, or suppers to private entertainments or for balls and parties'.[10] His venture proved successful, and eventually Crump was able to open a hotel – serviced by electricity.

The allegorical figure of *America* with her electric bulb appears to have been lost many years ago.[11] However, another symbol of electricity – sculpted in the same period – is still preserved in a detail of masonry outside the museum where the inaugural ball was held.[12]

The American physicist – sometimes called America's first 'pure' scientist – Joseph Henry, had died in Washington DC on 13 May 1878. The bronze statue to his memory was not erected outside the Smithsonian Institution Building until five years later, in 1883. It deserved this pride of place because he had been made the founding director of the Smithsonian when, in 1846, the British chemist James Smithson endowed it with the then-fabulous sum of half a million dollars. Joseph Henry was not given to making pronouncements about art, but he called the Smithsonian a 'monstrous catafalc' – words which were later proved to be prophetic when Smithson's body was exhumed from a grave in Italy and laid to rest in an ante-room off the entrance to the Smithsonian.

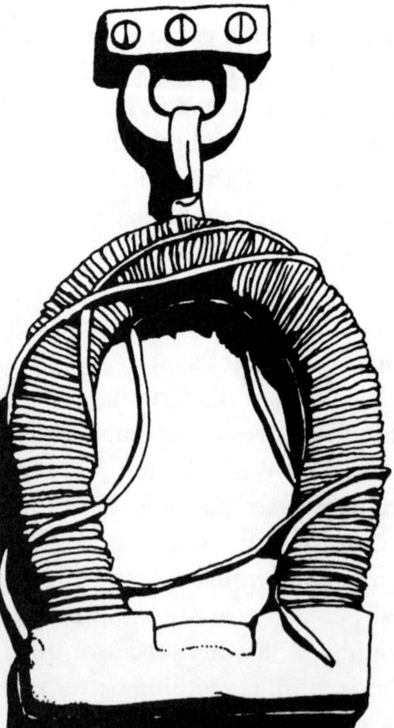

The sculptor of Henry's monument, the multi-talented William Wetmore Story, took pains to carve, on the classical pedestal upon which Henry rested his left hand, a bas-relief of an electromagnet.[13]

Undoubtedly, Story intended this as a symbolic reference to the fact that Henry, while professor at Albany College and Princeton, had perfected the electromagnet. It was, indeed, Joseph Henry who had invented the electric telegraph which had informed Garfield of his future destiny. In fact, Joseph Henry had taken his studies in electromagnetism much further than his more famous English counterpart, Michael Faraday, for he had made far-reaching discoveries concerning the electromagnetic properties of solar radiation and sunspots. These discoveries reflected his own profound interest in astronomy, which inevitably percolated into the activities of those scientists employed by the Smithsonian.

The statue of Joseph Henry (figure 2) was held to be important enough to warrant a dedication ceremony. In preparation for this, John Philip Sousa was invited to compose a march to celebrate the unveiling. Sousa called his piece 'The Transit of Venus March' – on the face of it, a strange title for a piece of music to celebrate the life and work of a physicist. The piece was played as the dignitaries marched from the hall of the museum to the special platform which had been erected for the ceremony outside the Smithsonian: afterwards, music by Handel and Meyerbeer was played, and after the unveiling itself (perhaps in preparation for an exceedingly long oration by Dr Noah Porter, of Yale University) the massed choirs from many parts of the city sang 'The Heavens are Telling' from Haydn's *Creation*. Was it perhaps chosen to complement one of Porter's own quotations from Wordsworth?[14]

The unveiling had been delayed by the poor workmanship of the bronze-casters in Rome, and then by inclement weather in Washington DC. Finally, a date was set for Thursday 19 April 1883 at 4.00 in the afternoon, even though it was realized that the President of the United States would be away on business at that time. It proved to be a good choice: the ceremony attracted an audience of over 10,000, for, as the official report tells us, the day was 'clear, mild, and propitious'.[15]

Given the context, this word 'propitious' is interesting. The ceremony had been timed so that the most propitious of all planets – Jupiter – was exactly overhead. Rising over the horizon at that moment was the sign Virgo: it would continue to ascend during the whole of the ceremony. The planet Venus, which had figured in Sousa's title, was setting in the west, and had just disappeared over the horizon – as befits a funerary memorial.[16] Did Professor Baird and William R. Rhees, who arranged this ceremonial, know enough about the skies to arrange the timing in order to take advantage of this happy coincidence of planetary positions? Did the two officials who reported the exact time of the ceremony with such care use the word 'propitious' in its original augurial sense, as a reference to the benefices poured down on Earth by gods and planets?

Indeed, was there something astrological even in the choice of the title for the music? Was Sousa's distinctive title, 'The Transit of Venus March', an overt attempt to draw a connection between the work of Joseph Henry and the planet Venus, or was it merely a tribute to the physicist's interest in astronomy? Or, again, was it possible Sousa recognized that, in the astrological and alchemical tradition, Venus was the ruler over copper – the same metal which had enabled Henry to demonstrate the power of the electromagnet and the electric telegraph? Did Sousa perhaps know that Joseph Henry's first telegraphic messages of 1830 were conducted along copper wire over a mile long?[17]

It is not clear why Sousa chose 'The Transit of Venus' as the title for his march. The phrase evidently intrigued him, for he used it later for the title of his third, final and worst novel.[18] One suspects that there may be some esoteric or highly personal meaning in the title.[19]

Transits of Venus across the face of the Sun are very rare: they occur in pairs (separated by about eight years), at intervals of just over a century. They are so rare that none have occurred in the 20th century, and the next transits are not predicted until 2004 and 2012. However, there *were* two transits of Venus during Sousa's lifetime, and one occurred during the time he was composing the march to honour Joseph Henry.

The first transit, which was not visible from Washington DC, was on the night of 9 December 1874: it was the one the astronomer Halley had predicted, using his new astronomical tables, as early as 1691. The second transit of Venus was on 6 December 1882, and was visible from the city during its entire six hours of transit.[20]

If Sousa, by virtue of the title of his work, *was* acknowledging the role played by Joseph Henry in revealing the electromagnetic properties of the Venusian metal, copper, the explanation is probably arcane enough to satisfy our present inquiry. From one point of view, it is sufficient that the music was composed during the period when the transit took place, and while a number of influential Washingtonians (amongst them, individuals personally known to Sousa) were being sent to various parts of the world to observe and record the transit.[21]

Although the official Naval Observatory plans for recording the transit of 1882 were widely publicized, an observation unit was also fitted out at Princeton during the same year.[22] It was here that Joseph Henry had been appointed to the chair of natural philosophy, in 1832, where he lectured on (among other things) astronomy and architecture, and where he began his experiments in the increase of electrical potentials (once again with copper wires) and on inducted currents and ether waves. The electromagnetic horseshoe which Henry constructed at Albany Academy, and demonstrated at Princeton, could lift weights up to 750 pounds. I wonder if this is the electromagnet shown upon the pedestal to Henry's statue?

The truth about Sousa and Venus may be more complex than the above suggests. As we shall see, Sousa was interested in arcane lore, and it is quite possible that when he gave his music its intriguing title he had in mind a more general astrological use of the word 'transit'. If so, then the music was probably composed by him in the full knowledge of a cosmic reality which had been reflected in the life of Joseph Henry himself. Remarkably, during the period in which Henry demonstrated his most important discovery in physics at Princeton, there *was* an uninterrupted sequence of astrological transits of the planet Venus.[23]

Henry is generally supposed to have improved the earlier (1825) electromagnet of the English physicist William Sturgeon by wrapping insulated copper wire around the iron core, the silk insulation increasing the number of coterminous wrappings of copper, and thus increasing the efficiency of the magnet. He made this improvement towards the end of 1830.[24] Between December 1830 and January 1831, Venus was in transit over four planets in the sign Capricorn.[25] If Sousa's title does refer to this cosmic event, then the symbolism he intends is as much alchemical as astrological: he visualized the planet of copper 'wrapping' itself over the other planetary metals in the sign Capricorn in much the same way as the copper of Henry's electromagnet was wrapped over its own metal core.

Fortunately, we need not concern ourselves here with whether or not Sousa had this correspondence in mind, or even whether the astronomical or astrological transit of Venus was intended in the title of his music. What is of interest to us is very simple, and demands no specialist knowledge of astronomy or astrology – it seems quite undeniable that there was some cosmological connection between the music composed to celebrate the dedication of Henry's statue and the electromagnetic motif on that statue's pedestal.

Did the universal man – the brilliant lawyer, poet and author, William Wetmore Story, who sculpted the memorial – exchange views with Sousa about this symbolism? This is likely as Sousa had an amateur interest in astronomy, while Story was actually a star-gazer, and a keen correspondent with leading astronomers of the day. Among his friends were the Brownings, whom he had met in Florence, Italy, and Robert Browning was (somewhat uncomfortably) famous for his knowledge of arcane things, and infamous if not for his dabbling in the occult, then at least for his dabbling with well-known occultists.

However, whether Story and Sousa talked together or not, the implication is that whoever commissioned Sousa to compose a march with this title had a profound understanding of astrology.[26] Furthermore, this person was in a position to introduce an arcane significance into the celebrations attending the unveiling of the physicist's statue. This suggests that there was some extraordinary wisdom directing not only the symbolism of the statue, but even the choice of title for the music composed for the occasion. Moreover, it suggests that this wisdom was somehow rooted in a knowledge of the stars.

At that time, astronomy had not yet become so rarefied in specialisms as to have lost its popular appeal: during the last decades of the 19th century, most educated people still felt they could follow intellectually the discoveries being made in the skies by astronomers. It is partly this which accounts for the wide popular interest in the transit of Venus, which even people in the street recognized as offering an opportunity for scientists to resolve the enigma of just how distant the Sun was from the Earth.

Diagrams explaining such principles of measurement, and predicting the course that Venus would take across the face of the Sun, were published in hundreds of books and articles. The excitement was intense: the planetary world was opening itself up to the newly invented refractor telescopes with quite extraordinary results, and discoveries about the stellar world were being made almost daily. This explains why, in his official report for 1881 (made for the Smithsonian in Washington DC), the astronomer Professor Edward S. Holden admitted that a 'record of astronomical progress for 1881 must necessarily be a very condensed summary'.[27]

His report dealt with the photographing of nebulae, clusters and comets, with new statistics relating to the Sun, and with the preparations he had made to study the transit of Mercury which had taken place on 7 November 1881. Even his dry report could not disguise the excitement he felt for the preparations being made in Washington DC to study the transit of Venus which was to occur on 6 December of the following year.

Holden's report marked the tip of an iceberg, for astronomy was a popular science. Coloured drawings of the vast solar furnace – the so-called solar prominences, sheets of convoluting flames hundreds of thousands of miles high – were being published, the finest being those drawn in the 1870s by Trouvelot at Harvard College. Samuel Pierpont Langley – soon to be made professor of astronomy at the Smithsonian, with charge over the astrophysical observatory in the Smithsonian Park – was already publishing his exquisite drawings of sunspots (see below), perhaps the earliest 'abstract' drawings known.[28] As part of his intense programme to bring astronomy to the masses, these stunning drawings were reproduced in hundreds of popular magazines and scientific journals.

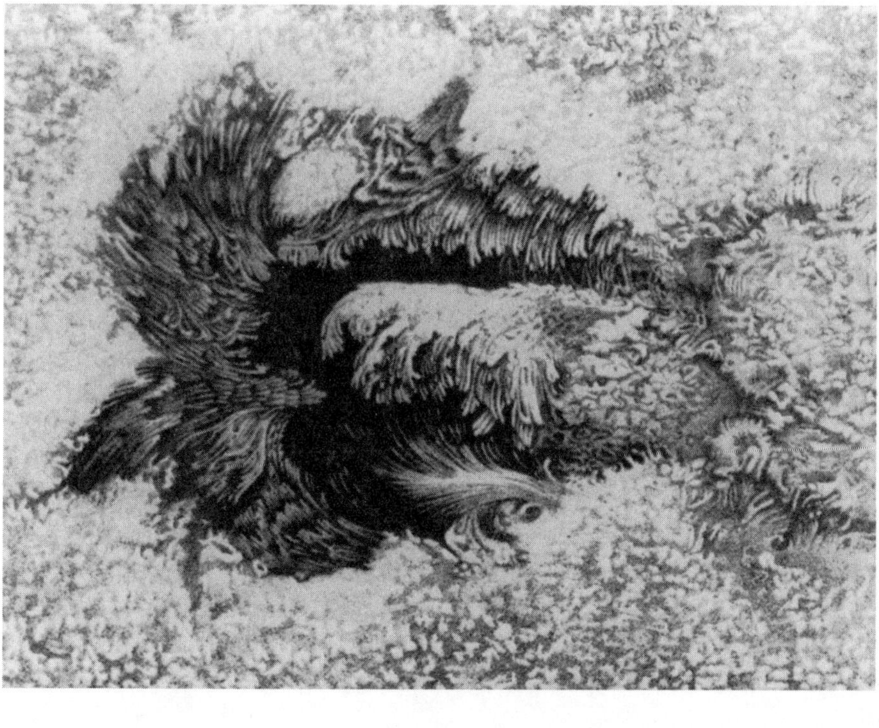

Even the surface of the red planet, Mars, was ceasing to be quite so remote as in earlier days. The discoveries relating to this enigmatic planet seemed to belong more to science fiction than to science itself, and mysteries were already being woven around what a handful of scientists had discovered in the late 1870s. By 1881, the surface of the planet was sufficiently accessible to the new telescopes for the Italian astronomer Giovanni Schiaparelli to begin to map it. His resulting chart was just about as adroitly abstract as anything that the Russian artist Kandinsky might draw, 20 years later. It was the Italian who first reported the existence of canals on the planet. His theories, which later turned out to be a combination of imagination and wishful thinking, were developed in 1877.[29] The exciting question sparked off by Schiaparelli at that time, and posed even in scientific works, was whether there was life on Mars.

Nowadays, popular astronomical books claim that it was Percival Lowell who proposed that there was life on Mars, but the fact is that the popular astronomical literature which flooded from the presses after the heady days of the early 1880s seemed not to doubt that the planet teemed with life. In fact, Lowell's *Mars and Its Canals* (1906), and the immensely popular *Mars as the Abode of Life* (1908), were merely exploiting the early theories of Schiaparelli and other astronomers. In this form of literature at least, Lowell was a popularist, riding a wave of popular interest: almost 30 years earlier, even such a circumspect astronomer as Professor Ball had been prepared to discuss seriously the possibility of there being human life on Mars.[30] In 1874, in a book which claimed to take us to the borderland of science, Richard A. Proctor – an astronomer and self-appointed scourge of astrologers – predicted that if life were discovered in outer space, then it would be on Mars. He recounted the story of Sir John Herschel's supposed discovery on our own Moon of the winged bat-man, *Vespertilio Homo*, as though this were science rather than science fiction.[31]

In fact, Proctor's borderland survey was tame in comparison with what had already preceded him. The clairvoyant William Denton had published his psychometric researches, at Wellesley in Massachusetts, in the previous decade – making clairvoyant readings based on the touching of rock samples, collected from different parts of the world. When holding a large slab of rock from Connecticut, he saw in vision a large animal which looked something like a frog, yet was as large as a cow. The creature had webbed feet, with five toes:

> The skin is bare, and spotted green and brown. It walks and sometimes hops. Sometimes it walks on its hind-feet, and sometimes it uses all

four. It has no tail. Its teeth are long and conical: they stand two inches above the gum.[32]

On 25 March 1869, Denton's friend Sherman, in a state of psychometric trance, claimed to have seen 'drawings like colored photographs' which were of Martians, some of whom had hooks on their feet, and had the ability to cover the ground very rapidly. These extraordinary creatures also had flying machines, rather like velocipedes with fans, which would fly not more than three or four feet in the air – though some could be made to fly over a Martian house.[33]

H. G. Wells' famous *War of the Worlds* (1897) may have been adapted in later film versions to show spacecraft hovering near the Capitol building in Washington DC, but even this classic was already merely part of a developing space-literature linked with the idea of Martian invaders. On the whole, the specialist astronomers sedulously avoided such nonsense, and decided that while there might be life on the red planet, it was unlikely to be human. In fact, the observers of the time were not even sure that there was water on Mars, and they were certainly not aware of the enormous and rapid fluctuations in temperature to which the planet's surface was subjected.

The impulse which such scientists as Langley, Ball and Proctor felt to popularize astronomy quickly seeped into the mediumistic circles which proliferated in both the United States and Europe at that time. The apotheosis of the science-fiction version of Martian life was marked by

Professor Flournoy's work with the medium Mademoiselle Smith, who, in 1894, claimed (in trance) to be in touch with Mars.[34] She was able to communicate with the spirits of deceased earthlings who found themselves on the red planet, and who could describe an all-too-earthly Martian landscape, set with oriental-style houses. More remarkably, the medium seemed to have the ability to write in Martian – in a script which suspiciously resembled in its grammar the French language. The script below, allegedly transmitted millions of miles from Mars, in 1898, says: 'My dearest, this is a farewell from thy child, who thinks so much of you . . .'[35]

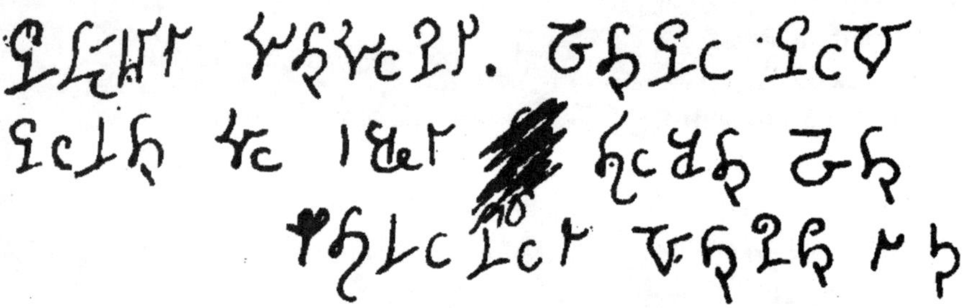

No mention here of the great mysteries – of the canals of Mars, dried up with age or still flowing streams of water; no mention of the white caps of the red planet, which puzzled the scientists of 1881. The Mars of one Martian (named by the medium as *Astane*) was too close to Earth for comfort, and revealed that, in some areas at least, Mlle Smith had little imagination. As Flournoy recognized, when writing in 1898, even the flying machines of the red planet 'will probably soon be realized in some form or another' on Earth. It is easy to be wise in retrospect, but one does wonder why the astute professor bothered to publish this nonsensical study of mediumship at all.

What was called the 'most important telescopic discovery of the century' was made by Professor Asaph Hall at the US Naval Observatory, in Washington DC, where, as chief observer, he had access to the colossal 26-inch refractor, made in the workshop of Alvan Clark and Sons. Taking advantage of a geocentric opposition which, in 1877, brought Mars in an unusual proximity to the Earth, Hall established for the first time (on 11 August of that year) that Mars had two satellites. The inner of these moons moved around its parent body almost three times in a Martian day. The satellites were named (perhaps unfortunately) Deimos and Phobos, supposedly with reference to a passage in Homer's *Iliad* –

reflecting the frequency with which Washingtonians resort almost automatically to classical literature for their mottoes, names, imagery and architecture.[36]

Had they not been so bound by classical learning, those astronomers might have chosen more appropriate names. Perhaps they could have called the satellites *Swift* and *Gulliver*. However, it was only some time after this extraordinary discovery that a few scholars began to reflect on what the English satirist, Jonathan Swift, had written, a century and a half earlier, about the astronomers his travelling hero Gulliver had met on the flying island of Laputa. These Laputian astronomers had told Gulliver that Mars had two moons, and that one of them revolved around its parent body in ten hours.[37] In 1726, when Swift had *Gulliver's Travels* published, no one knew that Mars had any moons, let alone at what speed they moved. As it is, Phobos actually revolves around Mars once in just over seven and a half hours, and Swift's insight remains one of the most interesting unexplained literary questions of English literature.

Deimos, which looks as much like an old misshapen potato as its brother satellite, orbits Mars in a little over 30 hours. This, the larger of the satellites, is about nine miles across at its widest extent. It is a credit to the power of the Naval Observatory's telescope in Washington DC that Hall could see these small cratered bodies at a distance of well over a million miles.

These, and other momentous stellar issues, were what occupied the astronomers who worked in the Smithsonian in 1881. What concerns us is that this interest in the stars poured out into the world around them – into the lapidary symbolism of the city in which they lived.

We do not have to wander very far from the Smithsonian Institution to discover further contemporaneous evidence of an interest in the stars and planets. Only a few minutes' walk along Jefferson Drive, in the direction of the Capitol, brings us to the imposing statue of Garfield (figure 3), who, in the same year that he was made President, was killed by two shots from the revolver of an unbalanced lawyer, Charles J. Guiteau, of Chicago.[38]

The night of Garfield's death, on 19 September 1881, Sousa – shocked to the core by the event – had wandered the streets of Washington, mentally composing a dirge, his 'In Memoriam'. This was played when the President's body was returned by train to Washington DC, and again when his coffin was buried in the cemetery in Cleveland. Nearly 50 years later, the same music would be played when Sousa's own body was buried in the Congressional Cemetery.

Sousa was among the immense crowd who saw the statue of Garfield dedicated on the road-island to the south-west of the Capitol. Just as he had known Garfield in life, so he had known the artist who had modelled this beautiful figure. The statue, set on its ornately decorated pedestal, was made by one of the most prestigious American sculptors of the day, John Quincy Adams Ward. On the northern side of the plinth which carries the statue is what appears to be an entire horoscope, cast in bronze, marking the signs of the zodiac and the planets (plate 5). It is perhaps the only such astrological figure on any public statuary in the United States. I shall deal with the secrets of this intriguing bronze cartouche later, as the mystery of Washington DC unfolds.

Had we wished to see another example of stellar symbolism, we need scarcely have left the new Smithsonian building. In one of the small offices perched in the upper part of the museum, the astronomer Edward S. Holden was already making notes for his annual report on developments in astronomy to the Regents of the Smithsonian, for the year 1881. He would observe with some pride that a new catalogue of 12,441 stars had recently been compiled, and that to ensure accuracy, each star had been observed at least three times.[39]

Alongside Holden's offices, the sculptor Casper Buberl had managed to finish his allegorical group, *Columbia Protecting Science and Industry* (plate 4), just in time for the inaugural celebrations for the election of President Garfield. It had been hoisted into place on the day before the planned ceremony.

The statuary is a tribute to the vision of architect Adolf Cluss, who commissioned it.[40] His allegorical Columbia – patently a symbol of the District of Columbia as much as of America – stands with arms outstretched protectively over two seated figures, which represent Science and Industry. Science is intent over an open book: the owl at her feet is Athena's bird, a symbol of wisdom, which (because of Man's ability to make permanent records) ranges through all history and time. Industry holds in her left hand a surveying instrument.

The hem of the cloak draped over the front of Columbia's figure is decorated with stars – the symbols of timeless eternity, set in a vastness of space. The starry hem is at an angle across Columbia's lower legs: the stars seem to point upwards, from the lowest part of the statuary group, where perches the owl of wisdom, up to the head of the female personification of Industry. It is as though the stars irradiate Industry with the power to transform that ancient owlish wisdom into tools of advancement for the good of mankind. The statuary assures the onlookers below that science, like the mythological Promethius, will bring down from the heavens great benefits for the future of mankind.

Even the metal which Buberl used to cast the statue has its own arcane meaning. In 1881, zinc was a metal rarely used for casting statuary, and its surface required painting to lend it a satisfactory appearance in a city already familiar with marble or bronze in sculpted works. Buberl's use of zinc was a homage to Smithson, whose bequest to the American nation had made the Smithsonian possible.[41] James Smithson had been the first to recognize (in 1803) that calamines were zinc carbonates.[42] In later years, mineralogists honoured Smithson's discoveries by naming zinc carbonate Smithsonite, and although this name is rarely used in modern times, the idea behind it lives on in the Buberl statue. In choosing the new casting metal for the statuary which represented sciences and the arts, Buberl was symbolizing through art the scientific prowess of the building's founder.

There was stellar symbolism to be found not only in bronze and zinc, but even in words during that momentous year in Washington DC. In 1881, the *Evening Star* – the finest of the city's newspapers – moved offices. It left behind the old building which it had occupied for many years on the south side of Pennsylvania Avenue, and relocated to larger premises on the Avenue's north side, on the corner of 11th Street. Business was good, and within eight years the management, at the behest of the brilliant editor, Crosby C. Noyes, had purchased adjacent property, razed the lot, and employed the architects Marsh and Peter to construct a splendid new building in the beaux-arts style, which, with further additions, still graces the site. The newspaper left the building in 1955, and went out of business a few years later, yet its name remains emblazoned on the marblework overlooking Pennsylvania Avenue.

Left behind also were the writings of the talented local reporter, John Clagett Proctor, who gazed with such sympathy into the lives of Washingtonians and the history of their city. He bequeathed us delightful snippets of arcane information which are still a joy to read.[43] It was Proctor's writings which first alerted me to the legend of Francis Pope naming Jenkins Heights after the city of Rome (see p.8), and it was Proctor who hinted at the profound symbolism in the fact that his newspaper, the *Evening Star*, overlooks Pennsylvania Avenue and the statue of Benjamin Franklin, the star-gazer and writer of almanacs.

*

In 1881, the planets were operative on a far higher level than any statuary or verbal symbolism might suggest. The year had a particular importance for those who were interested in the deeper traditions of astrological thought. Esotericists (of which there were many in the United States at that time) knew that this was the year which the great 15th-century abbot and occultist, Trithemius von Nettesheim, had predicted would mark a fundamental turning-point in history.

The Rosicrucian, Thomas Henry Burgoyne, one of the learned and perplexing esoteric writers working in 19th-century America, had already commented on the mysterious hypothetical planet, the 'Dark Satellite', which he insisted shadows the Earth, and which is linked with the undeveloped parts of humanity.[44] He informed his readers that, in the more glorious days of human history, known now as the Golden Age, the satellite was distant from the Earth. However, in the later Iron Age (through which civilization was now living) it was too close, so that its 'dark shadows became more and more bewildering'. In the year 1881, Burgoyne promised, this Dark Age would begin to recede, its malevolent influence having passed its darkest culminating point.[45] He was partly borrowing his ideas from the Roman poet Virgil,[46] but few of his readers would realize that. Most of them endorsed his enthusiasm for this new Age of Gold which would begin in 1881.

That it was to be an important year in the history of mankind was not doubted by the majority of people interested in arcane lore. In a rare book, which many occultists claim to have read, but few have even glanced at, Trithemius claimed that the era which had commenced in 1525, under the guidance of the planetary angel of the Moon, would come to an end in 1881. In this same year, a new era would begin under the control of the angel of the Sun, whom Trithemius named Michael (see opposite).[47] Far-reaching changes would result, for, in a previous age, the angel had been not only the institutor of many new arts, and the inventor of astronomy and astrology, but also of architecture – the very science in which Washington DC had striven to excel from its foundation.[48]

Trithemius – and, later, his followers – insisted that under the rule of this planetary angel there would be inaugurated an exciting change of direction for mankind.[49] The angel Michael was dedicated to the expansion of human consciousness, and freedom. Furthermore, it would be during the new Age of the Sun, which would begin in 1881, that the Jews would return to their homeland.[50]

It is quite certain that, because occultists were alert to the beginning of the new age, the year saw interesting changes in the history of esotericism and arcane movements. By that time, many leading occultists believed

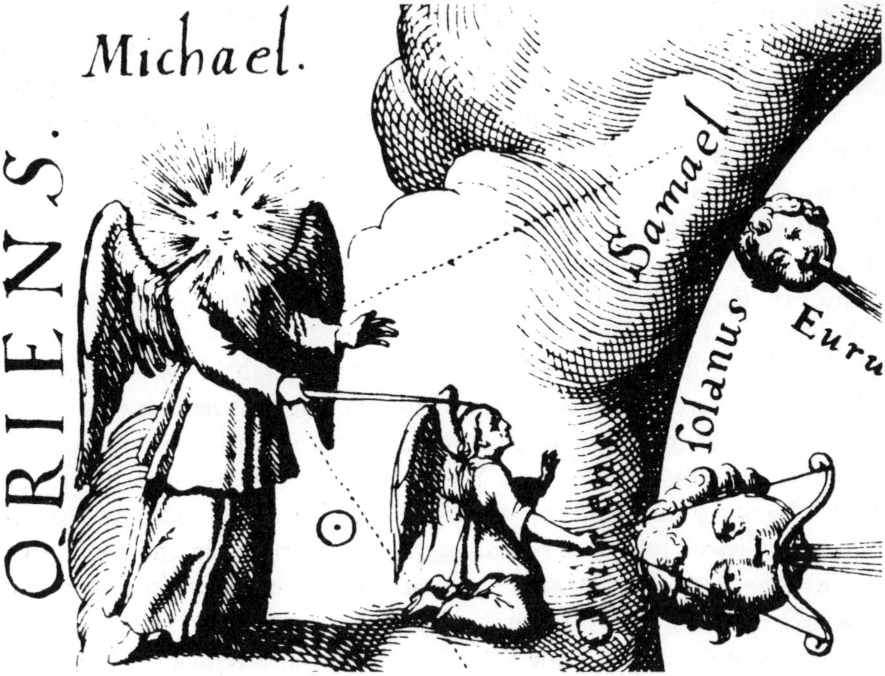

that the ancient Mysteries should no longer be reserved for the few, but should be made available to all who needed it. This gave rise to much heart-searching and schism among esotericists, who had, until now, believed that their secrets should be hidden from the masses. The protection of esoteric lore had been taken for granted in the past: 'People will always mock at things easy to be misunderstood; it must needs have impostures.'[51]

The Russian occultist, Madame Blavatsky, who had lived in America for a considerable time, was even then preparing her astounding revelation of the ancient Mysteries in her *Secret Doctrine* – a sequel to her study of the unveiling of the mysteries of the Egyptian goddess Isis, which had appeared in 1877.[52] She was sufficiently interested in the Trithemius text to recognize the importance of 1881 as a year of radical change.[53]

Perhaps urged on by such knowledge, the revisions made by the General Council of Theosophy (of which Blavatsky had been the seminal founder), held in 1881, formulated the notion that their organization was to become the nucleus of a Universal Brotherhood of Humanity.[54]

In Washington DC, Albert Pike – probably the most learned esotericist in the United States – was also familiar with the Trithemian doctrine of planetary angels. A decade before the great year dawned, when writing on the planetary angels, he had called them Amshaspends. Although he was familiar with the Trithemius literature, Pike spurned the name Michael, and harked back to an older tradition which named the leader of the angels *Ialdabaoth*.[55] Pike was using ancient terminologies from the ancient Mystery lore, but he knew full well from his wide reading of the French occultist Éliphas Lévi that Trithemius had called the angel Michael, and that he was the ruler of the Sun, and of fire. A translation into French of the Trithemius work on the seven planetary Rulers of the Ages is still among a library of books in Washington DC which once belonged to Pike.[56]

Actually, in 1881 Albert Pike's attention must have been on other things. His interest had been taken by the ancient Egyptian obelisk which Lieutenant-Commander Gorringe of the United States Navy had just transported from Egypt to New York, and which some scholars believed had hidden, for thousands of years, secret Masonic emblems beneath its base. After reading the description of the articles found by Gorringe, Pike came to the conclusion that they did not bear any resemblance to symbols used in Freemasonry.[57] In spite of this respected opinion, debate upon the monolith continued, and one Chicago attorney and scholar, Thomas A. M. Ward, made a translation of the hieroglyphics on the obelisk.[58] A copy of this translation is still in Pike's library in Washington DC.

However, this alert interest shown by specialists and scholars in the symbolism of the obelisk seems to have obscured the more pertinent question as to why, at this point in history, governments were troubling to employ such elaborate and difficult manoeuvres to carry from Egypt, to America and Europe, these massive monoliths. The flurry of literature concerning the magical importance of the monoliths, which has continued since the early 1880s, has never answered this intriguing question. Could those in charge of such enterprises have recognized the connection between the obelisks (dedicated to the solar god of the Egyptians) and the new planetary ruler Michael, who was ruler of the Sun?

Madame Blavatsky, writing at almost the same time as Pike, admitted that the spiritual beings who ruled the ages were the prototypes of the Seven Spirits of the Catholic Church: she saw Michael as the 'personified creation of the envoy of *Ilda-Baoth*', and guardian angel of the Jews.[59]

Helena Petrovna Blavatsky was often cunning with her secret lore, and the year gave her an opportunity to exercise this cunning. Although she was living in India by the March of 1881, she wrote a letter to the *Bombay Gazette* about the arcane significance of the year. She saw it as the 'correct number of the three figures which have most perplexed mystics and Christians for no less than sixteen or seventeen centuries' – including the great Newton. She insisted (in a somewhat tortuous argument) that the four-cypher 1881 was the equivalent of the three-cypher 666 – the number of the Great Beast of the biblical Revelation.[60]

Such numerologies aside, it is clear that whether, like Pike, one follows the Zoroastrian tradition, or, like Blavatsky, the esoteric stream of the Catholic doctrine, the Michaelic seven are very advanced spirits – well beyond the level of ordinary angels, and perhaps even beyond the understanding of the 19th-century occultists. Whatever names you gave to them, as Trithemius and his followers recognized, they are the builders, the 'Cosmocrates', who give new directions to civilizations.

Understandably, the fact that the leader of these mighty beings was due to take over the direction of Western civilization in 1881 caused considerable excitement in the esoteric circles of Washington DC, and of the occult world in general. A few scholars hunted among dusty books that mentioned the Seven Angels, and found little of worth, save a rare engraving (rare because it belonged to an esoteric literature which has not been widely published) of the seven planetary angels directing the movement of the zodiac (below), and influencing the life of mankind. It

is perhaps a good thing that the engraving was rare, for it was in a book which revealed – for those with eyes to see – all the ancient mysteries, mythologies, esotericisms and theophanies of the past in a series of arcane pictures.[61]

The Trithemius text, and the engraving based upon it, showed that Michael was a solar being, the ruler of the invisible *cosmic fire* to which the ancient arcanists had given many names, and it seemed not at all strange to the esotericists of the time that the year 1881 should see the first use of electricity in the federal city. All that really interested the arcanists of the time was the fact that Michael would work through cosmic fire, and through forms of electricity, which they saw as the workings of the sub-molecular world. They recognized that the new age which was to come would unfold new energies that would probably bring as many sorrows as joys. We shall have more to say about planetary angels and rulership in due course.

Even for those not learned enough to know of Trithemius and his seven planetary beings, it was as though the cosmos itself had announced 1881 as an important year. On the morning of 22 June appeared the brightest comet seen for many decades. It was successfully photographed by several astronomers – notably by the American professor, Henry Draper, in New York – the first time a comet had been recorded in this way. Scientists were surprised to find that even though the light of stars must have passed through over 100,000 miles of cometic matter, several of even the smaller stars were visible in the negative. This, they wisely concluded, proved the extreme transparency of the comet's tail.[62] The thing which seemed so splendid to the Earth scarcely had an existence in a material sense.

In 1881, Albert Pike's talented and beautiful friend, the artist Vinnie Ream (already famous in Washington DC for her bust and sculpture of Lincoln), finished the statue of the American naval hero, Admiral David G. Farragut. This was to be erected on 16th Street, in what is now called Farragut Square. She had won an open competition to sculpt the memorial, and it was widely rumoured that she had won more by feminine beauty and wiles than by talent. In fact, there may be little doubt that the model she submitted for the competition (though damaged during transit from her studio in Pennsylvania Avenue to the Naval Yards where the models were displayed) was among the best entered. Even so, the rumours *were* well founded – Vinnie did have influential friends in both the Senate and the House, and she never scrupled to use them. Even Senator John Ingalls of Kansas, though well aware of her feminine allurements, and recognizing her as the 'most delightful fraud' he had ever met, still participated in the political infighting to ensure that she was awarded the prize.[63] The modern historian Ruth L. Bohan, after examining many of the records relating to Ream's attempts to win the competition, could not deny that the young sculptress was selected at least as much because of the efforts of her friends in official Washington, as because of her artistic ability.[64]

In spite of the chicanery, there was an element of redemption in the work, for Vinnie's statue was cast from the discarded bronze propellers of the USS *Hartford*, which Farragut (below) had famously commanded with such extraordinary bravery.

A small model of the warship was placed in a time-capsule hollow within the pedestal of the Farragut memorial: it was a mark of the daring with which Farragut had led his fleet through the minefields and fortifications of Mobile Bay, in August 1864.[65] This had been the most courageous moment of a courageous life, for, in anticipation of reaching troops who, he hoped, would be able to cut off a tranche of the Confederate Army, he had decided to risk all by sailing over the submerged minefield. Almost immediately, his lead-ship, the *Tecumseh*, was blown out of the water by the mines. Farragut, now pushed to the lead himself, decided to ignore the danger, and somehow took his flotilla through the bay safely. It is said that so close to death were some of his ships, the mine cases could be heard scraping against their hulls.

The Farragut statue was dedicated on 25 April 1881. Astrologically, it might have seemed a curious day to honour a seaman, for there was an extraordinary gathering of planets in the Earth-bound sign of the Bull, Taurus. Indeed, the whole of April 1881 had witnessed a most remarkable and rare cosmic event in the skies, for there had been six planets hovering in the Earth sign for the best part of a week.[66] However, a discerning astrologer would have noted a meaningful relationship in the planetary pattern at the dedication ceremony, for Uranus was in the sign Virgo, and threw a trine aspect (the most harmonious of all relationships in the geometry of astrology) on to the planet of the sea, Neptune. Altogether, then, in spite of first impressions, it *was* a fine day on which to honour one of the bravest of all American sailors. Indeed, in contemplating such a chart, one cannot help wondering precisely who had such a profound knowledge of astrology in Washington DC, in that memorable year of 1881.

The redemptive message that Vinnie had intended by using the old propellers of the *Hartford* was simple and very ancient: the bronzes of war had been reforged into instruments of art, in a classical reshaping of guns back into ploughshares. Albert Pike, who had been writing love-letters and poems to Vinnie Ream for some years, would have likened this redemptive symbolism to the working of rough ashlar to make or reveal a perfect form.[67] The considerable difference in the ages of Vinnie and Pike had led to gossip and bad poetry.

When he met Vinnie in the Capitol of Washington DC, in 1866, Pike was 57 and she was 19. Vinnie was among the most beautiful women in the city, and certainly the most talented in the arts. Pike began writing poetry to her almost immediately, and their friendship seems to have been intense to the point of passion – if darkened somewhat by time's inequality, and Pike's own lack of feeling for the musicality of language:

> Darling! with what can I such love repay?
> What can October give to delicate May? –
> The afternoon hours of a waning day,
>   The saddening Autumn of Life's fading year . . .[68]

Whatever passed between them will remain secret, but one product of their friendship was a fine bust of the old man, which Vinnie modelled in her spare time (figure 4). In 1878, while she was sculpting and casting the statue of Farragut, Vinnie married the wealthy and brilliant Lieutenant Richard Loveridge Hoxie, who was in charge of the Washington DC Naval Yard sheds, where the casting of her work had been supervised. Her growing friendship with Hoxie had made Pike jealous at first, but it seems that when he was assured that the couple were really in love, he gave their marriage his blessing, and soon became a close friend of the Lieutenant.[69]

Hoxie was to play his own part in the development of Washington DC, for he was placed in charge of the water system for the city during the years of a strange interlude known as the 'Boss' Shepherd administration. During that time, Hoxie undertook many large-scale improvements to the city, including the building of underground aqueducts. In common with several other naval and military officers in the city, he was a keen astronomer, and was for some years professor of astronomy at Willetts Point, the postgraduate school for army engineers.[70]

In the Washington of 1881, then, there was a frisson of excitement concerning the beginning of a new age – whether it was one predicted by an abbot almost 400 years earlier, or one promised by this new invention, electricity.

Within less than a decade, hope for a bright new future – along with celebration of a distinguished past – had, as we have seen, drawn together a large number of diverse astrological symbols in Washington DC.

A statue of a lady with stars upon her shield seemed to augur another, more gigantic lady, who still stands overlooking New York harbour, with stars around her head. The larger figure realized the dream of a French sculptor, who liaised with a New York dignitary to ensure that the stars around her head would convey their message of hope to all who saw the statue. The planet Venus was represented in music, in a march composed by a native of the city, reflecting in its title an extremely rare cosmic phenomenon. The moment chosen for the unveiling of the statue celebrated by this music represented a propitious planetary time. A unique horoscope, clearly marked with zodiac and planets, was cast in bronze and raised on a statue dedicated to a president who had been assassinated in the city. A newspaper named after a star moved from one side of Pennsylvania Avenue to the other, and raised three versions of its own name to look down on those who walk or drive in the Avenue. A series of highly symbolic stars was cast in zinc as an integral part of the symbolism of a statue representing the District of Columbia. Furthermore, a besotted Confederate general, learned in the lore of the planetary angels, was writing love-poems to a female artist, who was for him 'the Star of one great love'; even as he wrote, his mind was on an Egyptian monolith being carried to the United States by an American sailor named Gorringe.[71] A scholar called Thomas A. M. Ward made a convincing attempt to translate the ancient hieroglyphics on the stone, to reveal their astronomical meanings, and published the results for an eager readership. An American senator who would eventually become the president, *pro tem*, of the US Senate helped a young woman to ensure that she, rather than her competitors, would be chosen as sculptress in a competition. The resultant statue was dedicated to a naval hero at a well-chosen astrological moment . . .

Who, in Washington DC during the 1880s, had the power to arrange and disseminate such arcane astrological symbolism, and to ensure that the statuary of the city should reflect the starry cosmos with such precision? The answer to this question, which takes us to the hermetic roots of Washington DC itself, hinges upon the one thing which bound all these people together.

Frédéric Auguste Bartholdi, the man who sculpted the Statue of Liberty, and the American William Brodie, who ensured that the gigantic lady was erected at an appropriate star-time; the official founder of the original Smithsonian, Benjamin B. French, and President James K. Polk, who had witnessed its founding; the artist Casper Buberl, who decorated the Arts and Industries building with allegorical figures; the genial composer Sousa, who celebrated such events in music; the unfortunate President James Garfield, and the sculptor of his monumental horoscope, John Quincy Adams Ward; Crosby C. Noyes, the editor of the finest newspaper in Washington DC, and his later journalist, John Clagett Proctor; the great esotericist Albert Pike; the naval hero who made his beloved Vinnie famous, the fearless Farragut; that other seaman, Lieutenant-Commander Gorringe, who brought back the hermetic stone from Egypt; the scholar Thomas A. M. Ward who read the ancient glyphs on the obelisk – the people in this long list *were all Masons*.[72]

The two heroines in this account of 1881 – Vinnie Ream herself and the portly Madame Blavatsky – were *also* Masons, as was the US Senator who had no illusions about Vinnie, yet helped her achieve her goal. Furthermore, private letters show that Vinnie's other friend, Abraham Lincoln, had intended to become a Mason when he relinquished the weight of office.[73]

Might we assume from this that the programme of arcane symbolism which may be traced in Washington DC was in the hands of the Masonic fraternities?

The answer to my question carries us back to the very beginnings of the federal city, when it was still little more than an idea in the mind of George Washington. Under his persistent and far-sighted direction, the city was surveyed, planned, designed and built largely by Masons. The drawing-up of plans for the city, and the recording of surveys, had begun in a small hotel in Georgetown – then a thriving port on the Potomac, three miles to the north-west of where Washington DC was eventually built. The hotel was called the Fountain Inn, and was owned by a Mason called John Suter.

Chapter Three

> Washington would be a beautiful city if it were built; but as it is not I cannot say much about it. There is the Capitol, however, standing like the sun, from which are to radiate majestic beams of streets and avenues of enormous breadth and astonishing length; but at present the execution limps and lingers sadly after the design.
>
> (Lady Emmeline Stuart Wortley, *Travels in the United States . . . during 1849 and 1850*, 1854)

In the National Gallery, Washington DC, is a painting by Edward Savage, which was bequested to the Gallery by Andrew W. Mellon (figure 5). The picture, painted during the 1790s, shows George Washington and his family at their home in Mount Vernon, gathered around a table on which is spread a large map of the federal city (figure 6).[1] Through the curtain which hangs between two columns there is a panoramic view, stretching 30 miles down the Potomac.

At first glance, this does not appear to be an especially remarkable picture: it would seem to depend for its fame more upon the subject matter than upon any great artistic merit. The grouping is stiff, and none of the family is paying much attention to the map of the federal city spread out on the table. I imagine that this lack of interest arises from the method of the painter, for modern infra-red reflectographic analysis has shown that Savage built up his picture as a composite from individual portraits he had painted of each person, looking into the middle distance, in the traditional way of formal portraiture.[2] One has the sensation that the map itself is a sort of afterthought – a painterly device intended to lend some cohesion to the scene.

For all its stiffness, the finished picture became very famous, if only because it was engraved many times during the late 18th and early 19th centuries – 'no engraving ever having a more extensive sale,' recorded the artist Rembrandt Peale. However, Peale could not resist adding rather wickedly, 'Savage had but little reputation as a Painter.'[3]

A careful examination of the picture reveals that its real meaning lies in the map, rather than merely in the illustrious family gathered around the table. Strange as it may seem, this bland-looking group portrait hides a great secret. The secret is so momentous that it has remained hidden until modern times, and its message may be understood only against a background knowledge of what happened in the years following the foundation of Washington DC, in 1791, under the direction of the Masons.

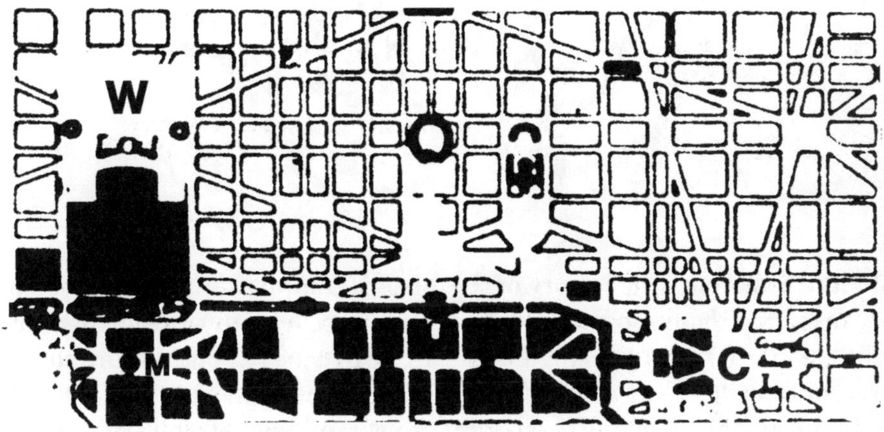

From what can be pieced together from historical records (some of which have been lost), the French engineer Pierre Charles L'Enfant chose the distribution of the three main sites for the city (above). These are what we now call the Capitol (C), the White House (W) and the Washington Monument (M). While the site of the last structure was changed considerably since those early days, the positions of the Capitol and the White House became the focal points for the city in the many maps which were drawn up during the next decade or so. The avenue joining the first two important sites (later called Pennsylvania Avenue) determined the approximate angle of the radiants from the Capitol. These radiants were imposed upon a grid of streets oriented on a north-south line, in a fashion which some historians trace back to ancient Roman foundations, and others to plans of Babylon.

As we shall see, the history of the 'plan' is complicated. Indeed, it is so complicated that in some respects it is more accurate to write of *plans* for the city, rather than of a single plan. All we may be reasonably sure about is that a plan for the city of Washington DC was drawn up by Pierre Charles L'Enfant in 1791, according to survey lines established a little earlier by the American, Andrew Ellicott, at the instigation of George Washington. In some cases, it is clear from Ellicott's working notes that the actual roads and avenues on the site were marked out to accommodate contours, and that this in itself fed back amendments to the form of the map.[4] In addition, George Washington and Thomas Jefferson contributed their own ideas, and in this way amended the original map considerably: Jefferson even went to the trouble of providing L'Enfant with maps of European cities which he (Jefferson) had considered to represent the finest ideals of architecture.

This intercourse of minds means that it is very difficult for us to establish who was responsible for different aspects of the plans which lay behind the design of the federal city. One distinction between the two early maps is that the L'Enfant plan shows no street or avenue names, while the plan which Ellicott drew up, after L'Enfant's dismissal from the project, gives names to the avenues and (to facilitate Washington's plans) numbers the lots, some of which were to be sold. If we bear this distinction in mind, we may be sure that the map painted by Savage, lying on the Washington table, is meant to represent the L'Enfant map – the result of the combined work and deliberations of the Frenchman and of Andrew, Ellicott, Thomas Jefferson, and George Washington himself.

Whatever its origins, L'Enfant certainly believed that the idea behind the plan was his own. Indeed, he was so convinced that the plan was his own that he believed he could do with it as he wished. When the builders of the city enforced changes upon his map, against his own judgement, the Frenchman's pride as an artist was disturbed: within a year of starting the enterprise, he had become so furious at the changes which were being made to his plan that he seriously proposed Congress should tear them up and start again.[5] Congress ignored his advice, of course. Time was short, and L'Enfant's angry outburst did not prevent further changes.

The design of Washington DC, then, though often attributed to one man, was actually the work of several, all of them geniuses in their own realms. Furthermore, the notion that Washington DC was built according to the so-called L'Enfant plan – though widely accepted in architectural textbooks – is something of a figment of the imagination, for within a year of designing the city, even L'Enfant was lamenting that his plan had been changed beyond recognition.

The irascible Frenchman would have been even more angry had he known what would happen to his 'idea' after his death. In later years, the city design attributed to L'Enfant was amended considerably – most dramatically in the early 20th century, when architects imposed their own artistic ideas on Washington DC – ironically, with the expressed aim of 'restoring' the city to its original 'L'Enfant vision'.

Andrew Ellicott and his co-worker, L'Enfant, are such important figures in the unfolding story of Washington DC that I must introduce them at this point.

Ellicott was born on 24 January 1754 in Bucks County, Pennsylvania. His father, like his Welsh-born grandfather a noted maker of clocks and astronomical instruments, bought a tract of land on the Patapsco River, from which the Ellicotts' flour mills eventually emerged, as the beginning of the modern Ellicott City.

Andrew Ellicott had been well educated by his father, Joseph (whose own father had come to America with his Welsh grandfather in 1731). Through the influence of his brother George, Joseph had kept a contact with the ancient tradition of astronomy. Andrew served in the army –

eventually rising to the rank of major during the war with Britain. At length, he became a personal friend of George Washington, Benjamin Franklin and David Rittenhouse. Perhaps this tie was strengthened by communal Masonic interests, but in the case of Franklin and Rittenhouse there was also an exchange of ideas relating to Ellicott's highly proficient knowledge of astronomy, which played such an important role in his pioneering work as a surveyor of uncharted lands. In his guise as civil engineer, Ellicott marked out the boundaries of such states as Virginia, Pennsylvania and New York. In 1785, he served in the Maryland legislature.

Undoubtedly, Andrew Ellicott was the most brilliant civil engineer in the colonies. George Washington, who had trained as a surveyor himself, was impressed by the young man, and invited him to survey the land lying between Pennsylvania and Lake Erie. This explains why Andrew Ellicott was the first to make accurate measurements of the Niagara River from lake to lake.

It is clear from Ellicott's fascinating journal – which reads partly as an adventure story set in the wilds, and partly as a cool scientific record of astronomical and thermometrical observations – that he had a profound knowledge of stellar observation.[6] Undoubtedly, this enthusiasm had been fostered by his father, who was so deeply interested in the subject that he built an observatory in one of the gabled bedrooms of his house a few miles from Ellicott Mills. Andrew's proficiency is evident from the many entries which intersperse his journals – a sample of which may be recorded from those taken on Union Hill, near the Mississippi, when he was determining the boundary of the United States, in May 1798. Using his six-foot Zenith Sector he recorded accurately the positions of the five stars, *alpha* Andromeda, Castor, Pollux, *beta* Pegasi and *alpha* Berenices.

In 1790, Ellicott was appointed by the government (undoubtedly at the suggestion of George Washington) to survey the new federal city: it is this phase in his life which interests us now. Two years later he was made Surveyor General of the United States. After his work in Washington, his growing fame led him into many useful enterprises: in 1817 he was appointed by the government to make certain astronomical observations necessary to the fulfilment of parts of the Treaty of Ghent. In his last years, he was professor of mathematics at West Point, where he died in 1820. His brother Joseph (born 1 November 1760) collaborated with him in the surveying of the federal city: this same Joseph later surveyed and designed the plan for what is now called Buffalo.

*

Pierre Charles L'Enfant was born in Paris on 2 August in the same year as Ellicott, the son of a painter to the French King.[7] In 1777, he obtained permission from the King to fight with the Americans against the British, and, once in America, was commissioned captain in the Corps of Engineers in 1779. In the terrible assault on Savannah he was left for dead on the field, but survived. At the siege of Charleston in 1780, he was captured and was not freed for two years. In 1783, George Washington recommended his promotion to major of engineers. Later, he undertook special duties for Washington in France, where (almost certainly being a Mason[8]) he organized a branch of the Society of Cincinnati, for which he designed its emblem. In return for remodelling the old City Hall in New York, then expecting to become the permanent capital of the nation, he was offered – and refused on the ground that it was an insufficient remuneration – ten acres of land around what is now Third Avenue and 68th Street.

In March 1791, George Washington commissioned him to plan the streets and public buildings for the new federal city. His struggles with the three Commissioners charged with the responsibility of overseeing and directing this endeavour constitute one of the great tragedies in the history of genius.

In truth, after the passage of the years, it may be difficult for us to understand the conflicts which George Washington and the Commissioners had with L'Enfant. There may have been some misunderstanding between the two parties, for while L'Enfant's spoken English appears to have been excellent, his written English was often excitable and verbose to the point of incoherence. It may have been this lack of ability to communicate, allied to his autocratic nature, which led him to believe quite sincerely that *he* was in charge of the design of the federal city, and that his direct responsibility was not to the three Commissioners, as representatives of Congress, but to George Washington. The story has been well told by many historians from many points of view, but not all the issues have yet been resolved.

As will be evident from what I have already said, it is no longer possible for us to determine with any certainty from surviving records whether it was the surveyor Ellicott, or the designer L'Enfant, who was responsible for the arcane significance of the city which will be revealed in the following pages. However, for the sake of simplicity, I shall continue to write of this design, from time to time, as the L'Enfant plan.

President George Washington arrived in Georgetown on 28 March 1791, and dined at Suter's tavern, the Fountain Inn, where he spent the night.[9]

He stayed in Georgetown for the following two days, discussing with various officials problems relating to the proposed site of the new city: to his intense disappointment, he was held back by bad weather from examining the future site.

About two months later, the artist John Trumbull, who had fought in the War of Independence and later built up a fine business painting events of that heady period,[10] met L'Enfant during his trip to Georgetown in May 1791. The artist found the Frenchman working at his famous plan in Suter's tavern.

When the three Commissioners in charge of the project authorized Andrew Ellicott, to survey the land for this great undertaking of a new federal city, it was almost inevitable that the engineer-surveyor should spend most of his nights in the same Fountain Inn. When the Commissioners themselves visited the yet-unbuilt city to investigate the early phases of its development and endure the autocratic insolence of L'Enfant, they too would stay at Suter's.

Even though Suter's was not the only hotel in Georgetown, it was understandable that these individuals should elect to stay there. As I have said, they were Masons, and Suter was a Master Mason. Indeed, a room in the hotel was used regularly by the Masons of Georgetown as their Lodge.

Suter's Georgetown inn had suddenly become a hive of activity in the otherwise sleepy port. During 1791 there was frenetic activity. The team headed by Ellicott, following a plan drawn up by L'Enfant (but not approved by the Commissioners formally responsible for the building of the city), had been setting stakes to mark out the roads and building areas of the new city.

The stakes had been driven into a landscape that was heavily wooded and, in places, very swampy: this rural quality would disappear only slowly. Almost a decade later, when the President's House and the Capitol buildings were taking shape (though neither was yet really fit for habitation), the city's main thoroughfare, Pennsylvania Avenue, was still a tangle of elder bushes, swamp grasses and rooted tree stumps.[11] Forty years later, when the artist William McLeod painted *A Glimpse of the Capitol*, it was still essentially a landscape painting, with the Capitol standing like some remote fairy-tale castle in a pasturage of grazing cattle, grasslands, trees and rough fencing.[12]

John Suter had died of cancer in 1794, but his namesake son decided to continue in the hotel business. Seeing the way the wind was blowing, he took advantage of increasing trade as the city developed and expanded by purchasing the Union Tavern, built in the previous year, on M Street, which was designed to become the main thoroughfare connecting the federal city with Georgetown.[13] He was not alone in such foresight: in the same year, his friend William Rhodes leased from Bennett Fenwick a building located on the corner of 15th and F Streets, to run it as the Rhodes Hotel: strangely, this was also to become linked with the name of Suter. After the death of her husband, Barbara Suter ran a boarding-house from Rhodes Hotel. In 1814, after the arrogant British officers had fired the major buildings in Washington DC, they insisted on lodging at this Suter establishment.[14]

It was George Washington's proclamation, dated 30 March 1791 and issued from Georgetown, which ordered that the ten-mile square marking the district should begin at Jones Point, at the mouth of Hunting Creek, to the south side of Alexandria.[15] It is this wise choice (which encompassed the river and river-banks) that explains why the early maps of Washington DC generally look like a bird's nest of criss-cross lines lodged in the cleft of a huge Y-shaped branch. This letter-form is made up of the Potomac River receiving the waters of the Eastern Branch, or Anacostia.

Perhaps such Masons as Benjamin Franklin, deeply interested in arcane lore, would have been amused by this aspect of the map (p.42). Doubtless, he would have recognized it as a form of what esotericists call 'the Pythagorean Y'. He might even have been inclined to see it as an elaborate joke. The Pythagorean Y is a vestigial drawing of a path through life, in which one is perpetually presented with a choice of symbolic directions. Should one move to the right, or to the left? Should one do good or bad? Should one be selfish, or generous? The Pythagorean Y represented all the dualities which the growing soul must bear with each passing moment of time. Benjamin Franklin, always alert to a good visual or literary joke, would have appreciated this outrageously open symbolism which supported the layout for a new city.

The southern pivot for this diamond shape was established on 15 April 1791. On that day, after awaiting the arrival of Daniel Carroll and Dr David Stewart (two of the Commissioners), the 'different Lodges of the town' met at the house of one Mr Wise in Alexandria, then made their way by the rough track leading to the area intended as the birthplace of the federal city. About 3.30 p.m., Ellicott – now revealed in the ritual as a Masonic brother of George Washington – symbolically confirmed the precise position on Jones Point, from which the first line of the district was to proceed.[16] This done, Elisha Cullen Dick,[17] the Master of Alexandria Lodge No. 22, along with Dr David Stuart, 'assisted by others of their brethren', placed the marker. Once the location was completed, a deposit of corn, wine and oil was made upon it, according to Masonic practice.[18]

It is highly likely that, among those who had participated in the surveying of this landscape prior to the ceremony, was a new associate of Ellicott – Benjamin Banneker, the mathematician and astronomer of racially mixed ancestry.[19] There is little doubt that Banneker was a good mathematician, but his reputation and ability have been greatly distorted by later writers and historians. Nonetheless, he undoubtedly had sufficient knowledge of spherical geometry and astronomy to produce tolerably accurate almanacs. He was certainly to achieve local fame as an almanac-maker in consequence of which he was dubbed, with respect, the 'Afric-American Astronomer'.[20] I suspect that it is very unlikely that the founding of a new city could have been undertaken without his erecting a horoscope to determine a suitable time, or without glancing at the prevailing planetary and stellar conditions.[21] Unfortunately, no such horoscope has survived. It is the appropriate planetary conditions attendant upon the foundation that leave us with no doubt that such a horoscope must have been cast, some time before the ceremony.

The lack of a horoscope should not disturb us, however: not a single document or contemporary record has survived this momentous event in the history of Washington DC. Not only are all the original documents lost, but there is no mention of Banneker's presence in the august company. Indeed, the only surviving contemporaneous witness of the event is a newspaper report, published 13 days afterwards (opposite).[22]

While any original horoscope for the occasion has been lost, there must have been a good reason for the haste with which the stone was laid, beyond George Washington's own sense of urgency that this rural landscape – rather than Philadelphia or New York – should be the site of the new city.[23] In fact, the cosmic setting on that day was so appropriate to the enterprise that one cannot imagine that Ellicott and Banneker – if not the three Commissioners in charge – were unaware of the stellar influences under which they worked.[24]

According to the published report, the group – consisting mainly of Masons – had met together at 3.00 p.m. They drank a toast, and then proceeded to Jones Point, where the stone was to be laid. When I walked from King's Street in Alexandria to Jones Point, it took just over half an hour, so I presume that the original founding took place between 3.30 and 4.00 p.m.

> Stewart at his right, and the Rev. James Muir at his left, followed by the reſt of the fraternity, in their uſual form of proceſſion, --and laſtly, the citizens, two by two.
> When Mr. Ellicott had aſcertained the preciſe point from which the firſt line of the diſtrict was to proceed, the Maſter of the Lodge and Dr. Stewart, aſſiſted by others of their brethren, placed the Stone ; after which a depoſit of corn, wine and oil was made upon it, and the following obſervations were delivered by the Rev. James Muir :
> " Of America it may be ſaid, as it was of Judea of old, that it is a good land, and

At exactly 3.30 p.m., Jupiter, the most beneficial planet in the skies, began to rise over the horizon. *It was in 23 degrees of Virgo.* If we assume that the unknown astronomer had selected this moment consciously, then he had seized on the moment when the zodiacal Virgo was exerting an especially strong and beneficial influence.

By this means, the zodiacal power of Virgo, which was called in later Masonic circles 'the Beautiful Virgin', was able to stamp her benign influence on the building of the federal city. Was this one of the contributing reasons why many astrologers have insisted that Washington DC is ruled by zodiacal Virgo?[25]

A few of the many Freemasons present at this ceremony would have been only too well aware of the profound implications of what they were doing. They were initiating the building of a new city that would serve not only the 15 states that had agreed to the creation of a new federal centre, but the whole of what would eventually expand into the United States of America. *It is quite clear that the ceremonial placing of the stone related to more than merely the founding of the federal district: it was somehow linked to the future destiny of America itself.* The Masonic toast they had drunk, prior to marching to Jones Point, had been quite explicit: 'May the Stone which we are about to place on the ground remain an immovable monument of the wisdom and unanimity of North America.'[26]

The land on which the federal city was to be built had not been absolutely desolate before the laying of the first stone. It was a thickly wooded wilderness of orchards, tobacco fields and swamp-lands, with one or two old farm-holdings dotting the land that would soon be examined for suitability as the site for the future capital. It would be examined first by George Washington on horseback, then by the visionary, Pierre Charles L'Enfant with his notebooks, and finally by the professional surveyor, Andrew Ellicott, with his marker poles and instruments. The land was already rich with history, but it was not the sort of history which usually interests modern people.

As is often the case, there were secrets in place names, but what the names evoked has largely been forgotten. When, in 1790, George Washington explored the area, and saw that it was good, the hill on which he thought of building the Capitol was called Jenkins Heights. Who was the Jenkins that lent his name to this hill? We do not know: the records which have survived reveal that a Jenkins family had lived in the area, but there is no indication that they owned the land. By the late 17th century, George Thompson and Thomas Gerrard held title to a considerable area of land which included Jenkins Heights. With mention of these early settlers, we go back almost to the first local pioneers, for George Thompson was the son of John Thompson, who accompanied the Jesuit missionary Andrew White across the Atlantic in the *Ark* in 1663.[27] At the time, the land was still occupied by the native Americans, though it had already been named *Terra Mariae*, or Maryland, after the beautiful young wife of the English King, Charles I. Though occupied by Indians who recognized (perhaps to their cost) that the lands belong to no one and to everyone, they were already a province named by foreigners. Amongst these was Cecilius Calvert, the Englishman who had become proprietor of the area in 1633. The deed of 1663, which granted Jenkins Heights in the name of Rome to Francis Pope, was bestowed in the name of Calvert.

The old names hover magically in the air, hinting at secrets long lost. If we were to look at history in the way of the ancients, as moral fables and spiritual instructions, we might find a quiet satisfaction in the story of a man named White sailing in a ship called the *Ark* to a land named after Maria, which is, after all, one of the names of the zodiacal sign Virgo. We no longer think in such moralizing terms, for they do not make much sense to us. Rather than attending to such sounds, we prefer to look into books and earth for our history. We think of history as stratifications in the soil, as a story long since overlaid and forgotten – when, in reality, history is all around us, and alive.

If you stand to the south-west of Capitol Hill, where Garfield's statue (figure 3) is located, you will be standing upon stratifications of long-forgotten pain. Your feet will be resting on a marble base designed to carry John Quincy Adams Ward's statue of an assassinated president, commissioned by his grieving army. The statue of Garfield turns its face away in studied nonchalance from the long-defunct Baltimore and Potomac railway station, where he was shot, and where a memorial tablet had been raised in his honour. The station was pulled down during 1907, in preparation for what one of his contemporaries described as the 'aggrandisement' of the city, but which others called 'the beautification'.[28] There was a kind of pain even in this undertaking. The Commission which oversaw the construction of the Federal Triangle that would replace part of the station insisted that they were returning to the 'plan' of L'Enfant. However, to achieve this end they destroyed most of the roads, avenues and building-lots which the Frenchman had laid out on this part of his map.

If you could remove the marble base of Ward's statue, you would probably find traces of the old brick-lined wharfage of the Tiber canal which skirted what was then called B Street (and which was later renamed Constitution Avenue). This made a sharp turn south, to run along a north-south axis at the foot of Capitol Hill. L'Enfant's map shows the canal very clearly. He had arranged for it to be dug to control the Tiber, for he had great plans for its waters: he had intended to place in this locality huge fountains fed by the river and its many tributaries.[29] L'Enfant's fountains never materialized, and, in consequence, the channelled but untamed waters wreaked their havoc with depressing regularity. In his diary, the early Washingtonian, Christian Hines, recorded graphically how, during one summer prior to 1805, the rain was so heavy that the Tiber flooded over into the streets, and several workers from the Capitol who had tried to wade through were swept away.

Below this herring-bone pattern of canal brickwork there might still be traces of rotten wood – the remains of the gallows on which felons were hanged in early federal days. In 1802, the murderer James McGurk gained notoriety when, on this very spot, he fell victim to the hangman: he was the first person to be executed in the federal district.[30]

The flakes of rotten wood from McGurk's gibbet may merge with the tips of the wooden sticks which Ellicott's workers had planted in the earth six years earlier, when they were staking out the avenues which now radiate like sunbeams from the centre of the Capitol. Below this wooden detritus you would have to dig deeply, but you would eventually come across the skulls and bones of Native Americans who had lived on these lands. Old records show that a village of tidewater Indians was once located at Carroll Place, near this spot, and it is known that they used the valley at the edge of L'Enfant's Grand Avenue as fishing grounds. As we noted earlier, some historians say that Jenkins Heights was the place where the Algonquins held their tribal conferences, but others insist that they met at Greenleaf Point: at all events, it would not have been possible to build Washington DC without disturbing the bones buried there long before the white man came.

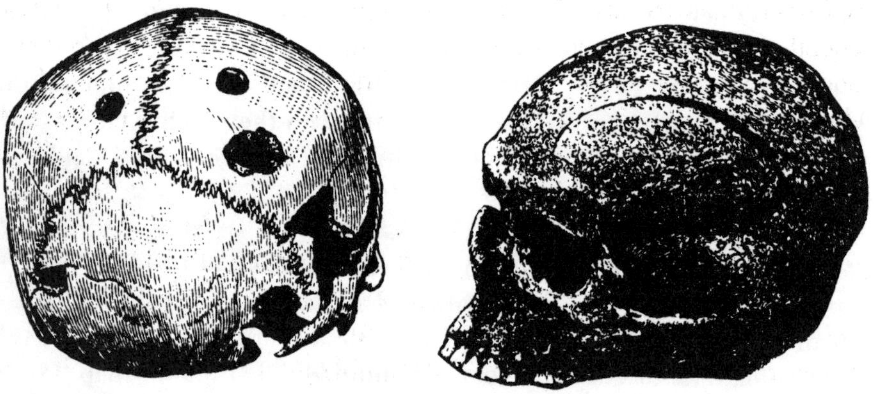

Among the curiosities once exhibited in the Army Medical Museum in Washington DC were numerous skulls of both races. Significantly, one which was identified after death – the squaw of Little Bear – and another of an unknown Native American, bore bullet holes and savage sabre marks. These were vivid reminders that over five million Natives were killed during the two centuries of European expansion in America.[31]

From this, it is evident that history did not begin with the coming of L'Enfant and Ellicott, intent on building a city. But it was a different sort of history that began to unfold after they had agreed a plan, as a working schema, at the behest of George Washington, in 1791.

The earliest reference to a future federal seat of government on the Potomac seems to have been made in a letter of 1783 from Jefferson and

James Madison to the Governor of Virginia, Benjamin Harrison. In this letter, they suggested that Virginia and Maryland might offer 'a Small tract of Territory . . . in the Neighborhood of George Town on Potowmack' to serve as the site for the new national capital. For some considerable time, both Philadelphia and New York were seriously considered as contenders for the honour, but George Washington wisely determined that the federal capital should be independent of any of the states it was designed to serve. In his diary for 12 July 1790, he wrote:

> . . . and about noon had two bills presented to me by the joint committee of Congress. The one, an act for establishing the temporary and permanent seat of the Government of the United States.[32]

This was a reference to what was to become The Residence Act, passed by Congress on 16 July 1790. In effect, the Act left a decade for the new federal site to be chosen, surveyed and built. The aim was to accommodate Congress by the beginning of the new century – on the first Monday in December 1800. It is a tribute to the labour and foresight of the early planners of the federal city that this plan proved effective. The public offices were moved there on 15 June 1800, and were settled in by 5 July, though the officials themselves soon complained of the want of proper accommodation for their own dwellings. Actually, these bureaucrats were secretly delighted that the move had taken place at that time – not because they were at all anxious to be in the new city, but because they were glad to see the back of Philadelphia, which had been subject to virulent attacks of the yellow fever.[33]

The federal city was an enterprise dear to the heart of George Washington, and he entrusted the making of its plan to L'Enfant, who had impressed him with some of his earlier designs. Washington did not realize what a hornet's nest the arrogant Frenchman would stir up in the close-knit community. Nor, I suspect, did he realize just how badly Congress would deal with L'Enfant, after his dismissal from the project. For years afterwards, the old man was a familiar figure on the streets, wearing his blue military coat, broadcloth breeches and cavalry boots – swinging, as he walked, a hickory cane with its distinctive silver finial. With the passage of the years, he became something of a nuisance, petitioning Congress each session for his fees. He died in abject poverty, dependent even for his food and lodging on the generosity of a friend, Thomas Digges.

*

In one of his diaries, George Washington describes his meeting with the proprietors of the land on which he hoped to build the federal city.[34] They met at Suter's, and after outlining his personal dream, Washington explained that he wished to purchase tracts of land which would, when taken together, be large enough to embrace both Alexandria and Georgetown. Eighteen proprietors signed the agreement to convey their lands by a proposed deed of trust, and few of them lived to regret this.

Almost 100 years after the idea of a federal capital had been mooted in Congress, a reconstructed map was painstakingly prepared to record the original ownership of the lands in Washington prior to this agreement, and before the surveyors were set to work on the federal city.[35] This 1874 map shows that the site now occupied by the Capitol was owned by Daniel Carroll. Half the site of the future White House was owned by Samuel Davidson. Pennsylvania Avenue, which would join these public buildings, ran mainly through the lands of David Burnes, who also owned the large stretch of land to the south of Tiber Creek, upon which the Washington Monument would eventually be raised.

Travellers of that period tell us that the area was beautiful – as lovely and sylvan as anything in America. A painting of about 1795, by George Beck, *George Town and Federal City, or City of Washington*, is probably idealistic rather than topographically accurate, yet it does catch the rural feeling of the place. It shows a rough road – almost certainly one of those built by 'wheelbarrow men'[36] – leading towards the land of Daniel Carroll, and to the ferry for Alexandria, sloping down undulating hills that border the Potomac. Perhaps the only thing which we might identify in modern times is the thickly wooded Masons Island, in the Potomac.[37] Beyond Georgetown, one catches a glimpse of a few houses dotting the hills which will become the federal city.[38] Among the distant houses are the remains of Charles Carroll's attempts to found a trading village, Carrollsburg, where the Anacostia joins the Potomac. By 1790, the Carroll plantation had extended to include Jenkins Heights,[39] upon which there had been a forest that Daniel Carroll had cut down to sell for timber.

The inhabitants of Georgetown had looked upon these rural transactions and transient ownerships with interest, for they were reasonably sure that the future of the federal development would influence their financial well-being.

Their own settlement, named in 1751 after George II – the grandfather of the British King against whom the Americans rebelled – had become a thriving port, and, for many, a useful outlet for produce grown in the Maryland farms. Indeed, because travel over such rough country was slow and laborious, it had been a most convenient port for those who farmed the stretch of cornfields and tobacco plantations among the woodlands and bogs where George Washington ensured the federal city would be built. The great man's plans had a profound influence on Georgetown, one which was mainly financial: the strain on local capital caused by land speculation prior to the building of the federal city cut the tobacco exports of Georgetown by three-quarters.[40]

Although things did not go quite so well as George Washington had expected, once it was reasonably certain that the area would become the site of the new city, speculators built a few houses, banking on the fact that federal land and property would soon be valuable. Shortly, a number of poorly constructed buildings would be erected to serve the men who were to work on the Presidential Palace and the north wing of the Capitol. A few brick houses, and a considerable number of wooden dwellings, were built very quickly – an augury of the problem which jerrybuilding would bring to the city, until regulations were finally brought in to limit the building of slums, as late as 1877.[41]

It had been George Washington's idea to do a deal with the landowners of the future site of the capital city: they would sell their land to the federal government, and participate in what was essentially a speculative scheme constructed around the sale of lots into which the land was divided. As it happened, this did not prove a good plan at first. At the auction of lots held in October 1791, only 35 out of the 10,000 available were sold. The plan which Washington had so carefully put into operation failed, and his Commissioners had to acquire loans from Maryland and Virginia for the public works to proceed.

The idea of selling off lots of land to provide working capital for building the city was enforced upon Washington, mainly because there were so few funds available from other sources. Even so, his plan brought him into conflict with L'Enfant, who had different ideas about the way things should be done.

In the early years of the Twentieth century, Herman Kahn, the Chief of the Division of the Interior Department Archives, discovered a tragic letter that L'Enfant had sent to the three Commissioners in May 1800.[42] This letter tells us a great deal about what L'Enfant had envisioned for the new city, and it reveals much of the frustration he felt that his vision was not translated into stone and marble.

The letter, which had remained hidden among other documents for well over a century, is in L'Enfant's inimitable English of almost incomprehensible obscurity. When studied carefully it is revealed as yet another spirited attempt to persuade the Commissioners to pay him for his services, as designer of the city. The letter tells the age-old story of a conflict between the powerless creativity of an isolated freelance genius and a powerful bureaucracy.

Many of the things which L'Enfant writes in this letter are of profound interest. It is clear that his difficulties were with more than the Commissioners themselves: one of his problems was that he found himself totally opposed to the scheme enforced upon the planning of the city by George Washington. L'Enfant thought that the sale of the lots should have come later – that is, once some of the buildings had been erected, and after the roads had been paved. Undoubtedly, he was right, but he did not have to face up to the problems which George Washington had relating to funding a project for which there was no adequate money supply.

My own interest in this document – which, I must emphasize, came to light only in the 20th century – is that it scotches one of the myths about the building of Washington DC. This myth (which exists in several versions) tells us that L'Enfant designed the plan, and that, with one or two amendments, his plan was laid down in stone and marble; that during the 19th century the builders of Washington DC lost their way, and deviated from the L'Enfant plan; that, in the early 20th century, serious attempts were made to rectify this by wholesale condemnation and rebuilding, in order to return to the sanctity of the L'Enfant plan. The conclusion to this myth is that Washington DC, as it exists today, is the brain-child of Pierre Charles L'Enfant. This is arrant nonsense. L'Enfant may well have been the designer of the federal city, but the city he designed is not the modern Washington DC.

The mythological version is corrected by L'Enfant himself, for even in 1800 he was not only lamenting the deviations which 'ruined the great end of the plan', but even pathetically suggesting to the Commissioners that it might not yet be too late to return to his original proposals. The pain of hurt pride and of fear for the future of the city shows through his clumsy words, and we may not doubt that he was writing in the spirit of 'one who feels for the Injury done to the Intention of the plan of the City':

> I take the occasion here to renew a warning . . . that unless . . . my notes and sketches, be Scrupulously observed and determined before tinking [thinking] of filling up or digging down any the by-streets – better would be at once to return the whole ground back to the plougher for maize and tobaco planting.[43]

While the Commissioners, and the later builders, did not adhere to

L'Enfant's plan, neither did they take his advice and plough up the federal city to grow tobacco. From the Frenchman's point of view, they did worse – they ignored him, and got on with building a city which had to be ready in embryo by 1800.

One problem with an idea as sophisticated as the one that L'Enfant created was that it was so integrated, so well thought out, that even a minor deviation was the equivalent of removing a card from the bottom storey of a house of cards.

'Having first determined some principal points to which I wished making the rest subordinate' L'Enfant begins his description of the theoretical basis for his design. The only rationale we are offered in the sequel is the means by which he located the site for the Capitol building. This, as we have seen, was the eminence called Jenkins Heights: he perceived it as though it were designed by Nature, to await a great monument. Since his words on the subject have often been misquoted, I insert here a line from a letter L'Enfant sent to George Washington in 1791:

the Western end of Jenkins's heights stands really as a Pedestal waiting for a Superstructure

His second principal point was the President's House, which has come down to us as the White House. The question which arises in our minds is, why did he locate the President's House where he did? What determined his choice of the angle which Pennsylvania Avenue subtended to the Capitol, and which is echoed in the angles of other avenues in his plan? Indeed, is it true that L'Enfant was the one who determined with such precision this primal angle – which was one of the acute angles that (as we shall see) Ellicott claimed *he* had established?

There seems to be no easy answer to these questions, but such answers as there are reach into the deepest secrets of Washington DC.

What were the main departures from the L'Enfant plan? The canal system he envisaged for the centre of the city has been filled in or converted into sewer systems. The two monumental columns – one an 'Itinerary Column', a mile due east of the White House, and a 'Naval Column' at 8th Street and K Street, SW – have been ignored, even into modern times. His proposal for a national church, on Pennsylvania Avenue, between the Capitol and the White House, has not materialized.

Few of the fountains he envisaged have been constructed, and only a third of the 15 state squares he designed have actually been incorporated into the city plan. The memorial he located for George Washington, following the dictat of Congress, was erected not as a human-scale equestrian statue, but as a gigantic reference to ancient Egyptian hermetic lore in the shape of the Washington Monument. Furthermore, even this giant stonework has not been placed in the position determined in L'Enfant's plan.

As we have seen, the building of the federal city began formally on 15 April 1791, when a number of Masons and local officials gathered together in Alexandria. Their purpose was the enacting of a Masonic ceremonial laying of the first marker stone for the new city, which would soon be called Washington.[44]

The original marker was almost certainly intended to be a temporary one, for it was replaced by a stone within a couple of years. This 'first stone' is probably still located somewhere at Jones Point, in Alexandria: a few years after the ceremony, a workman was reprimanded for moving it, or changing it. Later surveys reported that when the lighthouse was erected on the Point in 1855 it was encased in the sea-wall,[45] and the stone in the walled garden of the lighthouse seems to be strictly for the tourists.

Whatever its later destiny, the original was the first of many stones which Andrew Ellicott was to set down in his attempt to mark out a ten-mile square of land which had been set aside for the development of the Territory of Columbia. The marker stones were to be set at mile intervals along the surveyed boundaries: a count conducted in 1949 reported over 39 of the original stones still standing,[46] and their preservation is still discussed by interested Washingtonians.[47] Intriguingly, an earlier unofficial report had been critical of the general inaccuracy with which the stones had been laid: contrary to the general belief, the Territory of Columbia had not been a ten-mile square, and the stones were not even approximately at mile intervals.[48]

Even though the easily erected wooden houses were far more in evidence than stone ones, the development of the city was surprisingly slow. Statistics give a clear idea of its expansion. In 1790, there had been a handful of families living in the rural area which was to become Washington, while there were about 2,000 living in Georgetown. Although the speculators who had bought land on the projected federal area had been disappointed by the slowness of expansion and by the sparsity of returns, a decade later there were 3,210 people in the new city, of whom 623 were slaves. In Georgetown, the number was then 2,993, of whom nearly half were slaves.[49] By 1810, however, the population of the city had increased enormously to 6,771, with 1,437 slaves.

Such growth flew almost in the face of Nature. The deforestation contributed to a deterioration of weather conditions – humid heat in summer and intense cold in winter – but the tidal swamplands and the climate had never blessed Washington DC with perfect living conditions.[50] For some, the 'earthquake' which shook the city in February 1812 was almost the last straw.[51] More than one traveller during the 19th century found themselves wondering why George Washington had favoured this site for so great an enterprise. As late as 1835, the English writer Harriet Martineau was lamenting the difficulty of maintaining a social life in a city 'unlike any other that ever was seen, straggling out hither and thither, with a small house or two a quarter of a mile from any other . . . in making calls "in the city" we had to cross ditches and stiles, and walk alternately on grass and pavements, and strike across a field to reach a street.'[52]

The badly faded map of the future capital of the United States, attributed with good reason to L'Enfant and drawn about August 1791, has a notation alongside the location of the Capitol, designating it 'Congress House'. This designation, for what we now call the Capitol, is continued into a more famous map which is often (though wrongly) called the L'Enfant map. However, this second map (which I have reproduced on p.42) was made *after* L'Enfant's dismissal from service, and was in fact an amended version of his own, printed on behalf of Ellicott, in March 1792. Detailed comparisons have been made between the two maps, and it is quite clear that Ellicott amended many aspects of the original design – changing such things as the angles of avenues and the location of squares and circles.[53] On paper, these changes do not look very important (a degree here, two degrees there) but when such they are extended over miles of actual terrain, they become very significant indeed.

Careful examination of the changes made by Ellicott reveals that they are all, without exception, improvements, and are, more often than not, sensible adaptations to accommodate topographical requirements. This is especially evident in the adjustments he made to improve communications with Georgetown, which would surely have suffered had L'Enfant's plan been put into operation.

Although Ellicott did adjust minutely the orientation and the placing of squares along Pennsylvania Avenue, the one thing which the two men seemed to hold in agreement was that this avenue should link the Capitol ('Congress House' on the maps) with the President's House, affording a reciprocal view of each. Indeed, Ellicott (who was professionally very exacting) insisted in his version of the map that Pennsylvania Avenue should mark the line which joined *exactly* the centre of the Capitol (where the dome should be) and the centre of the southern portico of the President's House. One presumes from this that, although neither building was anywhere near completion, the portico of the President's House was to be an integral part of the design, while it was also intended that the Capitol should have a central dome of some kind, if not a massive portico.

Fortunately, as we are studying zodiacs rather than ancient maps, our own survey of the alterations which Ellicott made to the L'Enfant map can end here. The full genius of Ellicott's minor-seeming changes to Pennsylvania Avenue will become clear later.

L'Enfant does not appear to have left a record of the names he intended for the avenues which criss-cross his grid plan. However, it is safe to assume that the names now in use originated from his vision, since the 15 state avenues played a meaningful role in the symbolism of the city.[54] As one modern writer on the city, Pamela Scott, has pointed out, the distribution of the great avenues is significant, for the north-eastern state-names are clustered in the south-eastern quadrant, the mid-Atlantic state-names are in the centre, and so on. The three states which played crucial roles in the move towards independence (Virginia, Pennsylvania and Massachusetts) were honoured with avenues which cut across the entire city.[55] It was, however, the three Commissioners who determined that the federal city should be called Washington, and that the gridiron system of roads should be designated by numbers and letters.

In L'Enfant's faded map, and its later amendments, Pennsylvania Avenue was accorded the most important role, as mediator between Capitol and presidential home. In fact, the avenue was to play a more important role in the arcane symbolism of Washington DC than most people have ever realized. Initially, it became popular for good wholesome financial reasons: the visible link (opposite) afforded by the avenue between Legislature (Capitol) and Executive (President's House) explains why the earliest hotels in the city were located along its wide expanse, so conveniently close to the offices of both – but especially to the Capitol. In the years around the 1830s, when the city was beginning to take some sort of shape, those who could afford the rates would stay at the Indian Queen, the most splendid of the several hotels on Pennsylvania

Avenue. John Gadsby, famous for his tavern in Alexandria, where the Masons would meet, had established a less grand hotel in the avenue in 1826, when he converted a row of town-houses into the 200-room National Hotel, on the corner of 6 Street NW. It was here that the English writer Charles Dickens – who was always careful to ensure his comfort while sojourning abroad – stayed when writing about Washington DC.[56]

However, mention of such hotels should not give the wrong impression about the avenue in the first half of the 19th century: so far as architecture was concerned, Pennsylvania was in many respects like any other street in the city – a marble office, and a dozen good houses of brick, filled in with sheds and fields.[57] That stretch of Pennsylvania now overlooked by the two statues of *Past* and *Future*[58] outside the National Archives was occupied by the external stalls of the Centre Market, fronting the evil stench of the Fish Market. At the other end of L'Enfant's Grand Avenue, where Pennsylvania ran into Capitol Hill, things were even worse – a rank canal merging into the deep mud of the avenue itself. It is little wonder that Robert Ingersoll Aitken's modern statue of *Past* looks down so grimly upon Pennsylvania Avenue from a pedestal bearing the injunction, 'Study the Past'.

The impression one might gain from contemplating L'Enfant's map is that the early builders were ordered by Congress to get on with erecting their buildings along the lines laid down by L'Enfant and Ellicott, and –

given one or two later amendments – that was the end of the matter. Fortunately, the story of the building of Washington DC is far more complex, and entirely more romantic and creative than this. Although, as we shall see, the early architects responsible for individual buildings did attempt, with considerable success, to honour L'Enfant's masterplan, it took just over two centuries for an arcane schema to be established with the aid of interested Masons. In its final form, indeed, it would be a scheme so arcane that it would probably have surprised even those two Americans who were so deeply into star lore – Thomas Jefferson and Benjamin Franklin. Even so, working fairly closely to what the early designers had in mind, Washington DC *was* eventually turned into a city of the stars.

However it was designed, there is something magical about the enigmatic L'Enfant plan. Given its history, it is remarkable that it should have survived the depredations and cunning of speculators and iconoclasts during these two centuries, and given birth to one of the most intriguing cities in the world. L'Enfant's map may have curious origins, and the details he set out may have been ignored from the outset, yet his dream city seems to have led a charmed life. Perhaps it is because the map is faded that few historians have grasped the real cosmic magic behind it, and have consequently failed to appreciate just how romantic and enigmatic is the story of the building of this extraordinary city.

Eighteen months of planning, surveying and excavations were to pass after the laying of the first stone before substantial building works began within the bounds of the new city. A bridge had been built over Rock Creek to facilitate passage between Georgetown and the site, and the President's House was the first public building to be erected in Washington DC. A letter submitted 'by a gentleman' to a Charleston newspaper[59] offers the only surviving eye-witness version of the Masonic cornerstone-laying, which was held on Saturday, 13 October 1792,[60] when the Georgetown Lodge No. 9 of Maryland[61] gathered for the ceremony.

> On Saturday the 13th inst. the first stone was laid in the south-west corner of the president's house, in the city of Washington, by the Free Masons of George-town and its vicinity, who assembled on the occasion. The procession was formed at the Fountain Inn, George-town . . . The Ceremony was performed by brother Casaneva, master of the lodge, who delivered an oration well adapted to the occasion.[62]

Among the many toasts drunk in honour of the day (the first being to 'the fifteen United States') was one to: 'The city of Washington: may time render it worthy of the name it bears.'

It is in this newspaper report that the young architect, James Hoban, enters the public history of the city. Shortly before that time, Hoban had been living in Charleston, after emigrating from Ireland: he was already well known for his design of the South Carolina State Capitol. The date when Hoban became a Mason is not on record, but in the year following the laying of the cornerstone for the President's House he would become Worshipful Master of Georgetown Lodge No. 9. He came to the notice of those directing the founding of the city by winning a competition to design the President's House (below), and was certainly a speculative Mason at that time.[63]

Most of the walls of Hoban's original building have survived, though it has been found necessary to strengthen the foundations in modern times. This cannot be said of the interior: when the British burned the President's House in 1814, the innards were gutted and the walls badly damaged. Hoban was commissioned to undertake the extensive rebuilding work, and it was he who arranged for the external walls to be painted white to hide the scorch marks. This, as every American schoolchild will tell you, is the reason why the President's House was eventually called the White House.[64]

The story of the burning of the President's House is not one which should make Englishmen proud, yet it is equally true that the events leading up to this conflagration, and the even more shameful burning of the Capitol, are among those which most Washingtonians are anxious to forget.

The so-called 'defence' of Washington, under the command of the ill-prepared General Winder, was not the proudest moment in the history of Washington DC.[65] Almost no resistance was offered to the enemy, and when the cautious British general, Robert Ross, reached the city, he looked in vain for an officer to accept the terms of surrender.[66] The British marched into Washington DC in the evening, and Admiral Cockburn and his officers ate and drank in the White House before setting fire to it, leaving the walls cracked and blackened with smoke. The night sky was red with fires from public buildings, of which only the patent office was saved: 'The spectators stood in awful silence, the city was alight and the heavens reddened with the blaze,' wrote Margaret Smith, who had witnessed the destruction.[67] In spite of these 'usages of war', the British were otherwise restrained, and damaged few of the private dwellings.

Whatever this later history, Hoban's name was among those engraved upon the polished brass plate which was laid under the cornerstone of the President's House, set on the foundations that had been dug into the earth. Modern research with metal-detecting instruments has shown that the plate is still *in situ* and it is reasonable to assume that, even now, it records the day of foundation and the names of the officiating Masons.[68]

These events happened a long time ago, and any horoscopes cast for the foundations have not survived. However, in those days it was commonplace to relate new enterprises to the skies, as though seeking the benediction of gods, and it would not be inappropriate to resurrect such charts. Had the two horoscopes for the foundation of the federal city and for its first building survived, they would probably have looked like the two opposite.[69] The first is the chart for the founding of the federal city, in April 1791, the second that for the founding of the White House, in October 1792.

The two figures will not reveal much to those unacquainted with astrology, but there is no need to be perplexed by them. My purpose in reproducing these charts is to show the remarkable correspondence between them – a correspondence which can be grasped even by the non-astrologer.

Let us consider the second chart first. In the arch of skies on the day the foundation stone for the White House was laid, there was a most interesting conjunction. Shortly before noon, the Moon had entered the

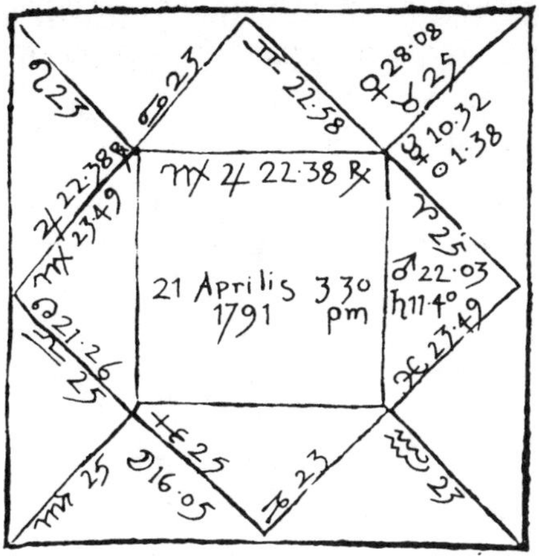

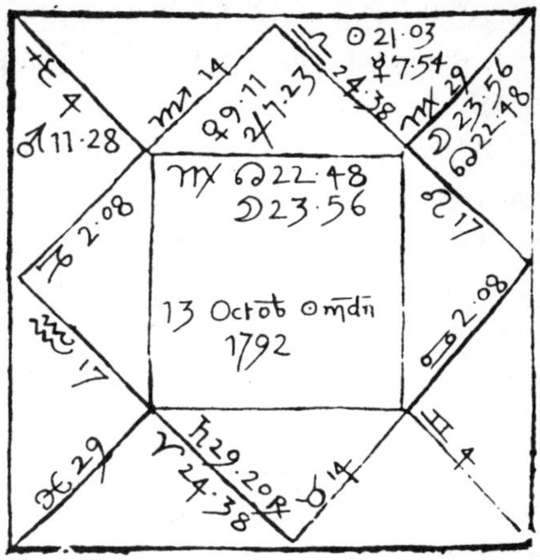

same degree as the Dragon's Head (a node of the Moon). *Both planet and node were in 23 degrees of Virgo.*[70] This close relationship is shown in the top of the central panel of the figure to the right:

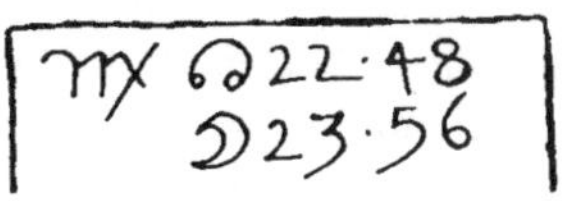

means: Virgo in: Dragon's Head 22.48
Moon 23.56

Now, incredible as it may appear, 23 degrees of Virgo was precisely the same as that occupied by Jupiter on the day the federal city foundation stone was laid.

This fact is recorded in the top of the central panel of the first figure:

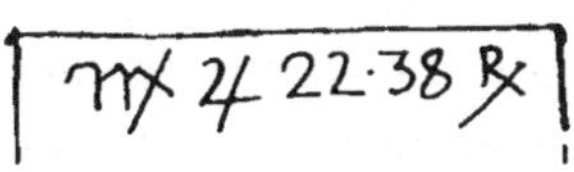

means: Virgo in: Jupiter 22.38 retrograde*

What the charts demonstrate is that a chart cast for 1791, and one for 1792, are related by a single degree, in Virgo. The chances of the correspondence being mere coincidence are so remote that we must assume that *whoever was directing the planning of Washington DC not only had a considerable knowledge of astrology, but had a vested interest in emphasizing the role of the sign Virgo.*

Time and time again, as we study the Masonic involvement in the building of this city, through almost two centuries, we shall see emphasis

*Do not concern yourself here with what 'retrograde' means.

placed on this sign Virgo. Time and time again, we shall see that a knowledge of the stars played an important part in every stage of the creative phases in the construction of the city. Indeed, as the story of Washington DC unfolds, we will be forced to the conclusion that the 13 approximately straight lines of avenues which L'Enfant planned for the city were symbolic of the stripes of the national flag, laid out to receive the impress of the stars.

Chapter Four

What, then, is this hidden language, and by what means can we, on earth, not only read heaven's golden alphabet but read the lessons, warnings and revelations aright?

(Thomas H. Burgoyne, *Celestial Dynamics: a Course of Astro-Metaphysical Study*, 1896, p.24.)

In August 1782, George Washington was in camp with his army at Newburgh, on the Hudson, directing the terrible war against Britain. He had just received, as a token of the admiration in which he was held in France, a gift from an old friend and brother Mason, Elkanah Watson, who lived in Nantes, in France.[1] Watson had sent him a lambskin apron, decorated with Masonic symbols. It has often been wrongly claimed that this was the apron worn by Washington at the ceremonial laying of the cornerstone of the Capitol of the United States of America, in 1793. However, on that occasion, Washington wore another gift from France – the apron presented to him in 1784 by the French general, Lafayette, which had been especially embroidered by the general's wife.

The design (see over) consists of a number of Masonic symbols – the radiant eye, which some call the 'Eye of Providence'; the Sun and Moon; the seven steps leading to the three primal symbols of Masonry, the open book, the compasses and the square. Between the two central columns are other symbols – the trowel, the ladder, the geometric representation of Euclid's theorem, and so on. At the bottom of the distinctive squared floor is a coffin from which a plant appears to sprout. Few people could fail to recognize this apron as 'Masonic', but I wonder how many people would understand just what those symbols mean?

An early wood engraving depicts Washington marching behind the

Masonic banner of Alexandria Lodge No. 22. His face, like the design on the apron he wears, is indistinguishable, but the 22 on the banner is quite clear: by a strange coincidence, it was this same Lodge which eventually inherited – and still possesses – the apron given to Washington by Elkanah Watson.[2]

The print which brings together this confluence of apron and Lodge is probably the most famous wood engraving relating to the early days of Washington DC (see opposite). It shows the procession making its way to the site of the future Capitol where George Washington will lay the cornerstone, standing in a trench cut into the south-east of the building site. The engraving is highly imaginative – perhaps because it was cut long after the event – and while the procession of Masons might have been portrayed with some accuracy, the houses behind were not.[3] In 1793, Washington would have been at best a shanty town, scattered around the slopes of Jenkins Heights on which the Capitol was built. All around, there were marshes and undrained land. Whichever paved street this procession of Masons marched along, it was not in the federal city, save in the imagination of the artist. Perhaps, indeed, the processional is

shown not in the federal city at all, as so many historians have surmised, but at its initial gathering, in Alexandria.

Be that as it may, there was one curious omission from the Masonic parade which made its way to the site of the Capitol on that day in September 1793. The first Masonic Lodge to have been formed within the federal city – the Federal Lodge No. 15 – did not join the parade. However, the Potomac Lodge No. 9, working from nearby Georgetown (and like the Federal, subordinate to the Grand Lodge of Maryland), *was* in the procession.

The Federal Lodge No. 15, with James Hoban as the Worshipful Master, had been formed in consequence of a petition submitted only a few days earlier, on 6 September, by three Ancient York Masons. The petition was granted on that same day by the Grand Lodge. One presumes that the Lodge had been formed precisely to ensure that a Federal group would attend the cornerstone ceremony, which had been widely advertised in Maryland and Columbia.[4] However, while the published records show that the three officers of the new Lodge – James Hoban, Clotworthy Stephenson and Andrew Eustace – were present at the ceremony, these same records do not show Federal Lodge No. 15 as taking part in the processional.[5]

The presence of the youthful Irish immigrant Hoban was more than a demand of Masonic protocol, for he was to be one of the architects of the Capitol, and was already architect of the unfinished President's House, to the west of the Capitol. That the Federal Lodge No.15 existed at all is significant. In particular, the fact that a Lodge had been created on 6 September indicates that not only were efforts being made to ensure that the new federal city was consecrated to the heavens, by way of a satisfactory foundation chart and ceremony, but that preparations had been made for the future spiritual life of the new city, in the form of a Masonic Lodge.

The horoscope for the granting of the charter for this first federal city Lodge is not without interest. I imagine that the petition must have been presented shortly after tea-time, when the Moon was still in Virgo. This meant that the chart had three planets (Sun, Moon and Mercury) in Virgo, along with the Dragon's Head, the *Caput draconis*. Perhaps it is merely accidental that the Latin name of this latter node is *Caput* – the word from which *Capital* and *Capitol* derive.[6]

George Washington probably never knew just how close he had been to losing the commanding site of Jenkins Heights for the Capitol building of his new city. Less than a decade before he rode over the land, dreaming of the splendid city which would be raised in the area, the richly wooded hill on which he finally located the Capitol had been proposed as the site for a school.

In 1784, Daniel of Duddington owned Jenkins Heights, and in the course of that year had proposed to his relative, John Carroll, that it would make an excellent location for the new college which the latter was anxious to build. Carroll – who was to become the first bishop of the American Catholic Church – turned down the gift, as it seemed to him that the spot was too far away from Georgetown to make a good boarding school for boys.[7] This story is illuminating, for it shows what foresight George Washington had: where lesser men would reject Jenkins Heights as being too inaccessible for a school or college, he could adopt it as the centre for a nation.

The design for the Capitol had been open to public competition. The chosen design was that drawn up by an amateur architect and professional physician, Dr William Thornton. However, the designs of the Parisian, Stephen Hallet, had impressed both George Washington and Jefferson.[8] Thornton, although a speculative Mason,[9] was not a practising architect, and from the outset his plan was criticized on very practical grounds by the only two trained architects involved – Hallet and James Hoban. Hoban was appointed superintendent on 21 November 1793, while Hallet was appointed his assistant – both supposedly to supervise the execution of Thornton's plan, which began to reveal difficulties from the outset.

Before the genius of the Mason Benjamin Latrobe[10] was released on the Capitol, a compromise had been worked out by which Hallet amended Thornton's design. This explains why Hallet's name, as well as that of Hoban,[11] was engraved on the silver plate that was placed upon the cornerstone which the Masons laid with such pomp and ceremony on 18 September, even though Hallet was replaced (in 1795) by the English-trained architect George Hadfield.[12]

The formal laying of a cornerstone was no new thing, even in America. It was already a ritual sanctified by Masonic tradition, a throwback to an age when it was believed that all human activities were overseen by the gods. In essence, the cornerstone ceremonial was designed not only to gain the approval of the spiritual beings, but also to ensure that these were content that the building was being brought into the world at the right time. That is one reason why it was a commonplace for those designing cornerstone rituals to examine the time of the ceremonial in the light of astrology.

In discussing the rituals used by Freemasons in respect of the ceremonial cornerstone and dedication of the Freemasons' Hall in London, in 1776, John Fellows traces them to the ancient Romans. He mentions that the writer Plutarch (who did more than most ancient writers to reveal the Mysteries of the ancient Schools of Initiation) recorded that Romulus, before laying the foundation of Rome, sent for men from Etruria, to find out how the ceremony of founding should be conducted:

> they consulted the gods, to know if the enterprise would be acceptable to them, and if they approved of the day chosen to begin the work . . . they invoked, besides the gods of the country, the gods to whose protection the new city was recommended, which was done secretly, because it was necessary that the tutelary gods should be unknown to the vulgar.[13]

Few authentic records of the splendid event on Jenkins Heights have survived, so we have to take a guess at the time when the stone was laid.[14]

At 10.00 a.m., the procession was gathering at Alexandria, on the south bank of the Potomac River, and people were exchanging Masonic greetings. A company of Volunteer Artillery had paraded to welcome the President of the United States, who shortly afterwards crossed the river with his suite, and was received on the north bank by two Lodges of Masons – No. 22 Virginia, and No. 9 Maryland. We can assume from this that the ceremonial did not reach Jenkins Heights until lunch-time, or even later. Afterwards, there were long speeches and considerable feasting – a 500-pound ox was barbecued – but, as there was no lighting on the Hill (or in the city of Washington as a whole) save for portable torches and the fire, we must imagine that the company departed before dark. This suggests that the chart for the occasion should be cast for shortly after midday.

The chart cast for this ceremonial is of great interest in view of the connection between Washington DC and the zodiac sign Virgo. Shortly before midday, Jupiter was rising in Scorpio, reminding us of the earlier chart for the founding of the district, which had allowed for Jupiter to rise in much the same way. This rising Jupiter is of considerable importance to the symbolism of American independence, and has continued in much-used emblems even into modern times.[15] In the Capitol chart, however, there is that emphasis on Virgo which, with good reason, we have begun to expect in horoscopes relating to the federal city. *The Sun and Mercury are in Virgo, as is the Dragon's Head.* It seems that whichever way we look in connection with the building of Washington DC, the beautiful Virgin always shows her face.[16]

With the third foundation in the city (the first being the for the city of Washington DC, the second for the White House), some of the historical obscurity is removed. The event of the founding of the Capitol building is not without its puzzles or controversies, but it was so public that it entered into history in a way that the two earlier occasions did not. The event was no semi-private enactment of interested Masons, who could appreciate the need to link their enterprises on earth with events in the heavens – the ceremonial at the Capitol was widely advertised in local newspapers. In addition, President Washington – undoubtedly the most famous individual in the United States at that time – lent dignity to the proceedings by his presence. The occasion has been recorded in many works of art in and near Washington DC, but perhaps the most famous are two bronze panels in the Capitol itself. On the left valve of the Senate doors of the Capitol is a panel, designed in 1868, showing George Washington laying the cornerstone (opposite).

The gentleman behind Washington is holding two forms of masonic square, while the President himself uses the trowel which later became so famous in Masonic circles that it was used whenever possible in important cornerstone ceremonials. The square and the trowel were emblazoned on the apron which Washington wore on this occasion, for these were the visible tools of the ritual and the inner work. Undoubtedly, invisible agencies were present at the cornerstone ceremonial, but they were made visible in the apron's symbolism.

The radiant eye represented the invisible presence of the Great Architect – the high Spiritual Being, who had been invited by prayer and ritual to oversee the ceremonial. The radiant eye was, as a later Masonic writer pointed out, the *Sol-œil* – the 'sun-eye', or Spiritual Sun, which lay hidden behind the French word for the Sun, *soleil*.[17] In dark contrast against this spiritual light was the coffin, with its botanic promise of developing life emerging from within, representing the telluric darkness of the Earth, from which this building was about to rise, true and well formed, thanks to the efficacy of the ritual and ceremony. If the radiant eye represented the brightest thing visible to our world, the coffin represented the darkness in which we earthlings are enclosed. The sarcophagus, or tomb, is from the Greek word *sarx*, meaning 'flesh'. It was appropriate that the light of the higher Sun should be at the top of the apron, and the darkness of the coffin be at the bottom.

The invisible Great Architect had been acknowledged in the

preliminary prayers of the ritual, while the invisible coffin was acknowledged in the 'cavation' made in the Earth. What the apron proclaims, and what can only be inferred from the panel itself, is that the ritual – like all human activities – took place between the light and the darkness, between Heaven and Earth.

The sculptor of the panel has exercised considerable artistic licence, for the early account insists that Washington descended into the trench (an indication, perhaps, that this was a foundation stone, rather than merely a cornerstone). Most of the images which depict this event fall into the same error – Allyn Cox's mural in the vaulted hallway ceiling of the House wing of the Capitol (executed in 1953) shows Washington on a lower level than the onlookers, but there is still no suggestion of a trench, or 'cavation'. The huge frescos which Cox completed for the George Washington Memorial Hall, in Alexandria, make a similar sacrifice of historical accuracy to attain pictorial drama.[18]

The second bronze in the Capitol is certainly less accurate in a historical sense. This is the bronze plaque of 1893 in the south-eastern corner of the Senate wing of the Capitol, which claims:

> Beneath this table the corner stone of the Capitol of the United States of America was laid by George Washington First President September 18, 1793.

The only problem is that extensive searching has failed to reveal exactly where the first stone was laid, and the plaque, for all the air of distinguished authority it exudes, is probably inaccurate.[19] Even so, the horoscope which must have been cast to determine the moment of foundation still encapsulates the same visionary precision as the others, and evinces the same concern for the importance of Virgo in the scheme of Washington DC.

We have seen, then, that the processional for the cornerstone ceremony had been Masonic. The architects and sculptors who erected the Capitol had been Masonic. The impression one might get from this glimpse into the early history of Washington DC is that the Masonic brotherhood was handing out jobs for the boys. However, the facts suggest otherwise: the facts suggest that destiny had brought together great men to do great deeds.

There is no doubt at all about Hoban's qualifications as an architect and visionary, while the reputations of Latrobe, who participated in the vision, and of L'Enfant who oversaw the planning of the federal city, are also beyond doubt. No one can question the merits and qualifications for the task assigned them by the President, of such men as Thomas Johnson, Daniel Carroll, Joseph Clark or Colleen Williamson – those other Masons who were mentioned by name on the silver dedication plate, laid by George Washington on the cornerstone. The achievements of all these exceptional men depended not on the fact that they belonged to a brotherhood, but upon their own abilities, their sheer professionalism and their spirituality.

This point must be made here because, as we trace the spiritual and esoteric traditions which underlie the modern structure of Washington DC, we shall constantly be meeting the names of individuals who were deeply committed Masons, and we might be tempted to imagine that the federal city was little more than a centre of Masonry. In fact, in terms of statistics, this would appear to be no more true for Washington DC than for any other major town or city connected with the original 13 states.

If, for fairly obvious reasons, Masonry was not officially active in Washington DC until a few days before the cornerstone ceremony, it had existed in the other states for well over 50 years. American Masonry was already well established in the last decade of the 18th century, and its connection with the revolutionary spirit has been examined by more than one historian.[20] In view of this, it is scarcely surprising that the esoteric planning, design, execution and rebuilding of the city should have fallen to the Masons. In some ways, given the early history of the United States, this could hardly have been otherwise. The federal city was intended to be an architectural symbol of independence, conceived and built at a time when most Americans still used an alternative calendar that marked their break from the tyranny of the British government. Even the silver plate which bore the records of the foundation ceremony for the Capitol used the dual dating system: the building was laid 'on the 18th day of September, 1793, in the thirteenth year of American Independence'.

By that date, there were already 19 states in the union, but few present at the ceremony would have failed to recognize the symbolic importance of the thirteenth year, which reflected the 13 states that had struggled through the fight for Independence to the ratification of the famous Declaration. It has been reported – though, I suspect, with little justification – that 44 of the 56 signers of the Declaration of Independence were Masons.[21] The very struggle for independence seems to have been directed by the Masonic brotherhood, and, some historians insist, had even been started by them. This historical fact was also acknowledged to some extent on the silver plate, for a third dating system was added to the two I have just quoted: it was 'the year of Masonry

5793', a date symbolically denoting the era following the supposed foundation of the Temple of Solomon. This third date was of considerable importance for, as we shall see, the building of Washington DC was itself involved with the idea of the completion of this great Solomonic enterprise. This was intrinsically involved with the completing of the unfinished pyramid – that other great symbol of Masonry.

The revolution against the British oppressors had begun in a warehouse owned by a Mason, and the group which had participated in the Boston Tea Party, in 1773, had been composed largely of Masons.[22] A great many of the officers who fought in the war against Britain were Masons, and those depleted numbers that did return to civilian life were anxious to apply their revolutionary fervour to the building of a new nation. As is well-known, the father of this nation, George Washington, whose magical hand may be traced in most of the wise undertakings at the end of the 18th century, was also a Mason – perhaps, indeed, the most famous Mason of all time. In the light of this, the obelisk to the south of the White House, which is dedicated to the memory of his political and military achievements, is in some ways less important than the later celebration of his Masonic standing: this is the George Washington Masonic Memorial in Alexandria, the portico walls of which are decorated with lapidary quotations from his pen, relating to the role of Masonry.[23]

It is possible that the story of Washington as a Mason has been overtold: even so, more often than not the telling of his story in popular literature has been inaccurate in detail. Washington was initiated on 4 November 1752.[24] Some historians have maintained that after his initiation, Washington showed little interest in Masonry, but this is completely untrue, as his surviving personal correspondence reveals.[25] He was the first Master of the Alexandria Lodge No. 22, from April 1788 to December 1789, and was therefore Master when inaugurated President of the United States on 30 April 1789. He was buried with Masonic honours at Mount Vernon: with one exception, the pallbearers were members of his own Lodge.

Some of the surviving correspondence shows that it was George Washington's vision which guided the planning and early building of the federal city which later bore his name.

There are good reasons why the newly formed Federal Lodge was not officially present at the ceremonial of the cornerstone in 1793, but there is no apparent reason behind another curious anomaly concerning the ceremony. Recorded on the suitably inscribed silver plate was the fact that instead of laying the north-east stone, in accordance with Masonic procedures and symbolism, George Washington laid a south-east corner.[26]

To understand the significance of this deviation, we must look at some of the secrets of the ancient practice of foundation ceremonials, which seem to have influenced Masonic beliefs and rituals.

In many respects, the very words 'foundation ceremonies' are something of a misnomer. Symbolically speaking, there is a considerable difference between the laying of a foundation stone and the laying of a cornerstone. As its name implies, the foundation stone was the one laid within the earth – it was the first masonry deposited on the footings of a particular building. And since it was buried within the earth, it was emblematic of darkness, and the chthonic. In contrast, the cornerstone was laid on top of an already founded wall – usually the wall of an underground cellar, or (in the case of a church) a crypt, which had been constructed prior to the foundation ceremony. The cornerstone symbolically represents the first transition of the building from the Earth plane into the upper realm. It is viewed in terms of the form the building will take as structure rising into the light, towards the eye of the Sun, away from the chthonic, coffin-bearing darkness of the Earth. This is probably one reason why the more careful Masonic writers usually refer to the ceremonial of the cornerstone-laying, rather than to the foundation stone – though the truth is that even in Masonic literature, the two are sometimes confused. The records often refer to the laying of the Capitol 'cornerstone', when surviving references suggest that it might have been a foundation stone.

In the mediaeval rituals, the cornerstone ceremonial marked the raising of the building *into the light of day* – into consciousness, or towards the heavens. It is probably in this that lay the importance attached to the cosmic moment – to the astrological or cosmic time – in so far as it reflected the influences of the stars and the planets, the omnipresent symbols and realities of the realm of light. There is much evidence to show that, in mediaeval times, the physical foundation of a building was regulated to correspond with certain cosmic events, reflected in the skies, with the Sun a being of light, surrounded by the 12 zodiacal signs and the 7 planets. Such cosmic symbolism explains why the foundation chart – or horoscope for the moment of the ceremonial laying – was held to be so important by mediaeval masons, for it recorded the moment when the darkness of the Earth was united with the light of God.

In mediaeval symbolism, where the fabric of a church building was seen not only as the body of Christ, but symbol also of Man, the crypt related to the hidden and unconscious part.[27] The crypt represented the dark unknown, while the fabric erected above it represented the consciousness. In terms of strict polarities, the 'dark' or 'lunar' crypt represented the feminine element, the upper 'solar' fabric the masculine. This much-needed balance between the male and female in every individual is, of course, expressed in different ways in the arts, but rarely more clearly than in the secret structures of architecture. The historian John James has suggested – with good reason – that the crypt which had been so popular in Romanesque art went out of fashion in Gothic architecture because the newly emphasized worship of the feminine Virgin provided a balance to the all-male Trinity, which had been so dominant in mediaeval liturgy and worship.[28]

Such associations explain why it was possible to equate the laying of a foundation stone with birth. In mediaeval lore, the fact of birth always demanded a horoscope – a symbolical record of the cosmic factors in attendance at that moment. The foundation horoscope is a chart for the 'birth' of a building, that is, a chart of the spiritual heavens at the moment that an idea is imprinted into the surface of the Earth. It reveals the moment when the spiritual and the chthonic meet: in the horoscope figure itself, the spiritual is symbolized by a circle, while the chthonic is symbolized by the cross:

○ + ⊕

This would suggest that the horoscope for a building should be cast for the moment of the laying of the cornerstone, rather than for the laying of the foundation stone, for this latter seems to relate to the idea of conception, just as evidently as the cornerstone relates to birth.

In mediaeval building, the floor marked the boundary between the chthonic and the earthly plane, where light became operative. The foundation point lay in the penumbric shadow realm between the two worlds of light and darkness. The Masonic insistence upon the north-eastern point for the laying of the stone reflects this penumbric realm, for it brought together light and darkness, since the east was the symbol of light, the north the symbol of darkness. Thus, the north-east corner was selected because it represented in horizontal space what the entire polarity of the building represented in vertical space. The horizontal space was that represented in the symbolism of the cardinal points: the north was in darkness, for theoretically no Sun shone from the north, while the east was symbol of light, as marking the point of Sunrise. The vertical space was the chthonic foundations, yet in darkness, and the light of day which would bathe the completed building. The north-east point marked the meeting of light and darkness, and was therefore symbol of the Earth plane, which is saturated with this duality.

Having taken that on board, we should now consider another element of Masonic lore. The *arch* of the Masonic Royal Arch Degree[29] has sometimes been equated with the rainbow, yet this is really the arch of the zodiac. In technical terms, it is the arch of the ecliptic which rises visibly in the heavens as the pathway of the Sun, and which is marked in some Masonic diagrams with the first seven segments of the zodiac, from Aries to Libra, as they emerge into 'the light of day' (alongside):

It might be argued by the purist that while Virgo is shown upon this arch, with its distinctive sigil ♍, the sign is not accorded any great importance. On the face of it, this is correct, yet when the arcane symbolism is examined more carefully it will be seen that Virgo is made emphatic by secret means. The Corinthian-like capitals on both columns each contain five-leafed floral devices: these, as we shall see are Virgoan symbols, which explains why the five-petalled rosette, and the related five-leafed palmette proliferate in so many forms in the lapidary symbolism of Washington DC.

At a later point, I shall show that the Virgo of the skies is closely linked with the Virgin of the Christian religion. For the moment, it will suffice if I demonstrate graphically that the five-petalled rosette and floral devices, which occurs so frequently in lapidary details of the city, is directly associated with both the Virgin Mary and Virgo. A fine example of the former is in a 16th-century Prussian woodcut (over), where the pentalphic flower is at her feet, and repeated five times as a

large flower amidst a floral surround of 50 roses, each with 5 petals.[30]

In view of such standard iconographic floral symbolism, we may begin to suspect that the entire stellar arc, or Royal Arch in the figure on p.79, is represented as resting, to some extent, upon the power of Virgo. This suspicion will be confirmed beyond doubt as we read on.

All the strains of cosmic symbolism outlined above played a part in the foundation ceremony of the Capitol building. However, as I have said, the early records indicate that the ceremonial at the laying of the Capitol cornerstone deviated from the accepted norm: instead of laying the north-east one, Washington and his fellow Masons laid a south-east cornerstone. At first glance, this would seem to have defied the speculative Masonic tradition, and to have thrown into disrepute the notion of the conflict between darkness and light which lies behind most esoteric speculation.

The records have been lost, and the original foundation stone has not been located. However, it is clear from internal evidence that George Washington, or whoever organized this ceremonial, instead of flouting established procedure, was actually being foresighted in the matter of the south-east cornerstone. The city of Philadelphia had been adopted merely as the temporary national capital for a specific period. By 1793, only seven years were left to run before all the federal offices would be located in the new city: time was short. In the knowledge that the important thing was to ensure that there would be sufficient space for Congress to meet in the federal city, the ceremonial was not intended to lay the cornerstone for the whole Capitol, but merely for the north wing.

One morning near the beginning of the 19th century, the Washingtonian Christian Hines walked through the rough woodlands where the Mall and the Smithsonian are now located, and stood on the new bridge at 7th Street. From this position, he could see the north wing of the Capitol, just beginning to rise from the ground. To his left was the President's House, perhaps half a storey high.[31] Hines' notes on the early development of Washington DC are among several surviving comments which demonstrate that the north wing of the Capitol was completed first.

It is in this fact that the secret of the south-east laying is found. It corresponded to the north-east of the building which would lie contiguous with it – that block which would form the central part of the Capitol, that would later carry the dome.

The south-east laying makes perfect sense within the framework of Masonic symbolism. The diagram below is intended to set out the underlying astrology and astronomy of the foundation-stone theory, in relation to the Capitol.

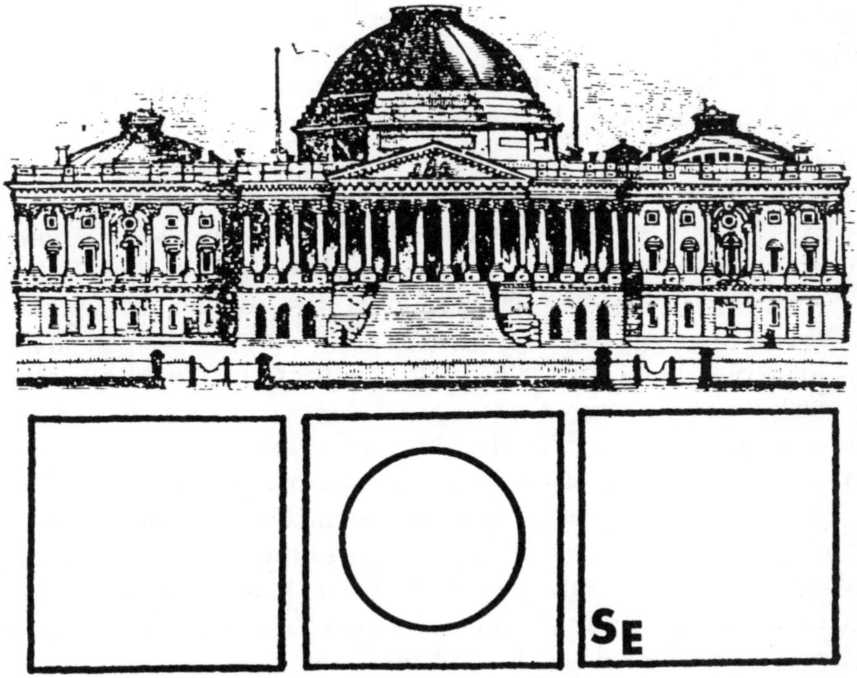

The important point is that the Capitol building was oriented by L'Enfant and Ellicott on an east-west axis. In doing this, they were arranging the building – and, of course, the entire city – in a particular relationship with the Sun. To understand this relationship, one need only imagine the Capitol building at the centre of the compass (left) and study the arc traced by the Sun as it sets throughout the year.

The external semi-arc (S-N) marks the range through which the Sun sets during the course of a year at Washington DC. Through the year, the points of Sunset over the west of the city move through this arc, starting at the south (S) in December and sweeping towards the north, where it reaches its furthest extent in June (marked N on the diagram).

To the south, is the extreme setting of the Sun, at 240 degrees, on 21 December (marked S on the diagram). To the north, is the extreme setting of the Sun, at 302 degrees, on 21 June. Now the Sun does not move through this arc at a regular speed: at the two extremes, the movement is very slight. For example, in December, the Sun hovers around the extreme southern 240 degree for 19 days: this is why the point is called the solstice, or 'standing-still of the Sun'. In a similar way, the Sun hovers around the extreme northern degree of 302 in June for 4 days – though it is in the neighbouring degree of 301 for about 12 days on either side, moving further south and then returning, after touching the solstice, or stand-still point. As the Sunset points swing between these two extremes to the median point, they gather speed, so that by March the Sun sets in a single degree for only 2 days.

To give you some idea of what this implies, I should point out that the diameter of the disk of the Sun itself measures approximately half a degree. This means that if you were to stand on the Capitol terrace on (say) 21 March, you would see the Sun set over a particular part of Washington DC (slightly to the north of the Washington Monument). On the following day, this Sunset point would have moved a considerable distance along the horizon, towards the north.

Astronomers can furnish very precise details of such local solar arcs, which are called *azimuths*, and it is therefore possible to work out, in theory at least, where the Sun will appear to set on any given day, in any place. Of course, astronomical data are based on spherical trigonometry, and do not always take into account variations in viewing points and horizons – for example, a tall building can obscure the actual setting of the Sun, and give an impression of an earlier Sunset than is suggested by the azimuth (I mention this because it is what occurs in Washington DC).

Now, architects who are interested in relating their buildings, temples and cities to the stars make use of the azimuth, no matter where they are building. With the aid of a local azimuth (which vary in different latitudes), they orient their buildings in order to relate them in a meaningful way to the Sunset, or the Sunrise, and to the fixed stars, which may also be measured against the azimuth. We shall see how L'Enfant and Ellicott used the azimuth of Washington DC at a later point. For the moment, it is sufficient to see that the entire city was laid out to a plan which accommodated the arc of Sunset to the west of the Capitol building in a very distinctive way. The east-west line on which the city is laid is halfway between the two extremes of northerly and southerly settings. The arc of the sunset at Washington DC is 62 degrees. The mid-point is therefore 31 degrees, which converts to 271 degrees on the compass bearing (marked E on the diagram opposite).

The Sun sets at this point on 21 March and 21 September, which marks the spring and winter equinoxes. What is important from our point of view is that the Sun sets to the due west, along the basic west-east line adopted by L'Enfant and Ellicott for their magnificent plan of the city.

The astronomy of this arc of Sunset, or azimuth, need not concern us deeply. What matters is that we grasp that, in a very simple way, the designers of the city oriented it to the Sun – specifically to the Sunset. Now, in Washington DC these measurements are made from the Capitol building, nominally from the centre of the dome, which we imagine as being at the centre of the compass. Symbolically speaking, this centre of the building is the point of stillness, where the arc of the Sunset is 'centred'. In these terms, the dome becomes a symbol of the half-arch of the visible heavens, which marks the point where the equinoctial and solstitial points meet, and are reconciled.

This consideration of the cosmic importance of the Sunset to the Capitol building shows that the dome – itself an image of the spiritual world above the city – was to be the spiritual fulcrum of Washington DC.

The centre of the dome was originally planned as the centre from which a whole sunburst of avenues and roads radiated (shown on p.42). It was also the centre from which the city was to radiate its spiritual influences. In view of this, we should not be surprised to find a zodiac (plate 21) marking the location of the furthest Sunset to the north, the space equivalent to the summer solstice.

Now, since the Masons recognized that the designs for the Capitol would eventually involve the construction of a dome, it was of great symbolic importance that this central point should be acknowledged in the foundation of the building. So, in founding the south-east part of the north wing, the Masons were acknowledging the importance of the central building, which was to carry the dome. To put it another way, the *south-east* founding of the north building was, at the same time, the *north-east* founding of the dome-bearing section that was to be the spiritual centre of the city. In this way, then, the south-east foundation-laying was not merely a matter of expediency, but an acknowledgement that a spiritually important dome would eventually grace the building.

This dome would be the centre of the horizon, in the western section of which the Sun would set in a regulated arch, and in the eastern section of which it would rise in a similar regulated arch. The dome would not only be the centre of the Capitol – it would also be the centre of the visible world. Thus, the original founding acknowledged the cosmic idea behind the building.

By this stratagem, the Masons lifted the Capitol into the sphere of cosmic stillness which is the centre of all well-planned buildings, and ensured that the Capitol dome was harmoniously related to the zodiacal arch in the skies.

Perhaps the Charles Bulfinch dome (opposite) is somewhat squat (the architect was not happy with it himself); nonetheless, its symbolism was much the same as the familiar, and more gracefully proportioned dome with which Thomas Ustick Walter replaced it in the middle of the century. Both Bulfinch and Walter were Masons, and we may be sure that the underlying astro-architectural symbolism was seen as being in many respects more important than questions of grace or proportion.

We have learned from the above that the apparent deviation from the norm in the ceremonial founding of the Capitol should not obscure the fact that the Masonic ritual of the cornerstone was linked with the union of the polarities of light-darkness, of Heaven-Earth.

At this point, further assessment of the concepts of east and light is required. The notion of the east as a source of light was as important in the Masonic rituals as it had been in the Egyptian, Greek and mediaeval European foundation rituals. The Sunrise was associated with the emergence of a new birth of spirit – in other words, with life. Indeed, the New Testament itself had supported the idea that light was the life of mankind.[32] One of the arcane Greek words from St John's Gospel is *zoe* (meaning 'life'): this word was the root of our own word *zodiac*, which did not mean 'circle of animals', as is so often believed, but 'circle of life'. It was the circle travelled by the greatest Light in our system – the Sun.

This Masonic idea is nowhere more fully recognized than in the familiar name 'Old East', which is still used to denote the cornerstone plate that formerly marked the foundation of the University of Carolina, at Chapel Hill, in 1793. The plate names the Grand Master supervising the ceremonial as William Richardson Davie,[33] the fraternity in attendance was from the Eagle and Independence Lodge, and the date was recorded as 12 October, in the Year of Masonry 5793, which is 'in the 18th Year of the American Independence'.[34] The foundation chart for this ceremony has not survived, but it is clear from a chart cast for the time that the astrologer waited for the moment when Mars was exactly on the beneficent Dragon's Head, along with Venus, in the sign Virgo. The Sun was exactly conjunct with Mercury, in Libra.[35] Virgo was a sign well known for its connections with studious application, while Mercury was the pagan deity who ruled over study. All in all, the stellar pattern of the chart reflected the mundane purpose of the building itself.

'Old East', and the planetary configurations which surrounded its ceremonial use, remind us that the magic of Virgo is not confined to the city of Washington DC, but has a wider application to the United States as a whole.

The foundation stone brings the building into the light of day, into the view of the cosmos.

As I have intimated, the historian of mediaeval architecture John James[36] was right to equate the crypt (its original Latin *crypta* was linked with the idea of 'hidden', or 'secret') with the unconscious – with the chthonic, and with the feminine side. This is tantamount to linking the crypt with the shadow realm, and regarding the building above it as representative of the heavens, bathed in the light of day. It is almost certainly in this cooperation between the dark chthonic of Earth and the fructifying power of the celestial heavens that the Masonic rituals of the Royal Arch were based. As we shall see, this goes a long way to explaining the importance of Virgo in speculative Masonry.

Symbolically speaking, the crypt is the burial place. It is the earth into which the seed of wheat must be dropped, to grow and resurrect, emerging as a sprouting plant from the coffin. In Masonry, the crypt is the burial place of the Master Mason, under the Holy of Holies. This burial can be symbolic rather than funerary, of course: certain levels of initiation are equated with death, often symbolized by a 'burial' in a tomb, or crypt. This idea of rebirth is continued even in modern times in the formal rituals of the Freemasonic cornerstone ceremonials, in which participants in the ritual scatter wheat upon the floor, and sometimes even link this seeding with the stars. For example, in the ceremonial for the dedication of the Supreme Council (Southern Jurisdiction) House of the Temple in Washington DC, on 18 October 1915, the Grand Minister of State consecrated the building by sprinkling wheat upon the floor, in the name of Justice, Right and Truth. He performed this ritual after pointing out that these three qualities represent the Three Stars in the belt of the constellation Orion 'in which, since the human race began, no man hath seen even the shadow of change'.[37]

So far, I have merely glanced at the symbolism of the architecture in Washington DC, but I think this has been sufficient to indicate that the idea of Virgo plays an important role in the astrological symbolism which dominates the city. I have also examined two foundation ceremonials in which the Virgoan element was of considerable importance. By taking this approach, I might have given the impression that the sole Masonic concern in these early years of the building of the federal city was with

Virgo. Certainly, as we shall see shortly, the symbolism of Virgo *was* intimately bound into certain Masonic symbols, and it is this fact – along with various other arcane matters which we shall examine – that accounts for the Masonic obsession with the sign in previous centuries.

The importance of Virgo, and her connections with the Egyptian goddess Isis, had been recognized in Masonic circles from the very early days of American Masonry. The French astronomer Joseph Lalande had been an important Mason, and his writings were widely read by Americans of the late 18th century. As early as 1731, Lalande had recognized that:

> The Virgin is consecrated to Isis, just as Leo is consecrated to her husband Osiris . . . The sphinx, composed of a Lion and a Virgin, was used as a symbol to designate the overflowing of the Nile . . . they put a wheat-ear in the hand of the virgin, to express the idea of the months, perhaps because the sign of Virgin was called by the Orientals, *Sounbouleh* or *Schibbolet*, that is to say, *épi* or *wheat-ear*.[38]

The spiritual growth which Masonry encourages enabled Masons to sense a profound symbolism in the stars and planets, and to relate these symbols to earthly events. This was nowhere more evident than in the symbolism of their foundation stone ceremonies, which they linked with the wheat-goddess, under her various names (the symbolic importance of wheat is very evident in the above quotation). However, their concern was not only with the power of the celestial Virgin, as tutelary zodiacal sign of the new city, but also with arcane astrological symbolism in general. A good example of this may be seen in one level of planetary symbolism which accompanied the ceremonial laying of the cornerstone of the Capitol in 1793.

The planet Uranus had been discovered by Sir William Herschel on 13 March 1781. At first, he did not recognize how extraordinary his discovery was: when, shortly afterwards, he addressed the Royal Society to inform them of his sighting, he claimed merely to have discovered a new comet. After a few more weeks' observation, he established that it was indeed a planet, and named it *Georgium Sidus* ('the Georgian Star') after King George III of England. The dedication paid off, for, in the following year, George made Herschel his private astronomer: however, the King was by no means popular – especially among the colonists – and not everyone was pleased with the new name for the planet.

The original name *Georgium Sidus* continued in use in the official *Nautical Almanac* and in popular almanacs for some decades after Herschel's death,[39] but not all astronomers had been happy with it. Indeed, Joseph Lalande (no doubt touched by Republican sentiment) proposed *Herschel* as the name for the new planet – a suggestion that still survives in its sigil, which incorporates the capital letter H for Herschel: ♅

The name *Uranus*, which had been proposed by German astronomer Johann Elert Bode, finally won the day. However, in 1793, at the beginning of the new federal dispensation, Georgium Sidus was in the heavens – a symbol of tyranny in the new nation, for it bore the name of the hated old King of England, who had done so much to obstruct that nation's birth.

It is my impression that the symbolism of this new planet was not missed by those Masons who were, at that time, already committed to the making of the new America. Understandably, they were probably tempted to see the planet as a herald of the birth of their own nation. If new comets and eclipses might be taken as augury of great events, how much more powerful an augury might be a new planet? The religious educator, Increase Mather, had imagined an eclipse visible in Massachusetts as evidence of Nature's grief at the death of President Chauncey, of Harvard College.[40] In fact, the Masons did not fall into this trap of anthropometric symbolism – instead they wisely decided to concentrate on the symbolism of the planet's unfortunate name.

What more cunning could these early founders of the nation – and of Washington DC – exercise than ritually to dispose of the planet and the kingly name in a Masonic ritual?

To grasp fully the event which befell the planet Uranus in the American symbolism, we must recapitulate.

On Wednesday, 18 September 1793, President George Washington, in his temporary role of Grand Master, laid the north-eastern foundation stone for the new Capitol building, which was to be the spiritual centre of Washington DC. The ceremony was partly designed to identify the Masonic movement with the new Republic, and towards this end the date of the foundation was noted according to two different systems – it was the thirteenth year of American independence, and the year 5793 according to the Masonic calendar. The historian Bullock is absolutely right to observe that the Masons did more than lay the Republic's physical cornerstones; they also helped form the symbolic foundations of the new order.[41] On that day, the Sun was in 24 degrees of Virgo, and thus reflected the Virgoan nature of the new city. However, by pure coincidence, the new planet Georgium Sidus, with its detested name, was exactly on the fixed star Regulus, the 'little king' star of the constellation Leo.[42] Its unfortunate link with royalty was redoubled by its name: indeed, it was a most curious coincidence that the planet bearing the name of King George should find itself on a star named after a king.

Through the conjunction of planet and star, the identification of the King with the new planet was more than nominal – it had become a cosmic reality. The Masonic astronomers had chosen the day of foundation for the city with great wisdom, for, as the ceremony was enacted, Georgium Sidus lowered in the west and disappeared from sight. As the planet fell into oblivion, beyond the view of those in the federal city, the Sun remained in the sky, set in the zodiacal sign Virgo – a triumphant symbol of the city which was being founded as the new administrative centre, to replace that of George III. Symbolically speaking, Virgo was in ascendancy, while the power of King George was in decline.

This curious arrangement of planets, with its exceptional power of symbolism, was not exactly unique, but it *was* extremely rare. Because, in geocentric terms, Uranus was such a slow-moving planet, a similar configuration had not been manifest in the heavens since 1708; it would not repeat until 1877. The Masons could not have chosen a more symbolically auspicious date for their all-important ceremony had they been able to manipulate the stars themselves.

The detail of the Masonic ritual symbolically rejected, or sent west, the kingly Georgius Sidus. This ritual banishing was paralleled in an earlier event, which had occurred in New York at the outbreak of the Revolutionary War. The rebellious Americans had overthrown the equestrian statue of George III, and melted it down to make bullets for their soldiers.[43]

When I discussed the apron worn by George Washington at the cornerstone-laying of 1793, I pointed out that some of the symbols were astrological. For instance, the seven stars on the radiant could be interpreted as symbols of the seven planets.[44] However, what I did not say, was that on the apron is an image of the zodiac – the archetype of all astrological symbols. This zodiac runs around the globe mounted on the pillar to the right of the apron (see over). Of course, in this crude woodcut the zodiacal arcs are not visible, but we know that the band represents the zodiac because this image of a zodiac-bearing pillar is one of the most widely used of all Masonic symbols.

This pillar (to the right, above) is distinguished by a zodiacal band which is wrapped around the globe. The band is intended to signify that the globe encompasses the spiritual world – not merely the stars and the planets, but the angelical beings who direct these orbs. The symbolism of this celestial pillar cannot be properly examined alone, as its meaning is intrinsically bound up with that of the pillar to the left.

The various arcane legends surrounding the two pillars are complex, but the underlying theme is that when the sacred knowledge was revealed to Man, it was carved upon two such pillars. One was of marble, the other of brick – to suggest that one was made by God, the other by Man. The knowledge pertaining to the cosmos was carved upon one – presumably the marble one – and is symbolized in the form of a zodiacal belt. The knowledge pertaining to the Earth – viewed in the mediaeval cosmoconception as the centre of the cosmos – was carved upon the other, symbolized in the form of an Earth-globe. The mission of all initiates was to find an inner balance between the two pillars – to relate harmoniously to the spiritual realm of the stars whilst remaining harmoniously linked with the material realm of Earth.

The legend insists that after the Flood, these two pillars were lost.

Eventually, the Greek philosopher-teacher Pythagoras discovered one, and the Egyptian magus Hermes Trismegistus found the other. It was the Egyptian initiate who discovered, and subsequently taught, the wisdom of the cosmos, or the inner and outer truths of the skies.

The specifically Masonic adaptation of the legend tells how both pillars (in this version of the story, now made of brass) were placed in front of the porch of the Temple of Solomon. One column was called *Jachin*, said by some scholars to be the Hebrew for 'he that establishes'. The other was called *Boaz*, perhaps meaning 'in strength'. Two pillars, each inscribed with one of these Hebraic words, erected in Würzburg Cathedral in Germany, are described by Stieglitz, and dated by him to 1042.[45] A 14th-century quatrefoil on the west front of Amiens Cathedral in France, carved about 1230, shows Solomon in front of his Temple, seemingly kneeling on one of the pillars at the west end of the edifice.[46] Something of the arcane significance of these columns may be inferred from a formulaic Masonic catechism of the 18th century:

Q. In what Part of the Temple was the Lodge kept?
A. In Solomon's Porch at the West-End of the Temple, where the two Pillars were set up.[47]

The catechism reveals that the Temple of Solomon is an archetypal image of the Lodge. To enter that Temple (that is, to enter into the domain of Secret Wisdom, by moving towards the east, towards the solar source of life, the solar eye, or *sol-œil*) one has to pass between the two columns. Those making the passing would be cognizant of the knowledge they displayed as symbols, respectively of cosmic and earthly wisdom. They were, in a word, guardian columns of the Spiritual Sun, in the Temple beyond.

If we reflect upon the nature of the two columns embroidered by Madame Lafayette on Washington's apron, we may see that while they look simple enough, in reality they symbolize the parameters of all esoteric knowledge. The column to the right is a splendid symbol of the same astrological wisdom implicit in the cornerstone ceremony which the first President of the United States enacted in 1793.

In view of the way such meaningful legends of the two pillars merge into recent history, a question comes to mind. If half the original knowledge of Masonry was concerned with cosmic lore (that is, with the sciences later called astronomy and astrology), then why is there such an inadequate expression of such cosmic lore in the modern literature of

Masonry?[48] Why is the modern Masonic literature so uneasy about astrology?

Is it possible that the operative Masons who built the mediaeval cathedrals, and imported into the fabric of such buildings as Chartres so many zodiacs and arcane planetary symbols, were satisfied that their astrology was expressed adequately in stone? The operative masons at Chartres left three zodiacs (one of which was a secret zodiac) on the west front of their great building, and a magnificent stained-glass zodiac in the 'zodiac window' in the southern wall, yet there is no indication that they wished to set down this cosmic knowledge *in written words*.[49] Did they feel that the cosmic lore could not be adequately expressed in words, and must be presented only in the form of images, set out in an architectural form, designed to serve rituals? Is this feeling behind the same reluctance of the Masonic fraternities – the speculative extension of the operative masonry which lay behind the glory of Chartres – to deal openly with astrological symbols?

By now, it must be clear that I am convinced that the symbolism of Masonry is replete with astrological lore, and this lore has overspilled into the cornerstone rituals. Even so, it would appear that the subject of astrology has not been examined with any real conviction in the Masonic literature itself.

In fact, there are exceptions to this inadequate treatment. When Albert Pike drew up the rituals for the Scottish Rite in the later decades of the 19th century, he made a serious attempt to examine the astrological and cosmological lore in the literature from which he took much of his knowledge. However, although Pike was a fine scholar in some areas, he was uninformed in astronomical and astrological matters, and he made significant mistakes in his writings on cosmological lore. For example, the analogy drawn between the three stars in the belt of the constellation Orion and the Three Kings of Christian biblical lore, introduced into the ceremonial dedication of the House of the Temple (see p.86), was due more to Pike's misunderstanding than to any cosmological or historical truth.[50]

Furthermore, even when Pike did deal adequately with astrology, he seems to have been satisfied by the classical literature, rather than by the astrological forms which had been preserved in the West through Rosicrucian and alchemical literature, and which were already beginning to find expression in popular astrological literature in America. I mention Pike in this context because I cannot help feeling that his own interests, and his own limitations, left their imprints on the later development of Masonic thought in the United States.

Albert Pike had learned French to help his legal business: in later years, he was given to introducing into his Masonic writings (often without attribution) ideas derived from French translations – not only from Masonic sources, but from the classics and both astronomy and astrology. This meant that his Masonic writings became deeply imbued with the Egyptology and pseudo-Egyptian mythology which permeated French esoteric literature at that time; the importance of this will be demonstrated in due course.

As I reveal the arcane structure of Washington DC I shall have occasion, from time to time, to refer to American astrology. This in itself raises difficulties, as, so far as I know, there is no published work of any quality dealing with the subject. In view of this – and in view of my conviction that the Masons introduced and controlled astrological symbolism in the building of Washington DC – I must examine here some of the astrological and arcane developments in the United States during the 19th century.

In a sense, it is possible to say that there was no specifically American astrology until the last decades of the 19th century. Until that time most of the astrological needs – both arcane and subcultural – were serviced by English astrology, which represented the last formulations of late-mediaeval tradition. The English master-works, such as the 17th-century works of William Lilly or John Gadbury (whose most important work on astrology was owned by Thomas Jefferson), and even the compendious late-18th-century work by the Mason Ebenezer Sibly would still be found on the shelves of American astrologers well into the 19th century. This means that the astrology practised in the United States in the mid-19th century was deeply rooted in the traditions imported from England. This truth was nowhere more clearly set out than in the notes left by an English astrologer who settled in New York about 1854, and found himself ruminating on the sort of books on astrology which were available in the States and suitable for his students.[51] All the titles he mentioned were published in England.

From a historical point of view, this English influence is of great interest, for it points to a deep conflict between the development of astrology in America and the development of astrology in American Masonry. The English tradition was very different from the French, but it was the *latter* astrological symbolism which was adopted into American Masonry during the middle decades of the 19th century. This certainly led to an uncomfortable schism between Masonic symbolism and the indigenous astrological symbolism, which was rooted in English cultural life.

English Masonry did indeed make use of astrological symbolism, but it was employed in a bland way, often without explanation. For example, the Sussex silverware given to the Duke of Sussex in commemoration of his completing 25 years as Grand Master of English Freemasons, in 1838, has a beautiful zodiac on the frieze of the model temple, within which are displayed the three great lights of Masonry. The catalogue printed to commemorate the gift refers to this purely as a zodiac, without any reference to its meaning:

> The principal feature of the design is a circular Temple of regular architecture, formed by six columns of the Corinthean Order, supporting an enriched dome, crowned by the figure of Apollo. On the frieze are represented the Twelve Signs of the Zodiac.[52]

As a matter of fact, this is one of the most beautiful English Masonic zodiacs to have survived from the 19th century.

In contrast, hundreds of zodiacs and planetary sequences have survived from French Masonic sources. To judge from such images, the French were far more inclined than the English to incorporate astrological imagery into their rites and Lodge decorations. For example, four of the lithographic plates in the Masonic *Le Soleil Mystique* of 1852 show zodiacs or planets as integral symbols within Lodges – as large-scale floor zodiacs and as decorations around the architraves and domes (figure 15).[53] It is certainly relevant that the general tenor of the symbolism of many of the plates in this French book is Egyptian, crowded with sphinxes, pyramids, obelisks and hieroglyphics: French Masonry had been inundated with pseudo-Egyptian symbolism, even before the Mason Napoleon had invaded Egypt, and encouraged his scholars to study and steal Egyptian artefacts.

This prompts a very significant question: to whom do we owe the allegiance to the French astrological and arcane traditions – at the expense of the English traditions – in the United States?

One influential American arcanist who wrote about astrology, and claimed to be a Mason, was the Rosicrucian Thomas Henry Burgoyne.[54] If he was a Mason, then he was quite certainly a maverick, deeply committed to esotericism. Burgoyne was involved with the Brotherhood of Luxor, an esoteric order dedicated to (among other things) counter-acting what they saw as the pernicious orientalizing tendency of the

Theosophical Society.[55] Burgoyne's major work *The Light of Egypt* was a profound study of esotericism, but his later books on astrology did not measure up to it in quality or insight. Even so, it is certain that his books were more widely read in American Masonic circles, because of his claims to being a Mason.[56]

It is difficult to know what to make of this man: it is quite possible that his contribution to American arcane thought is only just beginning to be fully realized by scholars. His writings about what he called 'the magnetic sphere of our planet which exactly corresponds to the animal soul of man' are the equivalent of what in occultism is termed the Eighth Sphere – until that time a closely guarded secret in the confines of the Secret Schools. [57] Burgoyne's prediction that a tenth planet would shortly be located has rightly been taken by some as a reference to Pluto, which was not discovered until 1930.[58] In the light of later developments, which led to a massive misunderstanding of the nature of reincarnation – a misunderstanding which is still current in English and American pseudo-occult circles. Burgoyne was undoubtedly right to point out that no truth has been more completely inverted by the ignorant, and concealed by the learned, than that of reincarnation.

Many of his observations on occultism and astrology are extremely profound, and he must have been the first American to write openly about the dangers of the orientalizing tendency of Theosophy, which he saw as the 'sacerdotalisms of the decaying Orient' poisoning 'the budding spirituality of the western mind'.[59] On the other hand, there is something distinctly materialistic in his view of the spiritual world, and all too often his version of the hermetic tradition is downright misinformed. Even so, as one reads his books, time and time again one finds oneself asking whence he derived his insights into the deeper levels of occultism.[60] Like most occultists, Burgoyne ascribed his power and knowledge to the *unknown masters*, the initiates he called the 'brethren of light':

> During these twenty years of personal intercourse with the exalted minds of those who constitute the brethren of light, the fact was revealed that long ages ago the Orient had lost the use of the true spiritual compass of the soul, as well as the real secrets of its own theosophy.[61]

Another astrologer whose work deeply influenced American astrology was Dr L. D. Broughton, who, although often referred to as the most influential American astrologer, was English by birth. Like the architect Benjamin Latrobe, Broughton came from Yorkshire. He was born in

Leeds on 29 April 1828 at (as he carefully records) 10 a.m.[62]

The biographical details he gives in his most important astrological work throw much light on how, in the early 19th century, arcane lore was often passed through the family line. His paternal grandfather, Luke Broughton, was a disciple of Nicholas Culpeper, and a keen astrologer. His father was a student of medicine at Leeds Infirmary, but also studied astrology. His uncle, the surgeon Dr Mark Broughton, used astrology in his medical work, while his aunt, Martha Broughton, was also an adept in the science. Broughton's father had married Mary Scott, the only child of Benjamin Scott (probably from the Yorkshire town of Wakefield),[63] and had six children: of these, Matthew, Mark and Luke studied astrology. Matthew and Mark went to America and practised astrology in Philadelphia.[64] For many years, Mark published a monthly periodical called *The Horoscope*, as well as an *Astrological Ephemeris*.

Broughton seems to have migrated to America in 1854, at the age of 26: he settled in Philadelphia, and graduated at one of the medical colleges in this city, then moved to New York in 1863. He was certainly the first astrologer in America to make wide use of the horoscopes of famous Americans to teach and illustrate his art.

This explains why Broughton's work, *The Elements of Astrology*, which owes a great deal to English writers of the period, must be classed as the first book to make a serious attempt to serve an American frame of mind.[65] I have already noted Broughton's widely discussed prediction of the death of Abraham Lincoln, in his *Monthly Planet Reader*, a journal which he began in 1861. This type of literature, which was addressed to the American consciousness and which (from an astrological standpoint, at least) may appear subcultural in content, was in fact both intelligent and informative by the standards of popular astrology.

In the light of all this, it is surprising that the horoscope Broughton cast for George Washington was inaccurate (opposite page). In truth, the data were so wrong that it would not be possible to blame the quality of available ephemerides, or planetary tables.[66] The unfortunate thing is that the series of errors in this figure is exceptional, for the horoscopic material Broughton supplied for other famous Americans and American events was usually accurate. For example, the chart he cast for the laying of the cornerstone of the School of Theosophy at San Diego, California, on 23 February 1897, was very reliable. He not only cast the chart accurately, but read it well: as he admitted, it would be difficult to choose a more unsuitable time to lay a foundation stone.[67]

Broughton was among the first astrologers in the United States to participate openly in attempting to establish astrology as a legitimate

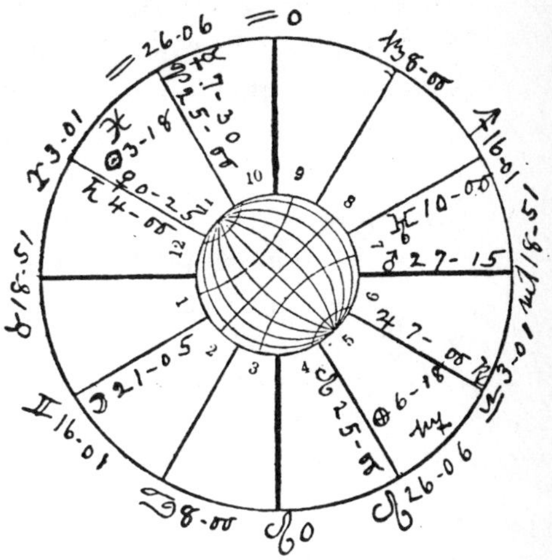

study in the face of both legal and academic prejudices. An instance of the former is his spirited defence of a certain Mr Romaine, who was sentenced in June 1886 at Philadelphia to 18 months in prison for practising astrology.[68] A good example of the latter is his defence of astrology against the repeated onslaught of Richard A. Proctor, the popular scientist who wrote widely on astronomy and uninformedly on what he called 'the humbug of astrology'.[69]

In spite of all these influences, some Masons did attempt to study the symbolism of the Craft in the light of astrology and astronomy, but these avenues of research appear to have been left to a handful of individuals who were probably regarded by their peers as somewhat maverick. Often this maverick approach led to real misunderstandings: such was the case when the scholar-Mason Christopher F. Nicolai claimed that the roots of English Masonry could be traced to certain astrologers of the 17th century, among whom was the well-known William Lilly.[70]

Among the most penetrating attempts to relate the Craft to astrology was Henry Pelham Holmes Bromwell's *Restorations of Masonic Geometry and Symbolism*, 1905. As the Past Grand Master of Illinois, Bromwell was deeply learned in Masonry: it is also clear from his writings that he had examined perceptively the symbolism of astrology. He approached the arcane lore of astronomy and astrology in an informed, open and original way, and it is not without significance that the subtitle of his fascinating work is *A Dissertation on the Lost Knowledge of the Lodge*.

In one particularly brilliant insight, Bromwell recognized that the projected celestial lines of the equinoctial and solstitial colures, which are fundamental to the foundation and cornerstone rituals practised by Masons, relate to the symbolic schema and layout of the Lodge. I have reproduced below Bromwell's original figure, which he intended for the eyes of fellow Masons. Alongside, I have offered a 'translation' of this figure, to show how it relates directly to the colures, the ecliptic and the four directions of space.

Within this structure is the fifth element (marked Q), which may be regarded as a fifth direction, vertically away from the planar surface. In

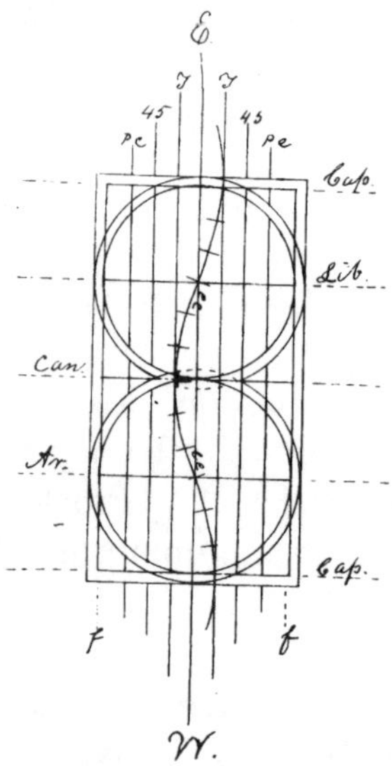

many hermetic systems, this Quintessential dimension of space is linked with the zodiacal sign Cancer. In esoteric astrology Cancer is recognized as being a sort of gateway, between the higher and lower worlds. It is Cancer which permits souls to descend into the material realm at the moment of incarnation. Whether or not this is a cosmic truth, the simple fact is that the idea of Cancer as a mediate point between two worlds has always been important in esoteric thought, and has entered into the symbolism of art. The idea of the upper reflecting the lower, with a space between them, is even illustrated in the traditional sigil, which is at least 2000 years old: ♋.

Bromwell's schema posits that the Lodge is a double square: an idea well in accord with Masonic traditions. Within this rectangle he assigned the projected circles of the two colures. These were so arranged to form a lemniscate (figure of eight ∞) within which is the ecliptic, or projection of the path of the Sun, through the zodiac.[71] Besides marking the path of the Sun, this sinuous line also delineates the path of initiation.

This astro-geometric plan of the Lodge is of great importance, since the series of initiations within the Lodge is regarded as a carefully orchestrated journey through symbols which are at once spatial and temporal.

My purpose in introducing this esoteric view of the Lodge is to indicate that Bromwell recognized that, even at the first initiation into Masonry (marked by the Entered Apprentice), the neophyte begins a journey which is symbolized as being planetary, against the pathway of the zodiac. There is nothing new in this vision of the hermetic journey, of course. Such a voyage is the bedrock symbol in the published hermetic literature of ancient Egypt and Greece: perhaps its most poetic expression is in Dante's poem, the *Commedia*. Almost every stage of Dante's journey through the three levels of Heaven, Purgatory and Hell is governed by initiation symbols expressed in terms of classical and mediaeval planetary or zodiacal imagery.[72] What does seem to be new is Bromwell's openly representing this cosmic astral journey in Masonic terms.

Furthermore, Bromwell injected a profound level of esotericism into the bland-seeming symbols used within the Lodges. These proliferate on the so-called tracing boards and carpets, which were probably at one time the equivalent of teaching boards, used by Master Masons to demonstrate Masonic symbols to the neophytes. When not used as an instrument of education, the tracing boards and carpets remain as symbols of the Lodge – of the inner and outer way of the Craft.

Almost in parenthesis, I should address a misunderstanding which may arise from mention of these symbols. It does not seem to be the purpose of the Master Mason to use tracing boards to *explain* the symbols they display. The true methods of initiation have always recognized that *it is harmful to explain symbols.* During the hermetic inner journey, the meanings of certain symbols well up within the neophyte, penetrating into the mind from within the hidden recesses of his or her soul, rather than being demonstrated by an outside agency. The personalized revelation is an integral part of the soul's growth, which usually accompanies initiation. This is one reason why those who conduct initiations rarely, if ever, attempt to explain symbols, for this can impede the neophyte's spiritual development.

The symbolism of individual emblems on the tracing boards has been dealt with very coherently by the Mason W. Kirk MacNulty, who recognized the dependence of these emblems on a well-established repertoire of mediaeval hermetic, Neoplatonic and cabbalistic traditions.[73] However, so far as I can establish, no serious attempt – other than Bromwell's – has been made to interpret the designs in terms of those cosmic symbols that reflect the path of the zodiac and the stars. Even though the structure proposed by Bromwell is linked with the simple-seeming tracing boards, is clear that whoever originated them had a profound knowledge not only of esoteric thought (which might be taken for granted in one advanced in the Craft) but also of astrology. This was a knowledge not only of the *outer* astrology – which may be learned through books or teachers – but of the *inner* astrology, which can be learned only by means of the inner journey, and the meditative life.

However, I do not wish to explore fully the connection between the Bromwell cosmic projection and the tracing boards. My aim is merely to indicate something of the esoteric astrology which lies behind early Masonry, my ultimate purpose being to demonstrate how this fits into the zodiacal symbolism of Washington DC. Hence I will restrict myself to looking at only three correspondences between projection and a tracing board.

First, I should point out that the tracing boards, like the Masonic carpets, are held to represent (among other things) the several levels of the Masonic Lodge. Now, in the Masonic rituals, the lodge floors are held to be symbolically different for each of the three degrees, and are regarded as multidimensional. In very simple terms, the floor is conceived as three-levelled, even though to outer eyes it appears to remain one and the same floor. Thus the hermetic and Christian concept of Three in One is reflected in the material realm through which the neophyte journeys during the process of Masonic initiation.

This triple nature of the floor explains why there are three designs for the traditional tracing boards, each corresponding to the journey symbolized and explored during the first Three Degrees. Within the hermeneutics of the Craft, these three boards must also be conceived as interpenetrating: in a sense, the Second Degree is a deepening or intensification of the symbolism of the First Degree. Just so, all the degrees which follow on the first Three Degrees are extensions, or deepenings, of these first degrees.

With this in mind, we are in a position to assess the deep connection between the first tracing board and the cosmic projection of Bromwell. The first tracing board (opposite) is designed to serve the initiation of the Entered Apprentice. Vertical to the centre of the tracing board is a ladder (in some images it is a stairway). This is partly a *scala* of the arcane tradition – a statement of the golden chain of being which connects Man to God, through a number of intermediate stages, or gradations. Prior to its adoption by Masonry, the ladder was a standard symbol of that form of alchemy which was concerned with rising, by way of self-perfection, to God.[74]

In the Bromwell projection (see p.98), we find that this same ladder is echoed in the winding ecliptic, with its 12 zodiacal divisions, which sinuate through the two great circles. The cusps of the zodiacal arcs are themselves so many stairs on this upward ladder.

In fact, this stairway points with remarkable clarity to the multi-layer significance of the Lodge floor. For the ladder of the tracing board is straight, since it describes, or represents, the 'straight way' of morality. In contrast, the ladder of the zodiac is curved. This is recognized in the tracing board for the *Second* Degree, in which the ladder is replaced, or extended symbolically, by a semi-spiral staircase – an even more direct evocation of the serpentine path of the ecliptic in the Bromwell projection. The apparent conflict between the straight and the curved pathways should not concern us unduly. The ladder describes the movement of the *inner* Sun, while the zodiac describes the *outer* Sun, but whether it is the Sun moving, or the observer who watches the Sun moving, is a moot point.

It is sufficient to note that within the tracing board and the Bromwell diagram there is a correlation which points to the inner and outer idea of a solar movement. A person following the sinuous path of the ecliptic is acting in imitation of the Sun. (This has both cosmic and Christological meanings which need not concern us at this point.)

At the top of the tracing board is an image of the Sun and the Moon.

These represent many things – in the cosmic Man, they represent the male and female elements which must be reconciled and distinguished if spiritual development is to be successful. In the esoteric cosmology they represent the extremes of creative solar power and undirected lunar imagination, which must be reconciled in the healthy human.

In Bromwell's projection we might easily miss the image of the Sun and Moon, but they are found in the two great circles which make up the figure of eight. In the esoteric tradition, the lemniscate marks (among other things) the meeting of the disks of Sun and Moon, with all the spiritual implications behind such a meeting. This symbolism takes advantage of the remarkable fact (what the ancients recognized as a cosmic mystery) that the Sun and the Moon of our skies appear to be exactly the same size.

The touching of the rim of the Moon with the rim of the Sun announces the beginning of an eclipse: that moment when the body of the imaginative Moon can darken the spiritual Sun. The esoteric tradition teaches that at such a time there are possibilities for inner development not normally available to mankind. The link I establish here between the luminaries and the two circles in the Bromwell diagram is presupposed by the zodiacal imagery inherent in his figure. The entrance to the Lodge (that is, to the Cosmos) begins at Capricorn and reaches the centre in Cancer. This explains why the great zodiacs which were laid down in the mediaeval cathedrals and basilicas were directed on an axis of Capricorn-Cancer.[75] This orientation followed not only the direction of the seasons, but also the direction of the neophyte in his or her search for God. Cancer was directed towards the altar – that is, towards the east (as in the Bromwell diagram on p.98). This reminds us that the gate of Cancer was called the Gate of Birth (a symbolism I shall deal with more fully below), an apposite term for an area designated for initiation, sometimes visualized as a birth into a higher realm.

As I have already made clear (diagram on page 98), this central point of Cancer is of profound importance within both the Lodge floor and the cosmic imagery upon which the floor is based. I have marked this node with the letter Q to remind us that it is here that the powers of the four elements meet to rise into the higher state of the fifth element, or *Quintessence*. The Quintessence is often used as a convenient symbol in esoteric literature to denote the access to higher realms which follows successful initiation. In this sense, the Quintessence is the higher plane of being contiguous to the normal one, and not subject to the normal elemental laws of gravity, time and so on.

It seems, then, that the nodal centre of the Lodge is a deeply significant place, reached by a zodiacal ladder. In the tracing board, this ladder reaches upwards towards the nominal centre of the image, which is a radiant star. As Kirk MacNulty points out, this star is an image of the Godhead: it is the thing to which all healthy men and women aspire.[76] The star seems to suggest something both remote and accessible – it is as remote as the confines of the cosmos, yet at the same time accessible, since it may be approached by means of a ladder which rests upon the Earth. It may be approached from the earthly realm of time and space, yet it leads to something which is itself outside time – that is, eternal.

This same stellar characteristic is found in the Bromwell diagram. The point where the two great circles seem to meet is called the node. For all this appears to be a mere linear intersection, it is really one of the most mysterious of areas, for it represents a meeting of time with eternity.[77] The deeper arcane symbolism of the area need not detain us here, but we should note that if the two circles are viewed as a figure of eight, *then they do not meet at all.* The two lines cross over, and must consequently describe different planes. If the circles are viewed as representing the meeting of Sun and Moon, then they certainly do not touch, for these cosmic bodies are separated by millions of miles. This mysterious point is a place where lines which appear to meet do not meet: it is one of the grand mysteries of the lemniscate.[78] It is outside time and space, like the star which occupies the central part of the tracing board.

Such an analysis as this cannot do justice to the multi-layered significance of either the tracing board or the Bromwell projection. However, we should now be sure that *underlying the Masonic symbolism of initiation is a profound grasp of the cosmic bodies which are the subject of astrology*. The examination of the symbolic power of Cancer, at the centre of the figure also introduces us to a concept which will become much clearer when we examine a zodiac in the Capitol building.

If we turn again to the apron which Lafayette presented to George Washington, and which was used in the ceremonial cornerstone laying of the Capitol building, we shall see that it was designed along the lines of the First Degree tracing board (page 101), though the ladder has given way to a stairway. On the apron are the stairs, the star and the luminaries, which have just been revealed as marking the soul's journey along the ecliptic, into the Quintessence marked by the mysterious nodal point. This apron design contains not only a model of the Lodge, but a model of the cosmos, as well as a path of initiation. The apron is revealed as emblematic of a deep astrological and cosmological lore.

*

Having examined something of the cosmological basis of certain Masonic symbols, we may pose a most interesting question which will take us back to the Capitol building. If the Masons who were involved in the foundation and building of Washington DC had access to this astrological symbolism, to what extent did they incorporate it into the Capitol building which was so much a product of Masonic activity? Indeed, did the Masons introduce into the Capitol any zodiacal or astrological symbolism at all? Following on from that, what is the earliest known zodiac, or planetary schema, to have been incorporated into the fabric of the city?

The answer is very surprising. The earliest zodiacal symbolism I know in Washington DC was incorporated into the fabric of the Capitol in 1819, shortly after the reparations made to the building after the British destroyed it.

In the Statuary Hall of the Capitol is the so-called *Car of History* made by the Florentine sculptor Carlo Franzoni (figure 7).[79] There are many beautiful sculptures in the Capitol building, but none so graceful or chaste as this, carved in 1819. The statue shows a female figure (said to be Clio, the Muse of History) standing in a winged chariot that is being drawn along spiritually – perhaps by its own wings, or perhaps by some invisible agency. The beauty of Clio's face is so perfect that she seems spiritually alive, reminding us that according to tradition, the model was a daughter of Franzoni's elder brother, Giuseppe.

Clio rests her left foot on the edge of the chariot, and looks down into the world, calmly recording in a large book what she sees. On the chariot is a bas-relief portrait of George Washington, with an angel holding a trumpet in one hand and an exquisitely carved palmette in the other. The chariot wheel, designed to hold the face of a clock,[80] rests upon a segment of the zodiac, as though to suggest that the Car of History stands outside the ordinary stream of time, as it is marked by the passage of the Sun through the zodiacal signs. The segment of the zodiac contains only three signs, picked out in marble relief. These (here represented in a mediaeval version) are Sagittarius, Capricorn and Aquarius:

The idea for this Car of History *may* have been suggested by Latrobe, for what appear to be prototypal drawings by the architect, predating the Franzoni work, have survived. [81] In this drawing, Latrobe portrayed Clio (or what has been taken to be Clio) seated in the winged chariot, facing to the left. In the final statuary, the goddess faced to the right, and was standing, her sandled foot on the edge of the car. Whichever way the goddess faced, and whatever her true name, the image is a striking one. If we can find a pre-1815 image of a goddess in a winged chariot, we might be able to determine what arcane notions Latrobe had in mind when he proposed this idea.

One possible source for his drawing is an engraving by the French artist F. A. David, among the portfolio of illustrations published by d'Hancarville in 1787.[82] This image portrays Triptolemus, whom the goddess Demeter had sought to turn into a god.[83] According to d'Hancarville, this scene represents a procession from the sacred rites of Eleusis, where the Mysteries of the corn-goddess were celebrated. The god in the winged car is taking part in a processional held in honour of the corn-goddess Ceres, the prototype of the zodiacal Virgo. Latrobe seems to have adapted the image by turning the god into a goddess, and putting in her hand one of Clio's attributes, a mirror, in place of the corn.

Many interesting conclusions could be drawn from Latrobe's surviving sketch, but as the early drawings do not appear to incorporate the zodiac, we must bypass this and pay attention to the statuary clock, which, whether influenced by the arcane mythology behind Latrobe's drawing or not, was certainly developed as an image of Clio, the Muse of History. In the light of this, it is probably Franzoni, rather than Latrobe, who first introduced astrological imagery into Washington DC.

The most obvious interpretation of this superb statue – and the one usually offered by non-specialists – is that the three zodiacal signs represent the three months of the year during which Congress was originally in session. I find this disappointing. If it was intended to be interpreted in this way, then it must be the most bland and unexciting zodiacal symbolism in the city. But is it possible to interpret this symbolism in some other way? Could the statuary have a deeper, arcane significance?

Yes, it could.

On one side of the car, facing in the direction of its imagined movement, is a bas-relief portrait of George Washington, with a goddess trumpeting his fame to the world (an image which the normally reticent Washington would scarcely have approved). This trumpeting of fame within a context of zodiacal symbols reminds me of another image, which would have been well known among Masons in 1819 – the angel trumpeting the fame of the horoscope of the United States in the illustration published by the Mason Ebenezer Sibly (figure 8). This angel holds in her hand a horoscope designed by Sibly to show Aquarius on the Ascendant and Capricorn on the MC (medium coeli), or zenith, at the top of the figure. The wheel of the Car of History rests upon the image of Capricorn, which is at the zenith, or top, of the globe.

We should not be surprised by these Masonic overtones in the Car of History, for although I have not been able to establish Franzoni's affiliations, Benjamin Latrobe certainly was a Mason, and the Italian was working under his control. In view of the Masonic association, we might reasonably expect a deeper level of cosmic symbolism than the idea of 'three months'. However, as there is no indication on the prototypal Latrobe sketch that he conceived of the figure being linked with the zodiac, or with any astrological theme, we must presume that it was Franzoni's idea to incorporate into the work an arc of the zodiac in order to convey a deep symbolic meaning.

While the use of a three-sign segment of the zodiac does not represent a major break with tradition, in all images where such a segment is used, an hermeneutic meaning is intended. In fact, whenever one encounters a section of a zodiacal arch in a Masonic image, one is drawn to thinking of the Royal Arch symbolism, which is redolent with zodiacal associations (shown on p.79).[84] Is it possible to trace such Royal Arch symbolism in this *Car of History*?

The first thing we should note is that the three signs of the zodiac do not figure on the seven stones which make the Royal Arch of the Masonic symbolism. Their peculiar symbolism is *that they are the threefold signs which are precisely the opposite of this arc*. The topmost zodiacal sign, which occupies the keystone of the Arch, is Cancer. Symbolically, this Cancer is in the full light of day: it is the sign in which the Sun is elevated at noon. The sign Cancer is opposite in the zodiac to Capricorn, which, in this clock symbolism, is the central of the three signs: as we have seen, the wheel of the chariot edges on to the raised cartouche which bears the sign. Is it possible that this curious three-sign segment of Franzoni's zodiac represents the telluric zodiac of the Arch – that which is hidden beneath the Earth, yet here made manifest in the march or flight of time? Is the symbolism so subtle and deep that it has been missed by all commentators? Indeed, is the Franzoni symbolism announcing that the passage of time – of history – is reflected not in the conscious decisions of Man (those held in the full light of day) but in unconscious decisions – those welling up from the hidden unconscious?

Strange as it may seem, this interpretation is entirely in accord with the Royal Arch. While the Royal Arch is topped by the keystone of Cancer, at its base is a coffin, the emblem of death. Death is ruled by, or represented by, the planet Saturn, the ruler of the zodiacal sign Capricorn.

The clock – such an evident symbol of the passing of time – raises Saturn to the heights, while the Royal Arch symbolism pushes it down to the nadir, or bottom, of the cosmic globe. (It is this cosmologically oriented symbolism which explains why there is a coffin towards the bottom of George Washington's apron – see p.68.)

Franzoni's *Car of History*, then, is beginning to emerge as one of the most extraordinary esoteric symbols in the Capitol building, intended to be a play on the contrast between Cancer, ruled by the Moon, and Capricorn, ruled by Saturn. In esoteric astrology, these are called the great Portals of Birth and Death. The relevance of this arcane doctrine (which is linked ultimately with the esoteric view of birth and death) to the *Car of History* will become clearer shortly, after we have glanced at two arcane engravings.

One of the most influential arcane texts from ancient times is the short essay, *On the Cave of the Nymphs*, written by the third-century AD Neoplatonist, Porphyry.[85] It is a commentary on the mysterious cave on the island of Ithaca, mentioned by the Greek poet Homer in his *Odyssey*.[86]

In section eleven of this essay, Porphyry recalls that the ancient philosophers insist that in the heavens are two gates, one of which is the Gate of Cancer, the other the Gate of Capricorn. Cancer is the gate through which souls descend into earthly birth, while Capricorn is the one through which they ascend in the post-mortem return to the spiritual realm. It is, Porphyry continues, the reason why the Romans celebrate their Saturnalia, when the Sun is in Capricorn, and why, during this festivity, the slaves wear the sandals of those who are free:

> the legislator obscurely signified by this ceremony, that, through this gate of heavens, those who are now born slaves will be liberated through the Saturnian festival, and the house attributed to Saturn, that is, Capricorn, when they live again, and return to the fountain of life.[87]

Something of the symbolism of this passage from Porphyry is reflected in the *Car of History*. It is this passage alone which explains why the Muse should be displaying her sandal on the edge of the chariot, above the head of George Washington (figure 7). She is showing that she wears the sandal of freedom, and at the same time indicating with her foot the human source of that freedom.

Those not conversant with esoteric symbolism may feel that this interpretation of the *Car of History* seems forced, and that the writings of the third-century Porphyry can have nothing to do with the statuary, or indeed with the Royal Arch symbolism of the Masons. In view of this, I would like to direct attention to two engravings, the first of which (opposite, top) is associated with Porphyry's vision of the cave.[88]

This illustrates the cave of the nymphs itself, and emphasizes the contrast between the light of day and the dark of the telluric. Two great arches circle the central images – one is an arch of light, the other an arch of darkness. The most interesting parallel between this engraving and the woodcut which represents the Royal Arch of Masonry is that, hovering above the Arch itself, *in the light of day*, is the Sun and Moon. Below and above the Arch are the five stars which represent the planets.

Here the darkness is represented by a mirror-image of the luminaries and planets, set in the darkened lower arch. This polarity of light and dark leaves us in no doubt that the two conjoined arcs represent the zodiacal circle, one half of which is in light, the other in darkness, when seen from any standpoint on the Earth.

I must also point to the remarkable correspondence in the two triangles in the hands of the two nymphs on either side of the hilltop. One displays a triangle resting on its base, the other a triangle resting on its apex. These represent the elemental powers of Fire-Air and Water-Earth, elements symbolized individually in the four corners of the engraving.

FIRE-AIR QUINTESSENCE WATER-EARTH

The two triangles meet and merge to form a six-pointed star on the roundel held in the hand of the central nymph: this star symbolizes the harmony of the *Quintessence*, within which the Four magically become Five (the Latin, *quintus* means 'fifth'). May we not trace a similar symbolism in the merging of the square and compasses to the right of the G for Geometry, beneath the Royal Arch of the figure on p.79? We can trace a similar symbolism in the arrangement of the seven stars within the radiant on George Washington's apron, for this forms a six-pointed star, with the seventh star at the centre.

The second engraving I would like to discuss in relation to the Franzoni sculpture is an arcane plate of 1788 dealing with the nature of the universal Mother Goddess, whose name is variously Isis, Virgo, Ceres and Maria.[89] The above detail of this cosmic woman (the whole engraving is figure 9) shows her seated within a curious zodiac. Although the connection with Franzoni's statuary appears to be slight, the image does illustrate many aspects of the Virgin of Washington DC, and partly explains much of the symbolism to be found in various federal buildings, such as the corn, the cornucopia and the Virgin herself.

In the present context of the Franzoni statuary, I would like merely to point to the goat on the wide band on the bodice of her dress. This is the goat of Capricorn, the representative of the gate which leads (after death) into the spiritual realms. Above the goat, beyond the halo-like form on the head of the woman, is the symbol of the fishes of Pisces, the zodiacal representative of Christ. An upper movement, from the goat of Capricorn, seems to promise a reunion after death with the spiritual domain of the Redeemer.

Below, on the hem of the woman's skirt, is the crayfish of Cancer, the symbol of the Gate of Birth. It is entirely consistent with the symbolism of the 18th century that this sign should be presented in the space between her legs and below her lap – suggestive of the location of physical birth, by which human souls descend into the plane of being. Perhaps, then, the flames which issue from between her legs are symbolic of the descent of the fire of spirit to the material plane of watery Earth?[90]

The contrast between the portal of Capricorn and the portal of Cancer might seem to exhaust the connection between this important image and Franzoni's work, but we should look a little more deeply into the engraving because of its relevance to Washington DC as a whole.

At first glance, the zodiacal circle appears absurd in its symbolism, for there is none of the usual progression of images from the Ram of Aries through to the Fishes of Pisces. All seems to border on chaos: the horseman of Sagittarius is next to the fishes of Pisces, while Pisces is followed by the Bull of Taurus, which is, in turn, followed by the scales of Libra. Is this image meant to represent the zodiac in disorder, ages in chaos?

In fact, a cool appraisal of the symbolism explains this apparent disorder. Under the impulse of Virgo, some of the signs (like the life forces they are) have descended to the Earth plane, and participate in the central action of the picture. Capricorn is on her breast, while the amphora on her shoulder, which gives so liberally of a stream of water, is Aquarius (itself missing from the zodiacal sequence in the circle). The female is, of course, Virgo, while the guardian lions at her side, the menacing guardians of the Virgin, represent the Leo of the zodiac who have stepped from the heavens on to the plane of Earth, through the invisible gateway which links the spiritual with the material.

We shall examine this fascinating picture in another context later. For the moment I would like to point out that the notion of birth and death, as expressed in Capricorn and Cancer, are given a unity of purpose in the female Virgo which represents ever-germinating life, under the dominant influence of the Moon (the inner concentric contains images of the Moon in different phases, symbolizing the dominion of the Moon over birth into form).

This woman also stands on the edge of a zodiac, as does the Clio of the Franzoni statuary. One might expect that she would be standing on Virgo (the opposite sign to the fishes of Pisces, above the Moon at her head), but this cannot be, for she represents Virgo herself. When fully appreciated, the symbolism almost soars beyond comprehension. In detaching herself from eternity to descend to the Earthly plane, Franzoni's Clio is turning herself inside out. She stands with her feet (that part of the body which is ruled by Pisces) on thc arch of the zodiac which is ruled by the opposite sign to Pisces: to emerge into time from eternity, she has had to dislodge herself so completely that she reverses her polarity.

A further connection with the Franzoni statuary is that this is a remarkable portrayal of a woman (representative of the soul) descending into time. The zodiacal circle represents eternity – that which (like Clio) is free of time: the Virgin herself, along with a number of associated zodiacal signs, has wrenched herself free, and has emerged from the archetypal world into the material realm. The Clio of Franzoni's work inhabits this half-incarnate world, for she too is a spiritual being who, by virtue of her destiny as recorder of history, has to stand half in the world, looking down upon its imperfections and perfections as dispassionately as possible.

The usual zodiacal symbolism of the Royal Arch seems to be reversed in the *Car of History*. The Saturn symbolism is at the top, at the zenith, of the statuary globe, while the Cancer symbolism is completed in the stonework of the Capitol below: in effect, *in the space of the doorway*. This is at once simple and profound: by this symbolic stratagem, the doorway in the Capitol, leading towards its centre, is invested with the notion of the Cancer doorway, which penetrates the two worlds and permits ingress from the heavenly into the earthly. It is therefore equated with a Door of Life. By means of this fascinating symbolism, the life force of Cancer is, so to speak, embedded in the fabric of the Capitol itself.

Perhaps this is a very suitable symbolism in a Statuary Hall given over to memorials in tribute to the lives of great men and women, who have passed into the higher world beyond the portal of death. Certainly from the Earth plane, this is symbolic of a passage into history. By this deeply conceived symbolism the Capitol is transformed in an image of the spiritual world, of eternity, while the bearer of the clock remains as a symbol of passing time.

Franzoni, then, appears to have reversed the accepted symbolism of the Royal Arch to reflect upon the true nature of time. History, the symbolism proclaims, is the record of death, of the evanescent – of those things subject to the passing of time. In contrast, the Capitol building (in which are embedded and hidden the lower segments of the zodiac) is a triumphant symbol of the eternal, of life, of those spiritual verities which cannot die. In other words, the Capitol – or the *idea* behind the Capitol – remains eternal and indestructible, while the world of Man that serves the Capitol 'in history' is involved in the mutations of time.

In view of these far-reaching conclusions, we must ask if Thomas Taylor's translation of Porphyry is likely to have been known to the Americans who were involved in the early stages of the building of the federal city. The answer is yes. Taylor, a friend of the poet William Blake, the artist John Flaxman and the writer Mary Wollstonecraft, was well known in America in the early part of the 19th century. His most important contributions to the literature of the period were new translations of the classical text of initiation, which he selected from a wide variety of sources.[91] In a later decade his writings had a profound influence on the Transcendentalists, such as Ralph Waldo Emerson and Bronson Alcott.[92]

If it *was* Carlo Franzoni who introduced the zodiac into this sculpture, is it possible to trace any prototypes with which he might have been familiar? The answer to this question is interesting, for it leads us to the origin of the idea of a zodiacal wrapping around a globe.

Franzoni was born into minor aristocracy,[93] and being a cultured individual must have familiarized himself with the rich sculpture of what was then, due to the mutations of Italian history, the Kingdom of Tuscany. When he was invited to work on the Capitol building by the American government, he was living in Florence. Among the ancient sculptures in the city museum was a Mithraic statue usually called *Kronos*, or 'Time' (left). The image is of a lion-headed human figure, with a serpent coiled around its body. The figure stands on a large orb, which must be a celestial sphere, because around it is a zodiacal belt. However, this leontocephalic image, derived from the ancient hermetic mysteries, is not really an image of time: it is an image of *Zervan Akarana*, a mighty spiritual being of the Mithraists who (like Clio) stands outside time.[94] However, this distinction – important to the understanding of Mithraism – is not of great importance in the present context. Ior if Franzoni did see the statue in the Florentine museum, he would have been led to believe by contemporary historians that it symbolized merely Time.

Since the theme of his superb *Car of History* is nothing other than 'Clio recording time', we may not be surprised that Franzoni should have remembered the earlier arcane image, in his beloved Florence, of a figure standing upon a zodiacal arch. Although I have no inclination to press this point further, it does explain how a symbolism once widely used in the ancient world should have found its way into the new federal city which – nominally at least – was concerned at that time exclusively with classical imagery.

If we reject this hermeneutic level of Masonic symbolism, we are still left with a deep meaning which relates to the foundation magic of the Masons. The fact is that the three signs of the zodiac, in the time when Franzoni carved this *Car of History*, were ruled by only two planets:

- Sagittarius was ruled by Jupiter
- Capricorn was ruled by Saturn
- Aquarius was ruled by Saturn

Even in modern times, astrologers regard the first two signs as being ruled by these same planets. However, in the last decades of the 19th century the rulership of Aquarius was changed, and given over to the 'new' planet, Uranus.[95] In 1819, there seems to have been no call for this amendment to the ancient tradition, and Aquarius was still under the rule of Saturn. In view of this, within the rulership with which the Masons of the day were concerned, two of the signs on the broken arch were ruled by Saturn, which was recognized as the planet of time.

This would be a fitting association for a Car of History, which marks the passage of time – especially as the chariot is represented as travelling in the direction marked out by the two Saturn-ruled signs, from the Jupiter of Sagittarius to the Saturn of Aquarius.

Given its dual function as clock-face and wheel, it is perhaps not surprising that the circular face has six bas-relief spokes radiating to the white 'wheel-rim' on which are depicted the 12 Roman numerals. What is of immediate interest is that each of these spokes is decorated with the five-leafed floral motif associated with Virgo.

It has been suggested that Franzoni's masterpiece inspired John Quincy Adams to write a humorous sonnet. About 1939, a workman is supposed to have found a 'yellow and dust-covered piece of paper' tucked securely into a corner crevice of the Willard clock framed by Franzoni's statuary.[96] It appeared to be an autograph sonnet by Adams, who had served the last 17 years of his life as Representative for Massachusetts. In this poem, constructed in the manner of a Petrarchan sonnet, Adams addresses the statue of Clio, who listens to 'the wordy war' born of the 'frantic reason of this wandering star', in the Capitol debating chambers. He begs the Muse to persuade these men away from mere words to deeds, that her volume may finally bear: 'one blessed page/Of deeds devoted to their native land'.

Genuinely by Adams or not, this poem does raise important questions. For instance, is it true that this Muse who drives over a zodiacal arch is nothing more than an allegory of a recording angel? Or is it possible (as I firmly believe) that Franzoni's female is of a much higher order, and should be ranked among the loveliest of arcane works in Washington DC? Furthermore, is it within the capability of spiritual beings – such as Clio, the cave nymphs or the archetypal Virgo – to participate actively in the life of Man? Or must these higher beings look on, in astonishment or awe, and merely record and observe, without participation, these antics which mankind calls history?

This question may have no answer, but one of the aims of this book is to look closely at an attempt which has been made to invite the stellar powers to radiate their benign influences the city of Washington DC. In the light of that inquiry, the Franzoni statuary may be far more important than has hitherto been recognized. From its secure place above a doorway in the Capitol building, it reflects upon the nature of the relationship which the spiritual world holds to the realm of mankind, where birth into Light and death into Darkness seem to be the beginning and end of all created things.

Chapter Five

> The Second Day of July 1776. will be the most memorable Epoca, in the History of America. – I am apt to believe that it will be celebrated by succeeding Generations, as the great anniversary Festival.
>
> (From a letter by John Adams to his wife, dated 3 July 1776, quoted by Charles F. Jenkins, *Button Gwinnett. Signer of the Declaration of Independence*, 1926, p. 86ff.)

The French astronomer Joseph Lalande, so used to standing in the darkness while looking up at the stars, would probably have thought of only one star as he stood in a darkened Parisian room on 28 November 1778. In his capacity as Master of the Lodge of Nine Muses, Lalande was mourning with his Brothers (of which one was the American, Benjamin Franklin) the passing of the writer Voltaire.[1]

Following Masonic tradition, the room had been completely hung in black, and was lighted only by candles. On transparent veils were inscribed quotations from the writer's books. Personifications of Poetry and History were weeping over the death of their son. These and other funerary symbols were guarded by 27 Brethren with drawn swords.

The number 27 is the Masonic three times three (3 x 3 x 3), a reference to the 'Living Arch' which, according to the revelations of the secrets of Masonry published by Avery Allyn in 1831, symbolized the human Royal Arch.[2] This was an arch formed by Masons when ritualistically pronouncing or portraying the secret name of God (see over).

The symbolism was fairly obvious. There was a triple bonding of right arms above the heads of the participants, a triple bonding at the heart level, and a triple touching at the feet, which were arranged to form a triangle upon the floor. Symbolically, the three levels of Creation united: the Trinity of Heaven passed through the Trinity of Man to form a Trinity on the Earth.

Among the symbols guarded by these 27 Brothers was a pyramid. Even the funerary pyramid was an arcane numerological arrangement: it consisted of four triangles, leaning upon each other. The four triangles (4 x 3) created an apex which slanted in a fourfold arrangement to trace upon the Earth the form of a square. Thus, the spiritual ternary (3) was being transformed into an earthly quaternary (4) – a standard symbolism of a union of Heaven with Earth.

As he gazed at the pyramid, Lalande would almost certainly have been drawn to thinking about the star Sirius. An astronomer who had shown great interest in ancient orientations, he could not help recognizing the importance assigned to this star by the ancients. If the Egyptian pyramids themselves were not aligned to it, he knew full well that a large number of Egyptian temples *had* been, and that an entire Egyptian calendar was regulated by it. In his massive four-volume study of stellar lore, Lalande had listed six alternative names for Sirius, and gave its position in 1750 with remarkable accuracy. His interest in Sirius was almost personal: he would have known that in the horoscope for his own birth, the Sun and Mercury had bracketed this powerful star.[3] Undoubtedly, the Egyptian pyramid and the star Sirius would have brought to his mind a surprising work by the man for whom the Lodge of Sorrows had been convened.

In his *Micromégas* of 1752, Voltaire had set the home of his giant-hero on the star Sirius. In this work – prophetic by almost a century – Micromégas notes that his stellar home has a huge satellite. Of course, in 1778 no one – not even Lalande – would know that Sirius really *did* have a satellite companion. Over half a century would pass before Voltaire's prevision was confirmed: it was not until 1844 that the Prussian astronomer Friedrich Wilhelm Bessel established that Sirius had a companion, and that this great dog-star, which a Roman poet had imagined as 'a distant sun', was really a binary, or pair of stars.[4]

Sirius, the dog-star, was called *Sihor* by the ancient Egyptians, who represented it as a dog-headed divinity, sometimes as a dog, representative of the god Anubis. The importance of the star in the ancient Egyptian culture cannot be overstated. Many Egyptian temples were oriented to the dog-star in ancient times. The astronomer Norman Lockyer studied many of these orientations, and among the most interesting he published was the orientation of the Temple of Isis at Denderah, which was directed to Sirius.[5] This Sirian orientation is of particular interest to us because three zodiacs have survived in the Denderah temple complex. As Lockyer points out, in the fourth century BC, Sirius rose with the sun on the Egyptian New Year. This, in mythological language, was the star-goddess Isis mingling her light with that of the sun-god, Ra.

The importance of the Egyptian star was recognized by Masons, who introduced its symbolism into their rituals, first in France and then in the United States. The American Freemason John Fellows wrote of Sirius as the 'radiant star', which was so widely used in the Masonic symbolism of America: 'The Blazing Star is Anubis, the Dog-star; whose rising forewarned the Egyptians of the approach of the overflowing of the Nile.'[6]

It was scarcely surprising that the most sacred star of the Egyptians should have found its way into the Masonic mysteries, for the speculative Masons who sought out the origins of their craft seemed always to perfect their studies in Egypt. There may be little doubt that this Masonic transmission explains why Sirius should have become important for the United States of America. The new world was tied to the hermetic ancient world by several symbols, but the most secret of these was the Egyptian star, the flaming star which the Mason Napoleon Bonaparte had emblazoned on his apron.

Alongside the Egyptian star, the triangle had always been a most important symbol in Masonic circles. That it was a cosmic triangle was rarely in doubt, because in certain symbolic forms it was represented

with the Eye of God (or the Eye of Providence) centred within the triangular space. In one fascinating pot-pourri of Masonic symbols (alongside), designed in 1865, the triangle takes pride of place. The scene is almost theatrical. Below a tympanum, on which sits a woman with corn and flowers on either side of her, is a dramatic scene: a modern Mason, with his apron much in evidence, draws back a curtain. Opposite, is a representative 'the keeper of the secret lore', an Egyptian Hermes, who draws back the other curtain. They are revealing the Mysteries. Beyond the curtain there is a dramatic focus which shows three men killing the Master Mason, Hiram, during the building of the Temple of Solomon. Revealed in a radiant glory of sunburst is the Masonic triangle: in this instance, it contains not the Eye of God, but the name of God, revealed in Hebraic letters.

Figure 10 is a little more sophisticated. Since it is from a French Masonic source, we might reasonably expect Egyptian symbolism to dominate, yet even here the triangle predominates. The entire plate is supposed to represent different aspects of 'Esoteric Masonry'. Above the head of the personification of Masonry is a double triangle, its rays illumining a pair of pyramids, symbolizing the idea of a celestial Trinity finding an expression on the Earth plane through triangular or pyramidic forms. Two of the cupids flying around the female are grasping triangles – one holds a drafting triangle, the other a Masonic square. The plate displays the three levels of being – the ideal, or *heavenly*, triangles in the light-filled skies; the *human* triangles in the hands of the cupids, and the *earthly* triangles in the pyramids.

Is it true, as this wood engraving (above) and figure 10 suggest, that the mystery of Masonic symbolism centres upon a cosmic triangle that finds harmonic expression on the plane of Earth?

*

In the years leading up to the 20th century, the Bostonian merchant and amateur architect Franklin W. Smith became obsessed with the notion that a cultural centre should be built in Washington DC. He presented the proposed idea to Congress in 1900, and it was taken seriously enough for plans to be drawn up, projecting the proposal.[7] It was an outstanding vision – a vast complex of 11 groups of buildings, each in a style he considered to represent the cultural achievements of a different civilization.[8]

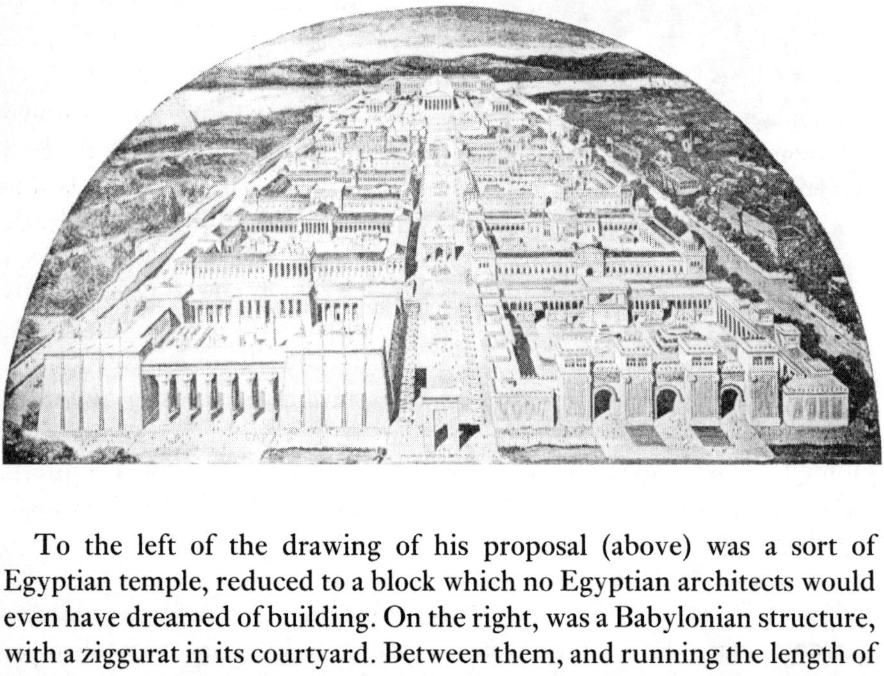

To the left of the drawing of his proposal (above) was a sort of Egyptian temple, reduced to a block which no Egyptian architects would even have dreamed of building. On the right, was a Babylonian structure, with a ziggurat in its courtyard. Between them, and running the length of eight eclectically designed cultural centres, was the equivalent of a *via sacra*, or sacred way. This led, by way of triumphal arches, to the Temple of the Presidents, which backed on to the Potomac.

As we shall see when we examine Smith's proposals in more detail, he had much support for this vast building programme, and some of his schemes did influence the later development of Washington DC. However, this complex of galleries was probably too extraordinary – too eccentric – to be taken seriously. Even so, there was one detail in the design which attracts one's attention, even today.

In the background to his drawing one can just make out three pyramids, ranged along the Potomac. It is these pyramids which explain my reference to Smith's brave, ruinously expensive and ludicrous plan: he may have been a Mason, and his plans were certainly supported by many Masons who were well aware of the significance of the pyramids in Washington DC. Like the pyramid on the reverse of the Seal of the United States (discussed later), those of Franklin W. Smith had been marginalized, as though they could have no significance in the cultural life of Washington DC.

I shall look at the symbolism of these pyramids in some depth later, and I shall examine in greater depth the ideas which Smith had for the improvement of Washington DC. For the moment, we should ask the rather obvious question: why should there have been so recurrent an interest in Egyptian symbolism – in such things as pyramids – in the non-theocratic Republic of North America?

Masonry's connections with the civilizing influence of the Republic were cemented to a great extent by the development of the new fraternal language, and by the encouragement of an aspiration to virtue, learning and religion. These two influences received ultimate expression in the spread of cornerstone ceremonies, designed to mark the foundation of important buildings or engineering projects. Symbolically, such ceremonials ensured that there was a relationship between Heaven and Earth: architecture was viewed as an instrument for permitting the unrestrained influx of heavenly virtues into the locality where cosmically oriented buildings were erected.

The problem was that the majority of foundation ceremonies in the ancient and mediaeval worlds (to which Masonry traced its operative origins) had been directed either towards pagan gods, or, with the development of Christian architecture, towards specific saints. This would not seem to be a suitable tradition for the new Republic to embrace. The ancient Egyptians and Greeks had oriented their temples and sanctuaries towards stars openly associated with such gods and goddesses as Osiris and Isis, which by modern standards were pagan.[9] The early Christians had oriented their churches and ecclesiastical buildings according to sunrises on specific saint-days – usually days linked with the saints after whom the edifices were named. This latter practice accounts for the importance which mediaeval builders attached to the ecclesiastical calendar – the named saint-days of which survived into almanacs used by 19th-century Americans.[10] The new Republic of the United States, while distinctly Christian in spirit and aware of the power of the symbolism of mythology, had no strong allegiance to either the pagan gods or the hierarchy of saints favoured by the Roman Church. Even so, the mediaeval religious notions of saint-days proliferated. A good example of this is in an almanac used by George Washington himself, to record (as he wrote alongside) 'Where and how my time is spent'.[11]

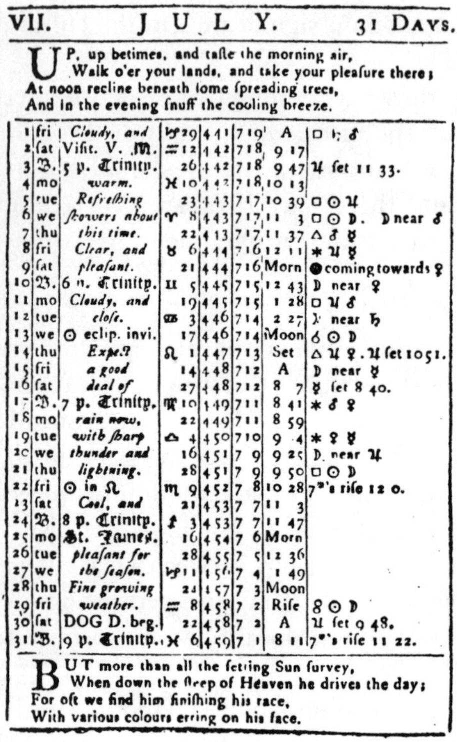

VII. J U L Y. 31 DAYS.

UP, up betimes, and taste the morning air,
Walk o'er your lands, and take your pleasure there;
At noon recline beneath some spreading trees,
And in the evening snuff the cooling breeze.

1	fri	*Cloudy, and*	♑ 29	4 41	7 19	A	□ ♄ ♂
2	sat	Visit. V. M.	♒ 12	4 42	7 18	9 17	
3	B.	5 p. Trinity.	26	4 42	7 18	9 47	♃ set 11 33.
4	mo	*warm.*	♓ 10	4 42	7 18	10 13	
5	tue	*Refreshing*	23	4 43	7 17	10 39	□ ☉ ♃
6	we	*showers about*	♈ 8	4 43	7 17	11 3	□ ☉ ☽. ☽ near ♂
7	thu	*this time.*	22	4 13	7 17	11 37	△ ♂ ☿
8	fri	*Clear, and*	♉ 6	4 44	7 16	12 11	✶ ♃ ☿
9	sat	*pleasant.*	21	4 44	7 16	Morn	● coming towards ♀
10	B.	6 p. Trinity.	♊ 5	4 45	7 15	12 43	☽ near ♀
11	mo	*Cloudy, and*	19	4 45	7 15	1 28	□ ♃ ♂
12	tue	*close.*	♋ 3	4 46	7 14	2 27	☽ near ♄
13	we	☉ eclip. invi.	17	4 46	7 14	Moon	☌ ☉ ☽
14	thu	*Expect*	♌ 1	4 47	7 13	Set	△ ♃ ♀. ♃ set 10 51.
15	fri	*a good*	14	4 48	7 12	A	☽ near ☿
16	sat	*deal of*	27	4 48	7 12	8 7	☿ set 8 40.
17	B.	7 p. Trinity.	♍ 10	4 49	7 11	8 41	✶ ♂ ♀
18	mo	*rain now,*	22	4 49	7 11	8 59	
19	tue	*with sharp*	♎ 4	4 50	7 10	9 4	✶ ♀ ☿
20	we	*thunder and*	16	4 51	7 9	9 25	☽ near ♃
21	thu	*lightning.*	28	4 51	7 9	9 50	□ ☉ ☽
22	fri	☉ in ♌	♏ 9	4 52	7 8	10 28	7*'s rise 12 0.
23	sat	*Cool, and*	21	4 53	7 7	11 3	
24	B.	8 p. Trinity.	♐ 3	4 53	7 7	11 47	
25	mo	St. James.	16	4 54	7 6	Morn	
26	tue	*pleasant for*	28	4 55	7 5	12 36	
27	we	*the season.*	♑ 11	4 56	7 4	1 49	
28	thu	*Fine growing*	24	4 57	7 3	Moon	
29	fri	*weather.*	♒ 8	4 58	7 2	Rise	☍ ☉ ☽
30	sat	DOG D. beg.	22	4 58	7 2	A	♃ set 9 48.
31	B.	9 p. Trinity.	♓ 6	4 59	7 1	8 11	7*'s rise 11 22.

BUT more than all the setting Sun survey,
When down the steep of Heaven he drives the day;
For oft we find him finishing his race,
With various colours erring on his face.

The July sheet from this almanac-diary is interesting because it records both Christian and pagan days of observation. For example, 2 July is the Christian festival of the Visitation of the Virgin Mary (abbreviated to *Visit. V. M.*). At the bottom of the same page, opposite 30 July, is a note that the dog-days begin (abbreviated to *DOG D. beg.*) – these were originally linked with the dog-star Sirius.[12]

It is not perhaps surprising that the ancient Egyptian god name for Sirius, *Spdt*  (which has come down to us in the Greek version *Sothis*), was represented by hieroglyphics which included a glyph of a five-pointed star. More remarkable is the fact that the first of these glyphs resembles an obelisk.[13]

Christian and pagan beliefs lived on together in the minds of most cultured men and women of the late 18th century, and this was no more true than in the realm of astrology, wherein even the names of the planets and the zodiacal signs could be traced back to pagan prototypes. It is true that the planets and signs had been sanctified and Christianized by the mediaeval Masons, who made extensive and imaginative use of both planetary and zodiacal symbols in their finest buildings. Even so, by the 19th century this sanctification and Christian adaptation had been forgotten, and there was a general feeling that the astrological symbols were somehow pagan. Fortunately, this feeling was not widespread among the Masons, who were inclined by disposition and spiritual training to seek new meanings in the old forms.

The leaders of the early Masons were well educated, and in the 18th century a well-educated person generally had some knowledge of the classics. This explains why, whenever a symbolism for the new Republic was discussed for practical purposes, ideas frequently circulated around ancient mythology. As we shall see, this also explains why the mottoes adopted by Congress for the Seal of the United States derived from the literature of ancient Rome. The same factor further explains why the planet Jupiter – the equivalent of the Greek Zeus, the chief of the ancient gods of Greece – should play such an important role in the horoscopes cast for the foundation charts and cornerstone ceremonies of the early Republic.

By the end of the 18th century, the cornerstone ceremony had become the most obvious public expression of the Masonic connection with the operative Masonry of the past – as the importance accorded to the square, the gavel and the trowel in such ceremonies attests. I do not mean to imply for a moment that there were not excellent Masonic scholars with an interest in traditional astrology – indeed, later we shall consider the work of one or two of these astrologers, to note their influence in the Craft. My purpose in emphasizing the cornerstone ceremony is to point to a rite that, in the early 19th century and earlier, formed a living spiritual connection between Masonry and mediaeval Masonic practices rooted in arcane schools.

Very few important buildings in the ancient world or the late mediaeval period had been constructed without the formality of a foundation stone ceremony as part of the dedication to a particular god or saint. This practice was continued into North American cornerstone ceremonials, which involved prayers, invocations to angelic beings, and religious rituals. There can be no doubt that the ancient practice of casting horoscopes to determine in advance suitable cosmic conditions for erecting a building was also continued into American rituals. By this means, it was intended that buildings should receive the blessing of the spiritual beings who dwelled in the heavens.

The ethos of Masonry encouraged Freemasons to see all worthwhile human activities as being spiritual in nature – activities that should be conducted in the belief that the Temple was the Self. In 1870, the Masonic author L. E. Reynolds wrote:

> Every one that has received the degrees of Ancient Freemasonry, is aware that they represent the building of a spiritual Temple, not made with hands; eternal in the heavens.[14]

The idea, which found sanction in Holy Writ, is still valid in modern

Masonry and was valid long before 1870, for, from its beginnings, Masonry was itself concerned with spiritual activity, and with the striving for inner perfecting.[15] Within this framework of belief, which held that the building of the Temple of Solomon was an expression of the building of the inner human being, the ceremony of the cornerstone rituals was conducted with some awareness of the exigencies of the spiritual world. This spiritual world was represented by the zodiac, planets, constellations and stars. It is therefore not surprising that stars should figure so abundantly in the early symbolism of American Masonry. The stars, being symbols of the eternal spirit – of the inaccessible stellar realm – were spiritual realities which might once have been pagan, but which were now thoroughly Christianized.

The 'open ritual' of the Masonic foundation ceremony is recorded in numerous documents, plates and memorial plaques in the United States. In the years following the Revolution, the Masonic fraternities held ceremonial layings for such new enterprises as bridges, locks, universities, government buildings, state houses, memorials and even churches. Such buildings were aligned with the stars, and with the spiritual beings who ruled the stars.

In most cases, the ceremonies were held in public, usually accompanied by considerable Masonic pomp, and sometimes with the unveiled plaques left to public view, announcing the speculative background to this operative phase of speculative Masonry. Usually the official records list the name of the officiating Grand Master, the Lodge present at the ceremony, and the date. As we have seen, the date was not always expressed merely in terms of the ordinary calendrical system, but in terms of the year of Masonry, dating from the year of the Declaration of Independence.

By contrast, the astrological conditions pertaining to the ritual of the cornerstone were rarely made public. This was nothing to do with 'Masonic secrecy' – it was merely a continuation of an ancient tradition. On the whole, only specialists such as astrologers were interested in the validity of foundation charts. They might be consulted, and hired to draw up a chart for a propitious moment, but their deliberations were usually too arcane to attract public notice.

Although a survey of the foundation charts used in the early phase of the building of Washington DC reveals the importance of astrology, and, indeed, confirms beyond doubt that astrology played a most important role in the early Masonic rites, the rationale of astrology was rarely discussed openly, even in Masonic documents. Knowledge of the stars – in so far as they were understood in Masonic circles – was preserved as secrets best left to those with specialist knowledge of such things.

One of my aims in this book is to reveal something of the extraordinary astrological symbolism contained within this arcane knowledge of the stars.

The cornerstone for the Washington Monument was laid at the north-east corner of the foundation in the early afternoon of 4 July 1848. As I have indicated, probably one reason why the Masons chose to lay the stone in the afternoon was because they wished to allow the all-important Virgo to become operative in the chart. Shortly before lunchtime on that day, the Moon went into Virgo.[16]

In fact, there was *another* Virgoan influence in this chart which might be missed by someone not familiar with the workings of astrology. The all-important Dragon's Head in the 1848 chart is in 25 degrees of Virgo.

Remarkably, during the morning of 18 September 1793, when the Capitol building was founded, *the Sun was also passing through this same degree of Virgo*. This could scarcely be accidental – it must have been arranged for astrological reasons by the Masons. Both placings – and hence, both charts – point to something of profound importance.

According to mediaeval Arab astrologers (who excelled in star lore), this degree had a particular importance: it marked that point in the zodiac where the Moon was thought to promote the greatest happiness and well-being.[17] We must presume, then, that the intention behind the choice of moment was that this beneficial influence would be transmitted into Washington DC.

The astrologer who erected the 1848 chart really knew what he was up to, and it demonstrates how the virtue specific to Virgo was allowed to pour into the stream of Washington DC's spiritual life. The in-streaming of an invisible virtue was reinforced, or made manifest, in the lapidary figures and Virgoan details, which were to become so much in evidence as the building of the city proceeded.

As I indicated in Chapter 3, the plan of Washington DC drawn up in 1791 by Charles L'Enfant and Andrew Ellicott, on the instructions of George Washington, set the theme for the building of the new city. The marker was laid with Masonic honours, at a moment which reflected the nature of Virgo. It was this marker that linked the space of the federal city with the time of the cosmos, which was to form the basis for orienting L'Enfant's plan. Given one or two deviations, it was this plan which formed the basic grid within which the federal city was built. Even the

Washington Monument, which L'Enfant had determined as an important nexus in his plan, but which had caused so many delays and financial heartaches in the building, was completed by 1884.

However, the Monument was *not* completed according to the L'Enfant plan. On 7 August 1783, the Continental Congress had voted unanimously for an equestrian monument to honour George Washington. L'Enfant, working, however reluctantly, under the directions of the Commissioners, who were aware of what Congress had intended, had visualized that the statue should stand on the Mall. The site for such a monument was marked by a pyramid of stones until well into the 19th century, and seems to have located exactly the axis of meridian and east-west point drawn up by Andrew Ellicott in 1791.[18] It was long believed that this point marked the exact centre of the old ten-mile square of the District of Columbia, though this was not the case.[19]

After his death, the idea was mooted in Congress of turning the site (or the central part of the Capitol itself) into a tomb for George Washington, whose body had, by this time, been buried at Mount Vernon. When approached by John Quincy Adams on this delicate matter, Mrs Washington, 'taught . . . never to oppose my private wishes to the public welfare', agreed to have the body transferred.[20] The Senate kept delaying the practical issues, however, until it was too late: after the death of Martha Washington, permission to remove the body of her husband was denied.

In spite of such delays and setbacks, a considerable change of vision was required to move from so thoroughly a neoclassical design as a horse-rider, to an obelisk which was essentially Egyptian in spirit. Historical documents indicate that this change was directed by Masons. Furthermore, not only was the form of the Monument different from that anticipated by L'Enfant, it was not even sited in the position he had visualized.

Since the Monument was to be massive in comparison with the equestrian statue ordered by Congress, it had been necessary to survey the land prior to locating it there. Engineers found that the spot central to the axis of the Mall (and then still marked by the pyramid of stones on the north-west line of the White House) would not be stable enough to support such a heavy building.[21] As it turned out, the site which was chosen, several hundred feet to the east of this axis, later proved equally unstable, and had to be shored up massively by pouring concrete into excavated channels. When we examine the implications of this change, we shall realize that it was probably not due to the official reasons given.

Another telling point is that the simple obelisk, now held in such esteem, was far from popular in the early days of its construction. The competition for the design of the monument, first announced in 1863 by the Washington National Monument Society, gave birth to many different ideas, several of which involved a pyramid or a series of pyramids.[22] In fact, there was nothing new in this approach, for within a year of Washington's death it was recognized that the great man could most fittingly be memorialized by means of a massive pyramid.

The committee appointed by Congress a few days after Washington's death seemed to have in mind the idea of a vast tomb as the Monument for the American hero. On 18 May 1800, the House of Representatives suggested the building of a pyramid, 100 feet square at the base and 'of proportional height' (a proposal not approved by the Senate). The notion that a pyramid would best represent the idea of George Washington extended even beyond the United States. In 1800, the American painter Benjamin West (then President of the Royal Academy in London) commissioned the English architect George Dance to design a monument to the former first President: the imposing design offered by Dance was an ornate wall, flanked by two huge pyramids.[23]

The Washington National Monument Society was founded by a group of people responding to the leadership of George Watterston, in 1833. The first design for the memorial, which is still preserved in the Library of Congress, was by Peter Force,[24] who clearly admired the proposal of 18 May 1800. Peter Force was then one of the most influential men in Washington DC – he was at one time its mayor, and in 1832 had written *The National Calendar* of the United States. His design – an enormous pyramid – is distinctly Masonic in concept, involving a 'human' pyramid contained within a greater 'cosmic' pyramid. The hollow interior of the larger pyramid contains a central triple-tier hollow, surrounded by four hallways and four corner rotundas. Since the light comes from an apex 'oculus', the pyramid is partly truncated. In many ways, Force's design is spectacular, and perhaps more noteworthy than any of the many other designs which followed – including the present memorial.

From the complex history of the Monument, it emerges that the finest design (a pyramid) and the one actually completed (an obelisk) were both distinctly Egyptian in conception. This leads us to ask, what does ancient Egypt have to do with the Washington Monument?

*

Before investigating the matter further, there is another factor to consider. Although the Washington Monument now has all the outer appearance of a gigantic Egyptian obelisk, this was not the original intention. The design produced by the Freemason architect, Robert Mills, and selected by the Washington National Monument Society in 1836, was to be surrounded by a colonnaded rotunda about 250 feet in diameter and 100 feet high.[25] Its entablature would carry statuary of four-horse chariots – the quadriga of the Sun-god, Helios. The driver of the chariot was to be a representation of George Washington: the Republicans who opposed kingship seemed quite prepared to equate their hero with the Sun-god.

This obelisk was not intended to be as tapered as the one which now graces the Mall: we owe this tapering to the military engineer, Thomas Lincoln Casey, who was also the moving power behind the building of the Library of Congress. In the original design, near the top of the obelisk, there was to have been an enormous five-pointed star, but no distinctive pyramid. In a sense, it was Casey who caught the spirit of the early designers, and, towards the end of the 19th century, ensured that Washington had a pyramid (of sorts) as a monument.

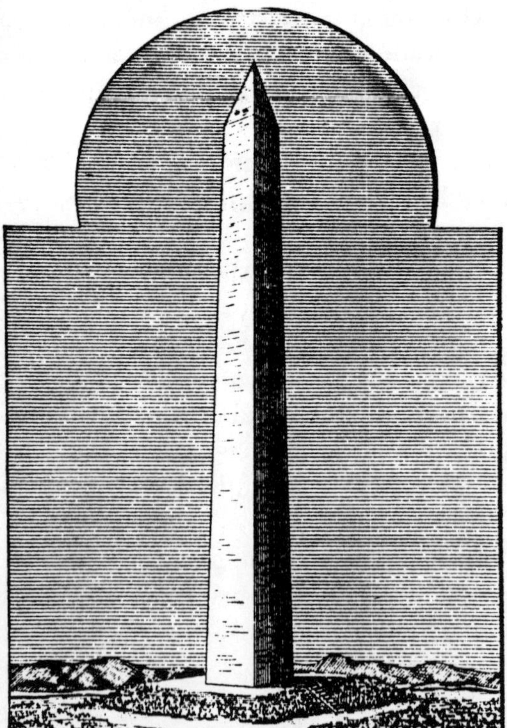

A further intriguing point is that the monument which finally emerged from this design is not technically an obelisk. It is not a single monolithic shaft but constructed from huge blocks of marble-faced masonry, granite and stone. The majority of these blocks for the first phase of building were carried from the Symington Beaver Dam quarries, in Baltimore County, while others were gifts from various parts of the world.[26] Among the many memorial stones which line the inside of the shaft are no fewer than 21 from various Masonic Lodges, with lapidary inscriptions.[27]

In accordance with Masonic practices, construction of the obelisk began on 4 July 1848 with a ceremonial laying of the enormous cornerstone, which had been donated by the Mason Thomas Symington who owned the quarries from which the Monument's marble was taken. The ceremony was conducted by Benjamin French, wearing the Masonic apron and sash George Washington had worn when he laid the cornerstone of the Capitol building in 1793.[28] The moment of the ceremonial cornerstone laying of the Monument has been preserved, and from this it is possible to reconstruct the foundation chart. I have already observed that the Moon and the lunar node were in Virgo at this moment. However, I should add that there were other important astrological factors at play, which we shall consider later. In many ways it is a remarkable horoscope, for it reflects precisely the same sort of stellar magic as was practised in ancient Egypt, millennia ago.

One hope behind the Washington National Monument Society's exertions had been that the structure would eventually reflect the idea of 'out of many, the one'. The Society had nurtured the forlorn hope that most Americans would contribute a small sum to honour the memory of their first President. This is why, in the initial stages, contributions had been limited to one dollar per person. The history of the funding of the Monument is in some ways a sad one; suffice it to say that the enterprise was halted by lack of funds. It took over 30 years for Congress to be bullied and cajoled into funding the operation to ensure completion, during which time the half-finished Monument remained fundless and stuck at 150 feet.

With adequate funding from Congress finally assured, the Monument was begun again. First, military engineers dug away the old foundations and bedding piers, and both extended and strengthened them, in preparation for taking the massive load which the eventual 550 feet of masonry would exert. Then a couple of courses (added by incompetent builders[29]) were removed, and the building of the shaft was begun again. The operation was in excellent hands: Thomas Lincoln Casey, whose influence on engineering and building in the federal city in the last decades of the 19th century was prodigious, had calculated that the Monument should be finished in just over four years. The time chosen for the laying of the 'cornerstone' is recorded in a most curious way: it is specified as though it were given in astrological terms. The event (remarkable as a cornerstone ceremony 150 feet above the city) was arranged for Saturday, 7 August 1880, *at one minute of 11 o'clock*.[30] This is a very specifically stated time, and implies that the moment was chosen because of some very precise astronomical or astrological phenomenon.

Before I examine the implications of this time, I should observe that once again the day seems to have been chosen because of its Virgoan links. On that day, three planets were in Virgo – the Moon, Mars and Uranus.[31]

The moment is quite fascinating from an astrological point of view, raising interesting issues. Rather than treat with complex issues, here, I deal with these in a note.[32] At this point, I will raise the question, what is the consequence of giving such a precise moment for a foundation? In terms of astrology, a minute does not usually make a great deal of difference to planetary positions: the most rapid-moving of the celestial bodies is the Moon, and in one minute its movement is measurable in seconds of arc which are not perceptible to the naked eye. However, the one thing which can change quite dramatically in a minute is the degrees on the Ascendant, and the other three angles of the chart. At the latitude of Washington DC, in the early days of August, every five minutes a whole degree of the zodiac rises over the horizon. Since the stars are conveniently measured against this zodiac, it is very likely that the time of 10.59 a.m. was chosen to point to a particular star.

A glance at the lists of star positions for the year confirms that, at that time, an important star was just rising over the eastern horizon, above the Capitol building. *This was the star Spica, the most important star in the constellation Virgo.*[33]

Spica is the prime star, the *alpha*, of Virgo, and among the most splendid stars in the skies.[34] It marks the ear of wheat in the Virgin's left hand (opposite), and many of the ancient names for the star (such as *Arista* or *Stachys*) reflect the idea of wheat or corn. The Arab astrologers who were reluctant to draw the human form represented the entire constellation as a sheaf of wheat, called *Al Sunbulah*. Its importance in the ancient Egyptian religion is attested by the fact that several temples in Thebes were oriented to its setting, about 3200 BC.[35] Because of its close proximity to the ecliptic (clearly marked in the illustration from an 18th-century sky-map, left) it has been used for millennia by sailors, which possibly helps explain the epithet *Stella Maris*, which is sometimes translated as 'Star of the Sea'. In the astrological tradition, Spica bestows success and great honours.

The true significance behind the engineered rising of this beautiful star on 7 August 1880 will become clear only much later. It is linked with the deeper mysteries of Washington DC which is the main theme of this book. For the moment, it is sufficient to see this importance accorded to Spica as yet another example of the importance accorded to Virgo, both as a zodiacal sign and as a constellation, in the symbolism of the city.

Although the usual processionals did not attend this curious sky-high ceremonial, in which the huge stone was swung by means of a derrick to the high building area, it was attended by President Hayes. He and his wife were witness to the actual cementing, along with selected members of the

Monument Society. The group had been carried to the construction level by means of a mechanical elevator.

As we have seen, Thomas Lincoln Casey ensured that the top of the Monument tapered to a point, and that it was, in effect, pyramidic. A close survey of this pyramid reveals that it is built up from 13 layers of stonework (the apex is made from aluminium). The symbolism reminds us of that found on the back of the dollar bill. However, the pyramid of 13 layers on the dollar bill is not complete – an incompleteness famously emphasized by the radiant triangle in the skies, enclosing the all-seeing Eye of Providence.

The pyramid of the dollar bill (see p.151) represents something unfinished, while the great pyramid atop Washington's Monument suggests something which *is* completed, even though not in marble or stone – the sacred and symbolic working matter, the *materia sacra*, of the Masons. This implies that Casey intended the pyramid which dominates the skyline of Washington DC to remain technically 'unfinished', while appearing to be completed.

The symbolism adopted earlier by Peter Force was perhaps a little more subtle, for he had allowed his truncated pyramid to be 'completed' by the light, like the one on the reverse of the Seal (and on the dollar bill). However, this symbolism took on a deeper meaning in his proposed memorial, for it permitted the influx of sunlight to render intelligible the dark realm within the pyramid. Within this darkness there was yet another pyramid – a truncated one of a sharper incline than the one that surrounded it. This Masonic symbolism was far more subtle than that exhibited in the 'completed' memorial on the Mall, for it reaches into the essence of the Masonic awareness of the struggle between light and darkness lies behind the symbolism of the cornerstone and foundation ceremonies.[36]

The Washington Monument, then, is not quite what it seems to be. It is a mystery, involved in some of the deeper mysteries of Masonic symbolism. Exactly what *was* achieved by the siting and building of the Monument will become clear later on, as we pursue the symbolism of Washington DC. For the moment, we should recognize that *the Monument represents, from almost every viewing point in the city, the same idea of a triangle hovering against the skies* that we saw in the wood engraving of 1865 (p.119). Was the Monument designed to point to something altogether higher than the memory of George Washington? Was it designed to point to something in the skies? If so, perhaps this stellar element was hinted at in the original Egyptian-revival symbol which was formerly on the false lintel over the eastern entrance to the memorial. This represented the great solar symbol of Horus – two mighty wings supporting an image of the Sun.

I have not been able to establish why Thomas Lincoln Casey removed the Egyptian-style frontage which had been placed on the east door of the Monument. Did he think that it interfered with the austere form of the obelisk?[37] Or did he have a feeling that the arcane symbolism was too obviously Masonic?

To judge from surviving prints, drawings and photographs, both the east and west doors had false lintels, beautifully decorated with an Egyptian motif – with the eagle-like wings of the Horus bird, supporting a solar disk.[38] This device, in a wide variety of subtly different forms, often appeared on doorways and stelae in the sacred buildings of Egypt, and was certainly involved with cosmological symbolism. In many respects, the device seems to be very simple: it consists of two pairs of

falcon-wings, carrying the solar disk. In some cases, two sacred cobras hang down from the Sun-disk, as for example on the limestone stela of King Ahmose, now in the Egyptian Museum at Cairo. Technically, such a device (above) is called the winged Sun-disk, with pendant uraei.[39] This symbol had been adopted, in a slightly changed form, in Western esoteric symbolism – including that of Masonry.

However, the Sun-disk on the lintel of the Egyptian-revival door of the Monument had been amended to make of George Washington a solar god: the initial W was emblazoned on the solar disk. Was it *this* aspect of the design which Casey objected to – the suggestion of deification? He can hardly have been objecting to the idea of the obelisk being linked with the Sun. A considerable esoteric literature (no doubt excited by the completing of the Monument) was being published in several esoteric communities, including the Masonic, emphasizing the solar nature of Egyptian obelisks.[40] Nor is it possible that Casey was objecting to the false lintel on the grounds that it savoured of paganism – which, of course, it did. He had so warmly embraced the 'pagan' element of the obelisk that he had gone to great trouble to ensure that the ratios of the Monument conformed to the ratios of ancient Egyptian obelisks.[41] In spite of this, some time after 1878, during which the foundations for the Monument were being strengthened, the Egyptian motifs were completely removed.

Whatever Casey's intentions, there can be absolutely no doubt that the idea of the winged-disk portal was favoured by Masons. Examples abound, but one in particular comes to mind. In England, the Egyptian-revival exterior of the Freemasons' Hall at Mainridge, Boston, constructed in the early 1860s, has a pylon-like front, with hieroglyphics on the architrave; above this is a curved frieze decorated with a gigantic winged disk around which are curled two uraeus serpents.[42]

At the time the Washington Monument was being completed, a woodcut of what was called an 'Egyptian temple gate', surmounted by a 'winged globe', was reproduced in a rare Masonic work on astrology by Robert Hewitt Brown.[43] Within a decade or so of Casey removing the offending item, an even larger Egyptian winged disk was erected in Washington DC, not far from the White House. When Franklin Smith built his extravaganza, the Hall of the Ancients, facing on to New York Avenue, its edifice was dominated by a colour image of the winged disk, replete with uraeus (plate 6).

Robert Mills' star has gone. His pantheon has gone. All that is left of his original idea is an Egyptian-like obelisk, towering over Washington DC. In many ways, the Monument is more American than Egyptian, but even to this day it seems to exude an Egyptian influence over the city. It would have been even more Egyptian had the designer, J. Goldsworth Bruff, had his way, for he had proposed to add a raised square surround to the base and to have its two entrances, to east and west, guarded by pairs of sphinxes.[44]

The Masonic dedication ceremony for the completed Monument was held on 21 February 1885, near to the anniversary of George Washington's birthday. It was in some ways an unusual day to choose for such a ceremony.[45] The weather was bitterly cold, the ground white with snow.[46] The presiding Grand Master was John S. Tyson, and the Senior Grand Warden Edward T. Schulz, who left a semi-official account of the ceremony in his history of Freemasonry: from this we can see just how deeply the Masonic Brotherhood was involved.[47] It was a well-organized affair, with the 21 Lodges of the District of Columbia, along with delegations from the Grand Lodges of Massachusetts, Rhode Island, Pennsylvania, Delaware, Maryland, Virginia, South Carolina, Georgia and Texas, as well as a considerable number of invited Brothers, at the head of the procession. The President of the United States and representatives of both Houses of Congress were waiting at the Monument, along with a vast crowd of guests and onlookers. The Marine Band, under the direction of the famous John Philip Sousa, played a number of rousing marches.

The date – so curious in many ways – must have been determined with great care. Whoever had arranged the time for the event had waited to ensure that the planet Jupiter should have just entered Virgo. It would *not* have been in Virgo if the ceremony had been held on the previous day – the *actual* birthday of the first President.

After the ritual testing of the corners of the obelisk, the Grand Master poured oil, 'an emblem of joy'. Then, using the same gavel which had been presented to George Washington for laying the Capitol cornerstone, and which was used for laying many other important public and Masonic buildings,[48] he consecrated the obelisk. The twenty-first President of the United States, Chester Alan Arthur – who had succeeded the assassinated James Garfield – then gave an address, dedicating the Monument to the name and memory of George Washington.[49] It had taken over a century for the will of Congress to be carried out: no one in that Congress of 1783 would have recognized the results of their edict.

The exceptional delay in the building of this federal monument contrasted unfavourably with the construction of other memorials in the United States. For example, the cornerstone of the Washington Monument in the city of Baltimore (also designed by Robert Mills) had been laid on 4 July 1815, with full Masonic ceremonial, in the presence of about 30,000 people.[50] It had been completed within 14 years, during which time the Masonry of the United States suffered greatly through the activities of the anti-Masonic movement. By the time the bust of Washington was lowered to complete the 15-ton statue (sculpted by the the Italian Henrico Caucici) on 25 November 1829, Masonry was under attack. One might be forgiven for thinking that this statue of Washington was to preside over the decline of the fraternity which had nourished him and his great enterprise.[51]

Given the unusual urge to introduce an 'Egyptian' element into Washington DC, we must ask if there is anything else pertaining to the Monument (without its winged-disk portal casing and its external star and sphinxes) which had an Egyptian flavour. The answer to the question is found not in the fabric or design of the monument – which constitute the spatial elements – but in the horoscope for its foundation, the temporal element.

I have already dealt with the horoscope cast for the laying of the

Washington Memorial cornerstone. It is sufficient to point out that on 4 July 1848 the Sun was in 12.45 degrees of Cancer.

The date for the founding ceremony for both Washington memorials, in Baltimore and in Washington DC, had been 4 July. This day was evidently chosen for its importance as a popular anniversary. Even an astrologer may be forgiven for thinking that the event at Washington DC, on 4 July 1848, was chosen for its historical importance, rather than for any deep significance in the cosmic moment reflected in the chart.[52] However, the fact is that the chart happens to denote a most important stellar event which links the Washington Monument with Egyptian mythology and religion.

The aluminium apex which completed the *pyramidion* may have been suggested by Geoffrey P. Marsh, who had made a special study of Egyptian obelisks and had communicated his knowledge of the subject to Casey on a number of occasions by way of a friend.[53] Marsh had pointed out that the Egyptians often covered the whole pyramidion with a close-fitting gilt bronze cap, 'the effect of which must have been magnificent'. The technique reminds one of the fact that the Pyramids themselves were faced with white marble, which must have been almost blinding in the intense brilliance of the Egyptian sun. However, Casey's intention was certainly not to blind: it is more likely that he was seeking to establish a sufficient protection from lightning, as his aluminium cap was connected to four well-earthed conductors. As it happened, the small right pyramid of pure aluminium, which weighed only 100 ounces and was just under 9 inches high, was the largest piece of this metal ever cast up to that time.[54]

On the aluminium surface were inscriptions recording the names of those who had participated in the various stages of the building, emphasizing the contribution of Thomas Lincoln Casey – who, incidentally, is named as architect. Whether it was intentional or not, the fact is that in consequence of this mention, Casey's name has the distinction of being placed on the highest point in the city. On the pyramidion is inscribed each of the dates for the cornerstone ceremonies, including the setting of the first stone at the height of 152 feet, in 1880, and for the setting of the capstone on 6 December 1884. The east-facing side of the aluminium apex was reserved for praise of God for the success of the undertaking, and for the dedication. The praise to God was recorded in Latin, as *Laus Deo*: it might just as well have been recorded in Egyptian hieroglyphics, as was the dedication on the two Egyptian sphinxes which front the Masonic Temple in Washington DC (figure 1).[55]

Interestingly, the Masonic name for God ('the Supreme Architect') did appear inside the obelisk, on one of the special dedication stones from a Grand Lodge.[56] Just so, the five-pointed star which had been rejected as a symbol for the exterior resurfaced among a number of Masonic symbols on the interior wall, on the stone donated by the Grand Lodge of Kentucky.[57] Most curious of all is the presence of a sculpted stone depicting a version of the Weeping Virgin, overlooked by winged Time and facing the broken column.[58]

The 21 Masonic dedication stones may be seen during the special tours of the interior staircase of the Monument.[59]

The extraordinary truth is that the very existence of the Washington Monument is intimately linked with the Egyptian star Sirius, the *Sihor* that the ancients represented in their sacred hieroglyphics as an obelisk-like form as well as a star. How is it possible that this most important star of the ancient world should find itself, as it were, resurrected in the architecture of the United States?

We do not have to resort to complex spherical geometry to examine the relevance of Sirius to several important charts in the history of the United States. For our general purpose, it is sufficient that we understand that, with the passage of the years, the stars appear to move against the ecliptic. This phenomenon, which is called precession, has been charted for centuries with more or less accuracy, and tables are readily available to show the positions of stars in any time during the past few thousand years. We may argue that in the 18th century the computations relating precession were not quite so accurate, or so universally agreed even among specialists, as they are now. The great French astronomer and Mason, Lalande, whose writings deeply influenced the early astronomers of the United States, gave the position of Sirius in 1750 as 10.38.22 Cancer.[60] Seventy years later, the 'philomath' Mason James Wilson gave its position of Sirius as 11.35.00 Cancer.[61] The difference in time between these observations is important, for in just over 70 years Sirius appears to move forward against the zodiacal belt almost one degree. These computations are not far off, when we consider that modern astronomical observations have established that, due to the precession of the equinoxes, the stars appear to edge forward in the zodiacal belt by 1 degree every 72 years.[62]

Sirius, which today we recognize as a binary, is set in 14 degrees of Cancer. This means that the following 72-year tabulation is reasonably accurate:

In 1992 Sirius was in 13.59 Cancer
In 1920 Sirius was in 12.59 Cancer
In 1848 Sirius was in 11.59 Cancer
In 1776 Sirius was in 10.59 Cancer
In 1704 Sirius was in 09.59 Cancer

These computations clearly show that on the day the Declaration of Independence was agreed in Philadelphia, the Sun was on Sirius.[63] Another important chart reflects the same influence. At the founding of the Washington Monument in 1848, the Sun was in 12.45 Cancer – and thus only 46 minutes from exact conjunction. Now, we must not forget that in the course of a day the Sun moves one degree in the zodiac. This means that, *in the course of that day, when the cornerstone of the Washington Monument was laid, the Sun would have passed over Sirius.*

The dedication of this same Monument was made after midday – perhaps shortly after 1.30 p.m.[64] As we have seen, this meant that the beneficial planet Jupiter, which has played such an important role in other charts connected with the city, was once again just in Virgo, in the first degree.[65] This was the very same degree occupied by the Moon at the foundation of the Monument, in 1848.[66]

Clearly this arrangement, by which Jupiter took over control from the Moon in such a precise fashion, was intentional. The prevalence of Jupiter in Virgo, in charts relating to the public buildings of Washington DC, is yet another reminder of the meaning of the Latin injunction in the motto of the Seal of the United States – *Audacibus annue coeptis* ('Favour our daring undertaking') – which is from a Virgilian invocation to the god Jupiter.[67]

Remarkable as this arrangement is, there was a far more important cosmic event at the moment of the dedication of the Monument: 13 degrees of Cancer was arising over the horizon. We see, then, that *in the course of that ceremonial, the star Sirius would have been on the eastern horizon. It would have been rising over the Capitol building, to the east of the Monument.*

We are touching upon mysteries which are so extraordinary that they seem to be beyond belief, yet one need only look to the skies, and to the records of stellar events, to realize that they are absolutely true.

In some ways, the Monument is an insipid thing, troubled by an unfortunate history. When I view it from this standpoint, I cannot help but agree with an architect who, shortly after its completion, wrote that it evoked in the spectator 'no necessity of analyzing details, no tumult of emotions', and inspired 'no thought worthy of thinking'.[68] However, when the Monument is viewed in the light of *its hidden arcane symbolism*, the insipidity of its design is suddenly illumined by a depth of arcane meaning that permits it to be ranked among the finest of modern works of art. We shall explore this at a later point.

The Mason who first signed the Declaration of Independence would have been aware of the particular significance of 4 July, as a cosmic event. The day was the second in the so-called dog-days, which, according to some American almanacs, began on 3 July. This traditional knowledge is no longer recalled with the same intensity as in the 19th century, but the majority of almanacs and planetary tables used then in both England and America all marked 3 July as the beginning of this important period.[69]

The term 'dog-days' is usually traced back to the Greek-derived *canicular* days, relating to the heliacal rising of the fixed star Sirius. However, historians are usually more inclined to trace the word back to the ancient Egyptian calendrical system, where its rising with the Sun was held to be of profound spiritual importance. It is an ancient Egyptian association which explains why there should be a dog carved on the chair of the goddess to the top right of the arcane engraving shown as figure 9. This connection with the dog-star Sirius is so important that we must assume that, whichever Mason elected this date for laying the foundation stone which was to form the spiritual hub of the city, knew exactly what he was doing.

Sirius, or *Serios*, was the most important star in the ancient world. It was so important during one period of Egyptian history that some documents refer to Egypt itself as the Seriadic Land, after the Greek name for the star.[70] Norman Lockyer, the 19th-century astronomer and specialist in temple orientation, surveyed no fewer than seven ancient Egyptian temples which were oriented to Sirius.[71] Among these were two at Karnak and one in nearby Dar el Bahri – the famous funerary temple complex of Queen Hatshepsut. Since the orientations were spread over a period of almost 3,000 years (the last pertaining to the Isis Temple, at Denderah, of 700 BC), the Egyptians gave different names to Sirius. At one time it was called *Sothis*, at another *Isis-Sothis*, and at yet another, *Thoth* – the name not only of an important Egyptian god, but also of the first month of the Egyptian year.

Each name of the Egyptian Sirius linked it with ancient wisdom, and in particular with the goddess Isis, who was the chief of the feminine mystery deities and the prototype of the stellar Virgo. Its importance in

Egyptian astrology is attested by the fact that it had a single hieroglyphic to represent it: the image of a dog. In terms of pictures, Sirius and its constellation were linked with the image of a dog long before the Romans gave it the name *Canis Major*, or 'Greater Dog'.

Because Isis is so important to Virgoan imagery, it is worth looking at her links with Sirius in greater detail. In the Egyptian mythology, the connection between the stellar goddess Isis and Sirius was expressed by the notion that Anubis (to use the Greek name for the star-god) was her guardian dog. The image of a celestial woman with a dog is not without hidden significance, for the dog exists on a lower plane of being than both humans and gods. It is thus intermediary between the goddess and 'those below her' – that is, the mass of humanity. In arcane art – as, for example, in the tarot pack – the presence of a dog is usually intended to point to the lower self. It represents that inner darkness which has not yet been sloughed off, to allow the inner light to intensify.

This connection between the goddess and dog survived into western esotericism in many interesting arcane devices and symbols. One striking 19th-century Masonic jewel (plate 7) has the delicately carved head of Isis, in black onyx, set in an ivory crescent Moon: below, pendant within the curvature of the Moon, is the five-pointed star that was the main form of the star Sirius. The jewel represents far more than Isiac wisdom, for the five-pointed representation of the dog-star reminds us that Anubis was the god who first taught mankind language, astronomy, music, medicine and the ways of worshipping the gods and God.[72]

That a goddess should be associated with a dog (however spiritual that creature might be) reflects the ancient idea that even the gods and goddesses are capable of spiritual development, and have pockets of 'darkness' which need to be redeemed. The Isis-dog is as much a symbol of that lower nature which has not been sloughed off by the goddess as is (say) the dog which accompanies the boy Tobias in the apocryphal 'Book of Tobit'. In this story, Tobias is guided on a journey by an angel, which represents his higher aspirations and possibilities: a dog trots before him, as symbol of the animal-like darkness of soul from which he must disentangle himself if he is to develop spiritually.

Isis had a fairly smooth passage into the new Christian dispensation, into the religious imagery of the Virgin Mary. The Egyptian Virgin-Queen had been too important and too popular a goddess to be demoted like so many other ancient gods and goddesses. Even her star survived as the *Stella Maris*, in the star drawn and painted upon her breast or on her mapharion (head-veil), well into the 16th century.

However, Anubis did not survive with such grace, and it is fair to say that the early Christians separated the Egyptian Isis from her dog. The creature continued in an almost shadowy existence for a while, in a number of pagan calendrical images and symbols linked with the Mystery lore. For example, when the Romans adopted the image of Mercury, as maker of the calendars and inventor of astrology, they retained the dog-head of Egyptian Anubis, and gave the figure the Greek caduceus. This partly explains why the 2nd-century AD Roman mosaic calendar, now at Sousse in Tunisia, portrays a dog-headed Mercury (clutching his caduceus) for the month of February.[73] This dog-headed figure remains shadowy because its role is that of psychopomp, who leads the newly deceased into the place of testing.

The early Christians (many of whom could neither understand nor sympathize with Egyptian symbolism) were less kind to the dog. In effect, they took it from the Virgin, and demonized it. The Anubis image was debased in a number of magical diagrams (perhaps of Ophite origin) which worried the third-century Christian writer Origen: among the seven ruling demons represented in these diagrams were animal-headed figures, including one of Erataoth, as a dog. In this way were the hermetic teachings of ancient Egypt demoted by ignorance.[74]

We started to examine the significance of Sirius because of the dog-days of July, and the importance of both 3 and 4 July. There may appear to be some chicanery in my linking the dog-days, which begin on *3 July*, with the important national day of *4 July*, as though one day made no great difference. However, I am not being meretricious – I am merely raising an issue which will lead us into curious byways of American history – into what modern astrologers have called the 'endless quest' for the birth-chart of the United States.[75]

At this point we need to ask, when did North America become the United States? In other words – given the nature of our astrological interests – what is the horoscope of the United States of America?

This question may sound innocent enough, and easy enough to answer, but it leads into a quagmire of conflicting historical data. Indeed, the issues raised by the question are so complex that I would not even pose it, were the answer not linked with the arcane significance of Washington DC.

The general assumption is that the new nation of the United States was inaugurated on the hallowed date of 4 July 1776, when, it is customary to argue, the Declaration of Independence was signed.

Unfortunately, on examination this date proves to be far from satisfactory: indeed, as we shall see, there is in the popular mind a radical misunderstanding as to what really happened on 4 July 1776, in Philadelphia. One thing which emerges from a cloud of uncertainties is that we may be quite certain that the Declaration of Independence was *not* 'signed' on that day.

There are well over twenty historical events to bear in mind, when considering the pros and cons pertaining to the moment when the United States was born.

The first Continental Congress met at 10.00 a.m. on 5 September 1774, in Philadelphia. On 14 October of that year, the first Continental Congress issued its famous Declaration that the claimed jurisdiction of the British parliament was invalid in America.[76] On the 20th October 1774, the 13 colonies formed themselves into a Continental Association. After new elections another Congress met, on 10 May 1775. Even at this time, after the Battle of Lexington (19 April 1775), when the first blood was spilt in the struggle towards freedom, some of the colonies were still opposed to a path which would lead to a final separation from Britain, with whom the fledgling Republic was at war. It was not until 23 August 1775 that George III declared the colonies to be in a state of rebellion.

On 15 May 1776, Congress noted that the colonies had been excluded from the protection of the British Crown, which suggests that a degree of independence existed at that time. On 7 June 1776, Richard Henry Lee introduced a series of resolutions which included a call for formal independence.[77] Although discussed over a period of four days, a postponement of vote was agreed: few in Congress could see any 'Wisdom in a Declaration of Independence' or in 'giving our Enemy Notice of our Intentions before we had taken any steps to execute them'.[78]

On 28 June, the draft of the Declaration was presented to Congress: it was not taken up and discussed until 1 July, when it was carried by nine colonies. Edward Rutledge requested that a formal vote be postponed until the next day.[79]

The formal vote for independence was not taken by Congress until 2 July 1776. The story of Caesar Rodney's heroic gallop through the storm to break the tie which existed in the Delaware delegation is a part of popular and accurate history. New York delegates did not vote, and thus only 12 of the colonies assented. Two days later, on the now famous 4 July, the unanimous Declaration of Independence of the 13 states was agreed – but the document drawn up in recognition of this was signed on that day only by the President and Secretary of Congress.[80] In spite of what is generally believed, the formal signing by all members of Congress took place later, at various times.

So far as historians of astrology are concerned, the mention of 4 July 1776 brings to mind a famous horoscope, which many believe is a record of the original horoscope for the founding of the United States.

The chart (above), cast by the 18th-century English astrologer Ebenezer Sibly[81] and published in 1784 as plate 53 in his book on the occult sciences[82] has caused much discussion among historians of astrology, but there remain many misunderstandings about precisely what the chart represents. We should observe that even this famous horoscope, cast for 4 July 1776, does not pretend to designate the signing of the Declaration, but refers merely to 'American Independence'. It seems to have been cast some time prior to publication, and is almost certainly the oldest surviving printed chart pertaining to American Independence.

I have no wish to descend into the minutiae of scholarship relating to the vexing question of the horoscope of the United States. Nicholas Campion's masterly survey in *The Book of World Horoscopes* (1988) contains a thorough and illuminating analysis of the many early charts relating to the new nation.[83] Fortunately Sibly's chart, so often taken as the founding horoscope of the United States, is discussed by Campion, who summarizes the confusion surrounding it. As he recognizes, when viewed from a traditional standpoint (that is, as a chart for the new United States), the horoscope does not make sense, and it is easy to see why historians of astrology have tended to condemn it as both inaccurate and careless. Certainly, the chart in the engraving does not relate accurately to the traditional day – 4 July 1776.

The problems attendant on attempting to determine just what the horoscope *does* represent have been compounded by the fact that many of those who have discussed this chart have so often not deigned to read what Sibly actually wrote about it.

In view of its importance to the history of arcane America, then, it is worth examining the chart in some detail.

Ebenezer Sibly was a Mason. He was initiated in 1784, in Lodge No. 79 of the Ancients at Portsmouth (England), and was first Master of No. 253, in London.[84] Even if this information had not been available, his Masonic connections could never have been in doubt: not only did he use certain Masonic symbols in some of his arcane plates, but he openly dedicated two of his books to the Masonic fraternity.

The 'Sibly Chart' (page 143) is carried in the right hand of a trumping angel, who hovers in the clouds above a mundane scene with sundry symbols relating to the new federal union (figure 8). There are many unresolved secrets in this chart, and one of them is found in a comparison which it offers with an earlier plate (opposite) in which Sibly published the horoscope for George III.

The Descendant point on this royal horoscope (the place where the Sun 'goes west', and sinks below the horizon) is the same at the lunar position in Sibly's chart of the United States. However, almost in contrast to this 'death element', the Moon of the USA chart is rising towards the horizon, and is only four degrees or so from the point of Moonrise. The symbolism intended by Sibly is quite clear – the *setting* of Aquarius for the British King is equated to the *rising* of the new American nation.

Sibly is disparaging about his King's chart, though in a distinctly arcane manner. He points to the placing of the fixed star *Algol* in the figure – emphasizing this to the extent of including it in the sigilization of the horoscope itself. Any astrologer of that period would have recognized what Sibly had in mind, for Algol is the most evil star in the heavens, and always brings bad fortune for those in whose chart it is operative.

In marked contrast, Sibly is extremely generous in his treatment of the chart of the United States. He writes:

> I shall now call the attention of my reader to that remarkable aera in the British history, which gave independence to America, and reared up a new Empire, that shall soon or late give laws to the whole world.[85]

His analysis of this situation follows a well-established mediaeval astrological system of examining what are called ingress charts – a system which is rarely used in modern astrology, but which involve casting charts for the ingress of the Sun into the signs Aries and Libra. Sibly compares the two ingress charts for the spring and summer of 1776, in order to study how the British government and the new United States will fare. He comes to the conclusion that America will come off best, and:

> the event shall be such as to cause a total and eternal separation of the two countries from each other; and that the congress . . . will establish an independent and complete revolution, which shall be built upon a firm and durable foundation . . . It is hence declared, that whatever is effected under this revolution of the Sun's ingress . . . by the

> Americans, shall not only be permanent and durable, but shall be supported by those three grand pillars of state, wisdom, strength and unanimity.[86]

In fact, on p.1053 of his work, Sibly admits that the famous chart was not intended as a standard horoscope for the United States, and describes in detail how he arrived at the chart.[87] By these means, he comes to the conclusion that it

> clearly evinces that the state of America shall in time have an extensive and flourishing commerce; an advantageous and universal traffic to every quarter of the globe, with great security and prosperity amongst the people.'[88]

Sibly's analysis and record of what he perceived in the chart were foresighted and original in view of the prejudices of the time in which he wrote. Without our benefit of hindsight, it might seem quite reasonable for an astrologer such as Sibly to pose a cosmic question, about the future of the Americas, from his base in London – the city from which the colonies had been administered until comparatively recently. The data in the chart certainly support this notion: the horoscope was cast for a latitude equivalent to that of London,[89] and the planetary positions confirm the London siting. Given this unconventional adjustment and one or two slight inaccuracies in planetary placings, the chart is tolerably accurate. However, though it does not pertain cosmically to the United States, as might be expected from its title, 'America Independence'.[90] My point is that the chart is intended as a record of a question, *posed in England*, about the future relationship between Britain and America. The form of the chart indicates that it is intended as a horoscopic examination of the future destiny of American independence.

From an astrological standpoint, the important thing is that the adjustments involved with time and space have placed the all-important Ascendant degree on 20 Aquarius. In this way, Sibly has linked the new country with the long-anticipated Age of Aquarius. This Aquarian impulse was a spiritual one which would encourage the federal union and its consequent spreading of the notion of the Brotherhood of Man – a notion so important to Masons. The idea of *Federal Union* is developed graphically in the lower part of the engraving (figure 8). The words are set out on an engraved scroll, overlooked by an infant – no doubt, a symbol of the newborn country – on the Earth below the horoscope.

In view of these facts, we would be doing Ebenezer Sibly a disservice, and adding confusion to the already confused history of astrology, if we insisted on believing that this engraving (figure 8) represents the horoscope of the new United States of America. Its importance lies in establishing the now widely held belief that the destiny of the United States is somehow involved with the nature of Aquarius, and with the notion of Federal Union. The readings appended to the charts by Sibly are probably among the earliest predictions, from the pen of an astrologer, that the Declaration of Independence would be successful.

Let us continue our brief survey of what happened in those heady years following American independence, to see if we can wrest from all the available information an accurate horoscope for the new country.

On 8 July 1776, the agreed Declaration was read out publicly, in Philadelphia's State House Square. This public avowal of independence, rather than the Congressional note of May 1776, may be regarded as the official birth of the nation.

The achievement of independence, won through not ink but blood, was marked by the surrender of the British at Yorktown on 17 October 1781, and formalized by the signatures of the defeated Cornwallis and the victorious George Washington two days later. The subsequent legalized statement of independence was ratified by the Treaty of Paris on 30 November 1782, which was not finalized until 3 September of the following year.

Thirteen individual states had declared their independence on 2 July 1776, and all significant powers had been kept by them. John Dickinson had made the first draft of Confederation, which would mark the emergence of the United States in 1776, but the exigencies of war precluded close study or agreement. In consequence, there was no federal power to raise taxes, to regulate currency or to defend the nation. Fairly quickly, pockets of chaos emerged. To rectify this situation, the Constitutional Convention was called in Philadelphia on 25 May 1787, with a quorum of delegates from seven states, to discuss Articles of Confederation. At length, 12 of the 13 states (with Rhode Island dissenting) were involved in this Convention. The Confederation Congress was held on 13 July 1787 in New York City, passed the North-West Ordinance, the Bill of Rights and its guarantee of religious freedom.

Thirty-nine of the forty-two delegates at the Convention signed the Constitution of Union in Philadelphia, on Monday, 17 September 1787.[91] Signature of ratification of the Convention, by the representatives of the individual states, followed, and when the last (Rhode Island) signed, on 29 May 1790, it was technically legal for the Constitution to become operative.[92]

The Rhode Island ratification (it was a close-run thing, with 34 for and 32 against) had been pre-empted. The first US Congress convened in New York City on 4 March 1789. It was arranged for the government to begin legislation within the framework of the Constitution on that same day, in Philadelphia, and George Washington was inaugurated as the first President of the United States on 30 April.

I have spelled out my understanding of the main events leading up to, and consequent to, the signing of the Declaration of Independence, because I am aware how difficult it is to pin down so momentous an historical event as the formation of the United States in a precise space and time, as required for a definitive horoscope. In spite of this, I should observe that at least 18 of the above 20 or so important historical milestones have been used, at various times, as the basis for horoscopes, speculative of the 'birth' of the United States.[93]

Given the complexity of the question, we may *still* ask which of the many charts claiming to represent the birth of a nation should be regarded as acceptable. In other words, what is the horoscope of the United States?

The chart for the first Continental Congress, which met at 10.00 a.m. on 5 September 1774 in Philadelphia, is outstanding for several astrological reasons. First of all, there is scarcely any equivocation about its timing or date. Secondly, the event it marks had very distinctive consequences for the history of the United States. Nicholas Campion is probably right in seeing the first Continental Congress as the ancestor of the later federal government.[94]

The emphasis of the chart is in Virgo: no fewer than four planets and one nodal point are in the sign, with the Sun exactly upon the Dragon's Head, in trine to Jupiter. At ten in the morning, Venus was exactly upon the mid-heaven. All in all, this is a very beneficial chart.[95]

This chart, which points to the first concerted attempt to turn a group of individualistic colonies into a federation, is dominated by Virgo. Would this help explain why the city which was built to serve this new federation, and which was first called 'the federal city', should also be ruled by Virgo? The designers of the city have always emphasized Virgo in its zodiacal architecture, and we must presume that this concern with the sign has some origins in the chart relating to the cosmic conditions which tied the states together in federal union.

*

The Sibly chart was cast according to the same prejudices that have held 4 July 1776 as the date of the signing of the Declaration of Independence.

Since the popular notion that this Declaration was 'signed' on 4 July evaporates on close examination, this date must be rejected as suitable for the casting of a national horoscope. On that day, Congress agreed the wording of the Declaration, and it was then signed by the President of Congress, John Hancock, who was a Mason,[96] and the Secretary of Congress, Charles Thompson. This signed declaration was nothing more than a partial ratification of something which had already been agreed – it was not itself a declaration of independence, but a formal presentation of a declaration now promulgated for the benefit of the world. There was no formal recognition and no other signatories on that day – the formal records (which were completed some time afterwards) state merely that the declaration was read and agreed. In other respects, the material is of considerable interest: the records show that the Declaration of 4 July 1776 was first signed by a Mason.[97]

What, then, *is* the horoscope of the new nation? Bearing in mind the contemporaneous exhilaration to which the event gave rise, I am minded to choose 2 July 1776. The journals of Congress are quite uncompromising about the fact that this constituted the date of the Declaration of Independence.[98] The relevant entry reads: '. . . these United Colonies are, and of right ought to be, Free and Independent States'.

'Yesterday, the greatest Question was decided, which ever was debated in America . . . A resolution was passed without one dissenting Colony that these united Colonies are . . . free and independent States.'[99] John Adams, who was to be the second President of the United States, wrote those words, later expressing the pious hope that 'The Second Day of July 1776. will be the most memorable Epoca in the History of America . . . the great anniversary Festival'.[100] A contemporaneous voice could not have recorded the birth of a nation with more enthusiasm or authority.

Of course, John Adams was to be disappointed, and it is the supposed signing of the Declaration of Independence two days later which is now the 'great anniversary Festival'. I must recognize that 4 July has been invested with an extraordinary outpouring of popular emotion, and is now deeply enshrined in the national consciousness. Even so, I cannot find in the chart for that day *any* trace of the nature of the federal agreement which has bound the states together in what has proved to be an enduring form.

In truth, I am not arguing about dates so much as about stellar influences. If my proposal that the chart should be traced to 2 July 1776 is accepted, *then the influence of the fixed star Sirius asserts itself in the horoscope of the United States.*

On 2 July 1776 – which I have argued is the *true* chart for the founding of the United States – the Sun was in 11.22 Cancer, which meant that it was in the same degree as Sirius.

This Sirian position was widely recognized in the entire range of astronomical literature with which Americans were familiar. The findings of Lalande in this matter have already been quoted, but Lalande wrote in French, and it might be unwise to assume a general familiarity with this literature among 18th-century Americans. However, among the books which had been in the personal library of Thomas Jefferson, and which were eventually purchased by the Library of Congress, was Robert Morden's *An Introduction to Astronomy* of 1702. In this were important tables of acronical risings of the stars, as well as a table of fixed star positions for 1700.[101] Morden specified that the star Sirius was in 9.58.50 of Cancer.[102] The African-American, Benjamin Banneker, may have been influenced by tables derived from Morden's calculations for, in his own tabulations for 1793 (which listed the positions of Sirius), Banneker gave the Sun as in 11 degrees on 2 July.

It is the case that, according to the tabulations available to those who were involved in this struggle to formulate a process of becoming independent, the star Sirius was even nearer to the Sun on 2 July 1776. In 1786, the French astronomer Montignot had published a list of stellar positions, to show how the stars had moved, in accordance with precession, since the first century of our era. As we have seen, this book also happens to have been in the library of Thomas Jefferson, who was deeply interested in astronomy, and who, of course, played a leading role in the events leading up to independence.[103] In a table of longitudes in his book, Montignot indicates that by 1786 Sirius was in 11.9.1 of Cancer. According to his own system of reckoning, in 1776 Sirius would have been in 11.8.56 of Cancer.[104]

We see from this that those Americans who were interested in astronomy at the time of the Declaration would have recognized that on 2 July 1776, the Sun was only 12 minutes away from Sirius: technically, in spite of a few minutes' difference, the Sun was definitely 'conjunct Sirius', in astrological parlance.

In a sense, these differences of minutes are not really important. The fact is that whichever of these degrees we take as being accurate, we must

recognize that *earlier in the course of the day, when the Declaration of Independence was agreed, the Sun must have passed over Sirius.*

Having considered these facts, we have to ask, what is this strange connection which Sirius – the most important star of ancient times – has with the United States of America?

Is it possible that the urge to introduce an Egyptian flavour into the spiritual life of the country, and into the monument which marks the hub of its federal city, has a deeper connection? Could this be linked with that other distinctively Egyptian symbol which has, in a curiously reluctant way, coloured the symbolism of the United States? By this, I mean the pyramid on the Seal of the United States, which is now found on every dollar bill (see previous page)?

From an arcane point of view, the answer to this question is in the affirmative: the only problem is that the design of this truncated pyramid is intimately bound up with the symbolism of the American eagle, which *also* dominates the dollar bill. When we look into these symbols, we may well be surprised to find that they represent polarities – the very polarities of east and north which the Masons used in their foundation ceremonies. It is almost as though this eagle – the ancient Sun-bird, with wings outstretched and vibrant with life – represents the consciousness and light of the American nation. In contrast, the pyramid, with its secret chambers buried in the rock-bed of Earth, represents its hidden darkness – the hidden fructifying powers at the spiritual roots of the nation, which are so desperate to reach the upper light of spirit.

Chapter Six

> Mercury ☿ hath signficance of all literated Men; as Philosophers, Astrologers, Mathematicians, Secretaries, Schoole-masters, Poetes, Orators, Advocates, Merchants, Diviners, Sculptors, Attorneys, Accomptants, Sollicitors, Clerks, Stationers, Printers, Secretaries, Taylors, Usurers, Carriers, Messengers, Foot-men . . .
>
> (John Gadbury, *Genethaialogia. The Doctrine of Nativities*, 1658)

During the Washington DC race riots of 1968, a city zodiac was destroyed. This was the zodiac on the bronze Noyes armillary sphere, which was torn down, carted away, and probably broken up for scrap. The sculpture has not been seen since.

This armillary – a skeletal projection of the heavens – was a beautifully crafted piece of sculpture set on a granite pedestal in the southern part of Meridian Hill Park (figure 11). Made in 1931, it had been commissioned of the sculptor Carl Paul Jennewein by the well-known Washington artist Bertha Noyes, and bequeathed to Washington DC in memory of her sister Edith.[1] As a model of the cosmic world, the armillary was, in many ways, far more symbolically appropriate than any gravestone marker of the physical remains of the deceased: in the esoteric view of things, the stars symbolize the spiritual home to which the living spirit returns, after relinquishing the body.[2]

Meridian Hill Park took its name from the elegant country mansion which was built in the area for Commodore David Porter, in 1817.[3] Financed by the prize money he won during the naval battles of 1812 against the British, Porter bought a farm of 150-odd acres on the wooded heights due north of the White House, with 'a splendid view to the south over rolling pastoral land to the President's House, the distant Potomac and the Virginia shores beyond'.[4] It is said that Andrew Ellicott raised the first meridian lines of the city on the stretch of what was then Robert Peter's land, and which later became the lawn of Porter's house.

Even though he was not particularly careful with his money, the Commodore's wisdom in choosing this site proved to be financially sound, for Meridian Hill, on 16th Street and Florida Avenue, became the centre of considerable speculation by builders in the 1860s.[5] In consequence, the district became sought after by the well-to-do: it was no surprise when, in 1888, a magnificent Romanesque-style mansion was built alongside the park for Senator John B. Henderson.[6]

Meridian Hill kept its name, but not its function. A letter in the Library of Congress records the efforts made by William Lambert to ensure that the prime meridian line should be determined from the Capitol. In consequence, by 1815, the longitude of Washington DC was recalculated, and this effectively moved the older meridional line from north of the White House to north of the Capitol building. A letter of William Lambert, dated 1815, sets out an abstract of the latest calculations made to determine the longitude of the Capitol. The result was 76 degrees 55 minutes 48 seconds. He wisely suggested that any variations in the figures adduced to support this longitude could be due to errors in the lunar tables.[7]

Besides being a memorial to a beloved sister, the Noyes armillary was a reminder of the foundation chart of the federal city. This truth had been reflected – whether consciously or unconsciously by the patron or the artist – in the symbolism of the sphere itself. In a photograph of the Noyes armillary (figure 11) taken in 1931, the zodiacal sign Virgo is portrayed in a distinguished position, exactly on the horizon.[8] She is shown as a naked woman, alongside a raised glyph of her ancient sigil, which looks like an M merged with a loop. As we contemplate this sigil,

we can understand why mediaeval scholars attempted to read in it the abbreviation MV, for *Maria Virgo* (the Virgin Mary).[9] These scholars may have been wrong about the graphic origin, yet they were not in error in tracing a connection between the Virgin of Christianity and the more ancient Virgo of the skies. This stellar Virgin had been the Mother Goddess of the pagan religions, the Isis of ancient Egypt. The image of the Isis-Virgo holding an ear of corn, on one of the Egyptian zodiacs at Denderah, is scarcely different in symbolic force from the more elaborate images of Virgo found on a thousand modern zodiacs. Even late-mediaeval images of Isis reflect the ancient tradition of the corn, for the goddess is depicted as 'the Great Mother of the Gods' with wheat-ears sprouting from her crown, the Moon covering her private parts, and her entire body flecked with stars.

The symbolism of corn so proliferates in Washington DC that we should pause to consider its importance. As we have seen already, in astrology the corn-sheaf is a Virgoan symbol, as the prime star in the constellation Spica represents the corn or wheat in the hand of the goddess (figure 13). This corn may be traced back to the ancient Mysteries of Ceres, and beyond, to the even earlier Egyptian Mysteries of Isis. Although seemingly divested of these astrological undertones, corn was held by the Masons as a particularly sacred symbol:

> The intelligent and worthy Mason cannot contemplate this simple symbol, the Ear of Corn, without lifting up his heart in thankful acknowledgement of the goodness of God, and of all the benefits bestowed by His hand.[10]

The Graeco-Egyptian symbolism still survives in the constellational Virgo. The stellar female is derived from Isis, who, even in late-mediaeval images, is depicted as studded with stars and holding a sheaf of corn. Only the magical *sistrum* – a uniquely Egyptian musical instrument – which Isis held in her right hand has disappeared from the image of Virgo.

As we approach the mysteries of Washington DC, we shall find that the image of Virgo, her symbols of corn and the cornucopia, takes on more and more importance. Indeed, we shall conclude that those who oversaw the design of the city adopted Virgo as its arcane leitmotif. Because of this, we should first look at a number of traditional images of the celestial Virgin to see something of the underlying philosophy hidden in her symbolism.

In the course of history, there have been very many variants in the zodiacal and constellational images, and throughout the past 2,000 years many attempts have been made to redefine the pictures drawn by ancient astronomers in their star maps – generally by recasting them in terms which reflected prevailing beliefs. There is no doubt that the early images in Greek and Roman times reflected the secret symbolism of the Egyptian Isis, which survives still in one or two ancient Egyptian planispheres.[11] When we considered the earliest surviving zodiac in Washington DC, we saw that Mithraic and Gnostic images projected the

'Mother Goddess' theme into the city. The Mithraic imagery was, of course, pre-Christian, and it was inevitable that through their influences the power of the corn image should be continued into the symbolism of the Virgin Mary. It was even more inevitable that the symbolism of the Isis-Ceres imagery – of a stellar goddess clutching corn – should also influence the symbolism of the Christian Virgin. Indeed, a survey of these early influences indicates that the symbolism of the pagan goddess and the Christian Virgin were at one time almost merged.

One extraordinary image of the Virgin, that appears in an arcane German woodcut of the mid-15th-century (left), shows her, replete with halo and attendant angels, wearing a dress emblazoned with wheat-ears. To judge from the badly damaged border inscription, the image portrays the Virgin carrying the newly conceived Child, as she was seen by Joseph in the Temple. The connection between the ancient Mysteries of Ceres and Isis could not be more evident. Just so, the connection drawn between Jesus and the Bread of Life, as is manifest in the Eucharist, is also part of the arcane meaning of the design.[12] Even the swirl of plants in the background, which display floral heads of five petals each, belong to the Virgoan imagery – which continued into the symbolism of Washington DC.

This ancient-Mystery association with wheat-ears in Christian imagery is not confined to the Virgin. In one extraordinary 15th-century fresco in Tessendorf, Austria, Christ is depicted with two streams of blood issuing upwards from his feet wounds, and forming a cross in front of Him. That issuing from His left foot turns into a vine, while that from

His right foot turns into wheat, which He is fingering delicately.[13] There are other Christian symbols in this church which make it clear that the painter was familiar with the arcane tradition.

By the mediaeval period, the pagan image of Virgo in star maps was thoroughly Christianized, if only because the monk-scribes who copied the ancient maps and diagrams rarely had a reliable tradition to go by, and fell back upon their knowledge of Christian symbolism. In some cases, the image of Virgo could not be distinguished in any substantial way from a picture of a winged angel.[14]

In one of the most important of all mediaeval astrological manuscripts, Virgo is shown as a winged maiden (alongside), grasping in her right hand three or four spikes of corn.[15] This has remained the essential symbol of Virgo since astrology was introduced into Europe by the Arab astrologers, in about the 10th century. Even so, within the astrological tradition, amendments and adjustments have been made to the image of Virgo on more than one occasion. For example, the wheat was sometimes transformed into a flower – very often into a five-petalled rose – in a symbolism which often had local or specifically religious significance.

In several delightful Christian images (see over), the Virgin Mary is shown supporting her suckling Child, while holding wheat in the other hand. This was an almost open reference to the fact that the pagan wheat (the star Spica, or wheat-ear) had been transformed by the power of Christianity into the Bread of Life.[16]

Given a familiarity with the fluctuations in style and symbolism, it is still possible for a modern astronomer to recognize in even the most obscure of the star maps the equivalent of a modern Virgo. The image for

Virgo has survived with more grace than many of the other constellation images, mainly because of her distinctive position in the skies. She is almost always depicted parallel to the ecliptic (the path of the Sun) to accommodate the placing of her primal star, Spica, which is close to this path, and also near the celestial equator. We see these characteristics of ancient Virgo in maps of the constellations close to the ecliptic drawn by the French astronomer Montignot in 1786. One shows the position of the stars according to Ptolemy in which Virgo's Spica is located in 27 degrees of the sign, where the ecliptic crosses the equator (see p.130).

In a beautifully illustrated manuscript describing some of the constellations according to the *Phaenomena* of Aratus,[17] written and illuminated at the end of the 12th century, the scribe described the 18 main stars in Virgo, and picked out as the clearest of these the one in her left hand, which he actually names Spica. This is an interesting use of the star name, for it shows that the scribe's sources have bypassed the post-Greek names derived from the Arabic tradition, and relied upon an unbroken tradition from the ancient world.[18]

The distinctive pair of scales in the right hand of the woman is what we would nowadays recognize as the constellation Libra, which in the ancient maps is almost always represented as part of the image for Scorpius.[19]

In some mediaeval images of Virgo, the ear of corn is virtually in the form of a palm-branch, held almost as a pointer across the ecliptic. This celestial Virgo looks distinctly male, and it is the gender which gives away its true origins, and reveals a confusion in the text. The Latin

manuscript[20] offers a description of Libra under Scorpius, yet, in spite of this, depicts Virgo holding the scales, as though the stars of Libra belong to Virgo. It is this confusion which leads me to suspect that this image need not be explained by Virgoan imagery at all. In my opinion, the monk-scribe who painted this picture was not sufficiently familiar with the astrological tradition. However, he was intimately familiar with the Christian tradition, and knew the standard image of the masculine archangel Michael, who holds in one hand the balance (in which the souls of the dead will be weighed), and, in the other, the golden sword, with which he drives back the demons who strive to obtain the newly dead souls, to carry them back to Hell. Under the brush of this mediaeval monk, the Spica of the corn-stalk (which was the Spike of early English astrology) has accidentally become a sword-like palm.

Early engraved gems – usually designed for magical purposes – often emphasize the power of the wheat, particularly in connection with the goddess Ceres, who was the Greek prototype of the Virgo of astrology. The three gems overleaf, taken from engravings in King's survey of magical gems, illustrate this very clearly. The first is a sardonyx, which portrays the head of Ceres with a wreath of wheat in her hair. The second shows Ceres seated, with the corn-measure at her feet and a cornucopia in her left arm: in her right hand she holds up a figure symbolizing justice. The third is a sapphire, cut with an image of the caduceus of Mercury between ears of wheat – a magical gem intended to attract prosperous trade.[21]

Those images which show Virgo clutching the caduceus (see page 162)

are surprisingly close to the most ancient literature pertaining to Virgo. In astrology, the planet Mercury is the ruler of Virgo.

This will prove important to unravelling the mysteries of Washington DC. In astrology, the term 'rulership' is used to denote the dominant influence of a planet over a sign (for example, the rule of the planet Mercury over Virgo). The same word is also used to denote the 'rule' of a planet or a zodiacal sign over a creature or thing in the material world. Everything in the mundane realm is ruled by a planet and (sometimes) a zodiac sign – for instance, dogs are ruled by the planet Mars, cats by the planet Venus. Mediaeval astrology was deeply involved in ascribing planetary rulerships to minerals, plants, animals, towns, cities and so on. These rulerships were sometimes described also as 'correspondences'. I will have more to say on this subject in due course.

In this simple-seeming notion we have intimations of the ancient power and longevity of the hermetic doctrines that touch upon initiation and the 'hidden knowledge' of *gnosis*. Plutarch, who was a priest and initiate in the service of Isis at Delphi, records the opinion, held by many, that Hermes (the Greek equivalent of Mercury) was the father of Isis.[22] This link, between the most important goddess of the ancient world and the secret hermetics (the word itself is derived from the name Hermes, the guardian god of the secrets), has echoed through the centuries, and is reflected now in the bland assertion of astrologers that Mercury is the planetary ruler of Virgo.

What do all these Virgoan traditions imply on a practical level? What is the supposed influence of this most feminine of all signs, Virgo, on the Earth plane? Why would the Americans of the late 18th century wish to associate this celestial Virgin with their new federal city? I shall return to this intriguing question more than once in the following pages, but here I shall offer an answer which relates to some of the images we have studied so far.

Virgo has always retained some of her pagan and Christian connotations of the 'Mother Goddess'. She is the 'nourisher' among the 12 signs, and, in Christian terms at least, a highly redemptive power: the Virgin who suckles the Christ Child is, by extension, giving suck to the whole of humanity. The Virgo of the skies is as redemptive of the human condition as the Virgin of Christianity was redemptive of the fallen Eve. The mediaeval mind – prone always to see every material thing as a symbol – made much of the fact that when, in the biblical account, the angel Gabriel announced to the Virgin Mary that she was to have a child, he began his speech with the word *Ave.* This *Ave Maria*, which has reverberated through Christian churches and private prayer ever since, was recognized as a reversal of (and therefore a redemption of) the Fall set in motion by *Eva.* The reversal was not particularly subtle or arcane, but it carried a deep message of hope for millions of souls.

This same sense of spiritual redemption was presaged in the ear of wheat, the Spica, in the hand of the stellar Virgin. The wheat signalled the germinal power that would grow from that Virgin into the Bread of Life. It was the Plant of Life which had been opposed by the Tree of Death – the wheat which could grow from the darkness of the grave. The symbolism proclaims that it is through Virgo that conflict is resolved, prior to being handed over to the next sign – to the equanimity of the balance of Libra. Virgo is the cosmic nurse, the *nutrix* of the alchemical imagery, which is the redemptive imagery of the arcane tradition.

There is a striking similarity in the *pelanos*, or sacred bread of the ancient Mystery lore, and the holy bread of the host in the Christian Mysteries. This point has often been developed by scholars.[23] The idea is clearly indicated in the 18th-century engraving, alongside, which portrays the World Mother, the Virgin goddess, not only with her many corn-ears, but with a version of the holy bread (top left) marked with what may be interpreted as a wide cross.

The characteristics associated with the Eternal Woman or the celestial Virgin have poured into the stellar Virgo who represents the federal city. In fact, in one beautiful glass zodiac in Washington DC, designed by the artist Sidney Waugh, Virgo is represented with a halo – perhaps even as the Christian Virgin herself (plate 3).[24] In such imagery, the redemptive power is recognized directly, for *the pagan Isis has been transformed into the Virgin Mary of the new Christian Mysteries.*

When the idea of the federal city was first formulated, shortly after the war with Britain, the United States was in need of healing, of organizing, and of redemption. The theme of the alchemical *nutrix* (the female nourisher), as a source of nourishment for the rest of the country, was one which would have been dear to the hearts of many Americans at that time. Mars had laid down his weapons – seemingly for all time – and the new states anticipated with relief a long period of recuperation and growth. How sensible, then, to adopt for the federal city the spiritual mascot of a pagan goddess who still retained all the attributes of an angel. Like the eagle which had been adopted as the primal symbol of the emergent nation, Virgo had wings. Because of her undeniable association with the Virgin Mary, this virgoan lady of the Mysteries was not quite so pagan as she might initially appear.

There was also another reason why Virgo would be a suitable tutelary spirit for the new federal city: the ruler of Virgo was Mercury, the planet of communication and commerce. The founders of Washington DC recognized that the hard-won independence of the United States would flourish only if the commerce and trade of the country flourished. Just as Virgo had wings, so she carried the caduceus, or magical wand, of Mercury (opposite). Such an image is found in an extraordinary number of places in Washington DC.[25]

The ancient hermetic literature recognized the power of Hermes to teach spiritual things to mankind, and this is still one of the attributes of Mercury. This chapter's epigraph, from the 17th-century English astrologer John Gadbury, indicates that the Mercury of astrology is the communicator between Man and God – as well as being ruler over the nerve-centre of the body politic. It was intended that the city of Washington DC should become the nerve-centre of the body politic of the United States, and it is perhaps this which explains the proliferation of the caduceus and other images of Mercury in the city. The fleet-winged Mercury is the messenger of the gods, the one who communicates between the realm of matter and the realm of spirit, the one who leads the dead to the Underworld, communicating with the lower world of spirit with the same ease with which he communicates with the upper realms of the gods. This multiple function as 'communicator' is usually the level of symbolism implied in the many images of Mercury, or his caduceus, in Washington DC.

The link which the lapidary images of Washington DC draw with Mercury – and which is sanctioned by astrological tradition – is nowhere more beautifully developed than in the old planetary images called 'the Children of the Planets'. The 'children' of Mercury are the human progeny of the Mercurial impulse – which is towards literature, music and the arts.[26] An early woodcut (figure 14) shows Mercury in his chariot, drawn by two cocks, the wheels of the chariot emblazoned with the image of the signs over which he has rule – Virgo and Gemini. Below, from left to right, reading downwards, we see the artist in his studio, the doctor examining urine, the astronomer-astrologer with his celestial sphere, and the merchant. On the next line of images we see a sculptor working a piece of wood, a scribe and a money-changer; to the extreme right is a man pumping at the manual bellows of an organ, to allow the musician to play. These associations, which fall under the influence of Mercury, are roughly the same as those recognized in modern astrology, except that in most cases the impulse has been brought up to date: for example, the scribe is now not only a writer, but a stenographer and one proficient with computers, while the lone money-changer has been extended into bankers, bank assistants and, indeed, almost anyone who handles money, or finance.

When a modern astrologer asserts that Virgo is ruled by Mercury, he or she may not be aware of the hermetic depth behind the statement, but the reference will generally be to the *sign* Virgo – to the Virgo of the zodiac. In ancient times, this rulership was extended also to the stellar pattern – to the *constellation* of Virgo, which is why some portrayals of Virgo as an asterism show her clutching the caduceus as a wand of her initiation (figure 13). It should not surprise us that the ancients believed that almost all the stars in Virgo exuded the nature (or planetary influence) of Mercury.

This star-lore tradition – which emphasizes that each of the stars exudes an influence that equated to a planet, or to a combination of planetary radiations – is no longer much used in astrology, but in ancient times it was of profound importance. In the second century AD the Egyptian astronomer Ptolemy, reporting the traditions of ancient star lore, set out the natures of each of the main stars in the constellations. In doing this, he described the stellar influences in terms of planetary powers or virtues. He recorded that the stars in the constellation Virgo were mainly of the nature of Mercury, in some cases touched with an admixture of Mars or Venus.[27]

Given the undeniable Virgoan symbolism of Washington DC – it is significant that we find in the city a considerable number of arcane images involving Mercury. In one arcane high-relief we even find a planetary symbolism in which Mercury is portrayed as feminine.

One extraordinary and beautiful sculpture in Washington DC may be ranked among the most remarkable pieces of modern arcane statuary in the city. In this, Mercury is shown flying over the back of the goddess Vesta, who is tending her altar flame (figure 15). Although our attention is here drawn to Mercury, the entire relief on this granite panel demands careful examination. It is an outstanding example of just how esoteric are certain public images of planets and zodiacs in the federal city.

This figure is part of a high-relief carved in 1941 by John Gregory,[28] on the southern face of the wall overlooking the gardens of the Municipal Centre Building, in Indiana Avenue. For all the simplicity of the granite sculpture, and for all the official interpretations of the symbolism offered by the government bodies, that symbolism is profoundly arcane.[29] The right foot of Mercury merges with the veil-like clothing drawn over the back of Vesta, reminding us that Mercury is identical to Hermes, the 'keeper of the secret veil', 'guardian of the ancient Mysteries'; it is Mercury who holds the veil before the eyes of the profane. Behind, his cloak trails in an undulating rhythm of six folds, uniting his form with that of the demi-god of healing, Asculepius, and merging with the feet of the goddess Maia, who was Mercury's mother. The trail of Mercury's cloak reveals his origins, and reminds those who are interested in mythology that the name of his mother is linked with the Greek meaning 'nurse', 'nourisher', and 'midwife'.

There is something altogether profound in this strange relief, with its almost incomprehensible references to ancient Greek sculpture. Why should an artist depict Mercury flying over a fire-sacrifice? Why should the healer Asculepius be gazing so intently upon the face of the youthful Maia, who sits in such dignity on the raised chair? The hierarchical intensity of the moment suggests that we are on the edge of a mystery, or at least gazing upon imagery that pertains to the Mysteries.

In truth, the mystery here is astrological in nature. Although Maia was a relatively unimportant goddess, there was, in ancient times, one day in each year during which a fire-ceremony was performed in her honour by those responsible for the sacred flame: on the first day of May, the Roman *flamen Volcanalis* (priest of Vulcan) sacrificed to her. This linked with the magic of the name *Maius*, which eventually became the fifth month of our own calendar, under the name May – the first day of which is still associated with special May Day celebrations. However, this calendrical date has little to do with the mystery in John Gregory's statuary, for the artist is intent on pointing to an altogether more significant cosmic event in space and time.

The month of May, as Chaucer's *Canterbury Tales* reminds us, is the month of Taurus – which is to say, it is the time when the Sun passes through that arc of the zodiac dedicated to the stellar bull. The remarkable thing is that on 1 May 1941 (the year when this relief wall was finished, and put in place), there was a configuration of no fewer than six planets in Taurus. These were, Mercury, the Sun, Venus, Saturn, Jupiter and Uranus. The six were harmoniously related (by a trine aspect) to Neptune and the Dragon's Head, in Virgo.

The relief was carved in full knowledge of the Cosmic event it would finally represent. The fact is that the unique disposition of the planets at midday on 1 May 1941 is reflected in its stylized imagery.

In Gregory's relief the fire-virgin Vesta is kneeling on the Earth, and enacting her ritual to the west. At noon on 1 May 1941, the fire-planet Mars (literally, the 'fiery one' in the ancient astrologies) was setting on the horizon of Washington DC, to the west. That is to say, it was at the lowest level of the earth, just about to disappear over the horizon – more or less in the position held by Vesta's lamp.

Gregory has shown Mercury flying upwards over the head of Vesta, his feet well off the ground: just as Maia looks westwards, so Mercury flies to the west. On 1 May 1941, Mercury was exactly overhead in Washington DC, beginning its descent towards the western horizon. Just as Mars was about to disappear into the night, Mercury was at the highest point in the skies. This explains why Gregory's Mercury should be flying upwards, above the burning lamp.

Are we now in a position to understand that strange pattern of the cloak which Mercury trails behind him? Could the *six* streams of cloak or air be the *six* planets which were ranged in the same sign of Taurus, on 1 May 1941? Maia, the goddess of this May Day, sits in regal splendour, because she has all *six* planets in her month-sign Taurus. She is not merely to witness the fire-ceremony held in her honour raised upon the dais and throne-like chair: she herself is represented among the six planets which make obeisance to her name.

However we choose to approach the significance of this relief, the arcane importance of Mercury is beyond doubt, as is the fact that it relates to events that were cosmic realities on 1 May 1941. This statuary is one supreme example of the arcane use of Mercury (more specifically – in the light of what Ptolemy wrote – of 'Mercury with Mars'), in a city which is ruled by the same Virgo over which Mercury traditionally has dominion.

Under our gaze, the symbolism of the relief has changed. The almost Egyptian-like hierarchical quality of Maia, so redolent of hermetic images, reveals her connection with the planetary Mysteries.[30] Gregory's statuary turns into a pictorial horoscope – a homily on the nature of the skies on that extraordinary day of 1 May 1941. Vesta is suddenly released from her official symbolic role as representative of the Sanitation Department of Washington DC. She has been transfigured by the genius of John Gregory into the servant of Mars, on the western horizon of the city. Maia is no longer the mundane symbol of the federal courts: she is raised to the rank of a goddess, acknowledged by six other planetary gods, following in the train of Mercury.

Another carving with a Mercurial theme is the relief of the female *America*, holding the magic caduceus, which John Gregory carved in 1937, for the rear entrance to the Federal Reserve Board Building (figure 16).

According to some historians, this image identifies America with Mercury.[31] From an astrological standpoint, this is perfectly acceptable, since many specialists believe that the entire United States is ruled by the sign Gemini (itself ruled by Mercury, like Virgo). The hand of this female rests upon an aegis bearing the seal of the Federal Reserve Board, her fingers almost touching the wing of the eagle. We shall examine this Geminian rulership later, and discover that it was one proposed by the Mason-astrologer Ebenezer Sibly as early as 1784.

The point which this beautiful Gregory sculpture makes is that Mercury is truly an hermaphrodite. Although associated for thousands of years with the male Hermes, the planet is nonetheless said to take on the sexual colouring of the sign in which it is located. Thus, when Mercury is in the feminine sign Virgo, it demonstrates most completely its feminine attributes. This is one reason why the so-called *America* above the rear entrance to the Federal Reserve Board Building is as much an arcane image as the so-called *Urban Life* sculpted by the same artist for the Municipal Centre Building (figure 12).

By now, we have seen enough Washington zodiacs and horoscopes to begin to understand why the wingless Virgo should have been placed on the important horizon line of Jennewein's armillary (figure 11). The Noyes armillary was a memorial to a defunct soul, and it is therefore fitting that the most important zodiacal image should be portrayed sinking below the western horizon, into the Land of the Blessed. More usually, however, Virgo is located on the Ascendant, or is distinguished by a number of planets. Virgo is not the only female among the zodiacal images, but she is by far the most feminine. What does this mean, in spiritual terms, and how does it apply to the esoteric background of Washington DC?

To answer this, we must first study the nature of Virgo in greater detail. Each sign of the zodiac consists of two elements, which may be characterized in terms of light and dark. Behind the light image of the stellar goddess Isis – the prototype of Virgo – there lies the dark goddess Nephthys, her sister. Just as human beings have a darkness hidden within themselves, so do the gods and goddesses of mythology. The ancient Egyptians brought into the light of day temples in honour of Isis and her stars, but did not build to honour the dark sister. Our interest lies in the symbolism of the stellar goddess, but it must be remembered that the stars may only be seen against a backdrop of darkness, which is the Earth's shadow. Those who wish to study the zodiacs and astrology from any place on Earth should be grateful to the dark gods and goddesses who reveal those of the light.

The goddess Isis was symbol of both the past and the future, because she had knowledge of the secrets of time. Isis represented total consciousness, or those things which have been brought into the light of day, for contemplation by the observing mind: this probably explains why the ancient Egyptian builders oriented so many of their temples to her major star, Spica, at Sunrise rather than at Sunset.[32]

In contrast, her dark sister Nephthys represented that which is hidden, the obscured unconsciousness of Man. Did Jennewein, sculptor of the armillary sphere, intend his figure of Virgo to evoke this wakeful Isis, who, like the later sibyls, had knowledge of past, present and future?[33] If so, then it is an Isis who, in her nakedness, symbolically reveals her sacred wisdom *unveiled.*

The Isis of the Egyptian mythology did not have wings: the hieroglyphic *ast*, or throne, upon her head revealed her true royal identity. Like the later Virgin of the Christians, she was Queen of Heaven, and therefore merited a throne. Long before the Greeks called her Isis, her name in Egyptian was *Ast*, as she was the Lady or Ruler of the Secret Places. In many images, especially in the so-called Egyptian *Book of the Dead*, she is frequenly shown with her arms uplifted to indicate that she was a goddess of the defunct – of the secret world into which souls go after life.

In addition to reflecting funerary symbolism, the Jennewein figure was also intended to signify the importance of Virgo to Washington DC – an importance emphasized in the long-defunct meridional placing on 16th Street and Florida Avenue. In this, Jennewein seems to follow a well-established custom of emphasizing the role of Virgo, insisting that Washington DC is under her rule and patronage.

But what exactly does this mean? How can a spiritual being – a living spiritual archetype – have an interest in, let alone a rulership over, a city? In particular, can it be true that such esoteric bodies as the Masons regard these ancient gods and goddesses of the stellar pantheon as living beings, with the power to exude benefices and virtues on certain parts of the Earth? Were the Masons dealing not in abstractions, in past and pagan images, but in a world of living archetypes which really could penetrate the realm of mankind?

The idea that countries and cities are ruled by spiritual beings is very ancient. The earliest surviving comprehensive astrological text which deals with this in depth – the *Tetrabiblos* of Ptolemy – is clearly a summary of astrological lore much earlier than the first century, when the text was compiled. In this work, Ptolemy lists the zodiacal rulerships over the main countries of the ancient world. Although several such lists have come down to us from that time, it is Ptolemy's which was most widely accepted into the mediaeval astrology, and which has survived, only slightly amended, into modern books on the subject.[34]

Ptolemy's chorography,[35] or 'rulerships of places', has been misunderstood by many historians. To explain how tradition (that is, tradition in Ptolemy's terms, 2,000 years ago) arrived at the rulerships listed in his text, he offered a complicated description based on a cosmological projection. This is too antiquated and inaccurate to be of much interest to modern astrologers or geographers. His system has been explained in terms of four astrological trigons, which are projected on to a trapezoid map of the world Ptolemy knew.[36]

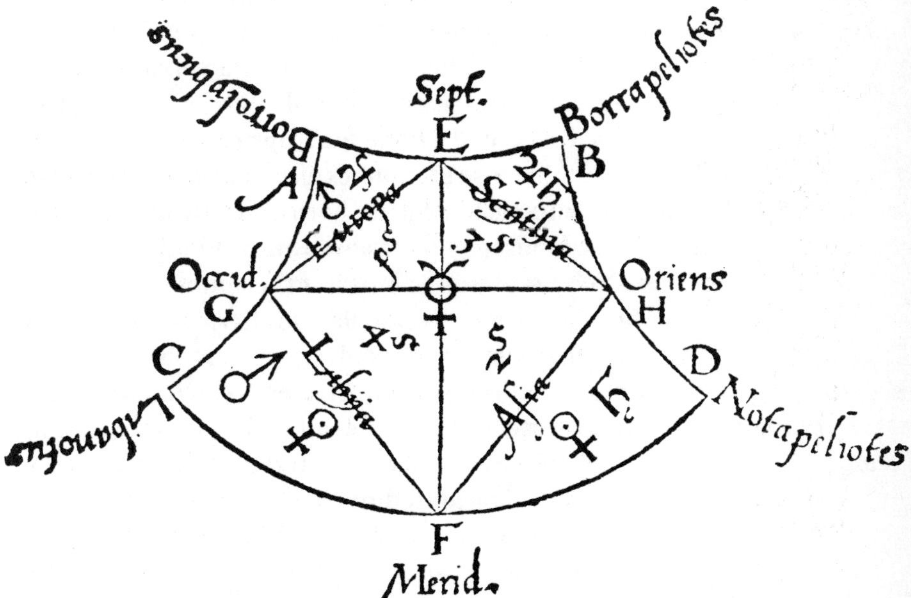

The complexities inherent in this analysis, and his extensive conclusions drawn from it, need not concern us here. The woodcut figure on the previous page is an attempt made by the 16th-century astrologer, Cardan,[37] to render Ptolemy's system in diagrammatic form. Ptolemy defines the areas marked out on his grid not in terms of topographical influences, but in terms of the temperaments and characteristics of the peoples living within these grids. Unfortunately, this is often overlooked, even by modern historians, who (in consequence) find it hard to penetrate Ptolemy's peculiar manner of thought.

What *is* of interest to us in our present research is an important rider which Ptolemy added, once he had listed the traditional chorographies.[38] At the end of his analysis, he moves from a consideration of countries, or domains, and passes to cities. He does not furnish a list of zodiacal rulerships for cities, but mentions, almost in passing, a tradition which was already old in his day and which later (partly thanks to Ptolemy) became so deeply enshrined in astrological lore that it has survived into modern times. He says that 'metropolitan cities' are sympathetic to the influence of the zodiacal positions of the Sun and the Moon, and in particular to that of the Ascendant. From his text, we must assume that he is claiming that the two luminaries and the Ascendant are of spiritual importance in the founding of a city.[39] It is important to remember that in astrology, the Ascendant is the eastern point – that part of the ecliptic which is rising over the eastern horizon at any given time. The Ascendant is said to be the most important single point in any horoscope.

Ptolemy was writing of a tradition which was ancient even in his day, but this same astrological belief underlies the important horoscopes I have cast for Washington DC, in the 18th and 19th centuries. For example, in the horoscope I recorded for the founding of the federal city, on p.65, it is evident that Ptolemy's rule applies, since the sign Virgo was on the Ascendant at that time. Equally, the horoscope we looked at in connection with the White House, on p.65, also confirms Ptolemy's rule, for the Moon (and its own node) were in Virgo at this foundation.

As we continue to investigate the stellar mysteries within this remarkable city we shall find that there is always an emphasis on the mystery of Virgo. The notion that this stellar Maiden is the zodiacal ruler of Washington DC echoes almost interminably in the zodiacs and lapidary symbols which grace the city, as well as in the foundation charts for each of its most important public buildings.

*

Now we should return to the second part of the question: the Masonic perception of rulership. The zodiac appears in Masonic symbolism with surprising infrequency. However, it is possible to interpret the specialist Masonic phrase 'Royal Arch' as a reference, among other things, to the arch of heaven – that is, to the zodiac?[40] In terms of symbolism, the Royal Arch is the vault of heaven, arising from one of the two Masonic pillars, founded at the eastern end in Aries, and on the western pillar in Libra (see page 79). Aries rests on the pillar called (in Masonry) Stability, while Libra rests on the pillar called Beauty. This symbolism is by no means superficial, for it can lead the inquiring mind into the very depths of hermetic thought. Nonetheless, within the framework of Masonic symbolism, this kind of astrology is rare.

In spite of this infrequent use of astrological symbolism in Masonic circles, if my thesis is correct – that is to say, if the arcane structure of Washington DC *was* designed largely by members of the Masonic Brotherhood – then it is reasonable to expect that we should be able to trace Masonic symbols relating to the zodiacal sign of Virgo. In other words, there should be some account in Masonic literature that points to the sign's arcane significance. I write these words with some diffidence, for the truth is that the Brotherhood – like any fraternity or sorority – guards its secrets well. While it is true that there are few hidden truths in the first three degrees of Masonry, it is equally certain that there are well-hidden secrets in the higher degrees.

To penetrate the true arcane knowledge of Masonry, one needs to approach symbols and hieroglyphics which do not reveal their secrets easily. Fortunately, in the 19th century one or two Masons did write about some of their higher secrets. Usually, however they wrote in a guarded way (mainly for a Masonic audience) and presented their arcane images in a similarly guarded way. Fortunately, it is possible to study these writings and images to learn something of their original arcane content.

What one finds is that, for all the reluctance with which the standard symbolism of Masonry approaches the zodiac, Masonic literature frequently refers to the hermetic importance of Virgo – if in suitably arcane and guarded phrases. Among the many symbols which pertain to Virgo, and which have been adopted into Masonry, are the sheaf of wheat (a representative of the star Spica, as we have seen) and the *cornucopia*. Each symbol points to a deep hermetic lore.

A 17th-century image of the Delphic Sibyl (over) shows the woman carrying a cornucopia, from which fall fruit and wheat. She is gesturing towards Christ, who sits on a hillside preaching: this image is connected with the mediaeval belief that the pagan Sibyl had prophesied the coming

III. SIBYLLA DELPHICA.

of Christ. In this sense, the cornucopia is no longer a pagan symbol, but representative of the fulfilment of time, when the spiritual fruit is pouring on to the earth, that the seeds within the fruit and wheat may grow.

Originally, the cornucopia was a symbol derived from classical mythology, and it was probably carried into Masonry from alchemical sources. It is literally the 'horn of plenty', from which all created things emerge. In the classical myth, the infant Zeus was fed by the virgin Amalthea with goat's milk. Zeus, to show his gratitude for this largesse, broke off one of the horns of the goat and presented it to Amalthea, promising that anyone who possessed it would have an abundance of all things he or she might desire.[41] Part of the esoteric secret behind this mythology is that the interior of the horn is dark, but from the darkness a largesse pours into the light of day, to enrich the living. Furthermore, the horn has come from a goat – the animal of Capricorn. When we examined the Franzoni zodiac on the *Car of History* (figure 7), we saw that one great cosmic duality within the zodiac – that of Cancer and Capricorn – relates to the idea of descent into birth (or life), and ascent into the spiritual realm (or death). The goat-horn cornucopia encapsulates both these extremes of darkness and light, of death and life.

The alchemists (whose symbolism influenced the development of arcane Masonic symbols) developed this mythology into various hieroglyphical forms, all touching upon different aspects of the maternal nature of the milky gift. In one alchemical image, published in an influential work by Michael Maier,[42] the world-nourisher Amalthea is shown feeding the child Zeus as a parallel to the story of the she-wolf feeding the two children who founded the city of Rome – Romulus and Remus. The cornucopia in both the sibyl image (opposite), and the alchemical imagery, points to the idea of 'the fruits of the land'.

Amalthea's cornucopia is said to have contained all the riches of nature, and was often shown as pouring forth corn, flowers and fruits. It is perhaps in this image of the cornucopia that we reach into the deeper meaning of one of the rituals in the Masonic cornerstone ceremonies.

We have briefly seen that the Masonic ceremonials of the cornerstone involve the depositing of corn, wine and oil upon the stone itself. In the 1793 foundation ceremonial at the Capitol, George Washington, along with the Grand Master Joseph Clark and three of the Worshipful Masters of the Lodges, descended into the cavasson[43] in which the stone was laid and put upon it corn, wine and oil. The entire congregation then joined in prayer, followed by Masons chanting honours, and a volley from the artillery.

This ritual seems to be linked with the idea of the cornucopia, with a lustration which will attract the benefice or largesse of the gods. Indeed, it is almost tempting to read into certain lines from Camoens' *Luciad* the origins of the three lustrations that figure in the Masonic cornerstone ceremonials: 'Amalthea's horn . . . scatters corn and wine, and fruits and flowers.'[44]

In ancient times, corn was the symbol of resurrection and rebirth. For example, the weeping Isis of the Egyptian mythology was linked with the story of resurrection and rebirth in the marvellous tale of her search for the severed body of her husband, Osiris – even in Egyptian astrology, Isis is figured as a corn-goddess. According to the Masonic writer Macoy, this explains the importance of corn in the Third Degree of Masonry.[45] It also explains the importance of corn to Washington DC, for the Virgin of the skies is always portrayed grasping a sheaf of corn or wheat, or with these attributes at her feet.[46] The sheaf of corn is one of the most recurrent symbols in the architectural sculpture of the city.

A more sophisticated example of this Virgoan symbolism in Masonic imagery was originally linked with the picture of a crying woman called *The Weeping Virgin*. Such an association reminds us that the Egyptian equivalent of Virgo – the goddess Isis – and her dark twin, Nephthys, were called in the hermetic literature, 'the weeping sisters'. The great Mason, Albert Pike, knew that the image of the Weeping Virgin was of Egyptian origin,[47] but also seemed aware that the connection between the image and the ancient hermeticism had been forgotten. He pointed out that one important branch of Masonry, though 'ignorant of its import', employed the image of the Weeping Virgin which was clearly linked with the profound myth of the Egyptian goddess Isis, and her search (in the company of her son, Horus) for the body of her slain husband. This Masonry

> still retains among its emblems one of a woman weeping over a broken column, holding in her hand a branch of acacia, myrtle, or tamarisk, while Time, we are told, stands behind her combing out the ringlets of her hair. We need not repeat the vapid and trivial explanation . . . given, of this representation of *Isis*, weeping at Byblos, over the column torn from the palace of the King, that contained the body of Osiris, while Horus, the God of Time, pours ambrosia on her hair.[48]

The symbolic importance of this female figure is enshrined in what the Masonic literature has called at times 'the Beautiful Virgin'. This is distinctly Egyptian in origin, but has its Masonic roots in early 19th-century literature and iconography.

Writing in the *Masonic Newspaper* for 1879,[49] the Mason Robert B. Folger offers a fascinating account of what he believed to be the 'invention' of this important emblem. In the middle of the century, his late friend and Brother, Jeremy L. Cross, used to run a wholesale paper business in Pearl, New York.[50] Cross, who had studied under the great Mason Thomas Smith Webb, began to lecture on the Masonic circuits in 1810. Early in this work, he found the literature relating to the Third Degree of Masonry wanting, and determined to produce a guide which would be helpful.[51] It was this endeavour which accounts for the contributions which Cross made to early American Masonry. Among the images he introduced – or perhaps borrowed from another Masonic source – was that of the Weeping Virgin.[52]

It seems that Cross believed there was a deficiency in the symbolism of the Third Degree, relating to the death of Hiram Abif, the 'son of the widow', who had worked for Solomon during the building of the Temple. To remedy this deficiency, Cross laboured to find a satisfactory symbol, or mnemonic, to be used in the degree rituals. By about 1819, he had evolved such an emblem (seemingly based on an earlier idea), involving the image of a broken column, as a memento of loss (above). When, in that year, Cross issued an edition of Thomas Smith Webb's *Freemasons' Monitor*, he added a large number of pictures to illustrate the text.[53] Among these was an image which eventually developed into the picture of a weeping, or silently lamenting, woman. A most interesting version of this Virgo image was republished by the Mason, Robert Hewitt Brown, in his study of Masonic astronomy in 1882.[54]

The amendment which Brown proposed has been called 'the Beautiful Virgin', but it is quite clear from his own commentary that it was supposed to represent the Virgin of the zodiac. In this respect, the Isiac

origins of the image were still being remembered, for in the Egyptian zodiac Isis had been the equivalent of Virgo. The version of the emblem published by Brown made no attempt to disguise the zodiacal origin of his figure (see above). Although he refers to the woman in his picture as *Rhea* (one of the Greek names for Virgo, as he admits), the sigil in the zodiacal arch above her head is certainly that of Virgo – a version of the familiar looped M. For some reason, Brown was referring to the zodiacal Virgo without using her name.

This design shows the Beautiful Virgin resting her right hand on a broken column, and holding up in her left hand a sprig of the acacia. If we follow conventional symbolism, and view the acacia as a classical symbol of death and mourning, then in this position it seems to echo the Spica of the more familiar Virgo imagery. In that case, it contrasts death with life. The image of winged Death behind her is a reminder that the device is intended to reflect upon mortality. The only significant deviation from the standard zodiacal symbolism in this design is in the substitution of the acacia for the wheat.

If we look at acacia on a deeper level of symbolism, then we may interpret this intriguing figure in a very different way. In the esoteric literature, it is maintained that the coffin or casket in which the pieces of Osiris (the husband of Isis) were kept was made of acacia wood. Since, in the mythology, his body was resurrected, we may see that the casket is far more than a tomb image – it is a resurrectional image. Archaeologists working in Egypt have observed that mummy coffins made of sycamore were often clamped shut with the harder acacia wood: perhaps this usage is reflected in the Greek equivalent for the tree, which means 'wood not liable to rot',[55] since it is certainly a wood that will not easily fall to the scythe of Time. Within such a framework of symbolism, the acacia in the hand of the Weeping Virgin is not an emblem of death, but a promise of resurrection – of a life after death.

The image of the Beautiful Virgin has caused dismay in some Masonic circles. Perhaps this is because its deeper strands of meaning have not always been fully grasped. Scholars have pointed out that the 'idea' behind the Weeping Virgin is much older than the Cross illustrations: a monument to mark the grave of the Temple architect (which is the main point of the Cross picture) was introduced into English Masonry as early as 1782. Cross merely seems to have fixed the form into its traditional symbolism. There are traces in earlier French Masonry of all the constituent elements in the Cross engraving, but we do not need to pursue the matter here: my own interest is in the later development, when the Virgin was transformed quite openly into Virgo, by means of the addition of the zodiacal arc and the sigil for Virgo.

The engraving of 1819, which first appeared in a Masonic work compiled by Cross, is different from the later version by virtue of the fact that it does not incorporate the zodiacal arc. How the zodiac was introduced into the later wood engraving is one of the mysteries of Masonic history, and it is an important one. Is there, then, any way of tracing possible astrological influences in this curious engraving, or in its later derivatives?

Folger's account of what he calls the 'Fiction of the Weeping Virgin' is well intended, but seems far from accurate.[56] He says that Cross, seeking a hieroglyphic to complete his series of mnemonics for the Third Degree, was inspired by a broken column – a memorial to a Brother,[57] in Trinity churchyard, New York City. Cross felt that to represent the idea of death, expressed in the working of the Third Degree, he should use an inscription, describing the merits and achievements of the dead. He then hit upon the idea of an open book. Taking this line of thinking further, he decided that there should also be a *reader* of the book. Cross selected a beautiful virgin, who should (in Folger's words) 'weep over the memory of the deceased while she read of his heroic deeds'.

The main problem with this account of the Beautiful Virgin is that it does not explain the later, distinctly arcane, development of the image, which is of such interest to us in our research into the mystery of Virgo. There seems an unbridged chasm between the crude imagery which Cross proposed and the more sophisticated image – clearly linked with Virgo – which emerged in Masonic circles during the 1880s.

Robert Hewitt Brown's discussion of the various amendments to Cross's images, and the symbolism of Rhea ('identified with Isis and Virgo'), is highly speculative, and does not explain the particular emphasis on Virgo, or even the introduction of the segment of the zodiac.[58] Nor does it explain the most intriguing and esoteric element in the design – the words 'Autumnal Equinox', which offer a symbolic reference to the West (the Descendant point of Libra), towards which Virgo looks as she brandishes her acacia. Anyone familiar with the theory of foundation orientation cannot fail to observe that the very phrase 'Autumnal Equinox' links the figure with orientation theory, and thus with architecture.

There is one very interesting idea which makes sense of the way the Weeping Virgin of 1819 developed into the Virgo (or Rhea) of 1882. Perhaps, given the antiquity of the title, we do not need to question why the Virgin does not appear to be weeping in any of the early versions. If the image is really linked with the hermetic tradition (as Pike has suggested), it is possible that the idea of a Weeping Virgin harks back to the weeping sisters, Isis and Nephthys, rather than the Virgin in the crude woodcut. The Virgin in the 1882 print is not weeping, and seems almost defiant.

One other important difference between the two images is that the Cross engraving of the Virgin shows her holding a book, while the 1882 Virgin merely rests her hand on the broken column. We have already seen an image of a woman holding a book, and linked intimately with the idea of time, in the Franzoni statuary clock, *The Car of History* (figure 7). This Clio might well weep at what she sees being done by mankind, yet she too is not portrayed as weeping. Franzoni's statuary was completed in 1819 – the same year that Cross's Virgin seems to have been developed. In the light of this, is the Cross emblem a little more sophisticated than has been recognized?

The three zodiacal signs on which the *Car of History* runs are Sagittarius, Capricorn and Aquarius. Are we being imaginative in tracing the image of Sagittarius to the acacia leaves,[59] the image of Capricorn to the time-god Saturn (who rules Capricorn), and the ambrosia that was poured over the head of Isis in the original imagery to Aquarius, the water-pourer? This latter idea will only make sense when we realize that the 'water' poured by Aquarius is not an ordinary liquid, but a celestial dew, a life force – in other words, ambrosia.

To take this further, did Hewitt Brown – deeply steeped in astrological symbolism – understand the hidden symbolism in this crude-seeming image, and reverse the zodiacal arc on which the *Car of Destiny* runs, so that it becomes an arch in the heavens? The encircled Virgin he pictures (p.176) is not weeping, yet is clearly identified as Virgo by the sigil ♍ over her head. Just so, the winged image of Time is marked with the sigil for Saturn ♄. In other words, just as there is a meaningful segment of the zodiac beneath the virgin Clio, so there is also one above the head of this feminine emblem.

I must make clear that these correspondences are not something I would wish to include as an essential part of my argument that Virgo is the ruling sign of the city of Washington DC. What I have proposed is more a tentative suggestion for further research, by interested historians. However, the truth is that there *are* other esoteric elements in the woodcut of 1882 that should encourage further analysis. Moreover, it is important that this image, which so clearly identifies the Egyptian weeping sister with the zodiacal arch of Virgo, *should have originated in 1881, the year which most esotericists and astrologers recognized would mark the beginning of the new age.*

While I was researching the origins of this curious Weeping Virgin, the Masonic historian Art de Hoyos suggested that I examine an 18th-century print which, while Masonic in subject matter, was partly derived from the alchemical tradition. This print not only appeared in a Masonic book, but was even engraved by a Mason, named Tringham, who openly asserted his affiliation in his signature.[60] Several details in this arcane engraving certainly seem to evoke symbols which might have been the source for the later Weeping Virgin that incorporated the arc of the zodiac above the head of the Virgin.

On the left of this alchemical plate is a seated Virgin. We may presume from the fruit and flowers which pour from beneath her dress, as though from a cornucopia, that she is a *stellar Virgin*. Behind her is Saturn, or perhaps Time, with his scythe. In his right hand, he dangles the circular ouroboros snake, biting its own tail. In his left is what appears to be a sprig of acacia leaves, which he is offering to the maiden. The pair are seated in the clouds – perhaps to show that they are archetypes, or stellar beings.

On the Earth plane is a considerable number of Masonic symbols, including many which found their way into American Masonry: the pyramid, the bees and beehives, and so on. At the bottom right, on a dais reached by seven steps, sits a king-like figure, with a celestial globe to his left: he is working on what appears to be a Masonic tracing board, drawing Euclid's famous theorem.[61] In the bottom centre is a sundial, the plinth of which is marked with Masonic symbols. At the bottom left are three broken columns, near the standard emblem of death – the skull and crossbones.

I know of several examples of pre-19th-century imagery which may have influenced Cross's visualization of this simplistic-seeming picture. The most likely source is the vignettes in a collection of engravings by Jacopo Guarana, published in 1792 under the title *Oracoli, Auguri, Aruspici*. Certain details in these vignettes lead us to presume that the mythological figure owe their symbolism to the German classical scholar, Johan Graevius, who was Historiographer Royal to William III of England.

Figure 17 shows a vignette which contains all the elements within the Cross design, though on a slightly different level of Masonic symbolism. It depicts winged Saturn with his scythe and hour-glass, the broken column, a clothed woman and the statue of a naked woman. The clothed one has fallen, and points with her index finger towards the letter G engraved on a stone – an obvious reference to the G for Geometry from the Masonic tracing boards and carpets. The superficial symbolism, announced in the Latin motto ('All things have an end'), approaches the theme of the impermanence of the material realm, contained in the Masonic Third Degree. It is worth noting that the wing-tip of Saturn points to the private parts of the statue above – perhaps to emphasize that she is a virgin? I suspect that we may trace in such a source as this the origins of the Cross emblem.

These symbols are far more complex than those in the simple device of the Weeping Virgin reproduced on p.175. Even so, the main symbols – broken columns, a (tearless) Virgin, Time with his scythe, the acacia, and so on – are continued in the cruder woodcut. We find in this engraving some intimation that those Masons who insisted that Cross did not invent these symbols himself were probably correct. There is little doubt that Cross (no intellectual or historian himself, as most Masons would admit[62]) had borrowed his symbols from a much earlier tradition, even if not specifically from the engraving by Tringham.

What I find of particular interest in the picture on page 176 is the segment of the zodiac, marked with the sigils for Libra, Virgo and Leo. Although the two prints have three signs of the zodiac in common, these are not the same in each case. The emphasis in the English print of 1650 is on Gemini – graphically demonstrated by the two cupids, one of which dangles a Masonic emblem: they are like flying twins, dangling between them a banderole inscribed with the wise saw, 'Silence and Secret'. The proximity of this aerial couple to the sign Gemini means that we must read them as pertaining to this sign. Gemini is renowned in the popular astrological books as the 'talkative sign', and (the emblem seems to suggest) it behoves the Mason to control his tongue, to preserve in silence the secrets he learns within the Fraternity. Is there a deeper significance in this Geminian symbolism, and does it bear any relationship to the symbolism of the crude cut of 1880?

The 1650 engraving was made by Masons, for Masons, in the city of London. This city was under the rule of Gemini, or the Twins. The year after the engraving was made, the astrologer William Lilly published a hieroglyphic predicting the coming Fire of London, conveying his meaning through the a 'hieroglyphic' image (below) of Gemini. Even

before the conflagration of 1666, this hieroglyphic was recognized as a prophecy that there would be a fire in the city of London. The meaning was evident from the presence of the Heavenly Twins (representative of the city) in the skies above the flames.[63]

The English Masonic images regularly emphasize the nature of Gemini, not merely because this is the 'zodiacal sign of London', but because it is the 'male' sign governed by Mercury.[64]

While my interest does not lie particularly in English Masonry, it is worth noting that its arcane symbolism is concerned with the masculine expression of Mercury. Mercury is notoriously a hermaphrodite, and when we turn to the symbolism of American Masons we do not find the Geminian Mercury emphasized. On the contrary, time and again, we find an emphasis being placed on the feminine side of Mercury – which is expressed by Virgo.

Almost certainly, it is this which explains why the arc above the Beautiful Virgin on p.176 displays Virgo rising above the head of the woman – for this image pertains to, and was developed exclusively within the confines of, American Masonry. The imagery of the Weeping Virgin helps explain why the majority of images of the personification of Masonry in the United States of America are female.

Whatever the real story behind the origins of Cross's hieroglyphic, it was eventually adopted by 19th-century Masons. Although the Grand Lodge of the State of New York would not countenance this new symbolism, it was finally established in 1826 in the Mystic Lodge of New York City,[65] after which it spread through the states. According to Cross, it was also received into the Grand Lodge in 1826. In spite of this acceptance, many Masons have remained unhappy with the image of the Weeping Virgin – perhaps because its open publication in illustrative form breaches one of their Mysteries.

In his own commentary on this symbol, published in 1882, Robert Hewitt Brown pointed out (somewhat archly) that had Cross 'been more familiar with the symbolism of those ancient Mysteries, from which Freemasonry is derived, he might have devised . . . [an emblem which] would not have . . . violated the traditions of our Order, and also, at the same time, have been in entire harmony with the astronomical basis of the third degree'.[66] Hewitt Brown has not been alone in deploring what appeared to be a personal addition to the repertoire of Masonic symbols. However, there is evidence that it was not entirely personal, and that Cross did not invent the image, following the process outlined by Folger, but merely amended an older symbolism. Much later, Masons may have lamented the fact of her 'betrayal', but this Beautiful Virgin did stem from a deep awareness within the Masonic tradition of the hermetic and sacred nature of Virgo.

There is something else we should consider in Hewitt Brown's words above: what did he mean when he intimated that there were secrets in the ancient Mysteries which Cross had missed? Perhaps the answer hinges on what is meant by 'weeping sisters'. As we have seen, both Isis and her sister Nephthys were said to be weeping for the death of Osiris. However, being goddesses, they could not weep ordinary tears. Is the secret behind this idea of weeping goddesses bound up with the nature of the liquid which they are supposed to have wept?

As is so often the case with Masonic symbolism, the secret seems to be involved with ancient Egyptian iconography and hieroglyphics. In such images, the gods are not portrayed as weeping, as throwing drops of sacred water. The Egyptian hieroglyphic *mst* which looks like the three-fold fall of water actually means 'dew', and portrays drops of water falling from heaven.[67] The same hieroglyphic also means 'instruction', or

'teaching'. The 19th-century Masonic scholar John W. Simons[68] believed that the sound-values of Egyptian hieroglyphics were more closely linked with the Hebrew language than with Coptic, as was widely believed. When examining the hieroglyphic *mst* (above) he pointed out that the Hebrew *ire* means 'to throw drops of water, to sprinkle, and to teach or instruct'.[69] He further pointed out that this hieroglyphic is linked with the Egyptian baptism, with the notion of shedding celestial dew on the head of the neophyte – that is, with initiation. In support of his argument, he examined a plate which showed an Egyptian initiation scene, where the gods Horus and Thoth pour sacred waters on the head of the neophyte (over).[70] The one initiated in this way, by water and fire, was called in Hebrew *msche*, meaning something like 'begotten', or 'born again' – a word relevant to the new state of the neophyte who has been initiated. According to Simons, the Egyptian hieroglyphic equivalent of this *Moses* incorporated the image for *dew*, *baptism*, or celestial tears.[71]

I am not for one moment claiming that this was the esoteric element behind the Weeping Virgin which Cross was not familiar with, or somehow missed (he did not appear to be deeply interested in such esoteric strains of thought). However, it *is* evident that the tears which Isis and Nephthys wept were not ordinary human tears, and were

certainly involved both with initiation and with instruction – the two, in an arcane sense, being quite inseparable.

It seems, then, that the Beautiful Virgin is a representation of the Virgin of the skies, the celestial Virgo, and that in certain Masonic contexts she is represented as weeping. The link between Virgo and Isis is nowhere more openly revealed than in this idea, for Isis was herself one of the two 'weeping sisters'. In some Masonic accounts, she is said to be weeping because she symbolizes the unfinished Temple – that is, the Temple of Solomon from which some Masonic fraternities still date the passage of the years. Since the Masonic symbolism sees the building of the *external Temple* as representative of the building of the *internal temple* of spirit, it seems that the Virgin weeps either for the imperfections still in mankind or because the Temple is not yet finished.

In the wood engraving used by George Oliver to illustrate his encyclopaedia of Masonry (opposite) the funerary symbolism is much in evidence. Not only does the Saturn-like image of Death play with the hair of the young maiden, in the manner of the cruel reaper of the mediaeval Dance of Death, but, as she reads the book (the memorial of a Master Mason in the early mythology of the Masonic Brotherhood, Hiram Abif), she holds high the *cassia* leaves.[72] The accompanying text tells us something we are now aware of: the virgin is weeping, and she is weeping for the unfinished state of the Temple. Oliver has captioned the picture *Burial Place – Time and the Virgin*, and his text indicates that the intended symbolism is a reference to the burial place of Hiram Abif, under the Holy of Holies:

> the open book implies that his memory [that is, the memory of Hiram] is recorded in every Mason's heart; the sprig of cassia refers to the discovery of his remains; the urn shews that his ashes have been carefully collected, and Time standing behind her implies that time, patience and perseverance will accomplish all things.[73]

It appears that with the passage of time, the wonderfully arcane symbolism of the Beautiful Virgin was demoted: she lost her celestial quality, and became little more than the equivalent of a Victorian funerary symbol of a lamenting woman. However, before this demotion

took place at the hands of such writers as Oliver, the celestial version of this Beautiful Virgin was the Virgin whom the Masons used in their mystery-symbols of Washington DC, the city of Virgo. The important point is this: in some way, the Masonic fraternities of the United States have visualized their federal city as the founding stone not merely for the United States, but for the Fourth Era, which will see the rebuilding, on the inner plane, of the Temple of Solomon.

Anyone who takes the trouble to examine the statuary and architectural details of the city cannot fail to note there the extraordinary number of Virgoan images (and hints of Virgoan imagery in such symbolic details as the corn-sheaf and cornucopia). It is worth pointing out that at least 50 public statues or buildings in the city are involved with the symbolism of Virgo, and each of the 23 public zodiacs emphasizes (in one way or another) this same Virgoan symbolism.[74]

Such imagery reflects the Masonic appreciation of the arcane significance of Virgo. It is in this pregnant myth of the Beautiful Virgin that we begin to see something of the arcane importance of the Virgo image to Washington DC. The image points – by inference – to the unfinished Temple of Solomon, that most enduring of Masonic symbols.[75] This means that the Weeping Virgin symbolizes, in a feminine personification, a lamentation at the unfinished pyramid on the Seal of the United States, and on every dollar bill. The pyramid is incomplete because it is the Egyptian Mystery equivalent of the Temple of Solomon: Virgo is the star-goddess weeping that so remarkable an endeavour still remains unfinished.

Chapter Seven

> Of all the noble sciences ever cultivated by mankind, Astronomy is acknowledged to be the most sublime, the most interesting, and the most useful . . .
>
> (Jeremy L. Cross, *The True Masonic Chart, or Hieroglyphic Monitor*, 1824, p.45)

The expressions of the sculpted lions which guard each end of the Taft Bridge in Connecticut Avenue, Washington DC, are rather supercilious. One wonders if they recognize just how important a role serendipity has played in their fame.

The original lions were among the first sculptures made from precast concrete in the United States. Unfortunately, the concrete was not as enduring as the sculptor had been led to believe, and by 1964 the lions had to be restored. When the precast lions and bridge were first constructed in 1906, the animals appear to have been intended merely as symbolic guardians. However, after the death of the former President of the United States, William Howard Taft, a decision was made to name the bridge after this popular man. Serendipitously, Taft's birth-chart had been dominated by a conjunction of three planets in the sign Leo, whose animal is the lion.[1]

In 1909, President Taft became one of the few people to be accorded the honour of being made a Mason 'at sight'.[2] If one were unduly imaginative, one might suspect that the artist and architect had somehow collaborated to create these supercilious lions precisely to honour a leonine Masonic President, rather than merely to decorate a bridge. But imaginative play with facts is not necessary to link three interesting men – architect, sculptor and President – in a different and far more creative astrological context. They each, in their own separate ways, contributed to the construction of Washington DC's most beautiful public building –

the Library of Congress, which houses two of the most impressive zodiacs in the world.[3]

The painter-sculptor Roland Hinton Perry had been born in 1870, the same year that the English novelist, Charles Dickens, died. This chance juncture of generations links these two men – Dickens, who examined the early library of about 50,000 books in the crowded north rooms of the Capitol building (some years before the fire which almost completely destroyed it), and Perry, who put the finishing touches to the purpose-built library which housed the millions of books that had outgrown the space available in the Capitol.

When Charles Dickens journeyed through America in 1842, he was writing to entertain his English readers, and would probably not see beyond the materials of stone and human flesh in Washington DC. He was impressed by the Capitol, and by Horatio Greenough's statue of George Washington, which looked for all the world like a Greek god inviting down lightning in retribution for man's cruelty to man. Did Dickens perhaps find himself wondering why the architect, Latrobe, had

designed some of the interior columns' capitals with a corncob and tobacco motifs (below), instead of with traditional acanthus? Probably not – Dickens, well schooled in the symbolism of Europe, would almost certainly have recognized the corncob as symbol of American farming, and the tobacco as symbol of the American mercantile system. The magnolia capitals might have presented more difficulty to an amateur symbolist, but it has been proposed that this American tree may have represented the arts and sciences of the New World.[4]

I doubt that Dickens would have sought the deeper meaning which Thomas Jefferson had read into the symbolism. Jefferson, a sophisticated and well-educated man, guessed at the underlying meaning of the corncob when he referred to Latrobe's design as 'the Cerealian capital'. It was, as Jefferson surmised, the symbol of Ceres, the goddess associated in Masonic literature with Virgo, the Beautiful Virgin.[5] Latrobe repaid Jefferson's recognition by sending him as a gift a model of the corncob capital, so that he could install it in his Monticello garden as the support for a sundial.

It is even less likely that Dickens would have perceived the esoteric meaning in the tobacco motifs which Latrobe introduced into his architecture. His designs for the library in the Capitol had been the first examples of the so-called 'Egyptian-revival' style in America.[6] The transition from archaic Egyptian-symbolism to a symbolism acceptable to the European vision was nowhere more apparent than in the capitals intended for the Library of Congress. Latrobe took an ordinary American tobacco plant and moulded from it a capital that not only looked distinctly Egyptian in style, but actually encapsulated something of profound esoteric significance (see engraving on page 188).

The tobacco leaf designs made by Latrobe have been discussed from many points of view, but the arcane symbolism behind them has not been sufficiently examined. One surviving sketch made by Latrobe of the tobacco leaf idea for his capitals included a drawing of the flower, beneath the projected design.[7] The flower is five-petalled (left). Anyone steeped in esoteric lore will recognize the

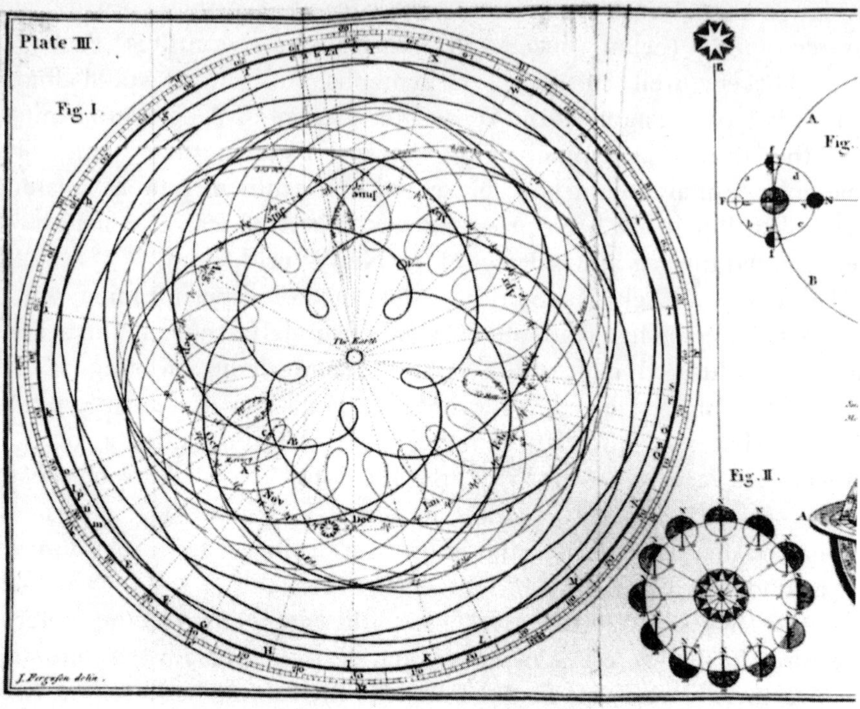

similarity of this pattern to that described in the skies by the planet Venus – a pattern which was illustrated beautifully by the astronomer James Ferguson in a well-known book on astronomy, with which Latrobe, as an amateur astronomer, would certainly have been familiar (see above).[8] This fivefold planetary rhythm explains why the planet Venus has been associated with the body of Man (and in particular with the *spiritual* body of Man) in a multitude of arcane diagrams that link the image of Man with the pentagram, or with a five-pointed star (opposite).

When we attempt to trace the graphic etymology of this 'occult man', or Venusian man, back to its ancient Egyptian roots, we generally finish up gazing at a hieroglyphic rather like the five-pointed star. This was originally the Egyptian *sba* star, which entered Masonic symbolism in the late 17th century. Latrobe must have been aware of the connection between the star and the rhythm of Venus. It required only a short leap of imagination to see this same five-pointed rhythm in the petals of the indigenous tobacco flower, and to transfer this to its Egyptian architectural equivalent.

The five-pointed star had been widely used in Masonic circles before the middle of the 19th century, but it was the Frenchman Champollion

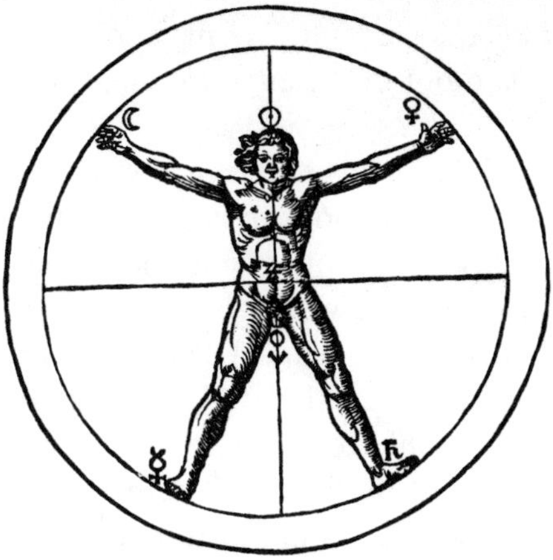

who confirmed its true meaning, and who linked it in one hieroglyphic form with the equivalent of Virgo.[9]

Reading between the lines, which one often must do with Dickens, I get the impression that he was not especially enamoured of the President, John Tyler.[10] Nor did Dickens seem to think much of the plan of Washington itself, for it was clearly not finished in any architectural sense. 'It is sometimes called,' he famously wrote, 'the City of Magnificent Distances, but it might with greater propriety be termed the City of Magnificent Intentions.'[11] Dickens surveyed the city from the top of the Capitol:

> Spacious avenues, that begin in nothing, and lead nowhere; streets, mile-long, that only want houses, roads and inhabitants; public buildings that need but a public to complete; and ornaments of great thoroughfares, which only lack great thoroughfares to ornament – are its leading features . . . To the admirers of cities it is a Barmecide Feast; a pleasant field for the imagination to rove in; a monument raised to a deceased project, with not even a legible inscription to record its departed greatness.[12]

He likened the city to the London slum of Pentonville, burned down, and built up again in wood and plaster, without even the mediocre harmlessness of the English climate: it would be scorching hot in the morning then freezing cold in the afternoon, with an occasional tornado of wind and dust.

The English writer's view is understandable. By 1842, Washington DC had lost its way. The original plans drawn up by L'Enfant had been mislaid, and the clarity of design marked out in the city streets, avenues and parks had become obscured.

Being a literary man, Dickens cast his eye over the library used by Congress, which he found pleasant and commodious. Being English, he might have felt a twinge of conscience, as it was not as commodious as it should have been: most of the book collection which had started this library had been destroyed by the British, on 24 August 1814.[13] Having entered the Capitol, Admiral Cockburn of the Royal Navy had arrogantly posed as Speaker, and after calling his rabble to order took a vote on whether they should burn the building and its library. There were no dissenting votes, and the books were used for kindling torches which were passed from hand to hand in an orgy of destruction.[14] The repairs were extensive. The central foundation of the Capitol of the United States was relaid on 24 August 1818, and as soon as the building was completed the books began to accumulate once more, to be put at the disposal of Congress. Then disaster struck again: ten years after Dickens had admired it, the 'second' library – which really comprised the national collection of books – was seriously damaged when, on Christmas Eve 1851, a huge fire broke out.[15] Astrologers have blamed both man-made and natural fires on the planet Uranus, which seems to bedevil American cultural life.[16]

Life was easy for members of Congress in the days when Dickens used the Library. The eccentric Philadelphian Ignatius Donnelly, elected to Congress as member for Minnesota in 1863, would spend many hours each week studying in its Library. He was to become (arguably, in the opinion of some historians) 'perhaps the most learned man ever to sit in the House'.[17] His researches and ruminations led to several literary works, the most influential (and perhaps the most imaginative) being his view of the lost continent of Atlantis which he revealed to the world in a readable but entirely unreliable book.[18] His influence was pervasive, and perhaps not altogether beneficial: the modern craze for Atlantis mythology owes more to Donnelly's enthusiasm in the Library of Congress than it does to the sedate Athenian academy of Plato.

Donnelly had been able to pass from the chamber directly to the Library, for, until 1897, the books were housed in a hall at the west front of the Capitol. However, the number of books increased dramatically due both to bequests and to improvement in copyright deposit arrangements, and, in that year, the entire collection was transferred to the new building

– an architectural wonder, with mysteries of its own – to the south-east of the Capitol.

In many ways, the new Library is the official architectural gem of Washington DC (plate 8). Specially designed to serve as the Library of Congress, its style is more flamboyant than any other building in the centre of the city. When it was completed, some Senators complained that the glistening golden dome (above the main reading room) detracted from the more famous dome of the Capitol building. Perhaps they were not concerned merely with the outer appearance of the Library dome – the inner dome, with its complex programme of symbolism, was in itself one of the wonders of the world.

The competition for the design of the new building had been authorized by Congress as early as 1873, when the pressure of books was already threatening to burst the Capitol Library and its various annexes at their seams. There were numerous submissions, but it was the design by the Viennese architect John L. Smithmeyer, the partner of the Washington DC architect Paul J. Pelz, was chosen.[19] As is usually the case in Washington DC, bureaucracy worked slowly, and the authorization for work to commence did not materialize until 1886. Two years later, an act of Congress put Brigadier-General Thomas Lincoln Casey, Chief of Engineers in the army, in charge of the project. It was while looking into the life of Casey that I made a far-reaching discovery, which helped explain why this remarkable man should have been appointed to such an important undertaking, and why the Library should have among its decorations so many zodiacs.

While examining the literature relating to the transit of Venus of 1882, which had so obsessed the Masonic composer Sousa, I read the reports of the Superintendent of the United States Naval Observatory, published in 1883.[20] In the course of this reading, I was astonished to learn that among the party of American astronomers sent to observe the transit in Wellington had been one Lieutenant Thomas Lincoln Casey, who was described in the offical records as 'assistant astronomer'.[21] These records show that he was assistant to the most brilliant astronomer of the day, Professor Simon Newcomb.[22] This information opened new vistas for me.

At first, though, the reference to Casey in this guise puzzled me. I had knowledge of him only in a later incarnation as Brigadier-General Casey, the Chief of Engineers of the army, a military man of fine American lineage who served in the Civil War, and who had participated in the completion of the Washington Monument, leaving his own name inscribed on its aluminium finial at the highest point in Washingon DC. He had also come to my notice as the army officer in charge of the construction of the new Library of Congress, with instructions to report directly to Congress annually, and to submit all plans to the Secretary of War and the Secretary of the Interior. Thus it is that from 1888 until his death in 1896, Casey was entirely responsible for the construction of the Library, and answerable directly to Congress. One of his wisest decisions (albeit nepotistic-seeming) was to appoint his son Edward Pearce Casey as architect, with the responsibility of overseeing the decoration of the Library.

It is in this chance listing of the official report on the transit of Venus of 1882 that I found my first clue to the extraordinary zodiacal imagery and secret orientations of the Library of Congress. From its inception, the design had been in the hands not so much of a military man and a Mason, as one who was interested in astronomy, and who was in regular contact with the most brilliant astronomer of the day – an astronomer well known among specialists for his seminal research into the planets and the lunar motions, and yet famous in a more general sense for his books on popular astronomy.[23] It is perhaps to the influence of this man on Thomas Lincoln Casey that we owe the erection, in Washington DC, of a beautiful building which not only contains seven zodiacs, but includes two of the most beautiful in America.[24]

The laying of the cornerstone for the new Library, on 28 August 1890, was almost a burlesque.[25] A surviving photograph, recently republished, shows the stone being craned into place at 3.00 p.m. on that day.[26] A sealed copper box, containing documents on the history of the building and newspapers for that day, had been put inside a special hollow in the stone, following the tradition of cornerstone-layings. However, nothing else that day seemed to follow tradition.

The mystery of this cornerstone laying is intriguing. It appears that in May 1890 the House of Representatives had passed a resolution that the cornerstone should be laid formally, under the direction of the joint committee on the Library, in cooperation with the US army Corps of Engineers – of which Casey was Brigadier-General. When Congress failed to act on the resolution, Bernard Green, the engineer overseeing the construction of the library, always impatient of delays, impetuously went ahead anyway with the unceremonial laying of the stone.

As the photograph reveals, it was certainly no formal cornerstone ceremony: indeed, the event seems to have been staged as an afterthought for the benefit of the camera. Much of the wall behind had already been raised to a height of four marble facing blocks – an estimated height of over 14 feet – with the support walls behind even higher.[27]

The question of why Green delayed his building programme by bothering to stage a photograph of this 'cornerstone ceremony' is a vexing one. Fortunately, the issues arising from the astrological conditions pertaining to the chosen time are not vexacious. Whoever chose the day (I would like to think it was Casey) must surely have realized what was happening in the skies at that time: the Sun and Saturn were in conjunction in the zodiacal sign Virgo. Was he aware of the importance of the Saturn-Sun conjunction, in an edifice which would contain so many zodiacs? If so, Casey's foresight (or Green's impetuosity) paid off. Had they waited until the next day, the chart would have pointed to disaster, from an astrological point of view.[28]

The spiritual deficiency behind this burlesque of 'ceremonial' is perhaps countered to some extent by the fact that two corner rooms of the building were later made the pivot for two sets of zodiacal arrangements, as though the north-east corner was the apex of a right-angled triangle, the subtended lines of which involved zodiacs. In the old map room to the north-west of the Library, are 12 zodiacal images, painted on the recessed window walls, while in the Pavilion of the Elements on the south-east corner is a magnificent ceiling zodiac painted by Elmer E. Garnsey (plates 9 and 10).

As the cornerstone was lowered on 28 August 1890, that acerbic critic of American life, the writer Mrs Anne Royall – a great lover of books – must have taken quiet satisfaction from her grave. The house in which she had lived on B Street had been removed in order that it might be overlaid by this north-east foundation stone for the national library of the United States.[29] Not being unduly egocentric, she would scarcely have taken much satisfaction in the association with this posthumous literary fame. Her pleasure would have been increased had the stone been laid with the cooperation of the Masons who had supported her, and whom she had defended with much courage during her lifetime.[30]

The architecture of the Library of Congress has never failed to attract favourable comment, and several excellent books on the sculptural programme have been published.[31] That this public building is the most beautiful in all America is almost beyond dispute. *What is not generally recognized, however, is that the Library is the hub of an arcane symbolism, which breathed a spiritual life into the city, and which had been planned about 1880, as an integral part of a new programme of rebuilding.*

As with all high-quality architecture, the symbolism of the Library of

Congress incorporates a system of exteriorizing space with a system of interiorizing time.

The façade is the Library's most exotic display, with beautifully carved spandrel figures by Bela L. Pratt (figure 19), and bronze doors by a number of American artists including Olin Warner, Frederick MacMonnies and Herbert Adams.[32] The richly designed fountain, which shores up the stepped courtyard to the west and represents a court of the sea-god Neptune surrounded by watery nereids, is Perry's masterpiece. The group recalls both Plato and Ignatius Donnelly, for the latter had noted that the Greek had surrounded the great statue of Poseidon (a most important god in his fable of Atlantis) with the image of 100 nereids, seated on dolphins.[33] In the crisp air of Washington DC, the god leans forward in animated contemplation of the world beyond; around him are fish-men Tritons and voluptuous nymphs riding seahorses – themselves the animals of the sea god (figure 20). In the water are dolphins and turtles. (Surprisingly, the trace of the exuberance of Nicolo Salvi's *Trevi Fountain* in Rome, which partly inspired the American sculptor of the Washington fountain,[34] is not out of place in this American clime.) No doubt the symbolism is there to remind us that Poseidon was ruler of the underground watery realms of the Unconscious, while the Library above was designed to service the intellect of man, which flourishes in open consciousness and light. This contrast of the 'lower deeps' of the unconscious with the 'upper sunlight' of human consciousness was a staple of esoteric symbolism in hermetic circles.

The idea of knowledge being concerned with consciousness and light is reflected in the symbolism of the exterior. To the east, above the second-storey pavilion windows, are a number of keystones, each sculpted to represent the face of one of the major races of the world. These were designed by Otis T. Mason, curator of the department of ethnology at the Smithsonian National Museum of Natural History. The significance of these ethnographic heads is distinctly arcane, for there is a symbolism in their number.

Altogether there are 33 heads: they are representative of the 33 degrees of Scottish Rite Masonry,[35] which strives to bind together all good men in universal brotherhood. These 33 keystones were sculpted by William Boyd and Henry Jackson Ellicott,[36] and, since they represent the nations of the world, it is evident that they symbolize the idea of space. From a Masonic point of view, the 33 ethnographic heads lend sculptural credence to a tenet expressed in the 1723 Masonic *Constitutions*, which insisted that the Craft was 'found in all Nations, even of divers Religions'.[37]

While some of these heads face in the four directions of space, another set of heads, in the portico, face only to the west. These are not racial types, but individual portraits – busts of famous men. The nine personalized heads represent literary genius and symbolize past achievements.[38] At least three were famous Masons.[39]

All of these heads – the 33 types and the 9 personalized geniuses – look out towards the four quarters of space. What are they trying to tell us?

The bearded Neptune, alert and poised in Perry's fountain, gazes towards the south-west, as though there is something of interest in that direction (figure 20). His gaze seems designed to symbolize direction, and therefore space – with the same insistence as the 42 heads above him. The outpouring of water symbolizes the distribution of knowledge and spirituality which is the purpose of all good libraries. The outflow of water, sprayed westwards by the personified water-gods and directed by turtles back towards the Library building (and thus in an eastern direction), represents the flow of time.

The Library is a celebration of space and time. The feeling for the dimensionality of space is reflected most dramatically in the symbolic details of the exterior, while the feeling for time is reflected most cunningly in the interior of the massive Library above. Time is emphasized inside this spectacular building by means of a number of zodiacs – those great circles against which the daily and annual movement of the Earth and Sun is measured. This symbolism was undoubtedly intentional, for in the very centre of the Library, within the great dome of the main reading room, is a huge clock (figure 21) designed by John Flanagan (and executed by him with a lack of regard for time which almost drove the superintendent of the construction of the Library, Bernard R. Green, to despair).[40]

Described as the most sumptuous and magnificent piece of decoration in the Library, it is a complex allegory of time, depicting a winged Saturn, scythe and hour-glass in his hands, striding over the top of the clock, accompanied by two women who are believed to represent the seasons.[41] The dial of the clock is about four feet in diameter, but the statuary is so high in the dome of the Library that it does not look over-imposing. The important thing about this clock is that the face itself is a sunburst, and that behind the rich assembly of mythological figures above it is a zodiac, picked out in mosaic, against a gold ground.[42]

Since the statuary above the clock obscures part of the zodiacal circle, only six of the images are visible. Moving from the left, in an anticlockwise direction, we see part of Capricorn, Aquarius and Pisces (as a single fish); to the right is Cancer the crab, its claws reaching up towards the lion of Leo, above which is the image of a naked Virgo.

Passing between Virgo and Leo is what appears to be the image of a comet, which may remain one of the mysteries of the Library of Congress in perpetuity. Records indicate that the clock was commissioned in 1894, but that it was not finally completed until 1902.[43] Since comets appear frequently in the skies, it is difficult to determine if Flanagan had any particular one in mind. However, the great comet which appeared in 1882 (the year of Franklin D. Roosevelt's birth) is said to have been the brightest on record during the 19th century.[44] It was visible even in broad daylight: in his diary for 8 October of that year the younger Casey – the future architect of the Library of Congress – recorded rising early to watch it from the front window of the family house.[45]

On the other hand, perhaps it is not necessary to identify the comet. It is quite possible that Flanagan did not intend to portray a historical cosmic event at all – perhaps his aim was merely to point to the notion that comets are meant to be the harbingers of change, of historically important events. This would tie in with his own intention, set out in a note to Green, proposing that the entire theme of the clock statuary should reflect the 'Flight of Time'. This theme is expressed on the Earth plane by a small roundel below the clock, which depicts what Flanagan called 'the swift runners . . . keeping the light of knowledge circulating': one runner is handing on to another a burning flame.[46] Just so, by means of a comet, the spiritual world hands on a burning flame in cyclical rhythm to mankind. If Flanagan wished to complete this sense of fleeting time on Earth by including an image which pointed to the idea of fleeting time in the heavens, what better symbol could he adopt than a comet, which looked so like a flame of fire streaking through the heavens?

Whatever the intended meaning of the symbol, it is entirely appropriate that his clock should be depicted with a comet in Virgo, as this sign is said to rule over such places as libraries.[47] Even if this were *not* the symbolism intended, there is a felicity in the fact that the central hub of the Library of Congress – itself redolent with zodiacal imagery – should be marked with a zodiac, the Virgo of which is emphasized by a reference to fleeting time. By such a symbolism, the eternity which is usually attributed to the stars is tempered by the brush of time, as it were, bringing Virgo down to Earth.

Flanagan's clock certainly symbolizes time. Furthermore, it reveals the zodiac as a symbol of time with the same arcane intent as the 33 faces on the outer walls of the Library proclaim themselves as symbolic of space.

The rich external sculptural programme above the three upper frontal doorways to the Library of Congress also contains the image of a zodiac. Anyone who enters by the central portal passes beneath the spandrel bas-relief of a zodiac, held in the hand of a woman who personifies Astronomy (figure 19). Immediately on passing through the deep arch into the centre of the atrium, or Great Hall, one finds oneself standing upon a marble floor into which are laid the 12 images of a huge brass zodiac. The arrangement of the 12 figures is in the form of a square, but at the centre is a huge sunburst, around which is a compass. This central design combines solar time with the directions of space, suggesting that the interior of the Library is dedicated to the same theme found on the exterior.

As the engraving from a Masonic textbook shown above indicates, the sunburst at the centre of a zodiac is no new thing – it was used symbolically in mediaeval art, even at a time when it was not recognized that the Sun was at the centre of the solar system. This may be traced back not to astronomical ideas, as one might imagine, but to Christian theological notions. From relatively early times, theologians seized on the cosmic idea that Christ was a solar being, with his 12 disciples in radiant attendance around Him.[48] In this notion, the central Sun has a much deeper symbolic meaning than any astronomical pagan imagery can convey, and almost certainly explains why so many late-19th-century zodiacs contain solar-radiant centres. The importance of this idea in the period the Library was being built, may be seen in a zodiac used in a book dealing with arcane astrology. This contained a solarized image called by the Masonic author Parsons 'the esoteric zodiac' (overleaf).[49]

Overlooking the marble floor zodiac, and facing west upon a parapet above the central archway, is a lapidary inscription, flanked by eagles: it names those responsible for this wonderful building.[50] Only one person among the four listed is known beyond doubt to have been interested in the stars – the army engineer Casey. However, he may have passed on his enthusiasm for such things to his son, who, as we have seen, was one of the chief architects of the building.

At first glance, the Great Hall zodiac seems to be very simple. Brass inlay silhouettes of the 12 signs, each lightly modelled and marked with intaglio to suggest form, are set into a dark-red French marble, circled by a lighter marble (plate 17). The zodiacal 12 are arranged on the floor of the Great Hall in a square (alternating with rosettes) at the centre of

which is a radiant sunburst, marked with the four cardinal points of the compass, intimating that orientation may be an important factor in the zodiac. The distribution of the zodiacal 12, and the rosettes, is interesting, for while the order follows the traditional sequence in a widdershins direction, the purpose of the orientation is not at first apparent. Indeed, only one practised in the secret arts of the Masons will recognize that its square form links this zodiac with Earth. Given such a linkage, is the compass it contains designed to indicate a hidden direction in space?

The zodiacal 12 are beautifully designed and crafted. Pisces (plate 17) is portrayed in the form of two dolphins swimming in opposite directions, but their mouths are not connected by a cord, in the traditional manner.[51] In the majority of mediaeval zodiacs, the two fishes are rarely represented as dolphins, but since the dolphin appeared frequently as a symbol of Christ in early Christian inscriptions and

literature,[52] we must presume that it was chosen to show that this floor zodiac is thoroughly Christian in spirit.

Opposite the dolphins is Virgo, portrayed as a seated Virgin, supporting a sheaf of corn against her right arm, and her elbow resting on a hand-scythe (above). This latter symbol is almost certainly intended to associate the Virgin of the skies with the ancient goddess Ceres, who was the link between the mediaeval Virgo and the Egyptian Isis.

In Pisces and Virgo we perceive at least one idea behind this square zodiac. The orientation produced by drawing a line through the centres of these two signs, when projected beyond the building, points to the Capitol Building, the dome of which is the cosmic centre of Washington

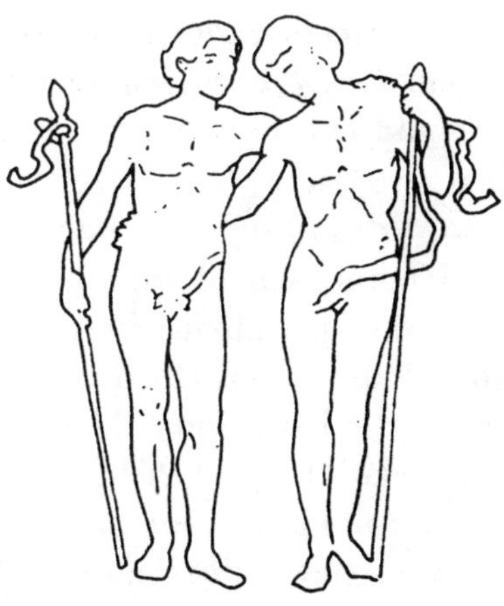

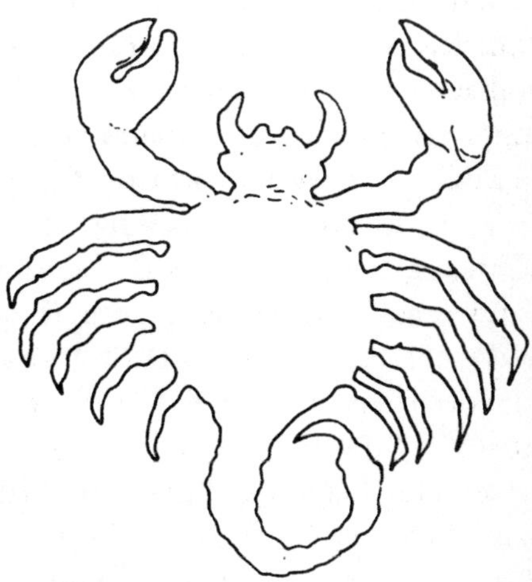

DC. *Once more we find a zodiac designed to emphasize the role of Virgo.*

Beyond this distinctive orientation, there is nothing overtly arcane about this zodiac, with the possible exception of the sign Gemini (alongside Scorpio on the previous page. Traditionally, this sign portrays two young men, representing the stars Castor and Pollux, the mortal and immortal Twins.[53] In the atrium zodiac, however, Gemini is represented by a young man and woman, their arms lightly embracing (figure 22). In the male's right hand, and in the female's left hand, thyrsus wands – in ancient times the emblem of initiation into the Mysteries.[54]

Since there is a zodiac embedded in the marble floor of the atrium – a zodiac which represents the Earth plane and, so to speak, supports the feet of those who walk into the Library – there must, following hermetic principles (which insist that the way up is also the way down[55]), be another in one of the ceilings above, representing the spiritual plane. This other zodiac would radiate stellar life into the intellectual realm of those in the Library, serving to remind one that the same contrast between lower and upper evident on the outside of the building also works on the inside. This upper zodiac is none other than the circular Garnsey zodiac in the ceiling of the Pavilion of the Elements, and it too has a solar centre.

We find that each of the 12 brass-inlay images of the floor zodiac is replicated on the beautiful roundel zodiac of the tondo painted on the ceiling of the south-east Pavilion (plate 19). This repetition implies that we are being invited to consider the floor zodiac as relating to the Earth (into which the figures are set), with the ceiling zodiac relating to the heavens. This distinction is partly confirmed by the fact that the Great Hall zodiac is arranged in a square, while the ceiling zodiac is arranged in a circle. This important difference is not without its esoteric import, for *in Masonry the square is taken as symbol of the Earth, and the circle as symbol of the spiritual world.* In view of this, we should examine the heavenly ceiling zodiac with some care.[56]

The painter of this ceiling, Elmer Ellsworth Garnsey, was born at Holmdel, New Jersey, on 24 January 1862. After art-school training, he became assistant to the painter Francis Lathrop, specializing in mural and architectural art. In 1892, he began work with Francis D. Millet on the decorative painting for the Columbia world Exposition. He was invited by the architect Charles F. McKim to take charge of the decorations in the loggias and the Bates Hall of the Boston Public Library. This remarkable artistic endeavour was one of the major achievements of American artists. Garnsey found himself working alongside the painter

John Singer Sargent, who was displaying his self-imposed programme of mythological-biblical subjects (including a mytho-poetic zodiac) on the ceiling and walls of the first floor of the Boston Library.[57] After this work – perhaps inspired by his contact with the sophisticated Sargent – Garnsey travelled in Europe, studying Renaissance decoration. Shortly after his return to America, in 1894, he was put in charge of the decoration of the Carnegie Institute in Pittsburgh, and then was appointed chief decorator of the new Library of Congress, where his learning in Renaissance fresco and decoration techniques was used to good effect; his masterpiece in this Library of Congress programme is the ceiling zodiac.

Fortunately, Garnsey was not persuaded by Sargent's unconventional style (at least, as exhibited in the pseudo-Babylonian and Egyptian themes of his Boston zodiac) to work in an openly unconventional style or imagery when he designed his Pavilion zodiac. Although the refined delicacy of his calm decorative quality is impressive, the zodiac appears at first glance to be quite traditional in its symbolism. It is only when it is examined in depth that its arcane associations begin to reveal themselves.

For all that the theme of the south-east Pavilion is zodiacal, the room is usually referred to as the Pavilion of the Elements, since it is dominated by the theme of the four Elements (Fire, Air, Earth and Water), which non-specialists do not usually associate with the zodiac.[58] Symbols pertaining to the Elements are repeated twice on the ceiling tondo itself, and the same elements are also the main theme of the four great frescos on each of the four walls of the Pavilion.[59] In the centre of the ceiling is an image of Apollo, driving his four-horse chariot. No doubt this painting of the Sun-god is at the centre of the zodiac as a humanized (or, properly speaking, a *deified*) version of the massive bronze sunburst in the centre of the zodiac in the Great Hall.

Two artists worked on the paintings in the Pavilion of the Elements. Elmer E. Garnsey painted the two sets of Elements and the surrounding zodiac within the tondo; while Robert Leftwich Dodge painted the central image of Apollo and the four wall lunettes, with their rich associations of the four Elements. There may be little doubt about these attributions, for both sections are signed and dated: the section on which Garnsey painted his name, along with the date 1896, even goes so far as to claim copyright on the work – no doubt a reflection on changes in artistic copyright laws which had recently been authorized by Congress. The date and signature for the zodiacal section is painted beneath the cartouche for Water, and above the roundel for Cancer (figure 23). I think that the choice of this cartouche for his signature reflects Garnsey's knowledge of arcane things. Cancer has nothing to do with his natal horoscope (as one might have expected), and I suspect that it was chosen because it is the sign of incarnation – the Portal of Birth in esoteric lore – the sign through which spirit descends into matter. In signing this cartouche, Garnsey is recognizing that his idea has found an incarnation in the material world.

Given the framework of the arcane structure of the Library, Garnsey's symbolism for the two sets of Elements is of great interest, as they reflect in a very distinct manner the two zodiacs we have examined: one set is depicted in roundels, the other in a square.

The roundel Elements are essentially personifications: Fire is represented by a goddess (probably Vesta, the goddess of the sacred flame) in front of a burning lamp behind which a tripod supports a flame of the type associated with the Greek Mystery centres, such as Delphi. Water is a mermaid. Earth is a maiden reclining in a field, alongside which is growing corn, while Air is a half-naked woman carried on the back of a great bird, which may be an eagle.

The Elements in the small square cartouche are symbolized in a most distinctive form: Fire is represented by a lamp, Air by a swan with large outstretched wings, Water by two interlinked dolphins, and Earth by a tortoise. These symbols have been explained in a number of ways: for example, it has been argued that the tortoise represents Earth because, in the Hindu mythology, the Earth itself is supported on the back of a sacred tortoise.[60]

The same arcane theme is repeated in a more subtle form in the beautiful ornate stucco decorations which frame the zodiac. Among the relief rosettes contiguous with the tondo of the zodiac are 16 five-petalled flowers. These are clearly linked with the arcane tradition of the five-petalled Venus symbol I discussed on p.190, as pertaining to the Egyptian hieroglyphic, the *sba* star. We may assume that Garnsey was aware of the significance of this star, for he was a Mason.[61]

As I have said, the 12 images are really painterly versions of the brass-inlay images in the Great Hall zodiac on the floor below. Since the Garnsey zodiac is dated 1896, and the tracings of the brass inlays are dated 1895, I am led to surmise that the designs for the Main Hall zodiac came first.[62] These were stamped (perhaps as authorization for use) by Edward Pearce Casey, and we must therefore presume that we owe the genius of the marble-work – and hence the designs of the figures – to the architect rather than to the painter.

The ceiling zodiac – which I shall name after Garnsey, even though it may have been Casey who designed it – is certainly the most beautiful and ornate zodiac in Washington DC. It was painted in thin oil directly on to the plaster dome (and cleaned and restored in 1986).[63] Its 12 images are picked out in white against circles of warm terracotta, and these roundels are in turn set against an ornate repeating floral scroll in green, blue and terracotta (plate 10).

As though to demonstrate the important connection with time, the 12 bronze images of the Main Hall zodiac square the solar circle, in the middle of which is a splendid sunburst in polished incised bronze. This is an *interior* Sun – one of the great Mysteries of the initiation schools. It is the inner version of that *external* rising, culminating and setting Sun to which the spatially oriented ethnographic heads look. Just as the external Sun is expressed in pagan terms, so is the internal and personified Sun, which centres upon the pagan mythological images of the ceiling zodiac.

The contrast between exteriorized space and interiorized time is in itself a subtle form of symbolism, of course, and it is tempting to assume that Casey intended to express nothing more than this in the designs he approved. However, he was a learned man with an interest in astronomy, and not surprisingly took the sophistication of time and space to their limits of symbolic expression. In collaboration with the architects Smithmeyer and (later) Paul J. Pelz, and, later still, his own architect son Edward Pearce Casey, he used the Library of Congress as the focal centre of the symbolism which radiates throughout the city. It is not too much to claim that *the Library of Congress was sited in this position, and its symbolic programme established, precisely in order to demonstrate the profound arcane knowledge of the Masonic fraternity which designed Washington DC.*

Why did Garnsey make so signal an attempt to link the ceiling zodiac symbolism with the marble zodiac below? As we shall discover, this question cannot be answered until we have traced the arcane structure of the Great Hall zodiac through a single radiant into the city.

In very simple terms, the Garnsey zodiac, painted on a dome which by its very nature represents the heavens, is contrasted with the Great Hall zodiac which is symbolized by a square form, and set in that part of the Library through which people walk. The symbolic connection between the two zodiacs is vertical: one represents the stars of the distant heavens, the other the stellar forces that have entered into the Earth. The heavenly zodiac represents the spiritual, excarnated powers, while the earthly zodiac represents the incarnated powers, enmeshed in the physical bodies afforded by materiality.

This vertical structure may be said to represent the spiritual line of the Library – that portraying ascent and descent through the spheres. In view of this, it might be rewarding to look for *another* orientation connected with these zodiacs, which points to a spatial, or earth-bound, orientation. Is there any direction implicit in the zodiacs which lead out of the building, into the greater space beyond? The very fact that the radiant sunburst in the centre of the Great Hall zodiac is marked with the four cardinal points suggests the idea of space, and of an outer orientation, beyond the confines of the Hall.

To trace a meaningful orientation from the Great Hall zodiac into the world beyond, we must stand in front of the west façade of the Library and examine the rich sculptural programme in the six spandrels above the portal. The six female figures above the doors of the Library of Congress, sculpted by Bela Lyon Pratt, were completed about 1895. We have already looked at one of these – the figure to the right of the central portal, depicting *Astronomia.*[64] This figure holds a celestial sphere marked with images of the zodiac (figure 19). Although only four zodiacal images are visible on this sphere, the sign of Virgo is rising just over the woman's hips. *Once again we have a subtle reference to the importance of Virgo.* Does this zodiac, to the south side of the central doorway, suggest that we should look towards the south of the building in front, to seek out a third zodiac?

We have already noted that the Pisces-Virgo axis of the zodiac is directed towards the dome of the Capitol. If you stand on the centre of the sunburst zodiac in the Great Hall and look through the central doorway, you will be looking towards the edge of the south wing of the Capitol. You will have a zodiac around you, and you will be looking through a portal which has another zodiac on its spandrel, above your head. Since you are, so to speak, looking along a line marked by zodiacs, you might reasonably expect to find a third zodiacal image, somewhere beyond, in the direction you are facing.

With this in mind, we might approach the south-east edge of the Capitol, and search for a zodiac – *but we would search in vain.* There is not the slightest trace of a zodiac on this part of the Capitol, even though there is certainly one in the interior of its north wing – a remnant of that painted by Brumidi on the corridor walls.[65]

Since we cannot find a third zodiac on the south wall of the Capitol, we should ask if there is one a little further to the west, on the edge of the Capitol grounds? In search of this, we descend the west stairway, and make our way along the south-west pathway that runs through the Capitol gardens, as far as the road which runs south-north at the foot of the gardens. From where we now stand, at the foot of the steep incline of the Capitol grounds, it is not possible for us to see the Library of Congress, which is hidden behind the hill. However, we do know we should be able to see its south wing, beyond the southern side of the Capitol. I say this to emphasise that we are (within a few yards) back on the line of orientation that sent us searching for a third zodiac.

We are looking for a zodiac which will contain a symbolism that points to the importance of Virgo, the Beautiful Virgin. In front of us is the memorial statue to President James Garfield, who, as we have seen, lost his life to an assassin's bullet in 1881 (figure 3).

Has this man, who was President for little more than a few months, anything to do with the zodiac we seek? If we are to fully appreciate the magic of this promised orientation, we must digress. We must examine in some detail the arcane associations which its sculptor wove into the statue that he raised on the far side of the Capitol, out of sight of the Library of Congress.

The bronze statue, sculpted by John Quincy Adams Ward, was erected to Garfield's memory in 1887, by the veterans of the Army of the Cumberland. Garfield was a native of Orange, Ohio: he achieved academic success in his youth, when he taught at Hiram College; military success in mid-life, when he progressed to being chief of staff of the Army of the Cumberland; and political success when he was elected President of the United States, in 1881.[66] These three phases of his life are symbolized in the three allegorical figures seated around the pedestal upon which his statue stands.

Garfield's life as a scholar is represented by a curly-haired youth, wearing a short tunic: he is reading from a scrolled parchment.

His life as a soldier is represented by a Hercules-like figure, with an animal-skin (is it a lion-skin?) over his head (figure 24). His lower legs are thonged, as though in preparation for marching. The distinctive posture of this soldier bears a very close resemblance to the pose of Michelangelo's figure of *Giorno* ('Day'), in the New Sacristy of San Lorenzo, in Florence. This is not surprising; the statue of *Giorno* is part of one of the most famous funerary memorials of the Renaissance. By echoing the pose, Ward seems to have been drawing a parallel between Garfield and Lorenzo de' Medici (beneath whose statue in the New Sacristy *Giorno* was placed): while Garfield once ruled Washington, the spiritual centre of the United States, Lorenzo ruled Florence, which, in the 15th century, was the spiritual and artistic centre of Italy.

In modern times, it has been recognized by art historians that the Michelangelo statue associated with Day is actually that of Giuliano, brother of Lorenzo. Giuliano was murdered during the Pazzi conspiracy, in 1478, at the age of 25, and was not especially distinguished for any military or political achievements.[67] It would strike us as curious, nowadays, that Ward should have sought to draw a connection between this youthful murdered Florentine and the high-achiever, Garfield – even though the two did meet a similar fate.

The statue to Garfield was erected in 1887, and at that time there was some controversy (based on a misunderstanding) about the identity of the Michelangelo figure. Ward was almost certainly following the claim of a noted German art historian, Herman Grimm, that the statue of Giuliano was really that of his more successful brother, Lorenzo de' Medici. Ward was giving a particular twist to the symbolism of his statue. Lorenzo had survived the assassination attempt of 1478, to become the most powerful man in late-15th-century Florence, and Grimm had written of that time that the 'struggles . . . show what courage it required to stand at the head of a State like Florence'.[68] Just so, Garfield's agonizing, drawn-out death, showed what courage had been required to stand at the head of the United States.

Grimm's *Life of Michelangelo* was not translated from German into English and published in the United States until 1896, after the statue of Garfield had been completed.[69] However, Grimm's view of the identity of the statue had influenced the thinking of an entire generation of cultured individuals, and was widely accepted by those interested in art and esoteric thought.[70] Presumably Ward had either read the original, or had learned of the German's findings during his visit to Florence. He kept small plaster-cast reproductions of the Michelangelo figures in his New York studio.[71]

Less complex than this symbol of military valour is the representation of Garfield's life as a statesman. This is symbolized by a figure in a long toga, with the draped *sinus* favoured by Roman senators. While less puzzling than the Michelangelo adaptation – but it does call to mind the readiness with which the sculptors of Washington DC were prepared to interpret contemporary events and symbols in the light of ancient Greek or Roman costumes and customs.

It is neither the statesman nor the soldier that demands our attention: we are seeking a zodiac upon this memorial. In fact, we seek a zodiac which has some connection with Masonry. Garfield was a Mason, who had been initiated into the very highest degrees. To judge from the richness and subtlety of the Masonic symbolism on this statuary, it is safe to assume that the sculptor John Quincy Adams Ward was a brother Mason.[72]

Now, above the head of the bronze scholar is a curious cartouche which seems, even on a superficial examination, to be of Masonic design (plate 5). On closer inspection, it turns out to be one of the most ingenious of Masonic symbols in Washington DC. It is, indeed, one of the best-kept open secrets of the city, in that it has remained unexplained until I discovered its meaning a few years ago.[73]

The cartouche is an elaborate horoscope, the outer concentric of which is in the form of a zodiac. The horoscope is displayed in bas-relief, hanging from a swag; it is overlaid with sprays of acacia leaves and palms. At the bottom of the figure is a writing-quill and a pair of Masonic compasses, no doubt symbolic of Garfield's scholarship and Masonic connections.

The seven planetary spheres are encompassed by an outer concentric on which are figured tiny sgraffito images of the 12 signs of the zodiac. The spheres are represented as channels, into which have been dropped a number of small globes that represent the planets. The planet-globes are located to denote a specific zodiacal position, against the 12 signs. For example, at the top of the figure (near the swag from which the zodiacal image is pendant) is the picture of a crab, indicating that the segment represents the sign Cancer. Just below this image is a tiny planet-globe. Since this ball is set in the outermost channel, or sphere, it must represent the furthermost of the seven planets, which is Saturn. We may surmise that whatever the horoscope represents, the planet Saturn will be in Cancer.

The second groove, which corresponds to the sphere of Jupiter, holds a tiny globe just below the extruding acacia leaf. The scales of Libra are visible alongside the ball, which suggest that Jupiter is in Libra.

The design of this horoscope figure is unique. The sculptor, instead of representing it as a standard horoscope chart (as one might expect), has resorted to a system of Ptolemaic spheres, favoured by late-mediaeval Rosicrucians and alchemists for their own arcane diagrams. In the centre of the seven spheres is a bas-relief image of the Earth, bearing a map of the Americas. The angle of the globe is adjusted to emphasize the latitudes of North America.

If this bronze bas-relief *is* a horoscope, what does it represent? The acacia leaves (a well-established Masonic symbol for the resurrection into the spiritual life, which is usually called death) suggest that this horoscope might be a death chart – that is, one cast to record Garfield's passing, or perhaps the moment of his assassination. Unfortunately, the mystery of the cartouche cannot be solved quite so easily: it certainly does *not* represent a death chart.

A close survey of this elegant device indicates that, for all its initial promise, it is not an accurate horoscope of any event in Garfield's life.[74] This much is evident from the information I have given pertaining to the positions of Saturn and Jupiter. While there was a period of just over two years in the life of Garfield when Saturn *was* in Cancer, this time did not correspond to a period when Jupiter was also in Libra.[75] Examination of the figure reveals that it cannot portray accurately any particular event in the skies, since one of the 'planetary orbs' is reduplicated. As a result, if we read the spheres as relating to the traditional astrology, we would be compelled to conclude that the horoscope has two Suns![76]

So, if the cartouche which includes a zodiac and planetary orbs is not a horoscope after all, what is it? The answer to this question does not involve us in astronomical gymnastics. One of the secrets of the Garfield zodiac lies in the demonstrable truth that it is a *copy* – and, furthermore, a copy of an illustration which was *not intended to be accurate in its portrayal of planetary positions.*

In the 1799 edition of James Ferguson's compendious book on astronomy[77] is a plate designed to illustrate an orrery, or working model of the solar system.[78] It is, like all orreries, a complex machine, intended to demonstrate the complicated motions of the planets in relation to the stars, zodiac and Earth. Ferguson, an adroit mathematician and talented in instrument-making, was certainly being disingenuous when he wrote of this 'simple Machine' (which he constructed in 1746). 'It may be easily made by any Gentleman who has a mechanical Genius.'

Our own interest in this mechanical contrivance is the supportive detail, which illustrates what Ferguson called 'the Planetary Globe' (opposite). This was an additional ingenious working mechanism, which consisted of a series of concentric channels in which were placed movable balls, inscribed with the planetary sigils and carried on wires. The device was really an adjunct to the Ferguson orrery, but its importance from our point of view is that it is quite clearly the original model for Ward's zodiacal cartouche.

In making a three-dimensional bas-relief of this illustration, Ward has changed very little. Given our own theme, and our interest in the spandrel zodiac which led us to the Garfield statue, we must regard it as significant that *the major change which Ward has countenanced was the moving of the all-important Ascendant away from Libra, into Virgo.* In addition, he has arranged the central map so that the figure pertains, with more or less accuracy, to Washington DC.[79]

Just as the plinth of Garfield's statue is surrounded by the three 'times', or stages, of his life, so does Ferguson's orrery detail represent three 'times'. On the base is clock time. On the outer concentric of the 'spheres' is the zodiac, representative of stellar time. Around the earth is the equator, which represents the time of the seasons. In turn, these three times are also symbolized in the cartouche, derived from the engraving.

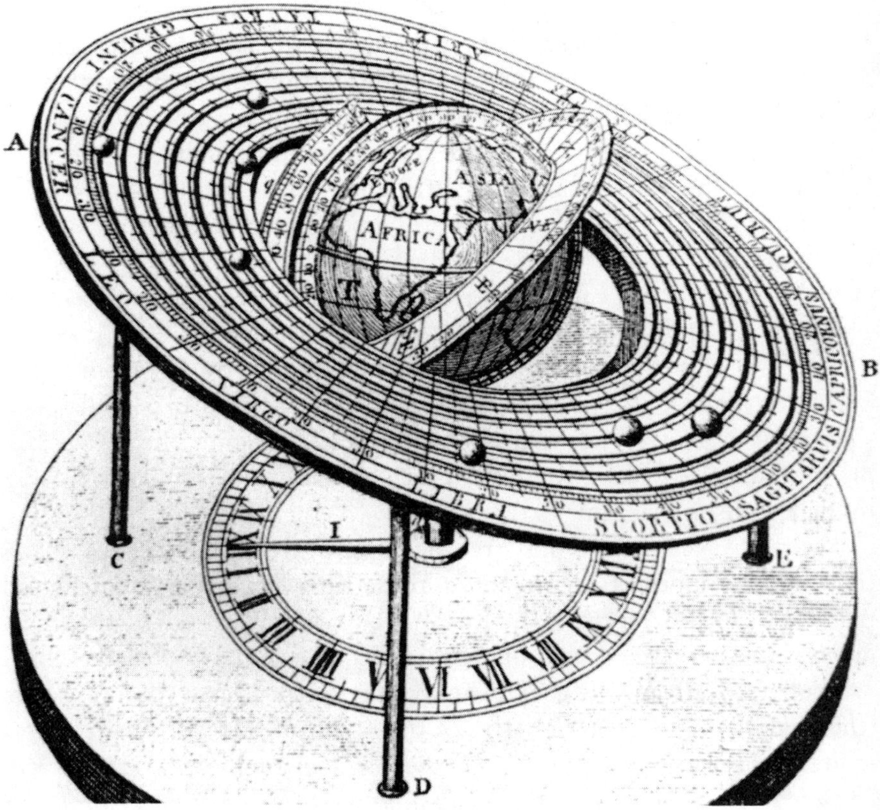

Complex as this cartouche is, we may take it as the third zodiac which we sought when we left the portals of the Library of Congress. From a point of viewing of the symbolism we are studying, it is sufficient that the Garfield statuary marks the termination of the line which we followed from the centre of the floor zodiac. *The Virgo on the spandrel of the portal zodiac has led us towards another Virgoan symbol.*

The line of direction connecting the zodiacs is not exact. The connection between the three zodiacs is continued in a specific direction, but not on a straight line. This in itself is curious. Given the architects were anxious to establish a connection between the three Virgoan symbols, it would have been relatively easy for them to adjust the positions of the symbols on a straight line. Or is it possible that there is some other connection between the three? Is there some other reason why the Great Hall zodiac should have been furnished with a compass indicating the cardinal points? In other words, is there a further mystery in Ward's statue and zodiac?

Having considered all these issues, what are we to make of Ward's choice of an 18th-century diagram as an arcane decoration for the pedestal of his statue of Garfield? There should be some deeper significance in the cartouche, for had Ward been interested only in introducing a zodiac into his statuary, he would have had little difficulty in locating, or having drawn up, a perfectly respectable horoscope for some important time in Garfield's life.

Ward does not appear to be interested in the personal potential in a zodiac figure at all: the cartouche is not a horoscope. Indeed, it copies almost precisely the same configuration set down by Ferguson, who purposely represented it as an impossible cosmic moment, in order to show that it had to be adjusted prior to rearranging the globes for practical display.[80] What are we to make of Ward's insistence on fidelity to the Ferguson diagram?

A spray of acacia leaves obscures the rising degree, yet it it is quite clear that the all-important Ascendant is in the sign Virgo. We should recall that the Beautiful Virgin of the Royal Arch symbolism carries not wheat or corn (as does the Virgo of the skies) but acacia. The plant which symbolizes death in this cartouche obscures that part of the horoscope (the Eastern angle, representative of the point of Sunrise) which relates to life, and the beginning of life. *This suggests that the bronze cartouche may be understood, on one level of symbolism, as reflecting upon the death of the great Mason. This symbolism works by linking the Beautiful Virgin that is Virgo with the spray of acacia, which obscures her own zodiacal sign.*

However, there is also a much deeper level of symbolism in Ward's reliance on Ferguson – on a diagram which is found in a book on astronomy that was once in the possession of Jefferson, a copy of which is, even now, in the Library of Congress.[81] Was Ward making merely a literary reference? It is very likely that through his graphic reference to the Michelangelo statue of *Night*, Ward was drawing a parallel between the destiny of Florence and the destiny of Washington DC. Is it likely that he was also drawing a connection between the Library of Congress and the Garfield statue, by means of his graphic reference to a diagram found in a rare book on astronomy in that Library?[82] While this may be part of the arcane symbolism, the truth is that the symbolism of the Ward cartouche is so sophisticated that it must rank among the most esoteric of all funerary devices in the world.

The underlying association which links the statue with the Library of Congress *is* important, for it points, once again, to Ferguson's book. It is in this book that we discover the deeper significance of Ward's symbolism. Having described the structure of the globe mechanism, with its seven 'Balls adjusted by sliding Wires', Ferguson writes:

> The Ecliptic is inclined 23 and a half Degrees to the Pedestal, and is therefore properly inclined to the Axis of the Globe which stands upright on the Pedestal.[83]

In the plate of concentrics about which Ferguson writes (diagram on p.211) the pedestal to which he refers is the base. From this pedestal-base project three upright columns, the fourth being hidden behind the mechanism itself. However, in relation to Garfield's bas-relief of 1887, the word 'pedestal' has a different meaning, for the statue of Garfield stands upon a pedestal: indeed, his zodiacal cartouche is affixed to the very same pedestal.

The fact is that Ward has treated Ferguson's text in an entirely arcane way, by reading it as though it were ambiguous. Ward ensured that the pedestal for his statue was so located that the angle it subtended between the *Astronomia*, on the spandrel above the door of the Library of Congress, and the centre of the Capitol dome was exactly 23 and a half degrees!

The similarity of arc implies that anyone who recognizes the context from which the bas-relief cartouche came (that is, Ferguson's engraved plate) would have little difficulty in tracing from it a meaningful orientation. This orientation leads one back, at a precisely stated angle, from its placing on the Garfield statue to the zodiac on the façade of Library of Congress. We are no longer dealing with straight lines connecting three points, but with precise angles connecting three points – the central communal angle being the cosmic centre of Washington DC.

Perhaps I need not dwell on the importance of the triangle which this arrangement traces on the Earth? Nor need I dwell on the fact that its angles are linked with cosmological measurements, one of which is subtended from the centre of the Capitol dome. It is intriguing that the centre of the dome, from which all radiants are supposedly measured in Washington DC, is tied in this arcane way to images of Virgo. The significance of this will become much clearer at a later point, when we examine the role of the Capitol dome in the arcane structure of the city.

Garfield was among the most talented of 19th-century American Masons. In 1858, immediately after graduating from Williams College with an essay on *The Seen and the Unseen*, he was invited to become professor of ancient languages and literature at Hiram College. He was initiated into Masonry close to his 30th birthday, on 22 November 1861, in the Magnolia Lodge No. 20, Columbus, Ohio. His rapid progress in Masonry need not distract us here,[84] but we should note that he was exalted to the Royal Arch Degree in Columbia Royal Arch Chapter No. 1, in Washington DC, on 18 April 1866.

This is significant, for, as we have seen, the image of the Beautiful Virgin, so adroitly represented as a rising Virgo on the Masonic cartouche, is a symbol developed in the Royal Arch Degree. We must assume that the cartouche is not intended to be a horoscope marking space and time, in the ordinary way of such symbolic devices, so much as a funerary acknowledgement of Garfield's achievements as a Mason.

On one level of Masonic symbolism, the Royal Arch represents the zodiac. The Virgo ascending on the cartouche is the Beautiful Virgin. What is the deeper significance of the acacia, which mingles with the palm leaves on the cartouche?

In terms of its mortuary significance, the symbolism of the acacia is fairly transparent. Acacia is the *shittah* of the Hebrews, from which the Arc of the Tabernacle was constructed.[85] The suitability of the acacia (which flourishes in barren regions) for such a spiritual purpose as the building of a most sacred ritual object is redolent with mystical symbolism. In terms of death rites relevant to the Masonic symbolism, Egyptian sycamore mummy-coffins were clamped shut with acacia wood. In the Masonic literature, the significance of acacia has been explained as originating in the Jewish custom of planting a branch of acacia on the grave of a departed relative.[86] It seems, therefore, that one might even trace in this desert tree (used as it is for sacred and funerary purposes) the idea of the physical human body, consecrated for some high spiritual aim involving redemption, regeneration, or rebirth.

In the cartouche, the acacia obscures the eastern angle of the 'horoscope', darkening the life force which the Ascendant symbolizes.

Ward has made clever use of a standard mortuary symbolism. He has represented the death-plant acacia as obscuring, or casting a shadow over, the Sunrise of life, in order to veil a much deeper symbolism pertaining to the Masonic symbolism of the Beautiful Virgin.

Within the context of our search for an image of Virgo, these issues are not of great relevance to us. Our concern with this cartouche is really at an end once we have observed that it contains a zodiac, and that the sign Virgo is not only given pride of place on the eastern horizon, but is even integrated into its deeply arcane symbolism. Complex as this 'horoscope' cartouche undoubtedly is, its importance for us lies in the fact that it performs much the same symbolic role as the bas-relief we examined on the portal of the Library of Congress: it affords a lapidary proof that an invisible radiant was intended by the designers, connecting the Library with Garfield.

The sculptor, Ward, must have known about the relationship which this memorial would bear to the Library of Congress. He completed the statue in 1887. The Library was not opened until 1897; even so, the plans for the buildings and the designs for the portal sculptures had been prepared some time earlier. In his capacity of president of the National Sculpture Society, Ward was often consulted by Casey on the sculptural programme, and for a considerable time sat on a special committee which directed that programme in minute detail.[87] He was also personally involved in the Library's artistic programme, for he modelled *Poetry*, one of the eight symbolic statues on the entablature of the Main Reading Room of the Library. Above this figure of *Poetry* is a quotation from Milton's poem *Paradise Lost*: 'Hither, as to their fountain, other stars/Repairing, in their golden urns draw light.'[88]

These connections suggest that the precise relationship between the Library zodiac and the Garfield zodiac cannot have been due to accident.

Our examination of the space-time complex which is the Library of Congress has permitted us to trace a line connecting three zodiacs which seem to encode a graphic reference to Virgo, the ruling sign of Washington DC. This must surely lead us to ask, are there any other Virgoan mysteries in this extraordinary city? Equally, the precisely formulated orientation of the Garfield zodiac leads us to ask a further question about the larger bronze zodiac in the Great Hall of the Library: is there any orientation in this zodiac which may also point to another secret in Washington DC?

The answer is *yes*.

However, before being able to understand fully this orientation, we must examine a number of other zodiacs in the city. A survey of these zodiacs will lead us to the greatest of all cosmic mysteries in Washington DC.

Chapter Eight

> The Pyramid, then, is below Nature and the Intellectual World. This is because it has above it, as ruler, the Creator-Word of the Lord of all . . .
>
> (Cyril of Alexandria – early fifth century AD; 'The Pyramid', quoted in R.R.S. Mead, *Thrice-Greatest Hermes Trismegistus*, 1964 ed., iii, p.164.)

Among the letters of the architect Benjamin Latrobe, relating to his design for the new Capitol building, is a sketch of 1806 which he made of an eagle that he intended to place in an entablature of the Capitol.[1]

The eagle was to be sculpted by Giuseppe Franzoni, who had arrived in America the previous month after being shipped over from Italy especially to work on the sculptures of the Capitol. Almost as soon as he arrived, Latrobe set Franzoni to carving the great eagle. However, although the Italian was an excellent sculptor, Latrobe was disappointed by the work: he found the eagle too conventional. The one he had visualized was to be distinctly American. Anxious to obtain guidance for Franzoni, Latrobe wrote to his friend, Charles Willson Peale, asking if one of his artistic sons could send him a drawing of the head and claws of the bald eagle.[2] Peale obliged immediately – not merely with the requested drawings but with an actual head and claw of a stuffed bald eagle from his museum.[3]

Over 70 years later, Latrobe's son – John H. B. Latrobe (also a Mason) – remembered the eagle which he had seen as a child, and which had been given pride of place in the old Hall of Representatives:

> I seem to see, even now, the speaker's chair, with its rich surroundings, and the great stone eagle which, with outspread wings, projected from the frieze, as though it were hovering over and protecting those who deliberated below.[4]

Latrobe finished off this account of his childhood memories by reminding his audience that when the British officer who had voted to destroy the Capitol building entered the great chamber over which this eagle presided, he had hesitated at first, for 'it was a pity to burn anything so beautiful'. Among the objects destroyed was the Franzoni eagle: only sketches of it survive. The one which replaced it, carved about 1816 by another Italian, Giuseppe Valaperta, is still *in situ*.

In 1828, the Masonic architect Charles Bulfinch had the Italian sculptor Luigi Persico place an eagle alongside his sculpture of the *Genius of America* over the central portico of the Capitol building.

When, in 1858, the great Columbus doors were cast in bronze for the entrance to this same central portico, the architect Thomas W. Walter placed an eagle immediately below the bust of Columbus.

When, in 1863, Thomas Crawford's giant statue of *Freedom* was mounted on the new dome of the Capitol, its helmet bore a crest of feathers. Although many people still believe this is the head-dress of an American Indian, it is the head and plumage of an eagle that dominate the planned centre of Washington DC, where the arch of heaven is reflected in the dome of a building. This symbolic crowning merely completed a sculptural programme which had begun with the building of the Capitol.

So it seems that, if one is going to study the arcane background to the formation of the United States, one should start with the eagle, which is also the heraldic bird on the obverse of the Seal of the United States of America. This fearsome-looking bird, so widely used in the symbolism of the States, is what esotericists have called an 'open mystery': by contrast the eagle as used by the early Masons, and by the Rosicrucians and alchemists before them, was an 'occult blind'. This means that it was designed to carry an open symbolism acceptable to the uninitiated, yet, at the same time, to hide a more profound meaning accessible only to those familiar with arcane symbolism.

The eagle originally proposed for the Seal of the United States was not an American (or bald-headed) eagle, but was crested. Furthermore, from descriptions and drawings left by William Barton,[5] we see that at one time he had proposed not only an eagle, but also a phoenix, which later gave rise to many misunderstandings in both Masonic and arcane literature.[6] When, in 1782, Charles Thompson was invited by Congress to revise the design, he insisted that it be an American eagle, not displayed, but rising (right). The phoenix was forgotten, as were many other elements in William Barton's design. Thompson also introduced the bundle of arrows (in the sinister talon) and an olive branch (in the dexter).

It is very likely that the idea of an armorial eagle came to the Americas by way of Masonic or Rosicrucian symbolism, although the bird was heraldic long before speculative Masonry was established in Europe and America. This same symbol, renewed by its Masonic context, was returned to Europe, slightly amended by the requirements of the American Fraternity, yet still recognizable as the eagle of the alchemical tradition. A fine example is a Sunderland jug dated 1804, bearing 'the armorial device' of the United States, now in the museum of the Grand Lodge, in Queen Anne Street, London. Around the image of the eagle is a quotation attributed to Jefferson: 'Peace, Commerce and honest Friendship with all Nations. Entangling Alliances with none.' This is no 'armorial device', but a design freely drawn from the obverse of the Seal, with little feeling for its symbolism. It shows 13 stars ranged in a curve above the head of the eagle: the stellar symbolism is spoiled by the addition of two other stars, one on either side of the eagle's neck. In its beak, the bird grasps a banderole bearing the incorrect motto, *ex pluribus unum*. I say that it is incorrect, but this is true only in terms of the Seal symbolism. The Seal motto insists on 13 characters for the three words, while this English version misses the point by presenting the phrase in good Latin, with the unabbreviated *ex*.

Despite the popularity of the eagle, its symbolism was not welcomed by everyone. Long before it began to dominate the symbolism of the new federal city, Benjamin Franklin had lamented that it had been chosen to represent his country. He recognized that the bald eagle was 'cowardly',

and claimed that it was 'by no means a proper emblem for the brave and honest Cincinnati of America.'[7]

Next to George Washington, Benjamin Franklin was probably the most famous of all American Masons, and was deeply learned in Masonic and Rosicrucian symbolism.[8] Undoubtedly, he would have known that the more intriguing symbolism of the Seal was that on the reverse – the unfinished pyramid (figure 27).

We have noted already how – in spite of the insistence on Egyptian themes within Washington DC – the pyramid has been marginalized: in the opinion of many, the finest design for the Washington Monument was the pyramid proposed by Peter Force, yet the more hybrid design of Robert Mills was accepted.

Whatever the underlying reasons – whether consciously directed by Masonic or other esoteric bodies, or a mere exigency of history – the pyramid on the reverse of the official Seal has remained obscure in the symbolism of the United States and Washington DC. In contrast, the eagle of the obverse, with its various permutations of 13, became part of the national consciousness.

The pyramid has remained something of an enigma. Partly by intent and partly by oversight, the arcane symbolism of the pyramid was allowed to languish in the shadows, while the obverse, with its bald eagle and its rather obvious symbolism of 13, was constantly paraded in the light.

Washington DC was a new undertaking. As L'Enfant himself had recognized, its construction marked one of those rare events in history when a city was planned and built for a specific purpose. At almost any stage of this construction, the sacred pyramid – its courses of masonry still unfinished – would have been a more satisfactory symbol for the city, and for the United States itself, than the predatory bird which did eventually take pride of place.

It is curious that the truncated pyramid on the reverse of the Seal of the United States is rare in the vast array of sculptural details which embellish the city. So far as I know, only two official buildings in

Washington DC include the image of a pyramid in their external decorations. However, even one of these has nothing to do with the truncated pyramid on the Seal,[9] and there seems to be only one official reproduction of that particular pyramid in the city itself.

In the frieze called *The Progress of Science*, carved by the sculptor Lee Lawrie in 1923 for the National Academy of Sciences Building, is a portrayal of the Greek philosopher, Thales of Miletus. Thales was one of the wise men of ancient Greece: he is supposed to have been the first person to predict a solar eclipse (possibly that of 585 BC) and to have been the founder of abstract geometry. What is of interest to us here is that behind his head are shown the three pyramids of Gizeh, in Egypt (figure 25). The pyramids are relevant in the context of science because Thales studied in Egypt under the priests (which is to say that he was initiated there) and subsequently imported the secrets of geometry to his native Greece. Further, he demonstrated that the height of a pyramid could be determined from the length of its shadow: the secret was to hold a stick vertical, and wait until the shadow cast by it was the same length as the height of the stick. At that precise moment, one could measure the height of the pyramid by its shadow. Lee Lawrie's bas-relief shows the Sun casting a shadow from the pyramid, while Thales holds a measuring stick.[10] There are a further three pyramids in a detail of the huge ceiling of the main hall of the National Academy: these may be taken as representative of the three huge pyramids at Gizeh.

One other pyramid occurs in the Library of Congress. In the wall mosaic by Frederick Dielman, in the Council of Scholars Reading Room, a portrayal of the Great Pyramid of Gizeh appears behind the personification of Mythology. This represents one of the three stages of antique architecture – or, indeed, the three founts of hermetic wisdom – for the central section depicts the Parthenon of Athens, while the right-hand section shows the Roman Colosseum.

The one official external reproduction of the pyramid image of the reverse of the Seal that I know is that embedded within the marble pavement of what is now called the Freedom Plaza, towards the western end of Pennsylvania Avenue, east of the White House (figure 27). Even this reproduction supports my argument that the pyramid has been marginalized, because on either side of it are *two* versions of the obverse of the Seal, illustrating the development of the heraldic eagle (figure 26).[11]

The only *architectural* pyramid in Washington DC which seems to reflect the Seal pyramid is distinctly Masonic. The great tower of the House of the Temple, designed for the Scottish Rite Freemasons,[12] at 1733 16th Street, consists of a truncated pyramid. Unfortunately, the location of this magnificent building does not permit one to view the pyramidal form with any ease from the west (to which it faces – figure 1). A good viewing point is from the east, from beyond the gardens, where the 13 stepped pyramid is revealed in all its splendour.

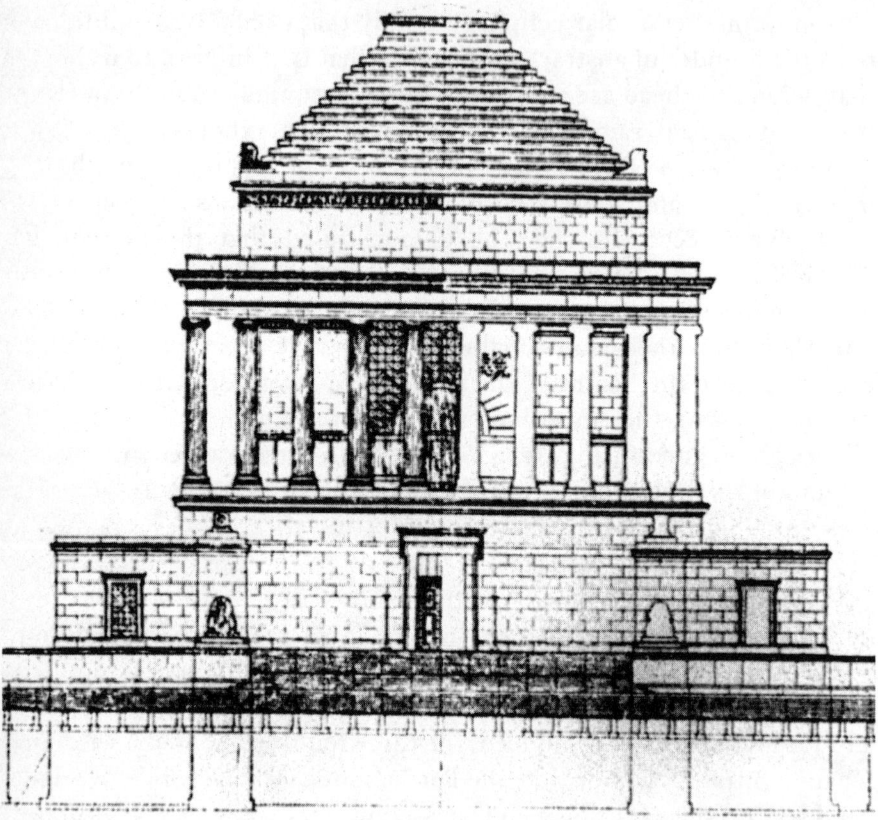

The exact time for the breaking of ground for the Temple was recorded as 9.00 a.m. on 31 May 1911, the ceremony being conducted by the Sovereign Grand Commander James Daniel Richardson in the presence of four other Masons.[14] In contrast, the exact time for the laying of the cornerstone held on 18 October 1911, attended by many hundreds of Masons, is no longer known. Even though the ceremony was extensively reported in the *Washington Post* (which had Masonic interests at heart), I have not been able to determine the exact time of the ceremony.[15]

However, it is possible to reconstruct the time with fair accuracy from the Masonic records. According to these records, the Supreme Council met at 10.00 a.m., and had occupied themselves with necessary business, including the granting of a charter to the New Bern Lodge of Perfection, North Carolina, before recessing to participate in the laying of the stone. After the procession to the new site and an invocation, there followed the *Festival Te Deum* (sung by the Scottish Rite Choir of St Louis) and a number of addresses and prayers before the cornerstone ceremony began. The ritual, along with the ceremonial laying, was completed under the supervision of the Grand Master of the District of Columbia, Most Worshipful Brother J. Claude Keiper – officiating with the original gavel used by George Washington in the Capitol ceremonial.[16] The ceremony was brought to a conclusion by Abram Simon, the rabbi of Washington Hebrew Congregation, and Earle Wilfey, minister of the Vermont Avenue Christian Church – both were Masons.[17] From such records, I must presume that the cornerstone-laying did not occur until after midday, and I have accordingly erected a chart for 1.00 – though the event may have been a little later.[18]

The chart for the laying of the cornerstone, on 18 October 1911, is very revealing from an esoteric point of view. *The Moon and Venus are together (conjunct) in Virgo.* Two planets which promote arcane endeavours (Neptune and Uranus) are in opposition, balancing over the horizon. Even more important, is the fact that the Sun was one degree from the star *Arcturus*, and less than two degrees from Spica. As we shall discover, both stars are of great importance to Washington DC. The selection of the day had involved a balancing act, for had the ceremonial been planned for the day before, the Sun would have been exactly upon Spica, but, on that day, the Moon would not have been in Virgo.

The Temple was dedicated four years later, on 18 October 1915, when the Sun was within the Arcturus degree.

Since the architect of this remarkable building was not a Mason (and indeed never petitioned to become one), Elliott Woods, then architect of the United States Capitol and a 32 degree Mason, formally acted on his behalf in the ceremony.[19] This recognition, that Pope did not belong to the esoteric body for which the building was being constructed, was extended into the actual design of the Temple: Woods' Masonic and architectural expertise was of such value to Pope that the two agreed to share the fee for the work, the greater proportion going to Pope.[20]

Woods contributed many important ideas to the design of the building – especially in regard to the demands placed upon the architecture by the interior demands of Masonic ritual. However, the notion of adapting the tomb of King Mausolus at Halicarnassus for the Temple was suggested by Pope. Whence came this idea of making a temple for ritual and worship from a mausoleum?

The only image of the reconstructed Mausoleum which I have been able to discover in Masonic sources, and which was also circulating in architectural circles prior to 1910, is a wood engraving in the *Hall of the Ancients* literature which had been promulgated by the Bostonian architect, Franklin W. Smith.[21] Not only was this one of the prints reproduced in the documents submitted to, and recorded by, the 56th Congress, but it was in the bound copy of Smith's pamphlets and writings, now in the Library of the Supreme Council.[22] It is almost inconceivable that Grand Commander James D. Richardson (a member of the House of Representatives for Tennessee until 1904[23]) and the architect of the Capitol, Elliott Woods,[24] both intimately involved in Congressional activities, could fail to have been aware of Smith's daring plans for what he called 'the aggrandizement of Washington DC', and consequently of the wood engraving in his published designs.

The collaboration between Woods and Pope seems to have been close. Because of this, it is now difficult to determine which of the two conceived the idea of adapting the tower of the Temple so that it was a truncated pyramid reflecting the pyramid on the Seal. The issue is complicated by the fact that the precise appearance of the Mausoleum at Halicarnassus was not known. The best description of it that has survived from the ancient world is from the Roman, Pliny,[25] who mentions that above the colonnade was a pyramid with 24 stages to the top of its peak. This 'peak' must have been truncated, for at the top was space for a marble statuary of a four-horse chariot, sculpted by Pytheos. In spite of infelicities in Pliny's description, most reconstructions of the Mausoleum have been based on his work.[26]

Although the many 'reconstructions' which proliferated in the 19th century were highly speculative, there were wise divergences from Pliny in such things as ratios, the number of steps on the pyramid, and the number of pillars in the colonnades. The German archaeologist Friedrich Adler had published his own reconstruction in 1899, and, to judge from the final designs, it was probably this which fired Pope's initial enthusiasm during his researches.[27]

Pope did not merely copy Adler. A comparison between the two designs reveals the genius of the former, not merely in the subtle proportions he established between the peristyle temple section and the pyramidic tower, but also in his allowing ingress through what had been the podium walls of the antique mausoleum. All one may trace in the

Pope design is the original *idea* behind the mausoleum: the subtle proportions of this major work of architecture, along with the distribution of masses, are entirely his own.

There is one more point to consider. The final scheme submitted by Pope on 6 May 1911 specified that the building be topped by a pyramid. However, there are many more than 13 steps in his preliminary blueprints and drawings.[28] I have not been able to determine which of the two architects determined that the tower should consist of precisely 13 steps – and thus link with the mysteries behind the foundation of the United States.

For all their intrinsic importance and beauty, these few examples of pyramids in Washington DC prove that while the eagle is everywhere in the city, the pyramid is obscured. It is clear that the histories of the obverse and the reverse of the Seal are very different. The obverse (see figure, p.219) was cut in brass as a die, in 1780, and was almost immediately put to use to authenticate an agreement governing an exchange of prisoners of war with the British.[29] In contrast, the reverse was never cut at all, even though there has existed, for over a century, an authority of Congress ordering the cutting of its die.[30]

The more one looks into this curious breach of law, the more obvious it becomes that there was some intention on the part of interested officials to ensure that the pyramid did *not* play an important part in the conscious symbolism of Washington DC. As late as 1883, the Secretary of State admitted: 'The Reverse of the seal has never been engraved by the Government.'[31] There was almost a conspiracy of silence mounted against the design. In January 1885, Theodor F. Dwight (in a letter to Whitmore) remarked of the reverse: 'It has been so long kept in the dark, a few months more of shade will do it no harm.'[32]

The reluctance to bring the pyramid into the light of day was not restricted to individual Masons: even bureaucrats seem to have been unhappy with bringing it forward. When the State Department prepared its exhibition display for the Chicago Exposition of 1892, it commissioned huge paintings of the obverse and reverse of the Seal. However, in the opinion of those responsible for the exhibition, the design of the reverse was so lacking in spirit, and so inappropriate, that it was not put on display.[33] The bureaucrats' objections – on aesthetic grounds – were clearly spurious: however we view it, the reverse design is neither 'lacking in spirit' nor inappropriate. Perhaps the truth is that the officials simply did not understand its complex hermetic symbolism, rooted in Masonic lore.

This curious outbreak of bureaucratic aesthetics wove its way into the fantasies of the Rosicrucian, Grace Kincaid Morey.[34] In her book, *Mystic Americanism*, she asks '*Why has the reverse or Pyramid side of the Seal been so long unknown?*', and, in the style of certain occultists, answered her own question. It has, she insists, remained unknown because it has not been understood by the people. She reminds us that paintings of it executed 'for exhibition at expositions of National importance' were rejected,[35] and sees this rejection as emanating from America's enemies, who have met no resistance from the people.

Morey's book is plagiaristic. She seems to have taken the account above without acknowledgement from Hunt's book on the history of the Seal.[36] It is also incomprehensible in parts. However, as with many writers who venture into the occult genre, she does at times exhibit flashes of genius. She responds to her own question about which 'starry groups of the Zodiacal Band' pertain to the symbolism of the Seal in an edifying way: she insists that this is the zodiacal symbolism linked with the knowledge of what she calls 'the Mother-side of God'.[37] There is only one 'starry group' which corresponds to the 'Mother-side' of God, and this is Virgo.

Morey, probably without realizing it, has strayed into what we shall eventually see as the great Mystery of Washington DC – a Mystery which takes the Egyptian pyramid as an ideal triangle, and links it with the zodiacal sign Virgo.

One has the feeling that the reverse of the Seal remained unfinished as a die for exactly the same reasons as the pyramid depicted upon it was unfinished – *because it pointed to a future development of the United States, rather than to the century following its design*. The promised 'New Age' (*Novus Ordo Seclorum*) set out in the banderole below the unfinished pyramid of the Seal is linked with a Masonic belief about the destiny of mankind since the destruction of the Temple of Solomon. Just as the Temple was unfinished, so is the spiritual development of mankind.

I must make clear that the idea of the truncated pyramid is not – and probably never was – a symbol *unique* to Masonry, or to that stream of Masonry which guided the development of the Seal. Indeed, the idea of the pyramid as a trinitarian symbol is easily accommodated into the Christian ethos, which is rooted in the Mystery of the Three in One, so beautifully represented in the form of the equilateral triangle. Not surprisingly, some American-based religious societies have adopted the truncated pyramid as a symbol of unfinished work – which takes it very close to the Masonic ideal.

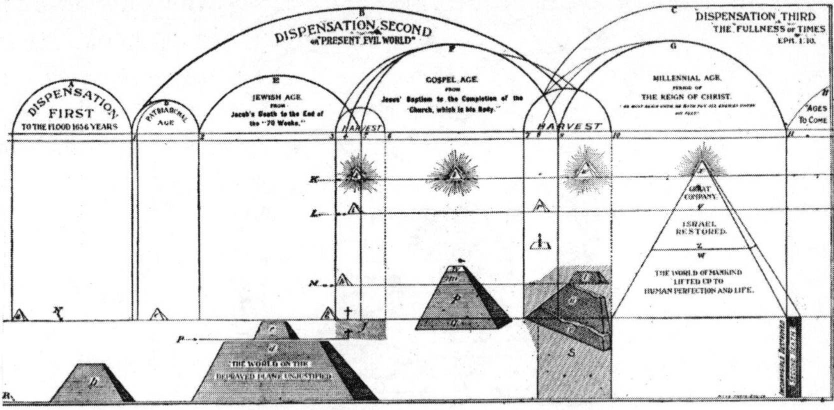

There is a most interesting frontispiece-foldout in volume 1 of the 1898 edition of the extensive Christian tract, *Millennial Dawn*, (above). This adopts the pyramid formation, in various stages of growth, as representative of the relationship between mankind and God in the various ages.[38] It is only in the future age that the pyramid will be completed: this is the Millennial Age of the Reign of Christ. Such diagrams may be hard to follow, and particularly difficult to relate to historical periods, but the idea is much the same as that contained in the original truncated pyramid of the Seal. It is surely no accident that the ideal pyramidion of this frontispiece, which hovers in what might be described as the ideal, or spiritual realm, is portrayed in a radiant auriol.

The precise origins of the pyramid design for the reverse of the Seal, with its three Latin inscriptions, are still steeped in mystery.

The very earliest deliberations about the Seal, between Adams, Franklin and Jefferson,[39] visualized (among other things) an Egyptian-biblical theme.[40] These deliberations of 4 July 1776 – which came so close to the famed Declaration – were not adopted for the final Seal. The only graphic survivals from this time were the Eye of Providence and the 13-letter motto, *E pluribus unum*.[41] There was no suggestion in these records of a pyramid. The national flag of 13 stripes and 13 white stars was adopted by Congress on 14 June 1777, but further deliberations on the much-needed Seal were not put in hand until 25 March 1780. The idea of a truncated pyramid for the Seal (over) was first proposed in 1782 by William Barton. The pyramid was already widely used as a symbol in Masonic fraternities in Europe, and we should therefore not be surprised that it should have been proposed in the context of a national symbol for a republic guided by so many Freemasons.

The designs for the obverse and reverse of the Seal were adopted by Congress on 20 June 1782. Although the obverse, with its dominant eagle, was later redesigned by the Secretary of State, Charles Thompson, who placed arrows and an olive branch in the talons of the bald-headed eagle, the reverse did 'not appear to have caused much discussion'.[42]

In fact, prior to the adoption of the design for the Seal in 1782, the two mottoes had been changed by Thompson. It was he who introduced the Latin scripts which now appear on the reverse (figure 27). When the two designs were passed by Congress on 20 June 1782, it was recognized that the motto *Novus Ordo Seclorum* signified (as Charles Thompson wrote) 'the beginning of the new American Aera'. This was supposed to have commenced from the date of the Declaration of Independence. Curiously, the account of this symbolism given by Thompson is left out of the journals of Congress – the first of a series of interesting lacunas which seem to bedevil the design for the reverse.[43] Nonetheless, the following questions arise: what was this *New Age* promised on the reverse the Seal, and why was the design to prove something of an embarrassment to officialdom?

On 7 July 1884, Congress alloted one thousand dollars to enable the Secretary of State to obtain new dies of the obverse and reverse of the Seal. In consquence, Theodor F. Dwight, Chief of the Bureau of Rolls and Library of the Department of State, consulted several specialist authorities for their opinions. Among these was the scholar Justin Winsor, who declared the design of the reverse 'both unintelligent and commonplace'.

Was Winsor also being disingenuous? If he really thought the design was unintelligent, then he had not looked at it with any care. Winsor was learned in American history,[44] and cannot have failed to been aware of the symbolism behind the 'unfinished pyramid'. He would have known of the design's antecedents, for a similar motif had appeared on a 50-dollar bill, issued in 1778, along with the motto *Perennis*, which had appeared in the first design. While the Barton pyramid also had the motto *Perennis* at its base, the upper part of the truncated pyramid was completed by the Eye of Providence, and bore the additional motto *Deo Favente*.

The fact is that Justin Winsor either failed to understand the symbolism of the pyramid, or elected not to write about it in letters which would undoubtedly one day become public. Yet in some ways one may sympathize with his view, since, from an exoteric point of view, the choice of a pyramid for the American Seal does seem curious. However, the pyramid, in a variety of forms, had been popular in Masonic fraternities in Europe for much of the 18th century. In particular, it had been used widely in British Lodges prior to the Declaration of Independence, and was certainly known and used in American Lodges during this period. Some of these pyramidic images are still preserved in public and Masonic museums, including a number in the museum of the Freemasons' Hall in London.

For example, a Spode ceramic of about 1790 has, imprinted within the bowl, a colour transfer of a Masonic design, which shows three pyramids, each separated by a foreground 'light', or candle. Here there is a clear aim of linking the three flames of the candles with the three pyramids.[45]

While there is distinct Masonic symbolism in this combination, it was once a symbolism rooted in the ancient Mystery lore. The Greek *pyroeis* (often used for Mars, the fire-planet) had a similar sound to the word 'pyramid', and seems to have been etymologically connected with it. On a more esoteric level, it is recognized that *pyrinos* meant not only 'fiery' but also 'wheaten' – recalling that the corn-goddess of the Egyptians, Isis, was sometimes called 'Mistress of the Pyramids'.[46]

From a slightly earlier period, *circa* 1770, is a first period Worcester tankard, which shows a pyramid with a stellar globe over the apex.[47] This calls to mind a number of engravings of about that period, which show pyramids with the Sun and Moon hovering over them. Also in the collection is an apron of *circa* 1789, painted for, and sold by, Brother Berring of Greenwich, displaying two pyramids.[48]

Such examples show that the idea of the pyramid was circulating widely in Masonic circles prior to the Declaration. However, while it is evident that the Seal design was directed and overlooked by a group of men that included Masons, the pyramid has never been widely used in American Masonic iconography.

A Lodge Summons of 1757, to Philadelphia Ancient Lodge No. 2, seems to incorporate virtually all the symbols pertinent to Masonry. Among these, we may trace one or two which were finally incorporated into the Seal: the Eye of Providence, in a Glory, and a constellation of stars. However, there is *no* pyramid in this complex symbolism. Even the *Master Carpet* print of 1819 (on p.90), which is recognized as an attempt to standardize Masonic symbols,[49] and which contains at least 40 distinct Masonic emblems, does not display a pyramid. This omission leads us to ask what was the arcane meaning of the pyramid, as it appeared in 18th-century Masonic contexts, prior to becoming part of the iconography of the Seal of the United States.

The Masonic pyramid appears to have derived from the 18th-century European fascination with Egyptian hermeticism, which resulted in several soi-disant 'Egyptian' hermetic Lodges being created. In consequence, the pyramid appears with startling frequency on 18th- and 19th-century French and English Masonic aprons. By curious good fortune, one beautifully painted Master Mason apron (famous for its depiction as a line drawing in Manley Palmer Hall's much-reprinted work on arcane symbolism)[50] is now in the collection of the Masonic Temple, Supreme Council, Washington DC (plate 12). The two pyramids on this apron are proportioned fairly closely to those at Gizeh, but not all Masonic aprons are of this ratio.

Of the many surviving examples of the Masonic pyramid from this phase of development, among the most fascinating (in that it clearly incorporates an enigma) is a beautiful Masonic medal minted in 1742. This displays on its reverse a pyramid between two columns (below). In the foreground is a sphinx, with a lunar crescent marked upon its side, revealing a symbolic connection with the Egyptian goddess Isis, whose significance has been discussed.[51] The bronze medal was designed in Rome by a body of practising foreign Masons, at a time when indigenous Masonry had been banned by the Catholic Church.[52] It was minted in

recognition of the appointment of the Englishman, Martin Folkes, as Deputy Grand Master of the Grand Lodge of England, on 24 June 1724,[53] and a bust of him is on the obverse. The Latin legend on the reverse may be intended as a recognition of this Mason's interest in astronomy and astrology, or it may apply to English Masonry in general, since *Sua Sidera Norunt* may be translated as 'They are acquainted with their own stars.'

The medal's Egyptian theme should not surprise us, for in 1742 there was a deep interest in Egyptology. Folkes, as a Fellow of the Royal Society, had been a friend of Sir Christopher Wren (a fellow Mason), and was acquainted with the antiquarian, Stukeley, who had been made a Mason of the Lodge in 1721.[54] Folkes also knew Sir Hans Sloane, who had been President of the Royal Society from 1727, and was almost certainly familiar with the private collection which eventually formed the basis for the British Museum, after Sloane died (at the age of 93) in 1753. In the collection which reached the British Museum was a remarkable Masonic document[55] and a selection of Egyptian antiquities, none of which appear to be of particular importance. However, in addition to this contact with Egyptology through his friendship with Sloane, Folkes was, at the time of his election, a member of the Egyptian Society, which would meet in Chandos Street, London, its purpose being 'the promoting and preserving of Egyptian and other ancient learning'. This Society was short-lived – it seems to have continued for only two years – and had ceased to meet shortly after Folkes was made Deputy Grand Master of the Grand Lodge. However, its influence had been considerable. Relevant to the medal was the fact that it had first met on the old-style date of 11 December 1741, regarded by those gathering as marking 'the Feast of Isis'. This ceremonial explains the crescent Moon mark of Isis on the body of the sphinx.[56]

However, the most intriguing mystery behind this medal is not the Isis-sphinx, but the shape of the left-hand side of the pyramid, which is notched and re-angled at the 13th course. This curiosity of design has never been explained. Could it have been the source of the inspiration of the 13-tier truncation of the pyramid which appeared on the reverse of the Seal (figure 27)? The curious notching has been 'amended' by later copyists of the medal, to imply that the crenellated wall to the left was actually built into the pyramid – but this is not in the original design, and is architecturally impossible.[57] Significantly, the original medal – or engravings after its design – would have been known in America, for by 1742 there were certainly at least six Lodges under the English Provincial Grand Lodge at Boston.[58]

A medal is a relatively formal thing, the design of which may be regulated by a small group of individuals conversant with esoteric symbolism: such designs are notoriously difficult to interpret, without the aid of a formal declaration of meaning, or some knowledge of the symbology adopted by the group. This is one reason why the meaning of the curiously notched pyramid in the Folkes medal remains elusive. In contrast, the designs of Masonic regalia are rarely intended to be quite so sophisticated or esoteric, and even when they are, it is generally possible to interpret their meanings within the context of Masonic symbolism. This is relevant to our search, as so many pyramids are found in Masonic regalia surviving from early European Lodges, and American Lodges after *c*. 1820 (though lost examples may have been older). For example, a Masonic apron, formerly in the collection of the historian Gould, and certainly from the pre-1790 phase of French Masonry (in that it pertained to the Grand Orient of France), displays a pyramid among its plethora of symbols.[59]

I should emphasize that, for all the pyramid was explored and exploited in a few European Masonic medals, in Romantic literature and operas associated with Masonry – most notably, in Mozart's Masonic *The Magic Flute*[60] – this kind of symbolism did not *extensively* permeate Masonry in America. The Masonic pyramid, while not widespread at the end of the 18th century, was a European Masonic symbol rather than one which had found popularity among American masons. Why did the Americans elect to graft on to their own influential Seal the symbol of the pyramid?

Were these American Masons perhaps impressed by the relevance of a particular variant of the pyramid to their project? In this context, the importance of the Seal pyramid rests in its incompleteness – it is in the process of being built, the Egyptian equivalent of the yet-unfinished Temple of Solomon. In the early days of the Republic, the United States was being built on a new and perhaps ill-prepared foundation of democracy: did it please the symbolizing propensity of the Masons to represent this building in terms of courses of masonry in a yet-incomplete building? In a slightly later phase, the new federal city was being built, as an extension of this new experiment in federalism. Could the unfinished pyramid refer to this notion of an experiment in democratic governance?

The symbolism – of a pyramid with 13 completed courses – was intended to point to the future. The courses were 'finished' by the triangular Eye of Providence. By means of this symbolic touch, the 13 courses of masonry were spiritualized by their union – they were, so to speak, given a cosmic purpose, or at least linked symbolically with the spiritual realms above. Alongside this symbolism was the notion that the 13 courses might be added to: there was ample room for other states to join the original 13. The space above the pyramid was a space *in potentia*, a spiritual area which would allow for federal expansion. Yet the space was ambiguous, for it also pointed to the idea that the building of the inner Temple was not yet finished.

The connection between America and Egypt is quite implicit in the imagery, and is a connection recognized by Masonic scholars.[61] We must assume that for all it was incomplete, the 13-layer pyramid was intended as a reference to the famous pyramid at Gizeh. This *was* completed – its present 'unfinished' appearance is due to the removal of its pyramidion in antiquity, and to the later use of its original marble covering as building materials by the Arabs who conquered Egypt. This much was recognized a century later by Tiffany and Co., when they were commissioned to examine the redesign for both obverse and reverse of the Seal. On 13 December 1884, in its report on the subject, this firm insisted that the pyramid of the reverse had been 'drawn to the scale of the great pyramid; the side seen in perspective to the right means East, this view being desired'.[62]

As a matter of fact, Tiffany and Co. were incorrect. The pyramid on the Seal is not in a proportion even remotely close to that of the Great Pyramid of Cheops at Gizeh. The proportions of the American pyramid are more closely linked with those of the pyramids shown on a French medal, cut to commemorate the Battle of the Pyramids of 1789, and reminds us of the close connection between France and America during the last decades of the 18th century.

During the 19th century, many proposals were made for changing both the obverse and the reverse of the Seal, but good sense prevailed, and the numerous suggestions of scholars and committees (including the proposals of Tiffany and Co.) were ignored. The Seal of 1884, cut by Messrs Bailey, Banks and Biddle, of Philadelphia, was as near as possible the version approved by Congress in 1782: this, however, was merely the obverse of the Seal, with its wide-winged eagle. *The reverse, with the pyramid, was not cut – still in open defiance of the orders of Congress.*

We must not overlook the fact that the pyramids of the Americas – those of the Mayans and the Aztecs – had always been truncated: on their levelled tops were groups of temples, or a single temple. In symbolic terms, therefore, the pyramid on the Seal seems more nearly represents the Central American temple-pyramids than those of Egypt. I personally do not believe that the truncated pyramid on the US Seal design was influenced by the meso-American temple-pyramids, yet this association has been suggested by some writers in the field. However, we may presume that, within the framework of this Mayan symbolism, the space above the truncation is awaiting the construction of a temple. This 'invisible' symbolism recalls one important strain of arcane symbolism within Masonry itself, which maintains that the present era is that during which the Temple of Solomon is being rebuilt. At the completion of this Temple, the present era will come to an end, and be succeeded by a more splendid spiritual era.[63]

It is only because the Masonic symbolism may be traced back to Egyptian Masonic models that we can accept with any sense of security the connection with Egypt. At the end of the 18th century, when the pyramid was first mooted by Barton for the Seal, the connection between Masonry and the ancient pyramid of Gizeh itself had not been explored with any depth in writing. It was not until the extraordinary investigative work of the Mason, Marsham Adams, shortly after 1894, that the intimate relationship between the initiation practices and the structure of the Great Pyramid was revealed.[64] In spite of this, it was widely believed by such Masons as Pike that certain Masonic hermetic beliefs, and even one or two rituals, could be traced back to ancient Egypt. There is some substantiation for this belief in the importance accorded to the Masonic square, which is the ancient Egyptian *kan*. In an article of the 1820s on 'Places of Initiation', the Reverend George Oliver, Provincial Deputy Grand Master for Lincolnshire, in England, had recognized that the pyramids of Egypt were initiation centres, even if he was erroneous in his view that they were built shortly after the dispersion of the Jews.[65] If this idea of the pyramid as an initiation centre had been around a few decades earlier, then we would have yet another level of meaning in the image of the truncated form – the unfinished pyramid would refer to an incomplete initiation into the Mysteries.

The idea of a truncated pyramid being completed by a spiritual being is simple, yet ingenious. Even were there not other arcane devices on the reverse of the Seal, the notion of a 'spiritual being' (symbolized by an auriolated Eye of Providence) would suggest a Masonic origin of the design. The symbolism of this Eye is profound and complex, but in essence it represents the all-seeing Eye of God. Its roots, in hermetic literature at least, may be traced back to the Eye of Horus imagery in Egyptian papyri.[66]

Thus, the spiritualizing 'completion' of the pyramid, like the material stratification of the pyramid itself, is Egyptian in origin. These Mysteries of Eye and Pyramid were appreciated even by the early Christian writers, who were disposed to reject most pagan-seeming ideas. Given the erudition of many early American Masons, it is inconceivable that some of the ideas expressed in ancient theological and hermetic literature did not circulate in Masonic circles.

Cyril of Alexandria, writing in the early 5th century AD, was a churchman enlightened enough to recognize the wisdom of the ancient Mystery Schools. Two surviving fragments of his writings deal with the appreciation of the Egyptian Mysteries: one is entitled 'The Incorporeal Eye' and the other, 'The Pyramid':

> If there be an incorporeal eye, let it go forth from the body unto the Vision of the Beautiful. Let it fly up and soar aloft, seeking to see neither form, nor body (nor even the types of such things), but rather That which is the Maker of these things . . .
>
> The Pyramid, then, is below Nature and the Intellectual World. This is because it has above it, as ruler, the Creator-Word of the Lord of all . . .[67]

In contrast to such flights of hermetic fancy, the numerology of the Masonic design seems to be banal: the 13 levels of the pyramid relate to the original 13 colonies. That these will be added to in the fullness of time is symbolized by the structure being perpetually incomplete.

However, there is a much more subtle numerology in the Seal pyramid than at first meets the eye. If the scroll-like section at the bottom (which contains the date 1776 in Roman numerals) is discounted, then *there are 72 bricks in the pyramid face.* This 72 is probably the most esoteric of all numbers (see p.290).

Nor are the two inscriptions and date without their own numerology. The top motto *Annuit Coeptis* consists of the obligatory 13. However, the bottom motto, *Novus Ordo Seclorum*, consists of 17 letters. Even so, if these are added to the 9 numerals in the Roman date, there is a total of 26. This means that the lower sets of letters and figures total 2 × 13. This simple numerology was certainly intentional, for, in order to introduce it, the designer cut a letter from the Latin word *saeclorum* (which is the most usual spelling of the word) to give *seclorum.* There are therefore 3 sets of 13 on the reverse of the medal. This 3 is so important that it is reflected in the trinity of the Eye of Providence, and in the nominal triangle from which the pyramid is constructed.

*

Perhaps this is an appropriate place to examine the arcane meaning in the two mottoes on the reverse of the Seal.

The motto at the top of the Seal, *Annuit Coeptis*, is from Virgil, adapted in order to give the 13 characters. It is from the *Aeneid*, the original of which runs, *Audacibus annue coeptis*.[68] This is a prayer to the god Jupiter, requesting that he 'favour my daring undertaking'. The change of person and tense in the American version introduces the requisite change in number of letters. We should observe that while the subject matter of the reverse of the Seal is undoubtedly pagan – if symbolic of hermetic Egypt – the superior motto is itself a prayer to a pagan god. Could *this* be the reason why there has been so much reluctance to bring the reverse of the Seal into the light of day? Whatever the nature of the god, the prayer directed in this way is a petition that the daring undertaking (symbolically, the building of the pyramid) may be completed, and that the new age will find fulfilment.

The motto *Novus Ordo Seclorum* has been adapted from Virgil's *Bucolics*,[69] where the relevant text reads *magnus ab integro saeclorum nascitur ordo* ('the great series of ages begins anew'). The 'Americanization' of the *seclorum* would be unforgivable in a classical sense, except that it was intended to incorporate a numerological meaning.

What is this Age that is about to begin anew? In order to understand the arcane significance of this motto, we shall have to examine what expectations those who designed the Seal might have had regarding the future of the United States. When we have grasped the importance of these New Age expectations, we shall be in a better position to understand why the design for this reverse has remained so consistently hidden.

As we have seen, the report by Tiffany and Co. on the reverse of the Seal recognized that in the pyramid, the 'perspective to the right means East'. What exactly did this mean? At first glance, the sentence does not make sense: there is no indication whatsoever that the pyramid is being viewed from its eastern aspect. It is true that the side to the left of the image is in darkness, and the larger face in light (see figure 27), but this could be just as well a reference to a western view as to an eastern.

The fact is that whoever recognized this 'eastern' view cannot have been familiar with some of the more obscure Masonic beliefs. The coloured picture used to illustrate the reverse of the Seal shows the left-hand side of the pyramid in shadow, with the facing section in the light.[70] This contrast of dark-light is primal to Masonic symbolism, and was enshrined in early American Masonry. For example, the membership certificate printed in 1780 by the famous Mason, Paul Revere, for the Rising States Lodge, began with a reference to the first verses of the Gospel of St John: 'And the DARKNESS comprehended it not. In the EAST, a place of LIGHT, where reigns SILENCE & PEACE.'[71]

The contrast between darkness and light is absolutely primal to the ancient art of laying foundations of buildings. We must look at this in connection with the pyramid under discussion. Traditionally, the first foundation stones is usually laid in the north-east corner of the edifice. This Masonic practice seems to be a continuation of the mediaeval tradition recorded by the mediaeval historian of architectural symbolism, Durandus.[72] Cosmologically, it seems to reflect the emergence of the light (Sunrise to the east) from the darkness (the sunless north). A well-laid cornerstone would daily reflect this symbolism of duality.

There are many explanations for this practice, which is enshrined in mediaeval architectural theory as indicated by Durandus, but the rationale taken over by the speculative Masons is that the north represents darkness, whilst the east (being the place of Sunrise) represents light. *In view of this, the image of the pyramid on the reverse of the Seal cannot represent an eastern Sunrise, but a western Sunset.*

It is evident, then, that the larger (frontal) face of the pyramid on the reverse is intended to represent the west, and is therefore symbolically bathed in the light of the setting Sun. This solarization is enshrined in the hidden numerology of the eastern face of the structure. This fact leads us to ask, why should the symbolism of this American Seal point to the setting Sun?

It is this solarization and orientation which demonstrate, more than any other element in the design of the Seal, that it evolved under Masonic control. The early visualization of the pyramid (see page 228) was entirely frontal. There was no attempt to instil a sense of orientation, with its consequent feeling for the majesty of conflict between dark and light. Equally, while the rather obvious symbolism of the 13 tiers was established in the first visualization, the secret numerology of the stones was missing. In so far as they may be counted, there appear to be 122 stones in this first pyramid design, which means that the symbolism of the mystery of the Sun is missed altogether. It was the later stage of the design of the reverse of the Seal which connected it with the mystery of the setting Sun. The relevance of all this to the story of Washington DC will become clear at a later point.

The triangular apex, or 'completion', of the seal pyramid was missing in the original design. The Eye of Providence, set in an aureole, was a Masonic symbol long before the Declaration of Independence, and has

remained so since that time. A medal (below) to commemorate the centenary of the Grand Master's Lodge, on 3 January 1849 portrays a speculative Mason in the operative phase of laying a foundation stone. Above his head is an aureolated eye very similar to that on the pyramid Seal sketch. It was when the eye was encased in a triangle, thus completing the shape of the pyramid and radiating a puissant spirituality, that the design became esoteric. In this a graphic recognition of the words of the Christian, Cyril of Alexandria, which I quoted on page 236:

> The Pyramid, then, is below Nature and the Intellectual World. This is because it has above it, as ruler, the Creator-Word of the Lord of all . . .[73]

The official explanation given by Hunt for the extraordinary combination of eye and pyramid in the original Seal design was intended for public consumption. I must emphasize that the design, whether derived from Masonic sources or not, is one of the most arcane of all American symbols. Albert Pike was writing almost 100 years after the design of the reverse's pyramid, but he nonetheless expressed sentiments about the truncated pyramid that were more accessible than those of Cyril of Alexandria. These sentiments had been around in esoteric literature for a very long time:

> And our expression, that our Lodges extend upwards to the Heavens, comes from the Persian and Druidic custom of having to their Temples no roofs but the sky.[74]

This pyramid, which extends upwards to the heavens, seems to advocate an unabashed reliance upon the wise spiritual direction of God in earthly affairs. No doubt this was the future spirituality which the founders hoped would find expression in the social and political life of the new America. Their dream – that the symbolic pyramid would be completed in America – probably explains the presence of the three pyramids outside the walls of the vast museum proposed by Franklin Smith in 1897. These were really the three pyramids of 18th-century Masonry, transposed to the banks of the Potomac: they were not emblems of the past, but a celebration of an anticipated spiritual future.

The examples above convey the true significance of the pyramid in the minds of those who founded the independent United States. In view of this, it would appear most unusual that the pyramid remained hidden in the symbolism of Washington DC. It is a mystery which can be understood, not in terms of the form of the pyramid itself, but in terms of the triangle into which it is resolved. No matter whether this form is inscribed with the name of God, or marked with the Eye of Providence, or whether it remains denuded of symbolism, it is still representative of the spiritual domain of the Trinity.

As will become evident a little later, the truth is that the arcane secret of Washington DC is deeply involved with the simple geometric form of a triangle. This triangle is so largely imprinted upon the map of the city that it is identifed by a name which emphasizes its function as much as its geometric shape. *I refer to the Federal Triangle, which runs its hypotenuse along Pennsylvania Avenue.* Before we examine the significance of this particular triangle, which is replete with cosmic and arcane meaning, we should look a little more closely at the symbolism of the triangle itself.

Chapter Nine

Wisdom was never more exemplified than when it adapted the pyramidial and triangular form, from the sublime architecture of the heavens . . .

(Madame Belzoni, 'My Unlettered Theory . . . dedicated to the Masonic brethren universally'. Quoted on p.32 J.Ross Robertson, *The Egyptian Obelisk! And the Masonic Emblems found at its base*, 1880.)

Perhaps it was of little public importance that Edwin Eugene Aldrin, who was one of two men to step on to the Moon on 20 July 1969, was a Mason.[1] However, it was public knowledge that he and his companion in the Apollo 11 spacecraft carried the Stars and Stripes. The photograph of Aldrin standing on the lunar surface, his globular visor reflecting the landed spacecraft, and the American flag set on a vertical pole in front of him, is probably one of the most famous in history.

What is not widely known is that alongside the national flag, Aldrin also carried a Masonic banner (plate 13). This had been embroidered especially for this strange journey by the librarian of the Masonic House of the Temple, in Washington DC.[2]

The popular name of the national flag of the United States leaves one in no doubt that there were stars upon it. These stars were five-pointed – and exactly like the secret star on the Masonic banner.

What is the mystery of this star which can be at once so public, yet so esoteric?

In 1821, the young French genius Jean François Champollion became the first man – in modern times – to read the secret name of an Egyptian queen in the form in which it had been incised upon basalt almost 2,000 years earlier.[3] Through spelling out the name of Cleopatra in this sacred writing, Champollion discovered the lost meaning of the Egyptian hieroglyphics. Within three years, he could read this forgotten language with sufficient ease to publish a book explaining his method of interpretation.[4] Among the hieroglyphics he revealed in this original and seminal work was one which, in several variations, had the form of a star:

Champollion, believing that most of the ancient Egyptian hieroglyphics had sound-equivalents linked with Coptic, proposed that this star had been named by Egyptian priests the *sioy*. Later Egyptologists recognized that the more ancient form was *sba*.[5]

Champollion proposed that in a combination of hieroglyphics the sound-equivalents was *sot-rnis*. He defined the image in terms which make of it the virtual equivalent of Virgo. The hieroglyphics *sot-rnis* meant:

> The star of midday: star or constellation represented in the form of a woman standing on a boat . . . raising her right arm towards her coiffure which is decorated with three long palm branches . . . holding in her right hand the sceptre, a Solus-flower . . .[6]

Later Egyptologists gave a different sound-value, but confirmed what Champollion had suspected while compiling his dictionary of Egyptian hieroglyphics – that the *sba* (above) was a 'determinative'. When found in a text, the star *determined* (or indicated to the reader) that the group of hieroglyphics associated with it was related to spiritual matters. It was related to the heavens, to invisible energies (which the Greeks later called 'aetheric'), to time, and so on. The *sba* hieroglyphic was a five-pointed star, within the centre of which was an encircled dot, somewhat like the modern sigil for the Sun. So far as the ancient Egyptians were concerned, this was a symbol of a high spirituality, which, while it might border on the familiar world, was quite inaccessible to ordinary vision.[7]

In 1821 – the same year that Champollion made his momentous discovery – a little-known Bostonian engraver, Amos Doolittle, attempted to standardize a large number of secret symbols used in the Masonic Lodges of America, in an engraving he made of *The Master's Carpet*. In a wood engraving based on this picture by Doolittle, pride of place was given to a particular symbol, which was centred beneath two other sacred symbols (above). These were the Eye of Providence and the secret letter G ('the most sacred of the the Masonic emblems', which represents, among other things, Geometry).[8] Below these was the five-pointed star – precisely the same as that which, thousands of years ago, the Egyptian priests had called *sba* – divested of its encircled dot.

Only two years earlier, in 1818, the American Congress had determined that the symbol of a five-pointed star should be adopted to represent every state joining the Union. They decreed that, as each new state joined, a new star should be added to the 13 state stars already on the flag. Thus the stars would increase in number, as symbol of this growing fellowship, while the 13 red and white stripes which had represented the original 13 states, would remain as symbol of the original union of states. This proposal was made by the Mason Senator Benjamin Latrobe. Latrobe was merely extending the heraldic use of stars on the Seal of the United States, as had been determined by a committee directed by Benjamin Franklin, in 1782.[9] According to Franklin's committee, there was to be a surround of '13 stars, forming constellation, argent, on an azure field'.[10] Latrobe's suggestion was adopted, and the stars began to appear upon the flag in ever increasing numbers.

Almost 50 years would pass before the massive statue of *Freedom*, sculpted by Thomas Crawford, would be raised to crown the new dome of the Capitol, in 1863. The statue is nearly 20 feet high, but from the ground it looks diminutive: as we have seen, the eagle's plumage on the helmet is often taken for the feathers of an Indian chieftain. So it is not surprising that the circle of stars set around the head of Crawford's statue should not be visible: it requires powerful binoculars to see that Crawford ensured that each of the stars was five-pointed.[11]

Thomas Crawford – like Champollion, Amos Doolittle, Benjamin Latrobe, and Franklin – was a Mason.[12] All five Masonic Brothers were interested in secret symbols, and must have been aware of the esoteric background to the star. It is unlikely that Franklin, who had lived for some considerable time in France, was unaware of the remarkable book by his brother Mason, Theodore Tschoudy,[13] which equated the French Masonic movement with a burning five-pointed star, *L'Étoile Flamboyante*, with the triangular Eye of Providence in the middle. In the 19th century, Albert Pike traced an even more specific Masonic meaning into the star, and linked it with the sacred Sirius:

> The Ancient Astronomers saw all the great Symbols of Masonry in the Stars. Sirius still glitters in our Lodges as the Blazing Star (*l'Étoile Flamboyante*).[14]

Pike borrowed very many of his literary ideas from earlier writers, and this particular idea he took from John Fellows – a Mason who had been deeply interested in the influence of the early Mystery lore on Masonry.[15] In linking Sirius with the five-pointed star, Fellows was merely continuing an idea which had its roots in early Masonry.

We have already looked at the significance of Sirius in the astrological tradition, and observed that it still carries some of its early Egyptian associations. These associations are even more deeply expressed in the Masonic view of the star. In his exposition of the ancient Mysteries, of 1835, Fellows not only linked the blazing star of the Craft with the 'Egyptian star', Sirius, but further explained the veneration in which this is held in Masonic circles by reference to the fact that the rising of the dog-star forewarned of the flooding of the Nile. The worship of the dog-star – the Egyptian Anubis – did not begin until about 3300 BC, when its heliacal rising began to mark the inundation.[16] Fellows was writing symbolically, of a non-liquid 'Flood' of anarchy threatening his own world.

In the same work, Fellows tells us that one of the mysterious symbols of early Masonry is the *key*, said to be an attribute of the dog-headed Anubis, who was for the Egyptians an emblem of the dog-star, and keeper of the ancient Mysteries. The key was meant to symbolize the closing of one year and the opening of another, because the Egyptians formerly commenced the year at the rising of this star. When Fellows adds that this marking of the year by the star was later extended to the opening and shutting of the place of departed spirits, he was reaching into the mystery of Cancer and Capricorn, which I discussed with reference to Franzoni's *Car of History*. From this single reference, we begin to see how important Sirius really is within arcane Masonic circles – not merely because it was a star of prime importance to the Masons, but also because it was linked with Masonic symbolism in such a simple-seeming device as a key.

This same key symbolism had been used in mediaeval Christian art, to portray entrance into and between two realms – into the higher spiritual realm of the living and the lower purgatorial realm. The idea is no more perfectly expressed than in an 11th-century drawing (overleaf) which shows a key in relation to what used to be called the 'three worlds' – the heavenly, the earthly and the demonic.[17] In the top register, which is the heavenly part of the triad, St Peter opens the gates of Heaven, represented as a walled city. In the earthly division, where the good angels of Heaven struggle with the evil of Hell, St Peter uses the same key to strike away a devil who contends with the angels for a soul (the book in the hand

of the angel is the Book of Life, while that in the claws of the demon is the Book of Death). On the bottom level of Hell, an angel uses the key to lock the gates upon the unfortunates thrown in there by the demons. This mediaeval key may not have been a descendant of the Egyptian star, yet it performed much the same function. It allowed access to the heavenly regions: it represented the archetypal realm of God.

In Fellows' revealing account of Sirius, we see the complete transformation of a symbol, to serve Masonic purposes. The original *sba* star was Egyptian. Indeed, it was the most important star in ancient Egyptian times, whether as symbol of Sirius or of the god-like spiritual realm. By a transformation which was not strictly accurate from a historical standpoint, the specifically Egyptian *sba* star (which related only to the heavens) was taken as representing entrance into both Heaven and Hell, and thus by extension, the realm of the Earth, where angels and demons might meet to contend for human souls.

The blazing star of the Masons is a symbol of an accessible Heaven. It is equated with the sacred key, which can unlock the mysteries of Heaven, Earth and Hell.

When it became possible to trace the influence of this ancient star to horoscope data relating to the United States, the transformation and

1. Statue of Albert Einstein by the modern American sculptor, Robert Berks. Einstein is seated before a granite horoscope of the heavens, cast for noon of 22 April, 1979 – the day on which the statue was dedicated. It is located to the south-west of the National Academy of Sciences.

2. Bronze image of Virgo, in Egyptian style (with an antique harp), designed circa 1924 – the fifth in the sequence of zodiacal images on the south door in the entrance hall of the National Academy of Sciences. The north door of the same entrance hall continues the sequence through to the last sign, Pisces.

3. Detail of the zodiac on the glass lamp-rim designed by Sidney Waugh for the Federal Reserve Board Building. The image of Virgo (with halo) is central to Leo and Libra.
4. Columbia Protecting Science and Industry, *sculpted by Casper Buberl in 1881 for the Arts and Industries Building, of the Smithsonian Institute.*

5. Bronze plaque, with Masonic symbols and a zodiacal device in the form of a series of roundels marked with balls representing planets. Designed and sculpted by John Quincy Adams Ward, for the marble pedestal supporting the memorial statue to President Garfield, 1887.

6. The mock-Egyptian façade of 'The Hall of the Ancients' – a museum designed by Franklin W. Smith in New York Avenue, Washington DC, about 1895. Smith worked assiduously for the 'aggrandizement' of Washington DC, and many of the rebuilding schemes which were put in hand during the early decades of the 19th century were envisaged and proposed by him.

7. Masonic jewel in the form of a lunar crescent, centred with the head of the Egyptian goddess Isis, carved in a semiprecious stone. The crescent enfolds a 'flaming star' – the five-pointed star so important in Masonic symbolism. The jewel is from the Museum collection of the Supreme Council (Southern Jurisdiction) Washington DC.

8. The western façade of the Library of Congress, designed by the architects J.L. Smithmeyer and Paul J. Pelz, and finished in 1898, under the direction of Edward Pearce Casey. The Library houses no fewer than five zodiacs (see plates 9–11): there is a sixth in a spandrel above the central door, carved by Bela L. Pratt in 1895.

9. The signs of the zodiac in the central tondo of the Southeast Pavilion ceiling in the Library of Congress, painted by Elmer E. Garnsey in 1896.
10. Detail of the roundel depicting the sign Sagittarius, from the Southeast Pavilion zodiac, painted by Elmer E. Garnsey in 1896.

11. Bronze image of the zodiacal sign Pisces, in the form of a pair of dolphins. One of the twelve signs set in marble in the Main Hall of the Library of Congress.
12. Hand-painted Master Mason's apron from the Museum of the Supreme Council (Southern Jurisdiction) Washington DC. Among the many Masonic symbols are pyramids (bottom left).

13. Embroidered silk flag which was taken by the Mason-astronaut, Edwin Eugene Aldrin, to the Moon in Apollo 11, in 1969. From the collection of the Supreme Council (Southern Jurisdiction) Washington DC.
14. Egyptian hieroglyphics from the ancient Temple of Amun at Karnak. To the left is the five-pointed star to which we may trace the origins of the Masonic star, linked with Sirius.

15. The eastern rim of the Mellon Memorial Fountain, outside the National Gallery (reflected in the pool of the fountain). Visible on the rim are the image and sigil for Aries. The zodiac was designed by Sidney Waugh, 1952.
16. Detail of Sidney Waugh's image of zodiacal Cancer, on the rim of the Mellon Memorial Fountain. Between the crab's claws is the sigil for Cancer.

17. The marble statue of Benjamin Franklin, in Pennsylvania Avenue, was sculpted in 1889 by Jacques Jouvenal, and donated to Washington DC by the newspaper publisher, Stilson Hutchins. The statue was unveiled on 11 January 1889 by Franklin's great-granddaughter, Mrs H.W. Emory.

18. Allegorical figures of America weeping on the shoulder of Clio (Muse of History) for the death of her sailors during the Civil War – sculpted by Franklin Simmons in 1877. The figures on the Peace Monument face west, down Pennsylvania Avenue.
19. The east-facing allegorical figure on the Peace Monument. To the right is corn, to the left a (now broken) triangle.

20. Detail of the allegorical Masonic figure at the foot of the memorial statue to Brigadier General Albert Pike, sculpted by Gaetano Trentanove, 1901. The flag in the hand of the lamenting woman is that of the Supreme Council (Southern Jurisdiction), of which Pike was Supreme Commander.

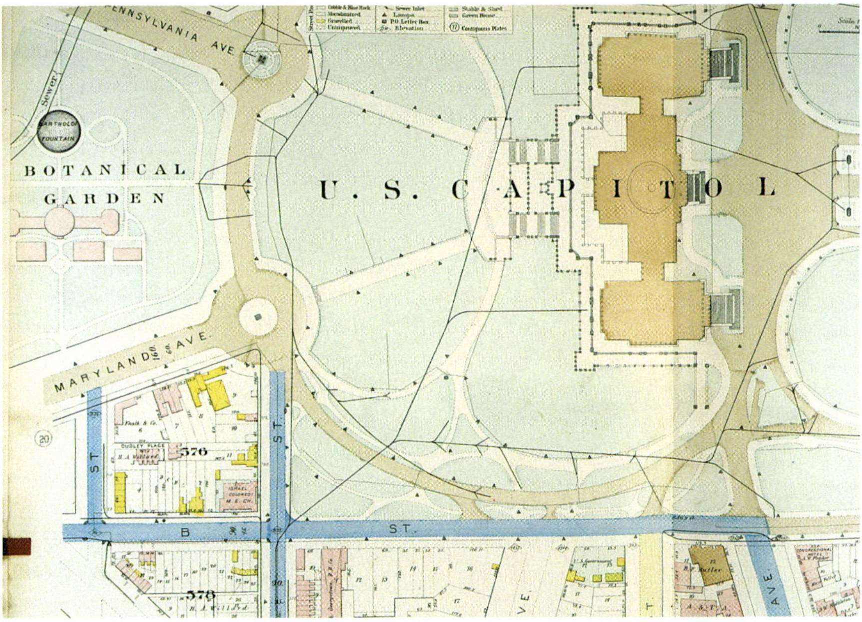

21. Sundial in Montrose Park (Georgetown) in the form of an armillary sphere, with zodiacal band. Dedicated to the memory of Sarah Louise Rittenhouse, in 1956, it marks the northernmost setting point of the Sun, as viewed from the Capitol building.

22. Plat (or plan) of the area to the west of the Capitol building, from G.M. Hopkins, Atlas of Washington DC, *1887. The circle to the top left is now occupied by the Peace Monument, and that to centre left by the Garfield memorial.*

23-24. Photographs taken shortly before Sunset on 12 August 1998, to record the extraordinary effect of the Sun's passage behind the Old Post Office tower in Pennsylvania Avenue, viewed from the high public terrace of the Capitol. The tower is of almost the same visual width as the Sun, and occults its passage only briefly, prior to its setting to the west of Pennsylvania Avenue.

adaptation of an Egyptian symbol to modern arcane purposes seemed to have been completed. As we learned on p.150, the day on which the Declaration of Independence was agreed saw the passage of the Sun over Sirius. The importance of that star was recognized in later major Masonic rituals. We saw that the laying of the cornerstone of the Washington Monument, in 1848, was arranged for the day on which the Sun passed over Sirius.

However, this development of the Sirian symbolism does not explain why a symbol which had been of prime spiritual importance to the ancient Egyptians should have been adopted (even under Masonic guidance) into the design of the national flag.[18] Nor could this communality account for the same star having been regarded as so important a device that, in 1789, it was incorporated into the obverse of the Seal of the United States.[19]

The five-pointed star – perhaps bereft of the meaning later placed upon it by the Masonic fraternities – certainly does trace its origins to ancient Egypt. It came to Europe by way of early-Christian, alchemical and Rosicrucian symbolism. The early history of the star is a romantic one, but, as it plays no further part in our study of the zodiacs of Washington DC, is not needed here. It is sufficient to note that the five-pointed star, pre-eminent in Egyptian tombs and pyramids, was eventually adopted by the Christians and appeared in their catacomb art. Thence it was preserved in the Gnostic and hermetic streams of symbolism which entered European esoteric thought in the 11th and 12th centuries. Even when the Americans began independently to forge their nation, the symbol still carried a number of arcane associations, some of which could be traced to ancient Egypt.

The idea of placing a head-girdle of stars on the statue of *Freedom* atop the dome of the Capitol had been proposed by Jefferson Davis. He said the stars would be 'expressive of endless existence and heavenly birth'.[20] This Masonic view is sufficiently spiritual for us to link it with the ancient Egyptian priestcraft. A more complicated and subtle explanation may be found in the later writings of Albert Pike, who had no hesitation in recognizing the Egyptian connection with Sirius. He could see the connection the star had with the important Masonic equivalent, the five-pointed star, which he described as 'an emblem of Fellowship'.[21]

Pike's words may appear undistinguished, but they point to considerable esoteric scholarship. The five-pointed star had been adopted into Masonry as an emblem of the 'five points of Fellowship'. Even earlier it had been used in ancient initiation centres to symbolize the

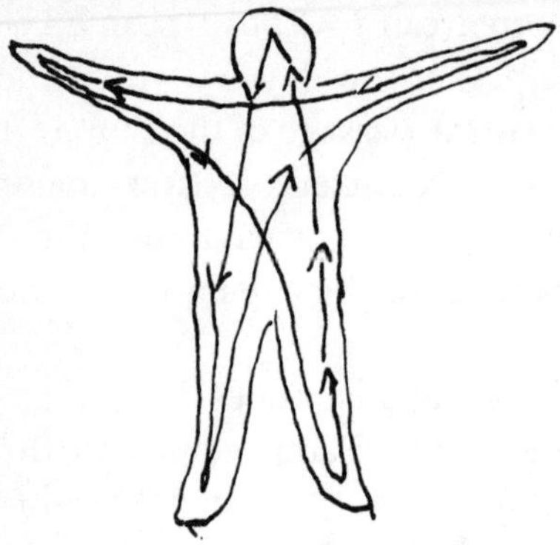

invisible spiritual world which may be penetrated by specially prepared – that is, initiated – human beings. Part of this symbolism was rooted in the esoteric teaching that the physical body of Man, as well as those spiritual bodies which sheathed the physical body, could be likened to a five-pointed star (alongside).

Pike, writing in 1871, was certainly familiar with the discoveries of Champollion, and even with the symbolism behind the proposal of Jefferson Davis. However, he chose his words with great deliberation, for he knew that within the Masonic tradition, the five-pointed star was regarded as a vestigial drawing of three men embracing in brotherhood (shown on p.117). He also knew that this symbol could be traced to surviving architectural details left by their fellow operatives, who built the great French cathedrals of the 13th century. These operatives (as the later 'speculative' Masons called them) wore tough leather aprons, for they dealt with raw stone, the rough ashlar of the later speculative Masons. Yet, for all the rudeness of their work, they were as learned in esoteric truths and in secret geometries as those later speculatives, who wore soft lambskin aprons in their rituals, and frequently had little need for physical labour. It is perhaps not surprising that when called on to devise a symbol of fraternity they should depict two men, feet apart, hugging each other, and whispering a secret word into each other's ear. Being versed in the secret geometry which was the very essence of cathedral-building, they interwove these figures so that they formed a five-pointed star.

When the mediaeval French operative mason Villard de Honnecourt drew two men embracing, enclosed within a pentagram, he was referring to this ancient hermetic device. Honnecourt's rough drawing is now famous, yet it is rarely recognized that it was merely a preliminary sketch for an idea which was often used by his contemporary Masons. The idea contained in this drawing is set in stone, not on the façade of Chartres Cathedral, as one might expect, but in the decorative stonework of a mediaeval building facing its west front. Moreover, this 'fellowship' star symbol is of such importance that it is even preserved in the stained glass of Chartres Cathedral itself, as well as in the glass of the nearby church of Saint Pierre.[22] From these survivals it is evident that the idea of the star of fellowship was ancient long before the Masonic fraternities became 'speculative', and turned the art of building with fabric into the art of building with spirit.

The Masonic explanation for this ritual star-like embrace is complex, and need not concern us here.[23] What is relevant to my argument is that such evidence as this star of fellowship suggests indicates that even if Masonry is not quite as old as some Masons claim, it is probably older than most of them believe.

The star-like gesture still called, in Masonic circles, 'the Five Points of Fellowship' is not without its more ancient significance, as Albert Pike recognized when he quoted the first-century BC Roman, Cicero, concerning the nature of the stars. Pike would have known that Cicero had many qualities in common with himself. Like Pike, Cicero was a scholar and politician, who had been swept into the maelstrom of a civil war against his will. Just as Cicero was a great speaker and lawyer, who served in the Senate and lived to see the assassination of his Caesar, so Pike was a great speaker and earned his living as a lawyer. He too lived to see the assassination of his President. Cicero, as Pike reminded us, claimed that the stars were living gods, beings 'composed of the noblest and purest portions of the ethereal substance'.[24] Pike must have realized that only an initiate could have really understood the truth of such words.

Is there a meaningful link between the ancient worlds of the Romans and Egyptians, and the symbolic credo of the Masons? Is it possible to trace the five-pointed star, stage by stage, century by century, through the secret schools which claim their own origins in ancient Egypt? To put it another way, is it reasonable to assume that the original meaning of the *sba* star had never really been lost? If so, may we recognize as legitimate the claims – frequently made in Masonic circles – that their esoteric traditions and symbols do go back, in an uninterrupted tradition, to the secret schools of ancient Egypt?

It is an interesting question, for if there is such a direct and tangible connection between the *sba* and the Masonic star, then there must be a link between the ancient Mysteries and the founding of the United States of America. Certainly, without some awareness of the extraordinary lengths which Masons and architects have gone to, to establish a connection between Washington DC and the stars, the city remains an enigma. *This is why, when we begin to look carefully at the architecture in the centre of Washington DC, we discover that it speaks an ancient language of the stars.*

*

In our own day, there is a danger that the wisdom of the stars (as opposed to the wisdom of the planets) may already be lost to astrologers. Modern astrology does not concern itself unduly with the fixed stars in chart interpretation. This was not so in the past, when the stars were held to be more powerful indicators of destiny than the planets. Even in the decades during which the federal district was being planned and the new city was being built, the ancient tradition of star-lore was still very much in evidence in astrological studies. For example, Thomas Jefferson's library included far more works on the stars than on the planets – far more works on astronomy than on astrology.[25]

This survival of the ancient star-lore (which may be traced back to 10th-century Arabic astrology, and even beyond) will become clear when we study a chart for an individual born before the siting of the federal city, who had some influence upon it in its early years of construction. Such a chart will enable us to see the extent to which fixed stars played their part in astrology at this time. What better horoscope may we take than that (below) of King George IV, the son of the British King whose maladministration lost the colonies, and who even contemplated abdicating because of that loss?

George Augustus Frederick was born on 12 August 1762, in St James's Palace, London. During the worst period of his father's insanity, in 1811, he became Prince Regent: he was therefore technically head of state when the British destroyed the official buildings of Washington DC in 1812. He became King of Great Britain and Ireland on 29 January 1820, when

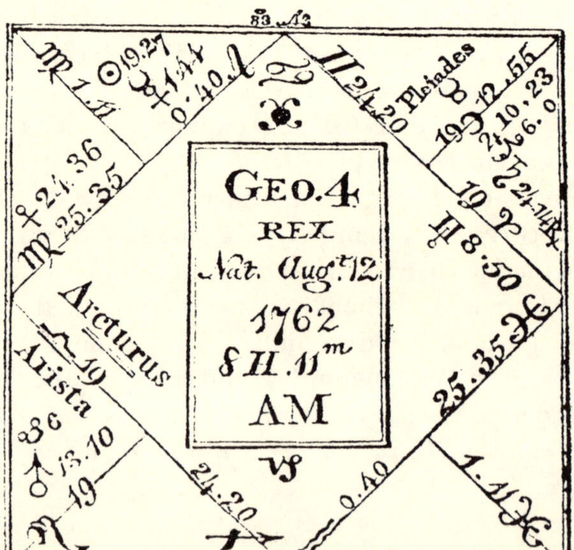

his father died, still insane. His natal horoscope, which I have selected here as an example of early-19th-century star-lore, is one cast by R. C. Cross, who has been called the first journalistic astrologer in Europe: it was published four years after George became King.[26]

The first thing we observe about this chart is that it contains the names of three stars: Arista, Arcturus and Pleiades.

When this chart was cast, it was believed that *Arista* (one of many names for Spica) was in 21 degrees of Libra in the year 1762.[27] This explains why the name of the star has been written below the symbol for *Libra 19* to the bottom left.[28] In the space above is the word *Arcturus*. This star is the *alpha* of Bootis, which in 1762 was believed to be in 22 degrees of Libra. Clearly, in the opinion of the astrologer who drew up the King's chart, Arcturus

was sufficiently close to Arista to become operative in the life of the King.

Arcturus is represented in the constellation of the giant, Bootes, as is evident from the engraving made for the astronomer Gallucci in the late 16th century.[29] The star, is located near the thigh of the spear-wielding giant (picture on page 251).

If we stick to the rounded off degrees in the King's chart, then in 1762 the star Spica was said to be close to 19 degrees Libra. The position of the star Arcturus was also given in the same degree of longitude, even though they are separated by a latitude of about 33 degrees.[30]

The majority of 19th-century astrologers who contemplated the chart of George IV would not have concerned themselves unduly with these matters: they would have read the positions of Spica and Arcturus from tables prepared by specialists, and that would have been sufficient for their purposes. Their main purpose would be to interpret the *significance* of these stellar placings. What, they might have asked, would the two stars mean when they appeared on the cusp of a king's horoscope?

A brief reading for this double placing would be that the stars would bring great popularity, but attract false male friends. The seven stars of the Pleiades (marked in the top right of the chart) would bring losses from legal affairs, and troubles with children. In sum, the fixed stars in the birth-chart do reflect some of the life events which the King later experienced.

In fact, the more proficient astrologers of the time would have considered as of greater importance a star which had been *omitted* from the horoscope. Robert Cross Smith had been delicate in his handling of the stellar influences. Perhaps wisely, given the rank of the native, the astrologer omitted the fixed star Pollux, which would have been in the same degree as the Sun in this chart. He left it out because of its evil reputation for bringing sickness and blindness, and because of the extent to which the Sun reflects symbolically the influence of the father – in this case, the insane George III, who died restrained and blind. It was mainly the working of this difficult stellar influence into the life and reign of George IV which accounts for his extraordinary unpopularity.

Fortunately, our present interest lies not so much in the accuracy of the chart, as in what we can learn from it. In fact, with one exception, the chart is reasonably accurate by modern standards, and even the reading which Smith published alongside it contained some insights.[31] What we learn from it, however, is that *in the early part of the 19th century, astrologers were just as interested in the influences of the fixed stars as in the influences of the planets.*

The chart offers us an insight into the fact that star-lore was still important at the end of the 18th century, when the grand schema for what became Washington DC was visualized, and laid out on the Earth. It is this, as much as the fact that the rising and setting of stars were linked with weather predictions, which explains why the astronomer Benjamin Banneker should have included so many references to the major fixed stars in his own almanacs.

It is almost accidental that the two stars marked on the chart of George IV – Arcturus and Arista – are of profound importance to the ground-plan of the federal city drawn up by L'Enfant in 1791.

The fundamental triangle visualized by L'Enfant when he planned the federal city was the one that may still be traced between the three most important architectural structures on his plan – the Capitol, the White House and the Washington Monument. Perhaps it was intended by L'Enfant, but if not, then history itself conspired to ensure that each of these three points of the triangle would be linked with the life and achievements of George Washington:

- The Capitol cornerstone was laid by Washington.
- Although he did not survive to live in the President's House, this did become a symbol of Washington's role as first President.
- Against all odds, the Memorial was erected to honour the achievements of Washington's life.

It is almost as though L'Enfant laid upon his virgin parchment the Masonic square as symbol of the spirit of George Washington, and dedicated its three points to the founder of the nation. In the early map of the city, these three points formed a right-angled triangle, with the 90-degree angle on the Monument, and the hypotenuse running down Pennsylvania Avenue, joining the White House with the Capitol. The longest edge of the triangle runs down the centre of the Mall (see over).

The three architectural structures which constituted the genius of L'Enfant's plan have been erected in *more or less* the same position which he suggested in 1791.[32] So fundamental is the idea of a triangle to the map of Washington DC that, in this present century, the triangular block to which this original L'Enfant gave rise has been condensed. It retains the hypotenuse of Pennsylvania Avenue, but has pulled in the right-angled triangle formed by the Mall with 15th Street, to make a smaller triangle appropriately named the *Federal Triangle*. I shall examine the symbolism of this Federal Triangle shortly: meanwhile, to distinguish it from its

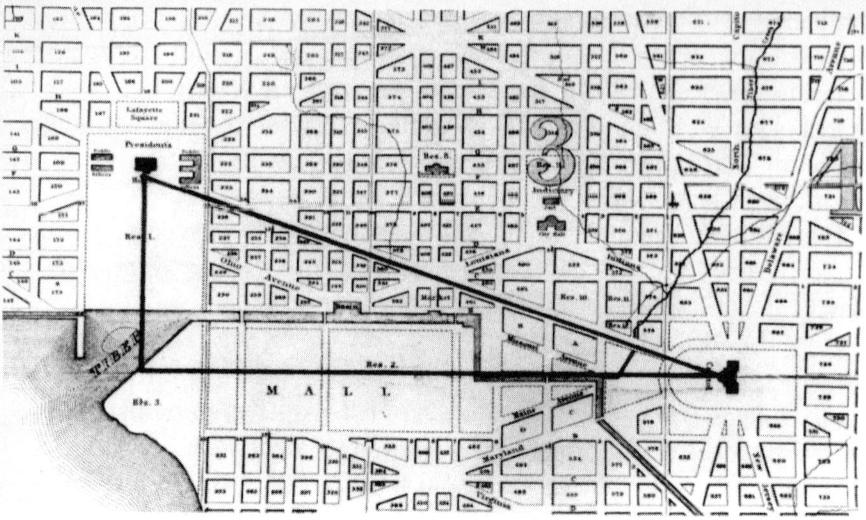

more expansive earlier original, I shall refer to this latter in future as the L'Enfant triangle.

The L'Enfant triangle is imprinted into the Earth, in much the same way as the three Masons draw a triangle with their shoes when they combine to make the Royal Arch (see p.117). The analogy might initially appear to be far-fetched. After all, the three Brothers, while drawing this earthly triangle, are also forming a triangle above their own heads, in the realm of the stars, and no doubt recalling the Trinity in the spiritual world. Their gesture was designed to unite the celestial realm of the stars with the Earth, through the medium of the human body. However, as we contemplate this drawing of a ritual embrace, we may begin to ask if the analogy suggested between this arcane gesture and the Federal Triangle is so far-fetched after all. *Is it possible that the earthly triangle of L'Enfant is also reflected in the skies?*

As a matter of fact, this idea of the duality of the upper spiritual and the lower earthly, which as we saw played a part in the light-dark symbolism of the Masonic cornerstone ceremonies, is also expressed through other Masonic symbols. The blade of the trowel, which is the fundamental implement of cornerstone-laying, and which is both an operative and a speculative Masonic tool, has two sides. When it is being used to lay the cement, one side is face down, directed towards the Earth, and literally covered in the dark matter of the Earth. In his book on Masonic symbols, the Reverend George Oliver discussed this duality, pointing out that the black trowel represented *darkness*, which was emblematic of the profound secrecy under which initiates were bound.[33] By extension of this symbolism, we must take it that the other side of the trowel represents *light*, and is presumably the light which the true Mason spreads by his example. It is certain that the Masons involved in the planning and building of the Federal Triangle who were aware of this duality.

It remains for me to demonstrate that this same triangle of light, with all its extraordinary levels of symbolism, is directly linked with that cosmic Virgin of light, the zodiacal sign Virgo.

By now, we should have few doubts that matters have been so arranged in Washington DC that Virgo – or the Masonic equivalent of Virgo, the Beautiful Virgin – dominates the symbolism of the city. This Virgoan symbolism is not restricted merely to details of statuary: it permeates even the basic planning of Washington DC itself, and reaches into the symbolism of obscure cartouches, light fittings and ceiling mouldings. Strange as it may at first seem, the Virgoan symbolism of the stars is also expressed through the triangle. The L'Enfant triangle, with its three primal buildings at its corners, is almost *the same as a right-angled triangle which may be traced in the skies, around the constellation Virgo.*

To appreciate this stellar symbolism fully, we must look first of all at the nature of the triangle, set out in L'Enfant's plan for Washington DC. Having done this, we must then relate it to a less obvious triangle, set in the stars around the constellation Virgo.

L'Enfant set down his triangle on the Earth with great care. His Masonic Brothers who continued his work ensured that each of the three points of the figure was consecrated, and linked in a meaningful relationship with the stars. I will recapitulate:

- The White House cornerstone was laid at noon on 13 October 1792. The Moon and the Dragon's Head were in Virgo.
- The Capitol cornerstone was laid by George Washington on 18 September 1793. At that time, the Sun, Mercury and the Dragon's Head were in Virgo.
- The Washington monument foundation stone was laid at noon on 4 July 1848. The Moon and the Dragon's Head were in Virgo.

Besides the obvious connection with Virgo, the one thing which these foundation charts have in common is that they each have the Dragon's Head in that sign. The Dragon's Head is the node marking the point where the path of the Moon intersects the path of the Sun. The term relates to an early phase of astrology when it was believed that the circuit of the Earth's satellite was the invisible body of a stellar dragon.[34]

In terms of the triangulation of the plan for Washington DC, this means that the corners of the L'Enfant triangle were symbolically fixed into the Earth when this beneficial point – the solar-lunar meeting point – was in Virgo.

This same triangulation is reflected in the stars gathered within and around the constellation Virgo.

One of the few modern Masons to write openly about the deeper secrets of astrology in the Craft was the Frenchman, Brunet.[35]

Among his many astute observations relating to esoteric astrology is that pertaining to the triad of stars surrounding the constellation Virgo. As Brunet points out, the constellation of Virgo is encased in a stellar triangle traced between the three first-magnitude stars, Regulus (*alpha* Leonis), Spica (*alpha* Virginis), and Arcturus (*alpha* Bootis).

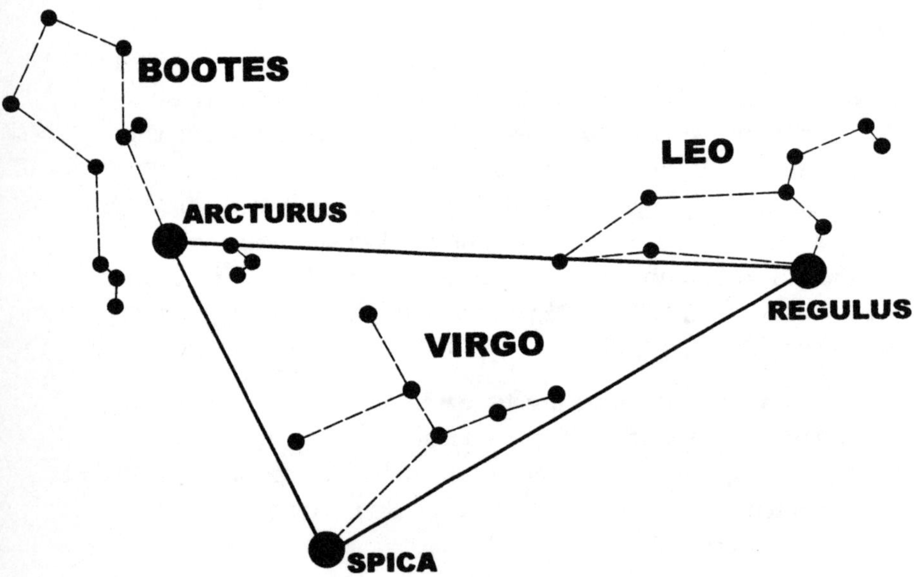

While one should not confuse the tropical sign Virgo with the constellational pattern Virgo, the undeniable fact is that this triangle of stars seems to reflect the central triangle in the plan of Washington DC. The stars of the Virgoan Triangle correspond with the L'Enfant triad, as follows:

- Arcturus falls on the White House.
- Regulus falls on the Capitol.
- Spica falls on the Washington Monument.

The White House star is Arcturus, a golden-yellow star which the Greeks called the Bear-watcher, and the Arabs, *Al Simak*, the 'one raised on high': it is a guardian star. It is also a beneficial star, which confers high renown and prosperity. Just as the White House was the first of the three to be founded, so is Arcturus said to be among the first stars to be named.[36]

The Capitol star is Regulus. As the Latin name ('Little King', 'ruler of a small kingdom') suggests, it is ambitious of power and command. It has lofty ideals and a developed sense of independence.[37]

The Washington Memorial star is Spica. This is the most powerful star in the constellation Virgo. It gives renown and advancement. In the star maps, it represents the wheat-ear held by Virgo, it also represents the largesse of nature, and its germinal power. Spica promises a future growth, nourishment, and wealth – the very things which George Washington bestowed upon the people of America.[38]

In terms of this stellar mythology, then, we can see that the symbolic relationship between the three is that Arcturus keeps its watchful eye on autocratic Regulus while, in turn, the largesse of Spica will vivify and nourish both. Although there is a limit to the application of such stellar mythologies to city planning, it is clear that the three stars typify, almost archetypally, the functions of the three material equivalents founded into the earth of Washington DC.

The following table sets down a synopsis of the archetypal relationship between the stellar triangle and the L'Enfant triangle, as mediated by the planets and nodes in Virgo:

STARS:	Arcturus	Regulus	Spica
NODES:	Node in Virgo	Node in Virgo	Node in Virgo
PLANETS:	Moon	Sun and Mercury	Moon
EARTH:	White House	Capitol	Monument

We have examined one stellar schema of the modern French writer, Brunet, to reveal something of the significance of a city plan drawn up by another Frenchman, in 1791. Is there any indication that schemas similar to that proposed by Brunet in 1979 were in existence earlier – perhaps in the late 18th century, when the L'Enfant plan was developed? Only if this is the case will it be possible for me to argue convincingly that L'Enfant (or whoever helped him with the astrology of his planning) knowingly set the three main buildings of his city according to the stars.

The idea of a stellar triangle enclosing Virgo is certainly expressed in the Masonic literature of the 19th century. In an obscure passage dealing with star patterns, Albert Pike traces several stellar triangles in the skies, and links these with Masonic symbols. He sees in one triad the Grand Master's square.[39] In another triad, which closely resembles the Virgoan triangle of Brunet – *Denebola* in Leo, Arcturus in Bootes and Spica in Virgo – he traces an equilateral triangle, which, he says, is a universal emblem of perfection.[40] It is quite possible that this specifically Masonic approach to triangular star patterns in Virgo is the source of Brunet's own carefully traced 'Grand Master's square' around Virgo.

A careful search reveals similar notions of star-triads in the astronomical literature of the 18th century. In truth, Brunet's sophisticated approach to the Virgo triangle (while perhaps sparked off by his reading of Albert Pike) was really developing very ancient astronomical ideas. Indeed, there is nothing very original in Brunet's Virgoan triangle. As early as the first century of our era, the Egyptian astronomer Ptolemy[41] gave many examples of how to distinguish stars by tracing straight lines between three or more stars, from constellation to constellation. These ideas were evidently old even in Ptolemy's day, for in his text on the stars he constantly acknowledges that his information was derived from the ancient Greek astrologer Hipparchus.[42] The method Ptolemy followed had been the accepted way of locating the stars or describing them, without the aid of diagrams, for hundreds of years, if not millennia.

Although the ancients used different names and followed rather cumbersome methods of describing the stars, they recognized that the simplest way of locating them was by means of imaginary straight lines. They knew, for example, that a line drawn from Regulus (in the heart of Leo) to Arcturus, in the lower body of Bootes, would pass through four stars (the *beta* of Leo, and the *nu* of Bootes). This line then provided a standard, or fiducial, for locating and describing the positions of other stars.

The importance of Regulus and Spica in star-gazing cannot be overemphasized. They are both so close to the ecliptic that they were often used in ancient astronomies as fiducials for tracing this hidden solar pathway in the night skies. The ancients took both these stars as markers of two of the so-called 'lunar mansions' – an ancient system by which the ecliptic was divided into 28 divisions, based on the mean daily movement of the Moon.[43]

The ancient star-gazers would have known that a line drawn from Regulus to Spica would pass very close to the *Zavijava* (*beta* Virginis), and that a line drawn from Spica to Arcturus would pass very close to the *zeta* of Virgo. In ancient times, the technique of drawing such straight lines was a useful way of locating stars against recognized stellar patterns. The implications of this will become clear when we look into the night sky, and study the stars ourselves.

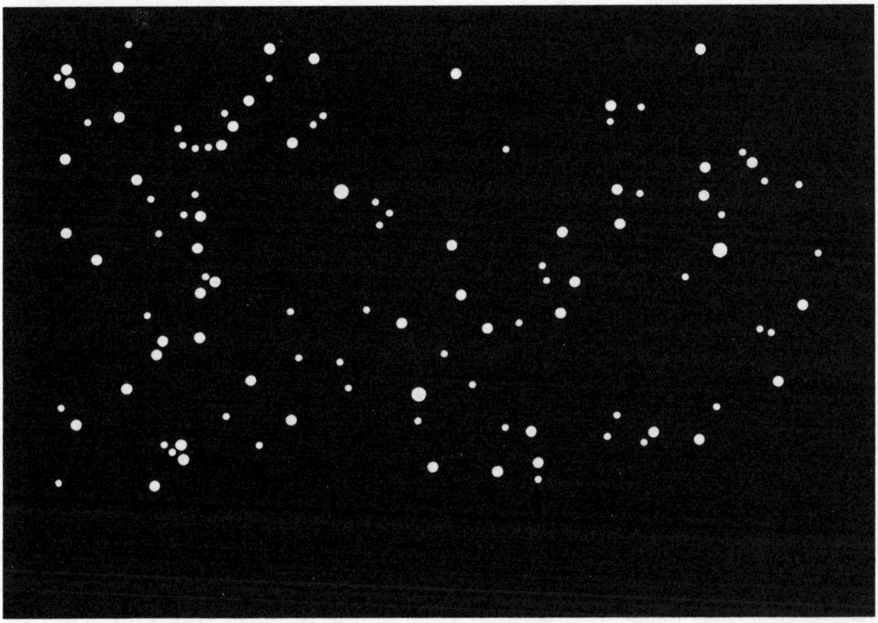

Undoubtedly, even a simplified image of a section of the night skies (see above) will look confusing to those not familiar with star-gazing. However, the minute such an identifiable pattern as the Virgoan triangle is drawn in (overleaf), it becomes relatively easy to distinguish the stars of the constellation Virgo, merely from the position of Spica at the right angle. It is just as easy to make out the constellations of Leo and Bootes (to right and left, respectively). Important to our study here is that a survey of the 12 constellational images along the ecliptic reveals that *Virgo is the only sign which may be described accurately as being located in a clear triangulation of first-magnitude stars.*

We know from such sources as Ptolemy that the ancients used this practical form of distinguishing the constellations. However, we must ask, is there any evidence that this form of star-gazing was known in the

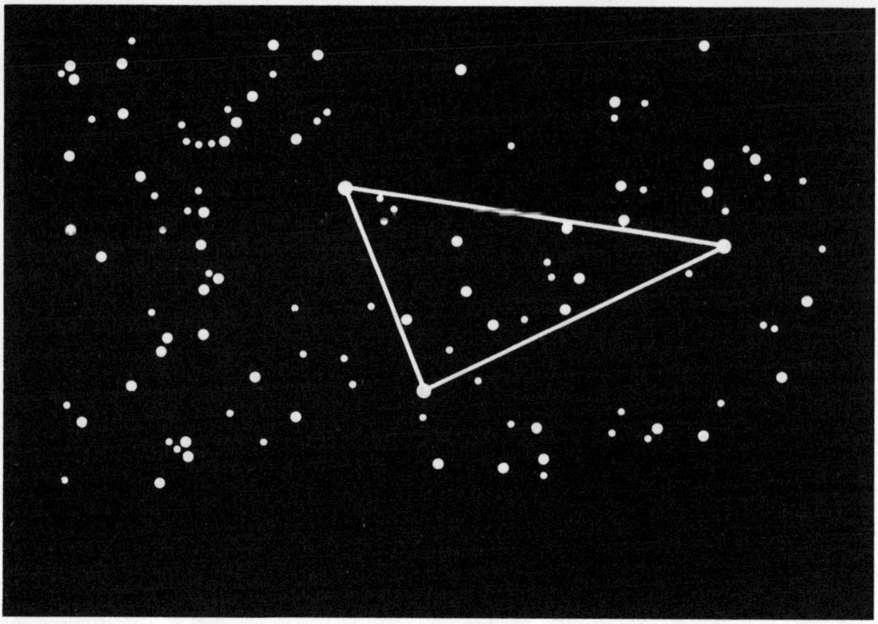

18th century? Or was Brunet's suggestion merely a clever yet archaic afterthought – a throwback to ancient astronomies, with no particular relevance to the building of such a city as Washington DC? To answer this, we need to turn to a late-18th-century account of such an approach to the stars, in a book known to have been available in Maryland. We can do no better than examine the study made by the French astronomer, Montignot, of Ptolemy's descriptions. This study is presented as a parallel translation into French of Ptolemy's original Greek work on the stars.[44] It will be recalled that this work was in the personal library of Thomas Jefferson, and eventually found its way into the Library of Congress.[45]

If we turn to what the Egyptian star-gazer had to say about Virgo, we shall see that Ptolemy (following Hipparchus, upon whom he leans heavily throughout) believed that a straight line drawn through two stars in Virgo would trace a line through the right foot of Bootes. There are, he tells us, two stars on that line which joins Arcturus and the southern foot of the Virgin. Having linked Virgo with the constellation 'above' it, Hipparchus then links her with the snake-like stars of Hydra below. Ptolemy also tells us that Hipparchus had observed that, between the star called Spica and the second star towards the tail of Hydra (*gamma*), three stars are touched by the same straight line.

From the analogies I have drawn between the three stars and the three points of the L'Enfant triangle, we may no longer doubt that the designers of Washington DC intended to draw a connection between a segment of the skies and their city. That they elected to use a triangle as the basis of this connection is perhaps a reflection of the importance of the triangle in Masonic symbolism. The question is, can we take this analogy further? Can we find *more* evidence of there being a direct connection between the stars and the triangle which lies at the heart of Washington DC?

The answer to this question is found in the *Federal Triangle* at the downtown heart of the city. However, before we look closely at the symbolism of this triangle, I would like to point to something else about the larger triangle which joins the White House, the Capitol and the Washington Monument into a three-in-one unity.

On the original L'Enfant/Ellicott maps, there is no doubt that the intention was to join these three federally important points into a perfect right-angled triangle. The maps and the accompanying descriptions are testimony to this. However, this did not happen. The three elements are *not* united by a perfect triangle at all. As we saw, when the site for the Washington Monument was chosen, it was decided that the foundations were not secure enough in the place indicated by L'Enfant. In order to ensure a secure foundation, the Monument was sited in such a position that it was neither on the north-south line from the White House, nor on the line extended due west from the Capitol building. It was set to the east of the north-west line, and to the south of the east-west line.

The displacement of the Monument from the position surveyed by Ellicott in 1791 was 371.6 feet east of the original meridian line (which ran through the White House) and 123.17 feet south of the east-west line, which was centred on the Capitol dome. These figures may not seem to be excessive, but there is one way to see just how massive they are in terms of orientation. It is possible to test the displacement from the meridian line by standing with your back to the centre of the Jackson equestrian memorial, 100 yards or so to the north of the White House, and centring your vision with the middle of the White House portico. You will now be looking exactly down the meridian line as set out by Andrew Ellicott, in 1791, before any important buildings were erected in the federal city. In theory – that is, in accordance with L'Enfant's own proposals – you should be able to see the Washington Monument towering over the centre of the White House. In fact, the Monument is displaced so far to the east, that it is hidden behind the trees. This experiment will give you some idea of just how far removed the Monument is from the site originally envisaged.

Unfortunately, it is not possible to play a similar sighting game with the Monument on the east-west line. Faced with the *fait accompli* of a displaced Monument on the important east-west line, when the Park Commissioners redesigned the Mall, under the impetus of the McMillan plan, they decided to *realign the Mall to the Monument.* This has been done with such consummate artistry that one becomes aware of it only when one learns the history of this orientation, or studies the map of Washington DC with great care. All this was very clever – and perhaps even necessary, in terms of park design – but if Ellicott and L'Enfant had intended the Monument to act as a solar marker (as I am sure they had), then the purpose of that orientation was completely lost. Even Jefferson's Pier was removed, so that anyone now wishing to establish what the true east-west line of the Capitol dome is, must carry a magnetic compass and adjust for true north!

Of course, all these apparently minor adjustments were made by architects who were not aware that Ellicott or L'Enfant had some cosmic plan in mind when they designed the city. Even so, we must ask: do these alterations imply that the sacred triangle visualized in the early plans was marred? Did they diminish the arcane significance of the original plan of Washington DC? Whatever the answer to this question, we must recognise that the original right-angled triangle designed by L'Enfant is no longer a perfect right-angle.

It is here that one of the true wonders of the city begins to emerge. My assumption is that the earthly triangle of White House/Capitol/Monument was intended as a reflection of the stars around the constellation Virgo. Now, the truth is that the three stars I have used to symbolize this triangle – Arcturus, Spica and Regulus – are not themselves arranged in a perfect right-angled triangle!

This deviation can be measured against the ecliptic. Regulus is, to all intents and purposes, on the ecliptic, but Spica is two degrees to the south. When these arcs are applied to the displacement of the Monument, the correspondence is so close that one has the impression that it must have been planned. When the sky triangle is measured against the earth-triangle, the correspondence between its two is almost exact.

Spica is not exactly at a right angle with Arcturus, as they do not set at the same time.[46] The differences are slight, yet highly significant. The distribution of the stars resembles closely the triangle drawn between the three federal points. In other words, *the deviation from the right angle made by the siting of the Monument is consistent with that found in the stellar triangle round Virgo.* Is it possible that someone involved in the original siting of the Monument knew about these cosmic alignments?

There are two tentative conclusions we may draw from these remarkable facts. First, the final placing of the Washington Monument may not have been determined purely by geotectonic motives, but in order to establish a closer correspondence between the earthly triangle and the stellar triangle around Virgo. Second, it is quite in accordance with the original plan of the federal city to regard the Mall, or the western projection of the Capitol grounds, as being symbolic of the ecliptic.

Chapter Ten

> The right angled triangle of unequal sides . . . which . . . squares the *south* and the *west* – the symbol of justice and representative in symbolic Masonry of Justice and Integrity.
>
> (Henry P. Homes Bromwell, *Restorations of Masonic Geometry and Symbolry*, 1905)

The Mason Dudley Clarke, a personal friend of President Theodore Roosevelt, was deeply interested in astrology, and discussed the President's own horoscope with him on several occasions.[1] The chart appears to have been cast at the request of Theodore's father when the boy was only ten hours old; he had been born at 11.03 a.m. on 27 October 1858, in New York City.[2] It seems that in later life Theodore Roosevelt mounted an enlarged figure of this horoscope on a chessboard, perhaps humorously relating life to an intellectual game.

Roosevelt, the 26th President of the United States, was a Mason of high initiation – a man of action, as well as of deep contemplation.[3] One imagines that it must have been inevitable that, on 8 June 1907, he should have been invited by the Grand Master Francis J. Woodman to spread the cement of the cornerstone and deliver an oration at the new Masonic Temple on 13th Street and New York Avenue.

This ceremonial was held in public, but it was only those in close proximity to the President who noticed that, as he tied his Masonic apron, he exposed the pistol he was carrying in his hip pocket.

Was the pistol a reminder of the fact that his predecessor, William McKinley – also a Mason – had been assassinated six years earlier while exposed to the public gaze in Buffalo, New York?[4] Given Roosevelt's knowledge of astrology, it is more likely that he was aware from a study of his chart that on 8 June 1907 his life would be under threat. On that day, Neptune was exactly upon his natal Moon, while

Mars was passing over its own place in his birth-chart.[5]

Roosevelt was already famous as a man of action and sophistication when he came to the presidency, and well-known for his interest in architecture. Plans to improve Washington DC had been in the air for some time, and it was probably nothing more than coincidence that the new Masonic Temple was not far from the Hall of the Ancients, where Franklin W. Smith, and a large number of well-disposed Masons, had fought so hard to put such improvements into operation. Roosevelt became President just in time to open the first exhibition of the McMillan commission, of 1901 – a commission which was to change the face of Washington DC. Thus it happened that it was a Mason with some knowledge of astrology who presided over the opening of a wide-sweeping plan, devised under the name of a brother Mason, to return Washington DC to the stars.[6] In particular, this involved developing a triangle of built-up land to the south of Pennsylvania Avenue and to the north of B Street (below). This triangle was inset in the same triangle that I have shown to have been connected with the three stars Spica, Regulus and Arcturus.

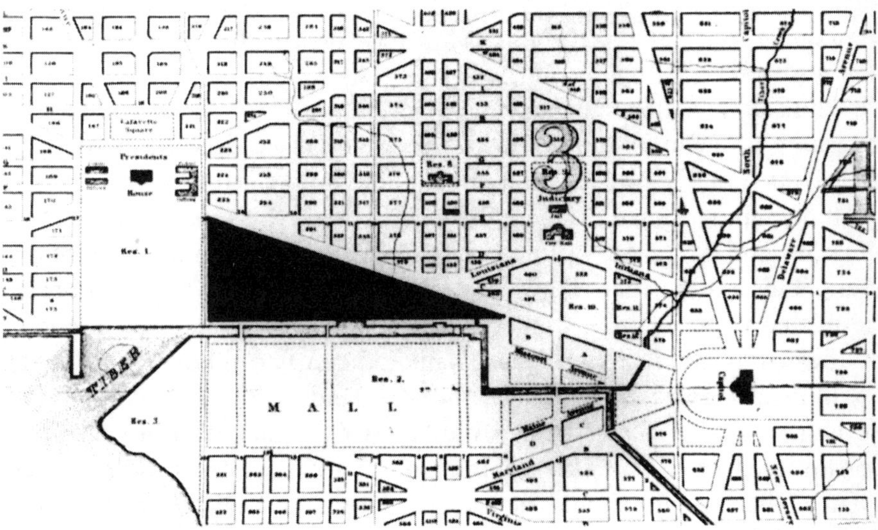

When L'Enfant laid down his famous map of the city, he designed the avenue which was first called B Street, and later Constitution Avenue, so that it ran from the east, along the northern edge of the Capitol and along the muddy flats called Foggy Bottom that bordered on the Potomac.

This avenue paralleled the Mall, which, in terms of the celestial science which we have just examined, was the equivalent of the ecliptic. So far as the early designers of the city were concerned, at the eastern end of the Mall was the star Regulus, in the form of the Capitol. Near the western end (overlooking the Potomac, in those days) was Spica, in the form of the monument site which was later dedicated to George Washington.

In his map of 1791, L'Enfant had not visualized a traffic-bearing road marking this route between the Capitol and the Washington Monument: he seems to have intended the Mall to be a garden-like promenade. He called this wide route the 'Grand Avenue'. It was a term that led to some confusion later, as George Washington had referred to Pennsylvania Avenue as the 'Grand Avenue', and placed great emphasis on the importance of this thoroughfare that was to link the Legislature with the Executive.[7]

This elementary design remained through the years as a warning that the Executive should keep a watchful eye on the Legislature (and visa-versa). It also laid the foundations for a meaningful triangle (see picture on page 265), capable of a wide range of terrain adjustments on the map of Washington DC. Howsoever this adjustment was made, the triangle would still reflect the stellar triangle formed by Regulus, Spica and Arcturus – provided, of course, the hypotenuse of the triangle lay upon Pennsylvania Avenue.

The original right-angle lay in the Mall, on the original site for the Washington Monument, yet it had been visualised even in the days of L'Enfant and Ellicott as susceptible to a more northerly line. In the relationship which had been established between the stars and the Earth, Regulus and Spica were placed close to the ecliptic, the pathway of the Sun. This means that the Mall itself was intended to be the Earthly equivalent of the ecliptic. The Mall was itself a sacred solar way: the Way of the Sun, while Pennsylvania remained the Way of Man.

The roadway which paralleled the Mall, and which was contiguous to it, was later called Constitution Avenue. It was a name derived from the most sacred of all concepts behind the spiritual concept of the United States, that people should be governed by a formulated constitution rather than by an hereditary tyranny. Constitution Avenue ran in parallel with L'Enfant's Grand Avenue, and was thus a *via sacra*, or sacred route.

Something of this sacred nature is still reflected in the symbolism which lies along Constitution Avenue. Indeed, it is quite astonishing that the section of the avenue which marks the eastern end of the Capitol grounds (at the intersection of Constitution with First Street) is occupied by the Dirksen building, which contains no fewer than 12 complete zodiacs, incorporated into 6 arcane patterns. On the other hand, near the western end of Constitution Avenue, are no fewer than three zodiacs, one huge horoscope and one planetary arrangement. It would appear that the designers of Washington DC marked off this central section of Constitution Avenue with a stellar symbolism which proclaims to those with ears to hear that the avenue is indeed cosmologically sacrosanct – confirming that it is a sacred road, linked with the stars.

Let us examine the nature of these stellar and zodiacal symbols more closely, starting with the one to the east, touching upon the grounds of the Capitol.

In September 1980, Cliff Young finished restoring the 19th-century paintings of the zodiacal signs by Constantino Brumidi in one of the northern corridors of the Capitol building.[9] Similar restorations had been made before, because in the room above the corridor was a Senators' bathroom from which water occasionally overflowed.[10] Even when Cliff Young began the work, the 12 images probably did not contain a scrap of the pigment applied by the genius Brumidi, who had used water-colour directly on the plaster, instead of tempera paints or fresco. Cliff Young later stated in a letter that the pictures had been repaired many times before and that 'the artistic standard of this work was very amateurish'.[11]

The restoration work had taken Young 16 weeks. If the records of correspondence in the files are anything to go by, the project had begun in the late 1950s. In 1957, a search had been made by the Acting Architect of the Capitol to obtain suitable astrological reference material for this restoration work.[12] Towards this end, the Office of the Architect wrote to the publishers of an encyclopaedia in Chicago, to see if their editor could provide suitable images of the signs of the zodiac. The publishers, in their innocence, sent back images not of the 12 zodiacal signs, but of the 12 constellations. The fact that some of the material provided as the basis for Cliff Young's restorations was inaccurate – being, among other things, images of the constellations rather than the 12 zodiacal signs – may explain why one or two of the 'restored' images in the Capitol corridor are inaccurate.[13]

As an outstanding example of how deviant the images of Brumidi have become, we need only glance at the zodiacal sign apportioned to December. This was certainly based on the image of the goat-fish (the traditional creature of Capricorn), save that, unaccountably, the artist has turned the horned goat into a unicorn. It is very likely that Cliff Young –

or one of his predecessors – had mistaken the tuft of hair on the forehead of the goat-fish for an incipient horn, and had extended it. Perhaps it had been extended slowly, over a period of decades, through a sequence of restorations.

A tracing taken from an 18th-century star-map engraving (above) shows the kind of material which was submitted to Young to aid his work: a person unfamiliar with the iconography of Capricorn might well be tempted to read the hair-tuft as a horn. This, in turn, might encourage him to turn the image into a fishy monoceros.[14]

The original Brumidi drawings have not survived, and so little of his original 'fresco' in the zodiacal corridors is from his brush that it is misleading to refer to them as Brumidi pictures at all. It has proved impossible to determine at what time the corridor Capricorn grew the horn. Research into the idea of a unicorn in zodiacal art has proved fairly unrewarding, though at least one ancient Roman gem – a cornelian – shows the sign Virgo with an attendant unicorn. This is perhaps not surprising, as there are mediaeval legends which tell of the taming of the unicorn by the Virgin Mary, in consequence of which the link between the Mother of Jesus and the stellar Virgin has always been strong. Were not the other 11 zodiacal signs also on the cornelian, then it might have been interpreted as being purely Christian.[15]

When we consider the rich astrological symbolism in Washington DC, we see that there was no reason why any restorer should have been so ill-provided for work on a zodiacal series as Cliff Young. Two of the seven zodiacs in the nearby Library of Congress are not only totally accurate in the representation of the zodiacal images, but are superb examples of the arcane tradition of astrology which has run through the design of Washington DC for over a century and a half. There is no shortage of zodiacal pictures in the city.

My main purpose in mentioning the 'months' of Brumidi is not to lament their destruction. My purpose has been to point to the fact that, in the north wing of the Capitol, there is a sequence of zodiacal pictures.

Across the avenue from the north wing of the Capitol is another building which contains a number of ceiling zodiacs. This is now called the Dirksen Office Building, after the politician Everett McKinley Dirksen. (It is interesting that the dedication to this remarkable man, cut into a marble block near the entrance to the building, should have been written by a Brother, to acknowledge his achievements.[16])

Before looking at these zodiacs, I would like to make the general point that the section of Constitution Avenue which runs contiguous with the Capitol grounds is edged on either side by zodiacs. It seems as though the designers of the city have gone to great lengths to ensure that this eastern section of the avenue is, so to speak, sealed off cosmically by stellar images. It is as though the sacred stretch of the *via sacra* is symbolically terminated at the Capitol building.

A further set of files in the archives of the Architect of the Capitol indicates just how easy it is for errors to be made in regard to images of the zodiac – particularly those which appear on public display in Washington DC.

In May 1974, one Senator Biden made an official inquiry about the astrological symbols on the ceiling of the Senate Post Office and the Civil Service Committee room. An employee of what was then called the Art and Research Staff in the Capitol responded.[17] She told the Senator's secretary that the symbols 'were just decorative devices that have been in use for many years in the Capitol Hill buildings'. The information was inaccurate: the symbols on the ceiling of this room in the Dirksen Office Building[18] are esoteric, and far from being merely decorative devices.

These 'decorative devices' were designed by the New York architects Eggers and Higgins in 1958.[19] It is evident from their work that this firm had considerable inside knowledge of the Masonic symbolism of the Beautiful Virgin. Of course, a person not expert in such matters may be forgiven for not realizing that the zodiacs of the Capitol buildings are more than merely decorative. Few people who live in Washington DC seem to be aware of just how much astrological imagery surrounds them, and even fewer are aware that most of these images are linked with the Mysteries of Virgo.

The extraordinary thing about these official misunderstandings[20] is that even as the Capitol zodiac was being restored with such ineptitude, and even as Senator Biden's question was being fobbed off, the arcane tradition of the zodiac was alive and well in Washington DC.

According to the records, the Additional Senate Office Building – in popular parlance the Dirksen building – was constructed between 1947 and 1958 to relieve the demand for office space in the Capitol. The site had been acquired for additional Senate office building, and had been cleared (in some cases forcibly, against the wishes of the owners) of 78 properties before 1949.[21]

By 1957, Fred Othman, a reporter on the *Washington Daily News*, was recording that the building – the very lap of senatorial luxury – would be finished within a year. Meanwhile, the journalist was picking his way through what he called 'debris deluxe' amidst the usual builders' chaos of a well-scaffolded site. In spite of his sense of public outrage at the costs, Othman could see that already the splendour of the building was beginning to show through: a huge zodiacal ceiling moulding was being lifted into place in one of the committee rooms.[22]

For all his skill as a reporter, Othman could not draw Harvey Middleton, the engineer in charge of these activities, into discussing the high costs or explaining why the building had been allowed to exceed by five million dollars the seventeen million allocated.[23] In retrospect, these sums of money do not seem so important. Certainly, few astrologers, and no one interested in the history of astrology, is likely to lament the vast expenditure. On six floors of this building are specially designed conference rooms, with podiums and ornate ceilings. In every case, their ceilings are inset with recessed square panels each containing a sign of the zodiac, along with its corresponding sigil (figure 28). However, this decorative arrangement is no simple sequence of 12 images – altogether there are 38 zodiacal images on each ceiling.

Since this curious zodiacal arrangement is found on 6 ceilings, the implication is that there are 38 × 6 recessed designs in the building – no fewer than 228 zodiacal images! The architects were clearly intending to make some zodiacal or cosmic statement about the building which they erected to the north-east of the Capitol, on Constitution Avenue. Did the architects feel that those in conference deliberating the future of the

United States should be aware that the spiritual world is above, and that its invisible exigencies should not be ignored?

Each of the zodiacal images and sigils is in bas-relief, with delicately modulated lines that pick out the salient points of the imagery, which is, on the whole, traditional. The sign Cancer (above, left) is represented in the usual guise of a crab, while the image for Libra (above, right) shows a pair of scales hanging from the horns of what might be a steer – perhaps a unique attempt to render a zodiacal image in strictly American iconography. As is usual in Washington DC, the image for Virgo is particularly well thought-out, and, to some extent, escapes the traditional form. The Virgin is represented playing a harp, a decorative item of which is a small ram or curly-horned sheep (figure 28).

The designs of the ceilings on the various levels of the building are identical in structure, but sometime in the mid-1990s were painted.[24] On all of them the zodiacal images have been left in white plaster, but their fields, or surrounds, have been painted in a flat matt monochrome, in a different colour for each ceiling.

At first glance, the order of these 38 signs appears to be meaningless. The full range of 12 signs is repeated twice. Running the longer length of each room are a series of 12 signs, starting at one side with Aries, the first sign, and on the opposite side with the last sign, Pisces (see over).

The two widths contain seven signs each, starting at one end with Gemini (through to Sagittarius) and at the opposite end with Sagittarius (through to Gemini). Although the images follow the natural sequence, the arrangement appears to be haphazard – indeed, the bas-relief zodiac signs seem to be merely 'decorative', without any of the usual hermeneutic qualities. One is left with the impression of considerable disorder – until the underlying structure is revealed. The entire sequence consists of 38 individual signs, arranged as follows, with a floral motif in each of the corners.

*	AR	TA	GE	CN	LE	VG	LB	SC	SG	CP	AQ	PI	*
GE													SG
CN													SC
LE													LB
VG													VG
LB													LE
SC													CN
SG													GE
*	PI	AQ	CP	SG	SC	LB	VG	LE	CN	GE	TA	AR	*

To the casual observer, this arrangement may appear to be haphazard. In fact the entire sequence has been arranged to place the sign Virgo in a very special position. The two pairs of Virgo (VG) face each other across the room.

Because of this careful arrangement, the four images of Virgo form a distinctive cross in the ceiling. It is as though the architect or designer wished to emphasize the Christian nature of this stellar Virgin. The fact that this cross may be traced in the decorative arrangement may explain something of the unusual symbolism in this image for Virgo (figure 28), who is playing the harp.

Part of the inner meaning of the figure may rest on the idea of the Virgin being involved in playing the music of the spheres. In addition, one cannot help observing the emphasis placed on the number four in the image. The Virgin's hair is divided into four falling ringlets. Her harp has four strings. Perhaps the sculptor chose an animal support in order to permit the harp to rest upon four legs? Even the distinctive sigil for the sign (left) emphasizes the four descenders in an un-traditional way.

May we take it that this emphasis on four is designed to point the way to the fourfold cross which lies behind the secret symbolism of this Virgoan arrangement? It would almost appear as though the architect had attempted to represent a Christian view of the early pagan imagery – sanctifying, by means of the cross, the pagan goddess of the skies. On mature reflection, however, it becomes evident that *the cross itself* is involved with orientation in space. Uniquely, we find that in this ceiling the four cardinal points are directed outwards, *as though Virgo were at every extreme of the cosmos.*

Since the Dirksen building is integrated into one of the grids laid down by L'Enfant, the long orientation of the ceiling is literally on the east-west orientation, which means that each of the images for Virgo is directed symbolically to one of the four cardinal points. Could there be any more obvious reflection on the dominance of Virgo over Washington DC?

If we are to read the Dirksen zodiacal symbolism correctly, we must see it as an injunction to study the orientation of Washington DC on cosmological lines. As a matter of fact, this same insistence on the fourfold is exhibited time and time again in the arcane symbolism of Constitution Avenue – mainly through a programme of symbolism based on the four Elements derived from the astrological repertoire.

In essence, the vast zodiacal cross of Virgo on the Dirksen building was a sophisticated attempt to reaffirm the importance of Virgo to the city, and perhaps to point to further secrets of orientation involving the great cross of the cardinal points against which Washington DC was aligned. The symbolism seemed to keep alive the great secret of the Beautiful Virgin which could be traced back for well over a century in the city.

This Dirksen astrology had really been the last flowering of a move to return Washington DC to the magical vision of L'Enfant and Ellicott, which we shall explore in the next chapter. The intention of the planners seems to have been to seal off the eastern end of Constitution Avenue, alongside the Capitol, with this influx of zodiacs. We shall see that they did the same thing with the western end of that avenue, which I have called the *via sacra* of the L'Enfant plan.

At the western end of Constitution Avenue are two beautifully designed buildings, with very different functions. One is the National Academy of Sciences, the other the Federal Reserve. Both buildings are replete with arcane symbolism, and both exhibit two delightful and unique zodiacs. The National Academy of Sciences, has an external zodiac in horoscopic form in the modern statue of Einstein, which was sculpted by Robert Berks in 1979. Perhaps we should begin our examination of the western symbolism of Constitution Avenue by glancing at this statuary, which includes what is probably the most remarkable horoscope in the world.

Earlier, I discussed the 'degree of felicity' which united the founding moment of the Capitol Building with the founding moment of the Washington Monument. What I did not say at that point was that, in addition to marking this 'degree of felicity', the Dragon's Head of the

1848 chart was *exactly* on a powerful fixed star. This star is the *beta* of constellation Virgo, which in the tradition is called *Zavijava*, and which was usually shown in the star maps set in the wing of Virgo (figure 13).[25]

In the astrological tradition, this star is entirely beneficial, and so one would wish to see it playing an important role in a foundation chart. However, it just happens that this was also the star used to re-confirm Einstein's theory, during the solar eclipse of 21 September 1922, which occurred in 28 degrees of Virgo. In view of this, it is probably no surprise that an imposing memorial to Einstein has been erected in Washington DC.

The sculptor Robert Berks represents Einstein sitting on a semi-circular bench of white granite (plate 1). The smooth surface in front of him is actually a representation of a sky map – a sophisticated horoscope – with the major stars and planets inset into the marble.

The marble surround on which the bronze statue is placed is marked out with stainless steel studs which reveal the positions of more than 2,700 stars and ten quasars, along with the Sun, Moon, planets and asteroids. It is in effect a 28-foot diameter horoscope for noon on 22 April 1979, when the statue was dedicated.[26] It is probably the largest marble horoscope in the world. Of course, I do not suggest that it is the largest

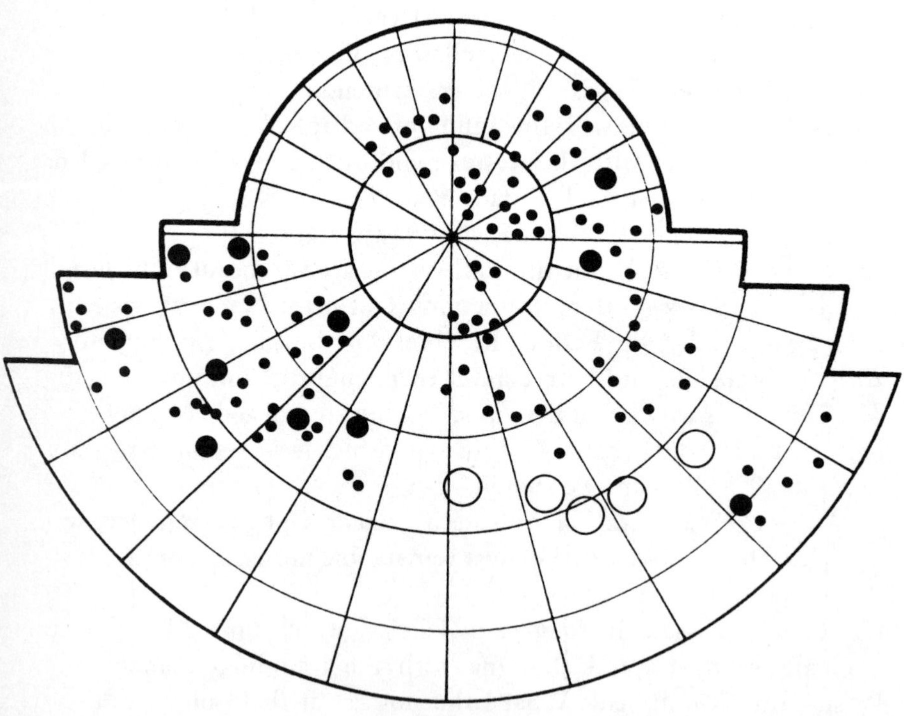

zodiac in the world (that in the Great Hall of the Library of Congress is much larger), but I know of no horoscope of this size.[27]

A simplified schema of this horoscope is set out opposite: the black dots represent the positions of important stars, while the circles represent the planets. Below is a graphic key to these stars and planets, with the stellar patterns marked out in the form of the familiar constellations.

These constellations, marked with their major stars, along with the visible planets, may be read from the following key:

1. The star *Sirius* in constellation *Canis Major*
2. The star *Procyon* in constellation *Canis Minor*
3. The stars *Betelgeuse* and *Rigel* in *Orion*
4. The star *Pollux* in constellation *Gemini*
5. The star *Aldebaran* in constellation *Taurus*
6. The star *Capella* in constellation *Auriga*
7. The star *Deneb* in constellation *Cygnus*
8. The star *Vega*
9. The star *Fomalhaut* in *Piscis Austrinus*
10. The constellation *Ursa Major*
11. The constellation *Ursa Minor*
12. The constellation *Draco*
13. The constellation *Hercules*
14. Sun in zodiacal Taurus
15. Mercury in zodiacal Aries
16. Mars in zodiacal Aries
17. Moon in zodiacal Pisces
18. Venus in zodiacal Pisces

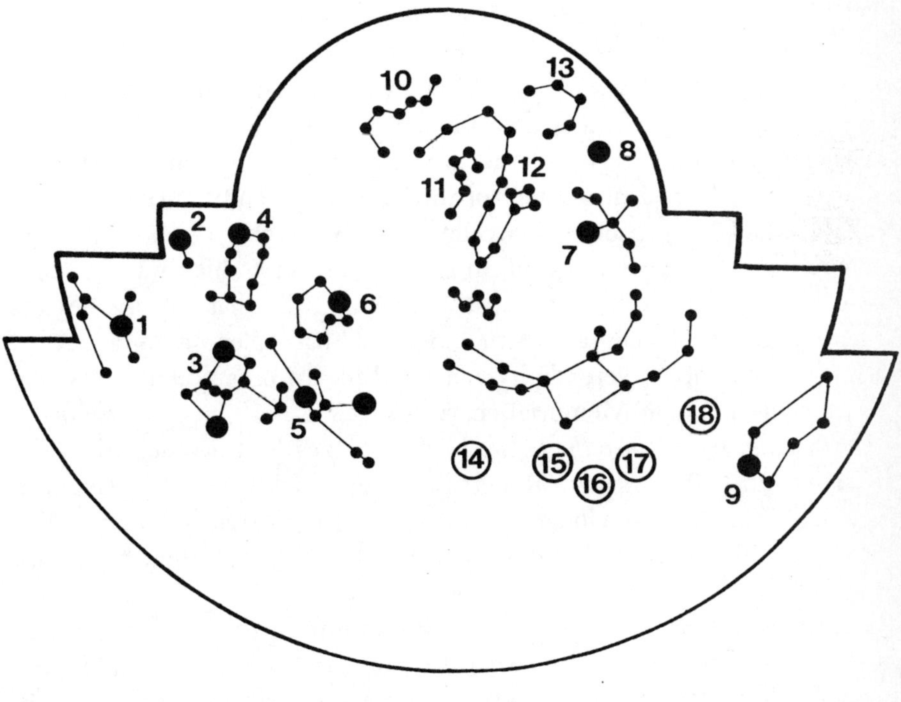

The bronze statue of Einstein looks in some puzzlement at the pavement of stars, and almost negligently tilts the side of his shoe over the northern stars of Bootes and Hercules. With his left hand, Einstein supports against his leg a sheaf of papers, on the top one of which are written the formulae which summarize his most important mathematical equations – the photo-electric effect, the general theory of relativity, and the expression of the equivalence of energy and matter.

Einstein, who applauded Berks' portrait of himself in 1954,[28] would not have foreseen that his 21-foot-high statue would become among the most popular of all photographic perches for youngsters visiting Washington DC. Children now scramble upon his back, more often than not wrapping their legs around his neck so that their knees touch his ample moustache, before smiling for the camera. The classical theme of the contrast between youth and age is delightful, and the freedom of the children to do these acrobatics seems to echo Einstein's expressed desire for freedom to seek truth in his own way. This desire is inscribed in a lapidary script on the back of the monument on which his statue sits. In truth, the children and Einstein owe their freedom to the Secretary of the Interior, who conferred on the National Academy of Sciences a title to the land on which the statue now sits only with the understanding that free public access should be available at all times.[29]

Since the sign Leo was rising over the horizon at noon on 22 April, the constellations Leo and Virgo were beneath the Earth, as were the planets Jupiter and Saturn. However, in keeping with the Virgoan tradition which we have repeatedly noted as the hallmark of Washington DC, Saturn and the lunar node (the Dragon's Head) were in Virgo at this foundation time.[30]

Remarkably, the real mystery of the Einstein Memorial seems to have been overlooked by scholars. The eclipse of 21 September 1922 saw the fixed star Zavijava being used to confirm Einstein's theory which was first confirmed by means of the solar eclipse of 29 May 1919, that fell on 8 degrees Gemini. The solar eclipse of September 1922 had fallen on 28 degrees of Virgo. Was it merely serendipity which led the astronomical advisers who erected the Einstein Memorial chart *to choose a time for the unveiling of their celestial figure when the planet Venus was exactly opposite this degree?*[31]

It is almost 20 years since Robert Berks designed this marvellous statuary and zodiac, and even longer since he modelled Einstein's head from life; yet he is still pleased with the work. When we spoke together, he seemed especially excited by the glyphs he had invented for the metal studs on the planisphere. When Berks undertook the commission there were no standardized symbols or sigils for such things as quasars, in consequence of which he invented some of the glyphs incised on the metal studs.

He shaped the studs in a particular bevelling of 6 degrees, to ensure that they could be seen at any human height, when viewed from beyond the marble surface. Berks confirmed that he had intended to reflect in miniature the circular harmonics of the planisphere and statue. He told me that the three wrinkles on Einstein's face – like the circular folds of his sweatshirt – were designed to emphasize the natural convexity of the studs. This convexity also was reflected in the shape of the flat planisphere (or exhedra) against which they lay. His design had been worked out with the profundity one might have expected of a statue of a genius like Einstein.

Robert Berks' fascination with the unity of time and gravity (which were the *materia philosophica* of Einstein) has led him to trace a connection between time and memory and between gravity and the human ego. He spoke quite openly of a sixth and seventh sense of time and gravity in mankind. In the light of this philosophy, one is tempted to see the Einstein zodiac as the brain of Man – literally, as grey matter – spread out on the floor, on the principle that Man's history is recorded in the stars, which have gazed down on mankind for millennia. Just as the planisphere is the memory of mankind, so the brain (ringed by the three creases on Einstein's forehead) is the personal history of this representative of humanity.

When I asked Robert Berks about the symbolism of Einstein's foot-rest, he confirmed that it had been his intention to have the genius stepping on to that particular area of the universe: the foot of this intellectual giant is on the cosmic giant, Bootes. In terms of Berks' graphic philosophy, Einstein is stepping out (that is, adjusting his centre of gravity) to rest his foot on the cosmic memory.

The connection between the Einstein zodiac and zodiacal Virgo may have been fortuitous.[32] Even so, if we wish to see yet another image that confirms the ancient role of Virgo in the city, we must turn our backs on this huge marble zodiac and follow the pathway to the steps that lead into the National Academy of Sciences itself.

On either side of the entrance hall (now used as a reception area) are two beautiful cast-iron gates. One is at the southern entrance, while the other is at the further end, opening on to an exhibition room, over which the symbols for the planets are painted on the octagonal dome.

Each of the four valves of the two doors is dedicated to three signs and sigils for the zodiac. These start at the top left of the first door with the panel depicting Aries, and end on the second door, bottom right, with Pisces. The three sigils for each sign run as decorations along the top of the corresponding valve. On the first valve to the left, on the entrance door, is the image of Virgo, represented as the Egyptian goddess Isis playing a harp (plate 2).

Is there some mystery in the fact that the two conventional zodiacs which seal off the eastern and western ends of Constitution Avenue (what I have called the *via sacra*) should portray Virgo playing a harp?

Between them, the entirely modern constellational horoscope of Einstein and the pseudo-Egyptian design of the zodiac in the National Academy, mark the western end of the Constitution Avenue symbolism. Beyond the Einstein figure, which is on the corner of 22nd Street, Constitution comes to an end, more or less where L'Enfant envisaged it should.

As I have already intimated, however, the building next to the Academy, on 21st Street – the magnificently designed Federal Reserve building – is also enriched by two zodiacs.

It may well be the placing of this building on Constitution which determined that it should be studded on the outside with Virgoan emblems, and that it should have two zodiacs on the inside. It seems to me there was a danger that this zodiacal theme, which has been represesented with consummate architectural skill, might not have been necessary. Originally, the building was earmarked to occupy the site of the historic home of John Hay, who had been Secretary of State under the two Masonic Presidents, McKinley and Roosevelt. Hay, who was himself a Mason (and an important biographer of Abraham Lincoln), had occupied a house across Lafayette Park, to the north of the White House.[33] My feeling is that if the Federal Reserve had been erected there, the architect, Paul Cret,[34] would not have felt the need to introduce such a high degree of zodiacal symbolism, to continue to emphasize the stellar theme of the *via sacra* of Constitution Avenue. It is fortunate for us that the building was finally located on this later prime site, rather than overlooking Lafayette Park.

The two Federal Reserve zodiacs (plate 3) are located on Saturn-like rings which run in planes horizontal to the Earth, around the star-studded globe of a light fixture. The 12 zodiacal images engraved on these glass rings were designed by the sculptor Sidney Waugh, and cut on the glass by Steuben. It is felicitous that the two glass zodiacs should be on a site contiguous with (and indeed at one time overlaid by) the glass-works which were built to serve the needs of builders, in the early days of the construction of the city.

The two Federal Reserve glass zodiacs are identical, and make wonderful use of the light which the glass ring both protects and embellishes. Did Waugh conceive of the light-bulb within the glass bowl as a Sun at the centre of the cosmos, rather than set in its traditional pathway of the ecliptic? There is a hidden meaning in this symbolism, for the halo around the head of Virgo is also a 'solar light' (engendered by the inner Sun), so that the light within the bowl falls upon the light of the Virgin in a magical alchemy of great profundity. The fact that in these images, Virgo is depicted with a halo (plate 3) also suggests that there has been the same urge to Christianize the zodiac at this western end of Constitution Avenue as we saw in the cross structure of the Dirksen zodiacs. Not only are both the central sections of Constitution Avenue sealed, as it were, with a multitude of zodiacal images, but these also include zodiacal images which point to the celestial Virgin in the guise of Mary, the Mother of Jesus and to the cross of Christ.

There are several other important Virgoan motifs in the Federal Reserve Building which should not go unnoticed. For example, on the ceiling of the first floor are two images of Ceres, with bas-relief images of corn on either side. The five-petalled devices, which we shall explore shortly in connection with Virgo, floriate everywhere in this building. For example, in the rear entrance rotunda ceiling are 96 soffits, above which is a continuous narrow frieze, showing a series of five-petalled plants. The same image is repeated on the lift doors.

Perhaps an even more surprising evocation of the sign is the Virgoan motifs around the top external frieze of the building: here, I have counted 590 wheat-ears in total. A more luxuriant form of the wheat-ear is found on bronze bosses in the window divides of the building (alongside): there are 34 such wheat-ears distributed around it. These alternate with two other images: one is of an unidentified Greek profile, and the other, tellingly, a profile of Mercury – the planetary ruler of Washington DC. I counted 15 heads of Mercury on the window divides around the building.

As though to emphasize the Mercurial presence on the exterior of this remarkable building, Paul Cret arranged for a marble image of Mercury to grace the north façade, on C Street. He commissioned the sculptor John Gregory to carve for the eastern of two high piers to the sides of the rear entrance a bas-relief of a *female* Mercury holding the sacred caduceus (figure 16). This bas-relief is seen to greatest advantage shortly before a summer Sunset, when the rays of the Sun dramatically contrast the low relief, showing the intensity with which the female (said by some to represent America[35]) is looking at the sacred caduceus.

I have already discussed something of the background to the notion of a female Mercury, but it may be of value to point out that from time to time the equivalent of the female Mercury has appeared in arcane contexts. One excellent example is this copperplate engraving of 1563, which shows a bare-breasted woman holding in her right hand the caduceus. In her left hand, she holds a compass and a square (which later became standard symbols in Masonry). She is surrounded by what are usually called 'the children of the planet'. This last group are individuals who lead their professional lives under the influence of the planet Mercury: we see the sculptor, the easel-painter, the cosmographer, the teacher and, in the background, the builder. Around this female Mercury are images of the seven Liberal Arts.[36]

It is now clear that both ends of the *via sacra* in the downtown section of Constitution Avenue are embellished with numerous zodiacs – 12 at the eastern end, and 4 at the western end. These zodiacs are surrounded by a plethora of related Virgoan symbols: we shall examine a few of these later. At this point, however, we must ask if there is any zodiacal symbolism between these two extremes, in that stretch of Constitution which forms *the southern side of the Federal Triangle*. Is there any indication of zodiacs, or of Virgoan symbolism, in this federal heart of Washington DC, along the stretch of the Triangle marked by Constitution Avenue?

The answer to this question is, unequivocally, yes. The acute end of the Triangle, where Pennsylvania runs through Constitution Avenue, is itself marked with one of the most splendid modern high-relief zodiacs in Washington DC.

About five years before work was begun on the zodiac ceiling of the Dirksen building, another architect was working on yet another zodiacal design for the city. The artist who designed this zodiac was commissioned to complete it in memory of a remarkable Mason.

In July 1947, Congress approved the erection of a memorial fountain to the late Andrew W. Mellon, one of the richest and most influential Masons of the first half of the century, who had died in 1937, leaving his important art collection to the nation.[37] It was Congress who ordered that the fountain be constructed in front of the National Gallery at the intersection of Pennsylvania and Constitution Avenues.[38] The fountain was completed by 1952, and located – as Congress ordered – in a triangular area at the eastern tip of the Federal Triangle. The water from the fountain's jets rains down into a raised inner bowl, which overflows to discharge into an even larger basin, whence it flows into a wide basin at ground level: thus, the water overflows three times from the central basin into the ground-level bowl. Below the lip of the second bowl, inset on the sides so as to be obscured by the flow of water, are the 12 signs of the zodiac designed by Sidney Waugh (plate 15).[39]

These zodiacal images were carved with considerable insight and feeling. It was probably the architect Eggers – aware of the Masonic tradition that permeated Washington architecture – who insisted that the image for the zodiacal sign Aries (figure 29) should be oriented so that it received the first rays of sunlight on 21 March, which marks the vernal equinox.

The United States Courthouse to the north-east of the fountain, across Pennsylvania Avenue, has shut off the complete effect of the first sunlight. The beams of the early Sun do light up the Aries segment and the two adjacent signs of Pisces and Taurus at this time of the year, but even this light is now filtered by the foliage of the trees to the east of the fountain. In spite of this, it is a delightful experience to study the way in which the zodiacal reliefs are pulled into life by the delicate early light (plate 16). This is exclusively an early-morning experience, as not only do the shadows of trees obscure the light as the Sun rises, but the pumps are programmed to work the fountain at an early hour, with the result that the images are hidden beneath the flow for the remains of the day.

This orientation of Aries towards the vernal equinox Sun may sound merely like sensible architectural planning, with no special arcane overtones, yet there *is* a secret in this design: a secret connected with Virgo.

If one draws an imaginary diameter across the 18-yard bowl of the fountain, from Pisces to Virgo, one finds that *the line follows the orientation of Pennsylvania Avenue*. The vernal orientation is designed to run directly down Constitution Avenue, with the fountain bowl acting, as it were, as the fulcrum of balance for the two massive groups of zodiacs which hang at either end of this section of the Avenue – the Dirksen building to the east, and the National Academy of Sciences to the west.[40]

It is evident, that Eggers must have known something of the mystery of the Virgo orientations which radiate through Washington DC. It is Virgo, to the west of the fountain, that participates in the arcane structure of the city, as she looks down L'Enfant's Grand Avenue along which could be seen the President's palace.

Since the tip of the Federal Triangle is so clearly marked with a magical zodiac, we might wonder if there is any other arcane symbolism in this Constitution Avenue side of the Federal Triangle?

In fact, the arcane symbolism touching upon Virgo is so extensive in this Federal Triangle that it would be beyond the scope of this book to analyse it completely. In view of this, in order to indicate something of the richness of the symbolism, I propose to discuss only the most salient zodiacal themes. I will limit myself to indicating only the Virgoan symbols found in the nine huge buildings in the Federal Triangle. At first, I will restrict myself mainly to examining only those buildings which front on to the Constitution Avenue side of the Federal Triangle, even though for the sake of completeness the map below shows the positions of all the buildings in it. I should point out that each building exhibits Virgoan, or other zodiacal symbolism, on a considerable scale.

The Federal Triangle has been over a century in construction. The Old Post Office, with its distinctive campanile-like tower, was completed in 1897, while the magnificent District Building (finished 1908) is presently undergoing extensive restorations (which fortunately are not in any way disturbing its external beauty). At least one structure (the Ronald Reagan Building) is not complete internally at the time of writing, in 1999. In consequence, I think that for the sake of clarity it will be as well to provide a diagram marking the ten main building-groups which now make up the Federal Triangle (opposite).

A comparison with any pre-1900 map (see, for example, the one on p.254) will show that in order to establish this massive triangular form, some of the original streets of the L'Enfant plan were removed. A comparison between this modern map, and the corresponding area in the Ellicott map, is revealing, against the background of the intentions behind the McMillan report.

Constitution Avenue was the old B Street, which was bordered to the south as far as the former Missouri Avenue, by the Tiber canal. The Central Market, where now stands the National Archives, fronted on to a huge square (inevitably, named Market Square by the mid-19th century) that destroyed much of the thrust of Pennsylvania Avenue. Across this Market Square ran Louisiana Avenue as far as the Tiber basin, which fronted the site now occupied by the IRS building. Running into this Basin from the north-west was Ohio Avenue, roughly parallel to Pennsylvania Avenue. For all the early-20th-century architects talked glibly of respecting the L'Enfant plan, in order to establish the Triangle they destroyed the entire length of Ohio. Along with Ohio went the south-eastern end of Louisiana and the north-Tiber ends of four streets (13th Street and its half-street, 11th Street and 8th Street, which ran through the Market). Somehow, this seems irresponsible planning by those assuring the public of their dedication to reasserting the L'Enfant plan! These architects and planners certainly had other aims in mind than merely returning to an idea drafted well over 100 years earlier. *In truth, to establish the Federal Triangle, these planners completely effaced the original plan laid out by L'Enfant and Ellicott.* This is not to suggest that what these architects did was not impressive – indeed, they added a new depth of arcane symbolism to the centre of Washington DC. However, I think that it should be recognized that this depth of symbolism had little to do with what L'Enfant had in mind.

To understand the arcane significance of the Triangle, we must take a look at the plan which has emerged in the course of the 20th century. The numbers in the diagram of the modern Triangle (below) refer to the buildings, not all of which I discuss in the text, my main interest being in those which front on to the *via sacra* of Constitution Avenue.

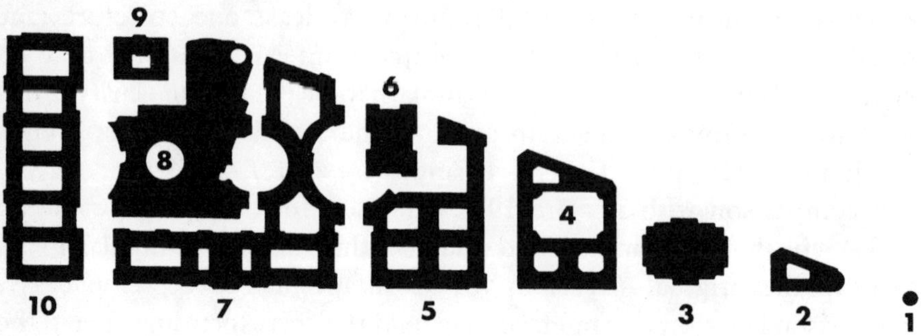

1. The Mellon Fountain zodiac
2. Federal Trade Commission
3. National Archives
4. Department of Justice
5. Internal Revenue building
6. Old Post Office building
7. Federal Triangle building, with the Departmental Auditorium
8. Ronald Reagan Building
9. District Building
10. Department of Commerce

It will be noted that the Mellon Fountain zodiac stands out somewhat from the general orientation line of the Federal Triangle – presumably in order to align its Aries-Libra orientation directly east-west, along the axis of Constitution Avenue. In this way, the zodiac invests the length of the Avenue with stellar power. As I have observed, an alternative orientation – that of Pisces-Virgo – is projected visually, if not geometrically, along Pennsylvania Avenue.

For historical reasons, the avenue which connected the Capitol with the White House was liberally scattered with hotels from the first decades of the 19th century. By 1900, no part of the avenue was more filled with hotels than that around the crossroads of 6th Street with Pennsylvania. On the four blocks of this were the National Hotel, the Fritz, the Reuter, the Metropolitan and the St James Hotel ('Electric Bus to and from new Union Station, 5 minutes', as a prospect of 1908 claimed), their sometimes patchy, yet always colourful, histories reflected in their changes of name.

The Metropolitan, on Pennsylvania, had begun life in 1802 as Woodward's Center Tavern, which was rebuilt as Davis' Hotel, renamed first the McKeown Hotel (*circa* 1815), then the Indian Queen (seemingly in reference to Pocahontas, to judge from the image on the signboard) about five years later. It was in this hotel that John Tyler was sworn in as President. After substantial rebuilding, it was renamed Brown's Hotel until after the Civil War, when it was refurbished (Some say, almost rebuilt) and christened anew the Metropolitan. In his account of a three-month tour in the United States in 1867, Henry Latham mentions in particular one famous barman at this hotel who was such 'a skilful compounder of all mixed drinks' that the hotel became a halfway house wherever one might happen to be going in the city.[41]

For such reasons, this hotel tended to remain popular with Congressmen, despite being outstripped in splendour, in the 1880s, by the neighbouring National Hotel. The manager of the day, G. F. Schutt, described this hotel as 'the only old time home-like hostelry in the city', even though, in truth, it was among the most expensive.[42] Mr Schutt was anxious to advertise its modernity (boasting electric light and heat in every room) yet it was probably the oldest of the still-operative hotels in the city. It was a five-storey building of whitewashed brick, marked by two commemorative tablets listing its earlier functions – first as a residence for General Roger C. Weightman, mayor of the city, then as mayoral offices. Later, up to 1832, it was the Bank of Washington, and became the National Hotel in 1826 (retaining a strange duality of function as a bank) – the largest in the city when under the management of John Gadsby.

In the twentieth century, all this bustle of commercial and Congressional life was removed to make way for staid and bureaucratic federal activities, leaving the area somehow desolate, even to this day. In later years – shortly before it was pulled down – the National Hotel witnessed the shameful treatment of the so-called 'bonus army' when (much to the horror of most Americans) unarmed veterans, demanding only their rightful pay, were routed by professional soldiers. The site of the St James Hotel is now occupied by the Mellon Fountain, with its marvellous zodiac.

To the south, cramped between Pennsylvania and B Street, was the splendid Howard, in the block adjacent to the Market. The same block had been overlooked by the towers of the Baltimore and Potomac railway station (overleaf), until, one by one, the lines of the stations in Washington DC were scooped up by 20th-century planners, and dropped into a centralized service at the single Union Station, its architectural front guarded by such giants as Thales, grasping the sharp bolts of electricity, and Prometheus with his stolen fire. On a wall of the Baltimore and Potomac railway station, near the spot where Garfield was

shot, a bronze memorial had been fixed. Although it gave only the date of his inauguration and made no mention of his murder, the old guidebooks suggest that by the end of the 19th century the plaque had become an object of pilgrimage among Americans.[43]

It was about this time, in the late 1930s, that something seemed to go wrong with the arcane symbolism of the Federal Triangle. Perhaps the original impetus of the McMillan Plan, and of the personal attention put into the Triangle by Andrew Mellon, was lost among the financial restrictions which hit the later development of the Triangle.

The Federal Trade Commission Building (2 on the map on p.284) was conceived from the very beginning as the eastern tip of the Federal Triangle, which is probably why it was called for a considerable time – even before its specific federal function was decided – the Apex Building. The designs first suggested by the architects, Bennett, Parsons and Frost, involved not only a suitably colonnaded rounded apex, but a large sculpture-wall and terracing, to offer an architectural finish to the idea of the Triangle.

Perhaps the mistake which was made in this crucial part of the construction of the Triangle was when, in July 1937, the Treasury Department decided to hold an open competition among American sculptors to provide two works to grace the eastern sides of the Apex Building. The brief offered to the competitors did not specify any details which were likely to inspire works with arcane undertones, and it is probably this which explains why such a wonderful opportunity to continue the esoteric Virgoan theme at this crucially important location was missed.[44]

The Apex competition was popular, and attracted almost 500 models from 234 sculptors. The winner was an unknown sculptor, Michael Lantz. His theme of a strong man subduing a horse, symbolic of 'Man Controlling Trade', might well have satisfied the banal requirements of official art, but resulted in two sculptures flanking the building (though not actually part of its structure) which stand out incongruously in the sophisticated symbolism of the Triangle. Fortunately, the symbolic weakness exhibited by Lantz's restrained horses on either side of the Apex Building was not allowed to touch the sculptural programme on the building itself.

As it happens, not all the competitors failed to grasp the Virgoan theme behind the Federal Triangle. For example, the sculptor Henry Kreis (who had the advantage of having worked on other projects in the Triangle) certainly grasped the opportunity to introduce a Virgoan theme at the Apex, in accordance with the nature of the Triangle. Kreis had submitted an agricultural theme with a standing woman, nude above the waist, clasping the head of a reclining bull, and sickle in hand, holding against her body a sheaf of wheat.[45] His plaster models received an honourable mention, and the judges passed over an excellent opportunity to continue the arcane theme of the Federal Triangle to its very tip.

In fact, Virgo has reasserted herself, and it is as though the Federal Trade Commission Building has received the zodiacal impulse of the Mellon Fountain at its eastern edge. Above the eastern doorway, overlooking Constitution Avenue, is a striking image of a woman holding a large sheaf of corn (figure 30). Thus, while a zodiac marks the furthest limit of the Federal Triangle, a low-relief carving of a corn-maiden (by the sculptress Concetta Scaravaglione) marks the furthest end of the most easterly building. Another bas-relief, to the west of the same façade, is by Carl Schmitz, and shows two men trading: one is an African holding a horn – perhaps the tusk of an elephant. The significance of this image within the context of the Virgin will emerge later.

Almost from the first stirrings of commercial life in the federal city, the south side of the plaza between 7th and 9th Streets had been the site of the famous Central Market, which had been not only spacious and convenient but one of the most 'picturesque establishments of its kind in the country'.[46] Like most markets, Central Market was not planned, but grew up out of local exigencies. In the first decade of the 19th century, a handful of traders began selling their wares on the north bank of the canal, conveniently near the hotels which were springing up around the Capitol. Gradually, the huddle of sheds was turned into a more permanent set of buildings, and eventually a formal market was constructed. Its proximity to the muddy banks of the canal, and the frequent flooding, gave it the more popular name *Mash Market* – a corruption of Marsh Market.

Slave auctions were regularly held there until 1850. Near the B Street side of the Market, and conveniently near the canal, had been what was probably the last slave-pen in central Washington DC. In her rag-bag collection of local city gossip, Mrs Chapin tells how an old Virginian once sold three of his own mulatto grandchildren here, 'within a half mile of the Capitol, whose dome was crowned with a 15-foot figure of the Goddess of Liberty'.[47] There was more irony in her words than even she realized, as the enormous statue of *Freedom* had been cast by means of slave labour. As a further irony, the splendid new Justice Department would overlook the site where such terrible things had been done with the support of the law. The huge and strangely beautiful Market was cleared in the late 1920s to make way for the 'Hall of Records' – the National Archives (3 on the map on p.284), which so many scholars and politicians had fought to establish in preceding decades.

The construction of the National Archives building was saturated in the Virgoan impulse. Both the formal breaking of ground for the structure and the formal foundation-laying were conducted under Virgo. The ground was broken on the morning of 9 September 1931, when no fewer than four planets were in the sign Virgo – these being the Sun, Mercury, Venus and Neptune.[48] The cornerstone for the National Archives was laid by President Herbert Hoover on 20 February 1933.[49] Once again, the emphasis in the chart was on Virgo. Three planets and one nodal point – Mars, Jupiter, Neptune and the Dragon's Tail – were in this sign.[50]

It was a curious moment for a foundation – not because there was anything outrageous or threatening in the cosmic moment, but rather because of the choice of the master of the ritual. President Hoover had lost the election in the previous year, and was just on the point of handing over the presidency to one of the most remarkable of all Masonic Presidents, Franklin Delano Roosevelt. Hoover had shown scant interest in the idea of the National Archives (his attention was taken up by the

Depression); by contrast, Roosevelt had recognized the need for such an archive for some years, and had been active in the extensive movement to persuade Congress of the need. One cannot help feeling (given Roosevelt's undeniable interest in the design of the building) that it would have been more satisfactory to have allowed *him* to preside over the foundation ceremony.

The Virgoan symbolism is reflected in several design elements on the façade of the building, but perhaps nowhere more openly than in the statue on the low terrace to the south-facing side of the National Archives, looking on to Constitution Avenue, to the west of the main entrance (figure 31). This is a bare-breasted woman cradling in her right arm a sheaf of corn and supporting against the corn a young child. The statue was entitled *Heritage.* It was modelled by David K. Rubins, after a design by James Earle Fraser, who had worked under the close direction of the architect of the building, John Russell Pope.[51] (This architect, it will be recalled, had designed the Masonic Temple on 16th Street.) The motto below the statue reads: 'The Heritage of the Past is the Seed that Brings Forth the Harvest of the Future.'

George Gurney, who has made a detailed study of the production of many of the sculptural designs in the Federal Triangle, offers excellent descriptions of their official symbolism. However Gurney's brief did not include an examination of their arcane meanings. For example, he interprets the sheaf of wheat as suggestive of a new generation and growth, and is under the impression that the urn supported by the left hand of the semi-naked woman is filled with the ashes of past generations.[52] The contrast between life and death is susceptible to many levels of interpretation, but within the framework of our own analysis we must see the woman with the child, backed by corn, as a prototype of the celestial Virgin, who bears so many different names throughout history – from Isis with her son Horus, through to the Virgin Mary with the Child. This arcane approach to the sculpture confirms the esoteric meaning of the inscription on its base.

Beneath this building ran the Tiber, which meant that the soil on which it stood was unstable. To get round this problem, the architects had over 8,500 concrete piles driven to a depth of 21 feet into the ground, to offer a specially secure foundation for the building, while the waters of the Tiber were used in the air-conditioning system.[53] Even as the builders worked, the vast armies of rats which had found sustenance in the old Market attacked the luncheon boxes set out by workmen, and caused consternation among pedestrians.

*

There is much in the symbolism of this building that reflects Pope's interest in the sacred buildings of the past. For example, he surrounded it with 72 colossal columns, with Corinthian capitals. No doubt he was aware of the sacred nature of the number 72, which we have seen in another context, is said to be the most arcane figure in numerology.

In truth, the number 72 appears in many traditions. In the Sufi tradition, which had developed the science of numerology to the highest level of sophistication, it is recognized that every number 'contains in itself an esoteric secret which is not to be found in any other number'. However, even within such a framework, the primal importance of 72 (and its derivatives, 18 and 9) was recognized. The number 72 touches upon the intimate connection between Man and the cosmos, for 72 expresses the esoteric secret of the circulation of human blood, and (at the same time) the cosmic drift of the stars, which is called precession. The average healthy heart beats 72 times in one minute: the Sun drops back against the zodiac one degree every 72 years. In this important connection which the number draws between the human blood and the drift of the stars we see something of the cyclic relationship between microcosm and macrocosm: a minute of human time is the equivalent of a year of cosmic time.

The recognition of the importance of 72 among esotericists has led some writers in the field to formulate their ideas in 72 paragraphs, or 72 chapters. For example, the 13th-century Sufi, Haydar Amuli, whose words I quoted in the previous paragraph, described his treatise on numerology, spirituality and the history of religion as the expression of 'the balance of seventy-two'. In 1128, the Knights Templars were officially recognized at the Council of Troyes, in consequence of which Bernard of Clairvaux drew up the Rule of Observances which was to guide them. From its inception, the Order had been rooted in esotericism, and it is therefore no surprise that Bernard's Rule should have contained 72 articles. As Albert Pike pointed out, it 'was not without a secret meaning, that *twelve* was the number of the Apostles of Christ, and *seventy-two* that of his Disciples'.[54]

Pope had been a member of the Commission of Fine Arts from 1917 to 1922, and was already well known for a number of exciting buildings in the city: in many ways he was ideally placed to find an arcane expression for the idea lying behind an archive. Although the new building was not begun until September 1931, the story leading up to this beginning of the Archives goes back very many years – the last phase of most active support for such an archive being under the direction of Professor J. Franklin Jameson, of Brown University. Jameson began campaigning as early as 1895, and saw Pope's magnificent building reaching completion only in the last two years of his life, while he was head of the Manuscript Division of the Library of Congress.[55]

In the early 19th century, the red-brick theatre popularly known as Butler's New Bijou (which replaced the old Bijou, destroyed in a fire shortly before 1873) was located near 9th Street corner on the lower reaches of Louisiana Avenue. This section of the avenue, along with the old theatre, was removed to make way for the new Department of Justice (4 on the map on p.284), which straddles the block, facing across Pennsylvania Avenue on to the Federal Bureau of Investigation Building, finished in 1975. To accommodate this austere structure, a whole block was razed. Among the buildings destroyed was the Franklin National Bank at one end, with the old and famous Droop's Music store, housed in a Romanesque-style building, at the other end.

The Department of Justice building was dedicated at 3.00 p.m. on 25 October 1934, in the presence of the Masonic President, Franklin Delano Roosevelt.[56] One suspects that the afternoon time had been selected because of its symbolical importance. At that moment, the sign Virgo was on the Descendant, with Mars and Neptune bracketing the degree. Jupiter, the planet usually associated with justice, was conjunct the Sun, in Scorpio.[57] There was a distinctly Masonic flavour to the event: the music began with 'Franklin Delano Roosevelt', composed by Woodin, and ended with the ever-popular march by Sousa, 'The Stars and Stripes Forever'.[58]

When we turn to the arcane programme drawn up for the Department of Justice we are, for once, in the happy position of being able to identify the source of the striking esoteric ideas which permeate it. Although the artist Jennewein was allowed considerable freedom to control the complex programme of sculptural symbols within and without the building, he was fortunate in having as an adviser the Mason Dr Harley B. Alexander, the former chairman of the philosophy department in the University of Nebraska.[59] Dr Alexander was profoundly interested in arcane symbolism, and this reflects in certain details of the symbolism adopted here.

The esoteric element nowhere plays such an important role as in the lapidary panels on the outside of the building. Among these panels is one designed by Jennewein, carved by the John Donnelly Company,[60] and installed in 1935 on the Constitution Avenue façade (figure 32). This work is a rarity in Washington DC, for it was designed to make a hermetic use of sunlight in the slow build-up towards an esoteric meaning. Given the context, this symbolism equates the sunlight with the light of justice, and deepens the significance of the Latin above the figures, *Lege atque Ordine Omnia Fiunt*: 'All things are created by Law and Order.'[61]

Since the façade (and hence the panel) is oriented on the west-east line, the morning sunlight falls upon the figures fairly evenly, picking them out dramatically, as the relief is highlighted above the shadows. However, the panel has been inset in such a way that, until the whole relief is lighted, a shadow remains over the stick in the hand of the nude figure to the extreme right. As the Sun moves higher up the skies, the hand of the man is eventually picked out. The sunlight then slides slowly down the stick in his hand until the bottom symbol is revealed by its rays. This last penetration of light reveals the intent of the symbolism – a serpent, coiled in the bottom-right corner. Such a light-darkness symbolism was widely used in Egyptian architectural devices.

The interpretation of the symbolism of this darkened snake seems to depend on the significance of the naked man who holds the staff below which the reptile curls. The official explanation is that the man represents Order, and that the serpent is 'the snake of Wisdom'.[62] However, it is clear that whoever wrote this had not examined the statuary with any care. The serpent is not wrapped around the stick, as is the case with the majority of religious or arcane symbols, but is actually *pinned to the Earth*. A close examination reveals that the man is holding not a stick, but a spear, the point of which penetrates the body of the serpent. This is no snake of Wisdom.

The significant thing is that the man is *standing* on the speared snake, to show that he has triumphed over it. Rather than being a snake of Wisdom, it represents the overcome lower nature – the dark chthonic forces which all men and women must overcome in their search for spiritual growth. However, remarkable though this relief is, it does not lie within my remit to examine its symbolism in further detail, for, while it clearly contains interesting Masonic symbolism of redemption, it does not represent the Virgoan theme which is my main concern.

As it happens, this Virgoan theme is represented splendidly in the aluminium doors below. These huge door-valves were designed and made by Jennewein in his own studio: each is decorated with lions, represented at the base of steps from which grow six robust ears of wheat.

The message of the symbolism is zodiacal, for the wheat of Virgo is a continuation in the zodiacal progression of the lion of Leo. The idea that from the bestial realm of animality (Leo) may grow the life-giving corn, with all the Christian implications of the *pelanos*, or sacred bread, is a profound reflection on the inner propensity of Virgo for order and perfection. This redemptive theme is also expressed in the spear in the hand of the man above, the bottom part of which transfixes the serpent.[63] Just as this portal imagery associates the snake with the lower lion, so it associates the growing wheat with the hand of Man, by which he remains creative in the world. The lion-guardians of the celestial Virgin are found in an arcane engraving which we have looked at before (figure 9).

The slow evolution of the image under the changing light confirms our interpretation. Just as the snake remains in darkness to the last, so the hand of man is first picked out by the light of the Sun – a sort of lapidary commentary on the words *Fiat lux* ('Let light be made'), in Genesis.[64] The snake is the dark inner serpent which must be overcome to free the inner light. The lions are the beasts within which must be pushed aside to allow the wheat-ears to flourish in the light.

With one or two exceptions, the murals and other paintings inside the Department of Justice are of a mediocre standard. Among the exceptions is the tempera mural by the Russian-born Symeon Shimin, who had become an American citizen only a decade before he painted it.[65] His *Contemporary Justice and the Child* (figure 33) shows the dispossessed and uneducated children on the left of the picture, the protected and educated on the right. In the centre, a young mother (albeit fearfully) directs her child towards the future. What is of profound interest to us is the presence (in the foreground) of a large triangle, in the guise of a set square, held in the hand of a figure that we must presume is the artist himself. Since the painting was not begun until 1936, the artist clearly had an opportunity to contemplate the symbolism behind the idea of the Federal Triangle, and its Masonic significance. Perhaps this is why he placed a blueprint of a building behind the square. In addition, since Jennewein's lapidary panel was *in situ* by 1934, it is reasonable to assume that Shimin had the opportunity to reflect upon the redemptive meaning of its inscription.

The creative human hand of Order, which holds the speared serpent, and which is linked with the idea of doing, or creativity (*Fiunt*, 'they are made'), is echoed in Shimin's picture. Just as the artist holds his own triangle, so the tempera itself is an example of the redemptive doing or creative work – and thus also of the Federal Triangle itself. It is surely no accident that the other hand of the artist holds a divider, and that both divider and triangle hover over the blueprint map for a building. We seem to have here a symbolic echo of the Three Lights of Masonry.[66]

I should point out that even the position of the triangle itself points to redemption. Its left-hand corner runs into the head of a sleeping boy (the 'sleeper' in arcane art is the one who is unawake to his or her own spirituality), while another points at the forehead of a young girl who is looking intently at a map. This is perhaps an analogy for the blueprint of her own wholesome future, doubling as the blueprint for the building itself, which is within the Federal Triangle. Whatever the content of the arcane symbolism, it is certainly intriguing to come across this creative reference to a triangle in the heart of a building which is itself set in the heart of a triangle.

The interior of the building is replete with further arcane symbolism, linked not only with the four cardinal directions, the four Virtues, the four winds and with an emphasis on the four Elements. Personifications of Fire, Earth, Air and Water, and of the four seasons, were designed by Jennewein in a variety of aluminium and lapidary details.[67]

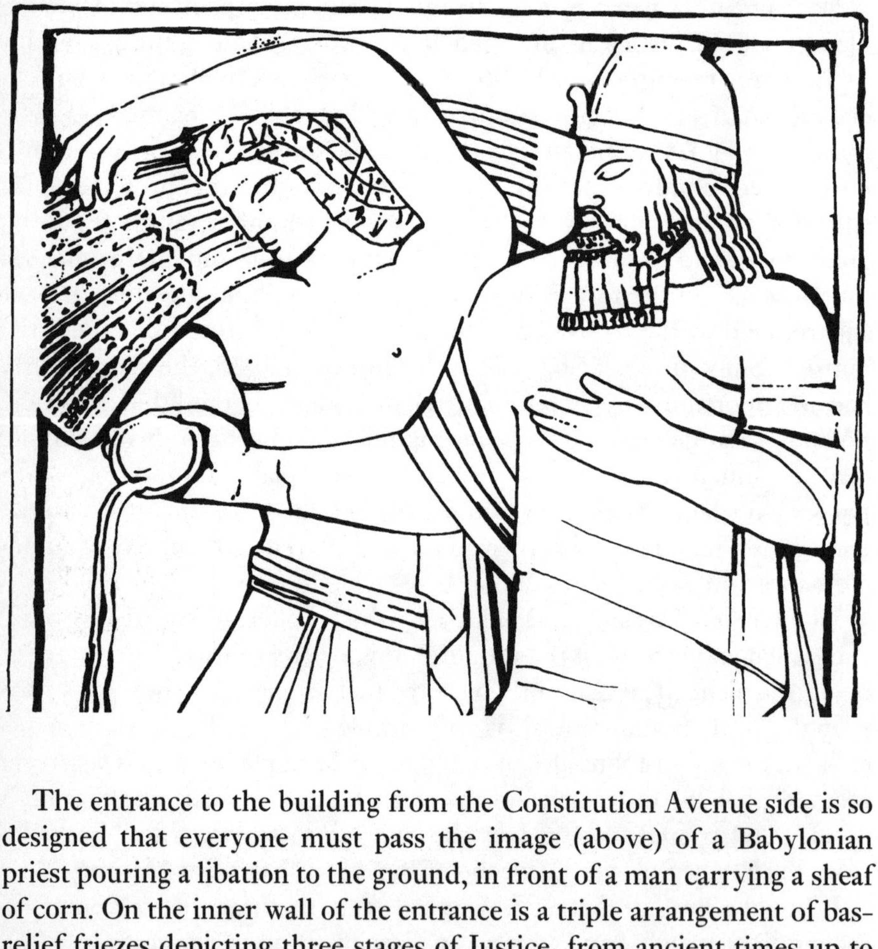

The entrance to the building from the Constitution Avenue side is so designed that everyone must pass the image (above) of a Babylonian priest pouring a libation to the ground, in front of a man carrying a sheaf of corn. On the inner wall of the entrance is a triple arrangement of bas-relief friezes depicting three stages of Justice, from ancient times up to the written constitution of 1789. These images were conceived by Dr

Alexander, and drawn by Jennewein.

The corn-bearer, representative of Earth, is in the form of a young woman holding up to her shoulder a child who is carrying a sheaf of corn. This image, though one of a series of four portrayals of the Elements, is distinctly Christian in form, yet it recalls the ancient imagery of Demeter, the corn-goddess also called Ceres.

In truth, Virgoan imagery so proliferates in the building that it is impossible to deal with it adequately within the framework of this book. However, worth special mention, are the American walnut roundels in the conference room of the Attorney-General. These were carved by Anthony di Lorenzo (under the direction of Jennewein) and portray splendid ears of corn. Even more noteworthy, in that they are quite obviously Virgoan, are the unique polychromatic terracotta snow cleats (designed to ensure that snow piled upon the steep roofs of the building does not slide off in massive tranches) wired to the roofs around the inner courtyard. These combine the sigil for Pisces (♓ – the sign opposite to Virgo) with the five-petalled symbol which are frequently associated with the corn-goddess of the skies. There are 1,100 such snow cleats affixed to the roof of the building.

One of the mysteries of the Department of Justice is the inscription over the pediment leading to the Great Hall. On either side of the image of an eagle, grasping in its talons a luxuriant olive branch, is a Latin motto, which has attracted the attention of many scholars because of its curiosity. It reads QUI PRO DOMINA JUSTITIA SEQUITUR, and has been translated as 'Who pursues [justice] on behalf of Lady Justice'. The scholar Sanches[68] has suggested that the Latin originated in Elizabethan England, and was used to denote or describe the Attorney-General of that time. However, we must recall that Elizabeth was frequently dubbed 'the Virgin Queen', and was linked not only with Astraea, the Greek corn-goddess, but also with the Virgin of the skies. In the light of this, we might interpret the Latin as reading 'He who follows Justice on behalf of the Lady' – the Lady being, of course, the stellar Virgin.

Within this translation is an arcane meaning with which I feel the architects must have been familiar. Astraea was said to have been the goddess of innocence during the Golden Age of the world. With the spread of sin among mankind, Astraea left the Earth, and metamorphosed into the constellation Virgo. The Latin might therefore be interpreted as implying a return to the spiritual archetypal world – the realm of ideas – away from the sins which beset the modern world.

Facing southwards, across Constitution Avenue, is what is often called the Federal Triangle Building (7 in the map on p.284), an immense structure incorporating the United States Customs Service, the Departmental Auditorium, and the Interstate Commerce Commission. The original design was not intended to house these three, however, and from the point of view of our own interests in arcane symbolism we may treat the building as though designed for a single purpose. This unified approach is supported by the fact that the building was designed by one architect – Arthur Brown of San Francisco.[69]

The central pediment above the portico, designed by Edgar Walter for Brown, is a formal allegory of *Columbia*. The bare-breasted figure of Columbia holds up a flaming torch – one of the attributes of the corn-goddess Ceres.[70] To her right, a totally nude woman clutches a sheaf of corn (figure 34). The bland 'official' interpretation of this figure, which seems to be based on the traditional image of Europa and the bull, is that she symbolizes national resources. However, her symbolism is rather more arcane than this would suggest, for while the wheat sheaves inevitably recall the sign and constellation Virgo, the bull she rides might remind even the casual observer of the other zodiacal Earth sign, Taurus.

On the Interstate Commerce Commission is another astrological symbol. The fourth pediment from the left, sculpted by Wheeler Williams in 1935, is a direct reference to the Elements. The male nude, reclining upon swirling clouds, holds a caduceus to show that he represents the god Mercury (ruler of Virgo). Like the eagle above the god, the two winged wind-gods on either side point to the symbolism of the pediment – it represents the Element Air.

On the same Commission building, the fifth pediment from the left shows a naked woman riding a sea-horse, with leaping dolphins to front and rear (figure 35). This tympanum, sculpted by Edward McCartan, represents the Element Water.

Like most of the sculptural programmes in Washington DC, these strange images are derived from classical sources. My impression is that many of the classical motifs and ideas which find expression on the exterior of the Federal Triangle building may be traced back to the illustrations in a single scholarly work which is still in the Library of Congress. This is a German lexicon of classical mythology by the classical scholar Roscher. Well illustrated with excellent wood engravings, it was certainly available to the architects and sculptors of Washington DC during the building of the Triangle.[71]

For example, in one volume of this work appears a picture of the fish-tailed horse carrying a woman who holds two torches (above). This could easily be the source for Edward McCartan's fish-tailed horse on the Interstate Commerce Commission Building overlooking Constitution Avenue (figure 35). The main difference is that Edward McCartan's female is nude, and since she is designed to represent Water, could not wisely be shown carrying torches, the attribute of Fire. The central figure of Columbia (by Edgar Walter) on the Departmental Auditorium *does* hold a torch, however. This symbolizes the light of knowledge.

On the Department of Labor Building, first pediment from the left, is a naked woman, sculpted by Sherry Fry. The woman rests her right arm on a jar, from which pour fruit, as though from a cornucopia (figure 36).

In terms of classical symbolism, she represents Spring, when Nature begins once again to reveal her bounty. This symbolism is confirmed by the two rams in each corner of the tympanum. Officially, these are supposed to represent 'Productivity and Security'. However, this piece of nonsensical officialese disguises the obvious fact (given the astrological background of the other three tympana) that these are the rams of the Fire sign, Aries. This tympanum represents the Element of Fire.

On the same Department façade, second pediment from left, is a naked man leaning against a bull (figure 37). He is stretched out upon rocks. At his feet is a millstone, and in the far pediment corner is a sheaf of wheat. The weight of rocks and millstone suggests the Earth, while the bull could be the bull of Taurus, which is an Earth sign, and the wheat is a product of Earth. Given the context of the other tympana, this is symbolic of the Earth Element, and confirmation that the central pediment represents something higher than merely the Earth Element. Being the fifth pediment, it is possible to read the symbols around Virgo (and Virgo herself) as pertaining to the fifth Element, the Quintessence.

It is clear that, on one level of symbolism, each of the four tympana represents one of the four Elements. However, as my analysis of the last one has intimated, they represent far more than merely the Elements – they represent the four initiation periods of the seasons, as determined by the tropical zodiac.

- The Fire tympanum represents the vernal equinox (Aries of 21/22 March – Aries being a Fire sign).
- The Air tympanum represents the autumnal equinox (Libra of 22/23 September – Libra being an Air sign).
- The Water tympanum represents the summer solstice (Cancer of 21/22 June – Cancer being a Water sign).
- The Earth tympanum represents the winter solstice (Capricorn of 22/23 December – Capricorn being an Earth sign).

I need hardly point out that these four orientations are expressed in the L'Enfant plan, and that the Federal Triangle building is itself squarely set in accordance with these orientations. These are the dates which determine the symbolic orientation of the major buildings in Washington DC, and which also play a most important role in Masonic orientation speculations. In view of this, we must ask, why are these points – best exemplified when distributed in the four directions of space – set in a single line? Why, one might ask, did Arthur Brown take the circle of the zodiac, and bend it into a straight line?

*

What the architects of the Federal Triangle – Arthur Brown among them – appear to have been doing is reflecting through their symbolism on the esoteric nature of the geometric triangle itself.[72]

They were constructing buildings which emphasized, through their decorations, the fourfold nature of the material world – Fire, Air, Water and Earth. That is to say, they were reducing the zodiacal 12 to the constituent 4. Where does this number 4 fit into the symbolism of a triangle? How can the earthly 4 be merged in a significant way with the spiritual 3?

This merging is possible through the famous Euclideian theorem, in which the relationship between the triangle and the square is demonstrated in a simple-seeming diagram.[73]

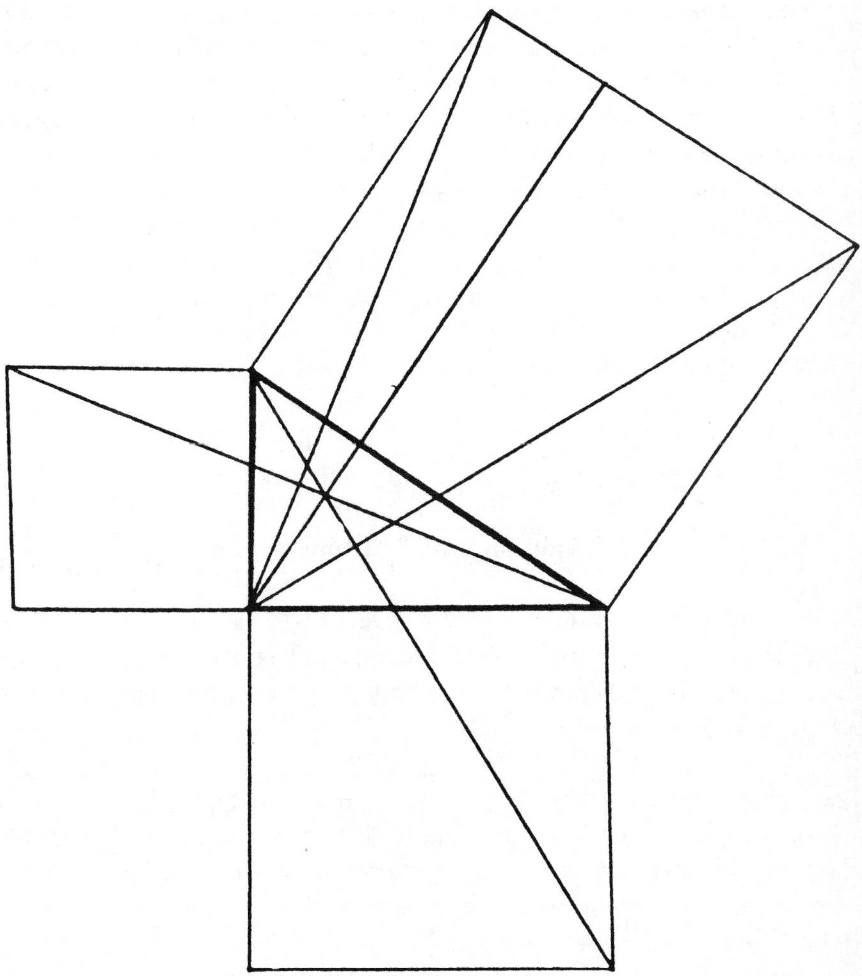

By means of this symbolism, the triangle, which is essentially a symbol of the higher spiritual world, is tied down to Earth. The elemental symbolism on the exteriors and interiors of the Federal Triangle buildings is intended to pin down the spiritual stellar triangle into the fourfold grid of the city.

Within certain arcane studies, the theorem of Euclid (which the Freemasons insist on calling the Problem of Euclid) is used as an image for contemplation, or meditation. Within the literature of Masonry, the fourfold nature of the square is extended into both mythological and archetypal regions: the four Elements are linked with the four Cardinal Virtutes, for example,[74] while the triangle is extended into the idea of the three upward-leading steps.[75] The square of elemental forces is sometimes changed, its four-fold nature transformed into the Cross of Matter.

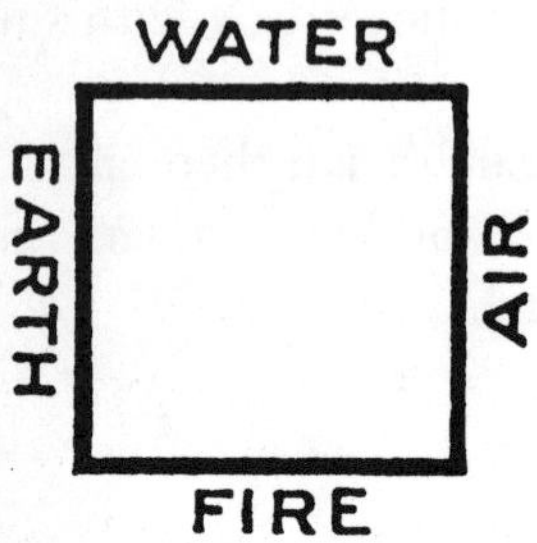

By drawing links between these geometric figures and the archetypes, a profound spiritual connection may be established between the nature of the spirit (the triangle) and the material plane (the square): within the Euclidean diagram is the 'solution' to the problem of how spirit may find a working relationship with matter. It is for this reason that Arthur Brown (among other architects) elected to take the zodiacal circle, and stretch it into a straight line. As a circle, the zodiac symbolizes time, and cycles and recurrence. When it is spread out into straight lines, to form a square, it symbolizes space. The triangle contained within the Euclidean diagram represents spirit dwelling within, and sanctifying matter. In this sense, it represents all living things, but especially the human being, who is a spiritual being dwelling for a limited time within the prison of the body.

This theorem of Euclid, which reverberates around the Federal Triangle, serves to emphasize the sacred and spiritual nature of the triangle itself. It is also imbued with philosophical ramifications which carry one well beyond such notions.

The four tympana we have examined – what we might call tympana of orientations – were sculpted by four different artists. Their unified symbolism is derived from the fact that they were designed to the specifications of a single architect, Arthur Brown.

The unity of the four tympana is undeniable. The meaning of the zodiacal symbolism is also undeniable. The two fishes of the Water tympanum represent the two fishes of Pisces. The two winged putti of the Air tympanum represent the twins of Gemini. The two rams of the Fire tympanum represent Aries. The wheat, and the millstone which grinds the wheat, of the Earth tympanum represent Virgo.

We may not doubt that Brown – who was, as we shall see, both a practising and a speculative Mason – sought to emphasise the fact that the Federal Triangle was somehow linked with the stars, and even with the sacred orientation points of sacred geometry and operative Masonic practices. This is confirmed by a wonderful statuary, partly hidden by the portico on the Departmental Auditorium.

Set back behind the columns of the Virgoan allegory of the huge tympanum of the Auditorium is a portal decorated with a beautiful panel and spandrels. This bas-relief, carved by Edmond Romulus Amateis, is one of the glories of the Federal Triangle sculptural programme, even though it is now in desperate need of cleaning. Because of its position, behind the massive colonnades of the portico, it is impossible to photograph, so we have to content ourselves with a line drawing:

The panel depicts George Washington during the Revolutionary War, before the Battle of Trenton. To Washington's left, is Nathanael Greene. To his right, carrying charts needed to direct the course of the battle, is John Sullivan. At first glance, this panel seems to be the only one in the entire decorative programme of the Federal Triangle which is historical, rather than allegorical, in theme.[76] In fact, the sculpture is both historical and allegorical, for the three main figures of this relief were Masons.[77]

Even this hidden Masonic theme is taken to a deeper level of symbolism than we are accustomed to. The face of Nathanael Greene is *not* a portrait. This is certainly not because of lack of authentic portrait models – many portraits and engravings of Greene have survived. The face is not authentic because the sculptor replaced it with a likeness of the architect of the building, Arthur Brown. This implies that Brown is revealed as a Mason, by means of one of those open secret symbols in which the Craft delights.

My purpose in examining here this George Washington relief is not to revert yet again to the enduring theme of the Masonic involvement in either the making of the Federal Triangle. My interest lies in the left-hand spandrel below the Greene-Brown figure in the Masonic group. Here, a bare-breasted woman reclines against a bough of foliage, her profile presented to the viewer. In front of her is a sheaf of corn and a drinking-horn.

Officially, the figure represents Agriculture, but this was not the arcane intention of the sculptor or the architect, both of whom were versed in esoteric symbolism. A deeper reading of the figure would suggest that she represents Virgo. She is another version of the Beautiful Virgin, and her corn and drinking-horn recall the corn and wine of the Masonic ceremonials. However, what is important about this Virgoan archetype is not the Masonic symbolism so much as her posture. She is in profile, on the façade directed along Constitution Avenue. This means that she is looking towards the west – towards the point of Sunset.

When we examined the Mellon zodiac, we found an image of Virgo directed towards the White House, and thus oriented towards the north-west, along Pennsylvania Avenue.[78] Now we find another arcane image of Virgo looking directly westward, along one of the other sides of the Federal Triangle.[79] The deep significance of this will become clear at a later point.

The Internal Revenue Building was the first new structure in the Triangle to be completed sufficiently for occupation. According to the original plans, the building was to be much larger. The entire block between Pennsylvania and Constitution was to be developed in at least two stages, the first (and major) section being completed on schedule by 1930.

The Internal Revenue Building is beautiful, though perhaps somewhat austere due to lack of external sculpture or ornamentation. However, records do suggest that a fairly extensive sculptural programme had been visualized by the architect, Louis A. Simon.[80] Unfortunately, this seems to have been discarded for financial reasons.

The few decorations which have survived from this vision are not particularly striking – four panels of eagles to the sides of the three central entrances to the building, designed by Simon and modelled by the firm Ricci and Zari.[81]

This paucity of sculptural detail would suggest that our own interest in the building should be limited. However, it is worth putting on record that the original plan had involved the destruction of the Old Post Office, to facilitate a later expansion of the Internal Revenue Building. An exploratory arm of this expansion survives in the extension (completed in 1935) reaching as far as, and angled along, Pennsylvania Avenue to the west of 10th Street. Fortunately, Congress wisely never gave approval for the demolition of the Post Office, with its wonderful Italian-style campanile, and the arm of this extension reached out to the Old Post Office in vain. Congress had made a happy decision, for, as we shall discover later, this campanile seems to play an important role in the mystery of Washington DC.

The north-west corner of the Federal Triangle was once the site of Albaugh's Grand Opera House – or Poli's Theatre as it was called by the general public. The building had been designed by the Washingtonian architect, Harvey L. Page, who was later responsible for the magnificent Masonic Temple in San Antonio, Texas. At the next intersection south, was the notorious red-light district of Ohio Avenue, which framed in its triangular intersection the Panorama Building, and other sleazy enterprises.

Most of these buildings were razed in the late 1920s to make way for the Triangle dreamed up by McMillan. No one seemed to lament the passing of the huge Navy Department to the south of the blocks, or the demise of Ohio Avenue, though many theatregoers did regret the passing of Poli's. The huge rotunda known as Manassas Panorama Building, between Ohio Avenue and C Street, had been razed in 1918, by which time it had been converted into Washington DC's first important automobile garage. Before that, it had been an exhibition hall for a vast panoramic mural painting of the second Battle of Manassas (1862). By 1892, the display had been changed to a panoramic of the Battle of Gettysburg, but, as one historian reports, business cannot have been all that good, for the management also sponsored midget shows and the demonstration of Edison's new phonograph.[82]

These curious snippets of history have been effaced, and the entire block is dominated by the seven-storey Department of Commerce (10 in the plan on p.284). At the time of building, this was the largest purpose-built office in the world.[83] Finished in 1931, it was the first building to be erected in accordance with the McMillan Plan, which was nominally concerned with an attempt to return, wherever possible, to the L'Enfant plan. General Hugh Johnson (one of the first to set up offices in the labyrinthine interior) called it 'the worst-planned and least efficient modern building in the world'.[84]

The newspapers which recorded the opening of the immense block emphasized its incredible cost. Seventeen and a half million dollars (one journalist recorded triumphantly) was a tenth more expensive than the price of bringing ten new states into the Union, by way of the Louisiana Purchase. In weak riposte, the official federal documents emphasized the massive amount of materials which had gone into the building ('There are 3,311 rooms, and 5,200 windows, containing 250,000 square feet of glass . . .').[85]

As with all those federal buildings which fronted on to the old Tiber, concrete piles were required to ensure a safe foundation:

> Here, through subterranean passages, ran almost forgotten Tiber Creek, still running towards the Potomac and draining as a wide area as it did in years long ago. So great is the flow from these old streams that it created a water pressure from below that seemingly impeded the driving of piles . . . a deep-sea diver was finally employed [to facilitate driving].[86]

Eighteen thousand piles, each 24 feet long, were embedded in the earth beneath the waters. Since these ran 16 degrees cooler than the temperature above ground, they were ducted into the building to serve as a cooling system.

President Herbert Clark Hoover laid the cornerstone on 10 July 1929, not realizing that in the 1980s the building would be renamed after him. The date was well chosen, for both the Moon and Mars were in Virgo.[87] There is in the chart for this event a most extraordinary coincidence. The planet Pluto, which was not discovered by Clyde Tombaugh until January 1930, had a most profound influence on this chart of 1929. Pluto, which happened to be in Cancer in January 1930, was exactly on the Sun during the laying of the cornerstone.[88]

As one might expect of so great an architectural undertaking, Hoover touched the cement with the same trowel as George Washington had used in the cornerstone-laying of the Capitol in 1793. Cornerstone ceremonies can be serious affairs, but for once, a delightful quirk of imagination was exercised. In the cavity of the cornerstone were placed documents of great interest, in the form of copies of important patents.

The earliest recorded patent – that issued to Francis Bailey on 29 January 1791 was enclosed, but the more interesting ones were those historic patents which influenced the course of history. Those for the telephone, the telegraph, the cotton gin, the sewing machine, the reaper, the incandescent electric lamp and a submarine were encased for posterity in this way.[89]

The Department of Commerce, built under the direction of the architectural firm of Cope and Stewardson, was completed in the first month of 1932. The long façade of this imposing building looks over the executive grounds which were once the private gardens of presidents. This façade marks the short edge of the Federal Triangle, and so its symbolism must be considered with the same care as those façades overlooking Constitution Avenue. Was there anything in the symbolism pertaining to this huge building which could be linked with the stars? Is it possible that this linear western edge of the Federal Triangle shows some sign of a zodiac, or the stars, in the way that its acute-angled apex does with the outstanding symbolism of the Mellon zodiac?

The answer to this question is surprising, for an initial examination of the façade does not reveal anything particularly astrological or astronomical. Nonetheless, on the western façade of this building is a series of pediments which offer a remarkable distillation of the star wisdom which we saw on the southern façades of the Interstate Commerce Commission Building. These were designed in 1934 by James Earle Fraser, who also sculpted them. Like the pediments of Arthur Brown, these represent the four Elements, but in a somewhat more forthright manner:

- The Mining tympanum clearly represents Earth
- The Fisheries tympanum represents Water
- The Commerce tympanum represents Fire
- The Aeronautics tympanum represents Air.

Once again, this is an expression of the elemental nature which lies behind the zodiacal signs.

There is a marked difference, in both imagery and symbolism, in the Department of Commerce tympana. While the Arthur Brown pediments drew on classical and zodiacal symbolism for their arcane meanings, these Fraser tympana are more humanized. This can be seen most clearly in the curious symbolism of the third pediment from the left – that designed to represent aeronautics by way of the theme of Air.

Two semi-nude aviators, wearing leather flying caps, support the raised arms of a third aviator who is strapped to artificial wings. The four eagles who look on from the corners of the tympanum are the only classical symbols of Air. What we have here is an entirely original symbolism, in which Air is represented as the boundless human desire to fly or soar. Undoubtedly, the symbolism was linked with contemporaneous elation about the success of flight: in the same year that the building was erected, a Curtis-Condor, operated by Eastern Air Transport Inc., had started flying a regular service between Washington DC, New York and Richmond. The Curtis-Condor was state-of-the-art, for it had been furnished with two-way radio telephones, and – being 'the largest passenger plane in the East' – was designed to carry 21 people, including the crew. The aviator who has been strapped to wings on the pediment is being urged to fly skywards in celebration of commercial aviation.

Dare we ask if there is any *overt* astrological symbolism in this somewhat austere and modern structure that is the Commerce Building? The answer is, yes. In the years following the completion of the building, a stellar observatory had been installed on its roof. This mechanism, accessible through a trap-door, was designed to facilitate the testing of instruments used in geodesic surveys involving the stars.[90] However, the trap door has been sealed, and the observatory is no longer *in situ*: its present whereabouts are not known.[91]

What is the force of symbolism behind this roof-top observatory? The Mellon zodiac, at the eastern end of the Triangle, is very specific – it measures the radiant of Aries at a specific point of Sunrise, and it signals the angle of Pennsylvania Avenue. These two measurements determine the acute angle of the Federal Triangle, radiating from the Mellon zodiac.

If the Mellon zodiac was designed to point to the two primal orientations of Constitution (with Aries-Libra) and Pennsylvania (with Virgo), then, in a poetic sense, the stellar device on the roof of the Department of Commerce wafted these points upwards, and back into the skies whence they came. The Mellon zodiac fixes the Federal Triangle to a point in space – to a position on the Earth. In contrast, *the instrument on the roof of the Commerce Building was designed to sweep through all the stars, in a symbolic flourish.*

There is an echo of this idea in one arcane plate which we have already examined (figure 40). To the right of the uplifted hand of the lunar-solar goddess is a celestial globe. Above it is what the text calls *einen schimmernden Triangel*, or 'a radiant triangle'.[92] The celestial globe grows from a seven-radiant star. It is clear that one's gaze is being directed upwards (by the force of the triangle) towards the large 'celestial image', which is the zodiac – in this instance, a great wheel directed by the seven archangels. This movement upwards from a model of the zodiac, towards the living zodiac in the skies, is precisely the same symbolism which the architects instilled into their own radiant triangle, the Federal Triangle.

If we imagine the Mellon zodiac at the sharp point of the triangle as being rooted in the Earth, then we see that the zodiacal power it engenders moves upwards, through the whole length of the Federal Triangle. Here, at the high western end of the Triangle, it radiates its stellar influence into the skies.

If we can consider the Federal Triangle in this way, we see not only that its lengths are punctuated by remarkable zodiacal symbolism, but that this symbolism is so directed as to link the Earth (the Mellon zodiac) with the skies (the roof-top stellar observatory).

The Department of Commerce observatory was a continuation of a long tradition. Its exquisite stellar symbolism is linked with the National Oceanic and Atmospheric Administration, which worked within the building. This was a modern version of the 19th-century Coast and Geodetic Survey (so named after 1871), charged with collecting data on the oceans, space and the Sun.[93] One delightful piece of information which emerged from my research into the Geodetic Survey is that it was the first of all federal government bodies to hire a female astronomer to work in its professional team. This young lady was Maria Mitchell, who joined the US Coast Survey in 1845. Born on Nantucket Island in 1818, Maria learned astronomy from her father, and in her 29th year discovered a new comet, so earning a gold medal from the King of Denmark. In 1861 she was invited to become the first professor of astronomy at Vassar, where she established an observatory.[94]

The architectural symbolism of the Federal Triangle, which we have considered in such detail, indicates that, in Masonic circles at least, the old magic of Virgo was not being ignored. During that period between 1930 and 1950, when the sculptural programme of the Federal Triangle was undertaken, zodiacal and Virgoan symbolism flourished. The Masonic Triangle, that tied down the triad of Masonic structures – the Capitol, the White House and the Washington Monument – was linked with the stars. It takes no great leap of imagination to see the Federal Triangle as the architectural equivalent, or reflection, of this symbolism. Without doubt, the major programme of sculptural decoration is zodiacal in character, and emphasizes the role of Virgo. The apex of the triangle, which points to the Capitol, subtends from a zodiac in which Virgo is emphasized. What more evidence would one need in support of the argument that the Masonic architects and planners, who have guided and guarded the city of Washington DC for almost two centuries, have attempted to stamp the Earth with the munificent power of the Beautiful Virgin?

The iconography of the Federal Triangle is so rich and varied that I find it difficult to summarize its meaning. However, it is evident that the one theme which dominates is that of Virgo – in her various disguises as Ceres, Isis and so on; in fact, in disguises so numerous that she was also called *Myrionyma*, the goddess with a thousand names.

If we were to seek a literary source for the various symbols of the Triangle, then we might be well advised to look into a work on sacred iconography which was standard in the late 18th century, in which the name Myrionyma appears.[95] Here are some relevant epithets, lifted by the author of this 18th century work from such classical sources as Apuleius. It is the Virgin Queen speaking:

> I am Nature . . . mistress of the elements . . . It is I who govern the luminous firmament of the heaven, the salutary breezes of the sea . . . the Egyptians honour me with peculiar ceremonies, and call me by my true name Isis . . . I am Isis, Queen of Egypt, instructed by Mercury . . . I first invented the use of corn . . . I shine in the Dog-star.[96]

The transition from words to images is not always easy to follow, so that it is not at first apparent that the four Elements we have seen repeated in the Federal Triangle should be ruled by Isis, the Virgin Queen. However, pictures speak more clearly than words, and anyone seeking to understand the rich symbolism of the Triangle could do no better than return to an engraving from one of the finest collections of esoteric engravings of the 18th century.[97] Figure 9 (from de Hooghe's engravings) is an exceptional image, a visual commentary on the nature of the Virgin Mother, the Isis or Virgo behind all things, 'mistress of the elements'. She sits with the cornucopia in her left hand, corn streaming from her lap and tumbling on to a scythe, such as we have seen in the hands of several Virgo images in Washington DC. Around her is a zodiac, with the signs in a curious order: Pisces is above her head, with Sagittarius, impossibly, next to the fishes. On her breast is the goat of Capricorn, while, on the hem of her dress is the crayfish of Cancer (an accepted alternative to the crab since the days of mediaeval astrology). This last pair show that beyond a shadow of doubt the zodiac is a sacred one, intended to be understood only by those initiated into the sacred wisdom.

Above is a plethora of symbols, all of which deal with the attributes of the 'many-named' Virgin, or with her various personifications. A considerable number of the symbols in this engraving can be found on the façades of buildings in the Federal Triangle, but virtually *all* the Triangle symbols may be found among the many plates within this work.[98]

The dog on the base of the seat towards the top right of de Hooghe's engraving reminds us of the important connection between Washington DC and the star Sirius, for this dog is nothing other than the star Sothis in its Egyptian hieroglyphic form. The two dogs in the corners of the pediments of the National Archives might be read on an ordinary level of symbolism as being 'guardians', for the building is dedicated to the idea of guarding the archives of the nation. However, given the Virgoan nature of the Constitution Avenue symbolism, we might be tempted to trace yet another connection with the celestial Virgin in these dogs. In some late-18th-century star maps (below), Virgo is depicted looking across the skies towards a nearby pair of dogs, the *Canes Venatici*, or 'Hunting Dogs'. These dogs (which are always represented in pairs) are usually shown in the hands of the giant Bootes.[99]

I am not suggesting that the architects of the Triangle were *directly* influenced by these arcane plates. Even so, this level of correspondence is sufficient to indicate something of the esoteric depth of its sculptural programme, and to emphasize the close relationship so many of the Triangle symbols hold to the esoteric tradition of the stellar Virgin. Note, for example, the black Virgin carrying the horn in the central top area of de Hooghe's engraving (figure 9), and the close connection this has with the African carrying a horn on the Constitution façade of the Federal Trade building. Although the graphic ideas were not copied, they certainly had a communal source in the flow of ideas relating to the stellar Virgin.

The question which remains amidst this plethora of symbols is, if the emphasis of Virgo is laid on the Federal Triangle, what was the purpose of this symbolism? *What is it about the Federal Triangle that it should seem to be designed as an ensemble with the symbolic power to lift man's gaze upwards towards the stars and towards Virgo in particular?* Is it possible that the angles of the Federal Triangle, when subtended into space, are somehow linked with the stars and the mythology of Virgo in some other way than merely as a reflection on the Earth plane of the stellar Triangle of Virgo?

The answer to this question brings us to the main arcane theme of my book, and pulls together most of the hermetic streams which we have seen flowing through Washington DC. The answer to this question about the stellar Triangle of Virgo, reveals the mystery of the city. It offers a glimpse into the secret of L'Enfant's plan, and explains why Virgo has remained such a fundamentally important symbol in the federal city for almost two centuries.

Chapter Eleven

> The selection of this site, the ground plan of this city, show the outline of a master, and years must elapse ere any school which we can found will be capable of worthily filling it.
>
> (Horatio Greenough, *Aesthetics at Washington. The Travels, Observations, and Experience of a Yankee Stonecutter*, 1852.)

From whatever direction one approaches the history of Washington DC, the processional avenue of L'Enfant seems always to find its way into the story, and the tale is usually linked with Masons. If we glance at the history of the capital from the viewpoint of, say, sculpture, we find a seamless fabric which joins together generations of artists through almost two centuries. And, this is a fabric woven in the vicinity of Pennsylvania Avenue.

Today, the Old Post Office is set back from Pennsylvania Avenue, oriented to the squares drawn on the original map along D Street, as though some planner had forgotten about what L'Enfant had indicated on his map. Across the road is the beaux-arts building which once housed the most influential of all newspapers in the city, the *Washington Evening Star*, its façade still looking on to the statue of Benjamin Franklin, who occupies the triangular-shaped declivity in Pennsylvania Avenue (plate 17). It is entirely fitting that this building, so intimately linked with a setting star, should look on to one of the most influential of early American Masons, one who had a knowledge of the stars and was a keen astronomer. The sculpture, commissioned of Jacques Jouvenal as a gift to the city by the newspaper proprietor Stilson Hutchins, was designed to look on to Pennsylvania from 10th Street, because in those days the avenue was flanked by printers and newspapers: within a stone's throw was the largest litho printer in the United States.[1] Now, the printers and newspapers have fled in the wake of threatened and actual development, leaving Franklin, displaced from his original symbolism, raising his right hand as though astonished at their disappearance. Nonetheless, there seems to be a destiny even in accidents, and this placing of a Mason on one side, and a building named after an evening star on the other, is propitious.

The *Evening Star* departed its famous building in 1955, leaving only its stellar name in metallic and lapidary inscriptions overlooking the Pennsylvania frontage. The reception hall of the newspaper has been revamped in modern times, but it is possible that a meaningful symbolism has survived from earlier days. In its marble floor is a huge sunburst, or starburst pattern. The five splendid radiants throw their beams out towards this magical avenue, encompassing in their angle the statue of Franklin on the far side, as though he were part of the profound secret of Washington DC.[2]

Pennsylvania Avenue is the spiritual centre of Washington DC. It is true that some of the buildings on the north side are without taste. For example, the hard-edged façades of the FBI building are far from pleasant, while the inside has been likened to a vast labyrinth that 'would make a minotaur beg for mercy'.[3] It is true also that on the south side of Pennsylvania, on 3rd Street, is what must be the most unpleasant building in Washington DC – the East Building of the National Gallery of Art. It is an affront to the city that such a structure should be allowed in the environs of the Capitol, and actually on an avenue which George Washington had visualized as a triumphal Grand Avenue, sacred in its arcane significance.

On the site of the awful East Building once stood the famous landmark, Mades' Hotel, owned and run by Charles Mades. The Mason John C. Proctor, who had worked as a journalist on the *Washington Sunday Star*,[4] reminded his readers that the unfortunate Augustus Sutter had died here. Born in Switzerland in 1803, Sutter had been one of the 'California pioneers', and it was in the millrace he had constructed that gold was discovered, in 1848. This discovery led to mass emigrations to the far west, resulted in the admission of California to the Union in 1850, and eventually spawned the myth of the cowboy.

In spite of his discovery, Sutter gained almost nothing, and even lost the considerable wealth he had owned before: questionable litigation about land rights handed his claims to others, and he finished up living on a pittance of $250 per month from the California legislature. According to the Masonic historian Denslow, Sutter's descendants were still seeking compensation from Congress for these losses as late as 1955, long after the hotel had been pulled down.[5]

*

When, in 1805, Thomas Jefferson did the obvious thing and decked out the wide expanse of Pennsylvania Avenue to serve as a route for his inaugural procession between the Capitol and what was then called the President's House, he was continuing a sort of tradition.[6] The processional which followed George Washington in 1793 to the laying of the cornerstone of the Capitol had picked its way up that same avenue in what was supposed to pass for a march – the progress made hazardous by the tree stumps which were still rooted in the avenue. In the later Jefferson procession, there was one advantage not offered to us moderns: it was still possible for an onlooker to stand on the western side of Jenkins Heights and see the President's House, just over a mile in the distance.

A charming engraving, dated 1839 and now in the Library of Congress (above), shows a view from the other side of the avenue – a prospect of the Capitol, seen from the balustraded terrace of the presidential home (already called the White House). In this picture, one has an unimpeded view up the avenue, to the splendid building on Capitol Hill: in the foreground are trees, and beyond, the straight avenue bordered by houses.

This pleasing view would have been the only advantage, however, for in those days Pennsylvania Avenue was little more than a rough trackway. A few years before this idyllic engraving had been made, and 20 years after Jefferson's parade, the irrepressible Anne Royall described

Pennsylvania Avenue – once L'Enfant's visionary *coup* – in trenchant terms:

> . . . the principal part of the city, Pennsylvania Avenue, being built in a marsh which a common shower overflows, and from want of sewers and proper attention, or rather no attention at all, it is overspread with standing puddles of water from year's end to year's end. From neglect of the corporation these puddles, as well as the gutters, are choked up with filth, which being acted upon by the heat of the sun becomes green and putrid. That is not all. The whole of the flat land between the settled part of the city and the Potomac, much of which is marsh, is also overspread with stagnant pools of fetid water . . . Over and above, there is a great, oblong, deep hole from which the earth has been scooped out in years past intended for, and called, a canal, but which has been the receptacle for dead dogs, cats, puppies, and, we grieve to add, of infants. This also contains green, stinking water which has accumulated for years, and doubtless has been the cause of annual bilious fever since this death-ditch, called a canal, was dug.[7]

Perhaps she was being ironic when she wrote, in a different context, 'Our Congressmen are too valuable to be killed off as rapidly as they are by the unsanitary conditions here at the capital city.'[8] By chance, one of the earliest photographs of the Capitol building, still in construction and without its dome, has survived. This confirms Anne Royall's depressing description of the chief axis of George Washington's dream city: in the foreground are the fetid waters which others – but not Anne Royall – called a canal, fed by the Tiber. The daguerreotype was taken in 1860, and Washington DC had to wait over a decade for the architect Adolf Cluss (who had also designed the first Masonic Temple in the city) to cover up this failed canal and drainage system, in preparation for the making of what is now called the Mall.[9]

A wood engraving, of the kind produced for popular guidebooks in the 19th century (see p.61), presents a view of the city as though the onlooker were standing on a raised garden in front of the Capitol building. Directly in front is the straight line of Pennsylvania Avenue, its great width shaded by poplars said to have been planted by Thomas Jefferson. All around are signs of rural contentment.

From the inset picture of the Capitol, we might imagine that the view was drawn before 1855,[10] when the rather squat dome designed by Charles Bulfinch was removed, and the architect Thomas U. Walter began to build his now-familiar and more splendid dome – undoubtedly

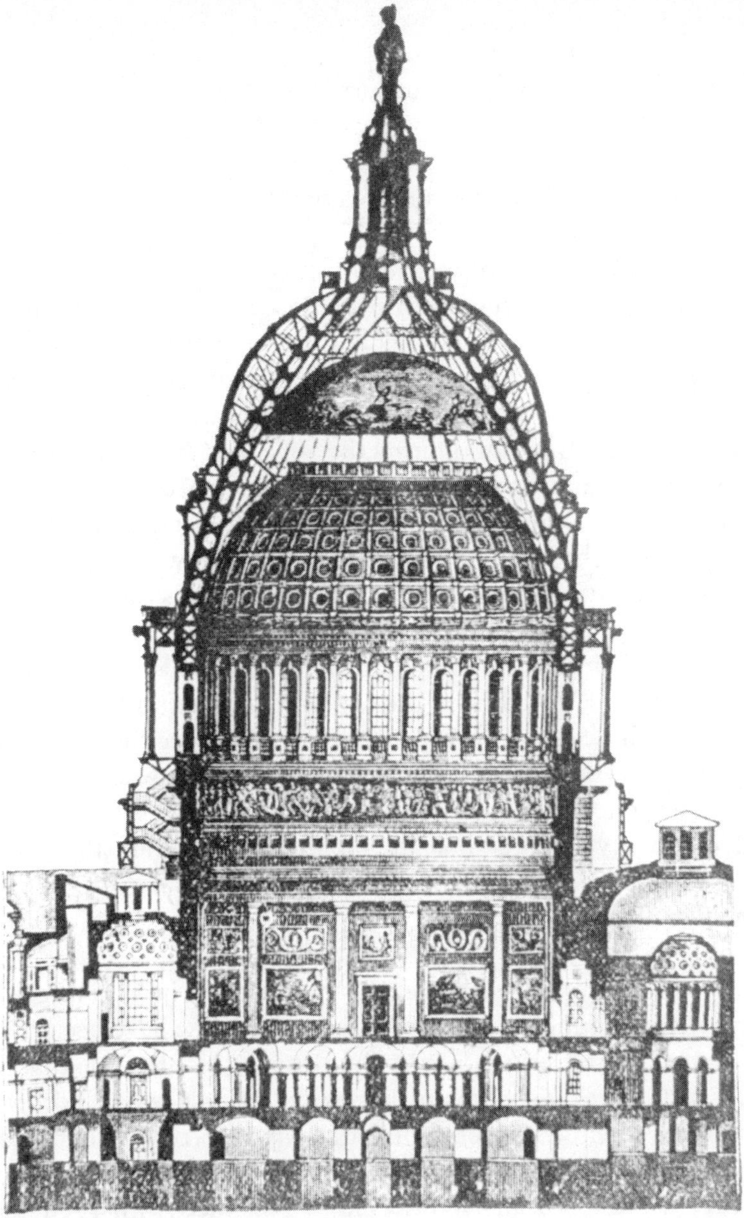

one of the architectural wonders of America – supported from the inside by a great network of cast iron.

In such early prints, the avenue seems to go on for ever – striking confidently towards the hills to the west. In the 1860s the visitor could visit the highest outer gallery of the Capitol dome, almost 300 feet above the ground. When Dr John Ellis made the climb in 1869, he recorded:

> The view is magnificent. The whole city is at our feet, with its long lines of streets, its splendid public buildings, its parks and gardens, and beyond is a panorama of unsurpassed beauty.[11]

Ellis looked to the west, over the Potomac, and following the insistent thrust of Pennsylvania Avenue towards the White House, saw beyond the soft hills of 'a vast tract of country in Virginia'. In modern times, the view for the casual traveller is very different. It is distinctly less rural, and on the lower terraces the vista towards the west is cut short at about a mile and a half by the high buildings behind the straight line of Pennsylvania Avenue. Even the prospect which has been left us has changed. The famous poplars have gone, and with them the shade which Jefferson had planned with such foresight. During the hot sun of July or August, a walk down the avenue may now be a distressing experience.

Virtually every building you see in the engraving on p.61 has disappeared – even the soft undulation of hills to the west are hidden by a skyline of buildings. The only thing which remains is the insistent rectilinear of Pennsylvania Avenue, with its view towards the White House.

The words 'White House' come almost unbidden at this point, for, as I have said before, it had been the expressed intention of the L'Enfant map to allow those standing on Jenkins Heights to see the White House, down Pennsylvania Avenue. However, something went wrong. The great edifice one sees in the wood engraving, marking the end of Pennsylvania Avenue, is not the White House, but the Treasury building. How can that be? *How can the early plans for Washington DC have been so radically changed?*

It is true that since the operative days of L'Enfant in Washington DC, both the Capitol building and the President's House have been rebuilt – most famously after destruction by the British. It is also true that, in the 20th century, a great many of the houses and markets which bordered on Pennsylvania Avenue have been pulled down to make way for offices and archives. Yet there should be no reason why the unimpeded 'reciprocal' view between Capitol and White House, planned with such care by L'Enfant and Ellicott in 1791, should not have been preserved to our own day.

The semi-official explanation for the symbolism behind this stretch of Pennsylvania Avenue was not particularly deep, yet, as George Washington recognized, it was important to the idea of democracy. L'Enfant – almost certainly following Washington's directive – had insisted that in an open democracy the Legislature, centred on the

Capitol, should be able to keep an eye on the Executive, centred on the White House. That is one reason why he had planned for the two buildings – though separated by well over a mile – to be visible to one another, along Pennsylvania Avenue.

Two sculpted women look down the length of the avenue towards the hidden White House, from the top of an ornate pedestal at the foot of Capitol Hill (plate 18). One is weeping, and a cruel historian might claim that she is weeping for what has been done to the city by some of its architects. The truth is less imaginative, for her sculptor had intended her to represent America weeping on the shoulders of Clio, the Muse of History, for the honoured naval dead of the Civil War. This naval monument was sculpted in Rome, in 1877, by the talented Mason Franklin Simmons,[12] following a sketch made by Admiral David D. Porter.[13] Since the monument was designated for the Capitol grounds, Simmons also had the benefit of guidance from Edward Clark, who was at that time the Architect of the Capitol.

On the eastern side of this statuary, facing towards the Capitol building, is the statue of a semi-naked woman (plate 19). Her right arm has been lost, but records indicate that she held up an olive branch, as symbol of peace. On the ground, to her left, are the well-established Masonic symbols of a sheaf of wheat and a cornucopia. It is not surprising, given these emblems of peace, that, as memories of the naval dead faded, the beauty of this woman with the olive branch should have been remembered, and Washingtonians began to refer to the entire sculptural group as the Peace Monument.

On the ground to her right is an assemblage of symbols which are ostensibly intended to represent the progress of literature and art. Alongside these is a huge cog-wheel which, like that on the Buberl statue (plate 4), probably represents industry – which, it is supposed, flourishes in times of peace. Of great interest, in view of what we have learned about the city so far, is the huge triangle in this amorphous mass of symbols. The apex of the triangle has been broken off in fairly recent times, but it is clearly intended as a Masonic symbol: it is the Masonic *square*, one of the working tools of the Craft.[14] What is left of this triangular shape lies almost in parallel to Pennsylvania Avenue – perhaps a reminder of the Triangle this avenue skirts.

With our own insight into the secret symbolism of Masonry, and the obvious Masonic influence in the design of the Peace Monument, we might reasonably ask if there is some secret behind this sculptural group. The answer is, yes. The sculpted figures may well symbolize peace on one level, but on another they point to something altogether different. As their position on an extension of one of the Triangle lines intimates, they are linked with the mysteries of Washington DC.

Sculpture and Pennsylvania Avenue were intimately woven together even from the early days. In 1783, the Continental Congress first voted to erect an equestrian statue to Washington. It was to accommodate this statue that L'Enfant set aside a point (marking the right angle of his triangle) to the south of the President's House and to the west of the Capitol, fairly close to where the Washington Monument was finally erected. However, in spite of this initial Congressional enthusiasm, the statue was not to grace the federal city for nearly 80 years – not until 1860, when the self-taught genius Clark Mills erected his statue. The sculptor visualized the great man at the decisive Battle of Trenton, catching the moment when the Lieutenant-General soothes the fear of his wild-maned horse. Mills' magnificent statue was erected on Pennsylvania Avenue, at the intersection with New Hampshire Avenue, now the Washington Circle. So far as Mills himself was concerned, the statue was only half-finished: lack of Congressional financial support had forced him to drop his sophisticated bronze pedestal, with its scenes from the life of Washington and its subtle Masonic symbolism. The statue has remained in this 'unfinished' state ever since.

The Mason Clark Mills[15] had come to the notice of Congress with his statue of Andrew Jackson, which had been raised seven years earlier to the north of the White House. This had been the first equestrian statue ever cast in the United States. To make the complex and difficult casting possible, Mills had built a private furnace alongside his studio on Pennsylvania Avenue, near the spot where the Sherman monument now stands.

In 1864, Clark Mills – by then the most famous artist in the city – took as student the young and beautiful Vinnie Ream,[16] who was to become the most celebrated female artist in Washington DC. Vinnie was employed as a clerk in the Post Office, but, in consequence of this meeting with Mills, she was to gain the attention of art-loving Washingtonians for her bust of Lincoln, which she modelled from life in a series of half-hour sittings. She was to become even more well-known – perhaps infamous – in Masonic circles through her friendship with the scholar Albert Pike, who fell in love with her, and began writing bad poetry in her praise.

Vinnie's bust of Lincoln had been modelled during lunchtime visits to the President in the White House (her studio was conveniently placed on

Pennsylvania Avenue[17]), and fortuitously was almost finished on 14 April 1865 – a Good Friday. Within three days, the living head she had modelled so lovingly in clay had been shot through and repaired with embalming waxes. It is said that she was one of the last people to speak with Lincoln, before his short carriage ride to the Ford theatre later that evening. Perhaps he had told her about his dream, from which he knew that something important was about to happen.[18] One wonders if she, in turn, had mentioned that there were rumours in Washington DC of an intended assassination.

THE NATIVITY OF

ABRAHAM LINCOLN,

President of the United States.

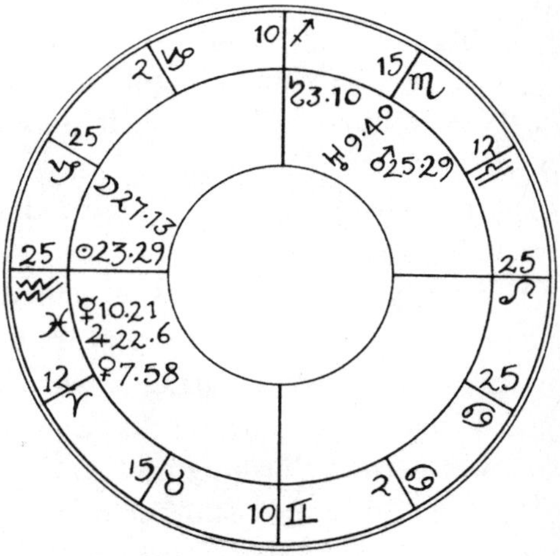

In his *Monthly Planet Reader* (above) for the last three months of 1864, the astrologer L. D. Broughton had unwisely read defeat for Lincoln in the coming election for the presidency. Even if Lincoln was not to be defeated, the stars still did not augur well:

> shortly after the election is over, Mr Lincoln will have a number of evil aspects afflicting his Nativity (I do not think that any of them will begin to be felt until the election is past). They will be in operation in Nov. and Dec. of this year. During these months, let him be especially on his guard against attempts to take his life; by such as fire arms, and infernal machines.[19]

In the same issue, under the heading 'Fate of the Nation for 1864', Broughton had written:

Let the President be careful of secret enemies, and also of assassination, during this and the next months.[20]

In his short 'Fate of the Nation' column for April 1865, he predicted:

some noted general, or person in high office, dies or is removed, about the 17th, or 18th day.[21]

Lincoln died on 15 April 1865.

By 1870, Vinnie Ream's success with the bust of Lincoln – and her familiarity with the assassinated President – led Congress to invite her to sculpt the full-length statue of Lincoln for the Capitol rotunda. In some ways, the statue is undistinguished: even given the general stiffness of late-19th-century male attire, it is overly stiff. Even so, the national uproar it caused was nothing to do with aesthetics. The tumult was due to the fact that many considered it indecent for a woman to model a human figure.

As often happens, one well-executed commission led to another, and to new opportunities. Her sculpture of the courageous Farragut was a sort of double-first – Farragut had been the first full admiral of the United States fleet, and his statue was to be the first ever erected to a naval war hero in Washington DC.[22] To design the statue as a full-scale model, she purchased another house behind her own in Pennsylvania Avenue, and knocked out a floor to give sufficient height to accommodate the huge figure.

Vinnie finished this statue in 1881, and married the wealthy Lieutenant Richard Loveridge Hoxie.[23] Her new status allowed her to foster the arts in Washington DC, and to promote women's rights. Her marriage did not appear to affect in any way her relationship with Albert Pike, whom she would continue to visit in his rooms in the House of the Temple, on 3rd Street.[24]

Shortly before her marriage, Vinnie made a bust of Albert Pike, in his role as the Sovereign Grand Commander of the Ancient and Accepted Scottish Rite of Freemasonry. She depicted the old man wearing his Masonic regalia, among the symbols of which are the radiant triangle enclosing the number 33,[25] symbols of his initiation into the 33rd Degree of Masonry (figure 4).[26] Just as Pike's poems reveal his love for the woman, the gentle light in his modelled face reveals Vinnie's admiration for him.

*

The friendship between Vinnie and Pike lasted, as all good friendships do, beyond death. Pike died in his rooms at the Temple on 2 April 1891. Seven years later, Congress approved the raising of the Albert Pike memorial, sculpted by Gaetano Trentanove. The statuary is imposing. A larger-than-life, full-length statue of Pike stands on a high pedestal, attended by a lamenting woman said to represent the spirit of Masonry (plate 20).[27] Both statues were completed by 1901, in time for the Masonic dedication ceremony.

Evidently, someone in the Masonic fraternity knew about astrology, for the day of dedication had been selected to reflect Pike's own birth-chart. This astrologer ensured that, at the hour of dedication, the beneficial planet Jupiter was exactly on the Sun of Pike's own horoscope, of 1809.[28]

Fortuitously, Pike looks northwards, towards the area where the dome of the new Masonic Temple would be raised on 16th Street, as a three-dimensional version of the radiant triangle she had modelled on Pike's bust. The pyramidic Temple was dedicated in 1915, the year that Vinnie Ream died.[29] Poignantly, the location of the statue has another significance: Pike has his back to that part of Pennsylvania Avenue where Vinnie Ream had once lived.

About 1929, the hotel which fronted on the house which Vinnie had owned, along with the smaller house she had renovated to make a studio, was demolished as part of a vast clearance plan. Not only was this section of Pennsylvania Avenue being rebuilt, but so was the entire area to its west, shortly to be known as the Federal Triangle. However, no buildings were erected to replace the line of houses which had included Vinnie's: the area is now a gardened adjunct to the Capitol grounds.

We have seen that Vinnie had been initiated by Pike, and was nominally a Mason: I wonder if, when she leaned out of the balcony of her house in Pennsylvania Avenue which fronted her studio and gazed to the west along the busy road, she would have known that she was looking on to the radiant triangle which L'Enfant and Ellicott had designed, less than 100 years before? Did she suspect that the radiant triangle she modelled on the bust of Pike was also modelled into the earth of Washington DC? Indeed, did she sense that her own studio, and the shop which fronted it, would be demolished at about the same time as this magical Triangle was developed, in order to bring Washington DC in line with modern misunderstandings of what L'Enfant and Ellicott had intended?

The name, Federal Triangle, is taken for granted nowadays, and few bother to question its origins. But, it is worth pausing to ask, why should

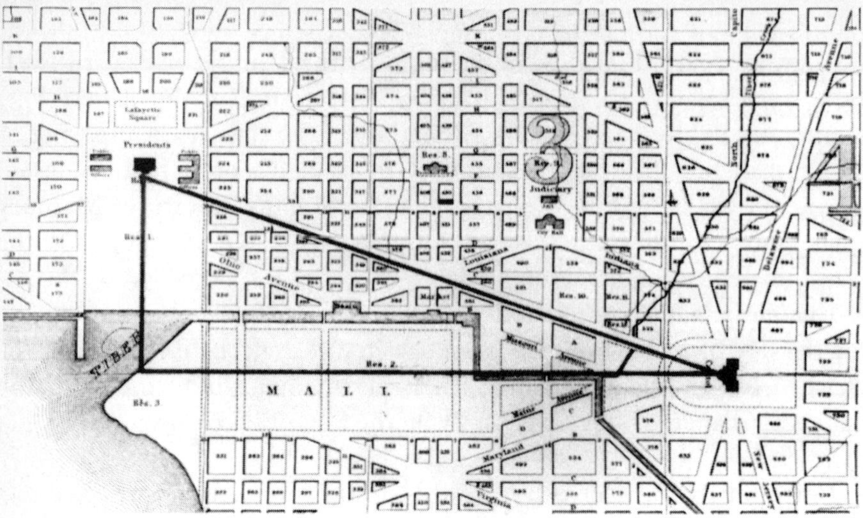

this part of the city be graced with the title *Triangle*, when the designers, L'Enfant and Ellicott, never referred to it in this way? Because of the way the map of Washington DC was laid out in 1791, there was a very large number of triangles in the city: why should this part receive so much attention, and *why should it be named after one of the most important of all Masonic symbols?*[30] The question must be asked, since Pennsylvania Avenue marks the longer line of the Triangle, and it is impossible to discuss the deeper significance of the Triangle without reference to the avenue.

We need not look for recherché architectural reasons to explain why the Federal Triangle should have been built on this spot. By the time the contemporaries of Vinnie Ream, Lincoln and Pike were living in Washington DC, the area had something of a bad reputation. There is an amusing map, published as the endpapers to Mary Cable's book on Pennsylvania Avenue, which tells all.[31] The short end of the triangle, which overlooked the swampy lands known as President's Park and which is now given over to the vast bureaucracy of the Department of Commerce Building, is marked at the south 'Murder Bay' (presumably because it fronts upon the rank-smelling canal). Adjacent to this is 'Freedmen Slums', alongside what used to be Ohio Avenue, the notorious Hooker's Division. This would scarcely appear a suitable area to lie within a stone's throw of the White House. Pennsylvania Avenue is marked as being the only paved street in Washington DC – and that is to say paved only with broken cobblestones.

Of course, within a decade or so this sink of iniquity would be cleaned up. Freedmen Slums were pulled down to make way for the United States Electric Lighting Company Power House, in 1897. The Hooker's Division must have been cleaned up somewhat by the building, two years later, of the fashionable Capital Bicycle Club – said at the time to have been the finest in America. Even so, neither the Electric Lighting building nor the Bicycle Club was a supreme example of good architecture, and both were razed by 1930 to make way for the first of the Federal Triangle buildings.[32]

The Federal Triangle has a curious history, and is one that could be written in moralistic terms of 'reform'. Although its real history does not appear in official accounts of the development of Washington DC, it is of interest to us because it demonstrates yet another phase of the benign interest shown by 19th-century Masons in the construction of their city.

If one reads the official history of the development of Washington DC in the first half of the 20th century, one learns that the great impulse for the demolition of slum areas, and the rebuilding of the city 'in accordance with the L'Enfant Plan', began with the McMillan Park Commission. This was set up in consequence of a movement among leading citizens and architects (of whom the most active was Glen Brown[33]) to change Washington DC for the better. It is the work of this body which is associated most closely with the development of the Federal Triangle.

The story goes that, during the 1900 celebrations to commemorate the centenary of the establishment of the seat of government to the District of Columbia, the American Institute of Architects (then in session in Washington DC) began discussions with the Senate Committee on the District of Columbia which led, ultimately, to an order of Senate that involved the preparation of a general plan for the development of a park system there.[34]

As a consequence to these political moves, James McMillan, chairman of the Senate Committee – and an influential Mason – submitted a resolution which was adopted by the Senate on 8 March 1901. The issues at stake involved more than merely the design of park lands and the development of the Mall: the location and design of new public buildings also fell under the terms of reference of the McMillan plan. Underlying this project was a growing recognition of the importance of the L'Enfant plan, and from this stemmed a wish to return as much as possible to this design.

Several commissions resulted from the work of construction subsequent to the McMillan Plan. The Fine Arts Commission, established in 1910 (largely due to the support of the Mason-President,

William Howard Taft, in a bill sponsored in the House of Representatives by the Mason Samuel W. McCall[35]), had the important function of surveying and approving all future public buildings and statuary intended for the city. In 1920, new legislation (which marked a return to a much earlier federal legislation that had been countermanded years before) led to a limitation of building heights, and to comprehensive zoning. In 1924, a National Capital Park Commission was formed, invested with the authority to purchase land for park purposes: two years later, this frame of reference was widened to extend the authority of the Commission over the consistent design and coordination of the architecture of the national capital.

There was an aesthetic method in all this planned destruction. What the historian Peterson has called, without a trace of irony, 'the resonance with the original L'Enfant plan', was part of the reason for the adoption of the McMillan Plan.[36] However, that is only part of the truth, for when we begin to examine the underlying stream of esoteric ideas which emerged during the execution of the plan, we are left in no doubt that the architectural development of the Federal Triangle (the later gem in the crown of the McMillan development) was under the control of individuals familiar with esoteric symbolism. We shall see, indeed, that the Federal Triangle, and Constitution Avenue which bordered it, while developed by the McMillan Plan, were used to incorporate an arcane symbolism of which L'Enfant and Ellicott would have been proud. Even so, we must bear in mind that this programme of arcane symbolism, which is perhaps the finest in the Western world, was not one visualized by L'Enfant or Ellicott. It was, however, made possible by the basic structures which these two great men provided at the heart of the city.

This is a brief official history of the events leading up to the National Capital Park and Planning Commission, which subsequently gave such sterling service to Washington DC, and which underpinned the innovation of the development of the Federal Triangle. Unfortunately, so far as I can see, this history is not wholly correct, for it fails to acknowledge the remarkable personality whose work *really* lay behind the movement towards redesigning the city.

The origins of most of the reforms set in action by the McMillan Plan, as a creative undertaking, may be traced to the far-sighted activities of a Bostonian, who had made Washington DC his home. The extraordinary thing is that the exuberant – if not to say eccentric – Franklin W. Smith has failed to receive recognition for what he did on behalf of Washington DC. He seems also to have been so ignored by later historians and biographers as to have almost disappeared from available published sources.

Franklin W. Smith seems now to be one of the enigmas of Washington DC. Although it is possible to trace to his enthusiasm and ideas most of the proposals which were put into operation in the city between 1900 and 1940, under the direction of the McAdoo Plan, the McMillan Plan, and the various committees which oversaw the building of the Federal Triangle, Smith's name does not figure in any of the biographical encyclopaedias relating to America. What we know about him is derived from the booklets which he wrote and published between 1896 and 1900, and which have survived in documents submitted to Congress in the latter year.

Franklin Webster Smith was born in Boston, about 1826, and must have settled in Washington DC in his 20s. He spent a good part of 60 years of his life in the city, or using his considerable wealth to travel abroad, studying ancient architecture. He perceived that the five grand constructions in the city served mainly to emphasize the surrounding shabbiness. He was adamant that the area to the south of Pennsylvania Avenue and to the east of the White House should be condemned, and turned into public parks and national buildings. Of course, he was not alone in this vision – several professional architects could see the need to embellish and change the city, but none seems to have had the grandiose vision of Smith.

I have not been able to find out precisely when he first started publicizing his plans for the development of Washington DC. However, by 1896 he was in a position to claim that he had lectured on the subject to over 50,000 people, who seemed to be supportive of his plans for the redevelopment of the city. His most productive period of publicization (which took his ideas to Congress) was under the presidency of William McKinley, who was a Mason.[37]

Smith's ideas for the alteration of Washington DC are enshrined in official Senate documents, and in booklets produced partly to augment these documents, and partly to popularize his view of how Washington should be designed. This sparse literature reveals Smith's foresight and brilliance. Even if it never proved possible to develop his main plan for a museum complex for the city, museums were built later, and almost every one of the clearance plans and rebuilding schemas he proposed were put into action in the first three decades of the 20th century.

The only proposals which he countenanced, but which were quietly dropped by those who followed up his ideas (usually without acknowledgement of Smith's originality), were the total rebuilding of the

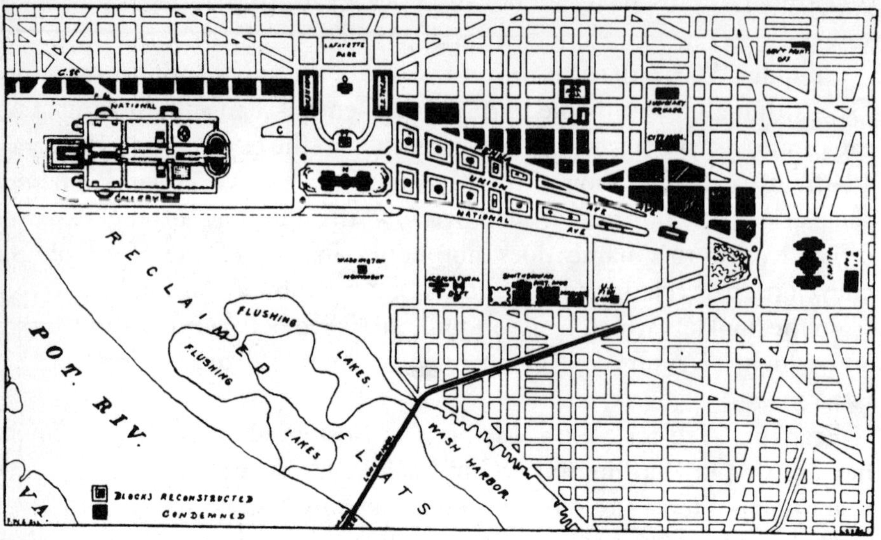

White House, and the raising of a second shaft, equivalent to the Washington Monument, in honour of Abraham Lincoln.

Although Smith's plans were steeped in a magnificent vision of the future, he did relate some of his ideas to the past. For example, in his report to Congress, he reminded his readers that George Washington had intended Observatory Hill to be the site of a university. To prove his point, he reproduced a letter recording Washington's instructions, appended to a detail of the early map of the numbered lots of the city. To sell this visionary idea of the vast complex of the National Gallery of History and Art (which had matured over a 50-year period) he had built in 1897, with the financial help of S. Walter Woodward, 'The Hall of the the Ancients' between 1312 and 1318 New York Avenue, to the north-east of the White House. A surviving lithographic colour print of a painting by W. F. Wagner (plate 6), shows it to be a full-size reconstruction of the hypostyle hall of Karnak, the columns of which were 70 feet high.[38] Below the frieze was a huge Egyptian winged disk, similar to that which Lincoln Casey had recently removed from the portals of the Washington Monument. According to descriptions, the buildings also contained Assyrian, Roman and Saracenic architecture. The Hall, which must have been bizarre in late-19th-century Washington DC, was well known enough to become part of a popular tourist itinerary, conducted through the city by trolley.[39] They seem to have been razed for redevelopment in 1926.[40]

I have not been able to establish whether or not Smith was a Mason, but there is no doubt that he was supported on a broad front by many Masons who saw the creative wisdom in his plans for the city. A letter of support for his massive project, dated 15 July 1897, was signed by seven Senators, at least four of whom were Masons.[41] His own correspondence relating to support for the plans for his national galleries and courts of history reveals at least two other Masons who were supportive of the project.[42] When an official resolution was signed by officials of the Washington Architectural Club, extending the good wishes of the Club to Smith in support of his scheme, one of the three signatories was certainly a Mason, and it is possible that all three were.

Something of the architecture of this building emerges from his collection of pamphlets, published under the general title of *The Halls of the Ancients*: this is now such a rare work that the only copy I know is in the Masonic Library of the Supreme Council, to which it was given by the Mason Dr Leroy Mortimer Taylor, who seems to have known Smith.[43] The irony is that among the engravings of remarkable ancient buildings in this book is one of the Mausoleum at Halicarnassus, which was the basis for the design of the House of the Temple, now known as the Supreme Council, Southern Jurisdiction.[44]

Smith was active in championing these reforms during the programme of public works begun in 1871 by Alexander 'Boss' Shepherd (said at one time to have been the most hated man in Washington DC), and bulldozed through against the objections of local tax-payers. Within four years, the Shepherd plan failed, due to fiscal corruption and incompetence, yet it did introduce lasting improvements. What Smith learned from seeing the personal losses and bankruptcies due to this excessive taxation was that, if the city of Washington DC was to be improved, then it would have to be done at the expense of the nation rather than at the expense of the local tax-payers. This important fiscal point was also incorporated into his plans.

L'Enfant had died in obscurity and poverty, in 1825, and was buried in Maryland. In 1909, his body was located and exhumed. With considerable pomp, his remains were carried to the Capitol rotunda, and then along Pennsylvania Avenue towards Arlington National Cemetery, where his coffin was reburied under a slab of marble on which was cut the plan he was supposed to have devised. As the coffin was carried along the stretch of Pennsylvania Avenue between the Capitol and the White House, L'Enfant's spirit might well have groaned, for, by 1909, the whole symbolism of Pennsylvania Avenue had been lost: there was no longer an unimpeded view between the Capitol and the White House.

The great mystery he or his associates had planned as an esoteric design for the city was lost. The irony is that this meaningful structure imposed upon Washington DC by the early Masons, with the grandiose purpose of lifting the design of the city to a high plane of symbolism, was disturbed and partly eradicated by a Masonic president.

Prior to being elected to the seventh presidency, Andrew Jackson had been the Grand Master of the Grand Lodge of Tennessee.[45] Even Masonic writers, who rightly never impugn their virtuous brothers, have wondered how to reconcile the fact that Jackson – who had been a Mason for at least 25 years, and had been initiated into the highest mysteries known to Masons – had a wickedly perverse and quarrelsome nature, quite out of character with the urbane and polite temperament which Masonry cultivates.[46] These aggressive qualities are no doubt excellent in a soldier, and they certainly served Jackson well when he was leading his men in battle, but at times his choleric nature overflowed to a point where he became belligerent with everyone – even with his best friends. His friend Anne Royall seemed to overlook some of his idiosyncrasies, and continued to admire him for his Masonic connections at a time when, due to the anti-Masonic movement which was still strong in the United States, such associations could be politically and socially harmful.

Anne Royall herself might have asked in her newspaper, at what point does courage descend into foolishness? It was well known in Washington circles that at the age of 13, Jackson was fighting with Davie and Sumter at Hanging Rock (1 August 1780) along with his brother Robert. In the following year, the two boys tried to capture British troops in Waxhaw Church, and were taken prisoner. When the commanding officer ordered Andrew to black his boots, the boy refused, and received a sabre blow, which left him marked on hand and face for the rest of his life.[47] Robert also refused, and he was less fortunate, for his wound was even more severe: he died shortly afterwards, either from neglect of the wound or from the smallpox which was rife in the prison.[48]

The four cannon around the Jackson statue, which symbolize his excellent belligerence, are rare pieces. They were cast in the royal foundries at Barcelona, and were captured by Jackson at Pensacola, Florida. Early prints show the statuary without the cannon and railings, even though these are an integral part of the design.[49] It is a curious fact that while we know almost everything about the early history of this equestrian statue – the first bronze casting of such in the United States – we know almost nothing about Jackson's own early years. Biographers have not been able to agree even about his place of birth.[50] The one thing we do know, from the adulatory letters and comments of friends, is that he was a very courageous soldier.

This statue certainly emphasizes Jackson's soldierly qualities. He is in his finest role, as Major-General Andrew Jackson, doffing his hat on a prancing horse as he reviews his troops before the Battle of New Orleans, in 1815. There would be no doubt in the mind of anyone contemplating the statue that this general could not fail to be victorious in the battle which was to follow. Dedicated on 8 January 1853,[51] the crowds cheered Clark Mills, recognizing the genius of a man who had no previous experience in this field yet had cast such a marvellous statue. Mills had caught the very essence of Jackson, with his belligerency directed in purposive control: it was evident that such a man of courage would serve the nation well.

It is true to say that by the time Jackson was made President of the United States, the L'Enfant plan had been mislaid and almost forgotten. Even so, Jackson must have recognized – if only because of the mythology and mystique built around it – that the wide avenue connecting the Capitol with the White House served a symbolic purpose.

According to a legend which may easily be believed, in 1836 the irascible Jackson lost his temper with bureaucrats and designers who could not come to a decision as to where they should site the new Treasury building. He cut through the impasse by ordering that it should be built to the east of the White House. Perhaps it was not his intention, but this meant that, once the structure was completed, it obstructed the prospect between Capitol and White House which had been so carefully engineered by L'Enfant and Ellicott in 1791. What L'Enfant had termed 'reciprocity of sight' was lost.

The great sadness about Pennsylvania Avenue is that it no longer offers that *reciprocity of sight* which the L'Enfant plan valued so highly. The 19th-century engraving (over) showing Washington DC in the days when it had horse-drawn trolleys, presents the problem all too clearly. From the steps of the Treasury Building, you can look directly up Pennsylvania Avenue and get a clear view of the Capitol building,[52] but this Treasury building obscures the view which was supposed to subtend reciprocally from the Capitol to the White House.

I can only presume that Jackson did not realize that he was tampering with a mystery – with what might, indeed, be called *the* Mystery of Washington DC. As architect for the new Treasury, Jackson chose the Mason Robert Mills, but the building we now know was constructed under the guidance of a number of architects, over a period of 35 years.[53]

*

The mystery with which Jackson tampered has remained a secret until now. This mystery lies in the orientation of Pennsylvania Avenue. This may well have been designed by L'Enfant and Ellicott to offer reciprocity of view between the Capitol and the White House, but its orientation was really a front for a deeper arcane intention. L'Enfant, or whoever put L'Enfant's design into operation, had intended Pennsylvania Avenue to link with the stars in a theatrical display which would rival the stellar achievements of Rome, Greece and Egypt.

To understand the secret meaning of Pennsylvania Avenue, we must first challenge a public misconception. The general belief is that L'Enfant designed Pennsylvania Avenue as a straight thoroughfare through the city, with its central orientation running through the Capitol building. It is supposed to continue as an avenue up to the White House, running as an orientation line through the centre of the White House, and to continue as an extended straight avenue through the Washington Circle, in the direction of Georgetown. *Unfortunately, this is not true.*

The most dramatic way to establish that it is not true is to fly in a helicopter over Washington DC, and examine Pennsylvania Avenue from the air. If this is not possible, then a less exciting alternative is to look closely at a copy of the map of the city. If you lay a straight edge along the length of Pennsylvania Avenue, you will quickly establish that it was never intended that it should be laid out on a straight line: the western extension of the avenue is subtended 3 degrees to the north on L'Enfant's map. From the air, this intentional deviation is even more

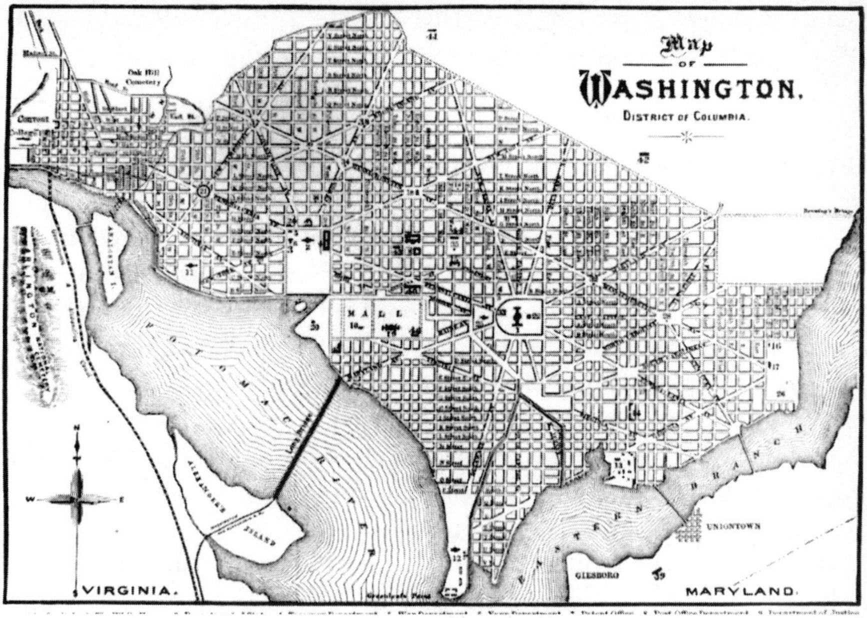

apparent, for the drama of foreshortening emphasizes the different angles: if you happen to be flying on the east side of the Capitol, you will see that the stretch of Pennsylvania Avenue to the west of the White House veers off from the straight line at an alarming rate. The simple fact is that Pennsylvania Avenue has been built (in accordance with L'Enfant's own map) as three sections which run at different angles to each other.

The one thing which L'Enfant's map does seem to establish is that he intended the central stretch of the avenue to connect the centre of the Capitol with the centre of the White House. His design was intended to permit an unobstructed view between the two – permitting that 'reciprocity of vision'. In addition, it is clear that the avenue connecting these two buildings was intended to run at a specific angle towards the west.

It appears that L'Enfant, and Ellicott (who adjusted the Frenchman's maps slightly – even in regard to this angle of Pennsylvania Avenue), wanted this stretch of the avenue between the Capitol and the White House to orientate differently from the rest of the avenue for very definite reasons. We shall discover what these reasons were, shortly.

The view down Pennsylvania towards the White House has been blocked by the intrusive façade of the Treasury. Now we have to add to this disorientation a further fact – the White House was not sited exactly where L'Enfant had planned. It was sited a little further to the north, which implies that even in the days when L'Enfant was alive, the orientation he had specified was not being precisely observed by the builders.

If Congress did not deal fairly with L'Enfant, history has perhaps been just a little over-fair, for he has gained a reputation for designing the city, and I have made it clear that, this reputation should be shared at least equally with Andrew Ellicott – if not with others. I realize that this view appears to fly in the face of the received wisdom of hundreds of historians, but, as I hope to make clear, the full majesty of Washington DC has not yet been appreciated, and so no historian has really been in a position until now to apportion credit for its design.

Let me record what was published in a report of 4 January 1792, adding my own italics for emphasis:

> In order to execute the . . . plan, Mr Ellicott drew a true meridian line by celestial observation, which passed through the area intended for the Congress house. This line he crossed by another due east and west, and which passed through the same area. The lines were accurately measured, and made the basis on which the whole plan was executed. He ran all the lines by a transit instrument, *and determined the acute angles* by actual measurements, and left nothing to the uncertainty of the compass.[54]

The report reminds us that Andrew Ellicott was one of the most proficient surveyors and astronomers in the United States at that time. Ellicott fixed the fundamental coordinates of the north-south, east-west lines, and the acute angles which ran between certain junctures of these, now called avenues. The nature of city planning demands that the surveying must precede the map-making – even though surveyor and designer must work in close cooperation.

The positions which Ellicott fixed were, by definition, determined by stellar coordinates. If the federal city was to become the City of the Stars, the City of Zodiacs, as I maintain, then it is more the doing of Andrew Ellicott than of Pierre Charles L'Enfant. In Washington DC, it is the acute angles which contain the greatest mysteries.

Why did Andrew Ellicott measure the length of Pennsylvania Avenue in such a way that its central portion, between Capitol and White House, ran at an angle different from the rest? The answer is that he did this in order to orientate this stretch of the avenue to a particular Sunset. From an arcane standpoint, this is what the design of the federal city was concerned with, – it was concerned with a Sunset. *By means of a Sunset, L'Enfant and Ellicott linked Washington DC with the stars.*

Naturally, I shall examine this Sunset shortly, but we should note that if a city (or, for that matter, a temple) is to be oriented to a particular and significant Sunset, or to a star, there are only two ways this can be done: by calculation, or by direct observation. Of the three people initially involved in the design of the city – George Washington, L'Enfant and Ellicott – two were professional surveyors, and well qualified to do both. However, while there are indications that Washington did ride over the grounds, looking at the land with a surveyor's eye, there is no indication that he was involved in the *details* of the design. There are specific records, in the journals to which we have already referred, that while Ellicott was quite capable of calculating orientations, he was more inclined and accustomed to establishing survey lines, meridians and the like by direct observation of the stars. There are no indications whatsoever that L'Enfant had this surveying knowledge, or that he had the sophisticated instruments which Ellicott owned. In view of this, my suspicion is that it was Ellicott who laid down the orientations to the Sunset and to the stars, which we are about to examine.

It is at this point – as we hover on the brink of revealing the stellar majesty of the original plan of the federal city – that we should return to the painting of the *Washington Family* by Edward Savage. This was bequeathed to the National collection by Andrew W. Mellon, who had been instrumental in establishing the Federal Triangle.

The picture was begun sometime before 1793: it shows George Washington, his wife Martha and her two grandchildren, Nelly and Washington Curtis, in the family home at Mount Vernon, gathered around a table on which is spread a large map (figure 6). Earlier, I claimed that this bland portrait group held a secret: the time has come to reveal what this secret is.

We are now in a position to appreciate the significance of the map on the table. We already know that it is a version of the so-called L'Enfant plan for the proposed city of Washington DC, but we do not yet appreciate its significance. Martha Washington is resting her closed fan on the site of the most important building in the city – the Capitol. The hilt of Washington's sword rests over Georgetown, but the pommel points in the direction of the President's House, which was later called the White House.

If we do not look carefully at the details of this picture, we shall miss its hidden meaning. The composition contains a most carefully arranged secret geometry, the meaning of which is revealed when one draws two diagonals from opposite corners: these cross exactly over Washington's hand. Perhaps this hidden geometry is intended to suggest that George Washington had a controlling hand in the design and building of the city? Such symbolism would be well founded, for, in the last years of his life, the city had been Washington's obsession, his dream-child.

However, there may be an even deeper level of symbolism in the centre of the picture. Nelly is making an odd gesture with her right hand: she is pincering her thumb and fingers in order to lift up the far edge of the map. The protective band of the sword edge seems to join the pincer movement at the point where the tips of her fingers meet. At this point, there is a jewelled bevel ornament, set in a radiant star, almost in the form of a sunburst. Nelly is touching the precise western point on the map – the place of Sunset in Washington DC.

Martha Washington is pointing to the Capitol, while her grand-daughter is touching the point to the west, where the Sun sets. If the bottom edge of Martha's fan is projected along the map, it cuts exactly between the pincered fingers of her grand-daughter's hand and the metal star. What are we to deduce from this symbolism? Is the artist, Edward Savage, telling us that there is some stellar or solar meaning in the line which connects the Capitol with the point of Sunset?

The answer to this question will become apparent if we examine a map of the city once more.

If we look at a 19th-century map of Washington DC (opposite), which is a later version of the one that the Washington family contemplates, we shall see that the map-maker had placed to the left a compass. This shows 'true' north, as opposed to magnetic north.[55] If we look to the centre of the map, we see the site of the Capitol – an arched space, with the black outline of the Capitol ground-plan in the centre. Directly to the west (by the compass) is an avenue, traced in white through a series of black garden spaces, and punctuated towards the end by a black spot. This spot marks the position where the Washington Monument was erected, in a slightly different position from that indicated in the L'Enfant map. It seems to be over this very point (to the west of the Capitol) in the painted map of Savage that the tip of Washington's sword hilt hovers.

The black circle is almost directly to the west of the Capitol building. This western point is the nominal place of Sunset – that is, to the *west*, at the equinoctial point. The Mall that was L'Enfant's Grand Avenue, connecting the Capitol to the Monument, runs almost on the east-west line that was determined by Andrew Ellicott, in 1791. This east-west line

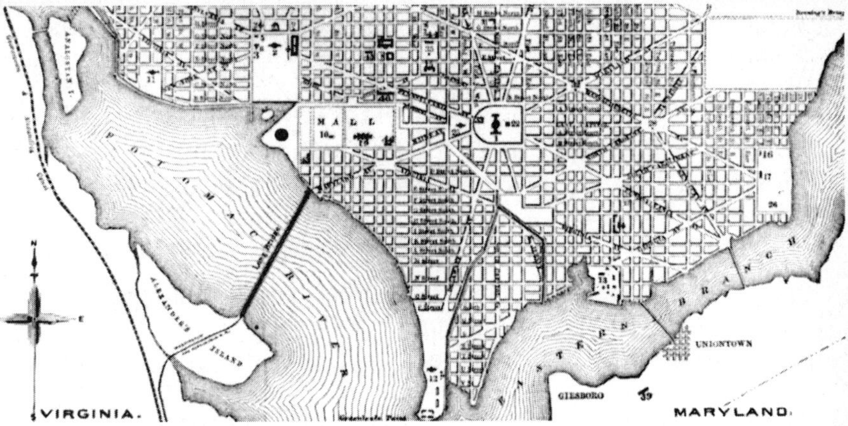

points the same area of sunset as is indicated on Edward Savage's map.

The point of Sunset does not remain constant. As the days pass, the Sun makes a gradual progression towards more northerly Sunset points, and then, after reaching its maximum point of setting (about 21 June), it begins gradually to return, in a southerly progression of Sunsets.

It is at this point, as we study the arc of Sunset over Washington DC, that we find ourselves confronted with yet another zodiac. The importance of this zodiac is derived from its siting in the city: this might most easily be understood in reference to the compass, reproduced on page 82.

The most northerly point of Sunset in Washington DC is almost 301 degrees, viewed from the Capitol.[56] On 6 June of each year, the Sun hovers around this extreme point for 13 days, and then on 19 June it makes one last thrust towards the north, just entering 302 degrees before making its slow but inexorable return to the south, remaining in 301 degrees for a further 13 days. This last thrust into 302 degrees is called the summer solstice, or standstill, for it marks the time and place where the Sun appears to stand still in its northern movement, prior to turning back towards a southern arc of Sunsets.

If you trace a line from the Capitol building, at 301 degrees, and extend it three miles or so into Georgetown, you will find that it passes through an area of parkland now called Montrose Park. Just to the north of Avon Place, on R Street, in a gardened area set inside Montrose, is a zodiacal band, an integral part of an impressive bronze armillary-style sundial (plate 21). This zodiac was placed there in 1956, in memory of Sarah Louisa Rittenhouse, who helped establish Montrose Park.[57] Once again, the Virgoan symbolism on the ecliptic band is interesting, for it depicts

Virgo with a harp, reminding us of the two Virgoan images at the extremes of Constitution Avenue (plate 2 and figure 28).

Was its position in relation to the Capitol planned? Was the zodiac located on this important solar angle to the Capitol by accident? I do not know. I am not even sure that, within the fulness of time, there is such a thing as accident. Whatever its origins, this zodiac stands as mute sentinel to the furthermost northern position of the Sun, at the summer solstice. One thing which does suggest that it was set down by someone aware of the importance of the orientation is that the sign of the zodiac oriented towards the Capitol building is Cancer. The solstice is, of course, *marked by the moment the Sun passes into Cancer, on 21 June*.

Are we to assume that the elaborate symbolism of finger-tips, sword hilt and fan in Savage's picture (figure 6) is pointing to a mystery linked with this Sunset – a mystery which the planners of the city elected not to speak of openly, yet encapsulated in the very fabric of the city? If this is the case, we must ask why the painting has given up its secret so easily. Did George Washington ask the artist to incorporate this symbolism into the painting? When we begin to look into such issues, we come up with some strange answers. For example, we discover that *all those involved in the painting belonged to the Masonic fraternity*.

Even in his day, it was widely known that George Washington was a Mason. What is not so well known, because it has only recently come to light, is that L'Enfant, who is reputed to have been the original designer of Washington DC, was probably a Mason.[58] Even the man who drew the version of the map on which the painted map was based – Andrew Ellicott – was a Mason.[59] By one of those remarkable coincidences which make history such an interesting subject, the 20th-century owner of the picture, who eventually bequeathed it to the American nation – Andrew W. Mellon – was a Mason.[60]

By a most felicitous accident (if it *was* an accident), the Andrew Mellon Fountain, erected outside the National Gallery in 1952 as a tribute to its benefactor, is decorated with a zodiac which is so oriented as to point to *exactly the same* western orientation of Sunset as is hinted at in the painting.[61] The sign Aries (figure 29) looks directly towards the east, while Libra is directed towards the west, in precisely the same orientation as is revealed in the symbolism of Edward Savage's map. When we examined this Mellon zodiac, we saw that the images of the 12 signs were so arranged that the orientation of Virgo is along Pennsylvania Avenue.

To return to Savage's painting: the grandson, Washington Curtis, does not appear to play an important role in the symbolism of the painting. However, in his right hand the boy holds a pair of compasses, as though about to measure something. Is he going to measure distances on the map around which the family are gathered? This is a faint possibility, for he appears to be the only one among them who is actually looking in the direction of the map spread out before them. On the other hand, are the compasses in his hand intended to symbolize the Masonic mystery of the sacred triangle?

Whatever the meaning of the dividers, the boy's right hand rests upon a globe. Edward Savage has not distinguished the surface of this globe with any clear markings, so it is not possible to tell whether this is a celestial or a terrestrial globe. It is my guess that Washington Curtis's hand rests upon a celestial globe, perhaps announcing the connection between the planned city and the stars, which we have seen symbolized time and again in the zodiacs of Washington DC. This notion is confirmed by a print of the painting, made by Edward Savage himself, in which the globe shows markings that confirm it is celestial, rather than terrestrial.[62]

For all the interesting game of symbolism, the role played by Washington Curtis is not primal in this painting. It is the boy's sister, Nelly, who has the most important symbolic role in the picture, for she is a young woman, a representative on the Earth plane of the archetypal Virgin. This may sound far-fetched at this stage, but, by the time we have finished our study of the skies above Washington DC, we shall no longer feel surprise that a young girl should have been represented indicating the western point of Washington DC.

For a period of about one week, the Sunset viewed from the Capitol seems to take place directly over the western end of Pennsylvania Avenue. From 6 to 12 August the disk of the Sun cuts into the horizon above the avenue, with an almost magical precision. Anyone who watches the Sunset, on any of these days, cannot fail to realize that the designers of this city intended this period – or perhaps *one day* in this period – to be an important element in the city's design.

Before we attempt to wrest from history the secret of this solar orientation, we must consider briefly the nature of Sunsets. We are so accustomed to think of a Sunset as an event in time, that many newspapers furnish the time of Sunset for particular localities in their information columns. However, in astronomy and astrology, time and space are interdependent. In order to define exactly the *time* of a Sunset, we must also define the *place* from which that Sunset is being observed.

This is important – the time of Sunset seen from the Peace Monument at the bottom of Capitol Hill, for example, is not the same as the time of Sunset seen from high on the dome of the Capitol.

Just so, the place where the Sunset would appear to set over the western end of Pennsylvania Avenue would not be the same when viewed from such different heights. If, in August, we happened to view the Sun setting from the Peace Monument, it would appear to set *earlier* than if we viewed it from the height of the Capitol dome. The Sun viewed from the Peace Monument would appear to set further to the south than that same Sunset viewed from the top of the dome. In the study of solar, lunar or stellar orientations, time is as much a factor of space, as space is of time. It may well be that we are talking of only a degree in space (or about four minutes in time), but such differences are of profound importance in the measurements in orientations.

L'Enfant had set back the building of the White House very slightly to the north of Pennsylvania – presumably to permit the Sunset on a particular day to unite three points on a single line. These three points would have been the *Sunset* on the hilly horizon to the west of the *White House*, as viewed down the line of *Pennsylvania Avenue*, from the centre of the *Capitol building*. Due to the ignorance of architects who were not privy to these late-18th-century secrets of orientation, we are left in modern times with *only two* of these points – with the angle of Pennsylvania and the Capitol building. In other words, because of a radical misunderstanding of one important aspect of L'Enfant's plan, we are now left with only two of the original coordinates that annually reaffirmed the connection between the city and a particular Sunset.

If we really begin to consider the matter carefully, we would see that the only thing we know for certain is the orientation of this stretch of Pennsylvania Avenue. *We no longer know for sure where on Capitol Hill – that is, from what height – the original designers intended us to view this Sunset.* If the centre of the dome – or a high terrace near the centre of the dome – had been marked out for such a viewing, then a different date would have been the result, for (as anyone who has made an aeroplane flight at the time of Sunset will confirm) the higher one is, the more delayed the Sunset. Perhaps this is one reason why, as he watched the city take shape, L'Enfant became so deeply troubled by changes being made to the heights of the points from which his 'reciprocal views' might be seen.

By 1800, the poor French designer seems to have been choked with anger at what was happening to the designs he clearly believed to have been his own. If we grapple for a moment with L'Enfant's confused and confusing letter of 1800, regarding the mistakes he saw being made in the building of the city, we may recognize that he was objecting to other things than merely the changes in the directions of avenues. He was objecting to *changes in heights*, to the fact that the hills set aside for the main buildings have not been raised, to improve what he called 'the variant angles of the Sights'.[63] The Capitol and the President's House are, as he expresses it in his quaint English, 'ridicully sunk', and both still 'wanted a considerable raising, at both places, before fitted for the bases of any stile of buildings . . .'.[64] The President's House in particular is still too low-sited, and should be raised, as he indicates in his coded English: 'That of the executive especially being upward of twenty feet idly sunk . . .'.[65]

Bearing in mind how L'Enfant was attempting to establish a precisely ordered arrangement of the two main buildings in the city, we can understand his chagrin. Things have not improved since his day. Not only has the view of the President's House been completely blocked, but there has been a systematic planting of high trees around it, which has further obscured the horizon. In addition, there has been the crass siting to the west of the White House, on Pennsylvania Avenue, of the World Bank building, the upward curvature of the roof installations of which completely dominates the skyline.

All these factors – which no good architect should have allowed – have contributed to the destruction of the orientation magic planned by L'Enfant or Ellicott.

In some respects, time has remained constant, while space has been manipulated by architects not privy to the great secret of L'Enfant and Ellicott.

The Sun continues to set in the arc of two or three degrees above the White House end of Pennsylvania Avenue, but the message in the stars which the two great designers wished to convey seems to have been lost. Both L'Enfant and Ellicott would have insisted that only one day (which is to say, one particular Sunset) would mark precisely the orientation between the Capitol and the President's House: exactly *which* day they intended is no longer known.

A great many things have changed since 1791, when the Capitol was still a wooded area (L'Enfant called it a 'savage wilderness'), and there were no buildings on the skyline to the west. Even as late as 1867, the barrister Henry Latham could estimate that the view from the steps of the Capitol stretched to about four miles.[66] Of course, by that time, the

Treasury, which he called 'the great manufactory of greenbacks',[67] had been extended so as to destroy the reciprocal view between the Capitol and White House along Pennsylvania, but the panorama beyond would have been more extensive than it is today. Certainly, with such an extensive view across the Potomac, it would have been possible to see from the Capitol the soft undulating horizon of the hills of Virginia. Such rural horizons are portrayed in the early drawings and engravings which have survived of the old Capitol building. Since that time, the extensive terracing around the Capitol has changed the shape of the hill, and the height from which the Sunset might be viewed. In addition, modern building beyond the White House has raised the skyline almost one degree above the horizon that would have been visible in 1791.[68] This means that all hope of our witnessing the solar symbolism designed by L'Enfant or Ellicott, on the day they intended, has been lost.

Is it possible that, from our own modern experience of this sequence of Sunsets in the second week of August, we might resurrect exactly what the original designers intended?[69]

Are we right in assuming that Pennsylvania Avenue was designed in such a way as to extend, as a projected line, through the centre of the Capitol – through the dome? This is a reasonable expectation, but it is not justified. The plan of the Capitol and grounds made by Robert King in 1803 show that the avenue did not extend as a trace-line through the centre of the Capitol.[70] Detailed plans made almost a century later, in 1887 (by which time the Capitol had been virtually rebuilt), also show that Pennsylvania was not intended to run through the Capitol dome. In each case, the line of Pennsylvania does not cross the dome.[71]

Although it is useful to have maps to study in such contexts, no amount of map-reading can ever be a substitute for direct experience. If you stand on the central pedestrian island in the centre of Pennsylvania Avenue, near that awkwardly planned open space which accommodates the Freedom Plaza, you will be able to look exactly up the centre of the avenue towards Capitol Hill. If you do this, you will discover that the dome, with its statue of *Freedom* on top, is slightly to the north of this central line. *The centre of the dome is not exactly on the orientation line of Pennsylvania Avenue.*

If the centre of the dome was not the hub of the city, then what was?

My own answer to this question is very simple: the centre of the city was *a viewing point*, located near the western front of the Capitol building. My answer is supported by old maps, and (more usefully) by direct experience. There exists a beautifully produced series of what

Americans call *plats*, or plans, of Washington DC, which are so detailed and informative that they give even the names of the house-owners. In this series, the ground-plan of the Capitol was drawn with such care that it is possible to follow it even today, over a century later (plate 22). We shall explore certain aspects of this plat shortly. At this juncture I would like to use this plat as evidence that if the angle of Pennsylvania Avenue is projected into the Capitol building, it does not project into the centre of the dome.

Why should I be showing so much interest in the old maps of the Capitol, and in the angle of Washington's Grand Avenue? My interest lies in determining *precisely* at which point (and therefore at what height) along this line we were intended to stand in order to view the Sunset along Pennsylvania. The Capitol building has changed radically since 1791, and its original design bears little relationship in terms of ground-plan, height or mass, to what L'Enfant or Ellicott visualized. The one thing we might have taken for granted as marking a point of convergence for orientation lines – that is, the centre of the dome – is no longer such a faithful measure. We must attempt to discover what alternative there is to the dome. *We must ask, what is the spiritual centre of Washington DC, if it is not the dome?*

There is still a number of vantage points from which a tourist can watch the Sunset, from the west of the Capitol building.

The higher terraces of the west wing, accessed from inside the building, are not normally open to the public. In modern times, the highest of the so-called public terraces are generally cordoned off for security reasons. In view of these limitations, the highest viewing point is the wide terrace above the western fountain. This terrace is certainly a few feet higher than the ground to the east, but this should not make a great deal of difference to our view of the Sunset, provided we are looking in the right direction, and provided it was from this 'ground level' that we were supposed to view it. From this, there is only one point from which one may gaze directly down the orientation line of Pennsylvania Avenue.

This viewing position is in the north corner of the central balustrade of the public terrace, by the bronze lamp situated on the wall of the northern ceremonial stairway (plate 22). From this position, it is possible to centre visually the vertical thrust of the Peace Monument so that it aligns directly with the centre of Pennsylvania Avenue.

Modern limitations – generally enforced by sensible security requirements – have resulted in members of the public having only this one position in which to stand to view the solar phenomenon during the week the Sun sets over the western end of Pennsylvania Avenue. This implies that the height from which they view is fixed, even if this was not the height intended by L'Enfant or Ellicott. From this single position, the viewing *height*, or elevation, might not be correct in terms of the 1791 plans, but the viewing *position* (which L'Enfant inelegantly worded, 'angles of Sights') undoubtedly is.

By strange good fortune, this ground-level terrace viewpoint is confirmed in in the plat in plate 22, to which we have already referred. If you draw a line through the centre of Pennsylvania Avenue on this plat, you will find that it passes exactly through the centre of the circle in which the Peace Monument, and continues into the corner of the terrace I have recommended as a point to view the Sunset.[72]

It is probably not too imaginative to consider this as being *somewhere* near what L'Enfant or Ellicott regarded as the spiritual centre of Washington DC.

Whatever its spiritual significance, this position does happen to be the only convenient viewing point from Capitol Hill. This is why I have studied the Sunset from this location on a great number of occasions during the month of August.[73] As the weather in Washington DC rarely admits of perfect Sunset-viewing, I have also made photographs, of the last hour or so of Sunset in order to study the angles of descent at various times. From these photographs, I have been able to record the path of the Sun in order to estimate which day L'Enfant or Ellicott would have had in mind. These estimates have, of course, been made with the astronomical data for the official azimuth, and for times of Sunset for the Capitol building constantly in mind.[74] In addition, I have checked my own observations with simulated Sunsets on computerized astronomical programmes. All these methods of observation and checking have been used in order to attempt to reach into the secret of the day which L'Enfant and Ellicott intended us to view the August Sunset.

Allowing for the changes which have occurred since 1791, I estimate that L'Enfant or Ellicott chose the Sunset of 10 August as the crucial symbolic moment. In modern times, the 10 August Sun sets towards the southern corner of the end of Pennsylvania Avenue. Modern building seems to have raised the skyline by about one degree, this would mean that in 1791 the Sunset would probably have been central to the angle of the avenue on 10 August, when its disk touched the horizon. You will observe that I assume this 'touching of the Sun with the horizon' to be the phenomenon that Ellicott and L'Enfant had in mind when they were relating Washington DC to the skies: however, even this assumption might be questioned.

Since, at this northern latitude, the Sun does not set vertically in the skies, we may watch the last hour of the setting Sun as it follows an angular descent through the skies, on a south-to-north incline, on 10 August.

I now want to look more closely at a remarkable building in the Federal Triangle, which we have only glanced at thus far – the Old Post Office. This beautiful building, in the so-called Romanesque-revival style, with its distinctive Italianate campanile, was the work of the official 'supervising architect', Willoughby J. Edbrooke,[75] who was at that time responsible for the design of public buildings in the city. His influence, though short-lived, was exceptional. As Scott and Lee report, between 1891 and 1893 he was responsible for at least 86 government buildings.[76] Interestingly, this masterpiece of architecture was not well received at the time of its completion, and ever since has faced periodic attempts to replace it.

In modern literature on Washington DC, the Old Post Office is sometimes claimed to be a sort of 'survival' in the Federal Triangle. In fact, it was the first public building to be erected there (though, of course, *before* the Triangle was an official programme). This may explain why it 'survived' the thorough destruction of all the other old buildings in the Triangle – mainly because it was, at the time the McMillan plan was drawn up, so relatively new, and so obviously a product of somewhat lavish public expenditure. As a matter of fact, by the time the first plans for the Triangle had been sanctioned (*circa* 1926), and the new Post Office had been constructed, the removal of the Old Post Office *was* officially authorized. It appears to have been saved by the terrible economic crisis of the 1930s, which virtually put an end to architectural development, even in the federal city. In the 1960s, plans were revived to remove the building, but by this time tastes had changed, and local objections to such plans were sufficient to steer the government into preserving the outer fabric. The interior space was redesigned into what is a vast, if eerie, shopping centre.

Why do I show my interest in this splendid structure here? Because at this time of the year, before setting, *the disk of the Sun cuts through the Old Post Office tower*, to the south of Pennsylvania Avenue (plates 23 and 24). I doubt that this phenomenon is accidental. Indeed, it may go a long way towards explaining why the Old Post Office (for all its vast waste of internal space) was allowed to survive the bulldozers of the planners of the Federal Triangle.[77]

To watch this temporary eclipse of the Sun by the vertical masonry of the tower is itself a deeply mystical experience. It is almost as though the architects who designed the 315-foot mock-Italian mediaeval campanile knew about the mystery of this Sunset, for, from the distance of the Capitol terrace, the tower appears to be just about half a degree wide. That is to say, *the tower is just wide enough to occlude the disk of the Sun.* This is most dramatic on 12 August, for in its descent to the south of the tower, the Sun tips the simple crenellation of the tower on the side of the pyramidic bases. When the Sun has passed behind the tower, to reappear on the northern side, its first flash is on the lower moulding around the tower. (This may be clarified by consulting photographs I took on 12 August 1998, reproduced as plates 22 and 23.)

There are less than 5 seconds between the last flash of the Sun on the south side of the tower and its first flash on the north side. *Were one standing back a little further, the first and last flashes would be separated by an even shorter time span.*[78] I have often wondered whether the tower (completed in 1897) was designed with a knowledge of this stellar magic in mind. The question has occurred to me because the solar symbolism of this 'eclipse' is involved with other things than merely the visual width of the tower.

The fact is that *the silhouette of the upper part of the tower represents a pyramid.* This pyramid, which is of a ratio similar to that on top of the Washington Monument, rests upon a vertical shaft. Now, the proportion of this shaft is such that, viewed from the distance of the Capitol building, its bottom edge (which aligns exactly with the width of the campanile) appears to be the same width as the diameter of the Sun.

Because of this geometry, during the days leading up to the solar magic of 10 August, we have nothing less than a symbolic reversal of the pyramid image on the Seal of the United States. The solar light touches the top of the pyramid, on a later day slides through it, and then on subsequent days begins to pass *beneath* the pyramid, to be occulted by the masonry of the tower. Does the statue of Franklin, on its pedestal below the campanile, hold up its hand in amazement at this solar wonder?

We see, then, that the likely key date for understanding the stellar mystery of Washington DC is 10 August.

On the evening of that day, the Sun sets directly over the horizon where the line of Pennsylvania Avenue would have aligned with the White House grounds. In other words, at Sunset on 10 August, the Capitol and the White House are connected by the disk of the Sun as it sets over the western horizon.[79] Even if I am wrong in my estimate by as much as a day or so (the error could not be more than this), this does not materially influence what I have to say about the stellar implications of the Sunset, in the following pages.

It is this dramatic stellar event which explains the esoteric connection which I (and the original planners of the city) have drawn between Washington DC and Virgo. As we shall see shortly, it is also this significant Sunset which explains the stellar symbolism of the L'Enfant triangle, and its truncated form, the Federal Triangle.

The mystery of Washington DC is concerned with far more than the orientation of an avenue to a specific Sunset.

On 10 August, the Sun is in 17 degrees of Leo.[80] A few degrees above the Sun on that day, and very close to the ecliptic, or path of the Sun, is the star Regulus. As the Sun sets behind the buildings to the west of Pennsylvania Avenue, Regulus is almost 13 degrees higher in the skies, along the trajectory which has just been followed by the Sun.[81] It will be hovering to the south of the Old Post Office campanile. Of course, we can estimate the position of Regulus, but, because the sky is still bright, we cannot actually see it. Nor would we be able to see the magnificent triangle formed by Regulus, Spica and Arcturus, balancing over the west of Pennsylvania Avenue. Were we able to see the stars during daylight, the pattern above Pennsylvania Avenue would look something like the triangular pattern set out in the schema on the next page.

Immediately upon Sunset, even when the sky is clear of clouds, the first-magnitude stars are not visible: the sky is still too bright for their weak light to show. However, as the Sun sinks below the horizon of the Earth, the stars of greater magnitude begin to reveal themselves. On 10 August, the star Regulus would set over L'Enfant's presidential palace (the White House) just over half an hour after Sunset.[82]

What, then, is the significance of Regulus, in this context? You will recall that Regulus, set in Leo, marked the acute angle of the right-angled triangle which framed the constellation Virgo.

On 10 August, it is as though this triangle, spearheaded by Regulus, lies poised over the White House end of Pennsylvania Avenue. It is now that the extraordinary stellar symbolism of Washington DC reveals itself. With the Sun below the horizon, and the stars of greater magnitude beginning to show themselves as the night skies darken, a fascinating pattern is emerges. Regulus is at the acute-angled end of the triangle, which begins to slip into the backdrop of sky behind the White House, at

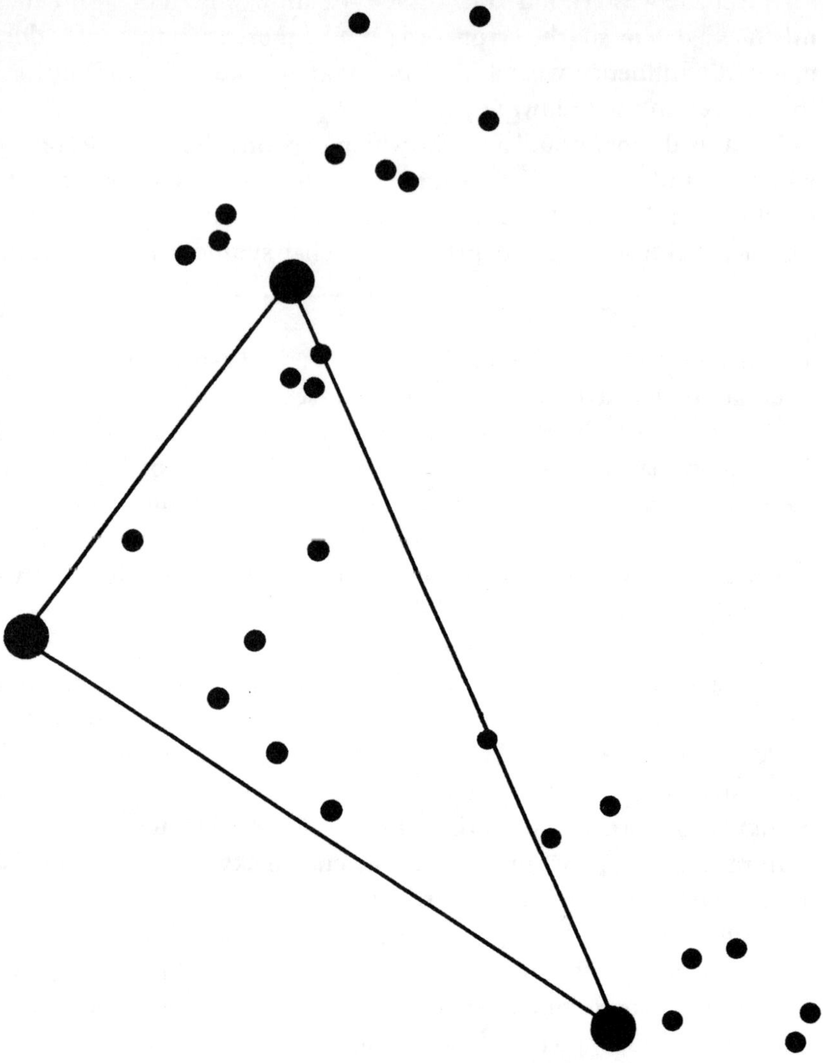

the end of Pennsylvania Avenue. Hanging in the skies to the west, above Regulus, are the two powerful stars Spica, in Virgo, and Arcturus in Bootes.

Where have we come across these three stars before? They were the ones that formed the L'Enfant triangle which bound together, in a meaningful symbolism, the Capitol, the White House and the Washington Monument. *They are the three stars which Masons such as Pike and Brunet recognized as enclosing the constellation of Virgo.*

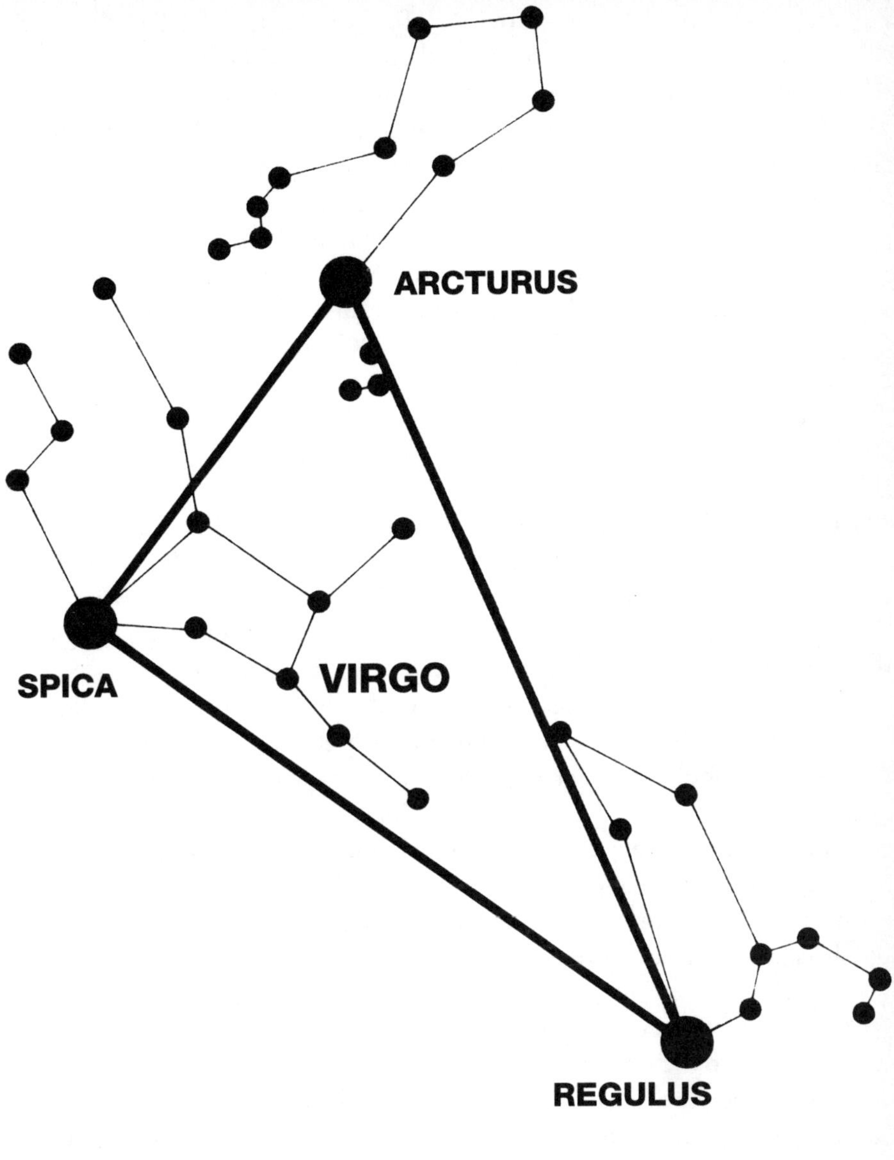

This, then, is the Mystery of Washington DC – that it was designed with its main avenue to point to a Sunset that would reveal in the skies the constellation Virgo.

On this momentous evening, we see in the skies – hanging over L'Enfant's grand ceremonial line of Pennsylvania Avenue – the inverted triangle formed by the three first-magnitude stars which embrace the constellation Virgo. The hypotenuse of this is formed by Regulus and Arcturus, while the right angle is marked by Spica. Due to the angle of the ecliptic, this spiritual stellar triangle literally hangs over the earthly Federal Triangle, to the south of Pennsylvania Avenue. If, shortly after Sunset on 10 August, we imagined the constellation patterns drawn among the skies, they would appear hanging above the White House end of Pennsylvania Avenue in the pattern shown on the previous page.

The three main stars that surround the constellation Virgo form in the skies a celestial triangle. The form of this triangle is precisely the same as that which the builders of Washington DC once impressed upon its streets and avenues, and which was later condensed into the Federal Triangle.

My conclusion, then, is that what we experience on 10 August of each year is a reconfirmation of the connection established at the foundation of the city of Washington with the stars of Virgo. On the evening when the Sunset is over Pennsylvania Avenue, the constellation of Virgo hangs in the skies above both the Federal Triangle and the White House.

This piece of astronomical data translates into a most extraordinary phenomenon in the skies – a phenomenon which is the source of much of the arcane symbolism we have traced in the architecture of the city. This symbolism pulls together the images of the triangle, the corn, the cornucopia, the zodiac and the refulgent image of the Virgin, in all her diverse forms. It is a Christian imagery which heralds the spiritual imperatives of that pre-Christian mystery lore which nourished the birth of Christianity in the secret schools of Egypt, Greece and Italy.

Now, as we have seen before, due to the precession of the equinoxes, the stars appear to be moving forward against the ecliptic. They move forward along the path of the Sun, so that the stars which now accompany the Sun during its setting are not the same as those which were with it in 1791. In the space of over 200 years, an adjustment of almost three degrees must be taken into account.[83]

In 1791, the most powerful star along the ecliptic, subsequent to the Sunset of 10 August, was Regulus. This first-magnitude star was then in approximately 27 degrees of Leo. That is to say that it was almost 10 degrees higher in the night sky than the Sun.

In modern times, due to the phenomenon of precession, the arc of difference has increased, permitting a longer time for the Sun to set and thus allowing Regulus to hover above the horizon for a slightly longer time. The longer Regulus can hover over the horizon after Sunset, the more chance there is of its becoming a visible part of the great cosmic triangle of Virgo before it sets.

This gradual lengthening of the time Regulus sets, born of precession, implies that as the years pass, *the visual impact of this cosmic triangle will become more and more powerful.*

The interesting thing is that this stellar triangle was evidently intended to remain invisible. It is a stellar figure or cosmic power that we *know* is there, yet which remains hidden from our sight. Below on the Earth, its equivalent form, the Federal Triangle, is plainly visible, with Pennsylvania as its longest side. Since the Constitution Avenue line of the Federal Triangle represents the ecliptic, the implication is that Pennsylvania Avenue was intended by L'Enfant and Ellicott as a sacred route, with its celestial equivalent an invisible pathway in the skies.

Perhaps it is clear now why the symbol-makers and architects of Washington DC concentrated their efforts on zodiacal symbols which reflect so deeply the arcane nature of the stellar Virgin? Perhaps it is clear now why the idea of an earthly triangle – encapsulated in the phrase *Federal Triangle* – should reflect this stellar form on the earth plane?

From the very beginning, the city was intended to celebrate the mystery of Virgo – of the Egyptian Isis, the Grecian Ceres and the Christian Virgin. This truth – and this truth alone – explains the structure of the city, and the enormous power of its stellar symbolism. Washington DC is far more than merely a city of zodiacs – it is a city which was built to celebrate a massive cosmic symbolism, expressed in stars. Its three main buildings – Capitol, White House and Washington Monument – mark on the Earth the annual renewal of that magical pyrotechnic display in the skies, which occurs on the days around the 10 August.

When we gaze upon this marvel of engineered starlight which is Washington DC, it is easy for us to forget how the city originated. It was engineered over two hundred years ago, when either Ellicott or L'Enfant drew a line from the top of a wooded hillside, and directed it towards a specific point of Sunset. From this single line, the planner subtended another which ran due west from the hill. At a certain point along this second line, he drew across it, at right angles, a third. He extended this, so that it cut the first line – the Sunset line. In this way, he formed a triangle on the earth. The planner had drawn this triangle with one angle pinned into the hill called Jenkins Heights because he knew that there was another triangle hidden in the skies, marked by pinpricks of starlight.

To reaffirm the connection between earth and skies, he ensured that on one day of each year the acute angles of the two triangles – the stellar and the earthly – would touch – triangle of light to triangle of earth – over the western rim of the city.

The designer intended this union of earth and skies to remain a secret. He knew how mysteries work. He recognized that it did not matter a great deal whether anyone who lived in his city discovered the meaning of his mystery: it was sufficient that he had bridged the material with the spiritual. He knew that the power born of this connection between earth and skies would continue to beneficially influence the souls of those who lived in the city, even if they did not know, with their conscious minds, whence this power came. His whole city was a Mystery, and he felt no need to explain it. He had taken for granted that the planner of a city should ensure that it was well designed on the earth, and that it was harmoniously linked with the skies.

A city which is laid out in such a way that it is in harmony with the heavens is a city in perpetual prayer. It is a city built on the recognition that every human activity is in need of the sanctification of the spiritual world, of which the symbol is the light of the living stars.

Postscript

> Who in his own skill confiding,
> Shall with rule and line
> Mark the border-land dividing
> Human and divine?
>
> (Longfellow, 'Hermes Trismegistus', poem of 1882)

I did not at first intend this book to be an account of the influence of Masons on the building of Washington DC.

When, more than ten years ago, I began my researches into the secret symbolism of the federal city, my interest lay in the stellar wisdom of the zodiacs which I encountered in the centre of the city. My attention had been drawn to the many zodiacs in the Library of Congress and in the Capitol buildings, and as I explored the meanings of these my attention was drawn to other zodiacs, in different parts of the city. Washington DC, which I had thought had only two or three zodiacs in its centre, soon revealed itself as teeming with zodiacs and zodiacal images – many of them in official buildings where one would never have expected to find such symbols of the spiritual world. Now I know that there are 23 important zodiacs in the city, and at least 1,000 zodiacal and planetary symbols. These figures may beggar belief, but the story behind them is even more incredible. It was only after some considerable time that I began to see the thing which drew most of these zodiacs together – the Mystery of the zodiacal sign Virgo.

It was my study of this stellar wisdom of Virgo – the Christian Virgin Mother in a later guise, a representative of Isis and Minerva, enshrined in zodiacs and symbols – which gradually alerted me to the influence of the Masons on the early growth of the city. I feel that I should make this development clear. I do this in deference to the many Masons who have helped build and preserve the city during the past two centuries, and in the hope that my approach may not be misunderstood by those who cannot find it within their hearts to approve of Masonry, for whatever reason. I did not start out by studying men, or their beliefs and moral codes – I started out by studying zodiacs.

I am not a Mason. The best I can say, in justification for daring to write a book which touches upon the wisdom of Masonry, is that I have read widely in the remarkable literature of the Fraternity. In addition, I have had the good fortune to pass a great part of my life acquainting myself with esoteric truths and mysteries, some of which, I find, are still enshrined in Masonic rituals and beliefs. Perhaps more important, I have met and talked with many Masons, in consequence of which I recognize that the true Masonry – like the true esotericism and like Christianity – is not found in books, but lives within the heart. Time and again, I have been deeply moved by the readiness of soul with which so many learned Masons have welcomed the questions of a profane, and have shown themselves prepared to discuss ideas and ideals, without revealing one whit of the deeper secrets behind their thoughts, words or deeds.

A man who is not a Mason, who dares to write of Masonry, risks making a fool of himself. The deeper secrets of Masonry have always been hidden behind instructions, rituals and epoptic symbols to which the unlearned profane are rightfully denied access. Beyond admitting this, I cannot imagine that I have spent these years in a foolish endeavour. If it seems to the Masonic reader that I have, then the best I may do is apologize, and listen attentively to any arguments that present a contrary view to the one I hold. Undoubtedly, the path which I have followed in fact and scholarship is beset with snares and pitfalls, for real scholarship is a parable of probity and life: it is only the truly blessed who do not fall at times.

Fortunately, this book deals with far more than Masonry: it deals with the product of a vast undertaking which, even now, lies spread out before the eyes of all those who can see. It is, as the ancient fire philosophers would say, 'a secret which is no secret', for it stands openly revealed in the architecture and sculptures of Washington DC, awaiting only the seeing eye to make its revelation known. 'It is by light we see; by eyes we naught behold,' runs the hermetic fragment.

It is to the foundation stones of this city, the first markers of which were pegged into the namesake-port of ancient Alexandria (famed for another lighthouse), that I have tied the lifeline which may save me from foolishness. With my eyes drawn constantly to lights in the skies, I have tried to keep my feet firmly on the ground. I have wandered through Washington DC with the open eyes of a historian and esotericist, drinking in its wonders, encountering intimations that my direction of thought – while not followed by the majority – is sound and level. In my account of what I have discovered, I have tried to offer only facts, rather than speculations.

My book is a footnote to the story of Washington DC, and anyone who wishes to check the credentials behind my ideas need only do what I have done, and examine the city itself. They need only wander through its streets, inspecting the same symbols and zodiacs which have excited me to write. These symbols silently reveal their secrets with a more assured authority than anything I am likely to muster in words.

The more I have explored the city, and the more I have been touched by the mysteries of the many zodiacs it contains, the more I have marvelled that so little research has been done into this arcane aspect of its design. One consequence of this scholarly silence is that the majority of my questions have remained unanswered. Why did the Italian sculptor Franzoni introduce a Mithraic zodiac into his Capitol sculpture, *The Car of History*? Why do two important zodiacs at the opposite ends of downtown Constitution Avenue portray the sign Virgo playing a harp? Was the zodiacal marker of the summer solstice, set in a park to the north of Georgetown, aligned so precisely *by design*, or was it merely a fortunate accident? Why did a sculptor elect to put upon the memorial to the assassinated President, Garfield, a horoscope that was meaningless, because it contained two Suns? It may be that I have not been able to provide answers to these queries, but at least I will have alerted the reader to the existence of the questions, and to the presence of the zodiacs in the city.

As the reader will have become aware, some of the highways and byways of Washington DC lead into the theory of astrology – into the scrutinizing of horoscope charts, almanacs and obscure-seeming astronomic lore. This is not merely because the Christian builders of the city have always held the arch of heaven in high esteem – it is to do with the fact that Washington DC was designed to grow with the stars, reflecting a very potent and specific stellar power. In the hope that my book may be enjoyed by the general reader, I have tried to bear in mind that few people are conversant with the deeper truths of astrology, and have accommodated my text accordingly. Even so, in order to reveal the full richness of Washington DC, I have been forced at times to discuss certain astrological theorems and traditions. Wherever it has been consistent with clarity, I have confined specialist terminologies – and such arcane things as horoscopes – to references in the notes. In this way, I hope that both the general reader and those familiar with astrology will follow the drift of my narrative without difficulty.

My main thesis – that Washington DC was designed by individuals interested in astrology and astronomy – should speak for itself. That some of these individuals were also Masons, or members of other fraternities, may need some explication. My research confirmed that some individual Masons played an important role in the development of the city, and led me to trace something of the background of the famous and less famous Masons who appear in these pages. Aware that the general reader may find this something of an irritant, I have put most of the Masonic biography to the notes, and, even there, have been as brief as possible.

It is not possible to work as a historian in the United States today without observing the understandable doubts which some Christian religious groups have concerning esotericism. If, as a Christian myself, I may venture an opinion in this context, it is that the Bible appears to have been written in such a way as to accommodate the understanding of a vast range of different beliefs, most of which find a meeting point in that seminal Mystery of the Christian religion, which is the Resurrection. Among this range of beliefs is one that might be typified as Christian esotericism, which approaches Christian texts and traditions in the light of hermetic thought. Generally speaking, an informed and well-intended analysis of esoteric Christianity is unlikely to unearth beliefs which conflict in any significant way with the traditions pertaining to the hallowed Mysteries of Christianity, or with the great cosmic and moral truths we find in the Bible. Beyond offering keys to such Mysteries, Christianity is a moral force, which should be capable of harbouring a wide diversity of opinions, and which should not harbour hatreds – especially hatreds directed at communalities of beliefs, in which differences are often peripheral or minor.

I introduce this thought because, given certain reactions to my previous works, I suspect that misunderstandings may arise about what I have and have not claimed in this present book. I have been surprised by the number of people who have taken it upon themselves to criticize some of my earlier writings without having done me the courtesy of reading what I have written. The general tenor of such criticism seems to arise from the misconception that any hermetic idea must be in some way diabolic, or linked with black magic. This is completely untrue.

In view of such misunderstandings, I would like to make it quite clear that I am not for one moment suggesting that it was 'the Masons who built Washington DC', or that Masons' Lodges ever had a coordinated, formulated plan to influence the growth of the city in any way. As a careful reading of this text will have indicated, I am claiming merely that Washington DC was designed and built on Christian hermetic principles derived from, or linked with, ancient cosmological ideas. In exploring this truth, I observe that some of the people involved in the building of the city, besides being architects, planners and artists, happened also to be Masons. I am reasonably sure that in just about every case these individuals were also committed Christians. It would be patently absurd (if only because it is so obvious) for me to labour the point that Washington DC was built by Christians.

In many ways, it is not surprising that Masons should have been so deeply involved in the city. Masonry is essentially a moral movement, and those who participate in it see the symbolic power in metaphors connected with building, improvement, architecture and art, if only because these activities offer rich parables for the conduct of the inner life. Speculative Masonry may have lost most of its contact with operative Masonry, and the soft lambskin aprons worn in the Lodges may not be sufficiently strong to stand the rigours of actual building, yet the symbols painted on these aprons are themselves the working tools of an inner activity. A wholesome interest in inner activity fosters an interest in the outer world, and in that partisan section of the outer world which is the village, town or city in which one dwells. I think this – rather than any large-scale communally formulated grand plan – explains why so many Masons have played such an important role in the development of Washington DC.

It is almost impossible now to say whence the zodiacal mysteries of Washington DC originated. If we feel the need to point the finger of admiration at one person, then it must be at that genius, George Washington. The principle underlying the cosmic design of Washington DC seems to have stemmed from his mind, for the city was his grand obsession in the last years of his life. His ideas and ideals – pooled with those of his immediate associates and friends, as was his wont – appear to have been put into their preliminary material form by Andrew Ellicott and Pierre Charles L'Enfant. The religious life of L'Enfant was outwardly Christian, but the man was something of an enigma, and it would be foolish of me to venture an opinion as to his moral or spiritual calibre. Ellicott came from a long line of Quakers: a reading of his journals suggests that his religious probity was beyond question. As for George Washington, it is evident from his writings and deeds that few men were as deeply Christian as he, in a moral, intellectual and intuitive sense.

I mention Ellicott, and the great genius Washington, to indicate the sort of men at whom casual critics of the ideas I have raised in this book may be tempted to throw stones. It is certainly our duty to root out evil, and reveal it to the light. However, there seems to be no purpose in dismissing the profoundly Christian actions of individuals such as Ellicott and Washington, merely because they happen to have been involved in the moral activity called Masonry.

Appendix

It is by light we see: by eyes we naught behold.

(Hermetic fragment, quoted by G.R.S. Mead, *Thrice-Greatest Hermes. Studies in Hellenistic Theosophy and Gnosis*, 1906, III, p.67.)

There is one final thing to consider: that is *why* should the designers of Washington DC wish to emphasize the role of the cosmic Virgin in this place and time?

The search for our answer will, once more, take us back to the mediaeval period, and beyond.

In the 6th century AD, the much-travelled Christian, Cosmas of Alexandria, heaped ridicule on those foolish enough to believe that the heavenly bodies revolved mechanically. He insisted that people who entertained such a preposterous idea would be amazed at the end of the world, when the angels ceased their ministry and the stars they had hitherto directed fell from the heavens.[1]

This late classical idea, which may sound so strange to our own ideas, was warmly welcomed into the mediaeval world-vision. The great Italian poet Dante had no doubt that the cosmos was directed by angels, and he called those who controlled the motions of the planets and stars the *angeli movitori*.[2]

The angels which hover on each side of the cosmos in mediaeval diagrams (overleaf) are not mere decorations. They are the spiritual powers who control the movements of the planets and the stars, and ensure that the creative enterprise of the cosmos is kept alive, and in good working order.

We moderns may be tempted to mock Dante's view of the heavens as

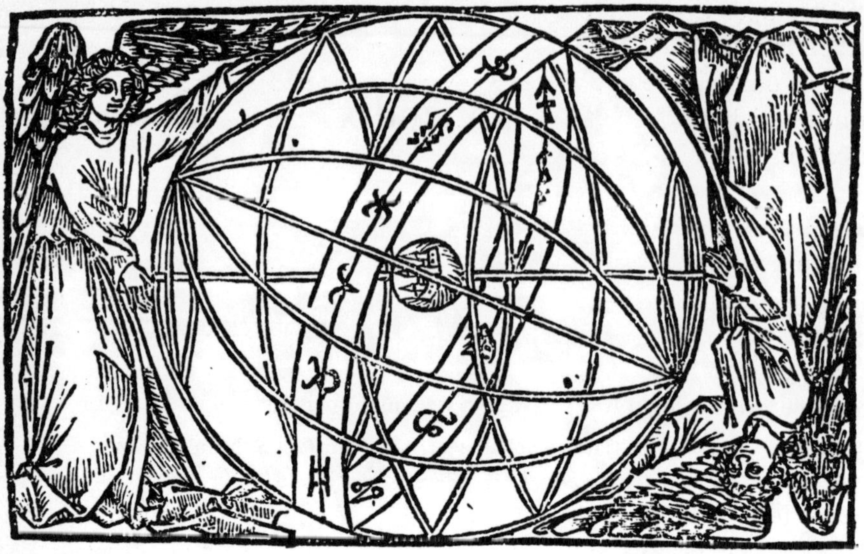

being hopelessly outmoded. We may be further tempted to challenge his belief that there were only 1,022 stars in the heavens, for do we not have a zodiac outside the National Academy of Sciences in Washington DC (plate 1) which reveals a segment of the skies set with over twice that number of stars, marked in metal studs on a marble dais? Yet, the truth is that Dante knew far more about the spiritual nature of the stars than any modern astronomer or astrologer, who thinks in terms of 'dead' matter, cosmic dust and laws of thermodynamics.[3]

Dante was deeply learned in astrology and he injected an extraordinary depth of meaning into his *Commedia* when he said that at the moment his vision began, the fishes of Pisces were quivering on the horizon.[4] With this phrase, he was indulging in a profound Christian symbolism which would have been immediately obvious to his contemporaries. Since the constellation Pisces was on the horizon, the opposite constellation Virgo must have been on the Descendant. In terms of stellar symbolism, Dante was saying that the moment his extraordinary vision began, the stars of the fish that was Christ, and the stars of His mother, the Virgin, were both visible, on either side of the heavens. So in terms of his Christian symbolism, at the time of his vision, the male and female representatives of God were cradling the Earth.

This level of symbolism is meaningful only within a framework of belief in which the stars are held to be living beings. In modern times, when such a belief is not much in evidence, it is difficult not only for us to understand the writings of Dante, but even to reach into the deeper mysteries of Christianity. Our own stars may be displays of high drama involving unbelievable velocities, temperatures and destructive flames, yet, in our minds and vision, they are as spiritually inert as the metal studs which mark the stars of the Einstein zodiac outside the National Academy of Sciences in Washington DC.

In simplistic terms, we may imagine that a good foundation horoscope, of the kind we saw in Chapter 3, is one which represents a cosmic ambience that protects the city or building to which it pertains. Traditional astrologers would support this notion, but those who have specialized in such matters (the art of determining satisfactory times for the foundations of cities, towns, houses, and so on) insist that of equal importance in such charts are not merely the Sun, Moon and Ascendant, but the fixed stars.[5] The great English astrologer William Lilly (who seems to have been a Mason) even went so far as to insist that stars, fixed as it seemed for eternity in the heavens, were important to cities and buildings because these were not as ephemeral as man:

> . . . no more can the fixed Stars compleat the effect of their impressions . . . with men, because men are of too small duration, and subject to a swift mutability in respect of their motion. And upon this is that Aphorism ground, that advises to make use of fixed Stars in the foundation of Cities . . . because Cities are generally of the longest continuance among corruptible things . . .[6]

This stellar tradition is given a practical form in many well-known foundation charts. A good example is that for the palace of the Escorial, built by King Philip II of Spain, which was elected a foundation time that involved the powerful fixed star, Fomalhaut. Philip's astrologer, Sumbergius, even adjusted the King's birth-chart (overleaf) so that it was related to this foundation, and also ensured that the double star *Ras Algethi*, the *alpha* of Hercules, was on the all-important Ascendant.[7] As we might expect, the horoscope factors attendant upon George Washington's foundation of the Capitol building, in 1793, also involved an important fixed star. The planet Jupiter, which was arising in the east at the time of the ceremony, was with the fixed star *Bungula*, the first-magnitude *alpha* of Centauri. We have looked at this foundation chart elsewhere, but we should observe here that Bungula is the nearest star to our own system, and that in the astrological tradition it is said to bring great success when it is with Jupiter. It is said to be particularly good for rituals!

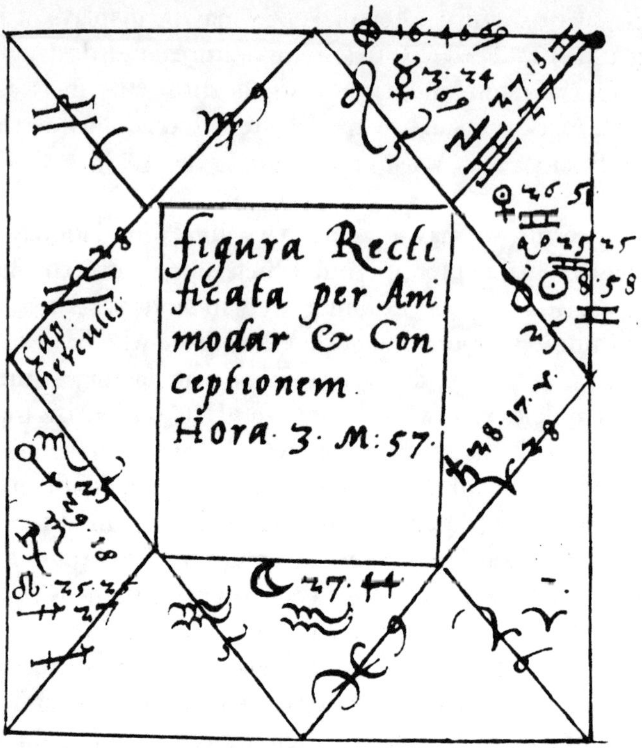

To understand the Masonic approach to this astrological use of fixed stars, we must make the effort to appreciate that all those schooled in esoteric lore – as we saw with Dante – visualize the cosmic bodies as living beings. Those architects who employ such elected moments for their foundations have, so to speak, invited living cosmic beings to participate in the moment of founding, which is the equivalent of the moment of birth.

I suspect that there is no more illuminating example of this than in the records of odes composed for a ceremonial observed by Masons on 23 May 1776, at the dedication of the Freemasons' Hall in London, designed by the outstanding Mason-architect, Thomas Sandby.[8] On that day, there were four planets in the zodiacal sign Gemini – twice as many as there had been at the foundation ceremony.[9]

After various perorations, a new ode, written by a member of the Royal Alfred Lodge at Oxford at the request of the Grand Master, and set to music by Mr Fisher, was performed. The ode was not the finest example of English poesy, it set out with little equivocation the notion that angels attend the laying of foundation stones, and participate in the ceremonials:

Heaven's rarest gifts were seen to join
To deck a finish'd form divine,
And fill the sov'reign artist's plan;

In a letter designed to explain this long ode, a Masonic Brother of the composer wrote:

> The Ode is designed to be sung at the consecration of a masonic hall; it is therefore addressed to those angelic beings who shouted for joy at the creation of the world: they are invited to attend the consecration of a building dedicated to the service of virtue, and sacred to the duties of charity and benevolence.[10]

I have already observed that when the ancient Egyptians oriented their temples towards specific stars, they were not dealing in abstractions – they were literally inviting the stellar gods to participate beneficially in their earthly life.[11] This same idea lies behind the hundreds of foundation charts which have survived from the mediaeval period.

We may take it that whoever arranged things so that the images of Virgo should predominate in the public zodiacs of Washington DC, and whoever arranged for Virgo to be so consistently operative during foundation and cornerstone ceremonies, must have been alert to the fact that *they were inviting some archetype, or spiritual being, to direct the destiny of the city.*

The first-century Egyptian astrologer Ptolemy did not actually say that spiritual beings rule places on Earth. However, this was clearly implicit in his lists of rulerships, for, even in his day, few astrologers would have denied that the stars, the zodiac or the planets were alive – were spiritual entities in their own right.[12] Indeed, Ptolemy knew what we have tended to forget in modern times – that *the very word 'zodiac' is from the the Greek root* zoon, *which means 'living beings'*. For the ancients, the cosmos was a living being.

In terms of the way Ptolemy thought, the impress or influence left upon a city by a sign of the zodiac, a fixed star or a planet, would be the equivalent of a deific influence. Since this cosmic influence involved the pagan gods (the planets and the zodiacal signs were given names and propensities by the pagans, long before Christ came to Earth), it may explain why the early Church was reluctant to embrace the astrological tradition, and lend it official credence. The names and functions of the angelic beings ruling the planets and zodiacal signs are derived not from the stream of pre-Christian literature, but from the arcane streams of Neoplatonic or Gnostic beliefs which the Church rarely hesitated to condemn as heretical.

Shortly before Ptolemy set down his compilation of ancient astrological lore, the spiritual ethos of the Mediterranean was subject to great changes. Christianity began to spread awareness of the new Mysteries. At first, the Christians did this with the willing compliance of the ancient Mysteries, which were headed by priests and initiates, many of whom knew that the old initiation systems were drawing to a close, and that their time had come to serve the new Mysteries of Christ.[13] However, within only three centuries, traditional astrology suffered a kind of eclipse, as the Christian religion – already Romanized to breaking point – established its own boundaries of acceptable knowledge, which involved the rejection of much considered to be designed to serve the pagan gods. Indeed, traditional astrology – formerly so important in Greece and Rome – was driven into the so-called 'heretical' enclaves, of the Gnostics, the Neoplatonists and the Mithraists, where it already had a substantial footing.[14] Although very many esoteric astrological ideas survived into Christianity, it was not until the 5th century AD that the 'living beings' which governed the planets were given names within a Christian context. There is much evidence to suggest that the spiritual hierarchies proposed by Dionysius the Areopagite, in that century, were derived from the ancient Mystery centres (though this need not concern us in the present context).[15]

The hierarchies proposed by Dionysius became a living part of the Christian tradition, and were rapidly assimilated into the art-forms of the religion. A rich fabric of associations and symbols was woven around the ancient planetary spheres, which had been so important in the hermetic Mystery Schools of Egypt and Greece.[16]

Dionysius had described the spiritual functions of the nine ranks of angels, and linked them with the nine heavenly spheres, inherited from pre-Ptolemaic astronomy. Only seven of these spheres were linked with the planets. Around the central Earth was the first sphere of the Moon, linked to the angels. In the next sphere, which in the ancient cosmology was that of Mercury, were the archangels. In the next – that of Venus – were the Archai. At the outermost planetary sphere, concentric to the Earth, was the seventh sphere of Saturn. The two outermost spheres marked the concentric of the zodiac and that of the fixed stars. The names and functions of the planetary hierarchies were listed and represented (see opposite), sometimes in diagrammatic form, and to these were added the names of the rulers of the fixed stars and the zodiac, under the control of the Cherubim and Seraphim, making a total of nine.[17] Not all the ancient cosmic systems consisted of nine spheres, but Dionysius adopted the ninefold system to promulgate his theologic vision of the cosmos.[18] The 17th-century engraving below gives, in descending order, the ancient names of the spheres, down to the Angels. It then repeats this hierarchy, with the names of the planetary spheres, from Saturn down to the Moon, or Luna.

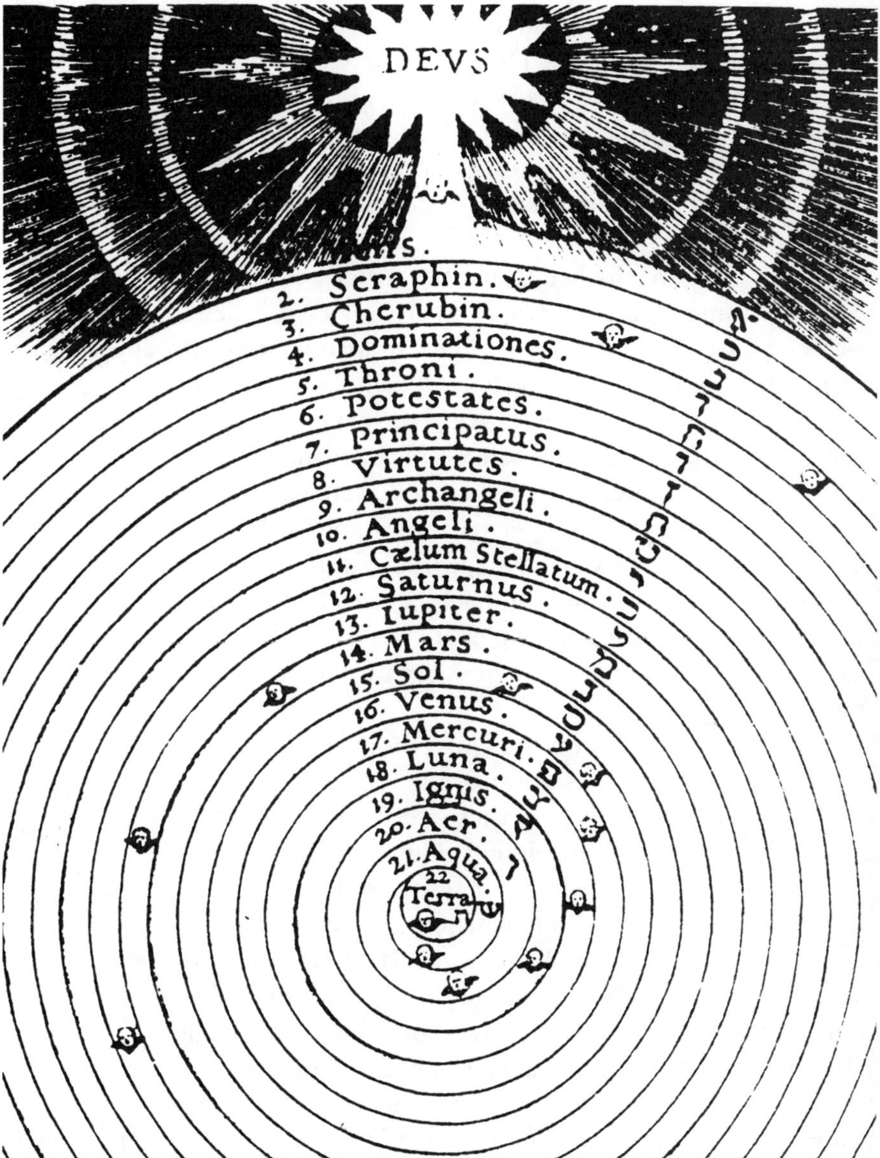

In later Christian speculations, this ninefold hierarchy of light (that is, the planetary seven, plus the Cherubim and Seraphim) was extended into another ninefold rank, projected into the lower, infernal darkness. To the Dionysian nine were added the dark distortions of the spiritual light, descending into the darkness of Hell. In this way, nine hierarchies of demons were visualized as the adversaries of the angelic hierarchies. Both groups of nine were struggling for the spiritual life that lay at the meeting point of light and darkness – which was the spiritual body of the Earth. The polarities were struggling for the souls of mankind.

It is a familiar idea that Dante's great *Commedia* set out, in poetic terms, the mediaeval ecclesiastical vision of the hierarchies of the Three Worlds. The invisible entities of Hell, Purgatory and Heaven, which Dante was permitted to see, and even converse with, had their origins in the wisdom of the pagan Mystery Schools, as much as in the theology of Aquinas.

What is often overlooked is that the structure of planetary hierarchies to which Dante paid lip service was already established long before the poet's own day. Not very long after Christianity was introduced to the world, the names of the angels and demons had begun to appear in literature. Among these names were those pertaining to the 12 angelic rulers of the zodiac, and the 7 angels of the planets.

Those unacquainted with the various systems of rulerships may find confusing the idea that an angel may be the spiritual guide of a planet, and that *another* angel may be the spiritual guide of a zodiacal sign. The confusion seems reasonable, for in the astrological tradition a zodiacal sign is said to be ruled by a planet, which suggests that the angelical beings may even be divided on how certain spiritual influences should be transmitted.

In fact, there is no division of power, or influence. The esoteric tradition teaches that it is not possible for the higher spiritual beings to have conflicting opinions – they work faithfully at the behest and command of the Supreme Being. However, it is convenient for us to think of the seven *planetary* beings as having a more direct and perceptible influence on human history, while the 12 *zodiacal* beings have a more remote (though no less powerful) influence on the ages, or cycles of civilization. The two groups of angels work in different cycles. The period governed by a zodiacal angel corresponds to a cycle of precession, which is 2,160 years. The planetary period is much shorter, at 354 years. In immediate historical terms, this means that our present Western historical development is under the guidance of the planetary angel Michael, the rulers of the Sun. The age in its zodiacal sense is presently under the guidance of the angel of Pisces, and will shortly be passing under the guidance of Aquarius.[19]

When, in the 14th century, Trithemius discussed the seven planetary beings, he used names derived from the Hebraic tradition – names which were already very old. These names – as well as the images of the zodiacal and planetary angels – were ancient when Dante began to use them in his great poem. Indeed, the octagonal baptistry of San Giovanni in which Dante was baptized, on the Saturday of Holy Week, 1266,[20] was already imprinted with a marble zodiac in the floor, as symbol of heaven come to Earth. It has been mooted that the Latin palindrome which circles the Sun at the centre of this 13th zodiac was linked with a hermetic alchemical school,[21] but, even if this suggestion is not accepted, it is still evident that the text is describing a spiritual experience involving the zodiac. Whatever the meaning of the palindrome, the names so crudely picked out around the zodiacal images were at least a thousand years old even in Dante's time.[22]

If there was a whirl of zodiacal rotation at the feet of Dante's parents at the baptism of their child, above their heads were the same tesserae decorations as still grace the great octagonal ceiling, depicting and naming eight ranks of the planetary hierarchies. Beneath each of the spiritual beings was the equivalent name – each from Dionysius' list.

Dante was christened with a marble zodiac at his feet and the hierarchies hovering above his head. When he grew to maturity, he wrote in loving terms about the Church of San Miniato, on the hill just beyond the gate of Florence, which had, set in its aisle, the most remarkable zodiac in the western world.[23] The image of Virgo in this zodiac was very little different in its symbolic force from that which had appeared in the zodiacs of Egypt, at least a millennium earlier.

In sum, the mediaeval mind recognized that, whatever the names or ranks of the angels, they were living beings – they were the servants of God, who participated in the spiritual evolution of the world. The angels were the messengers of God, their names and symbols reflecting their roles. What is important (perhaps even unique) in the Christian religion is that each of these mighty beings, who ranged from the *Angeloi* associated with the Moon through to the remote beings called the *Thrones* , who were the intelligencies of Saturn, was believed to participate in the personal life of mankind.[24] The whole spiritual hierarchy of Christendom conspired to oversee the development and evolution of mankind, whose home was strategically placed at the centre of the cosmos.

The above account is of immediate relevance to this book because, in the

Masonic tradition, the significance of the seven planetary angels was always acknowledged as a spiritual power. In some symbolic systems the planetary powers were accorded distinctive symbols which partly disguised their origins, yet continued to play an important role in the inner discipline of Masonry. It is not our place to reveal these planetary secrets here, but it is an open secret that the 'Working Tools', which vary with the first three degrees of Masonry, are linked with the three principles of alchemy, that were, in turn, linked with the three inner principles of man and woman. This continuity of tradition can be summarized in tabular form:[25]

ALCHEMY	PLANETS	MASONIC	MEANING
Sulphur	Mars	Gavel	Human passions
Salt	Saturn	Chisel	Human thinking
Mercury	Mercury	Gauge or ruler	Mediation

In alchemy, Mercury acts as a mediator which reconciles the wild burning of Sulphur with the cold aridity of Salt. In astrology, the mediator Mercury merges the aggression of Mars is tempered with the uprightness of Saturn. In Masonry, these alchemical-planetary forces are represented in Working Tools which permit the Gauge to measure accurately the rough ashlar, and the Gavel to be applied with the appropriate force, direction and weight to the Chisel. The artistic aim is to ensure that one cuts wisely and aesthetically, in shaping that rough ashlar which is the human psyche.

The tabulation may be misleading in some ways, for the symbols of Masonry are never fully explained within the rituals themselves. Even so, when they are examined in the light of hermetic history they reveal themselves as repositories of a deep arcane lore.

The learned Albert Pike (who, towards the end of his life, looked closely into Sanskrit to study the most ancient traditions behind such things) called the planetary angels Amshaspends.[26] Following tradition, he named the leader of the group with the Hebraic title *Ialdabaoth*. The mighty beings he commanded were said to be six in number, attendant upon the Sun-being Ahura Mazda, of which he is a synthesis, and numbered as the seventh.[27] In fact, Pike seems to have been more interested in the functions of the angels than in their many nomenclatures. He emphasized that the function of the angels was 'to furnish [mankind] the means of exercising [its] liberty'. He insists that those souls that are purified through this contact with light will rise heavenward, while those that persevere in evil will be chained to the body of the passions, from lifetime to lifetime. He recognized that, in this belief, he was not in any way diverging from the 'familiar lineaments' of early Christian doctrine.[28] The Russian H. P. Blavatsky, writing at almost the same time as Pike, admitted that these spiritual beings are the Cosmocratores, or builders. She seems to have been just as alert as Pike to the fact that the seven planetary angels had been dealt with by Trithemius, who had named the leader of his Secundadeians Michael. They both recognized that Trithemius had specified 1881 as marking an important turning point in Western civilization.[29]

The support of the superior archangel, Michael – who would be taking charge of the developing civilizations in 1881 – was clearly an important task which responsible humans might shoulder. It was a task shouldered to some extent by Theosophy, even though the most open preparations were put in hand by a German splinter-group, led by Rudolf Steiner.[30]

It was clear to both Pike and Blavatsky that the Michaelic seven are very advanced spirits, well beyond the level of ordinary angels. It was widely recognized by these two individuals, who so radically influenced the spiritual life of America in the last quarter of the 19th century, that in 1881, something of profound momentum was going to happen in the Western world, due to the change of planetary rulership envisaged by Trithemius.

In that shadowy hinterland which divided the acceptable theology of mediaeval Christian thought from the pagan-derived speculations of astrology, there developed a complex literature pertaining to the nature of the spiritual beings. Thomas Aquinas may have struggled to define the nature of the angels and demons,[31] yet even as he did so, the practical thaumaturgists were using the ancient documents to raise spirits and angels – even angels of darkness – to command them to do their bidding. It is unlikely that Aquinas ever doubted for one minute that the spiritual world was at the service of mankind, and would respond to human prayer: his difficulty seems to have lain in saying exactly what these spiritual beings were. In Christian esotericism, the angels and saints lived on in the calendars.

Some esotericists recognized that there was a spiritual connection between the calendar and the Christian festivities, which harked back to cosmological truths. The 19th-century Mason Ross Parsons commented on the link between an important Christian festivity in the middle of August and the constellation Virgo, when he wrote:

> The Assumption of the Virgin Mary is fixed on the 15th of August, because at that time the sun is so entirely in the constellation Virgo that the stars of which it is composed are rendered invisible in the bright effulgency of his rays . . . The misinterpretation of this sublime and ancient symbol . . . is as needless as it is shocking to an awakened mind. It is hard to say which degradation of Virgo is the worse, that by the Greeks into the Venus of erotic literature, or that of evangelical idolators, who . . . persist in viewing the Blessed Virgin simply as a Jewish maiden . . .[32]

The late-mediaeval arcanists searched through the ancient *calendaria*, occult documents, and arcane Christian literature, to produce a variety of lists proclaiming the names and functions of the spiritual entities. Lists of the planetary intelligencies, and of their corresponding antagonists (the planetary demons), were published in the earliest influential works on occult lore, compiled by Trithemius and other arcanists such as Cornelius Agrippa in the first decade of the 16th century. These names and functions are perhaps now of interest only to specialist historians, but the fact is that in compiling them, these arcanists rarely questioned that they were spiritual beings – that the angels, archangels and Archai whom they dealt with were gods in the pagan sense of the word. They had no doubt that these spiritual beings could be invoked to attract specific benefices.

Among the most interesting surviving *calendaria*, which arranged these associations in numerical sequences, is one (alongside) linked with Trithemius, and written in 1503, while he was still alive.[33] In the *scala* (ladder) of Twelve, which he drew up, are the 12 names of the ruling zodiacal angels. Among these is the ruler of Virgo, Hamaliel – a spirit which the *calendarium* identifies with the pagan corn-goddess Ceres.

This short mediaeval list of associations for Virgo – abstracted from a substantial document which gives the arcane associations for each of the zodiacal signs[34] – is worth translating, for it indicates how inclined were the mediaeval esotericists to hide meanings behind even simple words.

At the top is the angel-name *Hamaliel* – the high spiritual being who ruled the zodiacal sign Virgo. This is followed by the five sigils of the angel, which were to be used in making magical amulets. After this is the name of the month August, associated with Virgo. Then comes the name of the corn-goddess, *Ceres*, linked with Virgo – an association which, as the corn-sheaves of Washington DC have shown, survived virtually unchanged into the 20th century. Over four centuries after Trithemius compiled this list, Albert Pike, borrowing from ancient texts, wrote: 'Isis, the same as Ceres, was, as we learn from Eratosthenes, the Constellation Virgo, represented by a woman holding an ear of wheat.'[35]

The following word, *smaragdinus*, is the emerald, the sacred jewel of Virgo, presumably because it was supposed by mediaeval scholars to sharpen the intelligence. A sharp wit was an attribute of Virgo, and all who fall under the rule of her planet, Mercury.[36]

The preserve of the word *porcus* may surprise a modern reader, yet the same word that means pig was used in classical times to denote the private parts of the female (ruled, as some insist, by Virgo) and also had a special meaning in the ancient Mysteries.[37]

The *passer*, which is the sparrow, also has a double meaning, for it was a term of endearment. The mediaeval theme – once popular with artists – of the Virgin with the Sparrow is almost certainly a throwback to these lists. This Christian sparrow was the Jesus Child, the 'darling' of the Virgin Mary. The Latin was near enough to the word *passio*, or suffering, such as Our Lord endured in the Passion, to add overtones of arcane meaning to this symbol of a bird. The bird in the hand of the Virgin was a present joy and future sadness.

The double meaning in the tree (*pomus* – which, for all it may sound like an apple, is any kind of fruit tree) suggests that this Virgin will eventually produce fruit: in pagan times, the fruit would have been Horus, in later times, Jesus. This fruiting was developed into a powerful redemptive symbolism by the Christians who saw in the Virgin the woman who, through her fruit (Jesus) redeemed Eve, who had fallen through the forbidden fruit in the Garden of Eden.

The *calaminthus* (as we read the terminal abbreviation) is a wild mint: it was used in ancient times as a healing plant, and was under the rulership of Mercury, the planet of Virgo.[38] More important from the point of view of our present research is the extraordinary fact that *calamintha* was the herb used during the night of the Mysteries (the *Boedromion*) at Eleusis, in Greece, held in honour of the goddess

Demeter.[39] This mint was used to flavour the sacred drink (the *kykeion*) which the initiates received in the *cymbus* goblet, along with the sacred bread or *pelanos* – a reminder, perhaps, that the sacred rites in the Christian Church were adaptations of the rites from the earlier Mystery Schools.

The arcanists who constructed these lists of arcane associations recognized that they were not in any way haphazard minglings of names, but a portrayal of what were later called 'correspondences', or spiritual archetypes manifesting on the different planes of being. There was something in the animals, birds, plants and minerals listed below the angel Hamaliel which reflected, on its corresponding level, the spiritual working of Virgo. Thus, for example, a lady who wore the *smaragdinus* jewel – especially if this was incised with a suitable Virgoan image – would attract into her life the benefices bestowed by this sign.

In mediaeval magical lapidaries, the image of Virgo was usually associated with its corresponding '15 stars' – with the star Spica, which was set in the constellation of Virgo. The magical texts provided the appropriate sigils which were supposed to represent, on the material plane, the power of such stars. The one for Spica, the chief star of Virgo, is distinctive, with five terminations: that to the right (below) is a 13th-century variation:[40]

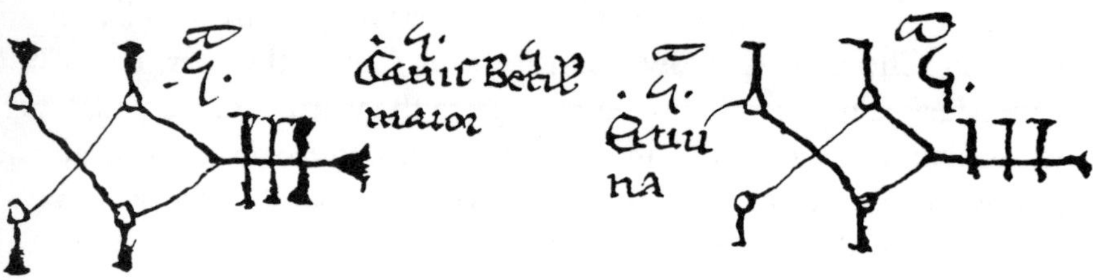

The corresponding texts recommend that the image of Spica be inscribed upon emerald (the *smaragdinus*) or that another image (of a bird, which could be the *passer* sparrow, or a man carrying merchandise – both images of the ruling planet Mercury) be inscribed upon the same stone. This would ensure the attraction to the wearer of the benefices of Virgo and her planetary ruler, Mercury.[41]

Of course, with the introduction of the spiritual and intellectual myopia which was called 'rationalism' into European culture, these attempts to link the Earth with stellar influences were rejected as superstitious. Those who worked within spiritual communities and secret societies, and who took it upon themselves to retain these spiritual communications with the stars, were compelled to do so in a different way. Instead of promulgating the virtues of amulets and talismans, they continued the secret laying-down of stellar influences by means of foundation and cornerstone ceremonies, and they began to ensure that appropriate images were distributed not upon the bodies of people, *but upon the outer fabric of the buildings around them.*

It is this admittedly somewhat simplistic account of one of the functions of the Secret Schools which explains why Washington DC has become a city dominated by the image of Virgo and Virgoan symbols.

What, then, was the nature of these spiritual beings who could be invited to oversee the destiny of a city?

On the whole, the mediaeval astrologers who wrote about such things as chorographies followed Ptolemy, or even earlier sources, and did not mention specifically that the rulers of countries and cities were spiritual beings. In doing this, they were probably staying on the windward side of the Church, which tended to smell heresy in any mention of pagan gods. However, it is clear that they took it for granted that the hierarchies – the angels, archangels, and so on – had a part to play in the cosmic realities reflected in astrological doctrines. It was the ancient Mystery Schools which had insisted that the planetary spheres were guided by 'intelligencies'.[42]

The tradition of godlike tutelary city-ruler was much older than this idea of planetary intelligencies, however. The ancient records indicate that it was a practice in former ages for the Mystery centres that directed civilization to hand out newly founded cities to the care of specific spiritual beings. As this practice was involved with the sacred lore, concerning which its adherents were not free to speak, few convincing examples of such rulerships are known. However, among those which have survived is one that is highly relevant to the city of Washington DC which was so frequently likened to ancient Rome.

There is a well-documented revelation that a specific goddess was linked with the foundation of Rome, which some Masons have visualized as the ideal of a Masonic city.[43] For many centuries the name of this goddess was kept secret, even from those who lived in the city. It was withheld for the same reason that the knowledge of the ancient Mysteries was kept secret – in order to protect the city from her enemies. However, at least one Masonic scholar believes that this sacred name was divulged when the Roman encyclopaedist Pliny revealed it as *Angerona.*[44]

Although I cannot agree with this opinion – which is to say, I do not think that the ancient sacred name of Rome *has* been divulged – it is interesting to examine the name Angerona because it indicates just how closely the ancient names of gods and goddesses were linked with cosmic phenomena.

Priests made sacrifice annually to Angerona on the kalends of January[45] – at what were called the *Divalia* or *Angeronalia.* The statue of the goddess, which stood on an altar of the *sacellum Volupiae*, on the Via Nova, took the form of a beautiful woman holding a finger to her mouth, 'the emblem of secrecy and mystery'. Was the goddess perhaps intimating her secret role as tutelary of the city which would foster the great new Mystery of Christ?

The name Angerona has been linked by scholars with the rare verb *angerere*, which means 'to raise up'. This meaning has in turn been associated with the time of the festival celebrated on the day that the Sun begins to raise itself from its ever-darkening decline. Prior to turning backwards towards more northerly sunsets, the Sun stands still, as it were: 21 December marks this winter solstice, or 'standing still of the Sun'. After this solstice, the Sun begins daily to climb higher in the skies until it reaches the full extent of midsummer.

Macrobius, in a work which dealt with the ancient Mysteries, revealed that it was common practice for ancient cities to be dedicated to a god or goddess:

> For it is well known that every city is under the protection of some deity: it is an established fact that it was the custom of the Romans (a secret custom and one that is unknown to many) by means of a prescribed formula to call forth the tutelary deities of an enemy city which they besieged and now felt confident of taking. This they did either because they believed that without this action the city could not be taken, or because they considered it an offence against the divine laws to make prisoners of gods.[46]

This should lead us to ask if the name of the goddess who rules over Washington DC is known. Or again, is it recognized in arcane circles just which zodiacal sign does rule over the city?

The modern astrologer Nicholas Campion has intimated that Washington DC is under the solar rule of the sign Virgo.[47] The Romans of antiquity might well have called the goddess Ceres, and celebrated her festival at the Cerealia, but their view that such a celestial being could be tutelary over a city would not conflict with that of a modern astrologer. However, a mediaeval esotericist – being by nature anti-pagan, yet by scholarly disposition a pagan – would have put this truth slightly differently. He would have said that Washington DC was governed by the intelligency Hamaliel, the spiritual entity which ruled Virgo, and which worked hand in hand with the planet Mercury.

The practice of assigning places to the rule of specific zodiacal signs (and thus, in mediaeval terms, to spiritual beings) is very ancient and has been extended into modern times. Since the rediscovery of America by the West, in the late 15th century, we are able to trace most of the sources for the zodiacal rulerships ascribed to the cities of the United States. The earliest valid ones I have been able to trace are from the pen of the English Mason Ebenezer Sibly, who seems to have been the first to deal publicly with the horoscopes relating to the destiny of the United States (see figure 8). In the same book in which he published these horoscopes, he mentioned that America (by which he meant 'North America') was ruled by Gemini.[48]

GEMINI, ♊.

Gemini is in nature hot and moiſt, like a fat and rich ſoil; and produces a native fair and tall, of ſtraight body and ſanguine complexion, rather dark than clear; the arms long, but oftentimes the hands and feet ſhort and fleſhy: the hair and eyes generally a dark hazle, of perfect ſight, and lively wanton look, the underſtanding ſound, and judicious in worldly affairs. Gemini is defined an airy, hot, moiſt, ſanguine, double-bodied, maſculine, diurnal, weſtern, ſign, of the airy triplicity. It is the day-houſe of Mercury; and conſiſts of eighteen fixed ſtars. The diſeaſes produced by this ſign are, all the infirmities of the arms, ſhoulders, and hands, phrenzy-fevers, corrupt blood, fractures, and diſorders in the brain. The regions over which it preſides are, the weſt and ſouth weſt of England, Brabant, Flanders, America, Lombardy, Sardinia, and Witternbergia; the cities of London, Mentz, Corduba, Bruges, Hasford, Norringberg, Louvaine, Mogontia, and Verſailles. In man he governs the hands, arms, and ſhoulders; and rules all mixed red and white colours.

Sibly was setting down this addition to the lore of chorographies in 1784, at a time when the federal city was little more than an astute idea in the mind of George Washington: Sibly was not therefore in a position to give the zodiacal rulership for what would eventually become the most powerful city in the world.

The astrological theory has to a very large extent succeeded in

Christianizing the pagan planetary and zodiacal gods, yet it still lives within a cosmoconception which recognizes the activity and participation of such gods and goddesses in the domain of mankind. It bears repeating that the astrological theory seems to hinge on the notion that the benign power of celestial beings may be invited to participate in the spiritual life of a city by means of astrology – through the medium of foundation charts, and related foundation rituals. After all, the horoscope may be viewed as a mark of a particular flow of virtues from cosmos to Earth. If an event (such as the laying of a cornerstone) could be precisely timed to control a particular influx of virtue, then specific spiritual beings could be invited to participate in the human world.

Foundation charts were the ultimate tests of the power of intercession. By means of the Masonic art, appropriate spiritual beings could be invited to participate in the life of a building or city with extreme precision. In this sense, the foundation chart – and its material expression, the foundation stone – were the outer forms of a prayer to the gods. We may not be inclined to follow this belief ourselves, in modern times, but there is ample evidence to show that the mediaeval builders did. Too many foundation charts have survived for us to believe otherwise. Undoubtedly, the mediaeval masons were following an ancient hermetic practice in inviting spiritual beings to pour their benefice and virtues into the life of their cities.

We may not know with any certainty the rank of the hierarchies which govern cities, but, as I have intimated, we do have some idea of the names of the spiritual beings who are supposed to govern epochs. It is worth our while contemplating these, because there is every indication that one of them – the representative of Virgo – was invited to participate in the foundation of Washington DC.

The connection between the idea of Rome and the idea of the new federal city for the United States was constantly emphasized by Thomas Jefferson. It is partly due to his influence that the first buildings in Washington DC were rooted in the classical idea of architecture. In the first few pages of this book, I observed not only that the hill on which the Capitol was sited had once been called Rome, but that, about the time this site was selected, there had been an eclipse of the Sun over the hill. This cosmic fact had been an echo of an event linked with the foundation of Rome itself.

In so far as there is an 'official' date for the foundation of that city, it is 20 April, 431 years after the Trojan War, which is the equivalent of 754 BC. Founded at that time was the original small castle on the Palatine.

There are many variations for this 'official' date. Cicero records that Varro asked the most reputable astrologer in Rome – Lucius Tarutius of Firmum – to cast the horoscopes of the founder Romulus and of the city of Rome.[49] Tarutius did so, working on the assumption that the birthday of the city had been on the feast of Pales (our own 21 April), and from that calculation he insisted that Rome was founded when the Moon was in the sign Libra. However, Plutarch (who was far more deeply learned in the Mystery lore than Cicero) recorded a tradition that the city was founded on the 30th of the month, when there was an eclipse of the Sun.[50]

It is these links with the classical ethos and literature of ancient Rome which explain why, *if we wish to understand the mentality of those who were involved in the founding and designing of Washington DC, we must look into classical literature, and into its late development – the arcane literature of the mediaeval period.*

The great 15th-century esotericist Trithemius, who has left his stamp on many late-mediaeval esoteric ideas, elected not to denote Christian rank when he described the seven rulers of the epochs.[51] He was recording a tradition which was already ancient – indeed, scholars now know that the literature to which he referred was pre-Christian.[52] Trithemius was probably not aware of the antiquity of the ideas he recorded, but he made it clear that he knew these seven spiritual beings were linked with the planets. He called them *Secundadeis*, a word which he did not explain, but which is probably a Latin-derived term meaning 'servants of God', or 'followers of God', and may be a translation of an Arabic term reflecting the cultural impulse through which the Secundadeian literature was preserved from ancient times. Trithemius followed an ancient tradition when he recorded the names of the seven Secundadeis – they were, indeed, names familiar to Bible-readers.[53]

Perhaps these reflections on the rank and powers of such exalted beings as Michael or Raphael are not all that important. Perhaps it is sufficient that we recognize as true the mediaeval arcane notion that such beings could be invited to participate in the life of a city, by means of the spiritual art of astrology.

In earlier times – before preparations for the Michaelic age became a matter of urgency – the majority of esotericists who were involved in the construction of Washington DC must have asked themselves frequently how it would be possible to invite the power or virtue of Hamaliel – of the intelligency of Virgo – into the life of the city which was to be the spiritual hub of their federal wheel. It was one thing to construct a city which, at its triangular hub, reflected in its form and symbolism the nature of a specific constellation; it was another to ensure that this 'house of the gods' would be worthy of a particular god. The ancient Egyptians, and after them the Greeks and Romans, had constructed temples in such a way that these could become the physical body of the god or goddess they invited by means of prayers and supplications to live within. The esoteric builders of the magnificent Christian structures also constructed their churches and cathedrals in the certainty that these would become the centre of activity of the angels, and a suitable repository for the power of Christ. Had this not been the case, the cathedrals would have had no function other than that of ceremonial, bereft of true spirituality.

This art of building seems to have been lost – or at least to have been transformed, to meet the exigencies of our times. Nowadays we rarely build churches and cathedrals as the home of our God or Christ, and we rarely construct cities in the image of the stars. The urge to invite into the everyday life of mankind the participation of the angelic beings seems to have evaporated.

To those working within an esoteric tradition, it might have appeared a relatively easy thing to prepare for the new era of Michael, which was to begin in 1881. Besides enacting special rituals and prayers, designed to invite the participation of the archangel, it would also be propitious to ensure that Washington DC was completed, according to the original plans, in preparation for the New Age. This is exactly what certain individuals – including many in the Masonic fraternity – must have done, for, shortly before that year began a concentrated effort was made to complete the building of Washington DC, and return it to some of the arcane principles visualized by the founders of the city. After 1881, came a tremendous flowering of the Virgoan imagery in the city, and the widespread introduction of zodiacs. There are over 20 important zodiacs in Washington DC, and with the exception of the two in the Capitol building, all postdate the year 1881.[54] From that year, the Virgin began to display her beautiful form, her symbols of corn, and her cornucopias, everywhere in the centre of the city.

It is evident that images of Virgo dominate the city of Washington DC. Even if we discard the undeniable fact that this domination was often arranged by the Masons, we are still left with the question – what is the purpose behind this extraordinary display of hermetic wisdom?

We have looked at a considerable number of public zodiacs in Washington DC. Each one emphasizes the role of Virgo in one way or another by, as it were, imitating the mediaeval imagery of Dante, and presenting Virgo on the horizon line – usually on the Ascending horizon, but sometimes on its Descendant. What is the meaning of this?

While many of the Americans who directed the move towards independence, and towards the founding of the federal city, were deeply Christian, it might be rash to assume that their aim was to build a city which was to reflect the mediaeval view of Virgo in her role as the Mother of Jesus. What, then, does lie behind this undoubted prevalence of Virgo in the city?

As is so often the case when contemplating the symbolism of the 18th-century founders of America, one has to go back to the literature with which they were familiar to understand their way of thinking, and to appreciate the hermetic symbolism in which they expressed themselves. In the five books of the *Astronomica* of Marcus Manilius[55] is a description of Virgo which would explain why any urbane symbolist would willingly associate the sign or constellation with his or her city:

> But modest Virgo's rays give polished parts,
> And fill men's breasts with honesty and arts;
> No trick for gain, nor love of wealth dispense,
> But piercing thoughts and winning eloquence.[56]

I suspect that behind even the most arcane of the references to Virgo which may now be found in Washington DC, there is a continual harking back to the vision of a civilized mankind which these lines promise. The verse is, indeed, almost a poetic statement of the urbane, sophisticated, honest and socially polished behaviour to which Masonry aspired. Moral training and accomplishment have been an important goal in Masonic instruction since its very beginnings, but within a new social order such as that envisaged by Republicanism, moral development took on a new urgency. The fact that by 1825 there were more active Lodges in the United States than there had been in the entire world 50 years before was a reflection of this urgency.[57] The politician-Mason, De Witt Clinton, was not alone in proclaiming that the spreading of virtue should be the primary aim of the fraternity.[58]

The question of foundation charts is of profound interest to many astrologers, some of whom are deeply interested in such questions as how the triumphs and vicissitudes of Rome were reflected in the horoscope for the founding of the city.[59] Others have concerned themselves with assessing the influence of cosmic powers symbolized by such charts on specific buildings. For example, details of the foundation chart for the new St Paul's, built by Christopher Wren, after the old St Paul's was destroyed by fire in 1666, were recorded by his brother Freemason, Elias Ashmole. This chart has been tested and validated for its accuracy by the modern astrologer Derek Appleby.[60] Yet others are fascinated as to why a mediaeval church in Florence, which was built specifically to a foundation chart designed to permit it to survive the mutations of time, has indeed passed through almost eight centuries virtually intact, when buildings around it have been less fortunate.[61] The marble zodiac in the nave of this Church of San Miniato is an interesting example of symbolism within the context of our study of Virgo – not least because this zodiac was well known to Dante, who mentioned the church in his *Commedia*.

The hermeneutic significance of the San Miniato zodiac is very complex, but there is one very simple exercise to establish the nature of its sacred symbolism. When you rest your own feet upon Virgo, you are establishing a contact between the human plane and the spiritual plane of the zodiac – the Virgin of the Christian tradition. Having established this connection with the sign which, in mediaeval symbolism, represents the Mother of God, you should allow your eyes to rest upon the image of the Sun which is at the centre of the zodiac. On the further side of the Sun, you will see the segment of the zodiac representing Pisces. As Dante reminded us, Pisces is symbol of the Christ Child, the fish. If you allow your eyes to rise just a little higher, your attention will be directed across the nave of the church towards the distant wall. There – exactly across the axis of Virgo/Pisces which you have established on the marble floor – you will see a fresco of the Virgin and Child. It would seem that the axis of the zodiac has been used by a painter who understood its spiritual significance.[62]

The link between Virgo and the Child, recognized by the early Christians, was continued into esoteric literature and into the emblems used and studied by the Masons, sometimes in suitably obscured forms. We have looked at the connections between Virgo, Isis, and Ceres. Albert Pike tells us that, in Egyptian times, Virgo was Isis, and her child was Horus. He reminds us that the inscription in her temple announced: 'I am all that is, that was, and that shall be; and the fruit which I brought forth is the Sun.'[63]

It is in such hermeneutic imagery that the significance of the Virgo-Pisces symbolism begins to emerge from the Christian Mysteries. The image of Virgo may be seen as the archetype of the feminine, while the image of Pisces, with its associations with Christ, may be seen as the archetype of the male. Shorn of its distinctly Christian symbolism, the

Virgo-Pisces imagery represents the archetypal Eve and the archetypal Adam separated, yet gazing at each other across the cosmos.

Within the framework of this symbolism we see that whenever we encounter a symbol of Virgo, the presence of Pisces is implied. Within this truth lies a deep secret pertaining to the dedication of Washington DC to Virgo – it has undeniable Christian overtones linked with the Mysteries of Christ, which has been recognized for centuries as the redemptive Mysteries of Pisces.

It is when we contemplate the literature of such savants as Dante, or when we contemplate mediaeval foundation charts, that we begin to sense something of the difference between the mediaeval world and our own. When in modern times we look at an astrological figure, we tend to think in abstractions – we see numbers, zodiacal symbols and so on, describing temporal coordinates and spatial relationships. The finest of the mediaeval astrologers did not think in such terms. For them, the planets, stars and zodiac were not abstractions, but living beings. Unless we attempt to bridge this gap between the ancient and the modern visions of the cosmos, we shall fail to appreciate the excitement with which the Freemasons who oversaw the construction and decoration of Washington DC.

As we have seen:

- The imagery of Virgo as ruler of Washington DC is reflected in the considerable number of zodiacs and lapidary symbols which grace the city.
- The Virgoan connection has also been emphasized in a number of foundation charts which are of fundamental importance to Washington DC.
- The foundation of the city itself, and the three corners of the triangle which L'Enfant had marked out for its centre (the Capitol, the White House and the Washington Monument), were each set down on the Earth at a time when the constellation Virgo had a particular importance in the skies.

When we contemplate this Virgoan symbolism – whether in the horoscope charts, in the zodiacs, or in the numerous lapidary symbols on public buildings – we may have no doubt that the design of the city has been in the hands of people who are intimately familiar with astrological teachings, and with the need within mankind to seek its roots in the Spiritual World.

There are three distinct phases in the Virgo tradition of Washington DC. During the first hundred years of the city's history, Virgo was emphasized through the horoscopy of foundation and cornerstone charts. The four main Washington DC foundation charts of this period emphasize Virgo, and often (most remarkably) duplicate significant degrees:

- Founding of the federal city
- Cornerstone of the President's House
- Cornerstone of the wing of the Capitol
- Foundation stone of the Washington Monument

Near the beginning of this phase, the first specific zodiacal symbol was set down in the Capitol by Franzoni.

The second phase opens shortly after 1881, when a public programme was put in hand designed to establish within the city a number of zodiacs. In every case, Virgo is emphasized in some significant way. While it is difficult to give precise dates for these zodiacs, the sequence seems to be:

- Library of Congress Main Hall zodiac
- Library of Congress ceiling zodiac
- Library of Congress portal zodiac
- Library of Congress zodiacal clock
- Garfield zodiac
- Noyes armillary sphere.

The several other decorative zodiacs in the Library of Congress are of lesser importance to our specialist studies.

The third phase partly interlocks with the end of this second phase, during the programme of public works which established the Federal Triangle in the early part of the 20th century.[64] Behind the programme of architectural embellishment of these huge public buildings was a recognition of the Virgoan symbolism which was of crucial importance to Washington DC. This resulted in a number of images of Virgo and Virgoan symbols, along with extensive (though not always circular) sets of zodiacal images in the main buildings. The temporal sequence of the zodiacal images and the important wheat-sheaf symbols may be summarized as:

- Dirksen zodiacs
- Mellon Fountain zodiac
- Extended zodiac on the Federal Triangle building
- Corn-sheaf on the Federal Trade Commission building

- Corn-sheaf on the National Archives
- Corn-sheaf on the Justice Department
- Corn-sheaf on the Federal Triangle building
- Inner gateway zodiac in the National Academy of Sciences
- Light fixture zodiacs in the Federal Reserve Board
- Einstein zodiac.

The last two phases of symbolism, while shot through with esoteric nuances, hold no production secrets: usually we can identify the architect and the sculptor, and more often than not have access to records. From a survey of such records, it is quite clear that the post-1881 zodiacal symbols, and the Virgoan symbols of the Federal Triangle phase, were backed by the Masonic fraternities. In many cases, I have been able to trace the designs, if not the actual execution, back to the enterprise and foresight of individuals, some of whom were Masons.

In contrast, the first phase – that which determined the Virgoan nature of the foundation and cornerstone charts – does hold what might be called 'production secrets'. While it is quite evident that the Masonic fraternities were behind the ceremonials, and therefore behind their timing (which is to say, behind their horoscopes), there does not appear to be surviving evidence of which individuals controlled this programme. Is it too much to attribute the brilliance of the zodiacal planning in this early phase to the named Masons who inaugurated building programmes, or actually enacted the foundation ceremonies? The simple fact is that we do not know who cast these early horoscopes, or who determined the foundation times and Virgoan symbolism which play such an important role in authenticating the hidden symbolism of the Pennsylvania Avenue orientation.

In spite of this, I cannot help being fascinated by the question: *who did plan this sophisticated arcane programme which would enrich the federal city by linking it with the stars?*

There is no easy answer to this question, and I can only speculate as to the truth. So far as I know, not a single documented horoscope has survived from this early period – though it is evident that some of the times recorded are curiously specific, and all of them appear somehow to involve Virgoan associations. This is why the horoscopes which emerge from re-casting charts for the known days, and speculative times, show an altogether remarkable grasp of horoscopy. There may be no doubt whatsoever that astrology played an important role in the choice of the key moments for the laying down of the federal city. Even so, until an authentic and documented figure turns up – presumably in some unexplored archive – we are, in most cases, reduced to speculation as to which individual, or group of individuals, was behind this extraordinary undertaking.

We have looked at the roles of L'Enfant, Ellicott and Washington many times in this book, and in this final stage we need to scrutinize them one more time.

As we have seen, there is little doubt that, although L'Enfant's map was certainly altered even within a year or so of completion, it was L'Enfant and Ellicott who designed the earthly triangle upon which hinges the secret of Washington DC. This implies that it was this pair who proposed an underlying triad of symbolism for the city itself. In view of the established chain of command, there may be little doubt that any major secret pattern will have been discussed with George Washington (perhaps also with the Secretary of State, Jefferson) and certainly with the Commissioners, for their approval. This chain of command was more than merely nominal, and L'Enfant was dismissed mainly because he was wilful enough at times to ignore it. Indeed, one of the issues which George Washington raised with him was that he (Washington) and the Commissioners had in mind certain things for the development of the city with which L'Enfant had not been acquainted. Unfortunately, this tantalizing militaristic *aperçu* is not developed further by Washington.

From reading into the reports and letters of those early days, I am left with the conviction that it was Andrew Ellicott who laid out the important direction of Pennsylvania Avenue, and linked it with the stars. In the course of doing this, he even amended to a small degree the plan proposed by L'Enfant. My conviction is supported by the fact that Ellicott was superbly qualified, through his knowledge of astronomy, to effect this marvellous orientation, with all its arcane Virgoan implications. On the other hand, it was L'Enfant who, after his own preliminary surveys had been confirmed by Ellicott, suggested that the 'Congressional building' should be constructed on the west end of Jenkins Heights. L'Enfant's famous explanation for his decision has reverberated through the history of the city – he chose the site because, as he said in a letter to George Washington, '. . . the Western end of Jenkins's heights stands really as a Pedestal waiting for a Superstructure . . .'[65]

The name first used by L'Enfant to denote this superstructure was 'Federal House'. Later, in one of his maps, he named it 'Congress House', but Thomas Jefferson deleted this and replaced it with his own choice, 'Capitol'. This simple change was profoundly involved with the symbolism behind the development of the plan: the word reaffirmed

Jefferson's own feeling that the federal city should reflect the Augustan splendours of ancient Rome.

Jefferson's original sketches for the federal city reveal that he had in mind that its general ground-plan should echo the ancient Roman model of roadways set in a ground-plan of rectangular blocks.[66] This design had been adopted in ancient times to facilitate the movement of marching men and both military and civic processionals. No doubt, Jefferson had wished to establish a city which reflected the glories and achievements of the ancient world, and especially those of Rome, which (as he recognized) had prepared the way for the spread of Christianity through the agency of its European road system.

There were other reasons for this wish to link with, if not to actually excel, ancient Rome. When the English Mason the Reverend James Anderson, who was a member of the Royal Society and a friend of the influential Masons Jean Théophile Desaguliers and Stukeley, wrote the first account of speculative Masonry, he had emphasized the role of Rome. His account may have been entirely imaginary in terms of strict history, but it certainly entered into the mythology of Masonry. Anderson claimed that no less a personage than Augustus Caesar was 'the Grand-Master of the Lodge at Rome'.[67] It almost followed from this that 'the Pattern and Standard of true Masonry in all future Times . . .' should become the architectural style to which Masonry aspired.[68] It is partly this mythos which explains the extent to which Washington DC was built on the supposed models of Augustan architecture. Was there, at the back of Jefferson's mind, the notion that since Rome had been founded according to a very specific horoscope, so should the new federal city?[69]

Although the plan for a city based on the ancient Roman system of rectangular blocks was adopted by L'Enfant, he sensibly broke the threatened monotony of this (and also aided rapidity of communications) by cutting angular avenues through the blocks – nominally to effect communications with various parts of the city and the surrounding districts. These radiants were adapted very early to the symbolism of the city, when they were named after the states which had participated in the struggle against Britain.[70] Could it be that this idea of a stellar radiant was also suggested by certain arcane ideas linked with the history of Rome?

One such idea, ultimately derived from the ancient Mysteries, had become established in the newly Christianized Rome by the fourth century. Since it involves the notion of the Virgin – albeit the Virgin of the Christians – it is worth exploring the idea's implications.

I have shown in my final chapter that the stellar display over

Pennsylvania Avenue is centred on 10 August. The displacement of the Sun along the horizon is sufficiently slow for both the day prior to this date, and the day after, to reflect the identical magic of orientation. Now, although the phenomenon is used to encapsulate the secret design of the centre of Washington DC, a Christian festival does relate closely to one of these three calendrical dates. On 15 August the Catholic Church celebrates the Assumption of the Virgin – the translation of her soul and body to heaven.[71] It is undeniable that the image of a celestial Virgo, poised in the skies above Pennsylvania Avenue, may be interpreted in Christological terms.

Once again, we are brought face to face with the fact that whilst those who guided the development of the new United States had no wish to introduce sectarian religion into their programme, they found themselves facing certain difficulties. They found it difficult to institute models derived from the ancient Mystery wisdom of Greece and Rome without appearing to pay lip service to the later, Christianized, versions of this same Mystery wisdom. It is this which explains why, even today, it is possible to see Washington DC as a representative of both pagan and Christian streams of thinking.

The earliest zodiacal rulerships ascribed to the cities of the United States that I have been able to trace are from the pen of Ebenezer Sibly, written *circa* 1784, seems to have been the first to deal in public with the horoscopes relating to the destiny of the United States (see figure 8). In the same book in which he published these horoscopes, he mentioned that America was ruled by Gemini. He listed only three cities of North America, but the rulerships he proposed are still widely accepted by astrologers in modern times: New York was ruled by Cancer, Philadelphia by Leo, and Charlestown (later, Charleston) was ruled by Libra. Undoubtedly, Sibly's own interest in these rulerships stemmed from his Masonic connections, for at the end of the 18th century Masonry was well established in each of these cities.

It is not certain how Sibly deduced these associations, since he never visited America himself, but it is interesting to speculate on how he may have arrived at these rulerships. New York may have acquired its zodiacal rule from its namesake city in England. In the 18th century, the River Ouse was still tidal at York, which meant that the city was a well-protected port. Due to engineering regulation of the river, the tides have moved many miles towards the sea. Nonetheless, when Sibly named New York as a Cancer city in 1788, its proto-city was still a tidal port, and was traditionally ruled by the watery Cancer.

In spite of what is widely believed, William Penn did not devise the name of Pennsylvania, and nor was the place named after him. He had applied for the tract of land to be called Sylvania, and it was the British King who added the prefix 'Penn' to this – not in honour of the Quaker, but of his father, the British admiral. The date of the founding of Pennsylvania has been recorded as 7 December 1682. I suspect this could be the reason why Sibly elected to accord the city to the rule of Leo. On that day, Jupiter and Saturn were in near-conjunction, close to the Dragon's Head – all in Leo.

The source for Charleston being under the rule of Libra is more elusive. In 1670, Charlestown took its name from the reigning British monarch, Charles II, whose various charts show a connection with Libra.[72]

Of course, in the light of our own interests, this material is rather disappointing. The only evidence that the city of Washington was linked zodiacally with Virgo is from the numerous charts I have cast for its early phases of building – all of which emphasize the sign Virgo, and most of which fall within the parameters of foundations set down by Ptolemy.

In his detailed development of the Isis theme, Albert Pike shows that the complex rites of Isis throw a great deal of light on the later development of Marian iconology. As Queen of the Underworld, she was the Black Virgin of pre-Christian times. As goddess of maternity, and the Great Mother, she was depicted with the Sun-god Horus as a child – sometimes with the child clasped to her breast. As a deity of the sea, she was shown alongside sail-boats, reminding us of the later name for the Virgin as the *Stella Maris*. It is this which explains why a sail-ship is often found in images of Isis. In some images, Isis is shown with the dog-star Anubis, and with other stars as emblem of her celestial origins. Oddly enough – even though there is no indication that Pike was familiar with the work – each of these themes is set out in the engraving from De Hooghe's esoteric work, which I reproduce in figure 9.[73]

It is in such hermeneutic symbolism that the significance of the Virgo-Pisces symbolism begins to emerge from the Christian mysteries. The image of Virgo may be seen as the archetype of the feminine, while the image of Pisces, with its associations with Christ, may be seen as the archetype of the male. Shorn of its distinctly Christian symbolism, the Virgo-Pisces imagery represents the archetypal Eve and the archetypal Adam separated, yet gazing at each other across the cosmos. Above them, standing at the mid-heaven, above this horizon line, is God, the all-seeing mediator.

Within the framework of this symbolic triangle, we see that whenever we encounter a symbol of Virgo, the presence of Pisces, and the all-seeing eye of God, are implied. Equally, when we see an image of Pisces, both its opposite sign Virgo and the mid-heaven image of God are also implied. By extension, the mid-heaven symbol, of the Eye of God, implies the polarity of Virgo and Pisces. Virgo seems always to be connected with the idea of the triangle.

My attempt to find a connection between the triangle and Virgo-Isis may seem far-fetched to those unfamiliar with astro-hermetic literature. However, the truth is that even 1,000 years before the birth of Christ, the ancient Egyptian texts in the Temple of Isis at Gizeh called the goddess 'Mistress of the Pyramids'.[74]

To understand the secrets of Washington DC we have to take not a leap of faith (which is easy) but a leap of imagination (which is more difficult). We have to place ourselves in a way of seeing things which is essentially foreign to our nature. We have to try and imagine what symbols were being manipulated by those involved in Esoteric Schools at the end of the 18th century. This means attempting to put ourselves in a position where the cosmos is seen, not as a mechanical and materialistic system, but as a spiritual and creative activity, overseen by angels.

The one thing which we have established about 18th-century esoteric symbolism is that it was permeated with Egyptian, or pseudo-Egyptian, notions. There was an element of revivalism in this interest – a revivalism supported by the opening up of Egypt by travellers and by French invaders. This revival would give rise to a whole new body of architectural forms which still grace the inner and outer temples of many Masonic buildings. In Washington DC, the two guardian sphinxes on the outside of the former House of the Temple (figure 1) – the Supreme Council building on 16th Street – are perhaps the most obvious examples of this nouveau-Egyptian symbolism.

However, for the moment I would like to look not at 'revived' Egyptian lore, but at Egyptian lore as it survived into and through the Christian era by way of cosmic symbols. It may have surprised some non-specialists to discover earlier in this book that the five-pointed star which graces the national flag of the United States can be traced back to an Egyptian hieroglyphic linked with spiritual beings. Here I must stress that this *sba* star survival is by no means unique. The truth is that many symbols from the ancient Mystery wisdom of the Egyptians were adopted into Christian lore, and in an amended form – and all too often in hidden ways – insinuated itself into later Christian art. Almost all Christian symbols and art-forms were at one time or another pagan, simply because most of these were continued from the ancient Mysteries, which were dominant in ancient times in Greece, Anatolia and the Middle East. The source of most of the ancient Mystery symbols was Egypt – though even serious historians, like Strabo and Plato, were inclined to trace the roots of Egypt to Atlantis, which for them was not a mythical place at all.

Whatever its spiritual origins, this non-revival Egyptian lore is more powerful than the revival form, simply because it is still charged with the old Egyptian lore which has worked into the subconscious levels of Man rather than into the conscious levels, as revival symbols usually do. To take a pertinent example of what I mean, I would like to glance at yet another mediaeval image of Virgo, which (on a cursory examination) would appear to have nothing to do with Egyptian lore.

In the Manuscript Division of the British Library is a remarkable manuscript[75] in which are painted colour illuminations of the 12 constellations. The image of the winged princess that represents Virgo (figure 38) is of very great interest to me. It is of interest not merely because the tabular part contains very early sigils for the planets (the four to the top right are early forms of Saturn, Mercury, Mars and the Sun) – nor even because we have in these tables examples of the early so-called Arabic numerals which were soon to be widely adopted in Europe. It is of interest because of the intrinsic symbolism of the image of Virgo itself. The winged Virgin is shown with her feet on the Earth, and her crowned head against the star-studded skies. Near the bottom of her dress is a line of seven stars, which do not correspond to anything that may be seen in the constellation Virgo in the skies. This line of stars continued into the later mediaeval woodcut tradition (see p.162), and I have shown that its purpose is to suggest that the line represents one side of a triangle, which may be completed by joining the two outer stars to the central star between the breasts of the Virgin. If my theory is correct, we have not only a Virgin who joins Earth to Heaven, but *one who herself displays a triangle*.

Where have we seen a symbol of life and a sceptre in connection with a Virgo image? When we examined the Egyptian image of the sacred dew – the tears of Isis and her sister Nephthys – we saw that the stream of water (the *mes* of the Egyptians) consisted of a stream of the *ankh* and *uas* symbols. The *ankh* is the symbol of life, while the *uas* is a sacred sceptre.

In the mediaeval image of 1490, these two symbols survive in a slightly different form, consistent with mediaeval symbolism, but with much the same depth of arcane meaning. The Virgo in this illumination is offering *life and power*, which (in promissory symbolism) she can pour down from the heavens on to the Earth plane by virtue of her hidden triangle.

The Egyptian image of the celestial dew shows what is sometimes described as a baptism – redolent of a modern baptism, in which holy water is poured over the head of the child. However, it is more than a baptism scene – it is a portrayal of the initiation of a neophyte into the secrets of the higher world. The life and power that are being poured over his head are not in the least material – this is the *higher life* and the *spiritual power*.[76]

This graphic sermon could be preached over a multitude of Virgoan images. The lesson we might learn from all such homilies is that the time has come to reassess these ancient designs, which were rarely merely decorative, and which almost always pointed back to an ancient arcane wisdom. This rich symbolism reveals itself in the fabric of the city of Washington DC, which was built to serve the future, yet used with such consummate skill the arcane devices of an ancient past.

My present interest does not lie in these stellar symbols, but in the two things the Virgin holds in her hands. In her left hand (marked by a large star which represents Spica) she holds a sceptre. In her right hand she holds a plant, which has a spray of five floral heads. I have seen a similar flower in hundreds of images of Virgo: it is a version of the wheat-ears of Spica. Just as the wheat is a symbol of spiritual life, so is the flower *the plant of life*.

The significance of Spica in the ancient Mysteries is that it pointed to the sacred corn that was marked by the prime star. This was taken over by Christian symbolism to represent the holy wheat – the bread of life, which was sometimes given in the image of a Christ Child, and symbolized as the holy bread, or host. This bread was called *pelanos* in the ancient Mysteries.[77] It was the *pelanos* which was adopted by the later Christians as the *host* of the sacred Mass – which means that the *host* was associated with the Spica-bread of life. Just so, this five-flowered plant associated with the star Spica, which lies closer to the pagan world than to the Christian, remains a symbol of the plant of life.

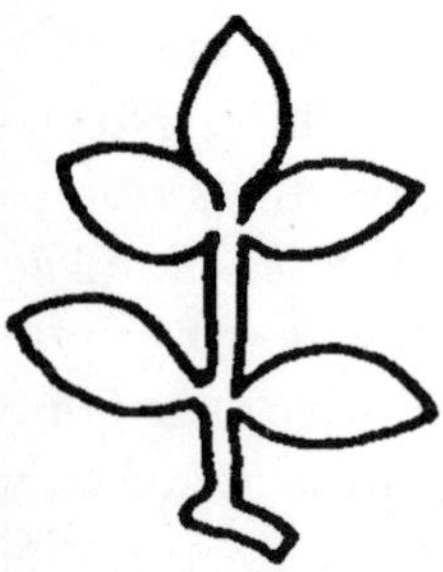

Images of the plant of life are found on a multitude of buildings in Washington DC – indeed, it is the most recurrent of all symbols in the city. Why should there be *thousands* of such flowers in the Federal Triangle, were it not in homage to the ancient Mysteries? After all, the architects must have known that such lapidary plants are still found in the ruins of the ancient temples and Mystery centres of Greece, Turkey and Rome. Why should the designers of the Library of Congress have chosen to have the sculptor Frederick MacMonnies decorate the dresses of both the maidens on the central doors (figure 39) with this same five-leaved flower?[78]. The dress of Minerva in the lunette above the two doors also bears this same five-leafed motif (opposite).

The two maidens on the bronze doors carry pairs of flaming torches, and are supposed to represent the Humanities and the Intellect.[79] However, their floral dresses, and their position below Minerva, indicate that the entire portal decoration is a paean to Virgo. The image of Minerva is intimately bound up with one of the great esoteric Mysteries of the ancient world, for it is said that the sacred Palladium was a carved image of Minerva, which in legend had been carried from Troy by the hero Aeneas.

The Palladium had two functions: one was to protect the city in which it was located; the other was to act as a spiritual centre for the dissemination of that esoteric lore which alone supports the growth of civilizations. This is why the Palladium was recognized as the supreme treasure of the ancient world. Legends tell how it was stolen by Odysseus, who carried it to Greece, to found the post-Egyptian civilization there. Later stories from the same legends tell how it was subsequently taken to Rome, in order that this city would then become the centre of the civilized Western world. In Rome, it was at first kept in the Temple of Vesta. However, because its presence was recognized as being of profound importance to the city, it was hidden away. After the Fall of Rome, the Palladium was carried to the new centre of civilization, which was to be Byzantium. Here it was buried beneath a column in the great Hippodrome. It is said that when Byzantium fell to the Turks, the Palladium was lost, and with it the power to direct the cultural growth of civilizations. However, some esoteric scholars insist that the Palladium of Minerva was not lost, but hidden away in another country, where the civilization of the future was to develop.[80]

The Palladium was a torch, passed on from dying civilization to embryonic civilization by the Secret Schools. Minerva, for whom a temple was built on the Capitoline Hill in Rome in very early times, was in the exoteric form of her worship the goddess of the arts and health – patroness of physicians. Exoterically, she was the goddess of wisdom, while in the esoteric tradition she was recognized as a later form of the Egyptian goddess, Isis.[81]

Whatever the present resting place of the sacred mascot of civilization, the Palladium, an image of its tutelary goddess Minerva, directing the

Humanities and the Intellect and openly linked with the symbolism of Virgo, is resplendent in bronze in the central doors of the Library of Congress. *Minerva, the Greek equivalent of the Virgo goddess, Isis, survives still in a prime position in Washington DC, still associated with a Capitoline Hill.*

Does it appear that I am being over-imaginative in tracing ancient esoteric symbols in Washington DC? To deny that the city is rooted in the ancient loam of the Mysteries is to fly in the face of fact. In this city, the triangulation of Virgo is undeniable: it can be seen picked out in pinpricks of light in the night sky, hovering over the White House at the end of Pennsylvania Avenue, for several days in the Virgo month of August. This star-shine, tied to the city by the orientation of Pennsylvania Avenue, is the recurrent mystery of Washington DC, and cannot be a consequence of accident. The federal triangulation, contiguous with the stellar Pennsylvania Avenue, is also undeniable, for as I have shown, a study of the many Virgoan symbols in that triangle reveals beyond a shadow of doubt that, while the buildings were nominally designed to serve vast bureaucracies, they were also quietly dedicated to the ancient goddess. The presence of Virgo in the lapidary symbolism of the city is equally undeniable. It is picked out in zodiacs and arcane devices so insistently and so openly that one is forced to conclude – and with good reason – that the zodiacs and symbols are there *both to reveal and to hide the power of the Virgin goddess.*

This city, then, designed to serve a great future, is firmly rooted in a wisdom of the past, and like many of the great cities of past ages has striven to unite itself with a tutelary goddess. The goddess may be traced back to origins in the earliest records of Western civilization – to the temples of ancient Egypt and to the oldest papyrus records known to Man. Because this is so self-evident, it is tempting to conclude with a reference to the angelic nature of Isis-Virgo – perhaps with a quotation from some arcane Egyptian source. Yet, for all the Egyptian imagery that is found in Washington DC, the city is Graeco-Roman in spirit. Washington DC has been constructed upon classical principles – from what is an Egyptian wisdom transmuted by the genius of the Greek Mysteries. It is therefore fitting that I conclude with a quotation from the arcane literature of the classical world. What, then, could be more appropriate than to quote from the great Roman poet Virgil, who helped Rome invent its own past? And what more appropriate a theme than the transition from the Dark Age of Iron, to the Light Age of Gold, which has been taken by some scholars as a pagan prediction of the new Mystery of Christ? Finally, it is fitting that it be Virgil seen through the eyes of a scholar who profoundly influenced the spiritual life of Masonry, in Washington DC, in the mid-19th century:

> Now the Virgin returns, the Saturnian reigns return:
> Now a new Offspring is sent down from high heaven.
> O chaste Lucina favour the Boy now being born, with whom
>   the iron race
> Shall end and a golden arise in all the world . . .[82]

Notes

CHAPTER ONE

1. From the 1853 edition of *The Poetical Works of Thomas Moore*, Vol. II, p.296. See also n.22 below.
2. Washingtonians may be confused by the former location of Foggy Bottom. The modern perception of the locality has certainly been changed by the positioning of the Metro station which bears its name. However, as the name implies, Foggy Bottom was originally towards the bottom of the sloping area which ran into the northern mudflat banks of the Tiber, and the north-east banks of the Potomac.
3. The drainage of the River Tiber began early. A hand-coloured manuscript map of 1797, in the National Archives, shows the intended reclamation of water lots near the juncture of the Tiber with the 'Potomack' (*Rec. Gp. 42*, in the Records of the Office of Public Buildings and Public Parks).
4. His name is recorded as Jacob Funk, and it is sometimes claimed that he was a Dutchman, though this scarcely accounts for his choice of the name, Hamburg. The story of the Funk ownership is a complicated one, but we should observe that Funkstown was part of a tract of 88 acres granted by Frederick Calvert in 1754 to one Henry Funk. *See* John Clagett Proctor, *Proctor's Washington and Environs*, n.d., but *c.* 1949, pp.305ff. Proctor tells us that the Maryland census of 1790 listed 12 different Funk families living within the state. In 1998, I counted 9 Funks in the Bell Atlantic telephone directory for the District of Columbia – a reminder of just how many of the names of the original settlers have survived in this city.
5. It was, as J.C. Proctor records, 'anterior to the drainage of the grounds, noted for its unhealthfulness'. See '"Foggy Bottom" or Hamburg', in Proctor (op. cit,. n.4 above), p.305.
6. For my detailed account of the Einstein zodiac, see Chapter 10.
7. More likely it was used to observe the coming of the ships along the Potomac, for even into the first decades of the 19th century ships could anchor at the wharfs.
8. Franklin Webster Smith is so ignored by historians that, in spite of his massive influence on Washington DC, I have found it difficult to locate even elementary information about his life and work.
9. As guardian star of the Nile, Sirius was called *Sihor*. I give some of the details of this ancient star because of its importance in some of the following chapters.
10. The vernacular *Sopet*, (or *Sed* or *Sot*) was continued into Roman astrology in the writings of the astrologer Vettius Valens, *c.*150 AD, but these terms are clearly derived from the original *Spdt*.
11. See Robert K.G. Temple, *The Sirius Mystery*, 1998 revised edition.
12. I write of the constellation *Cygnus* forming a cross over the island with some deliberation, since many of those who settled this area in the 17th century would have known of Julius Schiller's map of the heavens, which attempted to Christianize the pagan images by redefining the northern hemisphere in terms of

the New Testament personages and symbols. Schiller had proposed that *Cygnus* should be turned into the Cross of Christ. See J. Schiller, *Coelum Stellatum Christianum*, 1627.

This idea resurfaced in the cosmological map of the world constructed by Albert Ross Parsons, inset in his *New Light from the Great Pyramid*, 1893. The chart is designed to show Parsons' view of the distribution of the signs of the zodiac over the face of the Earth. Cygnus is over the eastern side of North America!

13. By a curious twist of history, President Roosevelt was a Mason. However, it is unlikely that Masons Island had anything to do with Masonry: it was purchased in 1777 by George Mason of the Virginia Legislature.
14. I recently had the good fortune to speak with a family member of descendants of the famous Dr Benjamin Rush, who was a contemporary of Banneker, and whom Banneker (see n.15 below) quoted in his almanacs. Our conversations revealed that only seven generations separate the living descendant from the illustrious Rush.
15. Since Banneker later did a reworking, or 'back-trial', of this eclipse, and since his companion Major Andrew Ellicott later dealt with it in surviving documentation, I assume that they both observed it. Certainly, they were both in the locality at the time: they had arrived at Alexandria on 7 February 1791, prior to laying out the boundaries of the new federal district. For reliable documentation of this event, see Bedini, Document 11, 'Projection of a solar eclipse . . .', *The Life of Benjamin Banneker*, 1972 ed., p.315.

    Of course, I do not know from what point within the federal district Banneker would have made the observation, but my guess is that he would have taken advantage of the highest point – Jenkins Heights, to the east of the Potomac site. Banneker had calculated the eclipse for 11.32 a.m. local time; James Ferguson had said that it would take place at 10.30 a.m., but there are differences in both time systems and spatial coordinates. As my own modern computer system records that the eclipse was exact at 07:36:30 a.m. local time for Jenkins Heights, bearing in mind time differences, Banneker seems to have been the more accurate of the two.
16. For an account of how Banneker did 'the vast amount of work . . . required to calculate a single eclipse,' based on calculations in his surviving notes and journals of Banneker, see Bedini (op. cit., n.15), p.203ff.
17. For a reproduction of the Franklin cut (of which the Banneker engraving is an unacknowledged copy) see C. William Mille, *Benjamin Franklin's Philadelphia Printing 1728–1766*, 1974, Appendix B (509), fig. 11.
18. See for example, A.J. Pearce, *Text-Book of Astrology*, 1911 ed., p.314, where the ancient rule is formulated: 'We do not believe that the mere eclipse portends anything, but that the relative planetary positions at the moment of ecliptic conjunction . . . of the Sun and Moon are indices of coming events: hence some eclipses are considered to portend evil and others good.'
19. As with most esoteric words, the meaning is a little more complex than I have suggested here. Even in Roman literature, the word *Aries* is sometimes taken as being synonymous with the 'golden fleece', even though it remains also the Aries of the zodiacal twelve. The Latin is derived from a Greek term which has an even more complex body of interrelated meanings.
20. The planetary positions for the 1791 eclipse were:

    SU 13AR42 MO 13AR42 ME 02AR56 VE 05TA45 MA 08AR03
    JU 24VG27R SA 09AR24

    Although Banneker knew of the existence of Uranus (which he called *Georgium Sidus* in his almanacs), he never gave its position. At the eclipse, the so-called 'new' planets were located: UR 10LE13R NE 26LI39R PL 21AQ36.
21. See the delightful work by William Tindall, *Standard History of the City of Washington from a Study of the Original Sources*, 1914, p.18. The story of the Pope

'prophecy' is repeated in many works – see, for example, Proctor (op. cit., n.4 above), p.289, and Willard Glazier, *Peculiarities of American Cities*, 1886, pp.529ff.

22. The second verse of Moore's poem, 'To Thomas Hume, from the City of Washington' (1804), makes sense only in the light of the story I have just told. In fact, an editorial note in the 1853 edition of *The Poetical Works of Thomas Moore*, vol.II, p.296, explains the lines by reference to *Weld's Travels* which records that 'the identical spot on which the capitol now stands was called Rome'. The 1853 version of this section compares in an interesting way with the 1862 edition. I give the 1853 version first:

> In fancy now, beneath the twilight gloom,
> Come, let me lead thee o'er this second Rome!
> Where tribunes rule, where dusky Davi bow,
> And what was Goose-Creek once is Tiber now!
> This embryo capital, where Fancy sees
> Squares in morasses, obelisks in trees;
> Which second-sighted seers, ev'n now, adorn,
> With shrines unbuilt and heroes yet unborn . . .
>
> In fancy now, beneath the twilight gloom,
> Come, let me lead thee o'er this modern Rome!
> Where tribunes rule, where dusky Davi bow,
> And what was Goose-Creek once is Tiber now!
> This famed metropolis, where fancy sees
> Squares in morasses, obelisks in trees,
> Which travelling fools and gazeteers adorn,
> With shrines unbuilt and heroes yet unborn.

23. Since so many errors have been made by historians prepared to write about the deed without troubling to examine it, I give its location in the Maryland State Archives, Annapolis.

The manuscript (in fair copy) is in *Liber AA* for 1664 (formerly *Liber 6*), at folios 318–321, and is dated June 5 1663. In the section wherein the 100 acres is granted to Pope, in consequence of his having transported two persons to the province in 1659, the text is marginally digested as *Francis Pope. 400 Acres. Rome*. I mention this because, in the preamble to the survey of the 'parcell of Land in Charles County', the site is actually called Roome: we must take this as a scribal error. On folio 319 the actual record of the deed in consequence of various grants and bequests reads:

> *Do hereby grant unto him the sd Francis Pope, a parcell of Land called Rome, lying on the East side of the Anacostine River Beginning at a marked Oak, standing by the River side, the bound Tree of Robert Troop, and running North up the River for breadth Two hundred perches to a bounded Oak standing at the mouth of a Bay or Inlett called Tiber . . .*

The one thing which does seem to be clear is that the names Rome and Tiber were used before Francis acquired the land.

24. See William B. Webb and J. Wooldridge, *History of Washington*, 1892, p.688.
25. The story was reported in the *Daily National Intelligencer* on 8 March 1854, and is told under the heading 'Stone from Rome', by Frederick L. Harvey, *Monograph of the Washington National Monument*, 1887, pp.52ff.
26. Hugh Y. Bernard in 'The Architectural Career of John Russell Pope', *The New Age*, vol.xcvi, no.8, August 1988, p.16. A John Pope (from Ashford, Kent) who settled in Dorchester is mentioned in Charles Edward Banks, *Topographical*

Dictionary of 2885 English Emigrants 1620–1650, 1981 reprint. However, the name Pope was not uncommon in the lists of immigrants: for some early settlers named Pope, see Peter Wilson Coldham, *Settlers of Maryland 1679–1700*, 1995, and Mrs O. A. Heath, 'The Popes of Northumberland County', in *Genealogies of Virginia Families. From the William and Mary College Quarterly Historical Magazine*, 1982, vol. iv, p.141.

27. Royal Cortissoz, *The Architecture of John Russell Pope*, 1928–30; Introduction to vol. II.
28. See, for example, the useful notes on the horoscopic figure for Rome in Pearce, (op. cit., n.18 above), pp.272ff.
29. The public zodiacs in Florence, the cradle of our modern Western civilization, are the marble versions in the baptistry of San Giovanni; in the nave of San Miniato al Monte (these are the oldest, the latter being dated 1207); and on the fountain in the Signoria Square. There are, however, painted zodiacs and horoscopes inside a number of Florentine churches, and in the Duomo.

CHAPTER TWO

1. Dennis Gabor, *Inventing the Future*, 1963 ed., p.204
2. L. E. Reynolds, *The Mysteries of Masonry. Being the Outline of a Universal Philosophy Founded upon the Ritual and Degrees of Ancient Freemasonry*, 1870, pp.426ff. The importance of electricity was recognized by non-hermeticists, too: as Paul Johnson says, in his *History of the American People*, 1997, p.574, it was electricity, more than any other single factor, which made California.
3. 'Rational Mystic', *Intellectual Electricity, Novum Organum of Vision, and Grand Mystic Secret*, 1798. It is quite extraordinary how electricity was adopted into arcane parlance – largely, one suspects, because its power seemed inexhaustible, yet its source remained essentially inexplicable. Among the interesting titles published at the end of the century, were: William Hemstreet, *Electricity and the Resurrection, or the Soul and Science*, 1900; G. W. Warder, *The New Cosmogony, or, The Electric Theory of Creation*, 1898; and his *Invisible Light, or the Electric Theory of Creation*, 1900, the title of which incorporated Nicola Tesla's interesting comment: 'My definition of electricity is invisible light'.
4. 'Rational Mystic', (op. cit., n.3 above), p.175:

   But when effete shall burst earth's womb,
   And wakes the universal shock* the tenants of the tomb:.
   Some Spirit kind, the long enigma solve!
   Shall back to Eden time revolve;
   And further yet 'fore angels fell
   And heaven was ting'd with smoke of hell?
   Was EIGHTEEN HUNDRED EIGHTY-EIGHT
   (Say) the hollow voice of fate?

   *(Poet's footnote: *Electric)*

5. See Paul E. Brierley, *John Philip Sousa. A Descriptive Catalogue of his Works*, 1973, p.53, n.38.
6. A presidential memorandum, dated 10 December 1987, designated the piece as the national march of the United States, because it had become 'an integral part of the celebration of American life'. See *The Scottish Rite Journal of Freemasonry Southern Jurisdiction USA*, May 1998, p.10.
7. Sousa did not divulge the name of the photographer, but from 1858 to 1881 Mathew Brady (famous for his dramatic photographs of the Civil War) had his studio in Pennsylvania Avenue, in the three floors above Gilman's drugstore, contiguous with the Metropolitan Hotel, between 6th and 7th Streets NW. Perhaps Sousa had a routine studio job done by one of Brady's many assistants.

This is guesswork, however, for there appear to have been half a dozen photographic studios in Pennsylvania Avenue in those days: photographers listed for 1881 include Johnson Bro's at 467–9 Penn., N.G. Johnson at 317 (who besides doing photos and tin-type portraits, also sold photographs of city views he had taken), M. Kets Kemethy at 1100 Penn., Thomas H. Marshall at 927 Penn., and E.J. Pullman (a photographer in Washington DC since 1866) at 935 Penn.

8. I call it (tongue in cheek) 'the year of darkness and light' because besides the launch of the Chaplin film, 1927 saw the first showing of Boris Karloff's *Frankenstein* and Bela Lugosi's *Dracula*. Lugosi was paid 500 dollars a week by Universal Studios for this, his most famous cinema role – even so, the fee was considerably more than that he received for his earlier stage version, in New York.
9. See *Annual Report of the Board of Regents of the Smithsonian Institution*, 1883, p.213.
10. Scc *Of Washington and Environs. Our Capital City, 'The Paris of America . . .'*, 1884, p.156, where a woodcut portrait of Crump, almost a double for Garfield, heads a description of the dining rooms.
11. An excellent photograph, taken *circa* 1881, has survived, and is now preserved in the archives of the Smithsonian (Arts and Industry Building).
12. A wood-engraving of thc inaugural ball, from the 19 March 1881 issue of *Frank Leslie's Illustrated Newspaper*, shows the statue in the distance, beneath the rotunda. There were over 5,000 guests. An intriguing exercise is to attempt to identify the portraits of those gathered in the foreground, around Garfield.
13. The statue was erected outside the Smithsonian because, from 1846, Joseph Henry had been the first secretary of the Institution – an administrative post which allowed him to revolutionize scientific research and the dissemination of scientific knowledge. The statue was erected by Act of Congress.

    William Wetmore Story, the widely talented sculptor, essayist and poet, was born in Salem (Mass.) on 12 February 1819. He studied law at Harvard, publishing a treatise on the law of Sales of Personal Property in the same year as his first collection of poems. On the death of his father – the famous Judge Story – he undertook to sculpt his memorial, and left to study sculpture in Italy (along with his wife and children) with this aim in mind. During the eight months in Italy, he prepared a collection of his father's letters, accompanied by a well-written Life, published in 1851. Eventually, he gave up his legal career, and devoted himself to sculpture and writing. His exquisite work, 'The Libyan Sibyl', in the National Gallery, Washington DC, is an example of his talent. He had a wide circle of gifted friends – he was close to the Brownings, in Italy, was intimate with Nathaniel Hawthorne, and knew Thackeray, Hans Christian Andersen, Charles Eliot Norton, Gaskell, Walter Savage Landor, Lady William Russell, and a host of other famous literati of the day. He was buried beside his wife (who predeceased him by a year) in the Protestant Cemetery in Rome, in 1895.
14. See Peter Parker and W.T. Sherman, 'Statue to Henry Unveiled', *Annual Report of the Board of Regents of the Smithsonian Institution, 1883, 1885*, p. xvii.
15. The time is given by Parker and Sherman (op. cit., n.14 above).
16. The horoscope data:

SU 29AR27	MO 01LB18	ME 03TA22	VE 20PI32	MA 29PI16
JU 27GE17	SA 25TA36	UR 19VG48R	NE 17TA47	PL 29TA03
Asc 28VG05	MC 27GE49	MN 12SC11		

17. Johnson (op. cit., n.2 above) estimates that by 1880 there were 234,000 miles of copper wire in use in the Western Union alone (p.482). The connection with Venus is more than merely 'astrological tradition' – it is even reflected in the name. The word 'copper' is from the Greek *koupros*, which also gave us the modern name Cyprus, 'the island of copper'. Cyprus was also the Island of Venus – the goddess is supposed to have been born of the foam near Paphos.
18. Sousa's last novel *The Transit of Venus*, 1910, is not well-constructed: the plot hinges unconvincingly on a survey seemingly sent to the Kerguelen Islands to

study the transit of Venus of 1882. Although no date is specified for this survey, one of the participants points out that 'the next transit after this one . . . will not take place until the year 2004'.

19. It is clear from Sousa's writings and music that he was interested in hidden meanings – for example, he delighted in the (false) story that his own name was a pseudonym, derived from the initials (SO, USA) stencilled on his luggage: in his last novel (see n.18 above) the hero's name, Stoneman, seems to be a play on 'Mason', while the name of the girl he loves – Miranda – is certainly a reference to the namesake daughter of the magician Prospero, in Shakespeare's play *The Tempest*. Hidden symbolism proliferates in his music and musical titles: for instance, the title of his 1888 composition *The Crusader* was arcane in the sense that it referred to his own acceptance into the Columbia Commandery No. 2 of the Knights Templars, in Washington DC. According to his biographer, Paul E. Brierley, this piece secretly incorporated fragments of Masonic music.
20. The following data for the astronomical transit of Venus are derived from material provided by the Royal Greenwich Observatory. These figures pertain to measurements based on the Leverrier motions, which were the basis of the 1882 *Nautical Almanac*. These vary by an extreme of just over three minutes from the modern system of measurements. The time is local to Washington DC:

    The external contact, when the disk of Venus was tangential externally to the disk of the Sun: 09:03:24
    The last external contact, when the disk of Venus was tangential externally to the disk of the Sun: 15:05:36

21. According to R.W. Shufeldt, in *The Report of the Superintendent of the Naval Observatory*, 1883, among those from Washington who went to foreign locations to study the 1882 transit were the astronomer, Simon Newcomb, and his assistant, Thomas Lincoln Casey. Three of the official photographers based at foreign locations were also from Washington DC. In charge of the observations in the city itself was Professor William Harkness of the United States Navy, along with his assistants, Joseph Rogers and Lieutenant Commander C.H. Davis. Their military ranks should remind us that the study of the transit was directed and funded by a military establishment – the United States Naval Observatory. From October 1880, Sousa was officially in the military, as the bandmaster of the United States Marine Corps (in the Museum of which some of his scores and manuscripts are still preserved). It is inevitable that he should have known about the extensive preparations being made to study the transit, both at home and abroad. To judge from his autobiography, Sousa either knew everyone, or had access to everyone, in Washington DC. He had met (in some cases, even become friendly with) five Presidents of the United States during his own lifetime. Relevant to the naval involvement with the transit of Venus, we should note that Sousa was friendly with Benjamin F. Tracy (Secretary of the Navy) who officially encouraged his book, *National, Patriotic and Typical Airs of All Lands*, 1890. Incidentally, it was Tracy who officially recognised Sousa's *The Star Spangled Banner* for naval use.
22. Under the direction of Professor C.A. Young. See Shufeldt (op. cit., n.21 above), p.xii.
23. In astronomy, the term 'transit' has a different meaning from the same term used in an astrological context. In astronomical terms, the word refers to a visible transit of the planet against the body of the Sun: in astrology, the transit does not need to be visible, nor does it need to be measured exclusively against the orb of the Sun: the word is descriptive of the passing of a given planet or node over a degree of the zodiac tenanted by another planet or node. In the light of this important distinction, the title of Sousa's march may take on a different meaning. In his novel, however, the hero makes his journey in order to be in the right position to observe an astronomical transit of Venus against the body of the Sun, and we may

not doubt that the novel title does refer to the astronomical idea of transit.

24. The discovery that a copper wire carrying an electric current had the power to magnetize steel and iron placed near it was made by D.F. Arago in 1820. The notion of coiling copper over an iron core – the basis of the electromagnet – was discovered by the Lancashire-born William Sturgeon, and described by him in 1825. Joseph Henry's development – spurred on by Sturgeon's reports – involved sheathing the copper wire in an insulating cover of silk, thus permitting a considerable number of wrappings around the iron core: this multitude of wrappings is emphasized in the sculptural detail on the Smithsonian statue. The horseshoe magnet which Henry constructed in this way, at Princeton, could lift weights of up to 750 pounds.
25. Henry gave the first practical demonstration of the electromagnetic telegraph in 1830–1, in Albany. His idea for the electromagnetic motor, with its automatic pole-changer, was the forerunner of all electric motors, and was published in 1831. On 17 December 1830, the planet Venus was just on the point of transitting the Sun, in 26 degrees Sagittarius. At this moment, no fewer than four planets were in Capricorn, while the Moon, Jupiter and Neptune were in the same degree of this sign. Later in the month, after Venus had transitted the Sun, on 24 December, there were five planets in Capricorn. By 15 January 1831, Venus had transitted the entire sign of Capricorn, during which time it had passed over the Sun, Neptune and Jupiter. Of course, during that period, the Moon had also transitted Venus. Astrologers will be interested to note that, in Henry's natal chart, Mercury was in 3.19 Capricorn, which corresponds closely with the degree of the Venus-Sun conjunction on 25 December 1830.
26. The rarity and importance of the transit were well known in the 1870s and 80s – see n.21 above. For example, Richard A. Proctor, a popular writer and Honorary Secretary of the Royal Astronomical Society, had included a paper on the transit in his *Essays on Astronomy*, published in both London and New York in 1872, and never failed to introduce commentaries about it in his many popular books that followed. Sousa seems to have chosen most of his march titles personally, and it is reasonable to assume that he was responsible for 'The Transit of Venus'. If this is the case, then he must have been the one to appreciate the arcane connection between the astronomical and/or astrological transit of Venus and Henry's use of copper in the electromagnet. However, the piece might have been named by either Baird or Rhees, of the Smithsonian, who were nominally in charge of the ceremony.
27. Edward S. Holden, 'Astronomy', in the *Annual Report of the Board of Regents of the Smithsonian Institution . . . for the Year 1881*, 1883.
28. The drawings predate the paintings of the theosophist John Varley and the Russian, Wassily Kandinsky (who was influenced by Varley into painting the first abstract picture). See Sixten Ringbom, *The Sounding Cosmos. A Study in the Spiritualism of Kandinsky and the Genesis of Abstract Painting*, 1970.
29. The canals he drew, and claimed to have seen, were very different from the winding channel of the 600-mile-long *Nirgal Vallis* revealed by the Mariner 9 photographs in November 1971.
30. See Robert Stawell Ball, *The Story of the Heavens*, 1886 – I have used the 1890 ed., p.190.
31. Richard A. Proctor, *The Borderland of Science*, 1874, pp.113ff.
32. William Denton, *Soul of Things: or, Psychometric Researches and Discoveries*, 1873, vol. II, p.97, reporting reading of 3 July 1873.
33. Denton (op. cit., n.32 above), vol. III, p.175, reporting Sherman's examination of 25 March 1869.
34. Theodore Flournoy, *From India to the Planet Mars. A Study of a Case of Somnambulism with Glossolalia* (trans. Daniel B. Vermilye), 1900.
35. Flournoy (op cit., n.34 above), p.223.

36. In Greek mythology, Phobos and Deimos were attendants of Mars, who (according to some accounts) yoked the fiery steeds of Mars to his chariot. The names in Greek mean 'panic' and 'cowardly', respectively. Phobos was sometimes personified as the son of Mars.
37. Jonathan Swift, *Gulliver's Travels*. The discussions about Mars are in Chapter 3 of the Laputa visit.
38. Guiteau is often described as a disappointed office-seeker, but it is more likely that he was simply insane. Detective McElfresh (one of the arresting officers), who searched him, certainly formed this opinion, mainly because Guiteau seems to have had no thoughts for his victim, and did not consider himself a murderer. After his arrest, Guiteau insisted on more than one occasion that his friend General Sherman (then still commanding General of the United States army) would be visiting him in gaol. Although deranged, he was, as Judge Cox recognized in his summing-up (delivered on 25 January 1882), 'of more than average mental endowments': indeed, Guiteau's knowledge of the law led to several disturbances during the trial. Although an alternative finding of 'guilty by reason of insanity' was mentioned in this summing-up, Guiteau was found guilty of murder. He was hanged on 30 June 1882.
39. Holden (op. cit., n.27 above) pp.191ff.
40. The German-born architect, Adolf Cluss, who went to live in the United States in 1848, had a profound effect on the development of Washington DC. His design for vaulted culverts to meet the rank nuisance of Tiber Creek, which assailed the nostrils of all who lived in the city, and his designs for the paving of avenues (not to mention the planting of 75,000 trees) were probably his most enduring public achievements in the city: he seems to have worked in close collaboration with Hoxie (see n.72 below), who became a special friend of Albert Pike. By 1890, he was the inspector of public buildings throughout the United States.
41. Smithson's original name was James Lewis Macie: he took the name Smithson about 1800. His bequest of about £100,000 to the United States led to the founding, by Act of Congress, of the Smithsonian Institution, on 10 August 1846. Smithson died in Genoa and was buried there, but the threatened destruction of his grave by industrial encroachment led to both body and tomb being moved to 'the Castle' at the Smithsonian, where they are still accommodated in a small annex to the left of the main entrance.
42. The name 'smithsonite' which was given to zinc carbonate in his honour by the French geologist Beudant, is now archaic.
43. See in particular the collection of articles he wrote for the *Washington Sunday Star* between 1928 and 1949, in *Proctor's Washington and Environs*, n.d. but *c*. 1949.
44. Thomas Henry Burgoyne was one of the pen-name of the Scottish Seer, Thomas Henry Dalton, whose spiritual descendants are still active in the Californian 'Church of Light'.See J. Godwin, C. Chanel and J.P. Deveney, *The Hermetic Brotherhood of Luxor. Initiatic and Historic Documents of an Order of Practical Occultism*, 1995, esp. pp.33ff.
45. T.H. Burgoyne, *The Light of Egypt, or The Science of the Soul and the Stars* (see p.135 in 1903 ed.). Burgoyne seems to have been the first to combine the Trithemian dating (see n.47 below) with the idea of the dark satellite (which is possibly his own understanding, or misunderstanding, of the eighth sphere of the theosophical literature). Like many esotericists of the time, Burgoyne did not claim originality for his ideas: he was markedly anti-Theosophical in his views, however, recognizing the dangers for Western occultism in the Theosophical programme of orientalization.
46. For an American version of this Virgilian prediction regarding the 'metallic' ages, see S.F.Dunlap, *Vestigates of the Spirit-History of Man*, 1898, p.253.
47. The year 1881 is mentioned in the Latin text, but Trithemius seems to have been lax in his sums, and a year on either side may be inferred from a careful reading,

when the months are taken into account. See Trithemius, *De septem secundadeis. Id est. intelligentis.*, 1525. The idea of the planetary rulers was by no means new when Trithemius published his book: on the first page of the work he admits that he has taken the information from 'the Conciliator' – one of the names of Peter of Abano, author of the influential *Conciliator differentiarum philosophorum* . . . I purposely describe the Trithemian beings as 'angels' because the rank of the Secundadeis is disputed by some specialists.

48. Trithemius (op. cit., n.47 above), paragraph 8, beginning: *Septimus mundi gubernator Michael fuit, angelus Solus* . . .
49. The Latin incipit (at a time when manuscripts rarely had titles) was *Joannis Trithemii abbatis divi Jacobi Herbipolensis: liber de intelligentiis caelestibus orbem post Deum gubernantibus.* It was later given the working title *De Septem Secundadeis.*
50. The prediction is partly bound up with the fact that Michael is the tutelary angel (*Sar*) of Israel, and partly with the numerology of the periodicities. The prediction would have been regarded as heretical in the early decades of the 16th century, which probably explains why it was mentioned almost *en passant* by Trithemius.
51. See C.G. Harrison, *The Transcendental Universe*, 1894. The quotation is after Synesius, Bishop of Ptolemais, from Pike's *Morals and Dogma*, 1906 ed., p.103.
52. H.P. Blavatsky's *Isis Unveiled: a Master-Key to the Mysteries of Ancient and Modern Science and Theology* was published in 1877, while her more astonishing orientalizing work, *The Secret Doctrine*, was not published until 1888.
53. The authors of *The Hermetic Brotherhood of Luxor* (see n.44 above), say that, in her diary for 9 October 1878, Blavatsky noted that the Reverend W.A. Ayton had sent her a translation of Trithemius' prophecies (which point to the importance of 1881). I can trace no reference to the receipt of such a translation in the Olcott/Blavatsky's diary for that day, though Blavatsky did send a letter to Ayton. However, on 20 November 1878, Blavatsky notes receipt of what she called 'the MSS of his translation of J. Trithemius's prophecies'. She was being uncharacteristically kind, for she must have recognized that this was not a translation from the original Latin – the only text worth translating – but a poor commentary. This was the day on which Blavatsky participated in the Vedic ceremony of casting the Baron de Palm's ashes into the waters of New York Bay.

    For some account of the reaction of Theosophists to the Trithemian predictions, and of what has been called 'The Key', see Godwin, Chanel and Deveney op. cit., n.44 above), pp.166ff.
54. This General Council was held on 17 February 1881. The other aims formulated at the Council make the hidden programme behind Theosophy quite clear – it was to be an exercise in orientalizing, which is to say that its avowed purpose was the introduction of oriental esotericism (including a version of Buddhist literature which few practising Buddhists would have agreed with) to the West, regardless of the spiritual value of such an introduction. See Josephine Ransom, *A Short History of the Theosophical Society*, n.d., p.155.

    There was nothing in the chart for that day to reaffirm the cosmic aims of these high-minded Theosophists, or to establish a connection with the angel of the Sun. A few minutes after lunchtime on 17 February 1881, the Moon would occupy the same degree in Libra as the contemporaneous astrologers believed was occupied by the Moon of Madame Blavatsky's chart. In 1881, Theosophy had not yet been subjected to the populist and entirely unesoteric astrology of W.F. Allen ('Alan Leo'), who had been drawn into the movement (to his own lucrative enjoyment) by his wife Bessie (née Phillips), an ardent follower of Blavatsky, who had settled in London in 1887. See, for example, Ellic Howe, *Urania's Children. The Strange World of the Astrologers*, 1967, pp.57ff.
55. See Pike, *Morals and Dogma*, 1871, p.563. The names of the six spirits were Iao, Saboath, Adonai, Eloi, Orai and Astaphal. Pike's account of the spiritual development of these beings explains why they should be called the Builders – a

term of considerable interest, even to a speculative Mason. Blavatsky's account of the Ophite name is more substantially accurate, however. In fact, Pike gives many equivalents of the seven, in a variety of world religions and mythologies: see, for example, pp.233,256ff.

56. This is the (extremely shoddy and incomplete) translation by Éliphas Lévi in his *Dogme et Rituel de la Haute Magie*, 1856, p.268ff. It was among the books purchased from Pike by the Supreme Council, Southern Jurisdiction, USA, on 14 May 1881 (no.133 in old catalogue).
57. See J. Ross Robertson, *The Egyptian Obelisk! And the Masonic Emblems found at Its Base*, 1880. For drawings of the 'Masonic' imagery, and a rapturous account, see John A. Weisse, *The Obelisk and Freemasonry according to the Discoveries of Belzoni and Commander Gorringe*, 1880.
58. See, for example, Thomas A.M. Ward, *A Translation into English of the Hieroglyphics upon the Egyptian Obelisk, Standing in Central Park, New York . . .*, *c.* 1881.
59. There are many references to the Amshaspends in H.P. Blavatsky's two seminal works, the *Isis Unveiled* of 1877 and the *Secret Doctrine* of 1888, but a comparison of her treatment of the archangel Michael in these two works shows how profoundly her conception of him changed in that decade, during which she had access to the Trithemius text. In the earlier work especially, some of the Michaelic lore is mentioned in her most infuriating eclectic manner, with little attempt to distil its true esoteric content: see, for example, *Isis Unveiled*, II, p.206, and *Secret Doctrine*, II, p.378, where Michael is thoroughly orientalized. For a useful digest, see her posthumous *Theosophical Glossary*, 1892, p.19.
60. 'See for yourself [Blavatsky writes]: 1 + 8 + 8 + 1 makes 18: 18 divided thrice gives three times six, or, placed in a row, 666.' Blavatsky knew very well that the 16th-century adept, Cornelius Agrippa, had equated the number with the Sun-demon *Sorath*, but, as is so often the case with the Madame, she was writing for the few – in this instance, pointing to the significance of the year 1881 for the solar angel, Michael. See letter to the editor of the *Bombay Gazette*, 29 March 1881, in *H.P. Blavatsky: Collected Writings 1881–1882*, 1968, vol. III, pp.84–5.
61. De Hooghe, *Hieroglyphica, oder Denkbilder der alten Volker*, 1744.
62. See (op. cit., n.27 above) Holden, pp.213 and 214.
63. John J. Ingalls (1833–1900) was Senator for Kansas from 1873 to 91, and from 1887 to 91 was president *pro tem* of the United States Senate. See n.72 below.
64. Ruth L. Bohan, 'The Farragut Monument: A Decade of Art and Politics, 1871–1881', in *Researches of the Columbia Historical Society – 1973–74*, p.243.
65. Along with the model were a number of documents, including some relating to Farragut's career, and to the history of the statue itself.
66. These were Saturn, Jupiter, the Sun, Neptune, Venus and Pluto, disposed as follows:

    SA 02TA30 JU 03TA19 SU 05TA35 NE 13TA41 VE 17TA39R PL 27TA19

67. Farragut was made Admiral in 1861; he died on 14 August 1870.
68. This poem was subtitled 'Vinnie' by Pike, in his *Hymns to the Gods and Other Poems*: originally in April 1869 it had been entitled 'Carisima' (see Lilian Pike Roome (ed.), *Lyrics and Love Songs by Gen. Albert Pike*, 1916). To his credit, Pike always insisted that he was not a poet: he could 'see what a poem ought to be, while unable to make it such': see Walter Lee Brown, *A Life of Albert Pike*, 1997, p.466.
69. See Brown (op. cit., n.68 above), pp.466ff. This is by far the best biography of Pike to date.
70. See the obituary in the *Evening Post*, 30 April 1930. After the death of Vinnie in 1914, Hoxie married (in 1917) Mae Ruth Norcross.
71. The quoted poem is from 'Mignonne' (one of Pike's pet names for Vinnie), 1868 –

see Roome (op. cit., n.68 above) p.52.

72. For the sake of convenience, I offer here brief notes of their Masonic affiliations (where known) in alphabetical order:

Frédéric Auguste Bartholdi was a member of the Lodge Alsace-Lorraine, in Paris: the Lodge was the first to see the Statue of Liberty, before it was gifted by the French people to the United States. Bartholdi had been encouraged to create the statue by the Frenchman Henri Martin, who was also a Mason, and a descendant of the great Lafayette, who had been such a close friend and brother Mason of George Washington.

William A. Brodie, who laid the cornerstone for the pedestal of the Statue of Liberty with Masonic honours, was at that time the Grand Master of Masons in New York. In 1984 a bronze plaque was set upon the pedestal recording the Masonic laying of the cornerstone on 5 August 1884.

Casper Buberl, a Bohemian sculptor, who had studied under his father and then in Prague and Vienna, went to live in the United States (mainly in New York City) in 1854. He revealed publicly his Masonic affiliations through the five reliefs he executed for the monument of his Brother Mason, James Garfield, in Cleveland, but I have been unable to identify his Lodge.

David G. Farragut (1801–70) was buried with Masonic honours by the Grand Master of New Hampshire and St John's Lodge No. 1 of Portsmouth. I have not been able to establish details of his own Lodge, but his contemporaries (in both letters and recorded conversations) recall him as a Mason, and as a keen promoter of Masonic interests.

Benjamin B. French was a Grand Master. In the Masonic ceremonial cornerstone-laying of the Smithsonian of 1847, over which he presided through the courtesy of Potomac Lodge No. 5, Washington DC, he used George Washington's gavel.

James Garfield was initiated 22 November 1861, and Passed on 23 December, in Magnolia Lodge No. 20, Columbus, Ohio. He received the Fourteenth Degree in the Lodge of Perfection, 2 January 1872. He was the 20th President of the United States of America. In Stefan Loran's *The Glorious Burden. The American Presidency*, 1968, p.359, there is a fascinating photograph of Garfield taking the Oath, on 4 March 1881. The young man leaning over the balustrade is Theodore Roosevelt, who would become President 24 years later, and a member of the same Lodge of which Garfield had been a charter member – the Pentalpha Lodge No. 23, Washington DC. Roosevelt did not become a Mason until the age of 43: he was initiated in the Matinecock Lodge No. 806 on 2 January 1901, and on 4 April 1904 was elected Honorary Member by Pentalpha Lodge No. 23.

Henry Honeyman Gorringe was a Freemason, aided in this project by a wealthy Brother, Louis F. White. See Peter Tompkins, *The Magic of Obelisks*, 1981, p.278.

Lieutenant Hoxie was probably a Mason. I have not been able to determine to which Lodge he belong; he certainly deposited in the Library of the Masonic Temple in Washington DC a personally signed, privately printed limited edition of eulogies and writings (mainly journalistic) relating to his wife: *Vinnie Ream. Printed for private distribution only: and to preserve a few souvenirs of artist life from 1865 to 1878*, 1908.

John J. Ingalls (see n.63 above) was a member of the US Senate during the political intrigue relating to Vinnie Ream's attempt to influence the decision-making concerning the planned Farragut statue. He was initiated in the Washington Lodge No. 5, Atchison, Kansas, in 1862.

Crosby S. Noyes, editor of the *Evening Star*, was a Mason, and was with the newspaper for almost 40 years, starting as a reporter in 1855. For a brief life, and for a brief history of the *Star*, see William Wirt Henry and Ainsworth R. Spofford, *Eminent and Representative Men of Virginia and the District of Columbia*, 1891, pp.228ff.

Albert Pike was the most influential (and certainly among the most erudite) of 19th-century Masons. He was the Grand Commander of the Ancient and Accepted Scottish Rite, in Washington DC, and, as an initiate into the 32nd Degree, was Master of the Royal Secret. His *Morals and Dogma of the Ancient and Accepted Scottish Rite of Freemasonry*, 1871, is a classic: it has been criticized because parts of it appear to be borrowed from other writers, but in his preface Pike himself admitted that the work was half-compiled. There is a small museum dedicated to the memory of Albert Pike in the Masonic Temple on 16th Street and R, Washington DC.

President James K. Polk was raised to the Sublime Degree in Columbia Lodge No. 31, Columbia, Tennessee, on 4 September 1820. Although many relevant Masonic records have been lost, it is known that he was exalted in the Lafayette Chapter No. 4, Columbia, on 14 April 1825. See H.L.Haywood, *Famous Masons and Masonic Presidents*, 1944, 1968 ed., pp.39–41.

John Clagett Proctor admits in his autobiographical notes which preface *Proctor's Washington* (see n.43 above) that he had been made a Master Mason on 5 October 1893.

John Philip Sousa was a member of Hiram Lodge No. 10, Washington DC, which he petitioned on 3 June 1881. He was a member of Columbia Commandery No. 2, Knights Templars, in 1886. (See Baldwin C.E. and J.H.Phillips, *History of Columbia Commandery No. 2 Knights Templar 1863–1963*, 1963). He is listed in the Eureka Chapter No. 4, in the returns of the *Proceedings of the Grand Royal Arch Chapter of the District of Columbia*, p.578, for the year ending 1891. In spite of this, Sousa, in his readable autobiography *Marching Along* (1927), makes no mention of being a Freemason. However, as the Mason Paul Brierley points out in his excellent *John Philip Sousa. A Descriptive Catalogue of His Works* (1973, p.40), some of his music may be fully understood only in the light of Masonry.

John Quincy Adams Ward must have been a Mason: this much is evident not only from the arcane Masonic symbolism of the Garfield monument, but from his involvement with the Library of Congress, which is riddled through and through with Masonic symbolism. However, extensive searches through Masonic Lodge transactions in both Washington DC have failed to reveal his Lodge, or date of initiation.

Thomas A. M. Ward was an attorney and counsellor-at-law: his connection with Masonry is revealed in the extended title of his book (see n.58 above) which offers a version of the hieroglyphic alphabet, and the resuscitation of the long-lost 'Third Degree' in the Egyptian Mysteries. There was no 'Third Degree' of the Egyptian mysteries, but there was (and is) in Masonry.

73. There is considerable literature relating to Blavatsky's Masonic connections. In her *Scrapbook*, vol.III, p.256, on January 1878, she recorded that she received a diploma of the 32nd Degree in the Ancient and Primitive Rite of England and Wales. In the following month the issue was raised in the *Franklin Register and Norfolk Country Journal*, the material of which has been published in *H.P. Blavatsky. Collected Writings. Volume One. 1874–1878.* On p.309, we learn that the Ancient and Primitive Rite was originally chartered in America, on 9 November 1856, with David McClellan as Grand Master, and that it submitted entirely in 1862 to the Grand Orient of France.

Vinnie Ream was initiated into Masonry in 1867 by Albert Pike – an action that caused considerable unrest among the Masonic fraternity, which did not espouse female membership. Perhaps this explains why Pike insisted that her degrees pertained to French Masonry, within which female members were permitted in certain Lodges. Vinnie was eventually initiated up to the eighth Degree. For a non-Masonic account, see the excellent biography of the artist by Glenn V. Sherwood, *Labor of Love. The Life and Art of Vinnie Ream*, 1997, pp.205ff.

As for the support which Vinne gathered around her to ensure that she won the competition, we have an insight into how deeply entrenched was Masonry in politics at that period of history in Washington DC. It is not possible to tell the story in full here, but it is worth pointing out that Bohan's article concerning events surrounding the Farragut statue competition (n.64 above), which was not written with Masonic influence in mind, unwittingly reveals the Masonic connections. The following individuals that Bohan names in her article were certainly Masons: Clark Mills; Charles Sumner; Simon Cameron; Charles B. Farwell; Eli Perry; S.A. Kimberley; John A. Dix; John Ingalls; David D. Porter; Alexander Ramsey and Godlove S. Orth. To his credit, Orth (US Congressman from Indiana) did not help Vinnie, on the grounds that it would savour of impropriety if a member of Congress were to influence a Cabinet officer.

As for the Masonic intentions of Abraham Lincoln, the historian H.L. Haywood records (in op. cit., n. 72 above, p.324) that a letter still exists which Lincoln wrote to a friend in the Lodge at Springfield, Ill., in which he states that he intended, at the end of his term of office, to petition for the degrees.

CHAPTER THREE

1. The date when the picture was painted is not known: however, it was exhibited in Philadelphia in 1796.
2. For an excellent survey of the curious origins of the painting, see Ellen G. Miles, *American Paintings of the Eighteenth Century*, 1995, pp.145ff.
3. For Rembrandt Peale's comments, see Miles (op. cit., n. 2 above).
4. For Ellicott's adjustments see the 'Comparative Map', with the Ellicott overprinted over the L'Enfant, in *Downtown Urban Renewal Area Landmarks, Washington DC*, prepared by the National Capital Planning Commission in 1970, p.28.
5. Herman Kahn, 'Appendix to Pierre L'Enfant's Letter to the Commissioners, May 30, 1800', in *Records of The Columbia Historical Society of Washington DC, 1942–1943*, 1944.
6. Andrew Ellicott's *The Journal of Andrew Ellicott*, 1803. It is quite clear from his surviving letters, and from his 'Journal', that besides being interested in all the usual geodesic problems of surveying, Ellicott was deeply interested in astronomy. He had personally made some of the instruments he used in his surveys and stellar observations.
7. H. Paul Caemmerer, *The Life of Pierre Charles L'Enfant*, 1950.
8. It is very likely that L'Enfant was a Mason.
9. For an account of this tavern, see Oliver W. Holmes, 'Suter's Tavern: Birthplace of the Federal City', in *Records of the Columbia Historical Society, 1973–1974.*
10. In his *Autobiography*, Trumbull records that he painted his *Battle of Bunker's Hill* (the battle at which the British definitively lost America) in London, in the studio of his mentor and friend, Benjamin West. Trumbull could not understand why the English engravers of the day refused to engrave it! I have not been able to determine whether Trumbull was a Mason – see, however, R.W. James and R. Case, *Freemasons Depicted in the National History Series of Colonel John Trumbull's Paintings,* 1959. Case shows that of the 175 well-identified individuals portrayed in these pictures (including 42 of the 56 signers of the Declaration of Independence), more than one-third were Masons.
11. See Constance McLaughlin Green, *Washington. Village and Capital, 1800–1878*, 1962, p.3.
12. William McLeod painted this picture about 1844. It is in the Collection of the United States Department of State.
13. The original tavern was destroyed by fire in 1832. The rebuilt version, in which Jerome Bonaparte stayed, is reproduced in Robert Reed, *Old Washington D.C. in Early Photographs 1846–1932*, 1980, p.148.
14. See the photograph in C.S. Kelly, *Washington, D.C., Then and Now*, 1984, p.58.

15. This information is taken from *Dunlap's American Daily Advertiser*, in the Philadelphia issue of 28 April 1791. There is a reproduction of the relevant newsprint page in R.B. Harris, *The Laying of Cornerstones*, 1961, p.21. I should observe that the date given here does not correspond to that recorded by Nicholas Campion, *The Book of World Horoscopes*, 1995 ed., p.424 (quoting Grant and Kraum in 'The Endless Quest for the United States Chart', *National Council of Geographic Research Journal*, Spring 1994)
16. He had already predetermined the spot, which was later overbuilt with the walled grounds of the old lighthouse. See n.23 below.
17. Cullen Dick was born near Marcus Hook, Pennsylvania, on 15 March 1762, and became a physician and plantation owner. One of his early medical undertakings was to superintend the health of convicts used in opening up the Potomac for navigation at Great Falls. He was a member of the Alexandria Lodge, and acted as its Grand Master both prior to and after George Washington. He was one of the three physicians who attended Washington at his death.
18. The symbolism of corn, oil and wine in such Masonic ceremonials is discussed at length in M. A. Pottanger, *Symbolism*, 1923.
19. Banneker was of English and African blood, born 9 November 1731: his grandmother was an Englishwoman who, after serving her five-year sentence for a crime which had led to her being transported, purchased a plantation near what became Ellicott's, Maryland.
20. Banneker's almanacs are now exceedingly rare. The most reliable modern study of his life and work is Silvio A. Bedini, *The Life of Benjamin Banneker*, 1971.
21. No horoscope has survived, but given the practices of the times, it is inevitable that such a chart would have been erected, even if not by Banneker.
22. The laying of the President's House was recorded in the *Charleston City Gazette* for 15 November 1792. Although there are many references to the subsequent work on what was later called the White House in private diaries, no record of the actual horoscope has survived. As with the Jones Point event, I am forced to recognize that a foundation chart must have been cast purely from the appropriateness of the planetary conditions of the time.
23. It was a temporary stone – the official monumental marker was not installed for another three years. The date for the 1791 ceremony appears to have been agreed in consequence of George Washington's visit to Georgetown, on 28 March, to discuss the project. There was some urgency beyond the need to establish a federal city by 1800 – many interested parties in Philadelphia and New York were anxious to attract the federal city into their own domains.
24. Dr Stewart, Daniel Carroll (both of whom were Masons) and Thomas Johnson were Commissioners appointed by the President under the Residence Act of 16 July 1790, intended to define 'a district or territory of the permanent seat of Government of the United States'. At the time of the ceremony, Philadelphia was being used as the temporary national capital. The Commissioners did not get on very well with L'Enfant – a man with an innate autocratic attitude – who, rightly or wrongly, was inflamed by the belief that he worked with a direct mandate from George Washington which allowed him to bypass the Commissioners.
25. I deal with this rulership of Virgo over Washington DC more fully in Chapter 6.
26. The toast is recorded in *Dunlap's American Daily Advertiser*, Philadelphia issue of 28 April 1791.
27. See J. Moss Ives, *The Ark and the Dove. The Beginning of Civil and Religious Liberties in America*, 1936, pp.108ff.
28. The enigmatic architect, Franklin W. Smith, used the word 'aggrandizement' when he began campaigning for the beautification of the city in the 1890s, and some seem to have taken objection to this word. However, the same word had been used by L'Enfant in his own notes on the design of the city.
29. L'Enfant further visualized five grand fountains, and marked these on his map.

30. McGurk, op. cit., p.21.
31. The two skulls are reproduced in Charles B. Reynolds, *The Standard Guide. Washington – a Handbook for Visitors*, 1900, p.480. Little Bear's squaw was killed in Wyoming Territory, while the unidentified skull, with nine distinct sabre wounds, was listed in the museum as '970 IB AG 3': in fact, he could have been killed anytime after the beginning of the 16th century. Of course, these skulls were not found at the bottom of Jenkins Heights, but the drift of my argument is clear. Native American tribes certainly lived along this part of the Potomac: it is said that the 'Maryland' Native Americans were descendants of the Algonquins. The name Anacostia (like Chesapeake and Potomac) was originally Native American, and offers confirmation that they lived below the Eastern Branch, as Captain John Smith reported.
32. See D. Jacson and D. Twohig, eds, *The Diaries of George Washington*, vol.VI, January 1790 – December 1799.
33. See Beckles Willson, *Friendly Relations. A Narrative of Britain's Ministers and Ambassadors to America (1791–1930).*
34. See John C. Fitzpatrick (ed.), *The Diaries of George Washington, 1748–1799*, 1925, p.142 – Monday, 12 July 1790.
35. This was the map entitled 'Sketch of Washington in Embryo', compiled by E.F.M. Faehtz and F.W. Pratt, based on 'the rare historical research' material assembled by Dr Joseph M. Toner. A copy is in the Library of Congress.
36. The *wheelbarrow men*, who are mentioned in early accounts of Maryland and the neighbouring areas, were convicts who served their sentences working on the construction of public roads. They were locked up during the night.
37. It is called Masons Island in the rough sketch drawn by Thomas Jefferson, in March 1791, and in the Andrew Ellicott topographical map of 1793. It was still Masons Island in the 1839 map drawn by William J. Stone. As I have said, the name has nothing to do with the Masonic fraternity, for it belonged to General John Mason. The later silting and artificial damming of the Potomac had resulted in a fundamental change in the topography of the island.
38. The print after the painting by Beck is by J. Cartwright, and, as the title suggests, is somewhat later. It was probably printed about 1798, when the city had already been named after George Washington.
39. The site is often called Jenkins' Hill in the early literature. However, in his letters and reports L'Enfant himself called it Jenkins Heights (sometimes, Jenkins's Heights), and I have retained this name as more evocative of the original location. See George W. Hodgkins, 'Naming the Capitol and the Capital', in *Records of the Columbia Historical Society*, 1961, p.44.
40. Constance McLaughlin Green, (op. cit., n.11 above), p.5.
41. James Borchert, *Builders and Owners of Alley Dwellings in Washington, DC, 1877–1892*, p.345.
42. Kahn, (op. cit., n.5 above),
43. Kahn (op. cit., n.5 above), p.203.
44. The three Commissioners named the federal city 'the City of Washington in the Territory of Columbia', and reported the decision to L'Enfant on 9 September 1791. See the *Papers of the Commissioner of Public Buildings, Letters Sent; Records of the Office of Public Buildings and Grounds, National Archives*, RG 42.
45. See Marcus Baker, 'The Boundary Monuments of the District of Columbia', *Records of the Columbia Historical Society*, 11 May 1897. See p.4 in particular: the 'marker stone' now in the walled lawn of the lighthouse is sometimes confused with it.
46. *Your Masonic Capitol City*, 1950, p.25. The District of Columbia Cornerstone section is abstracted from an article by G. Deane in the *Evening Star* for 2 January 1950.
47. See the *Washington Post*, 20 June 1998, 'Letters to the Editor' – 'Conserving the

Boundary Stones', by Silvio A. Bedini.

48. See J.C. Proctor, 'Laying of the First Corner Stone at Jones Point', in *Proctor's Washington and Environs*, n.d. but *circa* 1949, p.104. At the 200th anniversary of the foundation, the ceremony was re-enacted by the Alexandria-Washington Lodge No. 22. See S. Brent Morris, *Cornerstones of Freedom. A Masonic Tradition*, 1993.
49. Fifty years later, in the decade before the abolition of slavery, the population of Washington was 40,001, including 2,113 slaves. Not all the slaves were of African origin: some were British convicts. In those 50 years, the population of Georgetown had almost doubled, and the number of slaves had dropped to 725. Data compiled from USA Census 1800–1870, and published in table 1, p.21, of McLaughlin Green, op. cit., n.11 above.
50. In 1840, the French diplomat the Chevalier de Bacourt was assured by a friend that it would be dangerous for his health to live in Washington DC during July, August and September, because of the intense heat. See the letter of 28 June 1840 on p.46 of *Souvenirs of a Diplomat. Private Letters from America during the Administrations of Presidents Van Burne, Harrison, and Tyler*, Chevalier de Bacourt, 1885. Anne Royall, who lived in Washington DC for much of her life, is scathing about the city being unhealthy: see the quotation from her *Paul Pry*, in Sarah Harvey Porter, *The Life and Times of Anne Royall*, 1909, pp.153ff.
51. See the letter written by Mrs Latrobe (wife of John H. B. Latrobe) to Juliana Miller of Philadelphia, from Washington DC, on 17 February 1812. The letter is printed in John E. Semmes, *John H.B. Latrobe and His Times 1803–1891*, 1917, pp.15ff.
52. Harriet Martineau, 'Life in the Capital in 1835', from Allan Nevins, *American Social History As Recorded by British Travellers . . .*, pp.181ff.
53. See op. cit., n.4 above.
54. Pamela Scott, '"This Vast Empire". The Iconography of the Mall, 1791–1848', in Richard Longstreth (ed.), *The Mall in Washington, 1791–1991*, 1991, pp.39–40. Scott takes as evidence that L'Enfant himself named the state streets 'the inherent logic of the plan' (p.55).
55. Vermont (on 4 March 1791) and Kentucky (on 1 June 1792) had joined the original 13.
56. The National Hotel was demolished in 1942: a photograph of it, taken shortly prior to demolition, alongside a 1981 photograph of its replacement (the District of Columbia Employment Security Agency) is reproduced in Kelly (op. cit., n.14 above), pp.20–1.
57. I paraphrase from Henry Latham, *Black and White, a Journal of a Three Months' Tour in the United States*, 1867, p.59.
58. Carved by Robert Aitken in 1935, under the direction of the architect, John Russell Pope, who rightly insisted that the inscriptions remain on the north front of each pedestal.
59. The Charleston *City Gazette*, 15 November 1792. The letter was submitted by 'a gentleman in Philadelphia' on 20 October 1792. Harris (op. cit., n.15 above) reproduces the relevant section of the only known copy of this newsprint (now in the collection of the Charleston Library) on p.22.
60. The Potomac Lodge No. 5 archives began in 1795, and the records for this important ceremonial have not been traced.
61. This is now Potomac Lodge No. 5 of the District of Columbia. Although Georgetown was eventually included within the DC boundaries, it was not (in 1792) envisaged as a part of Washington DC. It would seem inevitable that this would happen in the future, however, as L'Enfant's plan connected the centre of the city with the Georgetown docks by means of Pennsylvania Avenue. For the Masonic details, see Harris (op. cit., n.15 above).
62. The Charleston *City Gazette* for 15 November 1792. The letter contains a few minor errors: for example, 'brother Casaneva' was actually Peter Casanave, Master of Lodge No. 9.

63. On 6 September 1793, three Ancient York Masons, then resident in the federal city, had submitted a petition, praying for a warrant to convene and work as Masons. These were James Hoban, C.W. Stephenson, and Andrew Eustace. The petition was granted, and Hoban became Master of the newly formed Federal Lodge, No. 15.
64. According to Harris (op. cit., n.15 above), it was Theodore Roosevelt (one of the many Masonic presidents) who first used the name on letterheads, thus putting an official stamp on an idea which was already almost 100 years old.
65. William H. Winder was Master of Cassia Lodge No. 45, Baltimore, in 1816, and Grand Master of the Grand Lodge of Maryland from 1822 to 1824 (the year of his death).
66. Donald R. Hickey, *The War of 1812. A Forgotten Conflict*, 1989, p.199.
67. Margaret Smith to Mrs Kirkpatrick, 30 August 1814. From the Bayard papers in the Library of Congress, quoted by Anthony Pitch in *The Burning of Washington. The British Invasion of 1814*, 1998, pp.120–1.
68. According to the Charleston *City Gazette*, the inscription on the brass plate ran:

    This first stone of the President's House
    was laid the 12th Day of October, 1792, and
    in the 17th Year of the Independence of the
    United States of America.
    George Washington, *President*.
    Thomas Johnson
    Doctor Steward *Commissioners*.
    Daniel Carroll,
    James Hoban, *Architect*.
    Collen Williamson, *Master Mason*.
    Vivat Respublica.

    All those listed were Masons, with the possible exception of Thomas Johnson. Harris (op. cit., n.15 above), p.15 records that the brass cornerstone plate is still where it was laid in 1792. It was left in place during refurbishments and investigations during the rebuilding of 1948, at the express commands of President Harry S. Truman, who was learned in Masonic matters. After his initiation in Belton Lodge No. 450, on 9 February 1909, Truman progressed to Grand Master.
69. I have reconstructed the charts using contemporaneous figures and sigils. However, the data are derived from a modern computer system, and are far more accurate than anything which would have been available at the end of the 18th century.
70. The data, in round-degree figures, for the federal city (FC) ceremonial and the President's House (PH) ceremonial are:

	SU	M0	ME	VE	MA	JU	SA	UR	NE	PL	MN
FC	02TA	06SG	11TA	29TA	23AR	23VG	12AR	11LE	27LB	22AQ	22LB
PH	22LB	23VG	08LB	10SC	12SG	08SC	30SA	23LE	30LB	22AQ	23VG

The time of the PH ceremony is not known, but since there was insufficient lighting available we presume that it began shortly after lunchtime. Even so, had it begun earlier, the conjunction would still have been operative, as the Moon would have remained within one degree either side of exact conjunction over a span of six hours. This means that the conjunction in Virgo would have occurred during the course of the ceremonial, if not at the precise laying of the foundation stone.

CHAPTER FOUR

1. Elkanah Watson was a friend of Washington, but in his letter addressed him as 'Most Illustrious and Respected Brother'.
2. The apron is now in the possession of Alexandria-Washington Lodge No. 22 at

Alexandria, Virginia. See Sachse, *Masonic Correspondence of Washington*, 1915, pp.19ff. The Lafayette gift is now in the Museum of the Grand Lodge of Pennsylvania.

3. There is a water-colour version of the scene by Latrobe in the museum of the George Washington National Masonic Memorial in Alexandria. In the background are poplars, not houses.
4. The *Columbian Mirror and Alexandria Gazette*, of 25 September 1793 guesses that the ceremonial was 'one of the grandest MASONIC Processions' *because* it had been advertised in several newspapers of the state.
5. Over 100 years later, when touching on this curious omission, Edward Schultz hazarded the guess that this was because the Lodge had not been fairly organized in the short time from receiving its charter and the cornerstone ceremony. See Edward T. Schultz, *History of Freemasonry in Maryland*, 1888.
6. See George W. Hodgkins, 'Naming the Capitol and the Capital', in *Records of the Columbia Historical Society of Washington DC*. 1961, p.43.
7. Margaret Brent Downing, 'The Earliest Proprietors of Capitol Hill' (1917), in *Records of the Columbia Historical Society, Washington DC*, 1918, vol.21, p.19.
8. In the *Columbian Mirror and Alexandria Gazette* (see n.4 above) report of the proceedings, his name is given as Stephen Hallate. As all the other seven names inscribed on the silver plate laid with the foundation stone were those of Masons, we must presume that Hallet was also a Mason. For an account of the competition, and the role played by Hallet in amending Thornton's plan, see Pamela Scott, *Temple of Liberty. Building the Capitol for a New Nation*, 1995. Hallet was dismissed as architect in November 1794.
9. William Thornton was born in the British West Indies, and eventually took American citizenship. He was the winner of the first architectural competition in the United States – to design the Public Library in Philadelphia. He had no training in architecture.
10. For his difficulties with the Thornton plan, see Talbot Hamlin, *Benjamin Henry Latrobe*, 1955, pp.261ff.
11. Both Hoban and Latrobe were Masons. As we have seen, Hoban was the Master of the newly formed Federal Lodge No. 15, then active in the city. He was High Priest of the Royal Arch Encampment of Washington in 1795. By profession an architect, he laid the cornerstone of the White House on 13 December 1792.
12. For a survey of the difficulties between Hallet, Hoban and the other early architects, see Glenn Brown, *History of the United States Capitol*, 1900, in which many misunderstandings regarding the design of the first Capitol are cleared up.
13. John Fellows, *Exposition of the Mysteries, or Religious Dogmas and Customs of the Ancient Egyptians, Pythagoreans, and Druids*, 1835, p.360.
14. The contemporaneous source for the ceremonial is the *Columbian Mirror and Alexandria Gazette* for Wednesday 25 September 1793, published from Georgetown. The relevant newsprint sheet has been reproduced by R.B. Harris, *The Laying of Cornerstones*, 1961, pp.32–3. From this report, it seems to have been a very fine occasion. It is fascinating to see the extent to which newspapers in those days (admittedly, often owned by Masons) were prepared to offer such minute details of Masonic ceremonies – even to providing lists of names of officiating Masons.
15. Jupiter rising on the Ascendant of a chart is regarded as being one of the most beneficent of influence.
16. The day is known, but the time is speculative. The data are:

    SU26VG10 MO08PI37 ME08VG38 VE14LE48 MA18LE33 JU27SC17
    SA15TA23R UR26LE05 NE00SC28 PL23AQ07R DH04VG48

17. 'Proteus', *A Dissertation on the Celestial Sign of the Rainbow*, 1879, p.2, etc.
18. Allyn Cox was not a Mason when he undertook the painting of the two huge

frescos in the George Washington Memorial Hall, in Alexandria. However, after completing the work, he petitioned, and was made a Mason.

19. For a discussion of the plaque, and the possible location of the first cornerstone, see S. Brent Morris, *Cornerstones of Freedom. A Masonic Tradition*, 1993, esp. pp.50ff.
20. But see especially Steven C. Bullock, *Revolutionary Brotherhood. Freemasonry and the Transformation of the American Social Order 1730–1840*, 1996.
21. One of the cards in the index of Masons in the Library of the Supreme Council in Washington DC records that John Dove's *Masonic Text Book* makes this claim (p.308). William L. Boyden, *Masonic Presidents, Vice-Presidents and Signers*, 1927, in his Foreword, is adamant that the statement that 50 of the 56 signers were Freemasons 'is absolutely without proof', though he admits that some of the old Lodge records have been lost, through fire, war and other causes. However, Ronald Heaton, in *Masonic Membership of the Founding Fathers*, 1988, p.cvi, was playing on the side of caution in listing only nine Masons.
22. The Mason John Rowe had shares in the cargo of the ship which sparked off the Boston Tea Party. See Bullock (op. cit., n.20 above), p.77.
23. See William Adrian Brown, *History of the George Washington Masonic National Memorial, 1922–1974. Half a Century of Construction*, 1980.
24. Washington was the first Master of the Alexandria Lodge No. 22, from April 1788 to December 1789. For a useful introduction to his Masonic affiliations, see Allen E. Roberts, *G. Washington: Master Mason*, 1976, and William Moseley Brown, *George Washington Freemason*, 1952.
25. For some of the correspondence, see Sachse (op. cit., n.2 above). Some correspondence in the Library of Congress, dealing with Washington DC, is written in such a way as to indicate Masonic interests.
26. See Schultz (op. cit., n.5 above), Period II, p.191. Schultz is quoting from the inscription on the silver plate, ordered to be read by the Commissioners at the ceremony.
27. The arcane mediaeval Latin *cryptus*, meaning 'secret', refers more to the secret places than to burial. The Latin *crypta* seems to have been the origins of our word 'crypt'. By extension, it refers to the secret places in the human body and psyche, of which the temple, church and cathedral are models. It is entirely reasonable to accept the dark crypt as a model of the subconscious, even though the mediaeval philosophers did not use this word. For further details, see James, n.28 below.
28. John James, *Chartres. The Masons who Built a Legend*, 1982.
29. Credit for the Royal Arch Degree, first practised in America in 1769, is traced back to Thomas Smith Wells. For a treatment of the Royal Arch which makes some attempt to deal with the astrology of the Craft, see George H. Steinmetz, *The Royal Arch. Its Hidden Meaning*, 1979 ed. of the 1946 version.
30. The print, from the *Psalter of the Blessed Virgin*, printed at Czenna, 1492, is reproduced in Thomas Inman, *Ancient Pagan and Modern Christian Symbolism*, 1884. In connection with the roses (the five-petalled flowers), Inman quotes Dante:

    Here is the Rose,
    Wherein the Word Divine was made incarnate.

31. James F. Duhamel, 'Tiber Creek', *Records of the Columbia Historical Society, Washington DC*, 1926, vol.28, p.204.
32. John, I, iv, in which the Greek *zoe* means 'life'. For the connection between this word and our word 'zodiac', see E.M. Smith, *The Zodia*, 1906, pp.81ff.
33. William Richardson Davie was one of the most interesting and powerful figures in the early history of North Carolina. He had been a member of the Federal Constitutional Convention, and was a friend of George Washington. Davie was elected Governor in 1799, indicating the close connection between Masonry and politics, in North Carolina. Bullock (op. cit., n.20 above) uses Davie's election to governorship as the basis for the surprising information that between 1776 and

1836, Masons served a total of 48 years in the governorship (p.228). Over half of Andrew Jackson's Cabinet members were Masons, from widely diverse states, including North Carolina. The oldest Brother in Andrew Jackson's Cabinet was Edward Livingston, who had been Deputy Grand Master of New York State. His brother, Robert R. Livingston, had been a member of the committee that had drafted the Declaration of Independence.

34. The plate known as 'Old East' is in the North Carolina collection of the University of North Carolina Library, Chapel Hill. The cornerstone to the later foundation of the main building was laid by the Grand Lodge of North Carolina on 14 April 1798, still under the direction of the Grand Master, Davie, who had been instrumental in founding the university. According to Bullock, a number of professors from the university were initiated into Masonry after the 1798 ceremony. The temporary University Lodge is discussed in Thomas Parramore, *Launching the Craft*, p.159. See also *Documentary History of the University of North Carolina*, I, pp.79–80.
35. The cornerstone was laid on 12 October 1793. The date appears to have been chosen to allow for Mars to conjunct the Dragon's Head, in Virgo. The conjunction was:

    VE 12VG57 DH 03VG31 MA 03VG19

36. For James and the crypt, see nn. 27 and 28 above.
37. See *Ceremony of Dedication for the HOUSE OF THE TEMPLE Ancient & Accepted Scottish Rite Masonry Southern Jurisdiction, USA. October 18 '15*, typescript in the Library of House of the Temple, p.9. The idea of the belt of Orion being a symbol of the Three Kings, or Magi, was probably suggested by the writings of Albert Pike (see n.50 below), for he moralizes upon this striking stellar triplicity on p.487 of his *Morals and Dogma* (1906 ed.). Almost everything he writes about the Three Kings is accurate, but he was in error in his following development, for the nearby *Hyades* are not 'five in number', which means that his Masonic thesis (in this context) is unfounded. The idea that the stars had not fluctuated in 4,000 years is poetic rather than astronomic: they are now 12 degrees further away from the celestial equator than they were in the heyday of Babylonian astronomy.
38. J.J. Lalande, *Astronomie par M. de la Lande*, 1731, 2nd ed. in 4 vols., vol.1.4, pp.245ff. The astronomer, Joseph Jérome de Lalande (one-time director of the Paris Observatory) instituted the Lodge *Des Sciences* in 1769, and is said to have been founder of the Lodge *Des Neuf Soeurs*.
39. In his almanac for 1795 the 'Afric-American astronomer' Banneker gives the name *Georgium Sidus* along with the sigil ⊕, which is incorrect. This sigil was already widely used in astronomy, astrology and alchemy to represent the Earth (the division of the circle into four reflects the fourfold Elements) and the *Pars Fortuna*. Fifty years later, 'John Partridge', in *Merlinus Liberatus . . . for 1848*, still gives the same term Georgium Sidus (e.g., p.26), but in the same year *White's Coelestial Atlas . . . for 1848* uses the word Uranus, though the editor, Woolhouse, is careful to designate it also 'Herschel's Planet' (e.g., p.26).
40. For a note on Increase Mather's view of the eclipse, see Andrew D. White, *A History of the Warfare of Science with Theology in Christendom*, 1955, p.173.
41. Bullock (op. cit., n.20 above), p.137.
42. Modern astronomy recognizes that the star is actually a triple. Although the name Regulus seems to have been first used by Copernicus, this was really a translation of the Greek used by Ptolemy in the first century of our era (as *Basilikos*, or King). Ptolemy, as a compiler, was rarely original, and we discover that the more ancient name used in Babylonia, *Sharru*, also meant 'king'. For notes on other names, and for the mediaeval *cor Leonis*, or 'heart of the lion', see R.H. Allen, *Star Names. Their Lore and Meaning*, 1963 reprint of the Stechert 1899 ed., p.255.

43. After the statue had been pulled down, some of the metal was used to make musket balls. The horse's tail – more or less intact – was discovered in 1871.
44. Of course, nowadays, we recognize that planets are not stars. However, in Greek astronomy, from which a great deal of astrology is derived, the planets were called 'wandering stars' (this is exactly what the word *planetoi* meant). In consequence it has been a formula for astrological symbolists to portray the planets in the form of stars – though it is more usual, and more directly informative, to portray them in sigils.
45. The Würzburg pillars are reproduced in J.S.Curl, *The Art and Architecture of Freemasonry*, 1991 p.00.
46. It is interesting that this image should be on the exterior when the dancing grounds inside the mediaeval buildings were often called 'Labyrinths of Solomon' – see Fulcanelli, *Le Mystère des Cathédrales*, 1971 English ed., p.48.
47. This 19th-century catechism is no longer used.
48. So far as I am aware (for all the promise of certain titles by Manley Palmer Hall), there is no work dealing reliably with Masonic astrology. However, in the section 'Knight of the Brazen Serpent', of his *Morals and Dogma* (1906 ed.), Albert Pike gathers together many astronomical traditions and links them in a most interesting way with Masonic rituals and beliefs. I mention other works on Masonic astrology in this present book.
49. The famous zodiacal window in the south wall of Chartres Cathedral sets out images of the 12 signs alongside their corresponding months. There are some high-quality reproductions of the entire window, as well as details, in Malcom Miller, *Chartres Cathedral,* 1996 ed., p.71, etc. For a survey of the arcane significance of the exterior zodiacs, see F. Gettings, *The Hidden Art*, 1978, pp.33ff.
50. Although Pike's belief that the three stars in the belt of Orion were once identified with the Three Kings was well founded, the idea never entered the mainstream of astrological or astronomical lore, and was already archaic in his day. In fact, by the 19th century, when Pike found the term in one of his books on astronomy, the terminology had been superseded, for *The Three Kings*, or the *Magi*, were names used in the constellational map by Julius Schiller in *Coelum Stellatum Christianum*, 1627. The term used by Pike is mentioned as one of many variants for Orion's belt in the encyclopaedic study of star names by Richard Hinckley Allen, *Star-Names and Their Meanings*, 1899, p.316. I am surprised that Pike did not see a more pertinent Masonic theme, in the fact that Weigel figured Orion (for which constellation the three stars form the belt) as the *Two-Headed Eagle*. Pike's own Lodge has been called the Lodge of the Double-Headed Eagle.
51. L.D. Broughton, *The Elements of Astrology*, 1898, for example, provided a list of books to be studied by his students. All save the ephemerides were English in origin. See Broughton's potted history of the English literary tradition, from Coley onwards, pp.viii ff.
52. Anonymous, *Masonic Offering to His Royal Highness Prince Augustus Frederick, Duke of Sussex, K.G., etc, etc, Grand Master of the Freemasons in England*, 1838, p.23.
53. *Le Soleil Mystique. Journal de la Maçonnerie Universelle*, 1852. The four 'zodiacal plates' include: Temple of Solomon, with a zodiac on the architrave; a Cubic Stone, with seven planets; the Temple of all the Mysteries, with a floor zodiac; and a Temple of Memory, with a zodiac around the base of the dome.
54. Thomas H. Burgoyne (the Library of Congress gives his name as Bourgoyne) authored *The Language of the Stars. A Primary Course of Lessons in Celestial Dynamics*, 1892, among other works. His most important book was *The Light of Egypt*, 1889.
55. See Joscelyn Godwin, Christian Chanel and John P. Deveney, *The Hermetic Brotherhood of Luxor. Initiatic and Historical Documents of an Order of Practical Occultism*, 1995.

56. In his *Celestial Dynamics; a Course of Astro-Metaphysical Study*, 1896, Burgoyne's earlier work *The Light of Egypt* is advertised as 'A Book no Mason can afford to be without'. His *Language of the Stars* (n.54 above) not only described the book as being designed 'For all Masonic Brethren', but claimed Burgoyne as 'A Master of Esoteric Masonry'. However, there does not appear to be much in any of these texts which makes any serious attempt to relate esoteric astrology to Masonry, and Burgoyne nowhere explains what esoteric Masonry is.
57. He calls the sphere 'the Lost Orb' and 'the Dark Satellite'. (*Egypt*, op. cit., in n.56 above, p.134) '. . . its dark shadows became more and more bewildering and potent until the year 1881, when it passed its grand perihelion point'. (op. cit., p.135)
58. Burgoyne's 'tenth planet' may have influenced Isabelle M. Pagan into making her own prediction, in which she named Pluto and even gave it a new sigil, after recognizing it as the new octave of negative Mars, the traditional ruler of Scorpio. For Burgoyne, see *Egypt*, op. cit., in n.56 above, p.264; for Pagan, see *From Pioneer to Poet*, 1911, p.101.
59. Burgoyne, *Egypt*, op. cit., in n.56 above, p.134.
60. None of his seminal ideas seemed to be circulating in Masonry at that time, and we can only presume that Burgoyne was alert to the advanced arcane ideas of C.G. Harrison, *The Transcendental Universe* (1894), and perhaps the clairvoyant methodology of the American seer, Andrew Jackson Davis.
61. See *Egypt*, op. cit., in n.56 above, vol.II, p.vi. In the second volume of this work (1900), Burgoyne revealed that the material had been issued to a few of his pupils as 'Private Studies in Occultism', several years earlier. It seems that Dr Henry Wagner had financed the publication of 'nearly all' of his writings, while Mrs Belle M. Wagner has been chosen by the Masters as his spiritual successor and 'representative of the Hermetic Brotherhood of Luxor', to perpetuate the chain of outward connection between those in the realm of the higher life and those upon the outward plane. The additions to the original manuscripts have been added by dictation from the subjective plane of life (to which he had ascended several years earlier).
62. Broughton's horoscope, which has the Moon and Saturn conjunct and rising in Cancer (Ascendant of 28 degrees), is printed as frontispiece to his work, *The Elements of Astrology*, 1898. Significantly, the book was published by the author (in New York).
63. His maternal grandfather, Benjamin Scott, resided in Wakefield.
64. Broughton's brother had formed an astrological society. There was another society, of which 'my cousin' William Broughton, W.J. Simmonite, and Mr Haywood were members (Broughton op. cit., n.51, p.395). Some of the horoscopes they studied were published in *Scientific Messenger*. Mr. Simmonite had an academy in Sheffield (in Yorkshire), 'The British Institution for the Education of Young Gentlemen and Ladies', where such things as astro-philosophy were taught – see Ellic Howe, *Urania's Children. The Strange World of the Astrologers*, 1967, p.48. Simmonite is still remembered in astrological circles for his important *Arcana of Astral Philosophy*, which has gone through many editions. Broughton tells us that Simmonite 'was the most learned and gentlemanly astrologer that England ever knew', and that he spoke, wrote, and taught eight languages, besides being a thorough scholar and mathematician.
65. Broughton informs us that the first book published on astrology in the United States was by Dr Roeback (not listed in the Library of Congress), and was based on John Gadbury's famous 17th-century work, *Doctrine of Nativities*.
66. The data in (A) below are given by Broughton, in his *Astrology*, op. cit., in n.51 above, pp.346ff. The data in (B) derived from the modern computer system Windstar.

(A)	SU03PI18	MO21GE05	ME07AQ30	VE00AR25	MA27SC15
	JU07LB05R	SA04AR55	UR10SG04	DH25SG41	

(B) SU03PI19 MO16CP58 ME06AQ34 VE29PI25 MA23SC14
JU08LB37R SA02AR42 UR10SG05 DH25AQ00

67. Broughton (op. cit., n.51 above), p.464.
68. Broughton (op. cit., n.51 above), pp9.380ff.
69. Broughton (op. cit., n.51 above), pp9.379ff. and p.405.
70. See Albert Gallatin Mackey, *The History of Freemasonry*, vol.II, ch. xxxiii. For a rebuttal, see ch. xxxiv.
71. One presumes that Bromwell was aware of the writings of Rudolf Steiner in this connection, and recognized that the Austrian had proposed that the movements of the planets are not in ellipses, as is proposed by modern astronomers, but in lemniscates. For an excellent study of Steiner's stellar symbols, including the lemniscate, see Joachim Schultz, *Rhythmen der Sterne*, 1963.
72. For a survey of Dante's astrology and its roots in Arab astrology, see Edward Moore, 'The Astronomy of Dante', in his *Studies of Dante. Third Series. Miscellaneous Essays*, 1903.
73. W. Kirk MacNulty, *Freemasonry. A Journey through Ritual and Symbol*, 1997 reprint.
74. In alchemy, the ladder is the central symbol on the title-page of the 'wordless book', the *Mutus Liber* of 1677. The sleeping man at the foot of the ladder indicates that the ladder is a scala of initiation. For a useful study, see Adam Mclean, *A Commentary on the Mutus Liber*, 1982, in the Magnum Opus Hermetic Sourceworks limited edition series.
75. So far as I know, no satisfactory survey has been published dealing with the esoteric zodiacs which appear in mediaeval Christian churches and cathedrals in Europe. For a study of the two mediaeval marble zodiacs in Florence, Italy, see F. Gettings, *The Secret Zodiac. The Hidden Art in Mediaeval Astrology*, 1987. The San Miniato al Monte zodiac (with which Gettings deals in considerable detail) is oriented with Capricorn to the west and Cancer to the east, and the entire secret symbolism of the church is directed towards this orientation.
76. See MacNulty (op. cit., n.73 above), p.27.
77. The symbol of the lemniscate is sometimes taken as a symbol of eternity, whilst in reality the only part of the image which points to eternity is the crossing point, or node.
78. For the lemniscate in astronomy, see Norman Davidson, *Astronomy and the Imagination*, 1985, pp.57ff. For the double point, see pp.137ff.
79. Carlo Franzoni came to the United States in 1816, at the request of government. His elder brother, Giuseppe, had arrived in 1809, and had already executed sculptures for the Capitol, only one of which survived the burning of 1814. Carlo was born in Carrara in 1785. His early death in Washington DC, in 1833, is said to have been due to overexertion while sawing wood – a practice recommended for health reasons by his doctor. Giuseppe, had lived for most of his time in Washington DC with his beautiful young wife on Capitol Hill, at 120 B Street SE.
80. The clock, designed by Willard, was not installed until 1837.
81. The Latrobe drawing was made before 12 August 1815, some time before Franzoni arrived in the capital. An inscription on the drawing says that a copy was delivered to George Blagden (the master stone-cutter of the Capitol) on that day. See Paul Foote Norton, *Latrobe, Jefferson and the National Capitol*. . ., p.239. It is possible that Giuseppe had earlier carved a figure of Time in a winged chariot, for a print has survived showing remains of a burned plaster model (this being seated) which was among the works destroyed by the British in 1814: see Elizabeth Bryant Johnston, 'The Seal of the Columbia Historical Society', 1902, in *Records of the Columbia Historical Society, Washington DC*, 1903, p.218.
82. D'Hancarville, *Antiquités Étrusques, Grecques et Romaines, Gravées par F.A. David*, 1787, vol.4, plate 16.

83. In Greek mythology, the goddess Demeter had tried to bestow immortality upon Triptolemus, but had been forestalled by the foolishness of his parents. She put Triptolemus in her chariot (drawn by winged serpents) and sent him over the world to instruct mankind in the culture and use of corn. We see from this detail of the myth that Triptolemus could have become an important personification in the symbolism of Washington DC.
84. Something of the connection between Royal Arch symbolism and astrological symbolism may be gleaned from Steinmetz, op. cit., n.29 above.
85. Porphyry, *De Antro Nympharum*. By far the best translation into English is that by Thomas Taylor: see n.92 below.
86. In the 13th book of the *Odyssey* Homer tells how Odysseus is carried from his ship, still sleeping, and set gently down on his native shores of Greece, at Ithaca. When he awakes, the goddess Athena appears to him. The period of sleep, and the awakening to the appearance of a goddess, are the basic mythology of initiation.
87. *De Antro* (see n.85 above), in Taylor ed. of 1991, p.45.
88. The plate, by Matthaus Merian, is from the alchemical work *Musaeum Hermeticum* of 1625, which does not contain the *De Antro Nympharum*, but it would be immediately apparent from its many contributors (including Nicholas Flamel and Lambsprinck) that the plate represented the famous cave. The later edition, of 1677 (the *Musaeum hermeticum reformatum et amplificatum*), also has the plate as frontispiece: not one of the writers whose works appear in this later edition (including Michael Maier and Helvetius) would doubt the significance of the engraving. As a matter of fact, the 1991 edition of the Thomas Taylor *On the Cave of the Nymphs*, with an introduction by Kathleen Raine, has the engraving displayed on the front cover.
89. De Hooghe, *Hieroglyphica, oder Denkbilder der alten Volker*, 1744.
90. The descent of 'fire' (which is light) into 'watery' plasms of body is entirely consistent with the hermetic view of incarnation.
91. His translation of Apuleius' story of initiation, *The Metamorphosis, or Golden Ass and philosophical works of Apuleius* (1822), is still justly famous. His *Iamblichus on the Mysteries of the Egyptians, Chaldeans and Assyrians* (1823) deeply influenced the later English scholar G.R.S. Mead in his own research work into the Mysteries. For an account of Taylor, see Kathleen Raine and G. Mills Harper (eds), *Thomas Taylor the Platonist: Selected Writings*, 1969.
92. See Kathleen Raine's introduction to the 1991 Phanes Press edition of the Thomas Taylor translation of Porphyry's *On the Cave of the Nymphs*, p.18.
93. His father was President of the Academy of Fine Arts at Carrara, and Carlo was nephew to the influential Cardinal Franzoni. The cultural level of the Franzoni family is intimated by the friendship Giuseppe, Carlo's brother, established with Jefferson, with whom he used to dine weekly.
94. For *Zervan Akarana*, see B.L. van der Waerden, *Science Awakening II. The Birth of Astronomy*, 1974, p.156. For its connection with the Greek *Chronos Ageraos* (unageing, or unmoving, time) see W.C.C. Guthrie, *Orpheus and the Greek Religion*, 1952, pp.79ff. The image of Zervan Akarana (actually entitled 'Mithraic Kronos') is reproduced in Franz Cumont, *The Mysteries of Mithra*, 1903, p.106 of the 1956 reprint. The important point is that Zervan stands *outside* time, and is not time. Just so, Clio is not a symbol of time so much as a recorder of phenomena born of time. This distinction is often recognized by Mithraic scholars who call the Kronos image *Aeon*, which stands outside time.
95. The rulership of Uranus over Aquarius seems to have percolated into astrology by way of Theosophy. Pagan, (op. cit., n.58 above) gave Uranus as ruler of the sign, and we must remember that she had been teaching in Theosophical circles for some time prior to writing this interesting book.

    In the United States, the rulership of Uranus was not widely accepted until the end of the 19th century. Neither L.D. Broughton (op. cit., n.51 above), p.237, nor the American astrologer, Ellen H. Bennett, *Astrology. Science of Knowledge and Reason*, 1897 (see p.124, for example), accepts the new rulership of Uranus. Hiram E. Butler's *Solar Biology* of 1887 (which was among the astrological material issued from Applegate, California) is something of a laughing-stock in astrological circles, yet for all his failings Butler did have some interesting views. For example, he proposed Uranus as ruler over Aries (op. cit. p.xxvi): however, he did not integrate this into his own system of interpretation.

For a survey of various rulership propositions, see Geoffrey Dean and Arthur Mather, *Recent Advances in Natal Astrology*, 1977, pp.203ff.

96. As with all such tales, the dates vary. The earliest account I know (derived from the Archives of the Architect of the Capitol) is in an article by the journalist, Will P. Kennedy, in the *Sunday Star*, 12 November 1939. The document, 'A Sonnet Saga', received from Carl Fogle, Architect's Office, in September 1962, says the paper was found by a workman in 1940. Methinks the poem too poor to foist on Adams.

CHAPTER FIVE

1. Voltaire had been initiated in *Les Neuf Soeurs* by Lalande on 7 April 1778, seemingly drawn to Masonry late in life by an article published in a newspaper by Franklin.
2. Avery Allyn, *A Ritual of Freemasonry*, 1831.
3. In July 1732, Sirius was in 10.26 Cancer, while Lalande's Mercury was in 5.48 of that sign, and his Sun 19.18.
4. We know nowadays that Sirius is 9 light years away from the Earth, and is moving towards us so rapidly that in less than 3,000 years it has changed its apparent position in the sky by the width of a full Moon (about half a degree). We know that its companion – called with little imagination 'Sirius B' – has a density of over 90,000 times our own Sun. We know also that Voltaire's hero was quite right – this Sirius B is a sort of satellite, for it revolves around the greater body once in about 50 years. Lalande was privy to no such knowledge, but it is evident from his writings that he recognized it as the most holy star of all in the god-filled skies of the ancient Egyptians.
5. J. Norman Lockyer, *The Dawn of Astronomy. A Study of the Temple-Worship and Mythology of the Ancient Egyptians*, 1894, p.197.
6. John Fellows, *Exposition of the Mysteries, or Religious Dogmas and Customs of the Ancient Egyptians, Pythagorens and Druids*, 1835, 'Explanation of the Frontispiece'.
7. For an account of Smith's 'Hall of the Ancients', see p.324ff.
8. An enlarged reproduction of the lunette drawing of this extraordinary proposal is reproduced on pp.174–9 of Joseph J. Thorndike (ed.), *Three Centuries of Notable American Architects*, 1981. The pagination is curious because the pages are wraps for the centrefold picture of Frank Lloyd Wright's design of 1956 for the mile-high skyscraper in Chicago.
9. For examples of Egyptian orientations, see Lockyer (op. cit., n.5 above). The calendrical and orientational importance of Sirius would have been recognized by the mid-19th-century architects and Masons through the writings of Lepsius (*Chronologie der Aegypter*, 1849, vol.1, pp.190ff.). However, Alexander von Humboldt (who visited Washington DC) wrote with considerable scholarly insight into the orientation and ancient traditions of Sirius in his *Cosmos: A Sketch of a Physical Description of the Universe* (trans. 1861), vol.3, pp.133ff. Humboldt points out that the importance of Sirius 'has long been acknowledged', and merely furnishes a digest of the most recent researches.
10. There are many useful works on Christian stellar orientations. For an early mediaeval study, see F. Gettings, *The Secret Zodiac. The Hidden Art in Mediaeval Astrology*, 1987. For a later study, see R. Taylor, 'Architecture and Magic: Consideration of the *Idea* of the Escorial', in *Essays in the History of Architecture*

Presented to Rudolf Wittkower, 1969 ed., pp.81ff.

11. Reproduced from John C. Fitzpatrick's *The Diaries of George Washington, 1784–1799*, 1925 imprint.
12. The dog-days are said to have taken their name from the period of six or eight hot weeks (the days of which were called the *caniculares*) begun at the rising of the star Sirius with the Sun.
13. I hasten to add that the ancient Egyptian for 'obelisk' is *thn*, and the 'obelisk-like' glyph is not part of the hieroglyphic group.
14. L.E. Reynolds, *The Mysteries of Masonry. Being the Outline of a Universal Philosophy Founded upon the Ritual and Degrees of Ancient Freemasonry*, 1870.
15. The Holy Writ support for the notion is in 1 Corinthians 3.10, and is delightfully illustrated in the frontispiece to Joseph Priestley's *Disquisitions Relating to Matter and Spirit*, 1777: 'I have laid the foundation & another buildeth thereon. But let every man take heed how he buildeth thereon.'
16. At midday, it was in the first degree of Virgo (in 00VG54).
17. It is interesting that the traditional significance apportioned to 25 degrees Virgo is echoed in the treatment of degree symbols in which 25.35 of Virgo is 'associated with the Holy Grail'. See Nicholas de Vore, *Encyclopedia of Astrology*, 1947 ed., p.102.
18. The pyramid of stones seems to have been removed *circa* 1874. Although some scholars are of the opinion that the meridional axis was first drawn through the White House by Nicholas King in 1804, Ellicott's own notes reveal that *he* was the first to establish this important line, as well as the precise east-west line on which the city grid was laid.
19. Some people are still convinced that the Monument marks the centre of the old District of Columbia. However, careful measurement shows that the centre was to the north-west of the Monument, on the corner of 17th and C. See *Geographic Magazine*, vol.6, p.149.
20. Letter from Martha Washington to John Adams, dated 31 December 1799, reproduced in W.B. Webb and J. Wooldridge, *History of Washington DC*, 1892, p.679.
21. Robert Belmont Freeman, 'Design Proposals for the Washington National Monument', *Records of the Columbia Historical Society of Washington DC*, 1973–4, p.170.
22. Freeman (op. cit., n.21 above), p.151.
23. George Dance (1741–1825) was from a long line of talented eccentrics: he had succeeded his namesake father as surveyor and architect of the City of London, at the age of 27. He was a founder member of the Royal Academy, and a Mason.
24. Peter Force was one of the most creative and influential people in the Washington DC of the first half of the century. He was a printer and publisher, and served as mayor of the city from 1836 to 1840. Although not a trained architect, his design for the Monument was among the finest proposed. Force was a founder-member of the Washington National Monument Society, and a Mason.
25. Robert Mills was clearly a Mason, but his Lodge is no longer known and documentary proof of initiation has been lost, save for the recorded fact that he would greet the Mason Lafayette as 'Illustrious Brother'. The President of the Washington National Monument Society which selected Mills' design was the noted Mason, Supreme Court chief justice, John Marshall.
26. Marble came from other sources, such as from other states, Switzerland, Turkey, Greece, China and Japan. Not all the contributions were welcome: for an account, see Peter Tompkins, *The Magic of Obelisks*, 1981, p.329.
27. For a list, with dedications, see *Your Masonic Capital City*, typescript of 20 April 1950, issued by the Masonic Service Association, pp.18ff.
28. Benjamin French was Grand Master of the Grand Lodge of Free and Accepted Masons of the District of Columbia. For details of this consecration and Masonic

ceremony, see Tompkins (op. cit., n.26 above), pp.322ff.

29. The 'Know-Nothings' party had taken over the building of the shaft in an attempt to complete it, but added only two ill-constructed courses. It has been suggested that the 'Know-Nothings' were responsible for the incident of the 'Pope Stone': see F. I. Harvey, *Monograph of the Washington National Monument*, 1885, pp.54ff.

30 See Senate Document No. 224, 57th Congress, 2nd Session; *History of the Washington National Monument and Washington National Monument Society*, compiled by Frederick I. Harvey, 1903, p.98. This official document was presented to Congress by the Mason Gallinger, and printed in 1903.

31. The data for 7 August 1880 are:

SU 15LE27	MO 02VG57	ME 11LE27R	VE 22LE16	MA 11VG03
JU 19AR33	SA 28AR57	UR 07VG51	NE 28TA18	DG 04CP21

Pluto, as yet undiscovered, was in 28TA18.

32. The main question seems to be, is the time related to observation from the ground, or from the considerable height of the Monument? It is evident from the calculations in n.33 below that whoever cast the chart to allow for the rising of Spica did so from the base of the Monument, as would befit a chart relating to a building.

33. My assumption, based on direct observation of Sunrise, is that the building line to the north-east of Capitol Hill is just over 1 degree higher than the horizon. In 1880, Spica was in 22.14 Libra. The Ascendant at 10:59 am at the Washington Monument was 25 degrees 11 minutes. Of course, given the time of day, Spica would not have been visible, but there is no doubt that the star had just risen. It might be argued that the official time of one minute of eleven was set down in order to point to the rising of the star: if the time had been formulated as eleven o'clock, it is likely that no one would have thought of considering the nature of the Ascendant.

34. It is a spectroscopic binary.

35. J. Norman Lockyer (op. cit., n.5 above), pp.318, 320, etc.

36. See Colin F.W. Dyer, *Symbolism in Craft Freemasonry*, 1976, pp.105ff, which is one of the most perceptive of modern books on Masonic symbolism.

37. Pamela Scott and Antoinette J. Lee are among the few modern authors even to mention the removal of the Egyptian-revival door frame. They are of the opinion that Casey removed it in order to obtain absolute geometric purity. See their work, *Buildings of the District of Columbia*, 1993, p.101.

38. Photographs of the solar-disk lintels (still in place in 1878) on both east and west portals may be seen towards the end of Senate Document No. 224: see Harvey, n.30 above.

39. See Philipp von Zabern, *Official Catalogue. The Egyptian Museum, Cairo*, 1987, Cat. no. 118. There is an interesting variation on the stela of Djedamoniuankh, Cat. no. 243.

40. T. A. M. Ward's *The Obelisks. Osiris and Isis, the Sun and the Moon*, 1880, displays on its cover two Egyptian obelisks which are named Boaz and Jachin, thereby linking together the Masonic mythology of Solomon's Temple with the obelisks.

41. The American ambassador at Rome, George P. Marsh, established that the ratio of base to shaft was one to ten. Casey therefore amended the projected height (set by the Society to 500 feet) mainly by placing the 50-foot pyramid on top.

42. This beautiful building is still well preserved. A picture is reproduced in James Stevens Curl, *The Art and Architecture of Freemasonry*, 1991, p.223. The winged disk is also part of the internal decorations of the House of the Temple, in Washington DC.

43. Robert Hewitt Brown, *Stellar Theology and Masonic Astronomy or, the Origin and Meaning of Ancient and Modern Mysteries Explained*, 1882, p.80. In fact, even in popular art-forms the winged-disk lintel or architrave became the standard symbol

of entry into the ancient Mysteries. An excellent example is in the drawing by Isabel de Steiger, 'A Neophyte in the Astral', which shows a supplicant at the door of an Egyptian temple, the portal of which has a winged disk on the lintel: see A. E. Waite (ed.), *The Unknown World*, vol.II, no.3, 15 April 1895.

44. The designs, which are preserved in the National Archives, are reproduced as fig.14, p.182, of Freeman (op. cit., n.21 above), p.151.
45. It was one day before the New Style date of George Washington's birth: he was born 22 February 1732, New Style.
46. Cold as it was, there was sufficient sunlight for the fall of shadow upon the Monument to indicate the approximate time of day: see n.64 below.
47. E.T. Schultz, *History of Freemasonry in Maryland, of All the Rites Introduced into Maryland, from the Earliest Time to the Present*, 1888. Schultz was at one time Master of Concordia Lodge No. 13.
48. For example, the cornerstone of the obelisk itself; the cornerstone of the statue of George Washington in the Washington Circle, 22 February 1860; the cornerstone of the extension to the Capitol, on 4 July 1851; the Yorktown Monument, Virginia, on 18 October 1881. The gavel is still in the possession of the Fredericksburg Lodge No. 4, where George Washington was initiated in 1752. For a well-illustrated account of some cornerstone ceremonials, see S. Brent Morris, *Cornerstones of Freedom. A Masonic Tradition*, 1993.
49. There appears to be no record of Chester Alan Arthur being a Mason.
50. Schultz (op. cit., n.47 above) gives an account taken from the *American and Advertiser* of 8 July 1815. For something of the Masonic background, see Schultz, Period III, pp.220ff.
51 For a balanced account of the anti-Masonic movement, see William L. Fox, *Lodge of the Double-Headed Eagle*, 1997, pp.42ff etc.
52. Saturn in Pisces is trine to Jupiter in Cancer, but this latter is squared by Uranus, in Aries. The modern astrologer has the advantage of seeing that Jupiter is exactly squared by Pluto, also in Aries.
53. See his letter from Rome, 9 February 1879, quoted in extract by Harvey (op. cit., n.29 above), p.121.
54. From Casey's report of December 1884, quoted by Harvey (op. cit., n.30 above), p.15.
55. The relevant part of the inscription on the sphinxes reads *smn.n.nf.* This translates approximately 'Made permanent for Him', which seems to be the equivalent of a foundation dedication to God. For a slightly different reading, see John J. Kessler, *Transactions of the Supreme Council*, 21 October 1963.
56. The dedication was in Latin (*Ad Majorem Supremi Architecti Gloriam* – 'To the greater glory of the Supreme Architect'), and was cut into the ornate stone presented by the Grand Lodge of Pennsylvania, in 1851.
57. The star appears as one of five Masonic symbols above a dedication to the memory of Washington as 'The Christian Mason'. These symbols are listed in a useful table in Gary T. Scott, 'Masonic Stones of the Washington Monument', in *Heredom*, vol.5, 1996, p.256.
58. The design, on the stone given by the Grand Lodge of Illinois, is dated 1853. It is incorporated into a formal blank arch cut into a surface of ashlars: the portal is flanked by two columns from which subtends an arch of 18 stones keyed by an additional central stone.
59. The gifting Masonic bodies and the positions of the stones are listed in another useful table in Scott (op. cit, n.57 above), p.262.
60. J.J. de Lalande, *Astronomie par M. de la Lande* (I have used the 1771 2nd ed., which is a corrected version, in the Library of Congress). For the position of Sirius, see the catalogue of stars on pp.202ff.
61. James Wilson, *Complete Dictionary of Astrology*, 1819, p.134.
62. I give the simplest of all explanations of the consequences of precession because I

am anxious to present the issue in such a way as not to disturb the general reader with unnecessary complexities. In view of this, there is no need to examine the issue of precession in terms of spherical geometry – or even to explain how the star positions are measured against the single fiducial of the ecliptic. The accumulated differences over a period of several centuries can lead to significant variations, but the figures I give are accurate enough to sustain my argument. Of course, the differences were well recognized in the late 18th century. For example, in, *État des Étoiles Fixes au Second Siècle, par Claude Ptolémée, Comparé à la Position des Mêmes Étoiles en 1786*, 1787 l'Abbé Montignot published a table of differences for the 24 main stars over the period of 1,646 years.

63. These statistics raise the intriguing question as to what the astronomers and astrologers of the late 18th century *believed* the position of Sirius (and, indeed, of other stars) to be. While the following observation does not affect my own conclusions, I should observe that the star-list known to Thomas Jefferson gives variant placings to the ones I list in this book – mainly because the true rate of precession had not been established. These star-lists appear in the work of Montignot (see n.62 above), which is now in the Library of Congress. On p.192 of this work, Montignot gives the rate of precession as one degree for every 70 years. This implies that the projections he has given from the Ptolemaic markings are only reasonably accurate. He claims that in 1786 Sirius (or, as he writes, *Syrius*) was in 11.9 Cancer.
64. The chart is 'speculative' in the sense that the precise moment is not known. However, the interesting thing is that the time can be worked out within a tolerable degree of accuracy from the photographs taken at that time. While it is a cold day, there is sufficient sunlight for the shadows to reveal that the Sun has passed the zenith. Photographs are preserved in the Library of Congress, and in the Library of the Supreme Council, Southern Jurisdiction.
65. Jupiter was in 34 minutes of Virgo, throwing its influence across the chart to the Sun and Mars. One presumes that this was the reason why the ceremonial was arranged for this day.
66. In 1848, the Moon had been in 00 degrees, 54 minutes of Virgo. In 1885, Jupiter was in 00 degrees, 34 minutes of Virgo. This indicates just how well planned, astrologically speaking, were such Masonic ceremonies.
67. The Latin is from Virgil, *Aeneid*, Bk 9, v.625.
68. See Freeman (op. cit., n.21 above), p.185.
69. See John Partridge, *Merlinus Liberatus. An Almanack For the Year of our Redemption, 1848*, 1847, p.14, and W.S.B. Woolhouse, *White's Coelestial Atlas; or, an Improved Ephemeris for the Year of Our Lord 1848*, 1847, p.14.
70. For an intelligent treatment of the Seriadic Land (the equivalent of the Sothiac Land) see G.R.S. Mead, *Thrice-Greatest Hermes*, 1964 reprint of the 1906 ed., vol.I, pp.76ff. In fact, Mead is referring to the rare work by Hekekyan Bey, *A Treatise on the Chronology of Siriadic Monuments*. . . , 1863. In this context, Siriadic is the equivalent of Sothiac.
71. For a summary of the Sirian temple stars, see the table on p.305 of Lockyer (op. cit., n.5 above).
72. For a Masonic account of this relationship, see Albert Pike, *Morals and Dogma*, 1906 ed., p.376.
73. In this mosaic of the months, formerly at Thysdus (el Djem), Mercury is the psychopomp of February, who has chosen to enter the lower door (Latin: *janua*) opened by January in the previous month.
74. The diagram is described by Lynn Thorndike, *A History of Magic and Experimental Science During the First Thirteen Centuries of Our Era*, 1923, vol.1, pp.366–7.
75. See Grant and Kraum, 'The Endless Quest for the United States Chart', *National Council for Geocosmic Research Journal*, Spring 1994, p.57.

76. For this Declaration, and for several of the following key-date proposals, see *Documents Illustrative of the Formation of the Union of the American States*, House Document No.398, Government Printing Office, 1927.
77. See Charles F. Jenkins, *Button Gwinnett. Signer of the Declaration of Independence*, 1926, pp.81ff
78. Quoted from a letter from Edward Rutledge to John Jay, mentioning the events in Congress up to 7.00 p.m. on 8 June 1776, reproduced in Jenkins (op. cit., n.77 above), p.82.
79. There is no known record of the nine-hour debate which was held on 1 July. For an account of this phase in the proceedings, see Jenkins (op. cit. n.77 above), pp.84ff.
80. A most useful study of the Declaration is John H. Hazelton's monumental *The Declaration of Independence*, 1906. The copy document is signed by the Secretary, John Hancock. The appended signatures of the 55 representatives are grouped according to the state they represent, with the exception of Matthew Thornton. See Hazelton, op. cit., pp.25ff. It was usual for such signatures to be added later. For example, the Articles of Confederation were agreed by Congress on 15 November 1777. These were signed at different times by the delegates: indeed, the delegates from Maryland, the last of the states to ratify, did not sign until 1 March 1781. See *Journals of the Continental Congress*, XIX (1912) p.214, and note on p.27 of House Document 398 (1927).
81. See Henry Sadler, in *Transactions of the Quattuor Coronati*, 1911, vol.xxiv, Pt 2, p.95.
82. E. Sibly, *A New and Complete Illustration of the Occult Sciences: or the Art of Foretelling Future Events and Contingencies by . . . the Heavenly Bodies*, 1784. The book is dedicated to 'The Ancient and Honourable Fraternity of Free and Accepted Masons'.
83. See Nicholas Campion *The Book of World Horoscopes*, 1996 ed. The only suggestion in Campion's work which seems to be susceptible to criticism is the claim (on p.424) that the first marker stone for the District of Columbia was laid on 15 March 1791: this is an error, for contemporaneous records show that the marker was laid (at Jones Point, near where the lighthouse was built in 1855) on 15 April of that year. See Brent Morris, *Cornerstones of Freedom. A Masonic Tradition*, 1993, which deals admirably with this first marker stone, and related issues.
84. In the Library of the Supreme Council, Southern Jurisdiction, is a first edition of Ebenezer Sibly's remarkable book, *A New and Complete Illustration of the Occult Sciences*, of 1784. The book was presented to the Library by A.L. Metz, in 1908.
85. Sibly (op. cit., n.84 above), p.1051.
86. Sibly (op. cit., n.84 above), p.1051.
87. The method he used was rooted in mediaeval astrology, and was based on a conversion of arcs of direction into projected arcs of time, according to prescribed and complex rules. Sibly was following a very advanced form of prediction employed in mundane astrology; even so, he seems to have been involved in some very sly conversions to achieve his aims.
88. For a survey of the technical issues, see Campion (op. cit., n.83 above), pp.414ff. See also Susan Manuel, 'Making Sense of Sibly', *National Council for Geocosmic Research Journal*, Spring 1994, vol.13, no.1, pp.35ff.
89. The house cusps of the chart are accurate if we assume that Sibly had used tables for the latitude of London calculated according to the Placidean system. The following data compare the houses of the Sibly chart of 1787 with a modern Placidean table of houses calculated for London:

SIB:	1: 19AQ49	2: 20AR	3: 23TA	10: 13SG22	11: 01CP	12: 20CP10
MOD:	1: 19AQ48	2: 20AR	3: 22TA	10: 13SG30	11: 01CP	12: 20CP

90. The data for the four charts I have mentioned are compared below. The Sibly data

(1) are from the engraved plate of 1784: the actual data (2) are cast for London, at the time and date specified in Sibly's horoscope. The data for (3) are for the planetary positions in Philadelphia on the same date and time; while the data for (4) are for London at 09.52 p.m. When comparing these figures, it is essential to bear in mind that the planetary tables available to 18th-century astrologers were rarely as accurate as those we use now. Even so, it will be seen that (1) and (4) are very close, even to the position of the Moon: we must presume therefore that Sibly cast his chart for shortly after 09:52:00 p.m. for London, and gave the time erroneously in his printed version.

1: SU13CN20 MN27AQ16 ME24CN12 VE03CN07 MA21GE23
JU05CN56 SA14LB48
2: SU13CN08 MN24AQ00 ME22CN21 VE02CN48 MA21GE17
JU05CN58 SA14LB50
3: SU13CN32 MN00PI16 ME24CN06 VE03CN22 MA21CN31
JU05CN59 SA14LB49
4: SU13CN19 MN26AQ58 ME24CN12 VE03CN05 MA21GE22
JU05CN56 SA14LB48

91. The delegates met in the morning, but had one amendment to carry and two agreements to countenance before signing the Constitution: we may estimate the time as being either about lunch, or shortly afterwards. See Gaillard Hunt and James B. Scott (eds). *The Debates in the Federal Convention of 1787 which Framed the Constitution of the United States of America*, 1920, pp.577ff.
92. Only 12 of the confederated states participated in the 1789 government.
93. An excellent summary of the numerous inquiries which have been conducted by historians and astrologers into the beginning, or 'nativity', of the United States has been presented by Nicholas Campion (see n.83 above). Campion gives data for 16 of these possible 'birth' dates, and offers several well-argued variations on times for them. In addition, he discusses other charts, such as the moment of international recognition, on 16 November 1776. Campion's summary, which sets out a considerable number of possible charts and discusses the taxing issues of precise times, is worth close scrutiny.
94. Campion (op. cit., n.83 above), p.402.
95. The data are:
SU13VG02 MO07VG43 ME25LE07 VE12LE48 MA18CN32
JU16TA08R SA27VG15 UR02GE25 NE20VG00 PL22CP40R
DH12VG59

Even the progressional promise within the chart, which will not be evident to non-specialists, proclaims the appositeness of the chart to American federalism. The major conflict of the Civil War, which tested the whole idea of federalism and split states, families and even Masonic Brotherhoods, is reflected in the progressions for the chart. (The following note is intended for specialists only.) I observe that the progressed chart, cast for the official beginning of the Civil War, on 13 April 1861 at Fort Sumner, has Pluto on the Ascendant (24 degrees Capricorn), sparking off the radical opposition between Pluto and Mars. The progressed opposition of Moon (07.08 Scorpio) and Jupiter (07.39 Taurus) is on the east-west axis of the radical chart. Venus, meridional in the radical, has just entered Sagittarius, to square with Mars, close to the natal Moon. The lunar node has retrograded to one degree of the radical Moon.
96. John Hancock is listed as a Mason in the useful file marked 'Declaration of Independence, signers . . .' in the Library of the Supreme Council, Washington DC.
97. Signed by the President of Congress and the Secretary of Congress.
98. Journals of Congress for 1 January 1776 to 1 January 1777, p.239.

99. See John Adams, in a letter to his wife dated 3 July 1776. Adams was not a Mason: indeed, his *Letters on the Masonic Institutions* reveal him to have been an anti-Mason. However, there has been understandable confusion about this in early literature: the John Quincy Adams who was initiated into Saint John's Lodge, Boston, on 5 December 1826 was not the famous John Quincy Adams.
100. Adams' much-quoted letter is published in full by Jenkins, (op. cit., n.77 above), pp. 85ff.
101. Robert Morden, *An Introduction to Astronomy, Geography, Navigation, and the Mathematical Sciences*, 1702. The table of acronical risings and settings is on p.81; the table of fixed stars for 1700 is on p.74.
102. Even if the erroneous precessional period of 1 degree per 70-year period were applied to this position, it would mean that, by 1776, the star was just at the end of the 11.00 Cancer, according to contemporaneous reckoning.
103. No. 28 in the Astronomy Section of the original Jefferson catalogue, as set out by James Gilreath and Douglas L. Wilson, *Thomas Jefferson's Library. A Catalog with the Entries in His Own Order*, 1989. The work is Montignot (op. cit., n.62 above).
104. The table is on p.192 of his work (op. cit., n.62 above) Montignot believed that the mean precession of the equinoxes was at the rate of 50 seconds per year or 'one degree for 70 years'. Astronomers now recognize that true mean precession is nearer to one degree every 72 years.

CHAPTER SIX

1. Bertha Noyes was born in Washington DC in 1876, and died there at the age of 90. Among many other achievements, she was founder of the Washington Arts Club at 1614 19th Street NW.
2. Because of its unfortunate history, I have examined this armillary sphere only in photographs. While the earth is not symbolized, on the base is a winged putto.
3. Commodore David Porter (1780–1843) was at that time serving on the naval commission in Washington DC. In 1824, he was in command of a large fleet dedicated to the suppression of piracy in the Caribbean. He resigned from the navy when he felt that the Department failed to support a personal action to remedy what he considered an insult to the American flag. He became subsequently commander-in-chief of the Mexican navy, then Consul to the United Barbary States. He was the author of two books. His foster-son was the famous David G. Farragut.
4. The quotation is from H.D. Eberlein and C.Van Dyke Hubbard, *Historic Houses of George-Town & Washington City*, 1958, p.450.
5. Meridian Hill House was demolished *circa* 1863.
6. It was demolished in 1935.
7. William Lambert correspondence, 20 May 1815, now in the Library of Congress. The longitude is now recognized as being W77 00′ 34″.
8. Virgo is shown descending over the western horizon. As is evident from other examples, the usual symbolism in the context of Washington DC is designed to show Virgo on the Ascendant, or eastern horizon. However, we should recall that this is meant to be a memorial, and the west is traditionally the place of death. Thus, even in this funerary context, Virgo remains the supreme symbol.
9. Richard Hinckley Allen includes this interpretation among several other etymologies in his *Star-Names and their Meanings*, 1963 ed. of the 1899 work, p.463. The quotation from Shakespeare's *Titus Andronicus* which precedes this analysis is neither recorded nor interpreted correctly. Equally inaccurate is Allen's attribution of the horoscope of Jesus to Virgo: the mediaeval symbolism recognized that Jesus was Piscean, born of the Virgin, on the opposite side of the zodiac. This is what Albertus Magnus had in mind.
10. Chalmers I. Paton, *Freemasonry. Its Symbolism, Religious Nature, and Law of Perfection*, 1873, p.139.
11. Although the Denderah planisphere has been discussed by many scholars, I know

of no satisfactory work on the subject. Of interest to astrologers is Cyril Fagan's original treatment of Egyptian astrology in *Astrological Origins*, 1971, but even Fagan calls it a zodiac. The original marble planisphere is now in the Louvre, Paris; a cast replaces this stolen planisphere in the ceiling of the shrine on the roof of the Temple of Hathor at Denderah. There is a magnificent full-scale cast of the planisphere in the Rosicrucian Egyptian Museum in San Jose, south of San Francisco. This is far more accessible than the badly located original in the Louvre. According to inscriptions, the zodiac is Ptolemaic, but it clearly contains data derived from very early ancient Egyptian stellar lore.

12. Among the several mediaeval prints showing the Virgin in a corn-dress is an interesting anonymous woodcut from the British Museum. Two angels hold behind the Virgin a screen on which are depicted 38 plants. Each of the flowers has five petals. This is reproduced in Richard Field (ed.), *The Illustrated Bartsch*, 164 (supp.), 1992; *Anonymous Artists*, p.8: The Virgin in a Robe Embroidered with Ears of Corn (S.1000b). For something of the background to the continuity of the Ceres Mysteries (through such spiritual facts as the Eucharistic bread) into Christianity, see n.23 below.
13. The Fresco is in the south wall of St Bartholomew's Church in Tessendorf, near Klagenfurt in Austria. There is a reproduction of the picture in Friedrich Zauner, *Das Hierarchienbild der Gotik*, 1980, p.209.
14. See, for example, the winged angel in the centre of the decan image of the *Sphaera Barbarica* (Reg. lat. 1283), reproduced as figure 30, F. Saxl and H. Meier, *Verzeichnis Astrologischer und Mythologischer Illustrierter Handschriften des Lateinischen Mittelalters*, 1953, p.lxi.
15. This is the 14th-century (Flemish?) manuscript, Sloane 3983, in the British Library, which is justly famous for its rich illustrations. The work is a truncated version of the Arabic astrological work of Albumasar, *Introductio in Astrologiam*. The image of Virgo is stellar (rather than pertaining to the sign) and is followed by the so-called Parantellonata, or constellations which rise with Virgo. For useful notes on this manuscript, see Saxl and Meier (op. cit., n.14 above), pp.247ff.
16. Plate 17 (Taf.VIII) of F. Boll, C. Bezold and W. Gundel, *Sternglaube und Sterndeutung. Die Geschichte und das Wesen der Astrologie*, 1966.
17. The manuscript is cod. 12600 (supp. 372) in the Nationalbibliothek, Vienna. It is not a complete *Phaenomena*, but a digest, identifying merely the stars in the constellations.
18. By the 13th century the Arabic versions of the names for the fixed stars were widely used in astrological and astronomical texts. If we glance only at the alternative mediaeval sigil for our Spica from the 13th-century *Liber Hermetis de XV stellis . . .* in the Bodleian Library, Oxford, we shall see a good example of this in relation to Spica. Alongside the sigil, the Latin text gives the interesting name *arkimech alazel* – showing just how much mediaeval astrology owes to the Arabic tradition. This is one of many garbled Latin variants of the Arabic *Al Simak al A'zal*, which means 'Simak unarmed', and was contrasted with the nearby 'armed Simak' which was the star Arcturus, 'the lofty lance-bearer'. A 1515 edition of Ptolemy's *Almagest* gives an equal distortion with the version *Aschimec inermis*.
19. In the classical stellar maps the constellation Libra rarely had a separate image, and was usually incorporated into the 'dread monster', Scorpius, placed in the grasp of its claws. These were *Chelae*, in Latin, and the constellation Libra was often designated by this word. However, in this 12th-century illustration, Libra (the 'faintly shining' *Chelae* according to the Aratus texts) is found in the hand of Virgo. In spite of this, the Aratus text is adhered to, and the stars of Libra are treated as though they are part of Scorpius.
20. This illustration from the 12th-century Aratus (cod.12600. supp. 372, from the Nationalbibliothek, Vienna) is reproduced by Karl Anton Nowotny, *Henricus Cornelius Agrippa ab Nettesheym, De Occulta Philosophia*, 1967, p.641.

21. The three gems are from C.W. King, *Handbook of Engraved Gems*, 1885 ed. The first and second gems are from plate xlvi, p.227, the third from plate lxxvi, p.239.
22. Plutarch, in *De Iside et Osiride*, discusses Hermes as the father of Isis, but in some versions of the myth she is 'unborn'.
23. For the symbolism of the threshing floor, where the wheat was chaffed to make bread, see Paul Schmitt, 'The Ancient Mysteries in the Society of Their Time, Their Transformation and Most Recent Echoes', in *The Mysteries. Papers from the Eranos Yearbooks*, 1971 ed., esp. p.100. Also, in the same 1971 work, Julius Baum, 'Symbolic Representations of the Eucharist'.
24. This is on the Steuben glass zodiacs on the two light fixtures in the corridor leading from the rear entrance of the magnificent Federal Reserve Board Building on Constitution Avenue and 20th Street NW.
25. I shall discuss some outstanding images of Mercury in Washington DC below: however, it is worth pointing to the striking example on the western corner of the United States Post Office in Massachusetts Avenue NE, designed by David Burnham.
26. Plutarch (op. cit., n.22 above), III.i. That this is entirely mythological is implicit in the extension proposed by Plutarch – namely, that the paternity was connected with Hermes as the discoverer of writing and the arts. An alternative father, the fire-bringer Prometheus, was the discoverer of wisdom and foreknowledge.
27. Ptolemy, *Tetrabiblos*, I.9. The two exceptions given by Ptolemy are the *eta*, which he called *Protrigeter* and linked with the nature of Mercury with Saturn, and the all-important Spica (Ptolemy called this *Stachys*) which was of the influence of Venus, perhaps with a touch of Mars. This Greek word in the original *Tetrabiblos* of Ptolemy was the *Protrigetrix* of the later star-lists, derived from the name used by Aratus (*Protrigeter*) in his *Phaenomena*. The word means, approximately, 'gatherer of grapes', and has been explained as being to do with the star rising in the morning just before the time of the vintage – though this would only be valid in ancient times. The Latin variations, such as *Vindemitor*, have much the same meaning. There is some indication that this yellow star (now relatively obscure) was much brighter before our own era.
28. John Gregory is perhaps best known for his wonderful series of relief panels on the north wall of the Folger Shakespeare Library, on East Capitol and 2nd Street. As with the Maia panel that I am about to discuss, these Shakespearian panels exhibit arcane insights.
29. Mercury is supposed to represent Commerce; Vesta the Sanitation Department; Aesclepius is supposed to represent Hospitals, and Maia the Courts. Fortunately, these explanations are at best occult blinds: John Gregory (or perhaps the architect, Nathan C. Wyath) has offered a splendid esoteric meaning on the huge panel which entirely supersedes the official explanation for the symbolism.
30. Gregory was clearly influenced by early Greek statuary. His seated Maia is reminiscent of the famous early fifth-century BC stela of Hegeso, now in the National Museum in Greece. Stylistic differences apart, however, the Hegeso stela is funerary, while the feeling of the Maia image is straight from the hermetic initiation lore: for example, her formal stiffness reminds one of such images as the seated Osiris in the Hunefer papyrus of the Egyptian *Book of the Dead*. I suspect that the secret of the Maia image will rest upon the significance of the object which she holds in her left hand. The fact that she is wearing the Mithraic cap indicates that Gregory wished to refer to the Mysteries, for this is the famous Phrygian initiation cap, an indicator of a grade in the Mysteries.
31. James M. Goode, *The Outdoor Sculpture of Washington DC*, 1974, p.442.
32. Norman Lockyer *The Dawn of Astronomy*, 1894, equates Spica with the Egyptian god, Min, and notes that the dedication of one of his temples at Thebes was oriented to Spica's setting in 3200 BC, while a temple at Tel al Amarna was similarly oriented about 2000 BC. Two temples in ancient Greece, at Rhamnus,

show variations in orientation which adapt to shifts in the setting of Spica, over a period of about 300 years, the earliest being about 1092 BC.

33. For Isis and Nephthys, see G. R. S. Mead, *Thrice-Greatest Hermes*, 1906 ed., I, p.224.
34. For a modern survey of the underlying distributions of the major ancient chorographies (including that of Ptolemy) see Nicholas Campion, *The Book of World Horoscopes*, 1988, App. 9, pp.508ff. On p.472, Campion places Washington DC under Scorpio, but it is difficult to see the validity of this: perhaps he has been misled by the error on p. 424 (seemingly taken from Kraum and Grant, 'The Endless Quest for the United States Chart', in *NCGR Journal*, Spring, 1994) which erroneously claims that the first marker stone *for* the District of Columbia was laid at 4.11.30 on 15 March 1791. This date is out by exactly one month, and one finds oneself wondering whence the precision of timing was obtained.

    In Nicholas Devore, *Encyclopaedia of Astrology*, 1947 reprint, p.344, Washington DC is given the ruler Scorpio by virtue of the Ascendant, and Virgo by virtue of the Sun. This suggests that modern astrologers are inclined to associate the foundation of the federal city with the foundation of the Capitol (when it was quite possible that Virgo, along with Jupiter, was rising in Scorpio, and the Sun was in Virgo). However, as we have seen, the Capitol was the *second* building to be founded, and records for the founding of the federal district are still preserved in contemporaneous records.
35. The word 'chorography' was suggested by the historian of early Greek astrology, Bouché-Leclercq, in *L'Astrologie Grecque*, 1899.
36. Ptolemy, *Tetrabiblos*, II.3.59.
37. I have taken the diagram from Cardan's commentaries on the Gogava translation of Ptolemy's *Tetrabiblos* of 1543, p.181.
38. Ptolemy, *Tetrabiblos*, II.3.74, in op. cit., in n.36 above, p.159.
39. Ptolemy, *Tetrabiblos*, II.3–4. It is evident that the Greek is corrupt: the translation offered by Robbins, in the Loeb version of 1964, certainly does not reflect what Ptolemy intended to say.
40. See for example, A.T.C. Pierson, *Traditions of Freemasonry*, 1865, pp.324ff. The earliest working in Europe seems to have been about 1740, but there are a variety of Royal Arch degrees. The so-called American Royal Arch seems to have come into use about 1796. However, what I have to say in the following text about the underlying symbolism of the Royal Arch seems to be fundamental to all the degrees.
41. In mythology, Amalthea was the nurse of Zeus, who was transformed into the star *Capella*, the little she-goat. She was associated with the 'horn of plenty', or cornucopia, which flowed with nectar and ambrosia, the food of the gods. She made a gift of one horn to Zeus, filled with fruits.
42. Michael Maier, *Atalanta Fugiens*, 1618 – emblem 2.
43. The *Columbian Mirror* uses the term 'cavasson': this is the cavation dug to permit access to the foundations.
44. Camoens, *Luciad*, II.
45. Robert Macoy, *A Dictionary of Freemasonry*, 1989 reprint, p.471.
46. James Gaffarel writes: '. . . the Ancient *Hebrewes* fancied not the Figures of any Living Creatures in the Heavens, as we do . . . Thus they represented the Signe . . . of *Virgo*, by a Sheafe of Corne . . .' James Gaffarel (Englished by Edmund Chilmead), *Unheard of Curiosities: Concerning the Talismanical Sculpture of the Persians; the Horoscope of the Patriarkes; and the Reading of the Stars*, 1650.
47. The weeping sisters in the hermetic tradition are derived from the Graeco-Egyptian hermetic texts: although the sisters are said to be weeping for the dismembered Osiris, the arcane mythology is intended to refer to something far deeper than grief. The clue to the idea of weeping is expressed in the secret meanings of such hieroglyphics as *aatet*, which represent the 'tears of heaven' or

sacred 'dew' so important in Rosicrucian literature.

48. Albert Pike, *Morals and Dogma*, 1906 ed., p.379.
49. *Masonic Newspaper*, New York, 10 May 1879. The commentary is reproduced in Robert Hewitt Brown, *Stellar Theology and Masonic Astronomy*, 1882, pp.65ff.
50. Jeremy L. Cross was made a Mason in 1808.
51. Thomas Smith Webb was initiated in 1792, in New Hampshire. By 1813, he was Grand Master of the Rhode Island Lodges, and has been described as 'perhaps the most influential Mason in post-Revolutionary America'. See Bullock, *Revolutionary Brotherhood*, 1996 p.253. In an attempt to settle a basic text for the Craft, after the Revolution, he modified for American use the influential work of the Scottish Mason William Preston (a friend of David Hume, Edward Gibbon, and the like), *Illustrations of Masonry* (1772), and published this in 1798. This became a classic among American Masons: it was a version of this book which Jeremy Cross published with 'hieroglyphics' (n.53, below).
52. The Masonic scholar Brent Morris tells me that his associate, Kent Walgren, has researched the early American imagery in considerable depth, and has come to the conclusion that Cross borrowed his illustration (which first appeared in his *Hieroglyphic Monitor* of 1819) from a copy of *The First Masonic Chart* which had been published earlier by Henry Parmele. The Parmele chart is known presently only through a copy of *circa* 1840, which (thanks to the generosity of Brent Morris) I have been able to examine: this does seem to support Walgren's thesis. The interesting thing is that Parmele writes of the woman as 'this virgin weeping'.
53. This was *The True Masonic Chart or Hieroglyphic Monitor*, 1819.
54. Brown (op. cit., n.49 above), p.69.
55. See Harold N. Moldenke and Alma L. Moldenke, *Plants of the Bible*, 1952, p.25.
56. Originally published in the *Masonic Newspaper*, 10 May 1879, and reprinted by Brown, 1882, pp.65ff.
57. The Brother was Commodore Lawrence. The memorial was set up in 1813, after Lawrence died in the battle between the *Chesapeake* and *Shannon*. Trinity Church was later rebuilt, and to Cross's chagrin, the Lawrence monument was replaced.
58. Brown (op. cit., n.49 above), pp.68ff. According to Brown, the image of the Beautiful Virgin, weeping over the broken column, denotes her grief at the death of the Sun, slain by the wintry signs. This is, to say the least, a crass interpretation of a deeply arcane symbol.
59. The various forms of acacia are ruled by different planets: for example, *Acacia aribica* is said to be ruled by the Sun, while *Acacia dealbata* is ruled by Saturn. What is of relevance to our theme is that the Egyptian acacia (which the ancient Egyptians called *Sn*t (*Sunt*, or *Sant*)), *Acacia nilotica*, is ruled by Jupiter, the planet of Sagittarius.
60. The print is discussed on p.68 of W. Kirk MacNulty's excellent study of Masonic symbolism, *Freemasonry*, 1997 ed. The print, from the library collection of the Grand Lodge in Queen Anne Street, London, is entitled *The Mysteries that here are Shown are only to a Mason known*. The engraver, William Tringham, inscribes what he calls the 'hieroglyphic' 'To the most Ancient and Honourable Society of Free and Accepted Masons' . . . by 'their most Affectionate Brother'.
61. The so-called 'Forty-Seventh Problem of Euclid' (it is a theorem, not a problem) is formulated by Euclid in Book 10 of his *Elements of Geometry*: the purpose is to show that in a right-angled triangle the sum of the areas of the two squares constructed on its sides embracing the right angle is equal to the area of the square constructed on the hypotenuse. The philosophy behind this 'Third Degree' emblem is susceptible to much esoteric enlargement when it is considered that within arcane symbolism the square represents the physical plane, the triangle the spiritual. In this sense, the triangle is seen as the spiritual working as a nutrix in the material plane. For a useful survey, see Charles Clyde Hunt, *Masonic Symbolism*, 1939, p.141.

62. In the introduction to a typescript copy of *A Diary Kept by Jeremy L. Cross from August 17, 1817 to April 2, 1820* in Washington DC (Class M.16.2), the anonymous writer of 1889 admits that 'Cross had but little education, though he had much good Common Sense, and a wonderful eye to business. He made his Masonry a very nice paying investment . . .'
63. For an account of the Lilly hieroglyphic of 1651, in his *Monarchy or No Monarchy*, see Ann Geneva, *Astrology and the Seventeenth-Century Mind. William Lilly and the Language of the Stars*, 1995, pp.47ff.
64. A good example of this may be seen in the horoscope 'portrait' of 'Mercuriophilus Anglicus' (or 'the English Mercury-lover' – which is the pseudonym of the author himself) from James Hasolle's *Fasciculus Chemicus* of 1650, a book which deals with 'the Secret Hermetick Science'. The horoscope shows the Sun and Mercury rising in Gemini: the book was printed and sold in London. The quotation on the title-page reads: 'Our Magistry is begun and perfected, by onely one thing; namely, Mercury.'
65. According to Folger, this was due to the attention paid to the hieroglyphics by Brother Henry C. Atwood.
66. For Robert Folger's representation of Webb's version of the Beautiful Virgin, see Brown (op. cit., n.49 above), 1882, pp.65ff. Folger was a 33rd-Degree Mason. while Brown was a 32nd-Degree Mason.
67. I am dealing here with historical perceptions which later research has shown not to be quite accurate. The idea that the hieroglyphic *mst* meant 'dew' is substantially correct, but the hieroglyphic itself seems to be a vestigial drawing of three fox-skins tied together, and Simons (n.69 below) might have been wiser to deal with the form *iadt* (below). However, it is clear from compounds that the hieroglyphic *mst* is linked with the idea of descent of spirit into matter – for example, it is the determinative in the phrase *mest*, which means 'to give birth to', 'to bring forth', and so on; *mesnekht* is 'birth-place'. However, another hieroglyphic form, linked with the sacred *A*, also means dew: this is *aatet*, which etymologically speaking, seems to be involved with praising or worshipping this influx from the heavens. Its hieroglyphic form is given in E.A. Wallis Budge, *A Hieroglyphic Vocabulary to the Theban Recension of the Book of the Dead*, 1911, p.14. A variant single form, *iadt*, is given by Alan H. Gardiner, *Egyptian Grammar*, 1927, p.533, as meaning specifically 'dew'.
68. John W. Simons was Past Grand Master of Masons, Grand Treasurer of the Grand Lodge of New York, Grand Treasurer of the Grand Encampment of the United States, etc. etc.
69. J.W. Simons (trans.), *A Comparison of Egyptian Symbols with those of the Hebrews*, 1878, pp.53ff. The book is a translation of a work by Frédéric Portal, which I have not had the opportunity to examine. Simons also points out that (– *mure*) means a doctor or professor, and 'first rains' (p.54).
70. The vignette which appears on the title-page of the translation by Simons (op. cit., n.69 above) is from Champollion's *Monuments of Egypt and Nubia*, vol. I, p.xlii. The rain which pours from the two jars is made up of the *ankh* (ansated cross) and the *uas*, the so-called 'hoopoe sceptre', meaning 'purity', 'happiness' and 'contentment'. This is to say that the neophyte is being baptized with the Waters of Life and the Fire of Joy: these, then, are the tears of the gods and goddesses.
71. Simons (op. cit., n.69 above) was keen to link the Egyptian initiation lore with the Bible. He points out that the name *Moses* was 'according to the Bible' an Egyptian name, signifying 'saved by water'. See Exodus, ii. 10.
72. See, for example, the work by the Mason, Alex Horne, *King Solomon's Temple in the Masonic Tradition*, 1972 ed.
73. George Oliver (n.75 below) seems to have made a mistake with his word 'Cassia'. We might assume that he intended to use the word 'acacia', which is the proper symbol for the Beautiful Virgin. Cassia is an inferior kind of Cinnamon, and has

nothing to do with the symbolism of the acacia. It is possible, however, that this mistake is a reference to a Masonic initiation ritual, for in his entry on Cassia (*sic*) in his dictionary (see n.75 below), p.452, he refers to the exclamation of the Master Mason, 'My name is Cassia' as being the equivalent of the phrase 'I have been in the grave; I have triumphed over it by raising from the dead . . .' I have not been able to trace how the acacia to which Cross refers became the Cassia of Oliver.

74. In this present work, I discuss 23 zodiacs and many more images and symbols of Virgo. There are well over 1,000 Virgoan images in the city, if the zodiacs, corn symbols and Mercury symbols are taken into account.
75. George Oliver, *A Dictionary of Symbolical Masonry*, in the version printed in Macoy (op. cit., n.45 above), p.445.

CHAPTER SEVEN

1. The conjunction at midday on 15 September 1857, Cincinnati, Ohio, was:

   VE 13 LE 43
   MO 17 LE 48
   MA 21 LE 57

2. William Howard Taft was made a Mason at sight by the Grand Master, C.S. Hoskinson, at an occasional Lodge formed for that purpose on 18 February 1909, in the Scottish Rite Cathedral, Cincinnati, Ohio. This honour, and Taft's subsequent degrees in Masonry, are traced by H.L. Haywood, *Famous Masons and Masonic Presidents*, 1968 ed, pp.60ff.
3. Edward Pearce Casey, the son of Thomas Lincoln Casey, was the Chief Architect of the Library during the final years of its construction. Roland Hinton Perry (1870–1941) designed and sculpted the remarkable *Court of Neptune* fountain below the west façade of the building. Taft had been Solicitor-General of the United States when the cornerstone of the Library of Congress was laid in 1890. He was technically responsible for its existence in law.
4. See, for example, Pamela Scott, *Temple of Liberty. Building the Capitol for a New Nation*, 1995, p.76.
5. For some of the classical associations within what the author calls 'the Sacred Zodiac', see Albert Ross Parsons, *New Light from the Great Pyramid*, 1893, pp.48ff.
6. This style is often traced back to D.V. Denon's illustrated *Voyage dans la basse et la haute Égypte pendant les campagnes du général Bonaparte*, 1802, but the Egyptian symbolism had already been revived in Masonic circles long before Denon's voyage.
7. Latrobe's marginal sketch is from a letter to Jefferson dated 5 November 1816, now in the Library of Congress.
8. James Ferguson, *Astronomy Explained Upon Sir Isaac Newton's Principles*, 1799 ed., plate III, opp. p.67.
9. For the encircled star, the *dwa*, which is among the most esoteric of all hieroglyphics, intimating at the astral nature of the Underworld, see Alan H. Gardiner, *Egyptian Grammar*, 1927, p.476. The *sba* star plays an important determinative role in terms relating to astronomy and astrology – for example, it is among the hieroglyphics for *khabesu*, which denotes the 36 decans of the Egyptian zodiac (a decan being a 10-degree division of a zodiacal sign) – see, for example, E.A. Wallis Budge, *A Hieroglyphic Vocabulary*, 1911, p.291.
10. In March 1841, Tyler was elected vice-president alongside W.H. Harrison: one month later, Harrison died, and Tyler was ushered forward as the tenth President. He was a conscientious and principled man: in 1832, he tried to introduce legislation to prohibit the slave-trade in the District of Columbia. He was unsuccessful, for as late as 1863 we find slaves being used to cast Thomas Crawford's statue of *Freedom*, which now dominates the skyline of Washington DC from the cupola of the Capitol.

Tyler was one of the non-Masonic presidents, which is perhaps understandable considering that he was politically active during the worst of the anti-Masonic upheavals. However, he was followed in the presidency by James Knox Polk, who *was* a Mason. Polk was raised to the Sublime Degree in Columbia Lodge No. 31, Tennessee, 4 September 1820. (For his further Masonic connections and degrees, see Haywood (op. cit., n.2 above), pp.40ff.

11. Dickens famously wrote it, and it is much quoted in his name, but the idea was not his own. Dickens is something of a Masonic mystery. There was a Lodge named after him in England (at Chigwell), but in his works he often seems to ridicule the ceremonials of the fraternity.
12. Charles Dickens, *American Notes and Pictures from Italy*, 1885 ed., p.81. A 'Barmecide Feast' is an illusion – a promised feast of nothingness, served on empty plates to a starving man. However, Dickens seems to be overlooking that in the *Arabian Nights* story, from which the phrase is taken, the illusion turns into a reality, and the starving man is fed.
13. The first catalogue, which appeared in 1802, listed just under a 1,000 books. By 1850, shortly before the fire, it contained 55,000 volumes.
14. For a graphic account of the incident, and the War of 1812 in general, see Anthony S. Pitch, *The Burning of Washington. The British Invasion of 1814*, 1998.
15. It is interesting to compare the two charts for these destructive fires. The one outstanding common degree is 13 degrees of Leo: on 24 August 1814 Mercury was in 13.06 Leo; on 24 December 1851, Mars was retrograde in 13.23 Leo. In the astrological tradition, this is the 'Degree of Literature'. See, for example, Nicholas Devore, *Encyclopaedia of Astrology*, 1947, p.100.
16. When the British defeated the Americans on 2 July 1814, Uranus was even more deeply involved. On that day, Uranus was retrograde in 28.55 Scorpio, and exactly square Saturn, retrograde in 28.46 Capricorn. Uranus was also in opposition to Venus in 28.30 Taurus. On the day of the fire of 1851, Uranus (which was retrograde, in 00.31 degrees of Taurus) was exactly in opposition to the radical Neptune (in 00.28 Scorpio).

    The American astronomer L.D. Broughton insisted that Gemini ruled the United States. He pointed out that when Uranus entered that sign in 1775 the American Revolution broke out. See *Broughton's Monthly Planet Reader and Astrological Journal*, 1 February 1861, vol.2, no.2.
17. Quoted without source by Paul M. Allen in the 1971 Introduction to Ignatius Donnelly, *Atlantis. The Antediluvian World.*
18. Donnelly's book (n.17 above), first published in 1882, was an overnight sensation: it has spawned hundreds of books about the mythic continent, even though many of the 'facts' he adduces are imaginative fictions or misinterpretations.
19. Between 1874 and 1886, John L. Smithmeyer and Paul J. Pelz submitted five distinct and very attractive designs to meet the varying demands of Congress and a number of Library committees. Later, and to their perpetual shame, Congress refused to pay the architects for all this work. Smithmeyer's life was ruined by his heartbreaking struggle with Congress, and he died in abject poverty. Relations with Pelz were strained towards the end, yet Pelz (himself in financial difficulties) borrowed money to bury his former partner.
20. *Report of the Superintendent of the U.S. Naval Observatory*, 1883.
21. Thomas L. Casey is mentioned as assistant astronomer to Professor Simon Newcomb of the United States Navy, serving in the foreign state of Wellington, on p.xii of the *Report* (see n.20 above).
22. Simon Newcomb (1835–1909), though born in Nova Scotia, had become a resident of the United States in 1853, and graduated from Harvard in 1858. He was made professor of mathematics in the United States Navy in 1861, and in 1877 was assigned to duty in charge of the Nautical Almanac Office – which explains his important role as foreign observer of the transit of Venus in 1882, with Casey as his

assistant. After he had been made professor of mathematics and astronomy at Johns Hopkins University, he continued to reside in Washington DC.

23. Newcomb's important popular works include *Popular Astronomy*, 1878, and *Astronomy for Schools and Colleges*, 1880. Among his important non-official publications is *The Elements of the Four Inner Planets and the Fundamental Constants of Astronomy*, 1895. His official publications include the far-reaching new theory of lunar perturbations, which showed that (even as late as the last decade of the 19th century) the motion of the Moon was not being predicted accurately. His work on Uranus and Neptune was seminal; he contributed largely to establishing an accurate constant for the precession of the equinoxes, and to the compilation of a new catalogue of stars. This, then, was the colleague and Masonic Brother of Casey, who was responsible for the design and building of the Library of Congress.
24. I shall discuss these zodiacs and their creators at a later point. They are located (1) in the Main Hall; (2) on the spandrel above the main entrance; (3) on the walls of the corridors of the east front; (4) on the window recesses of the north-west room (formerly the map room); (5) on the clock over the entrance to the main reading room; (6) in a mosaic detail of astronomy in the ceiling to the east of the Great Hall, and (most splendid of all – 7) in the ceiling dome of the south-east Pavilion.
25. At 3.00 pm, on 28 August 1890, the chart was:

AS29SG30	SU05VG25	MO16AQ03	ME01LB46
VE20LB01	MA14SG52	JU03AQ48R	SA05VG25
UR24LB03	NE47GE06	PL07GE53	MN19GE51

Whoever seized the moment might have recognized the importance of the developing harmonious trine between the Moon and Venus (on the mid-heaven). The person might even have recognized that Uranus was on 25 of Libra – a Degree of Literature – see n.15 above.

We should note that the planet Pluto had not been discovered in 1890, so that the threat of the conjunction between Neptune and Pluto would have gone unnoticed by a contemporaneous astrologer.

26. The photograph is reproduced on p.55 of the magnificent *The Library of Congress. The Art and Architecture of the Thomas Jefferson Building*, ed. John Y. Cole and Henry H. Reed, 1997. My impression, from studying the lighting on this photograph, is that it was taken sometime in the morning, and not at 3.00 p.m. (the time written on the bromide). Was the photograph perhaps staged, for record purposes, and a ceremony of some sort performed in the afternoon? An alternative thesis is that the number 3 in the inscription is actually an 8.
27. As Cole and Reed report, even the inscription on the face of the stone, 'August 28, 1890', was not inscribed until 16 January 1952 (op. cit., n.26 above), p.55.
28. The conjunction between Sun and Saturn would have been closer, more stable, but it would have been rendered harmful by the Moon, which was (24 hours later) 01PI17, and thus in opposition to the pair.
29. Anne Royall's favourite house had been on B Street near 2nd Street: it was here that she died. See Sarah Harvey Porter, *The Life and Times of Anne Royall*, 1909, p.153.
30. Anne's husband, William Royall, was a Freemason. As her biographer records, when she found herself a penniless widow, deserted by many who had been her friend during her husband's ascendancy, the Freemasons were among the few who stepped in to offer help in the form of shelter, food and clothing. For a study of her Masonic connections, see Porter, *Anne Royall* (op. cit., n.29 above), ch.vi, pp.93ff.
31. By far the best modern treatment is by John Y. Cole and Henry Hope Reed [editors] *The Library of Congress. The Art and Architecture of the Thomas Jefferson Building*, 1997.
32. Useful background information on the sculptors and artists who worked on the Library is given by Cole and Reed (op. cit., n.31 above).

33. Donnelly (op. cit., n.17 above), p.181.
34. Born in New York, Roland Hinton Perry studied in Paris under Gérôme and others.
35. For an account of the first 32 of the Masonic degrees, see Albert Pike, *Morals and Dogma*, 1906 ed.
36. Among other works, Henry Jackson Ellicott sculpted equestrian statues of Washington, Hancock and McClellan, for Philadelphia.
37. This statement is only politically correct: the fact is that the Craft is deeply rooted in the Hebraic and biblical view of mankind. Since it views Christ as the architect of the Church and the future Man, the development of the moral law which lies behind Masonry is essentially the development of a Christian moral law, and is involved with the Western image of the redemption of sin.
38. The busts of Demosthenes, Scott and Dante were carved by Herbert Adams (1858–1945), who did the McMillan Fountain in Washington DC; Emerson, Irving and Hawthorne were by Jonathan Scott Hartley (1845–1912), who also modelled the Daguerre monument in Washington DC; Goethe, Franklin and Macaulay were carved by Frederick Wellington Ruckstull (1853–1942).
39. Sir Walter Scott was initiated in 1801 in the St David Lodge No. 36, Edinburgh. Goethe was initiated in 1780 in the Lodge Amalia, in Weimar.
40. See 'Monument to Civilization. Diary of a Building' by Helen-Ann Hilker, *Quarterly Journal of the Library of Congress*, October 1972, p.261. In fairness, I must point out that the story has been told only from the point of view of Green, and other officials in charge of the sculptural programme. Flanagan, who was a highly gifted sculptor, was impeded by the contract, which sanctioned payment only on completion of the commission.
41. According to Flanagan's own written description, the zodiac is built up from mosaic tesserae: the belief that it was made from bronze seems to be derived from Herbert Small's *Handbook of the New Library of Congress*, 1901, p.66. See, however, Cole and Reed (op. cit., n.31 above), on p.243 of Thomas P. Somma, 'The Sculptural Program for the Library of Congress'.
42. Cole and Reed, (op. cit., n.31, above) p.128.
43. See Hilker (op. cit., n.40, above), p.261.
44. F.D. Roosevelt received his first degree in Masonry on 10 October 1911, and was conferred with the 32nd Degree in the Albany Consistory, New York, 28 February 1929.

    Curiously enough, Donati's comet, which reached its maximum brilliance in October 1858, is said to have been a factor in the birth-chart of Theodore Roosevelt, who was born on the 27th of that month. See Nicholas Devore, (op. cit., n.15 above, p.59). Theodore Roosevelt was initiated at Matiecock Lodge No. 806 at Long Island on 2 January 1901. He is said to have been one of the few Masonic Presidents who spoke from personal Masonic convictions in public addresses: see Haywood, (op. cit., n.2 above) pp.57ff.
45. Entry for 8 October 1882 (typescript in the Archives of the Architect of the Capitol).
46. Letter dated 22 May 1895, in the correspondence between the artist and Green: the relevant section is quoted on p.243 of Cole and Reed (op. cit., n.31 above).
47. See, for example, John Gadbury, *Genethaialogia*, 1685, as quoted in the epigraph to Chapter 6.
48. A personification of the Sun in the 11th-century codex in the National Library, Paris (cod. 7028), seems to be a copy of a much earlier zodiacal figure, seen through Christian eyes. Relevant to the important contrast in the Library design between time and space, matter and spirit, expressed through the zodiacs, we find, in the second century AD, Clement picturing John the Baptist surrounded by 30 disciples who represent the months (that is, time), contrasting with the idea of Christ surrounded by the 12 disciples who represents the zodiacal signs (that is,

spirit and space). 'Clement was merely following an established literary and iconographic tradition, itself rooted in occult lore, which links Christ with the Sun.' Quoted from F. Gettings, *The Hidden Art*, 1978, p.19.

49. See Parsons (op. cit., n.5 above), p.9.
50. Thomas Lincoln Casey, Chief of Engineers USA, is named as the one responsible for erecting the building. Bernard R. Green is acknowledged as superintendent and engineer; John L. Smithmeyer, Paul J. Pelz and Edward Pearce Casey were the architects.
51. This connecting cord was called 'the silver cord' by 19th-century astrologers, who insisted that it represented the cord which joined the soul to the spirit (in some cases, spirit to body), on the assumption that the two fishes represented these extremes. Mediaeval astrologers were less inclined to view the symbolism in dualistic terms, however. They called the knotted cord the *nodus*. In so far as Pisces was interpreted in esoteric terms, its dualism was treated in mediaeval esotericism as a reference to the twofold nature of Christ, who was both Man and God.
52. For notes on the dolphin in Christian literature, see Arnold Whittick, *Symbols, Signs and Their Meaning and Uses in Design*, 1971 ed., pp.231ff.
53. For useful notes on the Castor and Pollux tradition in astronomy, see Richard Hinckley Allen, *Star Names. Their Lore and Meaning*, 1963 reprint of the 1899 ed., pp.222ff.
54. For the thyrsus as emblem of initiation, see Mark Hedsel, *The Zelator*, 1998, pp.229ff.
55. The quotation is from the famous *Emerald Tablet* of Hermes Trismegistus. Among the excellent treatises on the Tablet (which do not breach the hermetic law) is Johann Daniel Mylius' *Opus medico-chymicum*, 1618, which includes an illustration of the tablet, as part of the *Basilica Chymica*: the engraving is by Merian. The text of the *Emerald Tablet* is included in many books on alchemy – even in those which do not view alchemy as a secret science of the soul. For example, it is included in E.J. Holmyard's *Alchemy*, 1957, p.95. In 1923, Holmyard discovered the first Arabic version of the text (until then known only in the mediaeval Latin) in one of Jabir's books. One must treat all modern translations with caution: the text was written for initiates who would understand the specialist words which are used within it. For example, in the Mystery literature, the 'Way Up' is *Anabasis*, sometimes equated with *Anaktoreion* – both words having very specific spiritual meanings connected with reincarnation; about which the initiate is forbidden to speak. For a version of the text which would have been known to Masons in Washington DC during the building of the Library, see Paschal B. Randolph, *Hermes Trismegistus: his Divine Pymander*, 1871 (which contains the text of the Smaragdine Table).
56. For an elementary approach to the meaning of the square and circle in Masonic symbolism, see M.A. Pottenger, *Symbolism*, 1905, pp.60ff. The significance of the square in Masonry cannot really be separated from that attached to Euclid's 47th theorem, wherein the squares grow from the triangle in a meaningful numerology: see, for example, Charles Clyde Hunt, *Masonic Symbolism*, 1939, pp.141ff.
57. I say that John Singer Sargent 'displayed' the zodiacal picture in the Boston Library because he did not actually paint it there. These arcane pictures were painted by Sargent in the studio of his friend Edwin Abbey, in Fairford, England, between 1892 and 1894, and were transported to Boston, where they were marouflaged on to the ceiling and walls of the upper chamber. It is my hope, one day, to reveal the extraordinary esoteric programme in these most remarkable of esoteric pictures.
58. The four Elements of the zodiac are called the triplicities in traditional astrology because they each repeat three times:

FIRE	Aries	Leo	Sagittarius
EARTH	Taurus	Virgo	Capricorn

AIR	Gemini	Libra	Aquarius
WATER	Cancer	Scorpio	Pisces

59. The four large lunette frescos of the Elements, by Robert Leftwich Dodge, do not fall into the area of our research, even though they evince arcane themes. For a brief analysis, see Cole and Reed (op. cit., n.31 above), pp.162ff.
60. Cole and Reed (op. cit., n.31 above), p.163.
61. For Garnsey's Masonic connections see *The National Cyclopaedia of American Biography,* p.349. Garnsey died in Atlantic City, 26 October 1946.
62. See sections 800 to 805 of the Casey documents in the Avery Architectural and Fine Arts Library, Columbia University. The plans, elevations and details of designs from the Library of Congress are stamped 'Edward Pearce Casey, Architect, 171 Broadway, New York', and signed by Bernard Green 'Superintendent & Engineer'.
63. See the *Examination Report, Library of Congress Murals*, by Perry C. Huston and Jay Kreuger, October 1986.
64. The official explanation is that she represents an aspect of science, but the leaves around the two figures in the spandrels indicate that there is an esoteric symbolism intended.
65. The 12 zodiacal symbols in the old map room are painted on the insides of the window recesses.
66. Garfield had been a successful and morally upright representative on a Republican anti-slavery ticket, and was elected to the Senate in 1880. He was inaugurated President of the United States on 4 March 1881. On 2 July, he was shot by a deranged office-seeker, Charles J. Guiteau, and died from his wounds on 19 September 1881.
67. Giuliano de' Medici was stabbed to death by a faction under the direction of the Pazzi family and Pope Sixtus IV. In drawing a parallel between Garfield the soldier and Michelangelo's *Giorno*, Ward might also be suggesting a connexion between the murders of Garfield and Giuliano. See n.68 below, however.
68. Herman Grimm's *Leben Michelangelos* was published in 1860 (2nd vol. 1863) in German: for obvious reasons, the quotation I give in the text is from the 1896 American ed., I, p.92. After dealing out terrible retribution to the Pazzi family, Cosimo de'Medici ruled Florence for many years. As it happens, Grimm misled a whole generation, for his suggestion had been misguided: an autograph fragment, in Michelangelo's hand – a prose project for a poem which is contemporaneous with the work on the statuary – shows that the figure above *Giorno* and *Notte* (Night) was intended to be that of Giuliano: 'El Di et la Notte parlano e dicono: Noi abbimo col nostro veloce corso condotto alla morte il duca Giuliano . . .' (Day and Night are speaking and say: We have in our rapid course led the Duke Giuliano to his death . . .)

    Like many 19th-century American artists, Ward travelled in Europe, paying especial attention to art and architecture: undoubtedly, he visited the New Sacristy in Florence.
69. Herman Grimm, *Life of Michelangelo*, trans. by Fanny Elizabeth Burnett, published by Little, Brown & Co., 1896.
70. The errors in Grimm's theory (which is contradicted by Michelangelo's own notes) were adopted by Rudolf Steiner, and have coloured the thinking of very many anthroposophists. See, for example, Rudolf Steiner, *Okkulte Untersuchungen über das Leben zwischen Tod und neuer Geburt*, 1970 ed., p.80.
71. A photograph of Ward's studio shows the casts on a shelf: see Lewis I. Sharp, *John Quincy Adams Ward. Dean of American Sculpture*, 1985, fig.38.
72. Ward had been a personal friend of Garfield, and was almost certainly a Mason, though I have not been able to identify his Lodge.
73. In the archives of the Architect of the Capitol, the plaque is merely described as 'a

cartouche', its astrological significance being unrecognized.

74. Long before I discovered the graphic source of the Garfield cartouche (see nn.77–80 below), I had cast horoscopes for all the major events in Garfield's life, and had compared these charts to the bronze plaque, but was unable to elicit any meaningful connection between events and the cartouche horoscope.
75. Saturn was in Cancer from 27 May 1856 to 10 July 1858, but during that time Jupiter was never in Libra. The lack of correspondence between planetary tables and the planetary positions on the cartouche was not the only problem I faced in attempting to reduce the cartouche to a workable horoscope. The diagram could not be reconciled in any way to known geocentric projections, for neither Mercury nor Venus could be so far distant (so elongated) from the Sun (see n.80 below).
76. One Sun (in the central sphere of the seven) was in Gemini, and one in Sagittarius. For the solution to this problem, see n.82 below.
77. James Ferguson, *Astronomy Explained upon Sir Isaac Newton's Principles . . .*, 1799. This useful book ran into many editions. My own researches are based on the British Library 1799 edition, and the identical edition in the Library of Congress. The *Globes* illustration is figure IIII (*sic*) of plate VIII, opposite p.217.
78. The name is said to have been derived from the title of Charles Boyle, as 4th Earl of Orrery, who made a clockwork model of the solar system *circa* 1700.
79. The Ascendant is marked by the flat strip (azimuth circle) which projects at right angles to the concentrics, and diagonally to these. This strip cuts the projection of the zodiacal segment at approximately 25 degrees Virgo (the actual intersection is, of course, covered by acacia leaves). The location is indicated by the half-armature (zenith) which projects over the top of the world-globe, below the swag. The similar projection on the Ferguson diagram corresponded fairly accurately to London, but the Ward bas-relief is not so accurate: the artist has simply superimposed a map of the Americas over the globe, and it is merely our assumption that he wishes to pinpoint in space the capital city. In any case, the schematic projections are of necessity highly exaggerated in both the diagram and the cartouche.
80. So far as can be estimated from the figure in Ferguson's plate, the sequence of planets is that given in the table below.

    MO CN 05
    ME LE 15
    VE GE 07
    SU SC 25
    MA SG 10
    JU LB 17
    SA CN 15

    Ferguson explains the meaning and utility of this detail of his plate in a special section ('The Planetary Globes'), on p.419.
81. We know that Ferguson's book was popular in the United States. It had been an 18th-century edition which Ellicott lent to Benjamin Banneker, and which deepened the latter's interest in astronomy. It is clear from surviving documentation and personal effects that Ferguson had been a Mason.
82. Once I had solved the problem of Ward's source, the reason why the planetary positions were so insistently impossible and unrealistic in terms of elongations became clear to me: Ferguson had never intended the planets to represent an event in space and time, for he had merely required the reader to adjust the globes to relevant positions with the aid of an ephemeris. He had placed his sigillated balls entirely at random.
83. Ferguson (op. cit., n.77 above), p.420.
84. His Masonic studies were interrupted by the war, but he affiliated with Garretsville Lodge No. 246 on 10 October 1866, in which he served as Chaplain. On 4 May 1869, he became a charter member of Pentalpha Lodge No. 23, in

Washington DC. His Masonic degrees were worked through to the Fifth Degree of the Ancient and Accepted Scottish Rite, in the Mithras Lodge of Perfection No. 2, Washington DC. He was initiated into the 13th Degree in the same year, receiving this from the hand of his peer, the great Albert Pike. He received the final degree in the Lodge of Perfection on 2 January 1872. See, for example, Ray Baker Harris, *History of the Supreme Council 33*, 1964, pp.222ff.

85. See H.N. and A.L. Moldenke, *Plants of the Bible*, 1952 ed., pp.24ff. This is not the shittim wood (*Bumelia*) of the United States. See also J.H. Philpot, *The Sacred Tree, or The Tree in Religion and Myth*, 1897, pp.11ff.
86. George Oliver, *A Dictionary of Symbolic Masonry*, in Robert Macoy's *A Dictionary of Freemasonry*, 1989 ed., p.402.
87. On the same committee were Augustus Saint-Gaudens and Olin Levi Warner.
88. The quotation, from *Paradise Lost*, Bk vii, 364, was selected by the Harvard University President, Charles W. Eliot. See John Y. Cole, *On These Walls. Inscriptions and Quotations in the Buildings of the Library of Congress*, 1995, pp.33ff.

CHAPTER EIGHT

1. Benjamin Henry Latrobe was born 1 May 1764 at Fulneck, the Moravian school in Yorkshire, England. His father was a master in the school, his mother was the daughter of John Frederick Antes of Pennsylvania. In March 1803, when Latrobe had been in America for only a few months, Congress allocated 50,000 dollars to start the south wing of the Capitol. He was appointed surveyor of the public buildings in the federal capital by Jefferson, to succeed Thornton, Hatfield and Hoban. He disliked the Thornton design, and insisted that most of the extant building was of such a low standard that it should be stripped back to its foundations.
2. Letter dated 18 April 1806 to Charles Willson Peale, in the Library of Congress.
3. For an excellent account of Latrobe, and this correspondence with Peale, see Talbot Hamlin, *Benjamin Henry Latrobe*, 1955, p.269.
4. From an address given by Latrobe to the American Institute of Architects, in 1881, as quoted by Hamlin (op. cit., n.3 above), p.292. John H.B. Latrobe was elected Grand Master, 22 November 1870: see Edward T. Schultz, *Freemasonry in Maryland*, Period VI, p.72.
5. Barton's written reports and drawings are reproduced by Gaillard Hunt, *The History of the Seal of the United States*, 1909, pp.24ff.
6. See, for example Manley Palmer Hall, T*he Secret Teachings of All Ages. An Encyclopedic Outline of Masonic, Hermetic, Qabbalistic and Rosicrucian Symbolical Philosophy*, 1947 ed. of the 1928 work, pp.lxxxixff. There are very many errors in this syncretic work, yet it has had a profound influence on modern subcultural occult literature.
7. Benjamin Franklin's letter to his daughter, 26 January 1784: in this he is discussing the eagle which figured on the badge of the Order of the Society of the Cincinnati, which had been made in France in 1784. The relevant section is reproduced in Bigelow, *Life of Franklin*, III, p.252. The Order of the Society of the Cincinnati had been formed in the previous year (1783) to perpetuate the friendships of the officers who served in the Revolutionary War.
8. Franklin was initiated into the Philadelphia Lodge in 1730, the year after it had been formed. Within a few years, he was Grand Master. His later titles in other Lodges were extraordinary in scope. He was a printer, and was responsible for the 1734 *Book of Constitutions*, the first Masonic book in America. In 1778, he assisted in the initiation of Voltaire. As H. L. Haywood *Famous Masons and Masonic Presidents*, 1968 ed., p.117 writes, Franklin, '. . . was one of the architects of the American Craft which was later to prove to be the best-organized and largest National System of Masonry anywhere in the world'.

   While in France, Franklin joined the Lodge of the Nine Muses, of which the astronomer Joseph Jérôme Lefrançois de La Lande was a member. On 17 November 1760, Franklin was present at a meeting of the Grand Lodge of England. In the minutes he is given the title of the Prov. Grand Master of Philadelphia.

9. The *Pyramid* – a ferro-cement sculptural memorial, made by Raymond John Kaskey, in 1972, in the Campus Drive of the University of Maryland School of Architecture Building – is not a true pyramid.
10. In the same panel by Lawrie is an image of Hipparchus, with the constellation Cancer above his head: a reference to his formulation of the hypothesis pertaining to the precession of the equinoxes.
11. The one to the left is the 1782 version of the obverse, the one to the right, the 1885 version.
12. The Scottish Rite is of Franco-American origin, and probably began in Paris in 1758. Its laws are said to have been formulated by Frederick the Great, who was, indeed, one of the most influential Masons of that century. The beginnings of the Rite in America are traced to Charleston, in 1783.
13. John Russell Pope was born in New York City, 24 April 1874, and after studying architecture at Columbia and the American Academy in Rome was awarded a travelling scholarship, which allowed him to journey through Italy, Greece and the Near East studying the ancient monuments, before finishing his studies at the École des Beaux-Arts in Paris, where he was the first foreigner to finish the three-year course in only two years. His major achievements in Washington DC, besides the Masonic Temple, include the Constitution Hall of the Daughters of the American Revolution (1929), the National Archives, the main building of the National Gallery of Art and the Jefferson Memorial.
14. See James Carter, *History of the Supreme Council, 33, 1891–1921*, 1971, pp.303ff. Richardson reported that he made plans for this ground-break, for the new Temple because it was the 110th anniversary of the founding of the Council. This probably accounts for the real strength of the chart, which lies in the position of the Sun. The Sun was exactly on the star Aldebaran, the *alpha* of Taurus, which is reputed to bring high honours and preferments. From an astrological point of view, however, the timing is less easy to understand, for it allowed the Moon to be very close to the harmful Procyon: on the other hand, by 9.00 a.m. the destructive Uranus had just set beneath the Earth. On p.304 of Carter (op. cit.) is a photograph of the five Masons attending the ceremony.
15. John R. McLean, who was a friend of John H. Cowles (who served as Grand Commander from 1921 to 1952, and may even have suggested Pope as architect in 1910), was a Mason in the Scottish Rite, and a member of the family which owned the *Washington Post*. This view of how Pope came to the attention of the Sovereign Grand Commander James Daniel Richardson was put forward by Hugh Y. Bernard in 'The Architectural Career of John Russell Pope', in *The New Age*, vol. xcvi, no. 8, August 1988, pp.13ff.
16. See Carter (op. cit., n.14 above), pp.320ff.
17. William L. Fox, in his eminently readable and authoritative work, *Lodge of the Double-Headed Eagle. Two Centuries of Scottish Rite Freemasonry in America's Southern Jurisdiction*, 1997, p.163.
18. Fox (op. cit., n.17 above), p.162, confirms that it was 'an afternoon ceremony'.
19. It is quite extraordinary that John Russell Pope should have designed buildings which evince such a feeling of esoteric lore, yet remained outside the Masonic fraternity. Hugh Y. Bernard recognized this in 'The Architectural Career of John Russell Pope' (op. cit., n.15 above), pp.5ff. Bernard was of the opinion that Pope was 'an operative Mason of the finest quality, who never saw fit to petition the speculative Craft'.
20. After the building was completed, Woods donated his share of the fee to the Supreme Council to purchase (among other things) the valuable collection of Goethe books of the Mason Carl H. Claudy of Washington DC for the Library,

acquired in 1919.

21. The mausoleum wood engraving is in the section dealing with 'Ancient Imitation of Materials', p.67. The engraving appears in the earlier booklets, and in the *Senate Document of the 56th Congress*, 1st Session, Doc. No. 209, 1900.
22. Franklin Webster Smith, *Halls of the Ancients*, 1900.
23. A brief personal and Masonic biography of James D. Richardson is given by William L. Fox (op. cit., n.17 above) pp.142ff. He was born in Rutherford County, Tennessee, 10 March 1843, and after service in the Confederate Army became an attorney. After election to the Tennessee legislature, he was elected in 1884 to the House of Representatives. He was Grand Master of Masons in Tennessee for one term in 1873, and in 1881 received the 31st degree in the Scottish Rite.
24. Elliott Woods was a Scottish Rite Mason.
25. Pliny, *Natural History*, xxxvi, 4.30–31
26. For a useful survey of the more important attempts at reconstruction, see Michael Ashley, *The Seven Wonders of the World*, 1980, pp.183ff.

    In 1856 Sir Charles Newton discovered the poor remains of the ancient building, above modern Bodrum in Turkey, and was able to determine the measurement of the base. Newton's reconstructions in his *A History of Discoveries at Halicarnassus* (1862) deeply influenced Pope's design, but there are very significant differences between the two. James Ferguson's reconstructions of 1862 may also have been influential on Pope.
27. Pope may also have been influenced by the Comte de Caylus' reconstruction in *Mémoires de littérature, tirés des registres de l'Académie Royale des Inscriptions et Belles-Lettres*, 1759.
28. Many of the original blueprints drawn up by Pope are still in a large bound scrap-book entitled *The House of the Temple* in the Library of the Supreme Council.
29. It was used by 16 September 1782, on a documented exchange signed by the President of Congress, John Hanson.
30. By law, it should have been cut in 1782, alongside the obverse. A later Act of Congress (15 September 1789) continued the legal need to cut the reverse, but this did not happen. When the obverse was recut in 1841, the reverse was ignored, and in 1883 it was decided to abandon all attempts to cut it. In the following year, an Act (7 July 1884) was passed to make dies of both the obverse and the reverse: once again, in spite of the act of Congress, the reverse was not cut.
31. On 10 January 1883, when the Secretary of State Theodore F. Frelinghuysen addressed the chairman of the Committee on Appropriations of the House of Representatives.
32. In a letter dated 6 January 1885. The relevant sections are quoted by Hunt (op. cit., n.5 above), p.57.
33. The story is told in Hunt (op. cit., n.5 above), p.61.
34. Grace Kincaid Morey belonged to the Grand Fraternity of the Rose Cross Order of America, the Supreme Grand Master of which was R. Swinburne Clymer.
35. Grace Kincaid Morey, *Mystic Americanism*, 1924, p.41
36. Hunt (op. cit., n.5 above).
37. Morey (op. cit., n.35 above), p.60.
38. *Millennial Dawn* is anonymous, but was published by the Watch Tower Bible and Tract Society.
39. Franklin was the only Mason of the three. There has been some confusion between the John Quincy Adams who was admitted into St John's Lodge, Boston, on 5 December 1826, and his namesake, the second President of the United States, who became the anti-Masonic writer. For a brief account, see Haywood (op. cit., n.8 above), p.317. There is no evidence that Thomas Jefferson, author of the Declaration of Independence, and of many published works – a scholar, an ambassador, and twice President of the United States of America, was ever a Mason.

40. In Jefferson's notes, now in the Library of Congress, 'Pharaoh sitting in an open chariot, a crown on his head and a sword in his hand passing thro' the divided waters of the Red Sea . . .' The symbolism is designed to express the idea that Moses' rebellion against the Pharaoh was obedience to God – an excellent parable for the rebellion of the colonists against George III.
41. According to Hunt (op. cit., n.5 above), p.13, the motto may have formed part of the design sketched out by the West Indian Frenchman, Eugène Pierre du Simitière, who was called in to do the drawings for the Seal, but is characteristic of the moral thinking of Jefferson. It was, in any case, a familiar motto among the American colonists, and has been traced in G. H. Preble, *History of the Flag of the United States of America*, 1880, p.694. See also Hunt (op. cit., n.5 above), pp.214–17.
42. See Hunt (op. cit., n.5 above), p.33.
43. Thompson's handwritten report, 'Device for a Great Seal for the United States in Congress Assembled. Passed June 20, 1782'. In the opinion of Gaillard Hunt, this lacuna is not important, for the commentary on the symbolism of the obverse and reverse constitutes an essential part of the fundamental law as Congress adopted it. But this is not necessarily a sound legal opinion.
44. Justin Winsor was born in Boston, 2 January 1831, and studied at Harvard and Heidelberg. His early employment was as a librarian – he was Superintendent of the Boston Public Library, prior to its rebuilding, and then Librarian at Harvard. Among his many works on American history was his editorship of *Narrative and Critical History of America*, 1884.
45. This is 87/81 in the collection.
46. See W. Marsham Adams, *The Book of the Master of the Hidden Places*, 1933. This combines Adams' two seminal works, *The House of the Hidden Places*, and *The Book of the Master.* Adams was a Mason, and sometimes strains the Egyptian symbolism to fit later Masonic rituals, but this is one of the most enlightened of all 19th-century works on Egyptian arcane thought.
47. P.67 in the collection. Its display entry informs us that the transfer for this design was based on an original engraving by James Ross (1745–1821).
48. B.116 in the collection, presented by Bro. W.A. Ashworth.
49. For the engraving by Amos Doolittle, for *The True Masonic Chart*, 1819, see Bullock, *Revolutionary Brotherhood*, 1996, p.249.
50. See Hall (op. cit., n.6 above), p.lxxvii. It was the learned Masonic historian, Art de Hoyos, who, while we were examining this French apron, drew my attention to the fact that it was the source for the Hall drawing.
51. The inscription *Romae.A.L.* is an abbreviation for *Romae Anno Lucis* ('At Rome, in the Year of Light'). The number below, 5742, is the Masonic calendrical equivalent of 1742.

    Masonic dating systems vary widely. In some documents and insignia, Masons date according to their concept of AL, or *Anno Lucis*, and sometimes AM, *Anno Mundi* – 'the Year of (the beginning of) the World', the supposition being that between the creation of the world and the birth of Christ passed 4,000 years. The system is, of course, now entirely symbolic. In the Rite of Misraim, the 'calculated' dating of James Ussher (calculated according to the scriptures, in his *The Annals of the World*, 1658) is adopted, which gives 4004. Robert Macoy, *A Dictionary of Freemasonry* 1989 reprint, offers a useful list of equivalents for the AD year 1866. However, these systems do not always share the same calendrical fiducial, and the common Masonic year has been widely adopted for some considerable time.

AL 5866	–	The common Masonic year
AL 5870	–	Rite of Misraim year
AM 5826	–	Scottish Rite year
AI 2396	–	Royal Arch year
AD 2866	–	Royal and Select Master year

AO 748 – Templars year
AO 552 – Strict Observance year

52. For the medal, see Menzdorf, *Denkmunze*, p.118, no.8. For an account of the influence of Roman Catholicism on Freemasonry, see Leon de Poncins, *Freemasonry and the Vatican. A Struggle for Recognition*, 1968 English trans. by T. Tindal-Robertson.
53. The Grand Master, Charles, the Duke of Richmond, was installed at the same ceremony.
54. R.F. Gould, *The History of Freemasonry*, n.d. but *c*. 1905, vols III, 6–7, and IV, 376.
55. This is now in the manuscript collection, catalogued as *Sloane 3329*. It is still an important source text for several streams of early Masonry. There is a litho facsimile produced by A.F.A. Woodford, 1872.
56. For the Society, see T.G.H. James, *The British Museum and Ancient Egypt*, 1981, pp.4–5. I can find no classical reference to a 'Feast of Isis' on 11 December, so I assume that the title is a blind. On the evening of 11 December 1741, the Moon conjuncted Venus, and while the members may have read some convenient symbolism into this meeting of two feminine planets, such a conjunction occurs at least once each month. Strangely enough, however, on that day the planet Neptune (in 8.57 Cancer) was close to Sirius, the *alpha* of Canis Major (then in 10.20 Cancer): however, Neptune was not known to astronomers at that time.
57. See William T. R. Marvin, *The Medals of the Masonic Fraternity*, 1880, plate xvi, and p.194
58. It is evident that there was an active Masonry in the Americas long before these assured and recorded dates. For example, at a Grand Lodge of England meeting, a health was drunk to the attending Daniel Coxe, as 'Provincial Grand Master of North America'. Cox was one of the Justices of the Supreme Court of the Province of New Jersey. Franklin himself appears to have been initiated at St John's Lodge, Philadelphia, in February 1731. A reliable list of Lodges, derived from entries in surviving official records, is given by Gould (op. cit., n.54 above), vol. VI, p.448. These were Philadelphia (1734), Portsmouth (1735), Charlestown (1735), Boston (Master's Lodge – 1738), Antigua (1738), Annapolis (1738). Each of these Lodges was closely connected with the mother-Lodge in England.
59. This Masonic apron is reproduced in colour in lithographic plate XVII, in Gould (op. cit., n.54 above).
60. For stage-designs for *The Magic Flute*, see James Stevens Curl, *The Art and Architecture of Freemasonry*, 1991.
61. See Norman Frederick de Clifford, *Egypt the Cradle of Ancient Masonry*, 1907. This wide-ranging work, not limited by a myopic search for Masonic origins, contributes greatly to a knowledge of the ancient civilizations.
62. Hunt (op. cit., n.5 above), pp.57ff.
63. Peter Tompkins, *Mysteries of the Mexican Pyramids*, 1976.
64. Marsham Adams, *The Book of the Master of the Hidden Places*, 1933.
65. See George Oliver, *On the Ancient Lodges, or Places of Initiation into the Cabiric Mysteries*, 1823. George Oliver (1782–1867) was born in Nottingham, England on 5 November 1782 (Haywood, op. cit., n.8 below), and was initiated at a very early age (his father was a Mason): he worked the Royal Arch and the Knights Templars, and was probably the most prolific writer on Masonry and arcane subjects in England during the 19th century.
66. In Egyptian mythology, the Eye of Horus was stolen by his evil brother Set, who threw it away and broke it. When Thoth found it, he made it whole before presenting it to Horus, which explains its name *udjat*, 'that which is sound'. This parable of healing could well be applied to the pyamid-eye symbolism, even though it takes us into the heights of esoteric thought.
67. For translation notes to this quotation from Cyril's 'The Incorporeal Eye',

Fragment xi, and for Fragment xiii, dealing with the pyramid, see G.R.S. Mead, *Thrice-Greatest Hermes*, 1964 version of the 1906 ed., vol.iii, pp.163–4.

68. *Aeneid*, Bk 9, l. 625. Very often, the variant *adnue* is given in the Virgilian texts, but the version on the Seal is acceptable Latin.
69. *Bucolics*, eclogue iv, v.5.
70. For the colour versions of the reverse and obverse, see Hunt (op. cit., n.5 above).
71. The Rising States Lodge Certificate is reproduced by Bullock, (op. cit., n.49 above), p.120. There is a rare copy in the archives of the Library of the Supreme Council, Southern Jurisdiction.
72. Durandus, *De Ritibus*, i. 18.8. For a brief survey, which sets out various beliefs about the north-east as the place of honour and offers examples of the north-east founding, see Alex Horne, *Sources of Masonic Symbolism*, 1981, pp.42ff.
73. Cyril of Alexandria, from 'The Pyramid', quoted in Mead (op. cit., n.67 above), 1964 ed., iii, p.164.
74. Albert Pike *Morals and Dogma*, 1871, p.366. For other pertinent references made by Pike to the pyramid in Masonic symbolism, see also pp.234,321,460,633 and 826.

CHAPTER NINE

1. Records in the Scottish Rites former Temple give Aldrin as a Mason of 32nd Degree. There is a signed photograph of him on the moonwalk in the Grand Master's room, in the Supreme Council, Southern Jurisdiction, Washington DC.
2. The banner was that of the Scottish Rite (Supreme Council, Southern Jurisdiction, USA). It is now on display in the Grand Master's room, in the former Temple, Washington DC.
3. Champollion was able to read parts of the Egyptian section of the triple parallel text Rosetta stone, which records a decree of the priests of Memphis, dated to *circa* 200 BC. The stone takes its name from the Europeanized version of the Arabic site-name, Rashid, where it was discovered by the French engineer, Bouchard, in 1799 during the Napoleonic expedition to Egypt. It came to England as war booty, in 1802, and is now on display in the British Museum in London. An excellent-quality cast is on display in the Rosicrucian Egyptian Museum, San Jose, California.
4. J. Fr. Champollion, *Précis du Système Hiéroglyphique*, 1824.
5. J.Fr. Champollion, *Dictionnaire Égyptien en Écriture Hiéroglyphique*, 1861, p.10 (the short-form is given on p.465). For the Coptic sound-equivalents which Champollion recognized, see Hans Jensen, *Sign, Symbol and Script*, 1970, p.487.
6. Champollion (op. cit., n.5 above), p.11.
7. The importance of the *sba* star in ancient Egypt may be dramatically illustrated by pointing to its myriad presence in the burial chamber (which, in accordance with Egyptian practices, was also an initiation chamber) of the ancient pyramid of Unas. Carved on the huge ceiling slabs of the inner chamber and antichamber of this pyramid are literally hundreds of *sba* stars. They are symbols of the pristine heavenly forces – of the spiritual realm beyond the grave, and beyond the illusory limitations of the physical body – which radiate into the sarcophagus. They are symbols which proclaim that the material realm is sustained and vivified by an invisible spiritual power.
8. Amos Doolittle's engraving was published in the 1819 edition of Jeremy Cross, *The True Masonic Chart*. The quotation pertaining to the letter G is from Robert Macoy, *A Dictionary of Freemasonry*, 1989, p.152.
9. Franklin is probably the best-known Mason among the group of Masons and esotericists who directed the design of official emblems, immediately after the Declaration of Independence. The story of the Seal is told by G. Hunt, *The History of the Seal of the United States*, 1909.
10. Franklin, from a letter dated 26 January 1784. See Bigelow, *Life of Franklin*, vol. III.

11. Thomas Crawford (1814–57) sculpted *Freedom* for the new dome, designed by Thomas U. Walter in the 1850s. As James Goode points out, it is ironic that this *Freedom* was cast in bronze, by means of slave labour. See J. Goode, *The Outdoor Sculpture of Washington, DC*, 1974, p.60.
12. The printer-publisher Amos Doolittle is described by Steven C. Bullock *Revolutionary Brotherhood. Freemasonry and the Transformation of the American social order, 1730–1840*, 1996 as 'the period's most active Masonic entrepreneur'. To date, I have been unable to locate details of his Masonic affiliations, though it is apparent that he was in a Connecticut Lodge.
13. Baron Louis Théodore Tschoudy was born at Metz (then in France) in 1720. He seems to have originated, or participated in forming, the Scottish Rite St Andrew Degree, the 29th. He was author of several books on Masonry, and involved in a long-running literary warfare with the papacy. However, so little is Tschoudy remembered now in Masonry that his name does not even appear in the well-researched and invaluable work by Léon de Poncins, *Freemasonry and the Vatican. A Struggle for Recognition*, 1968.
14. Albert Pike, *Morals and Dogma of the Ancient and Accepted Scottish Rite of Freemasonry . . .*, 1871, p.486.
15. John Fellows, *Exposition of the Mysteries, or Religious Dogmas and Customs . . . of Freemasonry*, 1835.
16. The heliacal rising at the summer solstice marked the New Year for the Egyptians, but precession has carried the rising well into August. For the *Sothic* Year, viewed in an esoteric context, see R.A. Schwaller de Lubicz, *Sacred Science*, 1988 ed., pp.26ff. De Lubicz points to the unique quality of Sirius as the only star which acted as a solar fiducial during the period of the entire Ancient Empire.
17. The drawings of which this is one are from the 11th-century *Register of Hyde Abbey*, Winchester, England, and are now in the Stowe mss. 960, in the British Library manuscript department. The entire manuscript was almost certainly prepared for King Cnut, a benefactor of the Abbey.
18. For a history of the Stars and Stripes, see George Henry Preble, *History of the Flag of the United States of America*, 1880.
19. See Hunt, (op. cit., n.9 above).
20. For Jefferson Davis quotation, see Goode (op. cit., n.11 above), p.60.
21. Albert Pike (op. cit., n.14 above), p.634. For an account of this genius, see Jim Tresner, *Albert Pike. The Man Beyond the Monument*, 1995.
22. Villard de Honnecourt's version of the greeting ritual is still preserved in the stained glass at Chartres Cathedral, with Christ as one of the participants.
23. For the mythology of the embrace, which is sometimes traced back to the story of the murder of Hiram Abif, and the attempt to pick up his body when the flesh fell from his bones, see Bullock, (op. cit., n.12 above), pp.25ff.
24. Pike (op. cit., n.14 above), pp.670ff.
25. See James Gilreth and Douglas L. Wilson, *Thomas Jefferson's Library. A Catalog with the Entries in His Own Order*, 1989.
26. This appeared in *The Straggling Astrologer of the Nineteenth Century*, no.12, 21 August 1824, a magazine compiled largely by Robert Cross Smith. Although it ceased publication two months later, Smith continued work in this field – the first of many to use the pseudonym 'Raphael'. He knew many occultists and astrologers of the day – among his friends was John Varley, remembered in astrological history because of his careful study of the new planet, Uranus (the *Georgium Sidus* of his day). At one point, Varley introduced Smith to the poet-artist William Blake, who had his horoscope cast by Varley and published in the magazine *Urania*, 1825. See F. Gettings, *The Hidden Art*, 1979, pp.117ff.
27. I refer to the tables and precessional data of Montignot (see n.44 below), which were still used in England and the United States at that time. By modern standards, these tables were slightly inaccurate, but our concern is not so much

with accuracy as to establish what these astrologers believed at the time when they cast the charts.

28. That is, on the second house cusp of the figure: Smith was anxious to point out that this powerful influence would be poured into the area of finance.
29. Giovanni Gallucci, *Theatrum Mundi*, 1588.
30. A modern astrologer is unlikely to have allowed an orb of over 2 degrees for a fixed star to become operative, as Smith has done. However, what we are interested in is, again, not so much accuracy, as what the astrologers of that period believed to be good practice. 'Raphael' was an advocate of the Placidean table of houses, which I am not usually inclined to use: however, my own check-chart was cast according to Placidus, to ensure conformity.
31. The figure is undoubtedly accurate in terms of early 19th-century charting, and is fairly accurate in terms of modern data. The major planetary error is the placing of Uranus in 8.50 Aries. According to modern tabulations, it was retrograde in 12.53 of Aries. For Smith's analysis of the chart, see *The Straggling Astrologer of the Nineteenth Century*, no.12, 21 August 1824.
32. In AD 2000 Arcturus will be said to be located in 24 degrees of Libra: it will be close to 31 degrees N in latitude. Spica will also be in the same degree of Libra, but its latitude will be 2 degrees south.
33. See George Oliver, *Signs and Symbols Illustrated & Explained in a Course of Twelve Lectures on Freemasonry*, 1857, pp.17–18.
34. In some ancient systems, the dragon was called Atalia. I cannot help wondering if the importance accorded the Dragon's Head in the astrology of Washington DC is linked with the fact that the Latin for 'Dragon's Head' is *Caput draconis* – the word 'head' of which gave us the English *Capital*, and the earlier Latin *Capitol*.
35. E. Brunet, *Maçonnerie et Astrologie*, 1979, pp.44ff.
36. R.H. Allen, *Star-Names and their Meanings*, 1899, p.98. In his *Tetrabiblos*, I. ix, Ptolemy says that Arcturus is of the nature of the planets Jupiter and Mars.
37. In his *Tetrabiblos*, I. ix, Ptolemy says that Regulus is of the nature of the planets Jupiter and Mars.
38. As we have seen in *Tetrabiblos*, I. ix, Ptolemy says that Spica is of the nature of the planets Mercury and Mars. Given the poverty of modern astrology (which has been severed from the Mystery Schools for almost 2,000 years), it is hard for us to perceive now the esoteric depth of the wheat symbolism behind the star Spica. The Graeco-Egyptian hermetic symbolism is discussed in 'The Myth of Man in the Mysteries' by G.R.S. Mead, *Thrice-Greatest Hermes*, 1964 ed., vol.I, p.123. Mead is commenting on the Mystery text which runs: '. . . in the secret rites at Eleusis, they show those who receive in silence the final initiation into the Great . . . Epoptic Mystery, a plucked wheat-ear.' Mead refers to Franz Cumont's *Mystères de Mithra*, 1898, in which the wheat-ears are represented as flowing from the heart-blood of the slain bull, and sometimes from its tail. He refers also to Eratosthenes, *Katasterismoi* (which deals with the symbolism of the stellar patterns), and concludes, perhaps somewhat weakly in view of the evidence he supplies, that the wheat-ear symbolizes the 'generative seed'. In the Mithraic Mystery the wheat-ears seem rather to represent the power in the spinal marrow, which is a seed of inner absorption rather than one of ejaculative power: in the Eleusian Mysteries its significance was so profound that it still remains a total secret.
39. According to Pike (op. cit., n.14 above), p.487, the stars marking this triangle are Algenib, Almach and Algol. However, this is such an unlikely tracing of a triangle that I can only presume that Pike was in error. This suspicion is supported by the fact that he specifies that Algol is in Andromeda: in fact it is the *beta* of Perseus. The other two stars, Algenib and Almach, are not especially distinctive, and it is difficult to work out what Pike had in mind. If stellar magnitude, brilliance or distinction are disregarded, it is possible to trace right-angled and equilateral triangles in virtually every group of stars in the skies. From the point of view of my

own argument, it is sufficient to note that Pike follows his piece of inaccurate astronomy with a reference to three stars which surround Virgo in an equilateral triangle – this may well be the source of Brunet's own more thorough treatment of the symbolism.

40. In fact, these three stars do form, as near as is sufficient for symbolic purposes, an equilateral triangle.
41. According to Theodorus of Melitus, Claudius Ptolemy was born at Ptolemais, in Egypt. See F.E. Robbins (ed. and trans.), *Ptolemy Tetrabiblos*, 1964 ed., p.v. Alternative birth-places include Alexandria and Canopus, but still fix his birth in Egypt. From textual evidence, Robbins concludes that he lived between AD 100 and 178.
42. Hipparchus was making astronomical observations in Bithynia and Rhodes in the middle of the 2nd century BC: scarcely any of his writings survive. One exception is his commentary on Eudoxus' *Phaenomena*. Much of what we know about this once-influential astronomer is derived from Ptolemy's *Almagest*. It is clear from a surviving title of a lost work, and from subsequent tradition, that he had discovered the 'precession of the equinoxes' (the phenomenon by which the longitudinal positions of the stars seem to increase), and seems to have done this by comparing the earlier Babylonian and Greek fixing of the star Spica with his own observations. Hipparchus may have compiled a catalogue of the main stars. The image of Hipparchus, on the façade of the National Academy of Sciences in Washington DC, seems to refer to his discovery of the phenomenon of precession.
43. In mediaeval lunar mansions (the latter word is derived from the Arabic *manzils*, which did not mean 'mansions' as they have been mandated in modern astrology – the original meant something like 'marking places [of the Moon]') Regulus marked the 10th manzil, *frons leonis*, while Spica marked the 14th manzil, named after the star. In the Arabic system, Regulus marked the 8th manzil, *Al Jabhah*, 'the Forehead': it was a manzil said to 'strengthen buildings', and therefore an excellent choice for the triangulation planned in 1791. Spica marked the 12th Arabic manzil *Al Simak*, 'the Unarmed'.
44. The full title is, M. l'Abbé Montignot, *État des Étoiles Fixes au second siècle, Par Claude Ptolémée, comparé à la position des Mêmes Étoiles en 1786*, 1787. Montignot has made it easier for his readers by inserting stellar references which Ptolemy himself did not use – the Greek letter designations introduced in 1624 by Bayer. In regard to the three corner stars, in what I have called the L'Enfant triangle, Montignot recorded (on p.192) the progressional differences of 24 main stars, and gave their positions for 1786 – the year before he published his translation. In 1786, Spica was 20.51.21 Libra: Regulus was in 26.51.20 Cancer, while Arcturus was 25.4.35 Libra. These positions need to be adjusted only by minutes to fall into line with their computed positions for 1791. One point worth making is that Montignot used a mean progressional period of 1 degree to 70 years. I record Montignot's computations because they are an example of what would have been available to L'Enfant and Ellicott.
45. This is catalogue no. 28 in the astronomy books (Ch.28, p.97) in the first printed catalogue of Jefferson's library – see n.25 above.
46. As the ratio of the triangle has not changed I give approximate figures for 1998:

Regulus	Long.: 29LE43	Lat.: N 00.28
Spica	Long.: 23LB43	Lat.: N 02.03
Arcturus	Long.: 24LB07	Lat.: N 30.47

CHAPTER TEN

1. This information is from an article by Jane C. Hunter, 'Roosevelt and Astrology', quoted by Manley Palmer Hall in his *The Story of Astrology*, 1943, p.12.
2. According to Hunter (op. cit., n.1 above), it was cast by the father of Li Hung

Chang, the Chinese statesman and General. The data are given in Marc Edmund Jones, *The Sabian Symbols in Astrology*, 1953, p.360, no.806 (the position of Neptune is given incorrectly).

3. He received his degrees in 1901, shortly after being made Vice-President, and had an active, deeply committed life in Masonry: for a list of Masonic affiliations in New York and Washington DC see William L. Boyden, *Masonic Presidents, Vice-Presidents and Signers*, 1927, pp.22ff.
4. McKinley was initiated on 1 May 1865. For a full history, see Boyden (op. cit., n.30 above, pp.18ff.
5. On 27 October 1858, the Moon was in 11CN40, while Mars was in 17CP49. On 8 June 1907, Neptune was in 11CN40 and Mars was in 18CP49R, with Uranus 11CP42R. Uranus was opposed by Neptune in 11CN23. Roosevelt would not have known how threatening the situation, for Pluto (as then unrecognized by most astrologers) was on the Descendant, at 23GE06.
6. James McMillan, the United States Senator for Michigan from 1889 to his death in 1902, was initiated into the Pine Grove Lodge No. 11, Port Huron, Michigan.
7. In the description annexed to his plan, dated 4 January 1792, L'Enfant described 'A *grand avenue* 400 feet in breadth and about a mile in length . . . [which] leads to the monument . . . and connects the Congress garden with the . . . President's park'. In a report of August 1791, intended as a commentary on the L'Enfant proposal, George Washington wrote: 'The *Grand avenue* connecting both the palace and the federal house will be most magnificent & most convenient . . .' In both quotations, the italics are my own.
8. Spica is 2.03 degrees south of the ecliptic, while Regulus is 0.28 degrees north of the ecliptic.
9. Memorandum of 15 September 1980 of Florian H. Thayn, from the Architect of the Capitol. In the Brumidi files is a letter to the artist from W.B. Franklin, setting out the sequence of the zodiacal signs on the corridor walls. There is no doubt that 'zodiacal signs' was intended for the paintings, but these were later 'restored' as constellation signs. The intention of Franklin is to emphasize the sequence of the months, rather than the sequence of the zodiacal signs.

   Constantino Brumidi was the principal painter in the Capitol in the decades from 1850 to 1880. He had restored painting by Raphael in the Vatican, which probably explains why his ceiling in the President's Room in the Library of the Capitol is based on paintings by Raphael. See Pamela Scott, *Temple of Liberty*, 1995, pp.101ff. and plates 200 and 201. The rotunda frieze, depicting America and History, begins with the landing of Columbus, and ends with a scene of the birth of aviation in the United States. The series was finished by Filippo Costaggini.
10. For example, the artist Ron Combs requested information on the signs of the zodiac which he had to 'restore' in 1966, due to a leak from the Senators' bathing room. The same memorandum, in the files of the Architect of the Capitol, mentions a similar flooding in 1961.
11. Letter from Cliff Young to the Architect of the Capitol, dated 28 October 1980. While Brumidi had painted in water-colour on to the plaster, Cliff Young recorded that in these restorations, he 'Redesigned and painted 12 Zodiac signs (background and signs painted with artist oil paint)'.
12. Letter dated 26 November 1957, from J. George Stewart, Architect of the Capitol, to *Compton's Picture Encyclopedia* (Chicago). Letter dated 6 December 1957, from Arthur E. Cook to the publishers, F.E. Compton & Company. Originally under file: *Frescoes, Murals and Lunettes – (Corridors) – Signs of the Zodiac*.
13. It is probably with some justification that the Brumidi 'months', or zodiacal images, are not mentioned in the authoritative government publication, *Compilation of Works of Art and Other Objects in the United States Capitol*, 1965 (88th Congress, 2nd Session, House Doc. 362).
14. As a matter of fact, the tuft of hair was emphasized in the early images because it

was marked by the star *Dabih* (resolved by modern telescopes into a series of multiple stars). One cannot expect a restorer, unlearned in the history of the stars, to have known this, however. In Brumidi's day, *Dabih* was still believed to be a single star – its duplicity was not determined until 1883, as a prelude to recognition of its multiple nature.

15. Cornelian was the stone of Virgo – see F.F. Kunz, *The Curious Lore of Precious Stones*, 1913, in the 1971 reprint, p.346. For mention of the unicorn image on the stone (from *Lettres au R.P. Parrenin*, 1770) see p. 341.
16. The dedication was written by the Architect of the Capitol, G. M. White. See George M. White, *Under the Capitol Dome*, 1997, pp.90–1. White was a Mason.
17. Memorandum dated 14 May 1974, from Mary C. Long of the A and R Staff, in file: *Frescoes – Corridors, Senate – Signs of Zodiac.*
18. The Dirksen Senate Office Building is sometimes called the Additional Senate Office Building, but is nowadays generally referred to as Dirksen House.
19. For some note of the Dirksen zodiac in conception, see memorandum dated 14 March 1958 from Pauline T. Connell (with referenced sketch) in response to letter from Eliot B. Willauer of the architects Eggers and Higgins, to Mr Harvey Middleton, dated 12 March 1958.
20. I must record, with considerable pleasure, that these misunderstandings are unlikely to be repeated in the future, as the Library of the Architect of the Capitol is now staffed by professional archivists, well informed in such matters, and alert to the symbolism in many of the buildings which fall under their jurisdiction.
21. See Senate Document No. 143 of the 83rd Congress, 2nd Session, 16 July 1954.
22. In the files of the Archives of the Architect of the Capitol there is a memorandum, dated 11 December 1957, recording that the architects in charge of the project had approved the design for the 'medallions' of the zodiac for what was then called the Additional Senate Office Building. By 12 March 1958, a photograph of the 12 images which were finally installed on the ceilings was submitted to George Stewart, the Architect of the Capitol, by Eggers and Higgins. I have been unable to locate the graphic source for these interesting designs: the sigils for Leo and Pisces are inaccurate, however, and remain so on all the ceilings. The finished sculptures from which the moulds were made were photographed in the New York studios of Rochette and Parzini, which suggests that they were made in New York.
23. Fred Othman, 'Senatorial Lap of Luxury', *Washington Daily News*, 28 August 1957. Naturally, Middleton blamed delays on senatorial decision-making – one of the themes which echo down the years in Washington DC, in letters, diaries and recorded pronouncements of architects, designers and artists.
24. The colours are a recent welcome addition, as when I first examined the zodiacs in 1989 they were unpainted and difficult to distinguish.
25. *Zavijava* (sometimes, Zavijah, Alaraph, or Zarijan) is said to be from the Arabic *Al Zawiah*, which means 'the Corner', for it once formed the corner of a kennel traced by the Arab astrologers in the skies. In traditional astrology, it is said to be of the nature of Mercury – sometimes of Mercury with Mars. In the star maps *Zavijava* was usually shown set in the wing of Virgo (figure 13). This star, which in the astrological tradition is entirely beneficial – and hence one would wish to see it manifest in a foundation chart – just happens to have been the star used to confirm Einstein's theory, during the solar eclipse of 29 May 1919. See Nigel Calder, *Einstein's Universe*, 1979, p.66ff.
26. The stellar map was prepared with the expert assistance of two astronomers from the United States Observatory in Washington DC, P. Kenneth Seidelmann and Richard E. Schmidt. A pamphlet, *The Celestial Map at the Einstein Memorial*, with a truncated form of the map, is available from the National Academy of Sciences.
27. Several *frescoes* in Italy (for example) are much larger – the ceiling painting by Baldassar Peruzzi in the Farnesina (Rome) is a gigantic horoscope for his patron, Agostino Chigi, cast for 1 December 1466. Nor is the Einstein zodiac the largest

marble zodiac in the world – the San Miniato al Monte zodiac, in Florence, Italy, dated 1207, covers a much larger area; this however, does *not* seem to be a horoscope. The massive Egyptian marble planisphere from Denderah is not a horoscope.

28. In a letter to Robert Berks, dated 15 April 1954. The sculpted head to which Einstein refers had been made from life by Berks in 1953.
29. See 'Badlands National Park', sec. 611, in *National Parks and Recreation Acts of 1978 – Public Law 95–625. Congressional Record* – House H 11550/s 791, 4 October 1978.
30. The horoscope data corresponding with the Einstein Memorial are:

ASC10LE24	SU01TA58	MO10PI56	ME04AR43
VE29PI27	MA12AR08	JU00LE11	SA07VG19R
UR19SC43R	NE20SG15R	PL17LB27R	MN15VG19

The floor schema also gives the positions of the 'minor planets', Ceres, Pallas, Juno and Vesta.

31. The chances of Venus being on the same degree as an eclipse by accident are many thousands to one. An eclipse repeats its degree position approximately every four Saros cycles – which is to say, 4 × 19 or 76 years: Venus moves through the zodiac in approximately 224 days.
32. My study of Berks' Einstein zodiac has left me astonished at just how little was left to 'chance'. However, all works of art are made in collaboration with the spiritual, and what we call chance seems, at times, to be the working of the spiritual into the material realm, and one of the integral factors of creativity. No one familiar with the development of modern art can wisely dispense with the idea that chance plays an important role in art.
33. See Will P. Kennedy, 'Washington of the Future', in *The Book of Washington*, sponsored by the Washington Board of Trade, n.d. but pre-1929, p.105.
34. Paul Philippe Cret was born in Lyons, France, in 1876, and died in Philadelphia in 1945. His most remarkable work in Washington DC is the Folger Shakespeare Library.
35. For the statue as 'America', see James M. Goode, *The Outdoor Sculpture of Washington DC*, 1974, p.442.
36. The seven Liberal Arts portrayed in the print are Arithmetic, Astrology, Dialectic, Geometry, Grammar, Music and Rhetoric. The female Mercury seems to be a summation of all seven.
37. Andrew W. Mellon, Secretary of the Treasury under Coolidge and Hoover, and one-time ambassador to Great Britain. He gave 15 million dollars for the building of the National Gallery of Art, and his personal collection of pictures for permanent exhibition. Mellon was made a Mason in 1928, and received the Royal Arch Degree in 1931.
38. This was specified in Public Law 194, 80th Congress, 16 July 1947.
39. Waugh also designed the zodiacs in the light bowls of the Federal Reserve.
40. In theory, the orientation should not be accurate, for Pennsylvania Avenue runs from Constitution at an angle of 20 degrees, while each zodiacal sign covers an arc of 30 degrees. However, the size of the sculpted images permits this illusion of orientation, even though it is not (and could not be) accurate.
41. Henry Latham, *Black and White. A Journal of a Three Months' Tour in the United States*, 1867, p.79.
42. For Schutt's advertisement, see *Washington Standard Guide*, 1908, p.40.
43. *A Handbook of Useful Information Concerning the . . . City of Washington . . .*, published by the Washington Board of Trade, 1895, p.33.
44. Some architects did object to the way this symbolically important apex was being treated. Edward Bruce was not the only one foresighted enough to see that an elaborate terrace and 'as fine a piece of art as this country can produce' was

essential. Indeed, he maintained that it would be an anticlimax among a group of buildings on which the government had, even in the '1930s, spent 100 million dollars. For the quotation from Bruce, see George Gurney, *Sculpture and the Federal Triangle*, 1984, p.376. Photographs of the Kreis models for 'Agriculture' and the companion piece, 'Industry', are given in Gurney, fig.242, p.386.

45. For an account of the making of this figure, see Gurney (op. cit., n.44 above), pp.211ff. On the base of the sculpture, Fraser is named as the sculptor, and Rubins as his assistant.
46. Rand McNally, *Washington Guide to Places of Interest in the City and the Environs*, 1926, p.31.
47. E.N. Chapin, *American Court Gossip, or Life at the National Capitol*, 1887.
48. The ground-breaking data are:

SU15VG55	MN09LE41	ME07VG35R	VE16VG18	MA24LB49
JU11LE44	SA16VG46R	UR18AR36R	NE05VG55	PL21CN46
DG06AR17				

49. See Virginia C. Purdy, 'A Temple to Clio: the National Archives Building', in Timothy Walch (ed.), *Guardian of Heritage*, 1985, pp.22ff.
50. The foundation data are:

SU01PI38	MO12CP44	ME12PI01	VE16AQ34	MA14VG20R
JU20VG26R	SA10AQ00	UR20AR38	NE09VG01R	PL21CN36R
DH08PI38				

51. See Purdy (op. cit., n.69) p.23.
52. See Gurney, (op cit., n.44 above), p. 214.
53. The original system has been replaced, and the waters are no longer used in this way.
54. For an arcane account of the cosmological basis of the number 72, see Guenther Wachsmuth, *Reincarnation as a Phenomenon of Metamorphosis*, 1937 English trans., pp.65ff. For 72 as the precessional number, see F. Gettings, *The Arkana Dictionary of Astrology*, 1985 ed., p.397.

    Some of the ancient traditions relating to the number 72 are obscure in meaning, yet clearly linked with the idea that it is a solar number. The Egyptian priest Horapollo described the dog-headed ape as being reared in the temples, so that the priests might learn the exact time of lunar eclipses. This was possible, according to his explanation, because at the time of the eclipse the male ape would always become blind and would refuse to eat, while the female would menstruate. In an obscure passage, Horapollo insists that the cynocephalus represents the inhabitable world *which has 72 parts*, and dies in 72 stages. The priests bury the newly dead animal whole for 72 days, and then take it from its grave in the full knowledge that on that day the last remnant of life will have left its body (*Horopollo*, I, 16).

    When Nostradamus published his collection of prophetic quatrains, he paid lip service to this value of 72 by linking his most important quatrains with this number. (For example, the famous quatrain for the year 1999, often called the 'Great King of Terror' prophecy, is no.72 in book X.)

    On a level which may appear not so exalted as these examples, the standard textbooks of numerology recognize that 72 reduces to one of its divisors, which is 9 (7 + 2), and is consequently a version of the sacred 3 × 3.

55. See Donald R. McCoy 'The Struggle to Establish a National Archives in the United States', in Walch (op. cit., n.49 above), pp.5ff.
56. See booklet DOJ.KF.5107. A5.R4.1934, *The Dedication of the Building for the Department of Justice of the United States of America*, 1934.
57. The relevant Western arrangement was:
    DES07VG46, MA04VG29 NE13VG50 VE25LB38 SU01SC43 and JU03SC11.

58. The music was adopted as the national march of the United States on 10 December 1987. See *The Scottish Rite Journal*, vol.cvi, no.5, May 1998, p.10.
59. For notes on the role played by Alexander, see Gurney (op. cit., n.44 above). I have not been able to ascertain whether Jennewein was a Mason, but there may be no doubt from his extraordinary statuary that he was deeply knowledgable in arcane art and architecture: the general feeling among Masons I have spoken to is that he was involved in Masonry, but to date I have been unable to identify his Lodge.
60. The panel was carved by William Kapp, Bruno Mankowski, Roger Morigi and Otto Thielemann, who worked for the John Donnelly Company.
61. The Latin is from one of Pliny's *Epistles.*
62. See Antonio Vasaio, *The Fiftieth Anniversary of the US Department of Justice Building 1934–1984*, 1984, p.45.
63. The burned wheat is clearly an arcane reference to the sacred host of the Mass, which had its prototypes in the early Mystery lore.
64. Genesis, I, iii.
65. I have not been able to establish whether Shimin was a Mason or not.
66. The dividers, the right angle and the holy book (here, the map below the dividers and right angle).
67. They were carved by Oscar Mundhenk and Robert C. Wakeman. The 'official' explanations for the five bas-reliefs are questionable, however.
68. Joseph A. Sanches, 'Origins of the Inscriptions on the Justice Seal', in *Justice News*, 2 November 1979.
69. Arthur Brown designed the San Francisco City Hall and Opera House. P. Scott and A.J. Lee, *Buildings of the District of Columbia*, 1993, p.172, trace his involvement with the Triangle to these accomplishments.
70. See Bell's *New Pantheon; or, Historical Dictionary of the Gods, Demi-Gods, Heroes, and Fabulous Personages of Antiquity*, vol. 1, 1790, p.11.
71. Wilhelm Heinrich Roscher, *Ausführliches Lexikon der Griechischen und Römischen Mythologie*, 1890–94. See especially vol. I, p.2674, under *Hippokamp.*
72. Most of the sculptural programmes on the façades of the Triangle buildings are inset within *pedimental triangles.* I realize that triangular pediments are an essential part of the classical-revival style, but it cannot be without significance that these shallow triangles, replete with astrological symbolism, are ranged along the sides of the Federal Triangle.
73. See Colin F.W. Dyer, *Symbolism in Craft Freemasonry*, 1976.
74. For a Masonic treatment of the four Cardinal Virtues, see C. I. Paton, *Freemasonry. Its Symbolism, Religious Nature and Law of Perfection*, 1893, Chs xlvi–xlix – pp.143–53ff.
75. See, for example, Paton (op. cit., n.74 above), pp.161ff.
76. Goode (op. cit., n.35 above), p.169 sees it as purely historical.
77. This should not surprise us, of course. According to Steven C. Bullock, at least 42 per cent of the officers who served in the Revolutionary Wars were, or would become, Masons. See, for example, Bullock, pp.122–7. John Sullivan was in the Pennsylvania Lodge No. 19.
78. The Federal Triangle is 90 degrees at the intersection of Constitution Avenue with 15th Street, 20 degrees at intersection of Pennsylvania Avenue with Constitution Avenue, and 70 degrees at the intersection of Pennsylvania Avenue with 15th Street.
79. The figure in the right-hand spandrel looks directly east, towards Sunrise.
80. Louis Simon's first sketches are not available, but Gurney quotes evidence to suggest these incorporated sculptures in both stone and bronze for the exterior: see Gurney (op. cit., n.44 above), pp.89ff.
81. Ulysses A. Ricci had studied under James Earle Fraser: the commission for the Internal Revenue Building came to the firm only after the mounting of a competition for the designs, which proved unsatisfactory. Ricci and Zari probably underquoted for the work in order to land the more lucrative Commerce Building

commission.

82. James M. Goode, *Capital Losses, A Cultural History of Washington's Destroyed Buildings*, 1979, pp.360ff.
83. The eastern façade is decorated with eight relief sandstone panels, symbolizing the functions of the agencies which originally worked within the building. The Bureau of Foreign and Domestic Commerce shows a caduceus. The Coast and Geodetic Survey shows stylized sea waves and a sextant. The date above the panel of symbols is 1807 – a reminder that this was the year when Thomas Jefferson founded the Bureau to survey the coasts of the new nation. Even this caduceus – symbol of Mercury, the ruler of Virgo, and the sextant, the traditional symbol of the star-measurer, point to the mystery of Washington DC.
84. Arthur M. Schlesinger, Jr, *The Age of Roosevelt. The Coming of the New Deal*, 1959, p.107.
85. See Helen Bowers (ed.), *From Lighthouses to Laserbeams. A History of the US Department of Commerce*, 1995 ed., p.114.
86. The *Washington Post*, 31 December 1931, special edition, 'Department of Commerce'.
87. The cornerstone data for 12.30 p.m. are:

SU 17CN56	MO 11VG29	ME 28GE18	VE 02GE41	MA 03VG48
JU 06GE07	SA 25SG41R	UR 11AR22	NE 29LE34	PL 17CN56

88. For useful data relating to the discovery of Pluto at Lowell Observatory (especially useful because of the colour plates recording the discovery), see Mark R. Chartrand, *National Audubon Society Field Guide to the Night Sky*, 1996 ed., p.667 (for plates 376–7).
89. Graham Bell's telephone patent of 7 March 1876; Samuel B.F. Morse's telegraph patent of 20 June 1846; Eli Whitney's cotton-gin patent of 14 March 1793; Elias Howe's sewing-machine patent of 10 September 1846; Cyrus McCormick's reaper patent of 21 June 1834; Thomas Edison's electric light-bulb patent of 27 January 1880; Francis H. Holton (patent no. 1,000,000) for the vehicle tyre, of 8 August 1911; and Simon Lake's submersible vessel patent of 1 July 1924. Among these outstanding patents was one by Abraham Lincoln, for a boat-raising device, of 22 May 1849.
90. There is a (poor-quality) photograph of this instrument on p.29 of the special edition of the *Washington Post*, 31 December 1931.
91. The observatory was removed years ago, and I have been unable to locate where it has been preserved.
92. While it is tempting to read the G in this triangle as an early Masonic symbol – the G for Geometry – this is not the case. The G is merely a letter-key for the explanatory text. The plate is from De Hooghe, *Hieroglyphica, oder Denkbilder der alten Volke*r . . ., 1744.
93. The *Washington Post*, 31 December 1931, p.8.
94. See Phebe Mitchell Kendall, *Maria Mitchell: Life, Letters, and Journals*, 1896. She was born 1 August 1818, with Mars and Venus conjunct in Virgo.
95. Bell (op. cit., n.70 above), vol.1, p.11.
96. Digested from Bell (op. cit., n.70 above)) vol.I, p.12.
97. De Hooghe (op. cit., n.92 above).
98. The following examples from the print reproduced are almost randomly selected, and the list could certainly be extended (especially in connection with the standard zodiacal correspondences). It will be observed that of the symbols listed below are repeated many times in the Federal Triangle buildings.

SYMBOL	LOCATION IN PRINT	LOCATION IN TRIANGLE
winged disk	under seat of Philo	Archives
ram	above zodiac	Dept of Labour
fruit	to right of Virgin	Dept of Labour

dog	below seat of Philo	Archives
bull	above zodiac	Auditorium Dept
Pisces	in zodiac	Interstate Commerce
scales	in zodiac	Mellon zodiac
wheat	on lap of Virgin	Dept of Labour
large horn	on shoulder of top figure	Federal Trade
birds	above head of right lion	Dept of Commerce
plumed helmet	top left female	Archives

99. The figures, *Canes Venatici*, seem to have been invented by Johannes Hevelius, the Polish astronomer, in the late 17th century. The northern dog is called *Asterion* (meaning 'starry') while the other is *Chara* ('loved one').

CHAPTER ELEVEN

1. In that part of Pennsylania Avenue were firms such as Norris Peters photolithos and J. L. Kervand, engraver and lithographer. The largest, employing up to 100 workers, was G.B. Graham, a lithographic printer and engraver, founded in 1839, and the oldest lithographic printing house in the United States, supported for decades by many contracts with the government. On the south-east corner of 13th and Pennsylvania were the printers, Gibson Brothers, who operated six huge steam presses and numerous hand- and proof presses, the steam presses worked by a 15-horsepower engine.
2. I note with horror that this lovely building, in which resides so much unconscious symbolism, seems earmarked for eventual demolition under the Pennsylvania Avenue plan. See *Downtown Urban Renewal Area Landmarks, Washington DC,* prepared by the National Capital Planning Commission in cooperation with the District of Columbia Redevelopment Land Agency, Summer 1970, p.67.
3. Russell Baker, 'Moods of Washington', in *New York Times Magazine*, 24 March 1874.
4. John Clagett Proctor was a member of Federal Lodge No. 1, and was initiated Master Mason 5 October 1893. For full details of Masonic history, see the 'Autobiography' which prefaces his *Proctor's Washington and Environs*, 1949.
5. William R. Denslow, *10,000 Famous Freemasons*, 1961.
6. For notes on Jefferson in a Masonic context, see H.L. Haywood, *Famous Masons and Masonic Presidents*, 1968 ed., pp.319ff.
7. From Anne Royall's *Paul Pry*: see Sarah Harvey Porter, *The Life and Times of Anne Royall*, 1909, p.153.
8. Royall (op cit., n.7 above), p.154.
9. The photograph, now in the National Archives, is reproduced on p.204 of Richard Longstreth (ed.), *The Mall in Washington, 1791–1991.*
10. In fact, we cannot date the engraving in this way. The Walter dome was not finished until 1863, when Thomas Crawford's *Freedom* (cast in five separate pieces by Clark Mills) was eased into place. During the interim period, guidebooks and 'views of the city' would often show the old Bulfinch dome.
11. John B. Ellis, *The Sights and Secrets of the National Capital*, 1869, pp.75ff.
12. The American sculptor, Franklin Simmons, was a member of St John's Lodge No. 1, Providence. Considering that he spent many years of his life in Italy, he produced an enormous number of portraits of famous American contemporaries, including Farragut, Porter, Grant, Meade, Sherman and Thomas. The equestrian statue of Logan in Iowa Circle, Washington DC, is by Simmons.
13. For Admiral David D. Porter, see *Admiral David Dixon Porter: the Civil War Years*, Chester G. Herne, 1996.
14. For an examination of the symbolism of the Masonic square, seen as an elemental square, against an astrological background, see Milton Alberto Pottenger, *Symbolism*, 1905.

15. Clark Mills became a Mason in the Lebanon Lodge No.7.
16. By far the best biography is Glenn V. Sherwood, *Labor of Love. The Life and Art of Vinnie Ream*, 1997. A brief account of the life of this remarkable woman by a Mason, based on the doctoral dissertation of Walter Lee Brown (1955) and the letters which passed between Vinnie and Albert Pike, is in Jim Tresner, *Albert Pike. The Man Beyond the Monument*, 1995, pp.148ff.
17. In the useful plats engraved by Walter S. MacCormac for *Atlas of Washington District of Columbia*, published by G.M. Hopkins in 1887, Vinnie Ream is shown as owner of the entire house block at 235 Pennsylvania Avenue, the third house from the corner of 3rd Street, on the north of the avenue, between 2nd and 3rd Streets. Perhaps at this time, or a year or two later, this was fronted by the Hotel Brunswick, on the ground floor of which was a grocery shop. There is a photograph of this frontage on p.43 of Robert Reed, *Old Washington DC in Early Photographs 1846–1932*, 1980.
18. At the Cabinet Council held on that morning, Lincoln asked General Grant if he had received word from Sherman. Grant said that he had not. Lincoln said that he would hear very soon, and the news would be important. When asked to explain, Lincoln said, 'I had a dream last night, and ever since the war began I have invariably had the same dream before any important military event occurred.' Lincoln's assassin had regarded the deed as vengeance for the military actions in the South.
19. *Broughton's Monthly Planet Reader and Astrological Journal*, vol.5, no.1, Oct.–Dec. 1864, p.2.
20. Broughton (op. cit., n.19 above).
21. Broughton gave a summary of the several stages of this prediction in his *Monthly Planet Reader*, vol.6, no.3, Jul.–Sept., 1865.
22. David Glasgow Farragut was born 5 July 1801, near Knoxville, Tenn. He became a friend of David Porter, who had him entered into the navy at the age of ten. He learned French, Italian and Arabic. He served under Porter in 1823 when the Commodore was ordered to destroy the pirate strongholds which, at that time, dominated many of the islands in the West Indies.
23. Richard L. Hoxie (who was to become a brigadier-general) was an engineering officer, responsible, from 1874, for the construction of new sewage systems, and for the development of new avenues and squares during the expansion of the city which followed the Civil War.
24. The original House of the Temple in Washington DC was not purpose-designed. It was a Victorian-style mansion, at 433 3rd Street NW, which the Supreme Council remodelled internally in 1884 for use as a temple. Pike lived there, among the books (a Library addition had been constructed in 1898) that he eventually put in the care of the Temple, during the last years of his life.
25. Thirty-third Degree is the final degree of the Scottish Rite: although Pike provided background essays dealing with the first 32 degrees, in his *Morals and Dogma* (1906 ed.), he does not appear to have dealt with the final degree.
26. The bust is now in the collection of the Supreme Council (Southern Jurisdiction), on 16th Street, Washington DC. Anyone who has examined the letters which passed between Pike and Vinnie will be forced to admit that Pike was in love with her. Vinne's own attitude to him is more ambivalent, however: she seems to have been a consummate manipulator of those who could promote her upward mobility, and she must have seen Pike (perhaps the most influential Mason in the United States in those years) as someone from whom she could learn. Pike (separated from his wife, but never divorced) looked forward to 'the frequent presence of one sweet face' of his Vinnie, whom he wished to see at least once a week. He had met her when she was a young girl, and from the friendship had grown a remarkable correspondence and a considerable amount of bad verse. The manuscript letters and poems, along with all printed editions, are preserved in the Library of the

Supreme Council, in Washington DC.

27. James M. Goode, *The Outdoor Sculpture of Washington DC*, 1974 p.228, calls her 'the goddess of Masonry'. However, William L. Fox, *The Lodge of the Double-Headed Eagle*, 1997, p.135, suggests that she is the 'Mother' of the Supreme Council. Whatever her symbolic identity, she is holding aloft the Scottish Rite banner.
28. On the day of Pike's birth, 29 December 1809, the Sun was in 07 CP 30. On the day of the dedication of his statue, 23 October 1901, Jupiter was in 07 CP 30. The dedication took place in the middle of the afternoon. This is yet another indication that someone in the Masonic fraternity at that time had a profound knowledge of astrology: I have not been able to identify this individual.
29. This was the sphinx-guarded 'House of the Temple' of the Supreme Council (Southern Jurisdiction), designed by Pope.
30. It is true that the most frequently used of Masonic symbols is an equilateral triangle, and the Federal Triangle is right-angled. For the Masonic symbolism of the right-angled triangle, see Chalmes I. Paton, *Freemasonry. Its Symbolism, Religious Nature and Law of Perfection*, 1893.
31. Mary Cable, *The Avenue of the Presidents*, 1969.
32. James M. Goode, *Capital Losses. A Cultural History of Washington's Destroyed Buildings*, 1979. For the Capital Bicycle Club, see sect. 130: for the Electric Lighting Company, see sect. 152., pp.236ff. Cycling was a highly respectable hobby in the 19th century – it is likely that the first 'velociped' in the United States of America was ridden down Pennsylvania Avenue – no doubt because it was 'paved' with broken stones.
33. See, for example, George O. Totten, 'Exposition architecture in its relations to the grouping of Government buildings', in *Papers Relating to the Improvement of the City of Washington, District of Columbia*, 1901, p.86. This paper was among those presented to Congress by the Mason, McMillan, in December 1900 – the same year that Smith's proposals were published by Congress.
34. H.P. Caemmerer, *Washington. The National Capital*, 1932.
35. Samuel W. McCall, Governor of Massachusetts, US Congressman and editor-in-chief of the *Boston Daily Advertiser*, was initiated in the William Parkman Lodge, Winchester, Massachusetts, on 10 April 1888. He died in 1923.
36. A. Peterson, 'The Mall, the McMillan Plan, and the Origins of American City Planning', in Richard Longstreth (ed.), *The Mall in Washington, 1791–1991*, 1991, p.109.
37. William McKinley, the 25th President of the USA (1897–1901), was initiated 1 May 1865 at Hiram Lodge No.21, Winchester, Virginia. For the story behind his initiation, and the subsequent Masonic history up to his assassination, see Wm L. Boyden, *Masonic Presidents, Vice-Presidents and Signers*, 1927, pp.18–19.
38. Colour print of Smith's Hall of the Ancients, as title-page for *The Halls of the Ancients* in its reprint as Senate Document 209, 56th Congress, 1st Session, parts 1–3; Washington DC, Monday, 12 Feb. 1900.
39. See Katharine M. Abbott, *Trolley Trips in and about Fascinating Washington*, 1900, p.99.
40. See Goode (op. cit., n.32 above), p.280. Smith also has a brief mention in Mary Cable (op. cit., n.31 above), p.179ff.
41. Julius C. Burrows (Senator for Michigan) was Past Master of Anchor Lodge of Strict Observance No. 87 at Kalamazoo. Henry C. Hansbrough (Senator for North Dakota) was a member of Minnewaukan Lodge No. 21 at Devil Lake. Jacob H. Gallinger (Senator for New Hampshire) was raised in Eureka Lodge No. 70, Concord, NH. Orville H. Platt (Senator for Connecticut) was a member of the Meriden Lodge No. 77, Meriden, Conn.
42. The Mason Joseph R. Hawley had been a major-general in the Civil War, and US Senator up to his death in 1905. Another Mason who supported the project was the

architect Edward W. Donn Jr, the chief designer in the Office of the Architect of the Treasury in Washington DC.

43. Leroy Mortimer Taylor was initiated in the Federal Lodge No. 12 of Washington DC on 18 May 1858, and subsequently achieved many high honours in Masonic initiation. The became Master of the Royal Secret in the Albert Pike Consistory on 1 October 1884. He died on 27 September 1904, and bequeathed his magnificent library of books to the Library of what is now the Supreme Council, Southern Jurisdiction.
44. Franklin W. Smith, *The Halls of the Ancients*, fig.44, p.67.
45. The records appear to have been lost, for H. L. Haywood, *Famous Masons and Masonic Presidents*, 1968 ed., p.35, reports the Grand Chaplain Philip Neeley (speaking after Jackson's death) as saying that in the early part of his life, Jackson attended the Philanthropic Lodge No. 12, under the Grand Lodge of Kentucky. This Lodge surrendered its charter in 1812, and Jackson's name is not on its rolls. However, he was present at the opening of a Lodge at Greeneville (Grand Lodge of North Carolina), on 5 September 1801. For details of Jackson's impressive Masonic career, see Haywood, pp.36–9. In fact, it was partly Jackson's famous bellicosity which helped steer Masonry through the disastrous period of anti-Masonic sentiment which was engineered in the 1820s and 30s.
46. Haywood (op. cit., n.45 above) is among those Masonic writers who raise this issue, though he does argue (pp.38–9), perhaps speciously, that there is really nothing to explain. Jackson's many enemies were not so kind.
47. He was born on 15 March 1767. For run-of-the-mill astrology, the presence of Mercury, Venus and Uranus in Aries in the natal chart would probably account for the bad temper. Even though the time is not recorded, the sabre blow allows one to create a speculative chart for Jackson. Undoubtedly, it is Uranus on the fixed star Alcyone which was responsible for the sabre cut, as the star (in the words of Robson, *The Fixed Stars and Constellations in Astrology*, 1969 ed.) gives 'accidents to the face'.
48. His mother died the same year from fever caught while tending Waxhaw prisoners on the British prison-ship in Charleston harbour. Her eldest son, Hugh, had already died at the Battle of Stono, which meant that Andrew was left to fend for himself at the age of 14.
49. The lithograph by Thomas Sinclair, printed in 1858, five years after the statue was erected, does not show railings or cannons around it.
50. See John Spencer Bassett, *The Life of Andrew Jackson*, 1916, pp.5–7. Jackson himself says, 'I was born in South Carolina . . . about one mile from the Carolina Road end of the Waxhaw Creek.'
51. This was the anniversary of the Battle of New Orleans.
52. In fact, if one stands on one of the crossing-islands in the middle of Pennsylvania Avenue and looks towards the Capitol dome, one will see that there is not an *exact* alignment of the avenue with the centre of the dome, even though the plans of Ellicott called for such.
53. Mills oversaw the construction of the central wing and the spine of the building (overlooking 15th Street) up to 1842. His original design has been radically amended, and the unpedimented Ionic colonnade along 15th Street is the only striking survival of his original plan. For a brief survey of the development of the building, and a note of other architects involved in the Treasury, see P. Scott and A.J. Lee, *Buildings of the District of Columbia*, 1993, pp.154ff.
54. The *Gazette of the United States*, Philadelphia, 4 January 1792. I have taken the passage from Mary Clemmer Ames, *Ten Years in Washington. Life and Scenes in the National Capital, as a Woman Sees Them*, 1874, p.44.
55. The emphasis on true north is marked on the zodiac in the Great Hall of the Library of Congress, and on the huge bronze compass set in the pavement on the Pennsylvania Avenue side of the United States Navy Memorial at 8th Street and

Pennsylvania. Another bronze compass is on the zero milestone, set up by Congress in 1920 to the south of the White House grounds, on the meridian of the District of Columbia.

56. At the latitude of Washington DC, the furthest degree north reached by the Sun is actually 302 degrees, in which it remains for 4 days. However, the Sun remains in 301 degrees for a total of 26 days during this period around the 'standstill', or solstice.
57. The lapidary text on the sundial support records the great age of this remarkable lady – she was born in 1845, and died in 1942. The armillary was raised in tribute to 'her vision and perseverance', through which the land on which it is sited became Montrose Park. So far as I can see, the armillary is unsigned, but its fixing indicates that it was adjusted for local setting. It was set in place by the Georgetown Garden Club, in 1956. See the *Washington Post*, 22 Nov. 1956, for the dedication ceremony.
58. The discovery of the manuscript revealing this information has not yet been reported in the Masonic literature, consequently I do not feel free to reveal the sources of this information, which came to me by way of private conversation.
59. Although I do not doubt that Ellicott was a Mason, I have not been able to discover to which Lodge he belonged.
60. The three degrees of Symbolic Masonry were conferred upon Andrew W. Mellon when he was Secretary of the Treasury, under the direction of the Grand Master of Masons of Pennsylvania, J. Willison Smith. The Royal Arch Degrees were conferred at the Grand Holy Royal Arch Chapter of Pennsylvania on 15 October, 1931. See *The New Age*, vol.xxxix, November 1931, no.11, p.689.
61. For more information on this zodiac by Sidney Waugh, see p.281ff.
62. See Gustavus A. Eisen, *Portraits of Washington*, 1932, vol. II, pl. xcix and pp.457ff.
63. See Herman Kahn, 'Appendix to Pierre L'Enfant's Letter to the Commissioners, May 30 1800', in *Records of the Columbia Historical Society of Washington DC 1942–1943*, vols. 44–45, p.200.
64. Kahn (op. cit., n.63 above), p.201.
65. Kahn (op. cit., n.63 above), p.201.
66. Henry Latham, *Black and White. A Journal of a Three Months' Tour in the United States*, 1969 ed., entry for 6 Jan. 1867, p.71.
67. Latham (op. cit., n.66 above), entry for 4 Jan. 1867, p.60.
68. The modern World Bank Building completely dominates the skyline to the west of Pennsylvania Avenue, beyond the White House, and is a further testimony to just how little the true import of the L'Enfant-Ellicott plan has been appreciated by modern architects and city planners. I find it interesting that the two major buildings that disrupt the stellar symmetry of Washington DC should have been built to serve finance.
69. In terms of the spherical geometry of astronomy, and the computerized programs available in modern times, there is no problem in establishing a 'theoretical' date for the significant Sunset. The Capitol is at longitude WO77 01, latitude N38 53. The azimuth for Pennsylvania Avenue proposed by Ellicott and L'Enfant was 290 degrees. This points to Sunsets around 11 and 12 August. However, our problem is that the perfection of spherical geometry offered by astronomy is, in this case, marred by high artificial horizons, and by variations in vantage points, such as are offered by the modern Capitol, as well as changes made to the duo's original plans. The simple fact is that we do not know what vantage point Ellicott and L'Enfant had in mind – in consequence, we do not know exactly what the horizon was in their calculations. This is why I decided to establish by direct observations the likely intentions behind the Ellicott orientations – or the specific 'acute angle' of Pennsylvania Avenue.
70. The relevant detail of the Robert King map is given by Glenn Brown, *History of the United States Capitol*, 1900. The ground-plan of the Capitol (since substantially

altered) did appear in the later Ellicott map. In 1926, William Patridge, who had been the chief draughtsman of the McMillan Commission, was asked by the National Park and Planning Commission to reconstruct the L'Enfant design from surviving maps, surveys and notes. In the course of this work, Patridge drew a comparative map, in which the amendments made by Ellicott to the L'Enfant plan are compared. This amended map is very revealing, and convinces me that Ellicott was responsible for the orientations.

71. This *Atlas of Washington District of Columbia*, published by G.M. Hopkins, with beautiful engravings by Walter S. MacCormac, of 1887, is extremely useful for the study of late-19th-century Washington DC. The colour plate from this atlas, a detail of which is given as plate 21 of this present book, is intended to help the reader determine the viewing point I have arrived at through my own researches.

72. If we draw a corresponding line through Maryland Avenue, we find that the two axes meet just inside the Capitol building, but not at, or within, the dome – let alone at its centre. Although L'Enfant designated the area, or grounds, for what became the Capitol building, he did not indicate its shape in this area. The later map by Ellicott shows the Capitol dome at the centre of this Pennsylvania-Maryland axis, but none of the early plans of the Capitol building show such an orientation. For a few of the early plans and elevations, see Brown (op. cit., n.70 above).

73. And, of course, in the corresponding azimuth period in early May (which, however, does not have a corresponding link with the constellation Virgo).

74. The azimuth for longitude W077 01, latitude N38 53, for the ten-day period under investigation is:

7 August	292	12 August	290
8 August	291	13 August	289
9 August	291	14 August	289
10 August	291	15 August	289
11 August	290	16 August	288

These data were provided by HM Nautical Almanac Office, Particle Physics and Astronomy Research Council.

75. Edbrooke (a Mason from Chicago) was the supervising architect within the office under the control of the Treasury Department.

76. Scott and Lee (op. cit., n.53 above), p.169.

77. Cable (op. cit., n.31 above), pp.207ff., suggested that the campanile was retained as a 'graceful gesture to the past'. It seems curious to me that Andrew Mellon, so deeply interested in architecture and Masonic symbolism, should have planned for the demise of the tower to complete his famous Triangle. Did someone perhaps tell him about the mystery of the tower, before he could destroy it? At all events, the real question is why it should have been built at all – especially with such a precisely measured pyramid at the top.

78. For very sensible security reasons, it is not permitted to mount tripods or other mechanical devices on the Capitol terrace. This has meant that all my observations and photographic records have been made with hand-held equipment. For this viewing of the sun flashes I have used a long-focus Zensa Bronica 250mm, with a 100 ASA daylight film.

79. Sunset on 10 August 1998 was at 20:04:48 PM EDT. See n.83 below.

80. In 1998, Regulus was 29:47 in Leo. It was only 28 minutes of arc from the ecliptic. See n.83 below.

81. Regulus will set almost 32 minutes after Sunset. We must recall that this is a horizon setting, which is lower than the visible horizon at the end of Pennsylvania Avenue. For details of setting, see n.83 below.

82. For more precise details of setting, see n.83 below,

83. The precessional equivalent from 1791 to 1998 is approximately 2 degrees and 53 minutes.

It will be evident to specialists that, throughout this section, I have elected to use a non-technical language, and to offer round figures, so as to be comprehensible to the lay reader. The following technical data are intended as a guide for those wishing to ascertain that my non-specialist generalizations in this section are in fact valid.

The azimuth at Washington DC (Capitol) for 10 days, centring on the phenomena, at longitude W077 02, latitude N38 53:

7 August	292	12 August	290
8 August	291	13 August	289
9 August	291	14 August	289
10 August	291	15 August	289
11 August	290	16 August	288

Positions of the three relevant first-magnitude stars in 1791 and 1999, rounded off to the closest minute, are as follows with precessional rate assumed in calculations as 1 degree in 72 years. While this is not precisely the precessional rate recognized by Ellicott, I feel that it is more reasonable to use the modern figure, given the brevity of period in question:

	1791	1998	Lat.
Regulus	26 LE 50	29 LE 43	N 00.28
Spica	20 LB 5O	23 LB 43	S 02.03
Arcturus	21 LB 14	24 LB 07	N 30.47

The following data, pertaining to differences in arc and time, were checked and adjusted against the Winstar computer program.

On 10 August 1791 the Sun set at 06:56:16 PM LMT, in 18 LE 11.
The star Regulus was in 26 LE 50, and set at 07:20:04 PM LMT.
The time difference between Sunset and star-set is 00:23:48.

On 10 August 1998 the Sun set at 08:04:48 PM EDT in 18 LE 09.
The star Regulus was in 29 LE 43, and set at 08:36:24 PM EDT.
The time difference between Sunset and star-set is 00:31:36.

On 14 August 1791 the Sun set at 06:51:15 PM LMT in 22 LE 01.
The star Regulus was in 26 LE 50, and set at 07:04:20.
The time difference between Sunset and star-set is 00:13:05.

On 14 August 1998 the Sunset at 07:59:50 PM EDT in 21 LE 59.
The star Regulus was in 29 LE 43, and set at 08:20:38 PM EDT.
The time difference between Sun set and star-set is 00:20:48.

APPENDIX

1. I have paraphrased this from Edward Moore, *Studies in Dante, Third Series, Miscellaneous Essays*, 1903, 'The Astronomy of Dante', p.26. Cosmas is perhaps better known by his ascribed name, Indicopleustes: the quotation is from his *Topographia Christiana*.
2. *Convivio*, II, ii, 62ff.
3. Dante had not counted them. In this, he was following the Arabic astrologer Alfraganus, who had not counted them. Alfraganus was following Ptolemy, who probably had not counted them either. Perhaps it was the numerology of the 1022 which attracted Dante (and presumably the others), rather than any concern for the physical reality. The actual number was irrelevant: Dante recognized that even in the *Via di San Jacopo* (our 'Milky Way') there was a multitude of stars.
4. *Inferno*, canto xi, 1.113: *che i Pesci quizzan su per l'orizzonta* ('horizon'd the glistening Fishes swim'). Dante refers to the sign which is rising, to show his own spiritual severance from the stars – because he is about to descend over the chasm's edge, into Hell.

5. For a single example, see John Coley's *The Astrologer's Guide,* 1986 ed., pp.97–9. For the fixed stars, see no.141. A fine summary, linking Coley's observations with Cardan and the English astrologer William Lilly, is in Annabella Kitson, *History and Astrology. Clio and Urania Confer*, 1989, 'Some Varieties of Electional Astrology', p.183. The fixed stars played a much greater part in prediction in the mediaeval period, but relatively modern excellent examples of the successful use of fixed stars may be found in Alfred John Pearce, *The Text-book of Astrology*, 1911.
6. William Lilly, *Anima Astrologiae: or, a Guide for Astrologers*, 1676, p.102.
7. See D. Fraser, H. Hibbard and M.J. Lewine (eds), *Essays in the History of Architecture*, 1969 ed., René Taylor, 'Architecture and Magic: Considerations on the Idea of the Escorial', plate 32. Taylor does not discuss the chart in connection with fixed stars, but the data relating to the design of the Escorial and the hermetic thinking of Philip II are useful. This chart (which is a copy) was probably cast by the hermeticist Juan de Herrera, and does not reveal the fixed star. However, on 23 April 1563, Mars was on the powerful fixed star, Fomalhaut, the *alpha* of Piscis Australis. The astrologer was very clever, for this same position (28 degrees of Aquarius) was the position of King Philip's own natal Moon!
8. Thomas Sandby was professor of architecture at the Royal Academy, and (along with his more famous artist-brother, Paul) was a Mason.
9. The four were disposed as follows:

   SU02GE42 ME15GE05 JU26GE22 UR06GE31

10. Written from New College, Oxford, 1 April 1776. Quoted in George Smith, *The Use and Abuse of Freemasonry*, 1914 reprint, pp.63ff. The full ode is on pp.61ff.
11. See J. Norman Lockyer, *The Dawn of Astronomy. A Study of the Temple-Worship and Mythology of the Ancient Egyptians*, 1894.
12. See, for example, Tamsyn Barton, *Ancient Astrology*, 1994, pp.109–113.
13. A great deal of work has been done in the past century on the close relationship between the ancient Mysteries and Christianity. See, for example, Hugo Rahner, 'The Christian Mystery and the Pagan Mysteries', 1944, in *The Mysteries. Papers from the Eranos Yearbooks*, xxx. 2, 1971 ed., p.337. From an esoteric standpoint, many of the lectures of Rudolf Steiner and the books of Gerald Massey and H.P. Blavatsky deal with this important theme.
14. For Mithraic astrology, see (for example) R.L. Gordon, 'The Sacred Geography of a *mithraeum*: the example of Sette Sfere', in *Journal of Mithraic Studies*, vol.I, no.2, 1976.
15. In the non-arcane literature, Dionysius the Areopagite is often called the pseudo-Dionysius. For a modern readable account, see Arthur O. Lovejoy, *The Great Chain of Being. A Study of the History of an Idea*, 1960 reprint of the 1936 ed., pp.67ff.
16. See Jamie James, *The Music of the Spheres. Music, Science, and the Natural Order of the Universe*, 1995 reprint.
17. In the Dionysian list of angelic beings (for which there were several minor variants in the mediaeval period), the following planetary grades were recognized in mediaeval art, mainly through the writings of Gregory (*Homilies*, 34), wherein the Latin names were given in place of the original Greek:

Moon	–	Angels
Mercury	–	Archangels
Venus	–	Archai (Principalities)
Sun	–	Exsusiai
Mars	–	Dynamis (Virtues)
Jupiter	–	Kyriotetes (Dominions)
Saturn	–	Thrones

   The Cherubim and Seraphim were usually linked with the zodiac and the fixed stars.

18. An interesting study of the hierarchies, in relation to 16th-century paintings, has been made by Friedrich Zauner, who appears to be deeply familiar with the arcane tradition. See F. Zaunev, *Das Hierarchienbild der Gotik: Thomas von Villachs Fresko in Thörl*, 1980.
19. We have already seen that, in the Judaic nomenclature which Western esotericism inherited, the angelic ruler of Virgo is named Hamaliel. Within the same nomenclature, Pisces is ruled by Barchiel, and Aquarius by Gabriel. The list of names, which often vary slightly in orthography, were widely published in mediaeval arcane literature, and were collected by (among others) Agrippa, *De Occulta Philosophia*, 1532. For a modern listing of planets, zodiacal signs, and other rulerships, see F. Gettings, *The Arkana Dictionary of Astrology*, 1990 revised ed.
20. Dante served as a prior in the baptistry, and once saved the life of a child, who was in danger of drowning in the baptistry waters. See William Anderson, *Dante the Maker*, 1980, p.69. Like the basilican church of San Miniato, the baptistry of Florence is mentioned in Dante's poem, the *Commedia*. His astrology – like the astrological programmes being adopted by the European cathedral-builders – was deeply indebted to the Arabic systems, especially to the writings of Alfraganus.
21. F. Gettings, *The Secret Zodiac*, 1987, p.168.
22. The 13th-century Latin palindrome links the individual (*te* – thou) with the higher world-element (*igne* – fire) and with the Sun (*sol*) in a round-dance: *engi rotor te sol ciclos et rotor igne.*
23. The foundation moment for the zodiac in the basilican church of San Miniato, in Florence, was Sunrise 28 May 1207. This zodiac, which is intimately linked with the arcane symbolism of the church, is discussed at considerable length in Gettings (op. cit., n.21 above).
24. For a general view of spiritual beings in relation to astrology, see Rudolf Steiner, *Man and the World of Stars*, 1963 ed., English translation of 12 lectures delivered at Dornach, November–December 1922. The selection of letters, published under the title of *The Michael Mystery*, 1956 revised ed., pertains more to the Secundadeian tradition of the post-1881 Age of Michael.
25. The arcane traditions relating to these three groups are complex. However, for an introduction to each of the categories, see (for alchemy) Titus Burckhart, *Alchemy*, 1967 (for planets) C.A. Muses, *The Works of Dionysius Freher*, 1951; and (for First Degree Masonry) W. Kirk MacNulty, *Freemasonry. A Journey through Ritual and Symbol*, 1991, pp.20ff.
26. Albert Pike was the Grand Commander of the Ancient and Accepted Scottish Rite, in Washington DC, and, as an initiate into the 32nd Degree, was Master of the Royal Secret. His *Morals and Dogma of the Ancient and Accepted Scottish Rite of Freemasonry*, 1871, is a classic study of Masonic symbolism and hermeticism, deriving its immense power from the accumulation of arcane wisdom which Pike derived from books in his own library of esoteric books.
27. Albert Pike (op. cit., n.26 above), gives many equivalents of the seven, in a variety of world religions and mythologies: see, for, example p.233. The names of the six were Iao, Saboath, Adonai, Eloi, Orai and Astaphal (see p.563). Pike's account of the spiritual development of these beings explains why they should be called the Builders. *Ahura Mazda* is the solar being, or light being, confronted by the dark Ahriman in the Zoroastrian religion.
28. Pike (op. cit., 1906 ed., n.26 above, p.252.
29. There are many references to the Amshaspends in H.P. Blavatsky's two seminal works. For a digest, see her *Theosophical Glossary*, 1892, p.19.
30. Steiner formally seceded from theosophy, and established his own arcane philosophy, Anthroposophy. He has lectured on the planetary angels – the Secundadeis of Trithemius – recognizing the importance of the change of rulership for Western civilization: see, for example, n.24 above. He has intimated that the planetary rulers were indeed archangels, but that they have evolved (or are

on the point of evolving) into the next higher rank of Archai.

Steiner – aware that Trithemius had made an error in calculation – placed the beginning of the epoch of Michael in 1879: however, he delivered this opinion in a lecture in the first decade of the 20th century, and his views could not have influenced the anticipation of the date in the Masonic tradition prior to this time.

31. Aquinas, *Summa Theologiae*, 1a.50–64. For a useful translation and commentary, see the Kenelm Foster ed. (vol. 9) of 1967.
32. Ross Parsons. *New Light from the Great Pyramid*, pp.49–50.
33. The *calendarium* of 1503, which contains a remarkable variety of angelic names and associations, has been reproduced in full as Appendix V of Karl A. Nowotny's 1967 edition of Agrippa, *De Occulta Philosophia*, p.615.
34. In the late-mediaeval arcane tradition (n.17 above), the 'angels' of the planets were named as Oriphiel (Saturn), Zachariel (Jupiter), Samuel (Mars), Michael (Sun), Anael (Venus), Raphael (Mercury) and Gabriel (Moon). These were the names used in the Secundadeian literature.

    However, the *calendaria* also gave another system of 'planetary spirits', named as Aratron (Saturn), Befor (Jupiter), Phalec (Mars), Och (Sun), Hagith (Venus), Ophiel (Mercury) and Phul (Moon). In the 1503 *Calendarium* of Trithemius there is also a third list which unfortunately confuses the solar being with the Mercuric (for which reason we have not reproduced this).
35. Pike (op. cit., 1906 ed., n.25 above), p.506. Pike borrowed a great deal, without acknowledgement (a method also followed by Blavatsky, but well in accord with esoteric principles): this material is lifted from Dunlap (op. cit., n.82 below), p.252, who was in turn quoting from an earlier French source.
36. George Frederick Kunz, *The Curious Lore of Precious Stones*, 1971 ed. of 1913, quotes Cardan to this effect, and adds some interesting notes on the emerald. See p.78.
37. The sacred pig (*porcus*) was sacrificed during the initiation rites at Eleusis. See n.39 below.
38. It is often difficult to identify modern plants from the ancient lists. This could also be a wild basil (the American dittany), but its Martian rulership (along with its infamous links with the flying-drinks of the witches), would suggest that Trithemius had in mind the mint.
39. This direct line between *calaminthus* and the Mysteries of Demeter should remind us that the pig, or *porcus*, of the Virgo lists in the Trithemian scalae, was also used as part of the sacred ceremony at Eleusis: the drink was a libation, while the pig was a sacrificial victim.
40. For a modern treatment of the 15 stars, see Joan Evans, *Magical Jewels of the Middle Ages and the Renaissance*, 1976 reprint of the 1922 ed., p.246. The 13th-century version in the figure is from the oldest known *Liber Hermetis* in the Bodleian Library – Ashmole 341. The names must be read downwards, as in three columns:

Canis	Beril(us)	Savi
major		na

    The two small figures to the top right of the sigils are numerals (recently introduced to Europe from Arabic sources): they represent the No.5. A later copyist failed to understand this, and incorporated the numbers into the sigils.

    The relevant section, relating to stars, stones, herbs and sigils, is reproduced as Appendix XXV in Nowotny (op. cit., n.33 above), and discussed on p.913.
41. The modern tradition of astro-gemology has become confused due to the intermixing of many traditions. Very often, the stone of Virgo is said to be the cornelian – a suggestion which does have its roots in mediaeval lore derived from Arabic sources. See, for example, Kunz op. cit., n.36 above, pp.307ff.
42. The occultist Cornelius Agrippa, in making his selections from a rich mediaeval

tradition, simplified and categorized these beings in a way which has influenced fundamentally the late-mediaeval arcane view. He gave the names, sigils, sacred numbers and magical squares for the planetary intelligencies in *De Occulta Philosophia*, 1534, II, cxlviii. Karl Anton Nowotny's facsimile edition of 1967, with extensive notes and commentaries, reveals something of the richness of the tradition in which Agrippa worked. One work in which the planetary Secundadeians were dealt with, which was also circulating in Masonic groups in the mid-19th-century, was De Hooghe's remarkable arcane work *Hieroglyphica, oder Denkbilder der alten Volker*, 1744.

43. See S. Russell Forbes, 'A Masonic Built City', in *Ars Quattuor Coronatorum*, vol.IV, 1941, pp.86ff. Unfortunately, my impression is that Forbes did not look closely at what Pliny actually wrote (*Historia*, Bk III v.655) and this led him astray. Pliny wrote:

> . . . Roma ipsa, cuius nomen alterum dicere (nisi) arcanis cacrimoniarium nefas habetur. . . . non alienum videtur inserere hoc loco exemplum religionis antiquae ob hoc maxime silentium institutae: namque diva Angerona, cui sacrificatur a. d. xii kal. Ian., ore obligato obsignatoque simulacrum habet.

The following translation is my own:

> . . . Rome itself, whose other name it is held to be a sin to utter save in the ceremonies of the Mysteries . . . It seems pertinent here to give an instance of an old religion established to institute such silence: the goddess Angerona, to whom sacrifice is offered on December 21, is represented in her statue with a sealed bandage over her mouth.

It is clear from this that Pliny is *not* saying that the ancient secret name of Rome was Angerona. So far as I know, the secret name of Rome has never been divulged.

Equally, Forbes seems to have made a mistake about the image which he claims to be that of Angerona. There is no internal evidence that the image of 'Angerona' in Robert Walsh, *An Essay on Ancient Coins, Medals, and Gems as Illustrating the Progress of Christianity in the Early Ages*, 1828, plate 9 is that of Angerona.

44. For Pliny, see n.43 above. While Macrobius insists the priests sacrificed in the Volupian shrine, Varro says that the sacrifices were made in the Senate House.
45. This date for the *Angeronalia* corresponds to our own 21 December.
46. Macrobius, *Saturnalia*, III.9. Some accounts insist that the basalt image of the goddess had her mouth bound with a filet, to demonstrate the same principle of secrecy.
47. Virgo is given as the solar ruler of Washington DC by Nicholas de Vore, *Encyclopedia of Astrology*, 1948, p.343. The tradition that Washington DC has the ascendant ruler as Scorpio back to Devore, 1948). This is continued through many other works into the substantial and scholarly survey by Nicholas Campion, *The Book of World Horoscopes*, 1988. However, I can find no support for this Scorpionic rulership, neither in the various foundation horoscopes, nor in the feeling of the place: as the Mason, Manley Palmer Hall admits in his *Astrological Keywords*, 1959, which continues this Scorpio-ruler tradition (p.68), the available lists are 'both archaic and incomplete'. It is a great pity that the learned astrologer A.J. Pearce, who had so much to say about astrological influences on the United States, did not extend his own chorography: he follows Sibly in listing the United States as under Gemini, New York as under the rule of Cancer, but otherwise repeated the usual associations: see *The Textbook of Astrology*, 1911 ed., pp.274ff.
48. Ebenezer Sibly, *The Science of Astrology, or Complete Illustration of the Occult Sciences*, 1788, p.101.
49. Cicero, *De Divinatione*, ii, 47, 98.
50. For a good account of the astrology behind the founding of Rome, see Frederick

H. Cramer, *Astrology in Roman Law and Politics*, 1954, pp.65ff.
51. Trithemius, *De Septem Secundadeis*, 1522.
52. In the short introduction to his text, Trithemius tells us that he had the lists and traditions for his secundadeis from the writings of 'the Conciliator'. This was the familiar title of the Italian philosopher, alchemist and astrologer, Peter of Abano (1250–1316). The tradition may be traced through the Abano text to Arabic to Gnostic literature, and probably beyond. Peter of Abano was singled out by the Inquisition for the distinction of having his dead body exhumed, that it might attend a public proclamation against him.
53. See Daniel, x.13, where Michael is 'one of the foremost princes'. In Jude, 9, Michael is 'the archangel'. In Revelation, xii, 7, Michael is the leader of the angels.
54. The two Capitol zodiacs are the Brumidi frescoes of *c.* 1860 in the north-wing corridors and the zodiacal arc beneath the statue of Carlo Franzoni's *Car of History*. The remaining 18 zodiacs are the six in the Library of Congress, the six sets in the Dirksen, the one in the National Academy of Sciences, the Einstein zodiac, the two in the Federal Reserve building, the Garfield zodiac and the Mellon zodiac. There are other zodiacs in Washington DC (there are a couple in Georgetown, for instance) but the ones listed are certainly the most important ones in the central part of the city.
55. While the 1579 edition of the Scaliger translation of Manilius' *Astronomica* was still available, the 1739 English translation by R. Bentley, and the 1786 French translation by A. G. Pingree, would have been better known to 18th-century Masons.
56. Manilius (op. cit., n.55 above).
57. S.C. Bullock, *Revolutionary Brotherhood. Freemasonry and the Transformation of the American Social Order, 1730_1840*, 1996, p.138.
58. For De Witt Clinton's Masonic connections see *An Address Delivered before Holland Lodge, December 24, 1793*, 1794, p.4.
59. There are some useful notes on the figure for Rome in Pearce (op. cit., n.47 above), pp.272ff. The rule of Leo over the city is very ancient, and the star Regulus (which is said to have entered the sign Leo in 293 BC) seems to be the guiding star of the Eternal City.
60. See Kitson (op. cit., n.5 above), 'The Foundation of St Paul's Cathedral after its Destruction in the Great Fire of 1666. An Astrological Investigation,' by Derek Appleby, pp.199ff.
61. See F. Gettings *The Secret Zodiac*, 1987, pp.118ff. The curious colophon in the Latin lapidary inscription indicates that the foundation-chart zodiac of 1207 was elected in order that the church would endure.
62. When, some years ago, I discussed this symbolism with the Abbot of San Miniato (which is still a monastic establishment) he told me that it was not an artist who had worked this Virgo-Pisces magic. Apparently, a 19th-century Benedictine abbot had ordered the fresco – then in a different part of the church – to be relocated on this important axis. Whether artist or abbot is irrelevant – what matters is the symbolism.
63. Pike (op. cit., 1906 ed., n.23 above), p.455.
64. Only two major buildings prior to the McMillan commission of 1901–2 survived the rebuilding programme. These were the Post Office building, designed by Willoughby J. Edbrooke and finished in 1899 – the 'Old Post Office'. The first official Federal Triangle building was the District Building, designed by Cope and Stewardson and finished in 1908. It was the Public Buildings Act of 1926 which made possible the massive rebuilding of the area we now call the Federal Triangle. This work, nominally under the control of Andrew W. Mellon, was overseen by Edward H. Bennett, who had been involved with the City Beautiful plans for San Francisco in 1905, and Chicago in 1908–9. In some ways, it is sad that the original L'Enfant plan has not been adhered to, and that the irritating kink in Pennsylvania

Avenue, between 13th and 14th Streets, was not ironed out. It is this kink, and this alone, which prevents the cosmic vision of the original builders being realized.

65. The letter was inscribed at the top (near now virtually illegible script) 'Georgetown March 1791'. The section I quote and reproduce is halfway down (the unnumbered) p.5. The original is in the Manuscript Division of the Library of Congress.
66. An autograph manuscript from Thomas Jefferson, dated 18 August 1791, contains a small diagram, sketched out in his hand, showing how the angles of the main avenues should run across the main grid of streets.
67. It is perhaps easy to deride Anderson now, but the fact is that Caesar *was* initiated into the ancient Mysteries, and may well have been head of one of the Schools in Rome. The real issue is whether it is historically accurate to equate the so-called Lodges of the ancient world with the Lodges of 18th-century English Masonry.
68. James Anderson was an influential fellow of the Royal Society. The quotation is from Bullock (op. cit., n.57 above), p.35. However, in this connection see H.D. Weinbrot, *Augustus Caesar in 'Augustan' England: The Decline of a Classical Norm*, 1978.
69. The Roman astrologer Tarrutius (first century BC) linked the conception of Romulus, the mythical founder of Rome, with the total eclipse of the Sun on 25 June 772 BC. According to Plutarch, Tarrutius gives the foundation of Rome itself as 4 October 754 BC. For modern notes, see Rupert Gleadow, *The Origin of the Zodiac*, 1968, p.67. There are, however, several variant horoscopes for Rome, and while some astrologers suggest Libra as the ruling sign, others suggest Leo and some Virgo.
70. Jefferson, in his capacity as Secretary of State, along with James Madison and the three Commissioners, elected to name the streets alphabetically one way and numerically the other, from the Capitol, on 8 September 1791.
71. The festival has been celebrated since at least the seventh century. Undoubtedly, this Christological imagery does correspond to the hermeneutic content of the stellar triangle of that period, as visible down Pennsylvania Avenue.
72. There are several versions of horoscopes for Charles II: see A. Leo [ed.], *Modern Astrology* (new series), IV, 314, 375, which gives a Libran Ascendant (well in keeping with his known personality). The chart is reproduced in Alan Leo's *1001 Notable Nativities*, 4th ed., no.648. However, the version of the horoscope which appeared in the collection of nativities published by Bonatus in 1687, would have been known to Sibly. This had a Virgoan Ascendant: see Leo, op. cit., IV, no. 649.
73. De Hooghe (op. cit., n.41 above).
74. Grant Showerman, 'Isis', in James Hastings, *Encyclopaedia of Religion and Ethics*, 1971 ed., vol.VII, p.435.
75. British Library Manuscript Department – Arundel 66.
76. The drawing is from *Monuments of Egypt and Nubia* by J. F. Champollion, I, pl.xlii. Portal (trans. Simons) in *A Comparison of Egyptian Symbols with those of the Hebrews*, 1878, calls the ansated cross (which is the European name for the *ankh*) the symbol of 'divine life', and the sceptre, symbol of 'purity' – which is the meaning given to it by Champollion.
77. *Pelanos* was made from wheat and barley flour, and used in the Mysteries rites – for example, following the sacrifice of the Great Bull at the *Boedromion* at Eleusis. It was barley bread that Ambrose equated with the bread of heaven, which was the body of Christ: see Julius Baum, 'Symbolic Representations of the Eucharist' (1944), in *The Mysteries. Papers from the Eranos Yearbooks*, Bollingen series xxx.2, 1971 ed., pp.264ff.
78. See John Y. Cole and Henry Hope Reed, *The Library of Congress. The Art and Architecture of the Thomas Jefferson Building*, 1997, pp.88ff.
79. The valve to the north represents the Humanities, that to the south, Intellect. This division is reflected in the Minerva symbolism in the tympanum above.

80. For a brief survey of the supposed journey of the Palladium, see Gettings (op. cit., n.21 above), pp.152ff.
81. For Minerva as a form of Isis, see *Bell's New Pantheon; or, Historical Dictionary of the Gods, Demi-Gods, Heroes*, 1790, p.11.
82. The translation is from S.F. Dunlap's version of Virgil's 4th Eclogue, in the former's *Vestigates of the Spirit-History of Man*, 1858, p.253. Dunlap had a profound influence on American esoteric Masonry, not only in his own right as an esoteric writer, but through the writings of Albert Pike who made extensive use of his book.

1. The Scottish Rite Temple (formerly the House of the Temple), designed 1911–1915 by John Russell Pope, on 16th Street, NW. The design of this building, now the Supreme Council (Southern Jurisdiction), was based on the ancient mausoleum at Halikarnassos, in Turkey.
2. Detail of the statue of Joseph Henry, sculpted by William Wetmore Story, and raised in 1883, outside the Smithsonian Institution Building, in Jefferson Drive. On the western side of the pedestal is a bas-relief of an electro-magnet.

3. Memorial statue to the assassinated President, James Abram Garfield, sculpted in 1887 by John Quincy Adams Ward, and located to the south-west of the Capitol. The plaque below the figure, and the three figures seated around the pedestal, are replete with Masonic symbolism.

4. Bust of the Grand Commander of the Scottish Rite, Albert Pike, modelled by Vinnie Ream, circa 1880. The bust is preserved in the collection of the Supreme Council (Southern Jurisdiction).

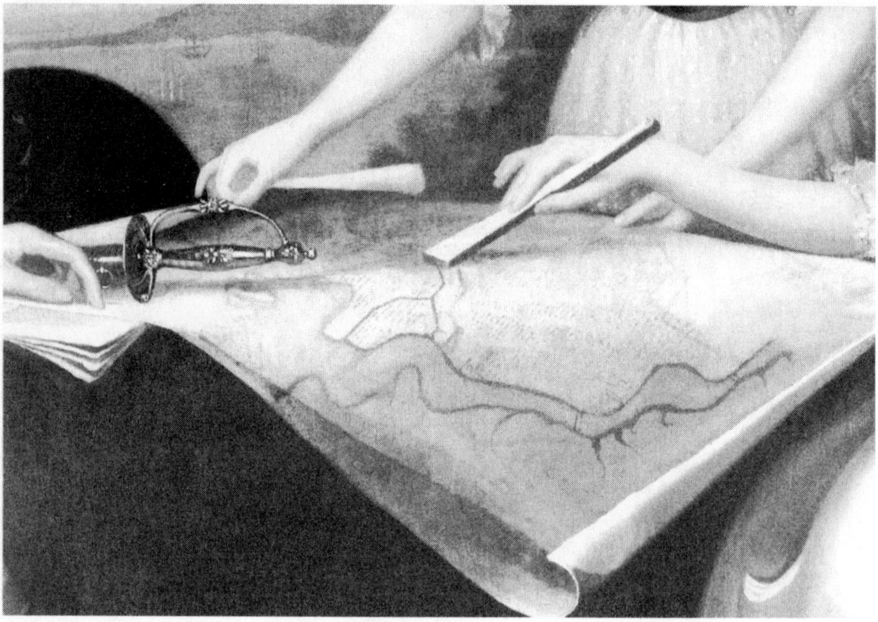

5-6. Oil painting (with detail) by Edward Savage of The Washington Family *(completed 1796). Reproduced with permission of the National Gallery of Art (Andrew W. Mellon Collection), Washington DC.*

7. Marble sculpture, The Car of History, *by Carlo Franzoni, completed in 1819 for the Statuary Hall of the Capitol. The clock-face wheel of the chariot rests upon an arc of the zodiac – from left to right, on raised relief panels, Sagittarius, Aquarius and Capricorn.*

8. Revolution of America – *engraved plate (no. 53) from the 1790 edition of Ebenezer Sibly's* A Complete Illustration . . . , *depicting an angel holding a specialist chart cast for a question concerning the outcome of the American Declaration of Independence.*

9. Representative of the Universal Mother, as corn-goddess in a dislocated zodiacal band, surrounded by numerous symbols relating to the eternal feminine. Note the crayfish of Cancer on her dress-hem, and Pisces above her head. To the extreme right (top) is Isis, with her dog. From de Hooghe's Hieroglyphica, *1744.*

10. French esoteric Masonry symbolized, with pyramids and the two pillars of Jachin and Boaz behind the female personification of Masonry. In fact, the symbols do not appear to go much beyond the Third Degree. Lithographic frontispiece to the 1852 edition of Le Soleil Mystique.

11. The Noyes Armillary Sphere, *which was designed to emphasise the zodiacal sign Virgo, sculpted by Carl Paul Jennewein, in memory of Edith Noyes, in 1931. This was once located in Meridian Hill Park, but was removed and lost (presumably destroyed) during a city riot.*

12. Twelve zodiacal signs, designed circa 1937 by Sidney Waugh, on the glass flange of a light-fitting in the Federal Reserve Board Building. The image of Virgo is Christianized by means of a halo: the glass was cut by Steuben.

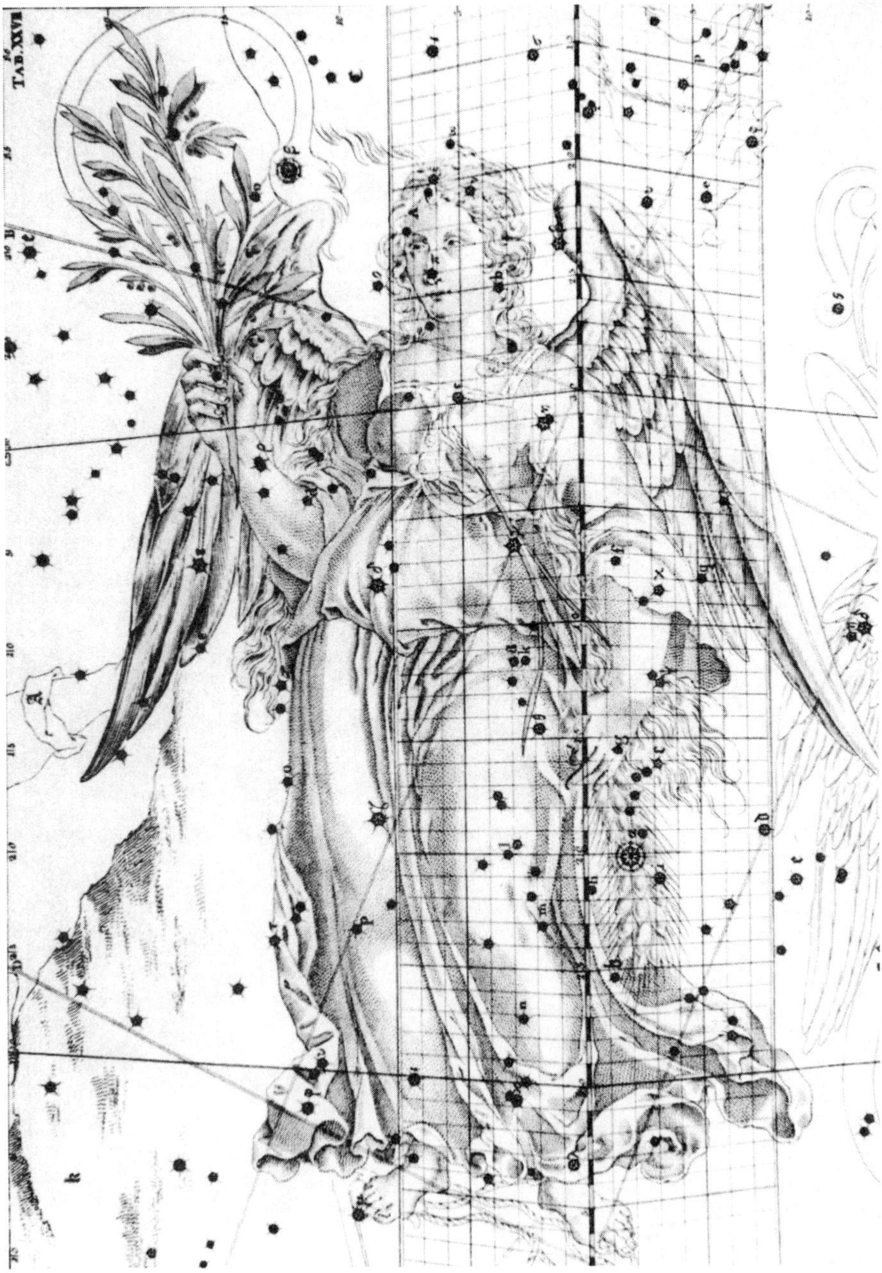

13. Sky map of the celestial Virgo, with corn in her left hand. The corn hangs vertical to the ecliptic (path of the Sun), and is marked by the large star Spica, 'the ear of corn'. The vertical lattice-work of lines on either side of the ecliptic marks the extreme limits of the zodiacal belt. After an eighteenth-century star-map by John Bevis.

14. In this early sixteenth-century woodcut by S. H. Beham, Mercury is shown in a chariot drawn by a pair of cocks. On the wheel of the chariot are images of the two signs over which Mercury has rule – Virgo and Gemini. Below are the 'children' of Mercury – those activities associated with the Mercurial impulse, such as drawing, painting, astronomy, music, etc.

15. High-relief granite sculpture, Urban Life *by John Gregory (finished 1941), in the grounds of the Municipal Centre Building. At the top left is Mercury in flight, below Vesta tending her lamp: to the extreme right is Maia, and in the centre, Aesculapius with his snake-entwined staff. The relief is among the most arcane in the city of Washington.*

16 Officially entitled America and the Federal Reserve Board *– sculpted in 1937 by John Gregory for that Board – the image is that of a female Mercury, with the Mercurial wand of office, or caduceus, derived from the ancient initiation symbol. Her right hand rests on the official seal of the Federal Reserve Board.*

17. Italian engraving from Jacopo Guarana's Oracoli, Auguri, Aruspici . . . *of 1792, which may be one source for the Masonic imagery of the 'Weeping Virgin'. Among the hidden Masonic symbolism is the fact that the fallen woman, at the feet of Saturn, is pointing to a displaced letter G – a symbol of Geometry, of considerable importance in Masonic symbolism.*
18. Interior of a French Masonic lodge, with a floor zodiac (probably set in incised marble), with the twelve images derived from the Egyptian zodiac (first century AD) formerly in the roof-shrine on the Temple of Hathor at Denderah, Egypt. At centre is the five-pointed star, within a triangle. Lithograph from the 1852 edition of Le Soleil Mystique.

19. Zodiacal band on a celestial globe in the left hand of a personification of Astronomy. *This sculpture, by Bela L. Pratt (finished about 1895), is in the southern spandrel of the bronze doors to the facade of the Library of Congress. The Virgo sign is just rising from the shadow, above the hips of* Astronomy.

20. Detail of Neptune and attendant, from Roland Hinton Perry's sculpture, The Court of Neptune *(finished 1898) in the fountain to the western façade of the Library of Congress. This 12-foot-high Neptune looks towards the zodiac on the pedestal of the Garfield Memorial (plate 5), to the west of the Capitol.*

21. Zodiacal clock in the main rotunda of the Library of Congress, designed and sculpted by John Flanagan. Behind the winged Saturn group are mosaics representing six of the zodiacal signs, including Virgo. Between Virgo and Leo is a comet, which is one of the mysteries of Washington DC's astral symbolism.

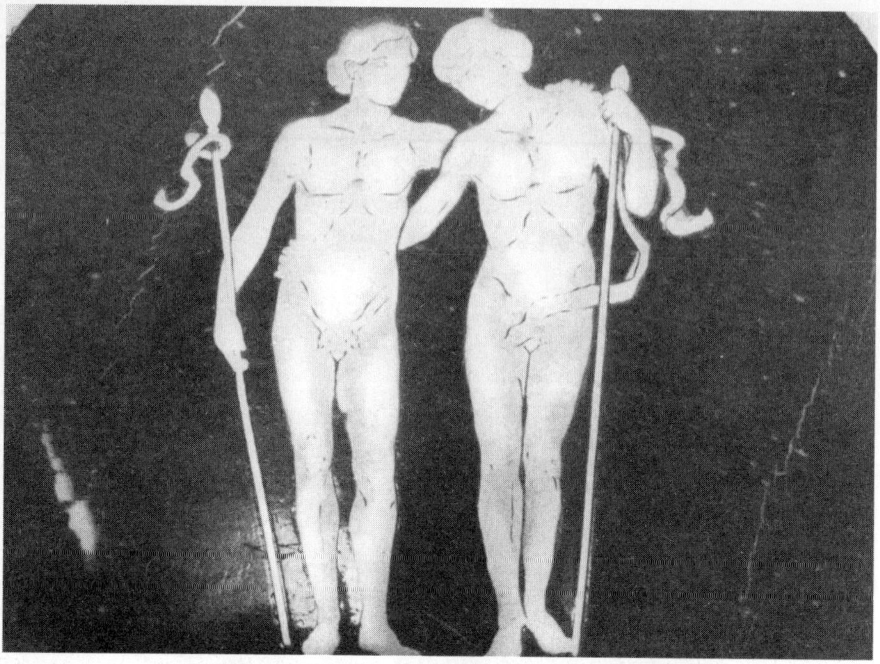

22. The bronze image of Gemini, from the zodiac set in the marble floor of the Main Hall of the Library of Congress, circa 1897 – perhaps to the design of Thomas Lincoln Casey. The staffs in the hands of these two males are derived from the sacred initiation staffs of the Greek Mysteries.
23. Detail of the ceiling zodiac from the south-east Pavilion of the Library of Congress, painted by Elmer Ellsworth Garnsey in 1896. That Garnsey should have elected to set his name and date above the sign Cancer is probably linked with the esoteric idea that Cancer represents the Gate of Birth.

24. Classical figure in bronze, at the base of the memorial to the assassinated President, James Abram Garfield, sculpted by John Quincy Adams Ward in 1887. The figure was based on a statue in the New Sacristy of San Lorenzo, Florence, and was intended by Ward to convey a secret meaning in harmony with the Masonic symbolism of the entire memorial.

25. The Greek scientist Thales, demonstrating how the height of the Great Pyramid at Gizah might be measured, with the aid of a shadow-stick. Detail from the bronze frieze, The Progress of Science *modelled by Lee Lawrie, in 1923, on the façade of the National Academy of Sciences Building, Constitution Avenue.*

26. Large bas relief bronze of the obverse of the Seal of the United States, set in the marble pavement of the Freedom Plaza! Washington DC. The symbolism of the Seal is among the most arcane of official devices linked with the origins of the United States.

27. Large bas relief bronze of the reverse of the Seal of the United States, set in the marble pavement of the Freedom Plaza, Washington DC. Unfortunately, this copy does not preserve certain of the esoteric principles in the design of the original pyramid – notably in the variation of the number of bricks in the western face of the structure.

28. A recessed bas-relief image of Virgo, from one of many ceiling zodiacs in the Dirksen Senate Office Building. These zodiacs, set in place about 1958, appear to have been designed especially for the Dirksen, but the image of Virgo, with the large harp, consciously echoes the Egyptian-style Virgo in the National Academy of Sciences (see plate 2).

29. Relief image of the zodiacal sign Aries, with sigil, from the rim of the bowl of the Andrew Mellon Memorial Fountain. This image, which faces due east, is one of twelve signs designed in 1952 by Sidney Waugh (see plate 15). As the fountain is located at the tip of the Federal Triangle, the image of Virgo is oriented along Pennsylvania Avenue.

30. Corn-sheaf held by a 'farm-worker', in the tradition of Virgoan imagery. Limestone relief panel, entitled Agriculture, *sculpted in 1937 by Concetta Scaravaglione on the south façade of the Federal Trade Commission building, overlooking Constitution Avenue.*
31. Limestone sculpture by James Earle Fraser, entitled Heritage, *in the form of a half-naked woman holding a sheaf of corn and a child. Completed in 1935 as part of the external decorative programme of sculptures for the National Archives, overlooking Constitution Avenue.*

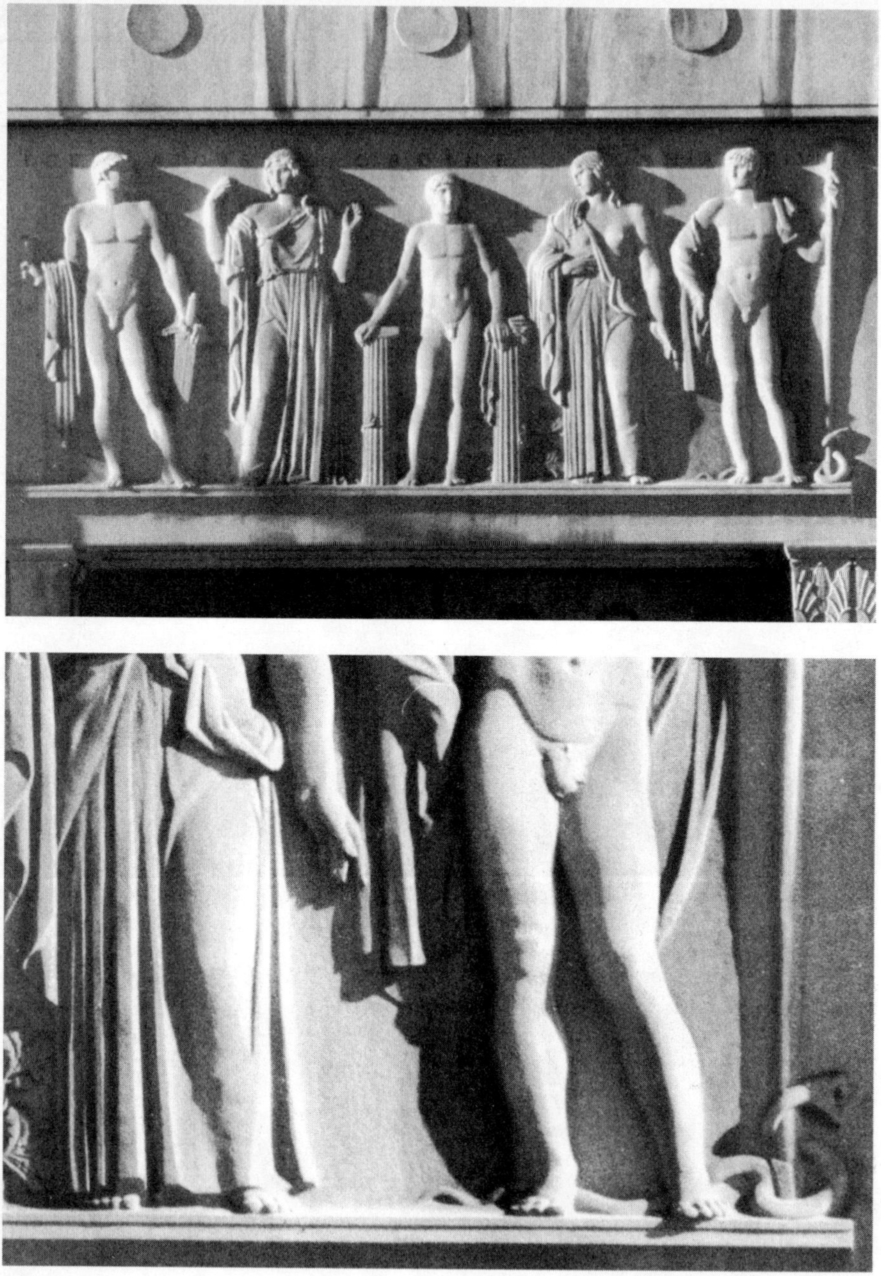

32. The Law and Order *limestone relief (with detail below) sculpted by Carl Paul Jennewein, in 1935. This is one of the few sculptures in Washington DC to make use of the movement of sunlight to express an esoteric message. The serpent impaled to the extreme right is the last feature to emerge from the shadows as the Sun moves to the south-west (detail).*

33. Tempera mural by Symeon Shimin, entitled Contemporary Justice and the Child, *completed circa 1940 for the United States Department of Justice Building. The draughtsman's square in the foreground (held by the hand of Shimin himself) is intended to echo the symbolism of the Federal Triangle in which the Department of Justice is located.*

34. Naked woman with sheaf of corn, seated on a bull – sculpted by Edgar Walter in 1935 for the central pediment of the Departmental Auditorium, overlooking Constitution Avenue. The detail is intended to represent the Earth signs of the zodiac – the other three elements also being represented in this central pediment.

35. Naked woman with a sea-horse, surrounded by dolphins – sculpted by Edward McCartan in 1935 for the former Interstate Commerce Commission Building on Constitution Avenue. The detail is intended to represent the Water signs of the zodiac – Cancer, Scorpio and Pisces.

36. Naked woman with a vase of abundance, and the Ram – sculpted by Sherry Fry in 1935 for the former Department of Labor, overlooking Constitution Avenue. The detail is intended to represent the Fire signs of the zodiac – Aries, Leo and Sagittarius.
37. Naked man with a sheaf of corn, sitting upon a rock, and leaning against a bull – sculpted by Albert Stewart in 1935 for the former Department of Labor, overlooking Constitution Avenue. The detail is intended to represent the Earth signs of the zodiac – Taurus, Virgo and Capricorn.

38. Fifteenth-century manuscript illumination of the constellation Virgo, from Ptolemy's Almagest. *The crown marks the figure as Queen of Heaven: the five-flowered plant in her right hand is derived from the hermetic tradition. The four sigils at top right are mediaeval symbols for Saturn, Mercury, Mars and Sun. Nineteenth-century lithographic print.*

39. Detail of the north valve of the central door of the façade of the Library of Congress. This bronze bas-relief was designed by Frederick MacMonnies, in 1898, as one of a pair of torch-bearing classical figures, below a lunette depicting Minerva and various constellations. The five-petalled floral devices on the dress of the maiden link with the symbolism of Virgo.

40. Engraved plate from de Hooghe's Hieroglyphica, *1744, showing the seven Planetary Angels that rule the periods of time (top half of engraving). In the lower half are numerous Masonic symbols, including an astrolabe completed by the radiant triangle, and marked by the letter G (alongside the raised arm of a lunar-solar personification).*